Understanding MACROECONOMICS

Ninth Edition

Robert L. Heilbroner
The New School for Social Research

James K. Galbraith
University of Texas—Austin
Lyndon B. Johnson School of Public Affairs

PRENTICE HALL, ENGLEWOOD CLIFFS, NJ 07632

Library of Congress Cataloging-in-Publication Data

Heilbroner, Robert L.
Understanding macroeconomics / Robert L. Heilbroner, James K. Galbraith. -
- 9th [ed.]
p. cm.
Includes index.
ISBN 0-13-933359-2
1. Macroeconomics. I. Galbraith, James K. II. Title.
HB172.5.H44 1990
339--dc20 89-15926
CIP

Editorial/production supervision: Susan Fisher and Anne Pietropinto
Interior design: Natasha Sylvester, Maureen Eide and Janet Schmid
Cover design: Bruce Kenselaar
Manufacturing buyer: Laura Crossland and Peter Havens

Printed in the United States of America

10 9 8 7 6 5 4 3 2 1

ISBN 0-13-933359-2

Prentice-Hall International (UK) Limited, *London*
Prentice-Hall of Australia Pty. Limited, *Sydney*
Prentice-Hall Canada Inc., *Toronto*
Prentice-Hall Hispanoamericana, S.A., *Mexico*
Prentice-Hall of India Private Limited, *New Delhi*
Prentice-Hall of Japan, Inc., *Tokyo*
Simon & Schuster Asia Pte. Ltd., *Singapore*
Editora Prentice-Hall do Brasil, Ltda., *Rio de Janeiro*

Contents

Section Four *The Macro Challenges*

PART IV *THE REST OF THE WORLD*

Preface

Here is the revised ninth edition of *Understanding Macroeconomics.* What is new and different about it? As always, the economic world has a way of changing faster than anyone expected. When the last edition went to press, people were mainly worried about inflation. As this one goes to the printer, inflation is less on people's minds than recession. In the last edition, the environment loomed very large. It is still there, but it is less ominous—perhaps because a new issue has taken its place, the world economy pressing in on us with its vast international capital reservoirs and its battering rams of international competition. Those changes in emphasis and concern are in themselves reason enough for a new edition, with new chapters.

Of course, the main framework of the book is still in place. We have altered the pace, speeding up the presentation of issues, and giving a lot more space to the still unresolved controversies of supply-side economics and monetarism and not-yet-dead "old fashioned" Keynesian economics. As before, we have tried hard to do justice to all sides, although we sometimes make clear our impatience with the ways things have gone. But we are careful to present our views as that, not as gospel.

To the best of our knowledge, this is the most interesting edition yet. At any rate, we have deeply enjoyed working on it.

About the Authors

Photo by Waring Abbott

Robert L. Heilbroner began his studies in economics at Harvard University, from which he graduated, summa cum laude, in 1940; and went on to complete his graduate work at the New School for Social Research in New York City. While still a graduate student, he published his first book, *The Worldly Philosophers,* which quickly became a standard introduction to economics in hundreds of colleges. Later books, including *The Making of Economic Society* and *An Inquiry into the Human Prospect,* together with a wide variety of articles in both scholarly and popular journals, won for him a wide audience as both economic historian and social philosopher. Dr. Heilbroner has been the recipient of numerous awards and honors, including election as vice president of the American Economic Association. He teaches at his graduate alma mater as Normal Thomas Professor, specializing in the history of economic thought. He is married and lives in New York City.

Photo by Maria de la Luz Martinez

James K. Galbraith is Associate Professor at the Lyndon B. Johnson School of Public Affairs, University of Texas at Austin. Before becoming a Texan, he served on the staff of the U.S. Congress, including as executive director of the Joint Economic Committee, where he was responsible for congressional oversight of monetary policy and of the Reagan economic program. He has been a Visiting Scholar at the Brookings Institution and a Marshall Scholar at King's College, University of Cambridge. He holds an A.B. from Harvard College and a Ph.D. in economics from Yale University. He is married to Lucy Ferguson Galbraith, a microeconomist. They have a son, Douglas, and daughter, Margaret, who shares her birthday (June 5) with Adam Smith and John Maynard Keynes. A prolific writer, Dr. Galbraith's most recent book is *Balancing Acts: Technology, Finance and the American Future.*

PART I

THE ECONOMIC BACKGROUND

CHAPTER 1

What This Book Is All About

A LOOK AHEAD

This is the chapter in which to get your bearings. As you read, keep in mind these objectives:

1. To get a feel for what is to come.
2. To learn how the book is organized.
3. Most important of all, to pick up a few study hints—you really want to pay attention to these.

THE ECONOMIC MYSTIQUE

Like most students who begin a first course in economics, you probably realize that economics is terribly important. You also probably have the uneasy feeling that it is terribly difficult. It may reassure you to learn that you are not alone in this frame of mind. Every year national pollsters report that economic problems, such as inflation or unemployment or taxes, rank high among the public's worries. But every year the pollsters also discover that the economics and business pages of newspapers and magazines are those that are *least* read. It seems that we all worry about economic matters, but throw up our hands at the idea of trying to understand what they are all about.

Why does economics have this curious mystique? Three reasons suggest themselves.

1. Mystery of Money

The first is that economics is intrinsically involved with money, and money is, well, perplexing. Why is a piece of paper worth anything at all? What do banks do with the money we put into them? Why isn't there enough money to go around at some times, "too much" money at others—to repeat the baffling opinions we hear?

Money is surely one reason for the economic mystique. But the problem with money is not just its inherent complexity. It is that we all use money, talk about money, worry about money, without ever having been educated about it. One purpose of learning economics is to repair that serious omission in our knowledge.

2. Language of Economics

A second reason is that economics speaks in a tongue we don't quite understand. "Prices are up because of rising demand," says the TV commentator, and we nod our heads. But exactly what is "demand"? What makes it "rise"? And those other words that the commentators use with such assurance—gross national product, consumption, investment—what do they really mean? Because we do not "speak" economics, we wonder whether we are being bamboozled; and when we ourselves use the words of economics, we often know that we are partly bluffing.

Therefore another purpose of this book is to introduce you to the language of economics. This language, like that of all disciplines, has a fair number of specialized terms, but it is certainly no more difficult to speak or to understand than the language of any of a dozen familiar subjects. By the end of the course, you should speak it pretty fluently.

3. The "Difficulty" of Economics

Last, there is the matter of the mystique itself, the reputation for difficulty that economics has acquired. It may come as a surprise to learn that in the 1830s economics was reputed to be a rather easy subject, especially suited to the education of proper young ladies. Later—indeed, up to the Great Crash of 1929—economics was still widely regarded as little more than common sense, instantly comprehensible by all right-thinking persons, especially if they thought along Solid Business Principles.

The aura of mystery that clings to economics today is mainly a product of the past generation or so, when economics itself came into national prominence. The aura is undoubtedly mixed up with the increased use of government powers in the economy, especially the use of spending and taxing to affect the level of national well-being. Here *is* something to be learned that is different from Solid Business Principles. But as you will discover, it is still nothing but logical thought, although applied from a national perspective, rather than from that of an individual enterprise.

Thus the overriding aim of our book is to demystify economics. Of course this does not mean that we can give you answers to all the problems of the economy. We don't know them. But we hope that when you finish the book, you will never again throw up your hands at the idea of *thinking* about economic problems. Once and for all, that should have lost its terror.

ORGANIZING THE SUBJECT

Economics is a very large subject with many aspects—economic history, economic statistics, economic theory, economic policy, and still others. We cannot study all these aspects in an introductory text, but it will help you grasp the larger subject of economics if we outline very generally what lies ahead.

We have organized our book into five major *parts,* each one of which has groups of related chapters or *sections.* The five major parts are these:

1. Economic history and background
2. Economic science
3. The study of the macro system of economic growth
4. The market mechanism, or microeconomics
5. International economics

Different instructors will have different inclinations about what parts to stress, and we have written the text to allow as much flexibility as possible in planning a coherent course. Even if there is no time to study all the parts of the text, you ought to glance at them to round out your understanding of what the dimensions of the subject embrace.

THE FIRST PART: ECONOMIC BACKGROUND

Many students would like to jump right into the midst of our current economic problems, and some instructors like to teach their courses that way. In fact, our book is organized so that a direct approach to major issues is possible by starting in macroeconomics or microeconomics.

But ideally we ought to acquire some perspective on our subject before getting embroiled in how things work. We ought, for example, to have a good working idea of economic history—of how our economy got where it is. We should know at least the rudiments of what some great economists of the past have said about how the economic system works. And we should be familiar with the economy in the same sense that we are familiar with the size and shape of the United States and where its great rivers and mountain ranges are.

That is what Part One is about. Chapter 2 gives you a jet-speed voyage through economic history. Chapter 3 takes you rapidly down the gallery of the world's great economists—the "worldly philosophers." Then, in three successive chapters, we fly you over the economic continent and then over the economic planet. *Try to read these chapters as background, even if your instructor doesn't assign them as classwork.*

NEXT: FROM FACT TO THEORY

In Part Two we turn to a very different subject—the core elements of economic "science." We put the word in quotes because, as you will discover, our subject both is and is not a science like the natural sciences. It has aspects that very much resemble sciences like physics, and aspects that are much more akin to studies like government or morality.

The science-like aspect has to do with the fact that the economic world, for all its variety and complexity, can often be understood in a highly generalized, abstract way. As a result, economists do not consider their task to be only that of describing phenomena, such as we have done in Part One. They also seek to find similar characteristics hidden within seemingly different problems or institutions, much as a doctor first takes a patient's life history and then examines him or her for signs of a general condition called a "disease."

In Chapter 7 we tell you something about the basis on which this capacity for generalization and abstraction rests. It is our introduction to the idea of *economic theory.* Then in Chapter 8 we go on to apply theory to the single most widely used generalization about economic life—supply and demand. Thereafter, to balance the picture, we look at another side of economics in a chapter whose subject matter you must surely have wondered about: "Why Economists Disagree." Finally, in Chapter 10 we add a kind of appendix to Part Two in a "Kit of Tools." Here is a brief introduction to the basic technical elements you will have to know, from how to read a chart to how to say some easy but powerful things in mathematical sentences. Many students will not need this chapter at all; others may find it a lifesaver.

PART THREE: THE MACRO ECONOMY

The subject we cover in the next 14 chapters is macroeconomics—the study of how the economy grows (and sometimes fails to grow), and of how and why it develops inflationary tendencies or unemployment. Note that there are very important issues which are not included in the macro point of view—for example, pollution and the problem of riches and poverty. These problems are best examined from the micro perspective that we will take up in the second major portion of the text.

Macro in Four Sections

It will help us organize the macro problem if we tackle it in four separate sections. In the first of these, covering Chapters 11 through 14, we learn about gross national product and the process of saving and investing that underlies growth. The second section, from Chapter 15 through Chapter 18, takes up the sectors of the economy in action, so that we become familiar with the workings of the household or consumption sector, the business or investment sector, and the government or public sector. At the end of this part we should understand how the level of GNP is determined.

The next section, comprising Chapters 19 through 22, fleshes out the macro picture by introducing us to the question of money—how it is "created," how its supply is regulated, how it affects the activity of the sectors and therefore the level of GNP itself.

Last but not least, in Chapters 23 and 24 we turn to the central challenges of macroeconomics—inflation and economic growth. We have put these chapters into a special section of their own. There is a reason for this. Up to this point we have mainly been explaining things about which there is a great deal of agreement. But when it comes to the big macroeconomic issues, disagreements are more readily noted than agreement. We have tried to point out the basis for these disagreements, as well as where our own judgment inclines us. But the unsettled nature of these questions seemed to us best emphasized by setting them apart.

THE REST OF THE WORLD: PART FOUR

Traditionally, there has been a terrible parochialism to American economics. It has tended to assume that learning about domestic issues, macro and micro, was really all a student—especially a beginning student—had to do. The rest of the world was relegated to the back pages of texts, and to the second and third years of economic studies.

As our text illustrates, this indifference to international economic problems is no longer the rule. Already in Chapter 6 we have looked into the ways in which the American economy is entangled with the economics of other nations, and an international theme has surfaced again and again in our studies of both macro- and microeconomics.

Nevertheless, there are aspects and elements of international economics that do have to be postponed until a student has some working grasp of the fundamentals. These are the matters we take up in this part, where the mysteries of the exchange rate and of international competition are examined.

HOW SHOULD YOU STUDY ECONOMICS?

Vocabulary

We have already stressed the importance of acquiring a new economic vocabulary. **To become economists, you will have to learn several dozen words and phrases that have meanings somewhat different from those of everyday usage: *capital, investment, demand,* for example.** You will have to master another dozen or so phrases that come awkwardly to the tongue (and sometimes not at all to the mind): *marginal propensity to consume* is a good example.

In economics, as in French, some people acquire new words and phrases easily, some do not; and in economics, as in French, until you can say things correctly, you are apt to say them very wrongly. So when the text says *gross private domestic investment* those are the words to be learned, not just any combination of three of them because they seem to mean the same thing. Fortunately, the necessary economic vocabulary has far fewer words than French has, and the long and awkward phrases seem shorter and easier after you've said them a few times.

Diagrams

Associated with learning the vocabulary of economics is learning how to draw a few diagrams. Diagrams are an immensely powerful way of presenting many economic ideas. Far from complicating things, they simplify them enormously. A supply and demand diagram makes things immediately clear in a way that a dozen pages could not.

So you must learn to draw a few diagrams. There is a great temptation to do so hastily, without thinking about the problem that the diagram is trying to make clear. A little care in labeling your axes (how else can anyone know what the diagram is about?) or in making lines tangent where they are supposed to touch, or cross where they are supposed to intersect, will not only make the difference between a poor grade and a better one, but will demonstrate that you truly understand the matter being illustrated.

You will also note that throughout the book, with each figure and most tables, a sentence or a paragraph highlights the point being made. This should help you in reviewing the material.

Key Ideas

Studying a vast subject requires organization. This means putting first things first and keeping details and secondary material in the background.

We've tried to simplify the task of learning by putting a highly abbreviated and goal-oriented "A Look Ahead" and "Looking Back" at the beginning and at the end of each chapter. These sections do not necessarily embrace all the vocabulary or ideas in each chapter; instead, they try to give you objectives to bear in mind before starting, and summaries to collect your thoughts when you're done.

At the end of each chapter, first read the general review. Then look only at Key Concepts to see if you can reproduce that review. Last, a glance at Economic Vocabulary will serve as a final test. Page numbers follow each word for easy reference.

Questions and Extra Words

Next, take time to answer all the questions at the ends of chapters. We have tried to make them few and central. If your instructor assigns the Student Guide that accompanies this text, do those problems too. There is no substitute for working out an example or for jotting down three reasons for this, four reasons for that. Learning is a process about which we know very little, but we do know that the physical and intellectual act of writing (or mumbling to yourself) is much more effective than merely thinking. Practice, as they say, makes perfect. You might reflect on the story of the sailor on a sinking ship. When asked if he knew how to swim, he answered, "Well, I understand the theory of it . . ."

Economics has to be learned by arguing about it. Therefore after many chapters you will find a few additional pages—sometimes to add to your historical, statistical, or analytic knowledge, more often to open for your consideration problems of public policy that are related to the issues we have studied. The policy issues are often controversial. We hope you will worry about them—not just read them. They are there to open debate, not close it.

Analysis and Abstraction

The idea of arguing brings us to our last word of counsel. Economics, as we have been at pains to say, is really not a hard language to learn. The key words and concepts are not too many or too demanding; the diagrams are no more difficult than those of elementary geometry. It is economic *thinking* that is hard, in a way that may have something to do with the aura of mystery we are out to dispel.

The hardness is not the sheer mental ability that is required. The reason lies, rather, in **a special attribute of economic thought: *its abstract, analytic character.*** Abstractness does not imply indifference to the problems of the real world. Economics is about things as real as being without work. Nevertheless, as economists we do not study unemployment to learn firsthand about the miseries and sufferings that joblessness inflicts. We study unemployment to understand and analyze the causes of this malfunction of the economic system. Similarly, we do not study monopoly to fulminate against the profiteering of greedy capitalists, or labor unions to deplore the abuse of power by labor leaders, or government spending to declaim against politicians. We study these matters to shed light on their mechanisms, their reasons for being, their consequences.

There is nothing unusual in this abstract, analytic approach. All disciplines necessarily abstract from the immediate realities of their subject matters so that they may make broader generalizations or develop theories. What makes abstraction so difficult in economics is that the problems of the discipline are things that affect us deeply in our lives. It is difficult, even unnatural, to suppress our feelings of approval or anger when we study the operations of the economic system and the main actors in it. The necessary act of analysis thus becomes mixed up with feelings of economic concern or even partisanship. **Yet, unless we make an effort to think analytically and abstractly in a detached way, we can be no more than slaves to our unexamined emotions.** Someone who *knows* that corporations or labor unions or governments are "good" or "bad" does not have to study economics, for the subject has nothing to teach such a person.

You must therefore make an effort to put aside your natural partisanship and prejudice while you study the problems of economics from its abstract, analytic, detached perspective. After you are done, your feelings will assuredly come back to you. No one has ever lost a sense of social outrage or social justice by taking a course in economics. But many students have changed or modified their preconceived judgments in one way or another. There is no escape, after all, from living in the world as economic citizens. But there is the option of living in it as intelligent and effective economic citizens. That is the prize we hope you carry away from this course.

CHAPTER 2

The Evolution of Capitalism

A LOOK AHEAD

There is one central idea this chapter will present—a very simple but exceedingly important idea. It is that capitalism—our Western economic society—represents a dramatic change in the way that humankind has grappled with its economic problems. In this chapter we will trace three main aspects of this change:

1 The emergence of a market system.
2 The development of a powerful industrial technology.
3 The assertion of political limits on the economic machinery.

The purpose of this chapter is not only to review these critical elements of economic history, but also to make you think about the subject of economics itself in a historical, evolutionary way.

WHERE DID CAPITALISM COME FROM?

The economic system we are going to study in this book is called **capitalism,** or sometimes the *free enterprise system.* In a way, we all know about capitalism because it surrounds us. It is the world we live in. But the question we are going to start with is far removed from our daily experience: Where did capitalism come from? How did the free enterprise system come to be?

People sometimes talk about capitalism as if it were as old as the hills, as ancient as the Bible. Yet this is clearly not the case. Nobody ever called the Egyptian pharaohs "capitalists." The Greeks about whom Homer wrote were not a business society, even though there were merchants and traders in Greece; neither was imperial Rome a capitalist system. Medieval Europe was certainly not capitalist. Nor would anyone use the word *capitalist* to describe the brilliant civilizations of India and China, about which Marco Polo wrote, or the great empires of ancient Africa or the Islamic economies of which we catch glimpses in *The Arabian Nights.*

We will make explicit why these were not capitalist economies in a moment. But we must begin by realizing that capitalism is a modern economic system—and furthermore, a geographically limited one. **Most of the people in the world's history never had any direct contact with it. Even today, less than half of the world's population lives in a system that we would call capitalist—though events could change that picture over the next few decades.**

The Elements of Capitalism

What is capitalism? The fact that the system appears in history only after many thousands of years suggests that we would do well to search for its identifying characteristics in historic changes rather than in specific institutions that exist today. Here are three of the changes that help us recognize capitalism as a unique development in the organization of human affairs.

1. Capitalism Becomes Visible When Economic Activity Becomes Detached from the Activity of the State. Economic activity refers to all the tasks carried on in society to produce and distribute wealth. Before capitalism, those activities were bound up with the exercise of rulership itself. Precapitalist societies were large, imperial kingdoms in some cases and small domains ruled by local lords in others. Yet in all these societies, large or small, production and distribution were carried on under the supervision of the ruler. The peasant working in the field and the artisan in his workshop were not working for their own account. They were directly or indirectly carrying out orders from overlords, for whose power and glory their labors would be used. Such societies have been described as "tributary" systems—a telling phrase that emphasizes the subordination of economic activity to the benefit of political elites.

Merchants, who *did* carry on economic activity for their own account, also existed in these societies. But they were at the fringes of society, not at its center. The provision of the essentials of state power and continuity—basic foodstuffs, for example, or weapons—was not entrusted to the pull and tug of mercantile activity.

So a decisive change that marks the emergence of capitalism as a new mode of social organization was the spread of market activity into every area of economic life.

Shortly we shall see how this took place. But here we need to note an important consequence of that spread. As buying and selling expanded, the authority of the state shrank. Within the state a new entity appeared—an *economy* whose function was to carry on the production and distribution of wealth. The economy thus appears as a kind of state within a state, a realm of society containing the vital activities formerly carried on as part of the overall exercise of authority from above. **Thus capitalism brings into being a new sphere of private economic activity—activity conducted for the self-interest of its actors.**

This new private sphere is the root of one of the most important political accomplishments of capitalism, the establishment of economic freedom, a theme to which we will often revert. But it is crucial not to think of capitalism as consisting only of private economic activity. The state persists under capitalism, not merely to carry on its traditional functions of waging war and maintaining peace and internal order, but also to provide essential services to the private sphere of activity—roads and ports, public works needed for health and safety, courts and coinage, to name only a few. Thus the public sphere shrinks as capitalism emerges, but it does not disappear. The state is indispensable for the operation of a market economy, in ways we will talk about many times in the pages to follow.

It is also clear, however, that there is a deep tension between the economic and political activities of a capitalist state. This tension is not just a passing "political" issue, but comes from the very nature of the system, which creates two realms of authority where formerly there was only one.

2. Capitalism Is Marked by Its Dynamic Search for the Accumulation of Material Wealth. The next historic change follows from the first. It is the extraordinary dynamism developed by capitalism, a dynamism that takes the form of an unprecedented piling up of wealth in a new form—not for consumption and display, but as capital.

Here a glance backward serves to illustrate the point. Precapitalist societies were certainly capable of accumulating staggering displays of wealth. No single creation of capitalism is likely to endure as long as the pyramids of Egypt, the Great Wall of China, the monuments of the Incas, or the stupendous cathedrals of medieval Europe.

Yet when we look back over the empires that built these monuments, what strikes us is how changeless was the tenor of most people's daily lives. The boundaries of empires might expand or contract, great works might take shape over a ruler's lifetime, but the level of mass existence varied little for generations. The diet, the housing, the clothing and material possessions of the Egyptian peasants at the time of Napoleon's invasion of Egypt differed little from those of the time of Cheops, builder of pyramids. The level of material life of the French craftspeople who labored on the cathedral of Chartres was not substantially different from that of their ancestors who helped the Roman legions construct the aqueducts through Gaul.

It is this basically static quality of life that capitalism removes. Economic historian W.W. Rostow has estimated that between the age of the American

Revolution and our own times, the volume of manufactured goods increased by *seventeen hundred times.** This is a display of expansion and accumulation beside which the achievements of prior civilizations pale into insignificance. Nothing resembling such a force for the creation of material wealth had ever existed before.

What was the source of this accumulative thrust? Essentially it was the very change we have just noted—namely, the emergence of a realm of economic life separated from the state itself. In the previous "tributary" mode of organizing economic life, the surplus of society's production was devoted to the construction of monuments to glorify its rulers or affirm its religious faith, or was used for arms to protect the kingdom or for the luxury goods through which imperial majesty displayed itself to the world.

For the new mercantile groups economic activity had a different aim—not to display wealth, but to accumulate it as a route to power and prestige. This required that wealth take the form of capital. What is capital? It is wealth that can be used to create still more wealth. The humblest commodities can be capital as well as the most dazzling jewels, as long as they are sold to gain still more wealth. **This use of wealth as capital rather than as a means of display or of luxury consumption was the vital difference brought about by the detachment of the economic sphere of life from the state.**

The consequences of the drive for the accumulation of capital are immense—indeed, capitalism derives its name from a recognition of the central importance of this propulsive force. One of these consequences is instability: The system is bursting with energy when the accumulation of wealth goes smoothly, wracked with economic and social troubles when it does not. A major theme of economics is to investigate this sequence of fast and slow accumulation—of growth and stagnation, boom and bust, prosperity and depression—that capitalism brings.

But another consequence deserves special attention at this initial stage of our inquiry: It is the encouragement given by capitalism to the development of technology as a principal means from which the expansive tendency of the system gains its momentum and through which it exerts its impact on daily life. At the end of this chapter we will look more closely into technology and its special significance for capitalism.

3. Capitalism Develops a New Mechanism for Its Internal Guidance. The mechanism was the market system—not just individual markets, but a network of interconnected markets that would guide the production and distribution of economic activity as a whole. We will spend much of this book learning how such a market system serves as a guidance mechanism for capitalism. Here we want once again to see the rise of such a system in a manner that helps us identify, and therefore understand, the larger historic change itself.

How did the market system come into being? The answer is that a vast revolution undermined an older world of tradition and command, and brought into existence a world in which not only goods, but also the services of labor, land, and capital were offered for sale. We have a name for the services of labor, land, and capital that are hired or fired in a market society. They are called the **factors of production,** and a great deal of economics is about how the market combines their

*W. W. Rostow, *The World Economy* (Austin, TX: University of Texas Press, 1978), p. 48.

essential contributions to production. But just because they *are* essential, a question must be answered. How were the factors of production put to use prior to the market system? The answer tells us a great deal.

There were no factors of production before capitalism. Of course, human labor, nature's gift of land and natural resources, and the artifacts of society have always existed. But labor, land, and capital were not commodities for sale. Labor was part of the social duties of a slave or a serf, a peasant bound to his lord and master, who was not paid "wages" for doing his work. Indeed, the serf paid fees to his lord for the use of the lord's equipment, and he never expected to be remunerated when he turned over a portion of his crop as the lord's due. Land was regarded as the basis for military power or civil administration, just as a state is regarded today—not as real estate to be bought and sold. And capital was thought of as "treasure" or as the necessary equipment of an artisan, not as an abstract sum of wealth with a market value. The idea of liquid, fluid capital would have been as strange in medieval life as we would find it strange to think of stocks and bonds as heirlooms never to be sold.

The Economic Revolution

How did wageless labor, unrentable land, and private treasures become "factors of production"; that is, homogeneous commodities to be bought and sold like so many yards of cloth or bushels of wheat? Beginning roughly in the sixteenth century—although with roots that can be traced much further back—a process of change, sometimes gradual, sometimes violent, broke the bonds and customs of the medieval world of Europe and ushered in the market society we know.

We can only touch on that long, tortuous, and sometimes bloody revolution here. In England the process bore with particular severity on the peasants, who were expelled from the common grazing lands, which were then "enclosed" to make private pasturage for the lord's sheep, whose wool had become a profitable commodity. As late as 1820, the Duchess of Sutherland evicted 15,000 tenants from 794,000 acres, replacing them with 131,000 sheep. The tenants, deprived of their traditional access to the fields, drifted into the towns, where they were forced, for the first time, to sell their services as a factor of production: *labor.*

In France the creation of factors of production bore painfully on the traditional landowners, less so on the peasants. When prices began to rise in sixteenth-century Europe as gold from the New World flowed in, feudal lords found themselves in a terrible squeeze. While the rents and dues they received from their serfs were fixed and unchangeable, the prices of merchandise they needed to buy were not fixed. Although more and more of the serfs' obligations were converted from "kind" to cash, and from physical duties to money dues, prices kept rising so fast that the feudal lords found it impossible to meet their bills.

Hence we begin to find a new economic individual, the *impoverished aristocrat.* In the year 1530, in the Gévaudan region of France, the richest manorial lord had an income of 5,000 livres; but in towns some merchants had incomes of 65,000 livres. Thus the balance of power turned against the landed aristocracy, reducing many to shabby gentility. The upstart merchants lost no time in acquiring lands that they soon came to regard not as ancestral estates, but as potential capital.

This brief glance at economic history brings home an important point. **The factors of production, without which a market society could not exist, are not eternal attributes of a natural order. They are the creations of a process of historic change, a change that divorced labor from social life, that created real estate out of ancestral land, and that made treasure into capital. Capitalism is the outcome of a revolutionary change—a change in laws, attitudes, and social relationships as deep and far-reaching as any in history.***

Freedom and Necessity

The revolutionary aspect of capitalism lies in the fact that an older, feudal way of life had to be dismantled before the market system could come into being. This brings us to think again about the economic freedom that accompanies the rise of a private sector of economic life, detached from the state. For we can now see that economic freedom did not arise just because men and women directly sought to shake off the bonds of custom and command. It was also thrust upon them, often as a very painful and unwelcome change.

For feudalism, with all its cruelties and injustices, did provide a modicum of economic security. However mean a serf's life, he could not be arbitrarily thrown off the lord's land, and in bad times he was guaranteed a small dole from his lord's granary. However exploited a medieval journeyman, at least he knew that he could not be summarily thrown out of work under the rules of his master's guild. And however squeezed a lord, he too knew that his rents and dues were secured by law and custom and would be coming in, weather permitting.

The eruption of the market system destroyed all of that. The creation of factors of production meant the end of assured livelihoods. If a landless laborer could not find work, his unemployment was not the responsibility of his lord, for he no longer *had* a lord. Nor was it the lookout of his former employer, who had no obligation to pay anyone who was no longer an employee. If a worker in the market system was fired, he or she could not complain to the guild, because there *was* no guild. For that matter, neither could an employer protest to the guild about some intruder who was "stealing" trade. And if a landlord's rents declined in a bad year, that was no one's worry but his own; there were no more "customary" rents to rely on.

Economic freedom therefore meant that each person was thrown into the marketplace to sink or swim. This freedom could be a precious achievement for individuals who had formerly been deprived of the right to enter into legal contracts. For many, it meant the chance to rise out of a station in life from which, in earlier times, there was no exit. But economic freedom had another equally important aspect. This was the necessity to stay afloat by one's own efforts in rough waters where all were struggling to survive, and where no one much cared when a

*One of the many fascinating questions that surround the origins of capitalism is why it arose only in Europe, and never in any other part of the world. The probable explanation is that the collapse of the Roman Empire left many towns without an allegiance to anyone. In time, these towns, which were naturally centers of trading and artisan work, grew powerful and managed to bargain for privileges with kings and lords. Capitalism thus grew up in the chinks and crevices of the medieval system. A similar opportunity and stimulus did not present itself elsewhere. Is it possible that capitalism is now appearing in the Soviet Union, Eastern Europe, and China? We will turn to this momentous question at the end of our book.

laborer, a landowner, or a capitalist disappeared from view.

The market system was thus the cause of unrest, insecurity, and individual suffering, just as it was also the source of progress, opportunity, and fulfillment. In this contest between the costs and benefits of economic freedom lies a theme that is still a crucial issue for capitalism.

THE UNLEASHING OF TECHNOLOGY

As we have already noted, the creation of a market society paved the way for a change of profound significance. This was the incorporation of science and technology into the very midst of daily life.

Precapitalist Technology

Technology is not, of course, a modern phenomenon. The arrangement of the gigantic stones that form prehistoric Stonehenge, the precision and delicacy of the monumental Egyptian pyramids, the Incan stone walls fitted so exactly that a knife blade cannot be put between adjoining blocks, the Chinese Great Wall, and the Mayan observatories attest to mankind's long possession of the ability to transport and hoist staggering weights, to cut and shape hard surfaces, and to calculate complex problems. Indeed, many of these works would challenge our present-day engineering capabilities.

Nonetheless, although precapitalist technology reached great heights, it had a very restricted base. The basic tools of agriculture and artisan crafts remained little changed over millennia. So "simple" an invention as a horse collar shaped to prevent a straining animal from pressing against its windpipe did not appear during all the glories of Greece and triumphs of Rome. Not until the Middle Ages was there a switch from the ox to the draft horse as a ploughing animal (a change that improved efficiency by an estimated 30 percent), or was the traditional two-field system of crop rotation improved by adopting a three-field system (see box).

Thus precapitalist technology was lavished on the needs of rulers, priests, and warriors; its potential application to the everyday work of ordinary people was virtually ignored.

THE DIFFERENCE TECHNOLOGY MAKES: THREE FIELDS VS. TWO

Until the Middle Ages, the prevailing system of cultivation was to plant half of a lord's arable land in a winter crop, leaving the other half fallow. The second year, the two fields simply changed functions.

Under the three-field plan, the arable land was divided into thirds. One section was planted with a winter crop, one section with a summer crop, and one was left fallow. The second year, the first section was put into summer crops, the second left fallow, and the third put into winter grains. In the third year, the first field was left fallow, the second used for winter crops, the third for spring planting.

Therefore, under the three-field system only one-third, not one-half, of the arable land was fallow in any year. Suppose that the field as a whole yielded 600 bushels of output. Under the two-field system, it would give an annual crop of 300 bushels. Under the three-field system, the annual crop would be two-thirds of the area, or 400 bushels—an increase of one-third. Further, in those days it was customary to plough fallow land twice and cultivated land only once. By cutting down the ratio of fallow to cultivated land, plowing time was greatly reduced, and peasant productivity even more significantly improved. For more on this and other fascinating advances in precapitalist technology, see Lynn White, *Medieval Technology and Social Change* (Oxford: Clarendon Press, 1962).

Why Technology Slumbered

There were, of course, good reasons why the technology of daily life was ignored. The primary effect of technological change in daily activity is to increase output, to enhance the productivity of the working person. But in a society still regulated by tradition and command, where production was mainly carried on by serfs and slaves and custom-bound artisans, there was little incentive to look for increases in output. The bulk of any increase in agricultural yields would only go to the lord, the king, or the church, not to the serf or the slave who produced them. Indeed, what would happen to the serfs if means were found to work the lands with fewer of them?

So, too, any artisan who altered the techniques of his trade would be expected, as a matter of course, to share these advances with his brethren. And how could his brethren, accustomed over the years to disposing of a certain quantity of pots or pans or cloth in the village market, expect to find buyers for more output? Would not the extra production—and the artisans responsible for it—simply go begging?

Thus productive technology in precapitalist societies slumbered because there was no incentive to search for change. Indeed, because technological change could only introduce an unsettling element into the world, powerful social forces were ranged against it. A society whose whole way of life rested on the reproduction of established patterns of existence could not even imagine a world where the technology of production was constantly in flux and where limits were no longer recognized in any endeavor.

Economic Life in the Middle Ages, Illustrated in the Breviarium Grimani
(The Bettmann Archive, Inc.)

The Incentive of Capitalism

These inhibiting forces were ruthlessly swept away by the emerging markets for labor, land, and capital. Serfs were uprooted to become workers forced to sell their labor power for wages; landlords were rudely shouldered aside by money-minded parvenus; guild masters and artisans watched commercial enterprises take away their accustomed livelihood; a new sense of necessity, of urgency, altered economic life. What had been a more or less unchanging routine of life became increasingly a scramble for existence.

The growing importance of the market, where a producer had to win a place for himself every day, radically altered the place of technology, especially in the small workshops and miniscule factories that were the staging areas of the capitalist revolution. Here the economic free-for-all forced people to look for toeholds in the struggle for a livelihood. And one toehold available to any aspiring capitalist with an inquiring mind and a knowledge of the actual processes of production was technology itself—some invention or improvement that would lower costs or change a product to give it an edge on its competitors.

This is where the appearance of wealth as *capital* made an enormous difference. It brought into being a wholly new personage in economic history—the *industrial capitalist* who made his wealth in pursuits that would never have led to riches in another age.*

For example, there was John Wilkinson, son of an iron producer who became a driving force for technical change in his trade. Wilkinson insisted that everything be built of iron—pipes and bridges, bellows and cylinders (one of which powered the newfangled steam engine of James Watt). He even constructed a much derided iron ship—later much admired. There was Richard Arkwright, barber by trade, who made his fortune by inventing (or perhaps by stealing) the first effective spinning machine, becoming in time a great mill owner. There were Peter Onions, an obscure foreman who originated the puddling process for making wrought iron; Benjamin Huntsman, a clockmaker who improved the method of making steel; and a score more. "A wave of gadgets swept over England," in the copybook phrase of an English schoolboy. A few of the "gadgeteers," like Sir Jethro Tull, a pioneer in the technology of agriculture, were great gentlemen, but most of the technological leaders in industry were men of humble origin.

*This is not a text in economic history, and therefore we must pass too quickly over a change of great importance in the evolution of the system. It is the leap from the earliest form of *merchant capitalism* into *industrial capitalism,* the form of the system on which we will henceforth concentrate our attention.

The crucial change is the rise of industrial activity, with its key institution of labor working for wages in factories. As a consequence of that new institution, the focus of profit-seeking shifted from mercantile trading to the production process itself. That is, the main source of profits was no longer sought in profitable exchange but in profitable production, brought about by driving and disciplining labor and developing its productivity through machinery.

That change did not occur everywhere. For instance, the shift from mercantile to industrial capitalism was not made in early-eighteenth-century Holland, so that the Dutch—formidable rivals of the English in the seventeenth century—were bypassed when England became an industrial society and Holland remained a trading one. Anyone interested in this chapter of the history of capitalism should look into Jan de Vries' marvellously interesting book, *The Economy of Europe in an Age of Crisis: 1600–1750* (New York: Cambridge University Press, 1976).

The Industrial Revolutions

The new dynamism revealed itself in a series of technological "revolutions" —periods in which the basic ways of making things suddenly underwent startling changes, and in which new kinds of goods and services entered, and radically changed, daily life.

The first of these periods is often called *the* Industrial Revolution, although actually it was only the initial rush of a long, multiphase process. Beginning in the late eighteenth century and continuing for over 25 years, the first industrial revolution mechanized spinning and weaving, enormously improved and expanded iron production, brought the all-important gift of power in the form of the steam engine, and introduced a crucial change in the application of technology to production—the large, controlled workplace we call the factory.

The second industrial revolution followed in the mid-nineteenth century, bringing railroads and steamships, cheap steel, agricultural machinery, and the first mass-produced chemicals. Then in the early years of the twentieth century, a third burst came with the development of the automobile, electrical power, and consumer durable goods; and in our own day we are witnessing a fourth—the revolution of computers, air transportation, medical science, perhaps genetic engineering.

The Effects of Technology

Many profound changes have followed in the wake of capitalism—no other socioeconomic upheaval has so fundamentally altered life in its every aspect. But of the changes wrought, none was more dramatic than the industrial revolutions. The new technology literally remade life, and we should take a few moments to clarify some of the ways in which it did so.

1. Output Increased Enormously, Raising Living Standards. First a few figures. Between 1701 and 1802, as the technology of spinning and weaving was gradually perfected, the use of cotton in England expanded by 6,000 percent. Between 1788 and 1839, when the process of iron manufacture passed through its first technological upheaval, the output of pig iron jumped from 68,000 to 1,347,000 tons. In France, in the 30 years after 1815, iron output quintupled, coal output grew sevenfold, and transportation tonnage mounted ten times.

But these figures do not convey a sense of the effect of technology on daily life. *Things* became more common—and more commonplace. As late as the seventeenth century, what we would consider the most ordinary possessions were scarce. A peasant counted his worldly wealth in terms of a few utensils, a table, perhaps one complete change of clothes. Shakespeare left Anne Hathaway his "second best bed." Iron nails were so scarce that pioneers in America burned down their cottages to retrieve them. In the wilder parts of Scotland in Adam Smith's time, nails even served as money.

Technology brought a widening and deepening and ever faster flowing river of things. Shoes, coats, paper, window glass, chairs, buckles—objects of solicitous respect in precapitalist times for all but the privileged few—became everyday articles. **Gradually, capitalism gave rise to what we call a "rising standard of living"—a steady, regular, systematic increase in the number, variety, and quality of material goods enjoyed by the great bulk of society. No such process had ever occurred before.**

2. The Scale of Economic Organization Grew Vastly Larger. A second change wrought by technology was a striking increase in the size of society's productive apparatus.

The increase began with the enlargement of the equipment used in production—an enlargement that stemmed mostly from advances in the technology of iron and later steel. The typical furnace used in extracting iron ore increased from 10 feet in height in the 1770s to over 100 feet a century later; during the same period the crucibles in which steel was made grew from cauldrons hardly larger than an oversized jug to converters literally as big as a house. The looms used by weavers expanded from small machines that fitted into the cottages of artisan-weavers to monstrous mechanisms housed in mills that still impress us by their size. Perhaps the thrust to bigness in machinery was best symbolized in the great Corliss engine (see illustration) that dominated the Philadelphia Exposition of 1876, perfectly illustrating the technological imperative for power and strength.

Equally remarkable was the expansion in the social scale of production. The new technology quickly outstripped the administrative capability of the small-sized business establishment. As the apparatus of production increased in size, it also increased in speed. As outputs grew from rivulets to rivers, a much larger organization was needed to manage production—to arrange for the steady arrival of raw materials, to supervise the work process, and to find a market for its end product.

Thus we find the size of the typical business enterprise steadily increasing as its technological basis became more complex. In the last quarter of the eighteenth century, a factory of ten persons was worthy of note by Adam Smith, as we shall see in the next chapter. By the first quarter of the nineteenth century, an ordinary textile mill employed several hundred men and women. Fifty years later, some railways employed as many individuals as constituted the armies of respectable monarchs in Adam Smith's time. And in still another 50 years, by the 1920s, many large manufacturing companies had as many employees as respectable eighteenth-century cities had people. The Ford Motor Company, for example, had 174,000 employees in 1929.

3. The Division of Labor Changed the Nature of Work. Technology also played a decisive role in changing the nature of that most basic of all human activities, work. **It did so by breaking down the complicated tasks of productive activity into much smaller subtasks, many of which could then be duplicated, or at least greatly assisted, by mechanical contrivances. This process was called the division of labor.** Adam Smith was soon to explain that the division of labor was mainly responsible for the increase in productivity of the average worker.

The division of labor altered social life in other ways as well. Work became more fragmented, monotonous, tedious, "alienated." And the self-sufficiency of individuals was greatly curtailed. In precapitalist days most people produced their own

The Corliss Engine

subsistence or made some article that could be exchanged for subsistence: Peasants grew crops; artisans produced cloth, shoes, implements. But as work became more and more finely divided, the products of work became ever-smaller pieces in an ever-larger puzzle. Individuals did not spin thread or weave cloth, but manipulated levers and fed the machinery that did the actual spinning or weaving. A worker in a shoe plant made uppers or lowers or heels, but not shoes. No one of these products, by itself, would have sustained its performer for a single day; and no one of these products could have been exchanged for another product except through a complicated network of exchange. **Technology freed men and women from much material want, but it bound them to the workings of the market.**

4. A NEW FORM OF ECONOMIC INSECURITY AROSE. Not least of the mighty effects of technology was its exposure of men and women to unprecedented change. Some of this was welcome, for change opened new horizons of material life. Travel, for instance, once the prerogative of the wealthy, became a possibility for the masses.

Yet the changes introduced by technology had their negative side as well. Already buffeted by market forces that could mysteriously dry up the need for work or just as mysteriously create it, society now discovered that entire occupations, skills acquired over a lifetime, companies laboriously built up over generations, even age-old industries, could be threatened by technological change. **For the first time in history, machinery appeared as the enemy, as well as the ally, of humankind.** No wonder that the textile weavers, whose cottage industry was destroyed by competition from the mills, banded together as Luddites to burn down the hated buildings.*

These aspects of change do not begin to exhaust the ways in which technology, coupled with the market system, altered the very meaning of human existence. But in considering them, we begin to see how profound and how wrenching was the revolution capitalism introduced. Technology was a genie that capitalism let out of the bottle; it has ever since refused to go back in.

THE POLITICAL DIMENSION

The disturbing, upsetting, revolutionary nature of the market and of technology sets the stage for one last aspect of capitalism that we want to note. This is the political currents of change that capitalism brought—political currents that are as much a part of the history of capitalism as the emergence of the market or the dismantling of the barriers against technical change.

Political Freedom

One of these political currents was the rise of democratic, or parliamentary, institutions. Democratic political institutions far predate capitalism, as the history of ancient Athens or the Icelandic medieval parliamentary system shows. Nonetheless, the rise of the mercantile classes was closely tied to the struggle against the privileges and legal institutions of medieval European feudalism. The historic movement that eventually swept aside the precapitalist economic order also swept aside its political order. **Along with the emergence of the market system we find a parallel and supporting emergence of more open, libertarian political ways of life.**

We should be cautious, however, in maintaining that capitalism either guarantees or is necessary for political freedom. We have seen some capitalist nations, such as pre-Hitler Germany and, more recently, Argentina and Chile, descend into nightmarish dictatorship. We have seen other capitalisms, such as Sweden, move toward a kind of socialism without impairing their democratic liberties. Moreover, the exercise of political democracy was very limited in early capitalism. Adam Smith, for example, although comfortably off, did not possess enough property to allow him to vote!

Therefore we cannot claim a hard-and-fast tie between capitalism and political freedom. It is true nonetheless that political liberties do not exist, or scarcely exist, in most nations that have deliberately sought to remove the market system. And today we see that even in the Soviet Union efforts to expand political liberty

*The word *Luddite* comes from a mythical General Ludd who supposedly led these raids of anger and desperation. The term has come to mean an "antimachine" attitude.

(*glasnost*) go hand-in-hand with the expansion of the market (*perestroika*). This suggests, although it does not prove, that some vital connection exists between democratic privileges as we know them and an open society of economic contract, whether it be formally capitalist or not.

Laissez-Faire vs. Political Intervention

Because of the economic freedom on which the market system rested, the basic philosophy of capitalism from Adam Smith's day forward has been laissez-faire—a French phrase, difficult to translate exactly, that means "leaving things alone."* But within a few years of Adam Smith's time, the idea of leaving things alone was already being breached. In England the Factory Act of 1833 established a system of inspectors to prevent child and female labor from being abused. The Ten Hour Act (1847) set limits to the number of hours an employer might demand of his work force. In the United States the Sherman Antitrust Act (1890) made illegal the banding together of large companies to create "trusts." In the 1930s the Social Security Act established a system of old-age pensions; unemployment insurance assured unemployed workers of incomes; the Securities and Exchange Act imposed restrictions on the issuance of new securities. And in our time a long roster of legislation imposes government regulations with respect to the environment, occupational safety, and nuclear power, to mention only a very few instances.

The effects of these interventions into the market process have become central questions for economics itself. As we study macroeconomics, we will be studying not only how the market system works, but also how various efforts to interfere with the market system exert their influence. Needless to say, government intervention in the market is one of the most controversial aspects of economics. But we are not interested at this juncture in taking sides, pro or con. Rather, we should understand that from the first Factory Acts, intervention has largely arisen out of a desire to impose corrective limits on the way in which the market system works or on the unwanted effects produced by technology.

Thus, if capitalism has brought a strong impetus for laissez-faire, it has also brought a strong impetus for political intervention. **Indeed, the very democratic liberties that capitalism has encouraged have been a main source of demands for political action to curb or change the manner in which the economic system works. The political economy of capitalism has always revealed a tension between laissez-faire and intervention—a tension rooted in the tug of war between the equal distribution of voting power and the unequal distribution of buying power.** That tension continues today, a deeply embedded part of the historic momentum of the capitalist system.

*It is said that a group of merchants called on the great Colbert, French finance minister from 1661 to 1683, who congratulated them on their contribution to the French economy and asked what he could do for them. The answer was *Laissez-nous faire*—"Leave us alone." Since Colbert was a strong proponent of the complex regulations and red tape that tied up industry in France at this time—a system we call *mercantilism*—we can imagine how gladly he received this advice.

LOOKING BACK

KEY CONCEPTS

The purpose of this chapter is to set our economic system into historic perspective. We have highlighted a few central ideas to give structure to this perspective.

Capitalism brings three historic changes:
- a private sphere
- accumulation of wealth as capital
- a market system

1 Capitalism is a complex system. We have sought to emphasize three striking changes that it introduces into economic history. First, it creates a realm of production and distribution that is no longer under state authority. This is the genesis of economic freedom. Second, the new economic sphere accumulates capital—wealth used to create more wealth, not luxurious consumption or public monuments. Third, the new manner of organizing economic life developes a new internal guidance mechanism—the market.

The market creates factors of production.

2 The market creates "factors of production"—workers who own and sell their laboring power, landlords who own and freely sell land, capitalists who own and sell capital. This means that labor, land, and capital have become commodities offered for hire in a vast market system where their owners are paid wages, salaries, rents, or interest. This way of bringing the services of these forces of production into social use contrasts sharply with the older means of tradition or command. Capitalism relies on economic freedom and its linked aspect, economic necessity.

The market contrasts with tradition and command. Capitalism encourages technology, which has come in waves—industrial revolutions.

3 Capitalism is closely entwined with technology. The market system encouraged the introduction of technology into everyday productive use by removing the inhibitions of serf- and slave-based modes of production and by thrusting responsibility for economic success or failure on the shoulders of each person. Technological advance has come in a series of great bursts or waves called industrial revolutions, beginning with *the* Industrial Revolution (spinning, ironmaking, steam power) of the late eighteenth and early nineteenth centuries.

Technology affects output, scale, and the division of labor.

4 Technology has profoundly affected economic and social life. It is responsible for the beginning of the rise in standard of living associated with capitalism. It is the main factor in the vast growth in size of business organizations. It is the source of a much greater division of labor and of a highly intensified interdependence of individuals.

The rise of capitalism is associated with political liberty; this has created tension between laissez-faire and intervention.

5 Capitalism is closely connected with political movements. One of these is parliamentary democracy, which arose out of the struggle to break the hold of feudalism. Another is an underlying belief in laissez-faire as a main principle of economic policy. A third is the effort to intervene against the workings of the market and technology whenever these powerful forces disrupt or endanger social life.

ECONOMIC VOCABULARY

QUESTIONS

1. Are there elements of tradition and command still visible in our market system? How important do you think they are? Can you imagine a system in which there was *no* guiding force of tradition and *no* exercise of command (government) at all?
2. What reasons do you think are plausible in explaining why it took so long for capitalism to burst on the scene; and how do you explain the fact that it emerged only in Europe, not in Africa, Asia, or South America? *Note:* The question is far from settled. If you devise a really persuasive answer, you will be well on your way to becoming a world-famous historian.
3. Profit-making is certainly as old as biblical man. Why are the institutions of capitalism not equally old?
4. Describe the social, political, and economic repercussions of the following: the typewriter, the jet plane, TV, antibiotics. Is the economic impact always greater than the social or political impact? Is the economic impact always favorable?
5. Do you think capitalism is necessary for political freedom? First frame your answer, and then test it against these facts: (a) There has been little political freedom in any modern nation that has decisively rejected capitalism (that lets out Sweden, which does not actively oppose capitalism). (b) The Republic of South Africa is certainly capitalist, and is not a politically free nation, especially for those who are not white. *Note:* These facts suggest that there are *no* open-and-shut answers to this question. The issue is a complicated one—more complicated than many people suspect.

CHAPTER 3

The Great Economists

A LOOK AHEAD

The rise of the market system brought with it a great puzzle: How did such a system "work"—what kept it together and in what direction was it headed? The name of this puzzle is economics.

In this chapter we learn more about the background of economics by looking into the ideas of three great economists whose thoughts still dominate our understanding of capitalism: Adam Smith, Karl Marx, and John Maynard Keynes.

As we study them, a few central questions come to the fore:

1 What holds the system together and gives it "micro" order?
2 Where is the system headed, giving it "macro" motion?
3 What should we do to improve the system's operations, or what policies should we pursue?

THE INVENTION OF ECONOMICS

The emergence of capitalism brought an extraordinary puzzle into being. The puzzle was to explain how a society could hang together when the time-honored mechanisms of tradition and command no longer played their accustomed roles. How could economic life unfold in an orderly and reliable fashion when each actor on the marketplace was out for himself, devil take the hindmost; and when it was already clear that change, not inertia, was to be the order of the day?

Mercantilism

Capitalism needed a philosophy—a reasoned explanation of how it worked. But the philosophy was a long time in emerging. All during the seventeenth and eighteenth centuries, for example, the understanding of market society was very imperfect. One group of British pamphleteers, whom we call the Mercantilists, tried to explain its workings in terms of a struggle among nations to gather "treasure"—gold and silver bullion. In this struggle, the Mercantilists saw merchants (hence *Mercant*—ilism) playing a central role because they exported goods that were paid for in treasure.

Early mercantilist policy was very simple: Let England sell as much and buy as little abroad as possible. In that way, its national wealth would steadily pile up. Later mercantilist theory was a good deal more sophisticated. Can you see why the earlier idea of amassing treasure could not successfully serve as a policy for *all* nations?

Physiocracy. In France during the eighteenth century an entirely different and equally inadequate explanation was called physiocracy. In many ways the French school of ideas was the opposite of the British school. Physiocracy taught that the real wealth of economic life lay in production, not in exchange—an important step in the right direction. But the Physiocrats believed that production was essentially a gift of nature (*physiocracy* means the order of nature), and that therefore only labor working with nature was truly productive. Thus, whereas the Mercantilists extolled the merchants as active agents in creating national wealth, the Physiocrats regarded them as a "sterile" class that did no more than handle the wealth produced by the agriculturalists.

Mercantilism and physiocracy are both indispensable steppingstones on the road to modern economics. Each yielded useful insights into the still unfinished economic revolution. But neither made the crucial breakthrough of seeing that the market was a *system.* That is, neither Mercantilists nor Physiocrats saw that the market network possessed an internal guidance mechanism to keep it on a steady course and that a society powered by the market was headed toward a visible destination.

These crucial insights came with Adam Smith, patron saint of our discipline and a figure of towering intellectual stature.

ADAM SMITH (1723–1790)

Adam Smith's fame resides in his masterpiece, *The Wealth of Nations,* published in 1776, the year of the Declaration of Independence. All things considered, it is not easy to say which document is of greater historic importance. The Declaration sounded a new call for a society dedicated to "Life, Liberty, and the pursuit of Happiness." The *Wealth* explained how such a society worked.

The Role of Competition

Smith set himself two main problems, one on the micro and the other on the macro level (although you will not find these terms used in his great, rambling, discursive tract). The first problem was to elucidate how a market-run economic system was articulated, how it achieved what we would call micro order.

Here Smith begins by resolving a perplexing question. The actors in the market, as we know, are all driven by the desire to make money for themselves—to "better their condition," as Smith puts it. The question is obvious: How does a market society prevent self-interested, profit-hungry individuals from holding up their fellow citizens for ransom? How can a socially workable arrangement arise from such a dangerously unsocial motivation as self-betterment?

PORTRAIT OF AN ABSENTMINDED PROFESSOR

"I am a beau in nothing but my books" was the way that Adam Smith once described himself. Indeed, the famous medallion profile shows us a homely face. In addition, Smith had a curious stumbling gait that one friend called "vermicular," and was given to notorious fits of absentmindedness. On one occasion, absorbed in discussion, he fell into a tanning pit.

Few other adventures befell Smith in the course of his scholarly, rather retiring life. Perhaps the high point was reached at age four when he was kidnaped by a band of gypsies passing near Kirkaldy, his native hamlet in Scotland. "His captors held him only a few hours; they may have sensed what a biographer later wrote: "He would have made, I fear, a poor gypsy."

Marked out early as a student of promise, at 16 Smith won a scholarship that sent him to Oxford. But Oxford was not then the center of learning that it is today. Little or no systematic teaching took place, the students being free to educate themselves, provided they did not read dangerous books. Smith was nearly expelled for owning a copy of David Hume's *Treatise of Human Nature,* a work we now regard as one of the philosophic masterpieces of the eighteenth century.

After Oxford, Smith returned to Scotland, where he obtained an appointment as Professor of Moral Philosophy at the University of Glasgow. Moral philosophy covered a large territory in Smith's time: We have notes of his lectures in which he talked about jurisprudence, military organization, taxation, and "police"—the last word meaning the administration of domestic affairs that we would call economic policy.

In 1759 Smith published *The Theory of Moral Sentiments,* a remarkable inquiry into morality and psychology. The book attracted widespread attention and brought Smith to the notice of Lord Townshend, one day to be the Chancellor of the Exchequer responsible for the notorious tax on American tea. Townshend engaged Smith to serve as tutor to his stepson, and Smith resigned his professional post to set off on the Grand Tour with his charge. In France he met Voltaire, Rousseau, and François Quesnay, the brilliant doctor who had originated the ideas of physiocracy. Smith would have dedicated *The Wealth of Nations* to him had Quesnay not died.

Returning to Scotland in 1766, Smith lived out the remainder of his life largely in scholarly retirement. It was during these years that the *Wealth* was slowly and carefully composed. When it was done, Smith sent a copy to David Hume, by then his dear friend. Hume wrote: "Euge!* Belle! Dear Mr. Smith: I am much pleased with your Performance . . ." Hume knew, as did virtually everyone who read the book, that Smith had written a work that would permanently change society's understanding of itself.

*Greek for "Well done!"

The answer introduces us to a central mechanism of a market system, the mechanism of competition. For each person, out for self-betterment, with no thought of others, is faced with a host of similarly motivated persons. As a result, each market actor is forced to meet the prices offered by competitors.

In the kind of competition that Smith assumes, a manufacturer who tries to charge more than other manufacturers will not be able to find any buyers. A job seeker who asks more than the going wage will not be able to find work. And an employer who tries to pay *less* than competitors pay will not find anyone to fill the jobs.

In this way, the market mechanism imposes a discipline on its participants: Buyers must bid against other buyers, and therefore cannot gang up against sellers. Sellers must contend against other sellers, and therefore cannot impose their will on buyers.

The Invisible Hand

But the market has a second, equally important function. Smith shows that the market will arrange for the production of the goods that society wants, in the quantities society wants—without anyone ever issuing an order of any kind! Suppose that consumers want more pots and fewer pans than are being turned out. The public will buy up the existing stock of pots, and as a result the price of pots will rise. Contrariwise, the pan business will be dull; as panmakers try to get rid of their inventories, pan prices will fall.

Now a restorative force comes into play. As pot prices rise, so will profits in the business of pot making; and as pan prices fall, so will profits in that business. Once again, the drive for self-betterment will go to work. Employers in the favored pot business will seek to expand, hiring more factors of production—more workers, more space, more capital equipment; and employers in the disfavored pan business will reduce their use of the factors of production, letting workers go, giving up leases on space, cutting down on capital investment.

Hence the output of pots will rise and that of pans will fall. And this is what the public wanted in the first place. **Thus the pressures of the marketplace direct the selfish activities of individuals as if by an Invisible Hand (to use Smith's wonderful phrase) into socially responsible paths. The Invisible Hand transmutes private, self-regarding motives into public, socially oriented behavior. The market becomes a mechanism for the allocation of resources into the channels desired by society.**

The Self-Regulating System

Smith's demonstration of how a market performs its social functions has never ceased to be of interest. Much of microeconomics, as we shall see, consists of learning again, or of examining more closely, how the Invisible Hand works. Not that it does always work. There are areas of economic life where the Invisible Hand does not exert its influence at all. In every market system, for instance, tradition continues to play a role in nonmarket methods of remuneration such as tipping or the sharing of incomes within a family. So, too, command is always in evidence within organizations or in the exercise of government powers such as taxation. Further, the market system has no way of providing certain public goods—goods that cannot be privately marketed, such as national defense or public law and order. Smith knew about these areas and recognized that such goods would have to be supplied by the government, not by the market.

Then, too, the market does not always meet the ethical or aesthetic criteria of society, or it may produce goods that are profitable to make, but harmful to consume. We shall look into these problems in due course. At this juncture, however, we had better stand in considerable awe of Smith's basic insight, for he showed his generation and all succeeding ones that a market system is a responsive and reliable force for basic social provisioning.

He also showed that it was self-regulating. The beautiful consequence of the market is that it is its own guardian. If anyone's prices, wages, or profits stray from levels that are set for everyone, the force of competition will drive them back. Thus a curious paradox exists. The market, which is the acme of economic freedom, turns out also to be the strictest of economic taskmasters.

Smith's Philosophy

Because the market is its own regulator, Smith vehemently opposed government intervention that would interfere with the workings of self-interest and competition. Therefore laissez-faire became his fundamental philosophy—not because Smith opposed the idea of social responsibility, but rather because he thought it would be most effectively provided by the Invisible Hand, not by the efforts of government.

His commitment to laissez-faire does not make Smith a conventional conservative. The *Wealth of Nations* is shot through with biting remarks about the "mean and rapacious" ways of the manufacturing class (Smith does not use the word *capitalist*), and the book is openly sympathetic with, and concerned about, the lot of the workingman, hardly a popular position in Smith's day. If Smith was passionately in favor of the "system of natural liberty"—the system founded on economic freedom—the reason is that he believed it would benefit the general public, not the interests of any single class.

Economic Growth

Smith's discovery of the self-regulating properties of a market system was his great "micro" insight (remember that is our phrase, not his). But his vision of an internally coherent market system was matched in importance by a second, "macro" vision. **Smith saw that the market system, left entirely to its own devices, would grow, that the wealth of a nation under a system of "natural liberty" would steadily increase.**

What brought about this growth? As before, the motive force was the drive for self-betterment, the thirst for profits, the wish to make money. This meant that every employer was constantly seeking to accumulate more capital, to expand the wealth of the enterprise. In turn, this led each employer to seek to increase sales in the hope of gaining a larger profit.

The Division of Labor Again

But how to enlarge sales at a time long before advertising existed as we know it? Smith's answer was to improve productivity: Increase the output of the work force. And the road to increasing productivity was very clear: **Increase the division of labor.**

In Smith's conception of the growing *wealth* (we would say the growing *production*) *of nations,* the division of labor therefore plays a central role, as this famous description of a pin factory makes unforgettably clear:

> *One man draws out the wire, another straits it, a third cuts it, a fourth points it, a fifth grinds it at the top for receiving the head; to make the head requires two or three distinct operations; to put it on is a peculiar business; to whiten it another; it is even a trade by itself to put them into paper.*

*. . . I have seen a small manufactory of this kind where ten men only were employed and where some of them consequently performed two or three distinct operations. But though they were poor, and therefore but indifferently accommodated with the necessary machinery, they could when they exerted themselves make among them about twelve pounds of pins in a day. There are in a pound upwards of four thousand pins of middling size. These ten persons, therefore, could make among them upward of forty-eight thousand pins in a day . . . But if they had all wrought separately and independently . . . they could certainly not each of them make twenty, perhaps not one pin in a day.**

Capital and Growth

But how is the division of labor to be enhanced? Smith places principal importance on the manner already announced in his description of the process of making pins: *Machinery is the key.* The division of labor—and therefore the productivity of labor—is increased when the tasks of production can be taken over, or aided and assisted, by the capacities of machinery. In this way, each firm seeking to expand is naturally led to introduce more machinery as a way of improving the productivity of its workers. **The market system thus becomes an immense force for the accumulation of capital, mainly in the form of machinery and equipment.** Moreover, Smith showed something remarkable about the self-regulating properties of the market system as a growth-producing institution. We recall that growth occurred because employers installed machinery that improved the division of labor. But as they added to their work force, would not wages rise as all employers competed to hire labor? And would that not squeeze profits and dry up the funds by which machinery could be bought?

Once again, however, the market was its own regulator. For Smith showed that the increased demand for labor would be matched by an increased supply of labor, so that wages would not rise or would rise only moderately. The reason was plausible. In Smith's day, infant and child mortality rates were horrendous: "It is not uncommon," wrote Smith, ". . . in the Highlands of Scotland for a mother who has borne twenty children not to have two alive." As wages rose and better food was provided for the household, infant and child mortality would decline. Soon there would be a larger work force available for hire: Ten was the working age in Smith's day. The larger work force would hold back the rise in wages—and so the accumulation of capital could go on. Just as the system assured internal micro order, so did it provide an overall macro dependability.

Smith Today

Of course, Smith wrote about a world that is long since vanished—a world in which a factory of ten people, although small, was still significant enough to play a central

*Adam Smith, *The Wealth of Nations* (New York: Modern Library, 1937), pp. 4, 5.

illustrative role; in which remnants of mercantilist, and even feudal, restrictions determined how many apprentices an employer could hire in many trades; in which labor unions were largely illegal; in which almost no social legislation existed; and above all, in which the great majority of people were very poor.

Yet Smith saw two essential attributes of the economic system that was not yet fully born in his time:

1. **A society of competitive profit-seeking individuals can assure its orderly material provisioning through the self-regulating market mechanism.**
2. **Such a society tends to accumulate capital, and in so doing enhances its productivity and wealth.**

These insights are not the last word. We have already mentioned that the market mechanism does not always work successfully, and our next two economists will demonstrate that the growth process is not without serious defects. But the insights themselves are still germane. Micro- and macroeconomics are about internal order and growth, even though we may come to different conclusions than those of Smith. What is surprising after two centuries is not how mistaken Smith was, but how deeply he saw. In a real sense, as economists we are still his pupils.

KARL MARX (1818–1883)

Every economist is roughly familiar with the ideas and influence of Adam Smith. Not so many recognize the degree to which economics also owes a debt to Karl Marx—not as the founder of a political movement that has troubled the world ever since, but as an economist whose dissection of capitalism has much to teach us.

Class Struggle

Adam Smith was the architect of capitalism's orderliness and progress; Marx, the diagnostician of its disorders and eventual demise. Their differences are rooted in the fundamentally opposite way each saw history. In Smith's view, history was a succession of stages through which humankind traveled, climbing from the "early and rude" society of hunters and fisherfolk to the final stage of commercial society. **Marx saw history as a continuing struggle among social classes, ruling classes contending with ruled classes in every era.**

Moreover, Smith believed that commercial society would bring about a harmonious, mutually acceptable solution to the problem of individual interest in a social setting that would go on forever—or at least for a very long time. Marx saw tension and antagonism as the outcome of the class struggle, and the setting of capitalist society as anything but permanent. Indeed, the class struggle itself, expressed as the contest over wages and profits, would be the main force for changing capitalism and eventually undoing it.

PROFILE OF A REVOLUTIONARY

A great, bearded, dark-skinned man, Karl Marx was the picture of a revolutionary. And he was one—engaged, mind and heart, in the effort to overthrow the system of capitalism that he spent his whole life studying. As a political revolutionary, Marx was not very successful, although with his lifelong friend Friedrich Engels he formed an international working-class "movement" that frightened a good many conservative governments. But as an intellectual revolutionary, Marx was probably the most successful disturber of thought who ever lived. The only persons who rival his influence are the great religious leaders, Christ, Mohammed, and Buddha.

Marx led as turbulent and active a life as Smith's was secluded and academic. Born to middle-class parents in Trier, Germany, he was early marked as a student of prodigious abilities, but not temperamentally cut out to be a professor. Soon after getting his doctoral degree (in philosophy), Marx became editor of a crusading newspaper, which rapidly earned the distrust of the reactionary Prussian government. It closed down the paper. Typically, Marx printed the last edition in red. With his wife Jenny (and Jenny's family maid, Lenchen, who remained with them, unpaid, all her life), Marx thereupon began life as a political exile in Paris, Brussels, and finally in London. There, in 1848, together with Engels, he published the pamphlet that was to become his best known, but certainly not most important, work: *The Communist Manifesto.*

The remainder of Marx's life was lived in London. Terribly poor, largely as a consequence of his hopeless inability to manage his own finances, Marx's life was spent in the reading room of the British Museum, laboriously composing the great, never-finished opus *Capital.* No economist has ever read so widely or so deeply as Marx. Before even beginning *Capital,* he wrote a profound three-volume commentary on all the existing economists, eventually published as *Theories of Surplus Value,* and filled 37 notebooks on subjects that would be included in *Capital*—these notes, published as the *Grundrisse* (Foundations), did not appear in print until 1953! *Capital* itself was written "backwards"—first Volumes II and III, in very rough draft form, then Volume I, the only part of the great opus that appeared in Marx's lifetime, in 1867.

Marx was assuredly a genius, a man who altered every aspect of thinking about society—historical and sociological as well as economic—as decisively as Plato altered the cast of philosophic thought and Freud that of psychology. Very few economists today work their way through the immense body of Marx's work; but in one way or another, his influence affects most of us, even if we are unaware of it. We owe to Marx the basic idea that capitalism is an *evolving* system, deriving from a specific historic past and moving slowly and irregularly toward a dimly discernible, different form of society. That is an idea accepted by many social scientists who may or may not approve of socialism, and who are on the whole vehemently "anti-Marxist"!

Capitalist Growth: Using M

A great deal of interest in Marx's work focuses on that revolutionary perspective and purpose. But Marx the economist interests us for a different reason: Marx also saw the market as a powerful force in the accumulation of capital and wealth. From his conflict-laden point of view, however, he traces out the process—mainly in Volume II of *Capital*—quite differently than Smith does. As we have seen, Smith's conception of the growth process stressed its self-regulatory nature, its steady, hitch-free path. Marx's conception is just the opposite. To him, growth is a process full of pitfalls, a process in which crisis or malfunction lurks at every turn.

Marx starts with a view of the accumulation process that is much like that of a businessman. The problem is how to make a given sum of capital—money sitting in a bank or invested in a firm—yield a profit. **As Marx puts it, how does *M* (a sum of money) become *M′*, a *larger* sum?**

Marx's answer begins with capitalists using their money to buy commodities and labor power. Thereby they ready the process of production, obtaining needed raw or semifinished materials and hiring the work capabilities of a labor force. Here the possibility for crisis lies in the difficulty that capitalists may have in getting their materials or their labor force at the right price. If that should happen—if labor is too expensive, for instance—*M* stays put, and the accumulation process never gets started at all.

Karl Marx
(Courtesy of the Library of Congress)

The Labor Process

But suppose the first stage of accumulation takes place smoothly. Now money capital, *M,* has been transformed into a hired work force and a stock of physical goods. These have next to be combined in the labor process; that is, actual work must be expended on the materials and the raw or semifinished goods transformed into their next stage of production.

It is here, on the factory floor, that Marx sees the genesis of profit. **In his view, profit lies in the ability of capitalists to pay less for labor power—for the working abilities of their work force—than the actual value workers will impart to the commodities they help to produce.** This theory of *surplus value* as the source of profit is very important in Marx's analysis of capitalism. But it is not central to our purpose here. Instead, we stop only to note that the labor process is another place where accumulation can be disrupted. If there is a strike, or if production encounters resistances, the *M* that is invested in goods and labor power will not move along toward its objective, *M′*.

Completing the Circuit

But once again, suppose that all goes well and workers transform steel sheets, rubber casings, and bolts of cloth into automobiles. The automobiles are not yet money. They have to be sold—and here, of course, lie the familiar problems of the marketplace: bad guesses as to the public's taste; mismatches between supply and demand; recessions that diminish the spending power of society.

If all goes well, the commodities *will* be sold—and sold for *M′,* which is bigger than *M.* In that case, the circuit of accumulation is complete, and the capitalists will have a new sum *M′,* which they will want to send on another round, hoping to win *M″*. But unlike Adam Smith's smooth growth model, we can see that Marx's conception of accumulation is riddled with pitfalls and dangers. **Crisis is possible at every stage. Indeed, in the complex theory Marx unfolds in *Capital,* the inherent tendency of the system is to generate crisis, not to avoid it.**

We will not trace Marx's theory of capitalism further except to note that at its core lies a complicated analysis of the manner in which surplus value (the unpaid labor that is the source of profit) is squeezed out through mechanization. A student who wants to learn about Marx's analysis must turn to other books, of which there are many.*

Instability and Breakdown

Our interest in Marx lies in his being the first theorist to stress the *instability* of capitalism. Adam Smith originated the idea that growth is an inherent characteristic of capitalism, but to Marx we owe the idea that that growth is wavering and uncertain, far from the assured process Smith described. Marx makes it clear that

*At the risk of appearing self-serving, a good first reader is R. L. Heilbroner, *Marxism: For and Against* (New York: Norton, 1980).

capital accumulation must overcome the uncertainty inherent in the market system and the tension of the opposing demands of labor and capital. The accumulation of wealth, although certainly the objective of business, may not always be within its power to achieve.

In *Capital* Marx sees instability increasing until finally the system comes tumbling down. His reasoning involves two further, very important prognoses for the system. **The first is that the size of business firms will steadily increase as the consequence of the recurrent crises that wrack the economy.** With each crisis, small firms go bankrupt and their assets are bought up by surviving firms. A trend toward big business is therefore an integral part of capitalism.

Second, Marx expects an intensification of the class struggle as the result of the "proletarianization" of the labor force. More and more small businesspeople and independent artisans will be squeezed out in the crisis-ridden process of growth. Thus the social structure will be reduced to two classes—a small group of capitalist magnates and a large mass of proletarianized, embittered workers.

In the end, this situation will prove impossible to maintain. In Marx's words:

> *Along with the constant decrease in the number of capitalist magnates, who usurp and monopolize all the advantages of this process of transformation, the mass of misery, oppression, slavery, degradation and exploitation grows; but with this there also grows the revolt of the working class, a class constantly increasing in numbers, and trained, united and organized by the very mechanism of the capitalist process of production. The monopoly of capital becomes a fetter upon the mode of production which has flourished alongside and under it. The centralization of the means of production and the socialization of labour reach a point at which they become incompatible with their capitalist integument. This integument is burst asunder. The knell of capitalist private property sounds. The expropriators are expropriated.**

Was Marx Right?

Much of the economic controversy Marx generated has been focused on the questions: Will capitalism ultimately undo itself? Will its internal tensions, its "contradictions," as Marx calls them, finally become too much for its market mechanism to handle?

There are no simple answers to these questions. Critics of Marx insist that capitalism has *not* collapsed, that the working class has *not* become more and more "miserable," and that a number of predictions that Marx made, such as that the rate of profit would tend to decline, have not been verified.

Supporters of Marx argue the opposite case. They stress that capitalism almost did collapse in the 1930s. They note that more and more people have been reduced to "proletarian" status, working for a capitalist firm rather than for themselves: In 1800, for example, 80 percent of Americans were self-employed; today the figure is 10 percent. They stress that the size of businesses has constantly grown, and that Marx did correctly foresee that the capitalist system itself would expand, pushing into noncapitalist areas such as Asia, South America, and Africa.

*Karl Marx, *Capital,* Vol. I (New York: Vintage, 1977), p. 929.

Marx's Socioanalysis

There is much more to Marx than the few economic ideas sketched here suggest. Indeed, Marx should not be thought of primarily as an economist, but as a pioneer in a new kind of critical social thought: It is significant that the subtitle of *Capital* is *A Critique of Political Economy.*

In the gallery of the world's great thinkers, where Marx certainly belongs, his statue would be centrally placed, overlooking many corridors of thought—sociological analysis, philosophic inquiry, and of course, economics. For Marx's lasting contribution was a penetration of the *appearances* of our social system, and of the ways in which we think about that system, in an effort to arrive at buried essences deep below the surface. That most searching aspect of Marx's work is not one that we will pursue here; but bear in mind, because it accounts for the persisting interest of Marx's thought.*

JOHN MAYNARD KEYNES (1883–1946)

Marx was the intellectual prophet of capitalism as a self-destructive system; John Maynard Keynes (the name should be pronounced "canes," not "keens") was the engineer of capitalism repaired. Today that is not an uncontested statement. To some people, Keynes's doctrines are as dangerous and subversive as those of Marx—a curious irony, since Keynes himself was totally opposed to Marxist thought and wholly in favor of sustaining and improving the capitalist system.

The reason for the present distrust of Keynes is that more than any other economist he is the father of the idea of a "mixed economy" in which the government plays a crucial role. To many people these days, all government activities are suspicious at best and downright injurious at worst. Thus in some quarters Keynes's name is under a cloud. Nonetheless, he remains one of the great innovators of our discipline, a mind to be ranked with Smith and Marx as one of the most influential our profession has brought forth. As Nobelist Milton Friedman, a famous conservative economist, once declared: "We are all Keynesians now."

The Great Depression

The great economists were all products of their times: Smith, the voice of optimistic, nascent capitalism; Marx, the spokesman for the victims of its bleakest industrial period; Keynes, the product of a still later time, the Great Depression.

*What about the relation of Marx to present-day communism? That is a subject for a book about the politics, not the economics, of Marxism. Marx himself was a fervid democrat—but also a very intolerant man. Perhaps his system of ideas has encouraged intolerance in revolutionary parties that have based their ideas on his thought. Marx himself died long before present-day communism came into being, so we cannot know what he would have made of it.

PORTRAIT OF A MANY-SIDED MAN

Keynes was a man of many talents. Unlike Smith or Marx, he was at home in the world of business affairs, a shrewd dealer and financier. Every morning, abed, he would scan the newspaper and make his commitments for the day on the most treacherous of all markets, foreign exchange. An hour or so a day sufficed to make him a very rich man; among economists, only the great David Ricardo (1772–1823) could match him in financial acumen. Like Ricardo, Keynes was a speculator by temperament. During World War I, when he was at the Treasury office running England's foreign currency operations, he reported with glee to his chief that he had got together a fair amount of Spanish pesetas. The chief was relieved that England had a supply of *that* currency for a while. "Oh no," said Keynes. "I've sold them all. I'm going to break the market." And he did. Later during the war, when the Germans were shelling Paris, he went to France to negotiate for the English government; on the side, he bought some marvelous French masterpieces at much reduced prices for the National Gallery—along with a Cézanne for himself!

More than an economist and a speculator, Keynes was a brilliant mathematician; a businessman who successfully ran a great investment trust; a ballet lover who married a famous ballerina; a superb stylist and an editor of consummate skill; a man of huge kindness when he wanted to exert it, and of ferocious wit when (more often) he chose to exert that. On one occasion, banker Sir Harry Goshen criticized Keynes for not "letting things take their natural course." "Is it more appropriate to smile or rage at these artless sentiments?" wrote Keynes. "Best, perhaps, to let Sir Harry take *his* natural course."

Keynes's greatest fame lay in his economic inventiveness. He came by this talent naturally enough as the son of a distinguished economist, John Neville Keynes. As an undergraduate, Keynes had already attracted the attention of Alfred Marshall, the commanding figure at Cambridge University for three decades. After graduation, Keynes soon won notice with a brilliant little book on Indian finance; he then became an adviser to the English government in the negotiations at the end of World War I. Dismayed and disheartened by the vengeful terms of the Versailles Treaty, Keynes wrote a polemic, *The Economic Consequences of the Peace,* that won him international renown.

Almost 30 years later, Keynes would himself be a chief negotiator for the English government, first in securing the necessary loans during World War II, then as one of the architects of the Bretton Woods agreement that opened a new system of international currency relations after that war. On his return from one trip to Washington, reporters crowded around to ask if England had been sold out and would soon be another American state. Keynes's reply was succinct: "No such luck."

The Great Depression hit the world like a typhoon. In America one-half the value of all production simply disappeared. One-quarter of the working force lost their jobs. Over a million urban families found their mortgages foreclosed, their houses taken from them. Nine million savings accounts went down the drain when banks closed, never to reopen.

Against this terrible reality of joblessness and loss of income, the economics profession, like the business world or government advisers, had nothing to offer. Economists were as perplexed at the behavior of the economy as were the American people themselves. In many ways, the situation reminds us of the uncertainty that the public and the economics profession share in the face of inflation or international competition today.

The General Theory

It was against this setting of dismay and near-panic that Keynes's great book appeared: *The General Theory of Employment Interest and Money.* A complicated book—much more technical than the *Wealth of Nations* or *Capital*—the *General Theory* nevertheless had a central message that was simple enough to grasp. The overall level of economic activity in a capitalist system, said Keynes (and both Marx and Adam Smith would have agreed with him), was determined by the willingness of its entrepreneurs to make capital investments. From time to time, this willingness was blocked by considerations that made capital accumulation difficult or impossible: In Smith's model, we saw the possibility of wages rising too fast, and Marx's theory pointed out difficulties at every stage of the process.

But all the previous economists, even Marx to a certain extent, believed that a failure to accumulate capital would be a temporary, self-curing setback. In Smith's scheme, the rising supply of young workers would keep wages in check. In Marx's conception, each crisis (up to the last) would present the surviving entrepreneurs with fresh opportunities to resume their quest for profits. For Keynes, however, the diagnosis was more severe. **He showed that a market system could reach a position of "underemployment equilibrium"—a kind of steady, stagnant state—despite the presence of unemployed workers and unused industrial equipment. The revolutionary implication of Keynes's theory was that there was no self-righting property in the market system to keep capitalism growing.**

The Role of Government

We will not understand the nature of Keynes's diagnosis until we get into our study of macroeconomics, but we can easily see the conclusion to which his diagnosis drove him. If there was nothing that would automatically provide for capital accumulation, a badly depressed economy could remain in the doldrums—unless some substitute were found for business spending. And there was only one such possible source of stimulation: the government. **The crux of Keynes's message was therefore that government spending might be an essential economic policy for a depressed capitalism trying to recover its vitality.**

Whether or not Keynes's remedy works and what consequences government spending may have for a market system have become major topics in contemporary economics—topics we will deal with later at length. But we can see the significance of his work in changing the very conception of the economic system in which we live. Adam Smith's view of the market system led to the philosophy of laissez-faire, allowing the system to generate its own natural propensity for growth and internal order. Marx had stressed a very different view in which instability and crisis lurked at every stage, but of course Marx was not interested in policies to maintain capitalism. Keynes propounded a philosophy as far removed from Marx as from Smith. For if Keynes was right, laissez-faire was not the appropriate policy for capitalism—certainly not for capitalism in depression. And if Keynes was right about his remedy, the gloomy prognostications of Marx were also incorrect—or at least could be rendered incorrect.

John Maynard Keynes
(The Bettmann Archive, Inc.)

Was Keynes Right?

But was Keynes right? Was Smith right? Was Marx right? To a very large degree these questions frame the subject matter of economics today. That is why, even if their theories are part of our history, the "worldly philosophers" are also contemporary. A young writer once remarked impatiently to T. S. Eliot that it seemed so pointless to study the thinkers of the past, because we knew so much more than they. "Yes," replied Eliot. "They are what we know."

LOOKING BACK

KEY CONCEPTS

This chapter has tried to give us a conception of capitalism as seen by the three greatest economists—whose ideas still powerfully affect our understanding of the system. Let us go over the main ideas that have emerged from this survey:

Mercantilists and Physiocrats extolled treasure and land.

1 Economics itself is a modern intellectual invention that awaited the advent of market society. Prior to Adam Smith, the main attempts to understand and explain the system were those of the Mercantilists, who stressed the importance of foreign trade as a means of gaining gold or treasure; and those of the French Physiocrats, who extolled the wealth-generating powers of the land and who dismissed the merchant class as sterile.

Adam Smith's Invisible Hand—competition plus self-interest

2 Adam Smith contributed two immensely important ideas to economic understanding. The first was the idea of an Invisible Hand by which the market system converted the selfish drives of individuals to a coordinated mechanism for social provisioning. Smith showed how this fortunate outcome arose from the workings of competition, which prevented the drive for profits or selfish interest from simply gouging the consumer or the worker.

Capital accumulation and division of labor bring growth.

3 Smith was also the first economist to explain how the market provided a powerful mechanism for accumulating capital. Smith's theory of economic growth hinged on the steady improvement in productivity that occurred when machinery was added to production, making possible a finer division of labor.

Class struggle

4 Marx was the great prophet of capitalism's doom. The essential cause of its demise would be the class struggle between workers and capitalists.

The unstable process of production

5 Marx also saw the market mechanism as inherently unstable—as tending toward crisis or disruption in the accumulation of capital. He analyzed this instability by tracing the obstacles faced by a firm as it sought to convert M, a sum of capital, into M', *a larger sum. This was done in three stages: first by using* M to buy labor power and materials, then by combining labor power with materials, and finally by selling the finished goods. At each stage the accumulation process was subject to disruption of various sorts.

Growth of monopolies and impoverished proletariat leads to revolution.

6 In Marx's view, the process of capitalist accumulation leads to the growth of big business and an "immiserated" proletariat. As successive crises wracked the system, the working class would eventually revolt, and a transition would be made from capitalism to socialism.

Marxism as a system of thought

7 Marx's system of thought was much larger than an analysis of the economic tensions of capitalism. Essentially it embraced a mixture of philosophy, historical analysis, and a critique of economic beliefs and forms.

Keynes's *General Theory* with its idea of underemployment equilibrium, ushered in the mixed economy.

8 John Maynard Keynes's *General Theory* (as it is widely called) was an attempt to explain how capitalism could have a *lasting* depression. In technical terms, Keynes's breakthrough was the explanation of underemployment equilibrium.

9 Equally important was Keynes's work in paving the way for the mixed economy in which government plays a crucial role in maintaining the economic growth of capitalism. Mixed economies are found in every capitalist system today; we will be studying them in depth in the pages to come.

ECONOMIC VOCABULARY

Mercantilism 30
Physiocracy 30
Invisible Hand 32
Self-regulation 33
Division of labor 34
Marx's circuit of production: *M*-into-*M*′ 38
Underemployment equilibrium 43

QUESTIONS

1. Why does Smith's model of the economy require *two* elements—the motivation of self-betterment and the restraining institution of competition? Explain why the system would not work with only one of the two.
2. Think of how the division of labor can increase productivity. Choose one example from agriculture, one from manufacturing, and one from a service industry, such as hotel management, transportation, or retailing.
3. Is the accumulation of capital needed for the improvement of productivity today? In what ways could additional capital—more machines, buildings, roads, etc.—improve the amount of production a typical farmer or worker could create?

4. Take any business you know about and see if you think that Marx's description of the circuit M-into-M' describes the way in which that business tries to accumulate capital. Which of Marx's three phases of the accumulation process is most likely to lead to trouble, in your opinion?
5. How do you feel about the idea of a mixed economy? Do you think it means an economy in which the government does a lot of interfering? Could a government simply spend money—for example, for social security—and not interfere in the market system at all? Could it interfere extensively, but not spend much money? Which of the two functions—interfering (regulating) or spending—is basic to Keynes's theory? Is it possible, do you think, to have a basically laissez-faire policy with respect to the market and yet use government spending to cure a depression?

AN EXTRA WORD ABOUT

Paradigms

How does science advance? The prevailing view used to be that it grew by accretion, gradually adding new knowledge and better-established hypotheses while shedding error and disproved hypotheses. That view has been seriously challenged by an influential book, *The Structure of Scientific Revolutions* by Thomas Kuhn, published in 1962.

Kuhn's view is that the growth of science is not a continuous, seamless extension of knowledge. Rather, science grows in discontinuous leaps, in which one prevailing paradigm is displaced by another. *A paradigm is a set of premises, views, rules, conventions, and beliefs that form the kinds of questions that a science asks.* For example, the Ptolemaic paradigm, with its view of the earth as the center of the universe, was replaced by the Copernican paradigm, which based its questions on the premise that the planets revolve around the sun. In cosmology the Newtonian paradigm was displaced by the Einsteinian, in biology the biblical paradigm by the Darwinian.

Paradigms change, says Kuhn, when the puzzles encountered by scientists become more and more difficult to answer within the existing set of ground rules. Then, usually in a short space of time, a new view of things comes to the fore, explaining the puzzles of the earlier paradigm and reorienting the questions for scientists, who then work within the new rules.

PRE-CLASSICAL AND CLASSICAL ECONOMICS

Kuhn's short, provocative book is worth reading by anyone interested in science or social science. The question it raises for us is whether economics also has paradigms. The answer seems to be both "yes" and "no."

First the "yes" answer. We can easily separate the history of economic thought into paradigm-like divisions that resemble the bounded inquiries of science. *One of the first such paradigms was the economics of the medieval schoolmen who argued and worried about the moral problems raised by the emerging market process.* For example, one of their main concerns was whether lending money at interest (usury) was in fact a sin (remember, in the early Middle Ages it had been considered a *mortal* sin); and they endlessly discussed the criteria for the "just" prices at which commodities should sell.

That view of the economic world was displaced by the Classical economists, whose most brilliant achievements were expressed in the works of Adam Smith and David Ricardo (1772–1823). The Classical economists had no interest whatever in just prices or in the sinfulness of usury. For them the great question was *how to understand, not evaluate, economic processes, in particular the accumulation and distribution of national wealth.* Smith, as we have seen, wrote an extraordinary exposition of how the members of society, although engaged in a search for their individual betterment, were nonetheless guided by an Invisible Hand (the market) to expand the wealth of nations. Ricardo wrote with equal force about the course of national economic growth, arguing that a growing population, pressing against limited fertile acreage, would drive up crop prices and divert the wealth of the country into the hands of the landlords.

MARGINALIST ECONOMICS

The Classical paradigm concerned large issues of national growth and dealt boldly with the fate of social classes. The Marxian paradigm, in turn, grew out of the Classical, differing from it in its much more critical approach to society and to thinking about society. Then, around the 1870s, a new angle of vision abruptly displaced the older one. The new view had numerous European originators, preeminent among them W. Stanley Jevons and Leon Walras. As a group they are referred to as the Marginalists, for *they turned the focus of economic inquiry away from growth and class conflict into a study of the interactions of individuals.*

The new paradigm explained many things that the older one did not—above all, the finer workings of the price system. But just as the Classical and Marxian paradigms had dropped all interest in the just prices that had so obsessed the medievalists, so the Marginalists paid little attention to the questions of growth and class fortune that had preoccupied the Classicists and Marxists.

KEYNESIAN ECONOMICS

Inherent in the Marginalist view of the world, with its extreme emphasis on interacting individuals rather than on classes, was a micro approach to economic problems. The next radical shift in view came from the work of John Maynard Keynes, whose perception of the economic system brought into focus a macro perspective on *total* income, *total* employment, *total* output. *The most striking result of Keynes's shift from a micro to a macro perspective was his discovery that an economy that worked well at the micro level did not necessarily work well at the macro level.* From the perspective of the Marginalists, such an economic state of affairs could hardly be envisioned.

PARADIGMS OR NOT?

Hence we can certainly discern sharp changes in the views and visions of economics.

The very definition of the economic problem alters as we go from the medieval schoolmen to the Keynesians. Classical economists, as we have said, forgot about economic justice; Marginalist economists, about growth or classes; Keynesian economists, about the inner working of the market.

These shifts in economic concerns resemble those of natural science. According to Kuhn, new paradigms bring new problems into focus, rather than resolving old ones within a new encompassing view. The camera of science is aimed, as it were, at a new subject and the former subject is relegated to the background, or drops out of the picture entirely.

Now the "no" part of the answer. Where economics differs from science in these paradigmatic jumps is that in economics we can relate changes in focus to a changing backdrop of social organization. Each "school" of economic thought reflects to some degree the historical characteristics and problems of its time; whereas a change in social structures generally plays a small role in causing one scientific perspective to replace another.

What "paradigm" rules economics today? A mixture of Marginalist and Keynesian thought lies behind most contemporary micro- and macroeconomics. A Marxian view underlies much of the radical critique of our time. Perhaps it is fair to say that no paradigm is firmly ensconced today. We live in a period in which much of the conventional wisdom of the past has been tried and found wanting. Economics is in a state of self-scrutiny, dissatisfied with its established premises, not yet ready to formulate new ones. Indeed, perhaps the search for a new vision of economics, a vision that will highlight new elements of reality and suggest new modes of analysis, is the most pressing economic task of our time.

CHAPTER 

A Bird's-Eye View of the Economy

A LOOK AHEAD

Before we begin our study of economics as a subject, we ought to know something about the economy. In this chapter we take a high-altitude pass over the terrain.

Things to watch for are:

1 The general dimensions of the two worlds of business—big business and small business.
2 The way in which income is divided up among households.
3 The size of the various government sectors. Note the plural—there is more than one meaning to "the government."

We can't begin to study economics without knowing something about the economy. But what is "the economy"? When we turn to the economics section of *Time* or *Newsweek* or pick up a business magazine, a jumble of things meets the eye: stock market ups and downs, reports on company fortunes and mishaps, accounts of incomprehensible "fluctuations in the exchange market," columns by business pundits, stories about unemployment or inflation.

How much of this is relevant? How are we to make our way through this barrage of reporting to something that we can identify as the economy?

BUSINESS

Of course we know where to start. Business enterprise is the very heart of an economic system of private property and market relationships. Let us begin, then, with a look at the world of business.

The first thing we notice is the enormous number of business enterprises—over 16 million in all. If we divide them into proprietorships (businesses owned by a single person), partnerships, and corporations, the world of business is classified in Table 1.

Small Business

Just looking at Table 1 makes one conclusion immediately clear: **There are at least two worlds of business.** One of them is the world of small business. It embraces nearly all proprietorships and partnerships, as well as a large percentage of corporations. Here are the vast bulk of the firms we find in the Yellow Pages of the phone book, the great preponderance of the country's farms, myriad mom-and-pop stores, restaurants, motels, movie houses, dry cleaners, druggists, retailers—in short, perhaps 95 percent of all the business firms in the nation.

Small business is the part of the business world with which we are all most familiar. We understand how a hardware store operates, whereas we have only vague ideas about how General Motors operates. But the world of small business

TABLE 1
Dimensions of Business, 1984
Note that corporations are overwhelmingly the most important, but by no means the most numerous, form of business organization.

	Total Number of Firms (000s)	*Total Sales (Billions)*	*Average Sales per Firm*
Proprietorships	11,262	$ 516	$ 45,817
Partnerships	1,644	318	193,430
Corporations	3,171	6,948	2,191,106

Sources: *Statistical Abstract of the United States;* Bureau of the Census, Washington, D.C., 1988.

warrants our attention for two other reasons.

First, small business is the employer of a substantial fraction—about half—of the nation's labor force. Second, the world of small business is the source of much "middle-class" opinion. As we can tell from Table 1, the 11 million proprietorships in the country have average sales (not profits) of less than $50,000 a year. These are tiny enterprises, but they certainly give a small-business point of view to over 11 million households—one out of every seven.

We should know something about what life is like in this world, and indeed, a considerable amount of economics is concerned with the problems of operating a small business. Later, when we reach microeconomics, we will study how small business fits into the economic picture.

Big Business

We have already glimpsed another business world, mainly to be found in the corporate enterprises of the nation. Compare the average size of the sales of corporations (Table 1) with those of proprietorships and partnerships. But even these figures hide the extraordinary difference between very big business and small business. Within the world of corporations, for example, 84 percent do less than $1 million worth of business a year. But the 16 percent that do more than $1 million worth of sales a year take in 92 percent of the receipts of all corporations.

Thus counterposed to a world of very numerous small businesses is a world of much less numerous big businesses. How large a world is it? Suppose we count as a big business any corporation with assets of $250 million or more. There are roughly 3,600 such businesses in America. More than half of them are in finance, insurance, and real estate. A fifth are in manufacturing. The rest are to be found in transportation, utilities, communication, trade. Just to get an idea of scale, the largest enterprise in the nation in 1987 was General Motors, with assets of $87 billion and sales of $101 billion.

Big business is to be found in all sectors; but its special place is the industrial sector, where manufacturing plays the predominant role.

The figures in Table 2 show once again the twofold division of the business world. If we subtract the 500 biggest industrial corporations and their sales from the total of all manufacturing firms and their sales, we find that the top 500 firms—not even one-tenth of one percent of the total number—accounted for more than three-quarters of all sales. **Indeed, if we take only the biggest 100 firms, we find that they are the source of just over half the sales of the entire industrial sector.**

TABLE 2
Industrial Sector, 1987
The 500 biggest firms—about .003 percent of all firms—account for three-fourths of all manufacturing sales.

	$ Billion
Total manufacturing sales	$2,268
Total sales of the 500 biggest industrial corporations	1,879

Sources: *Economic Report of the President,* 1988; Fortune 500.

A PARADE OF BUSINESS FIRMS

We shall have a good deal to investigate in later chapters about the world of big business. But it might be useful to end this initial survey with a dramatization of the problem. Suppose that we lined up our roughly 16 million businesses in order of size, starting with the smallest, along an imaginary road from San Francisco to New York. There will be 4,000 businesses to the mile, or a little less than one per foot. Suppose further that we planted a flag for each business. The height of the flagpole represents the volume of sales: each $10,000 in sales is shown by one foot of pole.

The line of flagpoles is a very interesting sight. From San Francisco to about Reno, Nevada, it is almost unnoticeable, a row of poles about a foot high. From Reno eastward the poles increase in height until, near Columbus, Ohio—about four-fifths of the way across the nation—flags fly about 10 feet in the air, symbolizing $100,000 in sales. Looking backward from Columbus, we can see that 12 million out of 16 million firms have sales of less than that amount.

But as we approach the eastern terminus, the poles suddenly begin to mount. There are about 850,000 firms in the country with sales over $500,000. These corporations occupy the last 71 miles of the 3,000-mile road. There are 505,000 firms with sales of over $1 million. They occupy the last 50 miles of the road, with poles at least 100 feet high. Then there are 1,500 firms with sales of $50 million or more. They take up the last quarter mile before the city limits, flags flying at skyscraper heights, 500 feet up.

But this is still not the climax. At the very gates of New York, on the last 100 feet of the last mile, we find the 100 largest industrial firms. They have sales of at least $11 billion, so that their flags are already miles high, far above the clouds. Along the last 10 feet of the road, there are the ten largest companies. Their sales are roughly $26 billion and up: Astronauts are the only ones who ever get a chance to see these flags.

HOUSEHOLDS

Business is not the only institutional feature we need to inspect in this introduction to the economy. How could business operate without a work force? Let us look at this work force as a collection of "households," as shown in Table 4.

The Work Force

Our table shows us an interesting fact about the household "sector." **There are more individual workers than there are households. This means that a typical household must have more than one member in the labor market.**

SECTORS

Economists are always talking about sectors. Sometimes, as is frequently the case in this book, they mean a part of the economy in which *motivations* are similar. For example, we talk of a private sector, made up of households and firms, and a public sector comprised of local, state, and federal agencies. The key difference here is motive. The private sector is driven by the desire for income or wealth. The public sector is directed by the aims and ambitions of people in political life. Private enhancement may be among these aims and ambitions, but usually much larger and more "public" issues motivate the lawmakers and administrators.

Sometimes, however, economists mean a *functional* division of the economy's activities. Then they typically speak of three sectors: (1) an agricultural sector that grows and harvests natural products; (2) an industrial sector that extracts and alters and assembles raw materials; and (3) a service sector that performs a miscellany of tasks: providing power and transportation, performing the tasks of storage and selling, and furnishing the thousand ministrations of personal service—legal services, maids' services, doctors' services, various governmental services.

Table 3 gives a general idea of the way in which employment and output are distributed among the three main functional sectors.

TABLE 3
Employment and GNP by Sectors, 1988
Most of the labor force works in stores or offices. Note how this ties into occupations, shown in Table 6.

	Employment	*GNP*
Agriculture	2%	2%
Industry	24	47
Services	74	51

Sources: *Survey of Current Business;* Bureau of Labor Statistics, *Employment and Earnings.*

Notice that roughly three-fourths of all employment and half of all output take place in the service sector. This does *not* mean that industry and agriculture are therefore unimportant. Try to imagine the consequences of one summer's shutdown in our smallest sector, farming!

TABLE 4
Household Characteristics, 1987
There are more workers than households.

	Millions
Total population	240
Number of households	89.5
Families	64
Nonfamily households	25.5
Individuals in work force	114

Sources: Census Bureau Reports *P-20* (March 1987); Bureau of Labor Statistics, *Employment and Earnings,* June 1988.

But what is a typical household? The answer is not easy, because there are many kinds of households: young or elderly households with only one individual in them; young married households without children; families with young children; families with offspring who are no longer young.

Economists look at the relation between households and work in terms of a **participation rate,** which shows the percentage of various groups who are working or looking for work. In the formal language of the statistician, they are "in the labor market." Table 5 shows how considerable is the variation of these rates.

Occupations

The table also shows us that sex is still a decisive element in determining the characteristics of the labor force. This has changed significantly and will probably change still further in the years to come: Women were only 31 percent of all workers in 1950; today they are roughly 50 percent.

What sort of work does our labor force perform? Table 6 tells us.

Later we will be looking more carefully into problems of occupations. Here we might note in passing that "white-collar" jobs—professional, managerial, sales, and clerical—employ over half the working force. Here is another strong root of the American middle class.

Distribution of Income

Households interest us not only because they are the source of our labor power, but also because they are the focus of our income and our wealth. Much of the buying

TABLE 5
Participation Rates, 1988
Participation rates vary greatly.

	Percent of Group in Labor Market
Males, 20 years and older	78.0
Females, 20 years and older	56.4
Both sexes, 16–19	52.4
Males, 65 and older	16.5
Females, 65 and older	9.3

Source: Bureau of Labor Statistics, *Employment and Earnings.*

TABLE 6
Occupational Distribution of the Labor Force, 1986
Over half the work force is white-collar.

		Percent	
Professional		13	
Managerial	White-	11	
Sales	collar	12	54
Clerical		16	
Craftsmen		12	
Operatives	Blue-	11	30
Nonfarm laborers	collar	4	
Farm workers		3	
Other service workers	Both	18	

Source: *Statistical Abstract of the United States.*

that powers the economic machine is cycled through the household, where purchasing power is collected as wages, salaries, dividends, interest, and rents, to be pumped out again as a flow of spending for consumer goods. Consumer buying, as we will see later, is a strong force for growth in our economy, although we should emphasize right away that it is not the only force. Business and government are also buyers in their own right and strongly influence the flow of purchasing power.

We focus on households at this stage of our inquiry because their function as buyers leads us naturally to inquire into the distribution of purchasing power among families. There are many ways of describing income distribution. We will use a method that will divide the country, like a great cake, into "quintiles"—five layers of equal size. The layers will help us give dollars-and-cents definitions of what we usually have in mind when we speak of the poor, the working class, the middle class, and so on. As we will see, the amounts are not at all what most of us imagine.

The Poor

We will begin with the bottom layer, the poor. Our definition will include as "poor" all the households in the bottom 20 percent of the income distribution. From data gathered by the Census Bureau, we know that the highest income of a family in this bottom slice of the five-layered cake was $13,886 in 1986. This way of defining and measuring income distribution gives us a picture of *relative* poverty, since the bottom quintile will always be considered "poor," no matter what its income. Government statistics often stress *absolute* poverty levels, calculated according to the cost of a minimal basket of consumption goods. The income figure calculated on an absolute basis is somewhat lower than the one done on a relative basis, and the number of households living in "absolute" poverty is lower than the number existing in relative poverty: In 1986 the Census Bureau calculated that 13.6 percent of the total population was below its absolute poverty level of $11,203 for a family of four.

The box titled "Who Are the Poor?" on page 58 shows us some of the characteristics of poor families, but there are two additional facts that we should note.

First, not all families below the poverty line in any given census are still

WHO ARE THE POOR?

Work and Welfare. In 1986 there were 32.4 million people living in "absolute" poverty in the United States, an increase from 24.7 million in 1977. Of these, many were poor *despite* holding a job: 41.7 percent of poor people over the age of 14 worked, and these "working poor" constituted the most rapidly growing part of the poverty population. Only one-third of poor people in the United States receive "welfare" (Aid to Families with Dependent Children) payments. Medicaid, the program that provides health insurance for poor people, reaches only 42 percent of the poor.

Age and Race. Until recently, the elderly were disproportionately poor. Today, however, the burden of poverty falls most heavily on children: 20.5 percent of all children were poor in 1986. Race is a major factor: Poverty afflicted 43.1 percent of black children and 37.7 percent of Hispanic children in that year. Still, the overwhelming majority of the poor are (and always have been) white: 69 percent, compared with 28 percent who are black and 3 percent of other races.

Homelessness and Hunger. A recent task force on hunger reported that 20 million Americans, including 12 million children, went hungry at some point each month. And then there were the homeless—in 1986, 28 percent of them with children.

Adapted from *Who Are the Poor?* by Michael Harrington, published by Justice for All; reprinted in *Dissent,* Spring 1988, 148.

there in the next. About one-fifth of all poor households are young people just starting their careers. Some of these low-income beginners will escape from poverty. In addition, about an eighth of the members of the poverty class are older people. Many of these were not poor in an earlier, more productive stage of their economic lives. At the same time, some families that are not poor when a census is taken will fall into poverty at a later stage of their lives. The moral is that poverty is not entirely static. At any moment, some families are escaping from poverty, some entering it. What counts, of course, is whether the net movement is in or out. This is important with regard to welfare, a problem we will take up in Chapter 35.

A second characteristic is that 60 percent of the families below the poverty line have at least one wage earner in the labor force. Thus their poverty reflects inadequate earnings. A considerable amount of poverty, in other words, stems from the fact that some jobs do not pay enough to lift a jobholder above the low-income level. In some regions certain jobs pay so little that even families with two jobholders (especially if one works only seasonally) cannot pull themselves out of poverty. This is often the case, for example, with migrant farm workers or with immigrants who must take the least desirable jobs.

The Working Class

We usually define the working class in terms of certain occupations. We may call a factory operative—but not a salesclerk—working class, even though the factory employee may make more than the salesclerk.

For present purposes, however, we will just add together the next two layers of the income cake and call them working class. This will include the 40 percent of the population that is above the poor. We choose this method to find out how large an income a family can make and still remain in the working class, as we have defined it. The answer for 1987 is just under $35,015. To put it differently, 40 percent of the families in the country earned more than $13,886 but less than $35,015 that year.

UNIONS

How many members of the labor force offer their services through labor unions? In 1987 there were 17 million. That was 18 percent of the work force.

These figures do not convey the power of labor unions because they do not point out the strengths of unions in the industrial sector. The table shows more accurately how labor unions fit into the overall work picture.

Like corporations, unions show great disparity of size and strength. In the mid-1980s there were some 50,000 local unions. Many of these small locals had memberships of 50 persons or fewer and were confined to a single enterprise. At the other end of the scale we find 210 large "national" unions, including such giants as the Teamsters or the United Auto Workers. In fact, the 10 biggest unions in the country account for over half of all union membership. Thus unions, like corporations, divide into a world of small and large operations, although the contrast in the unions is not quite so dramatic as in the corporations.

TABLE 7
Percent of Unionization, 1986
Unionization is very unevenly distributed by sectors.

Sector	*Employment (Millions)*	*Unionized (percent)*
Agriculture	1.4	2.4
Industry (manufacturing and mining)	21.1	23.7
Services and other	75.2	14.0
Government (federal, state, and local)	16.3	36.0

Source: *Statistical Abstract of the United States,* 1988.

The Rich and the Upper Class

With the bottom three-fifths of the nation located on the income scale, we are ready to look into the income levels of the upper echelons.

First, the rich. Where do riches begin? A realistic answer is probably around $200,000 a year, an income that usually means significant corporate responsibility. There are at least 500,000 such rich families in America, or a little under 1 percent of the total. They are the icing on the cake.

But under the truly rich is a considerably larger group that we call the upper class. This is the top 5 percent of the nation, its average doctors, airline pilots, managers, lawyers—even some economists. Some 4.5 million families are in this top 5 percent.

How much income does it take to get there? In 1987 a family made it into the 95th percentile with an income of $82,273. These numbers have a certain shock value. **It takes more money to be rich, but less to be upper class, than many of us ordinarily think.**

The Middle Class

This leaves us with the middle class—the class to which we all think we belong. By our method of cutting the cake, the middle class includes 35 percent of the nation—everyone above the $35,015 top working-class income and below the $82,273 threshold of upper-class income. In 1987 an average white married couple, both working, earned about $40,000, enough to enter middle class economic territory. No wonder that a middle-class feeling pervades American society, regardless of the occupation or social milieu from which families come.*

WEALTH

It is obvious that there are great extremes of income distribution in the United States. The famous economist Paul Samuelson has made the observation that if we built an income pyramid out of children's blocks, with each layer representing $1,000 of income, the peak would be far higher than the Eiffel Tower—but most of us would be within a yard of the ground.

Even more striking than the inequality of income, however, is the inequality of wealth—that is, the ownership of assets of all kinds. The latest survey by the Federal Reserve Board gives us the overall distribution of wealth, which we show in Table 8. It tells us that four out of ten American families in 1983 had little or no wealth. Their average holdings probably include a small bank account, a mortgaged home, perhaps some life insurance or pension rights. The next third of all

*Maybe you wonder how an "average white married couple" could enter an income group that we have defined as being not average. The answer is that not every household in our national layer cake is white or married, with both husband and wife working. Moreover, don't forget that these figures apply to 1987. To bring them up to date, increase them by the change in average prices since 1987. That won't be precisely accurate, but close enough.

TABLE 8
The Distribution of Wealth, 1983
We can see that wealth is much more unevenly distributed than income

Net Worth	*Percentage of All Families*
Less than $16,000	40
16,001 to 82,000	33
82,001 to 327,000	21
327,001 to 655,000	4
655,000 or more	3

Source: *Federal Reserve Bulletin,* March 1986, p. 167. All figures have been rounded for convenience sake.

families have modest assets—a larger bank account, a better home less encumbered with a mortgage, more insurance coverage. It is not until we reach the upper quarter (actually the upper twenty-eight percent) that we begin to find considerable personal assets, and not until we enter the top group that we encounter substantial holdings. Here is where the millionaire category begins.

A PARADE OF INCOMES

Suppose that like our parade of flags across the nation representing the sales of business firms, we lined up the population in order of its income. Assume the height of the middle family to be 6 feet, representing a median income of $29,458 in 1987. This will be our height, as observers. What would our parade look like?*

It would begin with a few families *below* the ground, for there are some households with negative incomes; that is, they report losses for the year. Mainly these are families with business losses, and their negative incomes are not matched by general poverty. Following close on their heels comes a long line of economic dwarfs who make up about one-fifth of all families. These are people less than 3 feet tall; some are shorter than 1 foot.

Only after the parade is half over do we reach people whose faces are at our level. Then come the giants. When we reach the last 5 percent of the parade—incomes around $82,000—people are at least 17 feet tall. At the very end of the parade are people towering 600 to 6,000 feet into the air—100 to 1,000 times taller than the middle height. What is the largest income in the country? We do not know: Probably our 15 or so billionaires have *incomes* of over $100 million.

*Adapted from the description of an "income parade" by Jan Pen, *Income Distribution,* trans. Trevor S. Preston (New York: Praeger, 1971), pp. 48–59.

Millionaires

How many U.S. families are millionaires—that is, own net assets worth $1 million or more? The Federal Reserve study shows that the number is considerably larger than was the case 20 years ago (allowing for inflation, of course) Four percent of all American families were estimated to be worth $500,000, and 2 percent (an estimated 1,310,000) had a net worth of $1 million in 1983. If we exclude the direct ownership of a home or personal business, about 376,000 families (one-half of one percent of all families) were worth $1 million or more in financial assets alone—stocks and bonds of publicly owned companies, mutual funds, insurance, bank deposits, and the like. This is about twice as large as a percentage of all families as in 1962—once again, taking inflation into account.*

America's millionaires own a very large proportion of the nation's financial assets. The Federal Reserve study showed that in 1983 the top one-half of one percent of families owned 56 percent of the nation's municipal (tax-exempt) bonds, 43 percent of all publicly traded stock, 69 percent of all trust accounts. The top *10* percent of all families owned 92 percent of all municipal bonds, 85 percent of all traded stock, and 88 percent of all trust funds, as well as about 40 percent of all checking accounts, almost three-quarters of all money market mutual funds, and almost two-thirds of all retirement or Keogh accounts.

How Millionaires Have Fared

There is no doubt, in other words, that the ownership of wealth is heavily concentrated. The *value* of this wealth can fluctuate considerably, however. Take a man who was a millionaire in 1970, and who invested his wealth in common stocks. He would have lost about one-half the value of this wealth by early 1982 because the cost of living doubled but the stock market stubbornly refused to budge.

Then came a great stock market boom in 1982 and a second, even more dramatic one from late 1985 through the summer of 1987. This was followed by the biggest selloff in history, when the market plunged by about a third in October 1987. At the end of this roller-coaster ride, our millionaire would have been worth approximately two and a half times as many dollars as he started with in 1982. Even after inflation, he would still have more or less doubled his real wealth. Of course, if our investor had had 20-20 foresight (there are not so many of those), he would have stepped off the train at the end of August in 1987. By then, he would have tripled his real wealth—always assuming that he had bought stocks that reflected how the market performed on the average. At any rate, we can see that the value of the wealth held by the top wealth-holders can change dramatically, even though the actual holdings of assets hardly changes at all.

*Financial Characteristics of High-Income Families," *Federal Reserve Bulletin,* March 1986, pp. 163–177.

TABLE 9
Size of Government Sector, 1986
Note that the size of the sector varies, depending on what function of government we emphasize.

	Percent of Total
Employment by government	15%
GNP bought by government	20
Personal income paid by government	26

Source: *Economic Report of the President.*

GOVERNMENT

We have almost completed our first overview of the economy, but there remains one institution with which we must gain an acquaintance: the government. How shall we size up so vast and complex an institution? Let us begin with the question of size: How big is the government within the overall economy?

The Size of the Public Sector

The question can be answered in at least three different ways, as Table 9 shows. **In round numbers government employs about one-sixth of the labor force; it buys about one-fifth of our total output (GNP); and it pays out about one-quarter of all personal incomes.** This is obviously big government. Is it too big? That is not a question that can easily be answered "yes" or "no." The following facts bear on our answer.

Government as Employer

When economists speak of "government" or the "public sector," they refer to *all* government activities, not just those of the federal government. For example, as Table 10 shows, state and local government play a considerably larger role than federal government when it comes to our first measure—public employment. Indeed, if we take away national defense, as a special kind of activity, state and local government becomes about *seven times larger* than the federal government as an employer.

Government as a Buyer of GNP

Next let us consider the size of government as a buyer of GNP—that is, as a direct purchaser of the goods and services counted within GNP. Here two considerations should be borne in mind. First, about 44 percent of the GNP bought by the public sector is purchased by the federal government. Three-quarters of this is for defense. Fifty-six percent of GNP purchases are bought by state and local

TABLE 10
Kinds of Public Employment, 1985
Most public employees work for states and localities, not for the federal government. The figure for national defense includes civilian employment only. It does not cover some 2 million in the armed forces.

	Federal	State (Number of Employees in Thousands)	Local
National defense	1,101	—	—
Postal service	754	—	—
Education	15	1,764	5,340
Highways	4	252	296
Health	263	678	712
Public Welfare	12	186	282
Police	66	81	613
Fire protection	—	—	317
Sanitation	—	1	220
Resources and recreation	241	196	269
Financial administration	118	131	190
Other	447	695	1,496
Totals	2,638	3,984	9,685

Source: *Statistical Abstract of the United States.*

governments for the kinds of purposes outlined in Table 8. Second, the fraction of GNP bought by the total government sector is roughly the same in this country as in European capitalisms, as Table 11 shows. Japan's percentage is smaller, mainly because it has so small a defense establishment.

Government as an Income Source

Finally, we have to consider the size of government measured by its contribution to income. As we have seen, the contribution of government to total incomes is larger than the value of public output. The reason is that government pays out some money to households other than the wages and salaries earned by public employees. The additional incomes are called *transfer payments* because they transfer incomes from some members of the community (usually taxpayers) to others—retirees, handicapped persons, disadvantaged citizens.

Transfers are almost entirely paid by the federal government. Of the many kinds

TABLE 11
Size of the Public Sector in Western Capitalisms, 1983
Measured by employment or expenditure, the United States public sector is well within the range of the public sectors in other major capitalist countries.

Country	Gov't Employment as Percent of Total Employment	Gov't Outlays as Percent of Total GDP*
United States	16.5	38.1
Japan	6.5	34.8
West Germany	15.9	48.6
United Kingdom	22.0	47.2

*GDP is gross domestic product (GNP less net factor payments to foreigners).
Source: *OECD Historical Statistics* (OECD, 1985).

of transfer payments, social security is by far the most important. Together with Medicare, this absorbs about a third of all expenditures made by the public sector. A quite different form of transfer is interest payments on the national debt or subsidies to farmers or businesses. Still another form of transfers is unemployment benefits or out-and-out welfare programs of one kind or another.

Welfare programs are a bone of contention among economists, as they are among politicians. We will just note here that the share of all transfer payments in GNP tends to be smaller in the United States than in other advanced capitalisms. We are not carrying a transfer burden that is heavier than that of, say Canada or West Germany or Italy.

Government Waste

Finally, in examining the size of the public sector, we have to consider its weight on our backs. Does government spending retard economic growth? Is it wasteful? That is a question we will meet many times as we go along. But in view of the heat it generates, we ought to state our own position now. **We believe that government can be a source of vitality and growth to the economy as well as a drag and a drain.** Everyone is acutely aware of the wasteful nature of many public projects, local as well as federal, civilian as well as military. On the other side of the coin, anyone who has ever gone to a public school, been treated in a public hospital, traveled on a public road, or flown in a plane guided by a public beacon system knows how useful public output can be. No simple judgment about the public sector can be an intelligent one.

LOOKING BACK

KEY CONCEPTS

The purpose of this chapter is not to load you with facts and figures, but to give you a sense of economic geography—a feeling for the terrain we call The Economy. The central ideas that we ought to have clearly in mind are these:

Business institutions:
- corporations
- partnerships
- proprietorships

1 Business is the most distinctive and important institution in a capitalist system. There are a very large number of private business organizations, but by far the most important of them are corporations, not partnerships or proprietorships. If you are not sure of the difference, read the important extra word following this.

Big business accounts for the preponderance of sales; small business is a substantial source of employment.

2 In the world of corporations there are clearly visible two subworlds of business—big business and little business. There is no official dividing line between the two. But if we take the top 500 corporations, we find that we account for 74 percent of all industrial sales, 60 percent of all industrial employment, and about 11 percent of all employment. Small business is also important because it is a big employer of nonindustrial workers, particularly retail or service workers.

Households are the source of labor.

3 Households are the source of the nation's labor force. Most households supply more than one worker, but participation rates vary widely among age and sex groups.

Income distribution: about one-fifth poor; about one-third middle class; about 5 percent affluent

4 For illustrative purposes we can classify one-fifth of all families and individuals as poor; two-fifths as working class; one-third as middle class; and 5 percent as upper class. While this classification gives us some idea of the ranges of family incomes in the different layers of the national income cake, we should note that the distribution of wealth is much more lopsided than the distribution of income.

The government sector varies in size, depending on what you measure.

5 Government is a very important but confusing institution to study. Its size depends on whether we assess its contribution to employment (roughly one-sixth); to GNP (about one-fifth); or to total household incomes (about one-quarter). Facts to remember: (a) State and local government is the main source of government employment and buys more of GNP than the federal government, whose purchases are mainly for defense; (b) transfer payments, largely for social security, swell the total of income payments above that of purchases of goods and services; and (c) the overall size of U.S. government in GNP, on any measure, is much like that of other advanced Western capitalist systems.

ECONOMIC VOCABULARY

Corporations 53
Sector 55
Poverty, relative and absolute 57
Participation rate 56
Quintiles 57

QUESTIONS

1. How would you explain the fact that big business has made so much headway in industrial production, but not in farming or retailing?
2. Do the facts of income and wealth distribution surprise you? Please you? Shock you? With what arguments would you defend the existing distribution: Fairness and equity? Efficiency? Natural differences among individuals?
3. When we say that the government is "too big" in this country, do we mean as a producer, an employer, or a payer of incomes? Is it possible to argue that the government is too *small* a producer, employer, or income payer? Suppose you wanted to increase our defense budget. Would you not be arguing just that?

AN EXTRA WORD ABOUT

Business Organization

Business is a central institution in our economic system, and all of us ought to know something about how business, especially the corporation, is legally organized. Although corporations are the dominant form of business property, too few people are well informed about them. Here is a brief introduction to the main forms of business organization.

PROPRIETORSHIPS

A proprietorship is the simplest kind of business organization. Usually it can be set up without any legal fuss at all, simply by opening a place of business. Sometimes one has to register or get a license, for instance, to open a liquor store or to set up practice as a physician or lawyer. But proprietorships are the easiest to understand of all forms of business.

They are also, as we have seen, the most widespread form (see Table 1). Why are not all businesses proprietorships? The answer lies in certain problems that proprietorships have.

1. A proprietorship has difficulty growing because its ability to borrow money is limited to the amount of credit its owner-proprietor can raise. Only a very rich man can borrow very much.

2. A proprietor is personally liable for all losses that his business may incur (he also gets all its profits). A rich man is not likely to open a proprietary business because if an unexpected loss is incurred—if his business is sued by an irate customer and loses the case—*the proprietor must pay from his own funds any obligations that the business cannot pay from its funds.* In fact, there is really no division between the property of the owner and that of the business.

3. When a proprietor dies, the business legally comes to an end. All debts must be paid, and a new business established to take over the old. This is hard on the spouse of the proprietor, the employees, and the creditors.

PARTNERSHIPS

Partnerships remedy many of these difficulties. Basically, a partnership is a combination of proprietors who have agreed, usually by legal formalities, to share a certain proportion of the profits and the losses of their business. The fact that there are now several people associated in the business obviously makes it easier to raise additional capital. Some very large businesses have been partnerships, at least until recent days.

Nonetheless, there are still problems for partnerships.

1. Partners are together responsible for all the losses or debts of the business. Like proprietors, partners jointly have "unlimited" liability, although some individual partners may have only limited liability.

2. The death of any partner requires that the business be legally reconstituted. When a partner of a firm dies, the firm usually has to undergo a reorganization.

CORPORATIONS

The corporation, as we have seen, is the most powerful, although not the most prevalent, form of business organization. Let us be sure that we understand exactly what a corporation is.

1. A corporation is a legal entity created by the state. Unlike a proprietorship or a partnership, all corporations must apply to their states for a charter allowing them to carry on business. The charter specifies in general terms the kinds of business they will carry on and the general financial structures they will have. Charters cost money, which is one reason that all proprietorships are not corporations. Another reason is that corporations pay income taxes on their income before it goes to stockholders.

2. Once a corporation is chartered, it exists as a "person." That is, the corporation itself—not the individuals who own it or work for it—can bring suit, be sued, or own property. This has the immediate advantage of limiting the liability of an owner of a corporation to the money he has put into the corporation. If the corporation is sued for more funds than the business possesses, the corporation will declare bankruptcy and the suer has no recourse to the private funds of the persons who own it.

3. Because the corporation is a "person," it does not go out of business when its owners die. The corporation is "immortal." It goes on until it fails as a business organization or voluntarily goes out of business, or until its charter is revoked by the state.

CORPORATE ORGANIZATION

Clearly, the corporation has substantial advantages over proprietorships and partnerships. But how does it run? Who owns it?

A corporation is owned by the individuals who buy shares in it. Suppose that a corporation is granted a charter to carry on a business in retail trade. The charter also specifies how many shares of stock this business enterprise is allowed to issue. For example, a corporation may be formed with the right to issue 100,000 shares. If these shares are sold to individuals at a price of $10 each, the original shareholders (also called stockholders) will have put $1 million into the corporation. In return, each will receive stock certificates indicating how many shares that person has bought.

These stock certificates are somewhat like a partnership agreement, although there are noteworthy differences. If you buy 1,000 shares in our imaginary corporation, you will own 1 percent of the corporation. You will have the right to receive 1 percent of all income that it pays out as dividends on its stock. You will also be entitled to cast

1,000 votes—one vote per share—at the meetings of shareholders that all corporations must hold. In this way, a shareholder is very much like a junior partner who was given a 1 percent interest in a business.

ADVANTAGES OF SHARE OWNERSHIP

But here are the critical differences between corporations and partnerships:

1. As we have already said, a stockholder is not personally liable for any debts that the corporation cannot pay. If the company goes bankrupt, the shareholder will lose his investment of $10,000 (1,000 shares at $10 a share) but cannot be sued for any further money. *Liability is thereby limited to the amount the shareholder has invested.*

2. Unlike partnership shares, which are usually very difficult to sell, corporation shares are generally easy to sell if one owns the stock of a company that is listed (bought and sold) on one of the nation's several stock markets. (The shares of a very small corporation are not as easy to sell, although they are less difficult to dispose of than a partnership.) Moreover, a stockholder may sell shares to anyone, at any price. If our imaginary corporation prospers, its shares may sell for $20 each. A stockholder is perfectly free to sell his or her shares at that price. As we have just mentioned, marketplaces for stocks and bonds have developed along with the corporation, to facilitate such sales of stock. The most important of these markets, the New York Stock Exchange, was organized in 1817. Today some 40 billion shares a year are bought and sold on the stock exchange. Thus, with the corporation comes the advantage of a much greater "liquidity" of personal wealth—that is, greater ease of turning assets into cash.

3. Shares of stock entitle the stockholder to the dividends that the directors of the corporation (see below) may decide to pay out for each share. But a shareholder is not entitled to any fixed amount of profit. If the corporation prospers, the directors may vote to pay a large dividend. But they are under no obligation to do so. They may wish to use the earnings of the corporation for other purposes, such as the purchase of new equipment or land. If the corporation suffers losses, ordinarily the directors will vote to pay no dividend or only a small one out of past earnings. Thus, as an owner of ordinary common stock, the stockholder takes the risk of having dividends rise or fall.

4. Corporations are also allowed to issue bonds. A bond is different from a share of stock in two ways. First, a bond has a *stated value* printed on its face, whereas a share of stock does not. A $1,000 bond issued by a corporation is a certificate for a debt of $1,000. The bondholder is not a sharer in the profits of the company but a creditor of the corporation—someone to whom the corporation is in debt for $1,000. In case of corporate bankruptcy, the claims of bondholders take precedence over those of shareholders.

Second, a bond also states on its face the *amount of income* it will pay to bondholders. A $1,000 bond may declare that it will pay $80 a year as interest. Unlike dividends, this interest payment will not rise if the corporation makes money, nor will it fall if it does not. Thus there is no element of profit-sharing in bonds, as there is in stocks. Like stocks, bonds can rise and fall in price when they are bought and sold, but bond interest does not change the way that stock dividends can. A bond's *coupon*—its stated interest payment—always remains the same; it is the *yield* on bonds—the ratio between the coupon and the market price—that varies. We will look into this again when we study interest rates in Chapter 21.

Bondholders are compensated for not sharing in profits. The risk of owning a bond is usually less than that of owning a stock. A bond is a legal obligation of the corporation, which *must* pay interest, and which *must* buy back the bond itself when a fixed term of years has expired and the bond becomes "due." If it fails to meet either of these obligations, the courts will declare the firm bankrupt, and all its assets will be turned over to the bondholders to satisfy their debts. If the firm's assets are not enough to repay the bondholders, they will suffer a degree of loss; but the shareholders will lose *all* of their equity, for a share of stock has no such obligations attached to it and never becomes due. No shareholder can sue a corporation if it fails to pay a dividend.

OWNERSHIP AND CONTROL

One last matter is of significance in discussing the organization of the corporation. This mode of structuring enterprise has made possible a development of great importance: the separation of ownership and control.

As we have seen, stockholders are the actual owners of a corporation, but it is obviously impossible for large numbers of stockholders to meet regularly and run a company. A.T.&T. has well over a million stockholders. Where could they meet? And how could they possibly decide what the company should do?

All corporations, small or large, therefore, are run by boards of directors (who may or may not own stock in the company) who are elected by the stockholders. At regular intervals, all stockholders are asked to elect or reelect members of the board, each casting as many votes as the number of shares that he or she owns. In turn, the board of directors appoints the "management"—main officials of the corporation; for example, its chief executive officer. Management hires the rest of the employees. As the number of shareowners grows, it is not surprising that power drifts into the hands of the management. (The extent to which managers can operate independently of, or even contrary to, the interests of stockholders is one of the hotly debated questions in economics.)

STOCK EXCHANGES

We have mentioned stock exchanges as the organized markets in which shares are traded. *An important thing to realize is that buying a share of stock does not put money into a corporation, unless the stock is newly issued by the company.*

Most of the shares bought and sold on the stock exchanges are old shares, issued years ago. When you buy a share of General Motors, the money you pay does *not* go to General Motors. It goes to the individual who sold you the shares. If you own shares in a company that produces cigarettes, and you want to get out of this business because you disapprove of smoking, you sell your shares. *But doing so does not take any money out of the cigarette business.* It simply transfers your shares to another person who will pay you for your stock certificates.

Does it then make no difference to a cigarette company whether you buy its shares or not? Not quite. Corporations like to have their shares well regarded by the public because from time to time they *do* issue new shares, and they want an eager market for these shares. If their shares are in general disfavor, they will sell for lower prices, and at a lower price a company is easier to "take over" than at a higher price.* Finally, managers usually own shares in their own companies. As the shares go up, they become richer. So companies are far from indifferent to the fate of their shares. Nonetheless, we should clearly understand that we do not put money into businesses when we buy their outstanding shares.

*A "takeover" is a concerted effort, usually by a small group of individuals who own a considerable amount of the company's stock, to round up enough proxies (votes) to oust an incumbent management and to install a management of its own. Takeovers are dramatic when they occur. They are not frequent, but they happen often enough so that corporations keep an eye out for "raiding" interests. If the price of the stock falls, it is often an invitation to be taken over, simply because it is cheaper to buy the votes (shares) when the price is depressed.

CHAPTER 5

The Trend of Things

A LOOK AHEAD

The last chapter was an aerial photo of the economy, giving us the lay of the land. Now we want to take a series of pictures over time to give us a sense of change in the economic landscape. This will fit into our first historic conception of capitalism, gained in Chapter 2, and will also give us a chance to test some of the theories about capitalism we covered in Chapter 3.

In particular, we are going to examine four major trends of modern times:

1 The growth of production measured by GNP—gross national product.
2 Trends in income distribution.
3 The drift toward big business.
4 The rise in government.

Warning before you begin: Don't get bogged down in facts and figures. Keep your eye out for trends and for explanations of trends. The facts are there to illustrate these trends and to test explanations, not to be learned for themselves.

THE PROCESS OF GROWTH

Imagine that we have had a camera trained on the U.S. economy over the last 60 years. What would be the most striking changes to meet our eye?

There is no doubt about the first impression: It would be a sense of growth. Everything would be getting larger. Business firms would be growing in size. Labor unions would be bigger. There would be many more households, and each household would be richer. Government would be much larger. And underlying all of this, the extent of the market system itself—the great ongoing flow of inputs and outputs—would be steadily increasing in size.

Growth is not, of course, the only thing we would notice. Businesses are different as well as bigger when we compare 1988 and 1929: There are far more corporations now than in the old days, far more diversified businesses, fewer family firms. Households are different because more women work outside the home. Labor unions today are no longer mainly craft unions, limited to one occupation. Government is not only bigger but has a different philosophy.

Total Output

Nonetheless, it is growth that first commands our attention. The camera vision of the economy gives us a picture that keeps widening. It *has* to widen to encompass the increase in the sheer mass of output. Hence the first institution whose growth we must examine is that of the market system itself.

More specifically, we must trace the tremendous growth in our total output. The technical name for this flow of output is gross national product (GNP), a term we will use many times in the future and will later define more carefully. Here we only note that it is the dollar value of our annual flow of final output. Figure 1 gives us a graphic representation of this increase in yearly output.

Correcting for Inflation

As we can see, the dollar value of all output from 1929 to 1988 has grown enormously. But perhaps a cautionary thought will have already struck you. If we measure the growth of output by comparing the dollar value of production over time, what seems to be growth in actual economic activity may be no more than a rise in prices. If the economy in 1988 produced no more actual tons of grain than the economy in 1929 but grain prices were double those of 1929, our GNP figures would show growth where there was really nothing but inflation.

To arrive at a measure of real growth, we have to correct for changes in prices. To do so, we take one year as a *base* and use the prices of that year to evaluate output in all succeeding years.

Here is an elementary example. Suppose our grain economy produced 1 million tons in 1929 and 2 million in 1988, but wheat sold for $1 in 1929 and $4 in 1988. Our GNP in the current prices of 1929 and 1988 is $1 million for 1929 and $8 million 59 years later. But if we evaluate the GNP *using only the 1929 prices* (i.e., $1

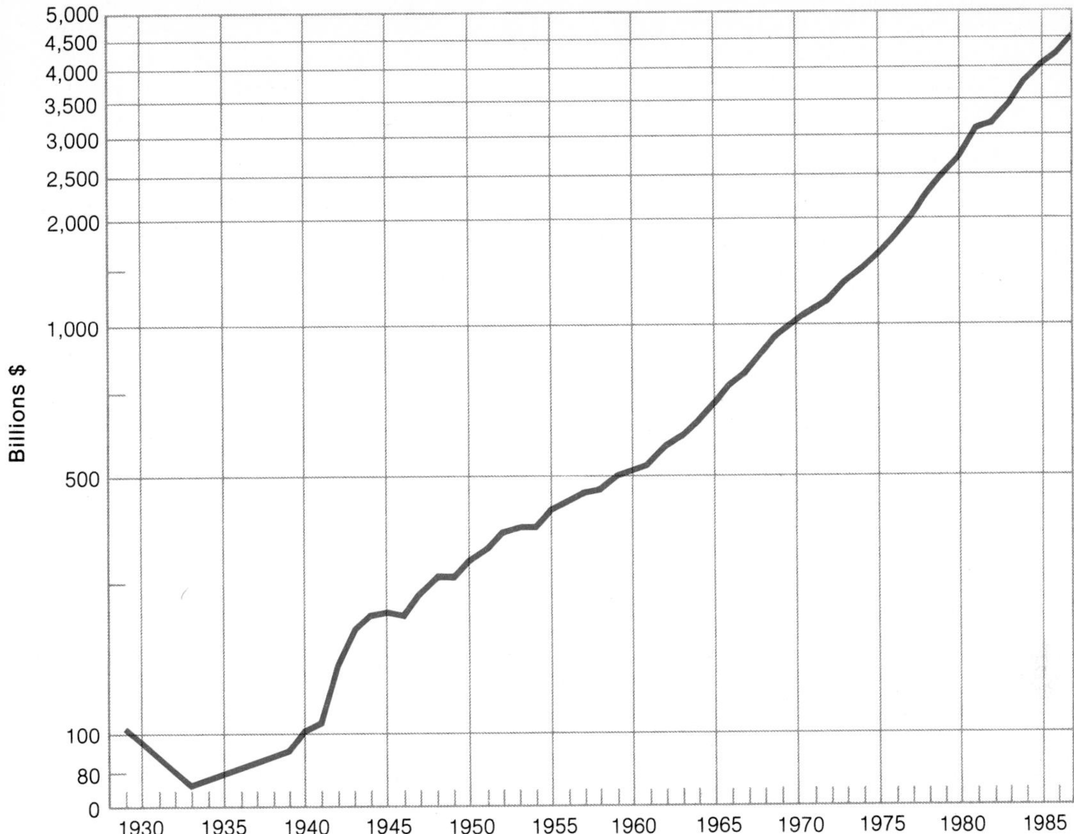

FIGURE 1
Value of GNP 1929–1988
Gross national product (GNP) increased 44-fold in 59 years, as measured in the prices of each year's production. In this graph we use a semilog scale because it shows more clearly the rate of growth *rather than the absolute dollar growth of GNP. Note how the rate of growth of nominal GNP has accelerated since 1940. From 1940 to 1965 the speedup reflects mainly an acceleration of real GNP growth. After 1965 the further acceleration mainly reflects inflation.*

per bushel), our GNP is reduced to $2 million in 1988. This constant-dollar GNP is often referred to as the *real GNP,* while the current-dollar GNP is called the *nominal GNP.* We can use the prices of any year as the base. The important thing is that all outputs must be evaluated with only one set of prices.

Figure 2 shows us the much-reduced growth of output when output is measured in 1982 dollars, the year now most frequently used as a base.

As we can see, growth in real (or constant-dollar) terms is much less dramatic than growth in current dollars that make no allowance for rising prices. Nonetheless, the value of 1988 output, compared to that of 1929, with price changes eliminated as best we can, still shows a growth factor of almost 5½.

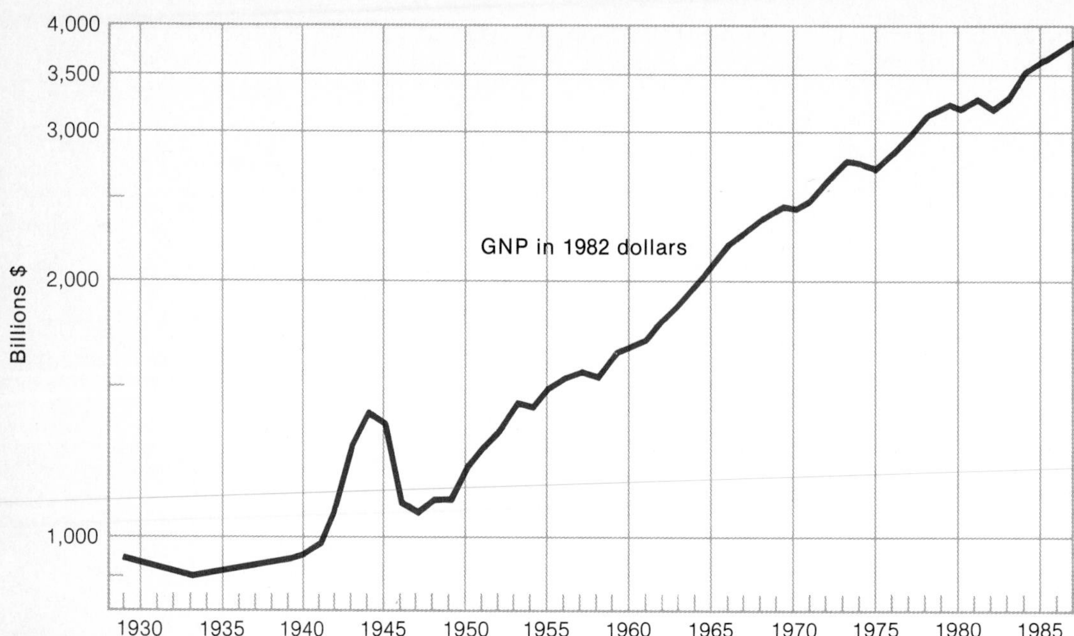

FIGURE 2
GNP in Constant (1982) Dollars
Measured in real terms, GNP increased only about 5½ times, not 44 times, between 1929 and 1988. Note that, except for the major interruption of the Depression and World War II, real economic growth has followed a nearly constant trend in history.
Source: *Economic Report of the President, 1986.*

Per Capita Growth

But there still remains one last adjustment to be made. The growth of output is a massive assemblage of goods and services to be distributed among the nation's households, and the number of those households has increased. In 1929 the United States population was 122 million; in 1988 it was about 243 million. To bring our constant GNP down to life size, we have to divide it by population to get GNP per person, or per capita.

Historical Record

In Figure 3 we see the American experience from the middle of the nineteenth century in terms of real per capita GNP, this time in 1929 prices.* Viewed from the long perspective of history, our average rate of growth has been astonishingly consistent. This holds true for an average over the past half century since the Great

*Why do we use 1929 as a base here and 1982 as a base in Figure 2? We do it to accustom you to the idea that different years can serve as the basis for comparison. Note, too, that our 10% bands are approximate—they should be wider in the later years, and narrower in the earlier, than they are drawn.

VOLUME AND VALUE

You should be warned that there is no entirely satisfactory way of wringing price increases out of the hodgepodge of goods and services called GNP, and so of measuring precisely the increase in the "real" volume of goods and services. That is because there is an unavoidable element of arbitrariness in grouping or adding together the various price changes that occur in different goods when the relative proportions of these goods in total output are also changing. This class of difficulties is known as "index number problems."

For example, consider an economy that produces two goods, wheat and steel, in two periods, 1900 and 1990. Suppose in 1900 the price of wheat is $1 per bushel and 100 bushels are produced, while the price of steel is $5 per ton and 100 tons are produced: 1900's GNP is thus $600. In 1990 the price of wheat is still $2 per bushel and 200 bushels are produced, while the price of steel is $8 per ton and 1,000 tons are produced: 1990's GNP is therefore $8,400 *current* dollars. But the *real* GNP in 1990 depends on whether you use the wheat-to-steel proportions of 1900 or those of 1990 as the "base" for your calculations of the price index. With 1900 proportions of 50 percent by value for each commodity, the price level has increased from 100 to 180, and the real value of GNP in 1990 is $8400/1.8 = $4666.67 1900 dollars. But using 1990 proportions (20 to 1), the price level change is calculated as approximately 1.6 times, since the smaller proportionate price increase (in steel) is given a greater weight. The result: Real GNP growth in one case is measured as [(8400/1.8)/600] = 7.77 times over nine decades, and as [(8400/1.6)/600] = 8.75 times in the other. A difference!

Index number problems arise *whenever* we try to group together commodities whose relative volumes of output are changing. So we cannot just add up tonnages of wheat and steel and rice and coal to arrive at approximations of real GNP. The best we can do is agree that we will use a *common* base year for calculations of price indices (usually the earlier year, or 1900 in the above example). That way at least our calculations will be consistent.

What about adding up, not the goods themselves, but the *labor time,* the millions of hours of work embodied in the production of those goods? By this means we might get a measure of the "pure volume" of output, independent of prices. But the problem is that we want our measure of GNP to reflect some measure of value—and not all hours of labor are valued equally. We would have to boil down all kinds of labor, skilled and unskilled, trained and untrained, manual and intellectual, to multiples of some "basic" kind of labor, representing an elemental amount of "economic effort." And how would we do that? By looking at the value, *measured in prices,* of the resulting output! Thus there is no way to escape the index number problem.

In the end, the task of measuring an aggregate of different things can never be solved to our complete satisfaction. Growth is a concept we constantly use, but it remains beyond precise definition.

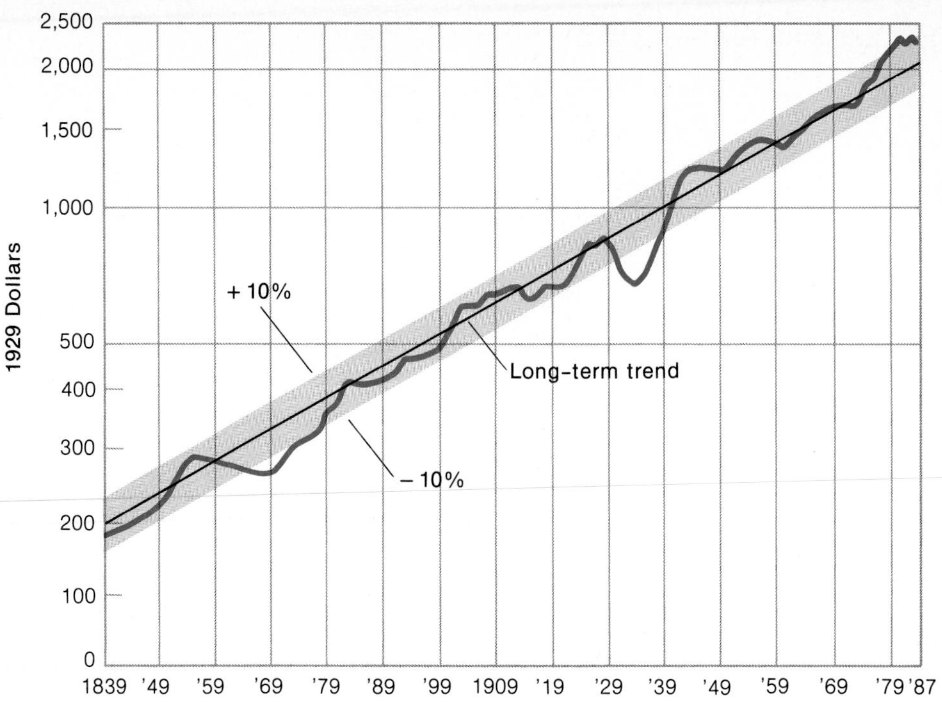

FIGURE 3
Real GNP Per Capita (1929 Dollars)
Real GNP per capita has shown a long, irregular, but fairly steady upward trend.

Depression or back to the 1870s (or even 1830s). As the chart shows, the swings are almost all contained within a range of 10 percent above or below the trend. The trend itself comes to about 3.5 percent a year in real terms, or a little over 1.5 percent a year per capita. Although 1.5 percent a year may not sound like much, remember that this figure allows us to double our real per capita living standards every 47 years. This is Adam Smith's growth model come to life!

Sources of Growth

How do we explain this long upward trend? Here we can give only a brief summary of the causes we will study more systematically later. Essentially, we grew for two reasons:

1. The Quantity of Inputs Going into the Economic Process Increased. In 1929 our civilian labor force was 53 million. In 1987 it was about 122 million. Obviously, larger inputs of labor produce larger outputs of goods and services. (Whether they may even produce *proportionally* larger outputs—i.e., larger outputs *per man or woman who works*—is another question we will investigate later.)

2. The Quality of Inputs Improved. The population working in 1987 was not only greater than in 1900, it was better fed, healthier, and above all better schooled. The best overall gauge of this is the amount of education stored up in the work force. In 1900, when only 6.4 percent of the working population had gone beyond grade school, there were only 223 million person-years of schooling embodied in the population. In 1986, when over three-fourths of the population had finished high school, the stock of education embodied in the population had grown to over a billion person-years.

The quality of capital has also increased, along with its quantity. Consider, for example, the contribution made to our output by the availability of surfaced roads. In 1900 there were about 150,000 miles of such roads. In 1988 there were almost 4 million miles. That is an increase in the quantity of roads of over 25 times. But that increase does not begin to measure the difference in the transport capability of the two road systems, one of them graveled, narrow, built for traffic that averaged 10 to 20 miles per hour; the other, concrete or asphalt, multilane, capable of supporting heavy trucks at 65 miles per hour.

Productivity

Improvements in the quality of inputs—in human skills, in improved designs of capital equipment—have been far more important than mere increases in quantity. Better skills and technology enable the labor force to increase the amount of goods and services it can turn out in a given time.

Figure 4 shows the trend in productivity since 1950. As you can see, the growth has been fairly steady up to the early 1970s, despite occasional dips. After 1972 the trend seems to shift downward, and in 1979 and 1980 it actually turns negative—we grew less productive! This may have been a short-lived phenomenon, having to do with the inefficient (unproductive) use of labor in a recession.

GNP AND QUALITY CHANGE: THE CASE OF COMPUTERS

One of the most difficult practical issues in measuring GNP concerns products whose quality changes rapidly from one year to the next. In principle, such quality changes are equivalent to a *decline* in the price of a "standard" or unchanged version of the product. But in real life it is very hard for national income accountants to estimate just how quickly such quality-adjusted prices are really declining.

In the case of computers, the Commerce Department's Bureau of Economic Analysis worked from 1969 through 1984 on the assumption that the price of a computer was unchanged, so that the nominal and the real measures of output in the computer industry were the same. Then, in 1985, the Bureau introduced new figures which showed that the price of computers (in terms of units of computing power embodied in the machines) had in fact fallen by *a factor of nine* over this period because of enormously improved productivity. The result: In 1972 dollars the real output of computers was reestimated to be *over $100 billion higher* than originally thought.

Such corrections are large enough to make a difference to measures of total output growth and of total productivity growth in the 1970s. Indeed, a significant part of the measured slowdown of productivity growth may be simply a failure to measure the effects of technological progress in a timely way.

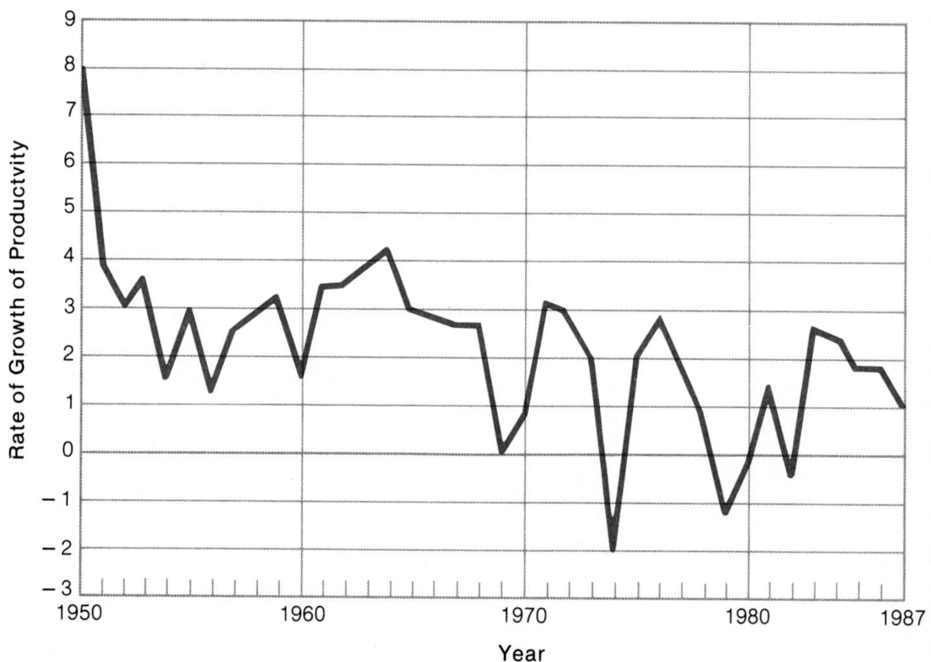

FIGURE 4
The Productivity Picture
These data show that measured increases in productivity have fallen precipitously in some recent years, especially in recession years, when the rate of output was also low (or negative).
Source: *Economic Indicators.*

Here we want to emphasize the contribution made to long-term growth by our normal steady improvement in our ability to grow and extract and handle and shape and transport goods.

CHANGES IN DISTRIBUTION

We have seen how striking was the increase in output in the twentieth century. But what happened to the division of this output? Have the rich gotten richer and the poor poorer, as Marx predicted? Or has the trend been in the direction of greater equality?

Changes in Dollar Incomes vs. Changes in Shares

The question is not easy to answer. Remember, we are interested in the changes in *shares* going to different groups, not just in absolute amounts. There has certainly

---

THE DIFFERENCE GROWTH RATES MAKE

The normal range in growth rates for capitalist economies does not seem to be very great. How much difference does it make, after all, if output grows at 1.7 or 2.7 percent?

The answer is: an amazing difference. This is because growth is an *exponential* phenomenon involving a percentage rate of growth on a steadily rising base. At 1.7 percent, per capita real income will double in about 40 years. At 2.7 percent, it will double in 26 years.

Professor Kenneth Boulding has pointed out that before World War II no country sustained more than 2.3 percent per capita growth of GNP. From World War II until 1973, Japan achieved a per capita growth rate of about 8 percent. Boulding writes: "The difference between 2.3 and 8 percent may be dramatically illustrated by pointing out that [at 2.3 percent] children are twice as rich as their parents—i.e., per capita income approximately doubles every generation—while at 8 percent per annum, children are six times as rich as their parents."

been a tremendous change in the dollar amounts that we have used to define different social classes, as Figure 5 demonstrates.

The figures show that growth has helped boost all income classes. But has the *proportion* of income going to the various classes also changed? That is not what we find. Figure 6 shows that the sharing out of incomes among social groups has been remarkably steady, at least until the beginning of this decade. Only if we go back to the 1920s do we find a marked change. In those days the share of the top 5 percent was perhaps twice as large as it is today, and, of course, such programs as Medicaid, food stamps, and public housing, which have significantly improved the real living standards of the poor in our own time, did not exist.*

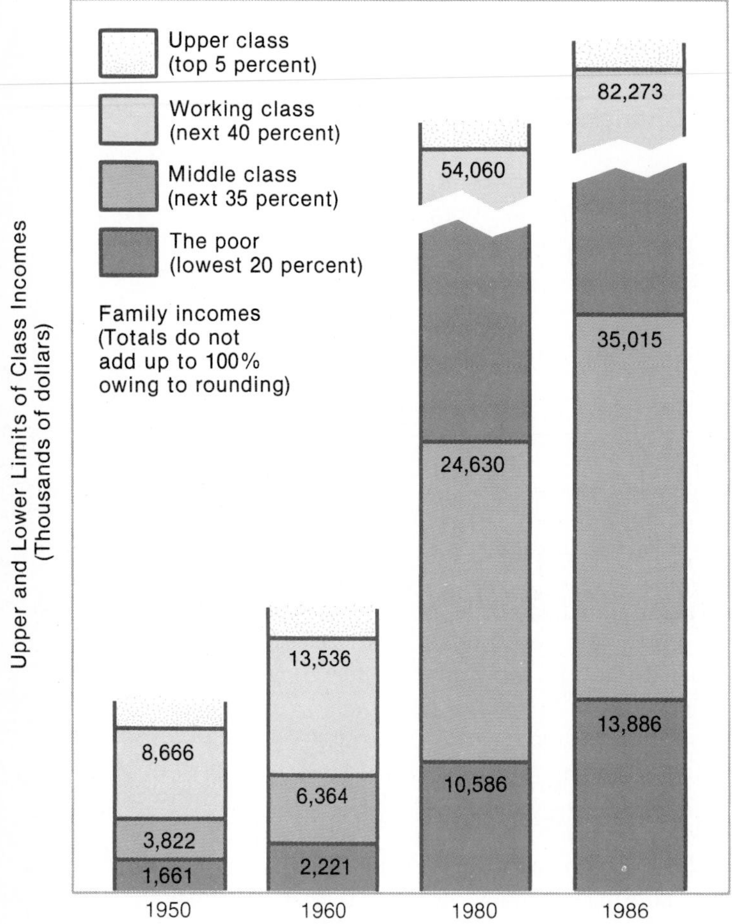

FIGURE 5
Upper and Lower Dollar Limits of Social Classes
The dollar incomes of all social classes have increased markedly. (Notice there is no upper hand in the topmost class. Do you understand why?)
Source: *Census Bureau P–60, 149.*

*A more detailed study of changes in income distribution would have to take into account some facts that are not included in the figures above. For technical reasons, the Census Bureau does not include most forms of capital income (such as capital gains on stocks or real estate) in its computation of incomes. If it did, the share of the top 1 percent would be larger. The Census Bureau also does not fully take into account cash and noncash payments to the poor, such as food stamps or welfare aid. This would add to the share of the poor. In other words, the Census figures are mainly derived from earnings, not returns on capital or "in-kind transfers" that may benefit high- or low-income groups.

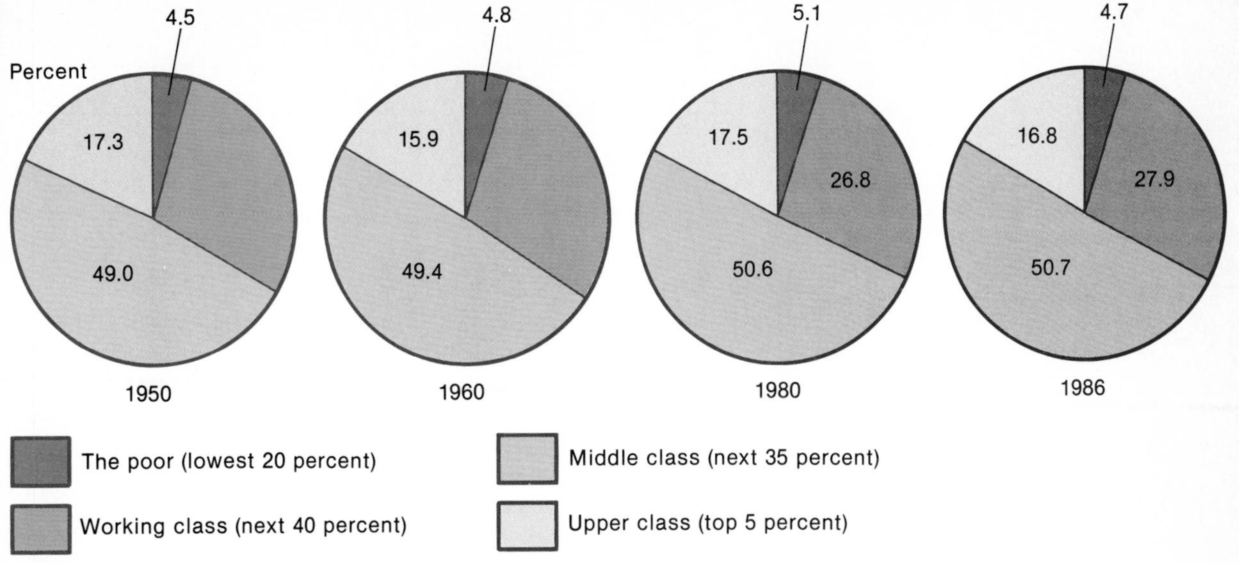

FIGURE 6
Shares of Total Income Going to Different Social Classes
The distribution of income among different social classes has shown very little change.
Source: *Census Bureau P-69.*

What has happened to the distribution of income since 1980 is not so encouraging. The deep recession of 1981 put a halt to further improvements in income equality, as large numbers of the newly unemployed slipped to the bottom of the income pile. Cuts in social programs further reduced the share of the poorest, while cuts in progressive tax rates and in capital gains and inheritance taxes raised the after-tax income shares of those in upper-income brackets. Economic recovery after 1982 restored some of the income share of the middle classes, but we remain today a less equal nation than we were a decade or two ago.

The Elimination of Poverty?

What about poverty? For many years the number of persons below the government's designated low-income level was dropping, both absolutely and in relation to the larger population. We can see this gradual shrinkage in Table 1, where poverty declines markedly from 1959 through 1969. By 1975 the decline has stopped owing to two recessions, in 1970 and 1974–1975. Thereafter poverty rises and falls with economic conditions: down in the recovery of 1976–1980, up sharply with the deep recession and cutbacks in antipoverty programs of 1981–1982. In the recovery since 1982 the *proportion* of the population defined as poor has fallen, in large measure because of the rise of the multi-income family unit as many more women entered the labor force. However, the *absolute number* of poor people was still higher in 1986 than in 1981. Thus social stagnation afflicting millions of poor people coincided with economic recovery; the rising tide did not "lift all boats."

TABLE 1
Persons Below Low-Income Level

	1959	*1969*	*1975*	*1981*	*1986*
All persons (millions)	39.5	24.1	25.9	31.8	32.4
Percent of population	22.4	12.1	12.3	14.0	13.6

Source: Census Bureau *P-60.*

What caused the decline in poverty up to 1975? The progress against poverty was heavily concentrated in one section of the population—the elderly. This was due primarily to a rise in the coverage and real value of social security benefits. By the mid-1980s, poverty among older people had fallen to historically low levels. On the other hand, conditions for single women with children and for minorities had not gotten better, and had perhaps even deteriorated. The advent of the homeless in the 1980s has been a new and shocking experience, showing that dramatic poverty persists among a small part of our population.

TRENDS IN BUSINESS

We have examined the main trends in personal income. Now let us turn to business. Here one change immediately strikes the eye. There is a marked decline of the independent small business—with its self-employed worker—as a main form of enterprise.

Decline in Small Business

In 1900 there were about 8 million independent enterprises, including 5.7 million farms. By 1986, as we saw in the last chapter, the number of proprietorships had grown to over 12 million, a figure that included some 2.1 million farms. Meanwhile the labor force itself more than tripled. Thus as a percentage of all persons working, the proportion of self-employed has fallen from about 30 percent in 1900 to under 10 percent today.

Rise of Big Business

With the decline of the self-employed worker has come the rise of the giant firm. Back in 1900, the giant corporation was just arriving on the scene. In 1901 financier J.P. Morgan created the first billion-dollar company when he formed the United States Steel Corporation out of a dozen smaller enterprises. In that year the total capitalization of all corporations valued at more than $1 million was $5 billion. By 1904 it was $20 billion. In 1986 it was over $7 trillion.

CAUSES OF POVERTY

In a box on page 58 we took a quick look at some of the characteristics of the poor. Here is a second, more systematic glance. It puts all households—families and individuals—into various categories and shows us the chance that someone in a given category will be a member of a low-income (poor) household (once again using the official definition).

TABLE 2
Chances of Being Poor, 1986

	%
All families	12.0
Single persons	21.6
White families	9.4
Black families	29.7
Families headed by females	
White	30.6
Black	53.8
Children	20.5
Elderly	12.4

Source: Census Bureau *P-60.*

But we must always be very careful before we impute poverty to any single source. One of the authors, sitting in a Ph.D. exam, was questioning a candidate about a dissertation on poverty. It seemed there were many causes for poverty, all impressively substantiated with evidence.

"But if you had to single out one cause as the *most* important," asked the examiner, "which would it be?"

The candidate hemmed and hawed. There was skill. There was health. There was culture. There was native ability. But if he *had* to choose, he would say that education—or rather, the lack of it—was the greatest contributory factor in poverty. Most poor people simply didn't have the knowledge to enable them to get high-paying jobs.

"And why didn't they have the education?" asked the examiner.

That was easy. Education was expensive. Poor people couldn't afford private schools. Their need for income was so great that they even dropped out of public school early to earn money.

"I see," said the examiner. "People are poor because they are uneducated. They are uneducated because they haven't the money to buy education. So *poverty causes poverty.*"

TABLE 3
Largest Manufacturers' Share of Assets (%)
The share of the biggest corporations grew rapidly during the 1950s and 1960s and stabilized in the 1970s. It may have risen since then.

	1948	*1960*	*1970*	*1981*	*1986*
100 largest corporations	40.2	46.4	48.5	46.8	55.0
200 largest corporations	48.2	56.3	60.4	60.0	66.0

Source: *Statistical Abstract of the United States*

It hardly comes as a surprise that the main trend of the past 80 years has been the emergence of big business. More interesting is the question of whether big business is continuing to grow. This is a more difficult question to answer, for it depends on what we mean by "growth."

Certainly the place of the biggest companies within the world of corporations has been rising. Marx was indubitably right in predicting this trend. Indeed, as Table 3 shows, the top 100 companies in 1970 held approximately as large a share of total corporate wealth as the top 200 companies in 1948.

Merger Mania

Until recently, economists generally believed that the concentration movement had leveled off. Between 1960 and the early 1980s, the percentage of assets held by the top 100 corporations remained fairly steady, and the concentration of sales likewise showed no signs of significant change.

Beginning in the early 1980s, however, this condition of overall stability changed suddenly and dramatically. A new merger wave broke out—a wave of such immense proportions as to dwarf all earlier periods of corporate acquisition (see Figure 7). During the quiet years before this wave, the annual number of mergers in the ranks of the nation's larger corporations averaged less than 100, and the total amount of assets involved in all mergers amounted to something like $5 billion per year. Then merger mania began. In 1984, 2,999 "big" mergers took place, involving $124 billion in total assets. In 1985 and 1986 the numbers were *still* higher—about $180 billion in each year—and 1987, despite the market crash in October, saw mergers amounting to over $150 billion. By that year billion-dollar mergers— **mergers that were individually larger than the merger totals of the premerger decade—had become commonplace.** (See box for details.)

Behind the Merger Wave

What brought about this extraordinary and quite unforeseen merger frenzy? Two factors seem to underline the boom—one financial, the other legal. The financial impetus came originally from the combination of high interest rates and slow

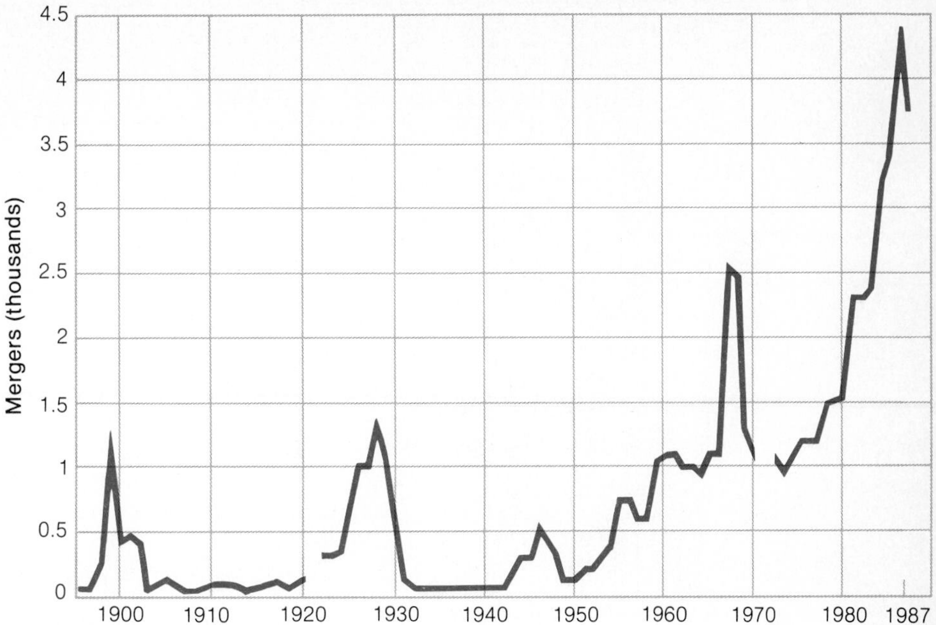

FIGURE 7
Number of Mergers 1895–1987
The number of corporate mergers has risen to new heights in the 1980s.
Source: *Cited in Barrie A. Wigmore, "Speculation and the Crash of 1987, "presented to the American Economics Association, December 28, 1988. From Devra L. Golbe and Lawrence J. White, "Mergers and Acquisitions in the U.S. Economy: Aggregate and Historical Overview," in Alan J. Auerbach (ed.),* Mergers and Acquisitions, *a NBER Report, p. 37; © 1988 by the University of Chicago Press.*

growth in the middle 1980s. Together these factors depressed profitability and the price of corporation shares to the point where the market value of the existing assets of many corporations (e.g., the oil reserves of the big oil companies) was far less than what it would cost to recreate those assets with new investments (oil exploration). This presented aggressive companies and shrewd financiers with the opportunity to acquire existing assets cheaply by buying out the corporations that owned them. Later in the decade, when the stock market began to boom again, a purely *speculative* motive made an appearance: Merger artists sought profits by bidding for companies that they could sell off later in the rising market. Even at the market's peak in 1987, it was still more profitable to buy existing assets on the stock market than to create assets with new investments.

The persistence of the merger mania may also be due to a changed attitude on the part of the federal government. Deregulation set the stage for a general competitive consolidation within the industries affected, such as trucking and airlines. And under President Reagan, the Justice Department effectively stopped enforcing the antitrust laws, thus removing an obstacle that had formerly dampened merger enthusiasm.

1988'S BILLION-DOLLAR DEALS

Announced Bids, Jan. 1 to Mar. 7

Buyer	Target	Price (Billions)
R. H. Macy	Federated Department Stores	$6.2
Eastman Kodak	Sterling Drug	5.1
Bat Industries	Farmers Group	4.3
Bernard F. Brennan	Montgomery Ward	3.8
Black & Decker	American Standard	2.3
Desert Partners	USG	1.9
Mesa	Homestake Mining	1.9
Pirelli	Firestone Tire & Rubber	1.9
Dun & Bradstreet	IMS International	1.8
Barris Industries	Media General	1.6
Beazer	Koppers	1.3
Kohlberg Kravis Roberts	Stop & Shop	1.2
American Brands	E-II Holdings	1.1
Forstmann Little	AFG Industries	1.1
New England Electric	Public Service of New Hampshire	1.0

Data: M&A Data Base, *Mergers Acquisitions Magazine; Business Week*

Hostile Mergers

The merger wave of the mid-1980s was often marked by "hostile" takeovers—purchases of one company by another, or by a financier, despite the objections of the first company's management. Hostile takeover bids succeed because existing shareholders find them profitable: The "raider" makes a buyout offer well above the current market price of the shares, and such lucrative prices cancel out whatever loyalty shareholders may feel toward existing management.

Where do the billions to take over a large company come from? Many hostile takeovers have been made possible because banks lent raiders very large amounts of money, often on frail security. After the takeover was consummated by buying out shareowners with the bank's money, the raider typically unloaded his debt on the company he had acquired, causing it to issue "junk bonds"—high-interest, ill-secured debt—whose proceeds were then used to reimburse the bank. Or the raider may have sold off the acquired company's assets to raise the cash to pay the bank that supplied the acquisition funds to begin with. Thus banks have provided the largest share of initial takeover financing.

Consequences of the Merger Wave

The effects of the merger wave cannot be described as clearly as its causes. It will be some time before we know to what degree the overall concentration of assets will be affected, or whether the domination of big companies in individual markets has changed. In the meanwhile the most important effect of the merger wave is likely to be on corporate profitability. Interest on the $173-odd billion of new debt that was issued in 1987 is an *expense* that must be met before profits can be realized. If this expense is not met—and in the case of junk bonds it may not be—any adverse turn of events, either in a single strategic company or in the overall economy, could possibly precipitate a panic comparable to those that shook the financial world in earlier periods of financial wheeling and dealing.

Is it possible that the merger wave may turn out to be a good thing, not a bad one? Its supporters claim that the effect will be the creation of larger, wealthier, and more efficient institutions, capable of better meeting massive competition from abroad. Its detractors worry about financial instability and about the wholesale elimination of jobs—including middle-management jobs—when companies merge. And in the background there is always the troublesome issue of the concentration of economic power. We are in the midst of a remarkable transformation of the corporate scene.

Explaining the Trend to Business Size

Can we explain the long-term trend toward the concentration of business assets, as we did the trend toward growth in GNP? By and large, economists would stress three main reasons for the appearance of giant enterprise.

1. Advances in Technology Have Made Possible the Mass Production of Goods and Services at Falling Costs. The rise of bigness in business, at least in the first instance, is very much a result of technology. Without the steam engine, the lathe, the railroad, it is unimaginable that big business would have emerged at all.

But technology went on to do more than make large-scale production possible. Typically it also brought an economic effect that we call **economies of scale.** That is, as production processes grew bigger, they also became more productively *efficient:* They came to yield more outputs in relation to the inputs of land, labor, and capital that they used.

THE RISE AND CRASH OF THE STOCK MARKET

The stock market is America's most closely watched, if not most reliable, index of economic performance. We watch the stock market not just from vicarious interest in other people's money, but also because it tells us (we think) about the prospects for a national economy that very much affect our own lives. A rising stock market reflects confidence: in future profits, investment, and growth. A falling market is depressing.

From the depths of recession in 1982, the stock market began one of its longest and most sustained recoveries in history: five full years of steady upward march. In 1987 the market soared to new highs, rising nearly 50 percent above its value on New Year's day, as measured by the Standard and Poor's index of 500 stocks.

Then, from October 13 through October 20, 1987, catastrophe struck. On October 19 alone the Dow Jones Industrial Index lost 508 points, or over 22 percent of its value. By whatever measure, all of the gains of a year were wiped out in a week. The total lost value of stocks in America's corporations was estimated at just over $1 *trillion* dollars.

What difference did it make? The answer, one year later, is: evidently not very much. Unlike the Great Crash of 1929, the Great(er) Crash of 1987 produced no recession, no panic, no wave of failures of brokerage firms and banks. In the words of President Reagan's Task Force on Market Mechanisms:

> *Two important points emerge from a comparison of the market decline of 1929 to that of 1987. First, structural change in the economy since the Depression—chiefly the changing composition of economic activity, the increasing roles of the government and the absence of chronic deflation—means that the economy now appears to be far more stable than it was in 1929. Second, the Great Depression appears to have been caused not by the stock market crash but by the interaction of a number of diverse circumstances (such as the declines in agriculture and housing) and misguided policies (such as the Smoot-Hawley Tariff, the tight monetary policy in late 1931 and the tax increase in the summer of 1932). Thus, as long as a similar set of circumstances and policy initiatives are avoided, a comparable economic contraction should remain only a remote possibility.*

Economies of scale are perhaps most easily visualized in the vast increases over the past 30 years in the size of tanker ships that transport petroleum. Supertankers, now ranging in size up to over 220,000 tons, use no more crew (labor) than far smaller vessels. And because the volume of a container rises more rapidly than its surface area, the capital costs (the steel that goes into the ship) are also less per barrel of capacity. **Thus both capital and labor are reduced per unit of output as the size of tankers increases.**

Economies of scale exist in many other types of processes, such as mass assembly lines, where the economies in the use of labor time and in the specialization of capital goods are key factors. These economies provided a further powerful impetus to the growth of size. **The firm that pioneered in the introduction of mass-production technology often secured a competitive selling advantage because, having used fewer inputs per unit of output, it could offer its outputs at a lower price.**

2. Concentration Is Also a Result of Corporate Mergers. We have just looked into the merger wave of the 1980s. But ever since J. P. Morgan assembled U.S. Steel, mergers have been a major source of corporate growth. At the very end of the nineteenth century there was the first great merger wave, out of which came the first huge companies, including U.S. Steel. In 1890 most industries were competitive, without a single company dominating the field. By 1904 one or two giant firms, usually created by mergers, had arisen to control at least half the output in 78 different industries.

Again, between 1951 and 1960 one-fifth of the top 1,000 corporations disappeared—not because they failed, but mainly because they were bought up by other corporations. **In all, mergers account for about two-fifths of the increase in concentration between 1950 and 1970; internal growth accounts for the rest.**

3. Depressions or Recessions Plunge Many Smaller Firms into Bankruptcy and Make It Possible for Larger, More Financially Secure Firms to Buy Them Up Very Cheaply. Certainly the process of concentration is abetted by economic distress. When industries are threatened, the weak producers go under; the stronger ones emerge relatively stronger than before. Consider, for example, that three once-prominent American automobile producers succumbed to the mild recessions of the 1950s and 1960s, and to the pressure of foreign competition: Studebaker, Packard, and Kaiser Motors. More recently, American Motors was absorbed by Renault, and Chrysler only escaped demise by congressional bailout in 1979.

A New Trend Toward Smaller Industries?

Last, a possible countertrend. The long movement toward bigness may be peaking because of new technologies that favor smaller, more flexible firms. Perhaps symptomatically, while the large integrated steel firms have languished, "minimills" have been flourishing. Some economists have suggested that perhaps the day of the industrial Goliath is over, and that the Davids of the future will be firms capable of highly computerized "batch" operations instead of long mass-production runs. It will be a while before we know if this is the case, but the trend alerts us once again to the strategic role played by technology in establishing the basic structure of the economy. Moreover, it may be that today's emerging flexible-production companies will become the industrial giants of tomorrow!

HOW BIG IS BIG?

Just to get an idea of scale, the 36th largest industrial corporation in 1987 ranked by sales was Unisys. Its sales that year were $9.7 billion. It was not the 36th largest in terms of its assets, which were $9.9 billion. The 36th largest firm in assets was Rockwell International, with assets of $8.7 billion. Rockwell's sales of $12.1 billion ranked it 27th in terms of sales.

Thus it makes a difference whether we rank companies for size by sales or assets. At the very top of the heap, the top 9 firms in terms of sales are the top 9 in terms of assets. This coincidence weakens as we move down the list. Some examples: Chrysler was 10th in sales, 15th in assets; General Dynamics was 39th in sales, 68th in assets; North America Phillips was 86th in sales, 117th in assets; Conagra was 41st in sales, 150th in assets.

Which is more important, sales or assets? Sales measure the dominance of a company within its field; assets measure its overall financial strength. Actually, both sales and assets measure size, but what counts in the marketplace is profitability. Here the correct measure is the net rate of return—the rate of profit earned per dollar of capital. The average big business earns two to three times the return of the average small business, but really spectacular rates of return are usually found in smaller businesses on their way to stardom.

Last rule of thumb: To make it into the top 500 companies, your sales have to be about $460 million; your assets, $200 million.

Labor Unions

What about labor unions? Have they also shown trends comparable to the big corporation? Their history is parallel in many ways. Over the last 80 years, the percent of the labor force belonging to a union has increased from 3.2 to 18. Thus the twentieth century has seen the emergence of big labor alongside big business. Yet, as Table 4 shows, the peak came in the 1950s and the percent of unionized nonagricultural workers has actually declined since then.

TABLE 4
Labor Force in Unions
The importance of unions in the labor force has been falling, although unions remain powerful in key sectors.

	1940	*1950*	*1960*	*1970*	*1980*	*1986*
Percent unionized	27.2	31.9	31.4	27.3	22.0	18.0

Source: AFL-CIO *Directory of Labor Organizations.*

FROM PIN FACTORY TO ASSEMBLY LINE

We recall Adam Smith's pin factory. Here is a later version of that division of labor, in the early Ford assembly lines.

> *Just how were the main assembly lines and lines of component production and supply kept in harmony? For the chassis alone, from 1,000 to 4,000 pieces of each component had to be furnished each day at just the right point and right minute: a single failure, and the whole mechanism would come to a jarring standstill. . . . Superintendents had to know every hour just how many components were being produced and how many were in stock. Whenever danger of shortage appeared, the shortage chaser—a familiar figure in all automobile factories—flung himself into the breach. Counters and checkers reported to him. Verifying in person any ominous news, he mobilized the foreman concerned to repair deficiencies. Three times a day he made typed reports in manifold to the factory clearing-house, at the same time chalking on blackboards in the clearing-house office a statement of results in each factory-production department and each assembling department.**

Such systemizing in itself resulted in astonishing increases in productivity. With each operation analyzed and subdivided into its simplest components, with a steady stream of work passing before stationary men, with a relentless but manageable pace of work, the total time required to assemble a car dropped astonishingly. Within a single year the time required to assemble a motor fell from 600 minutes to 226 minutes; to build a chassis, from 12 hours and 28 minutes to 1 hour and 33 minutes. A stopwatch man was told to observe a 3-minute assembly in which men assembled rods and pistons, a simple operation. The job was divided into three jobs, and half the men turned out the same output as before.

As the example of the assembly line illustrates, the technology behind economies of scale often reduced the act of labor to robot-like movements. A brilliant account of this fragmentation of work will be found in Harry Braverman's *Labor and Monopoly Capital* (New York: Monthly Review Press, 1974).

*Allan Nevins, *Ford, the Times, the Man, the Company* (New York: Scribner's, 1954), pp. 1,507.

This does not mean, of course, that all unions today are diminishing. The last two decades have brought a boom in unions for white-collar workers, such as teachers and office workers; in unions for municipal employees, such as police, firefighters, and transit workers; in diversified union organization, such as the powerful Teamsters. The declines have come where industries are declining, as among railwaymen, clothing trades workers, and auto workers. Unions are certain to remain a major force in crucial areas of the economy.

THE TREND IN GOVERNMENT

We pass now to a consideration of the last great trend in the economy—the trend in government, whose end result has been the emergence of the modern public sector.

From Small to Large Government

First we must try to explain the rise of the government sector from its relative insignificance at the beginning of the century to the general magnitude and importance it enjoys today. What follows is an analysis of the historic trend that we believe most economic historians, conservative or liberal, would agree on.

1. The Growing Size of Business Provoked a Demand for Government Supervision. As business firms increased in size, private decisions became fraught with much larger social consequences. As business increased in size, the social impact of its activities steadily widened. Building or not building a plant came to spell prosperity or decline for a town, even for a state. Cutthroat competition could mean ruin for an industry on which whole regions depended. At the same time, as companies emerged with many thousands of employees and millions of dollars' worth of capital, fears grew about the possible misuse of power that so great a concentration of economic control seemed to imply. Thus one important reason for the long-term growth of government has been the public demand that it prevent or cope with problems that arose from the sheer increase in business size.

2. Technology Brought a Need for Public Supervision. Much of the long-term growth of government stems from the impact of technology. Examples: As the automobile became commonplace, it created a need for traffic authorities to deal with it—some 10 percent of state and local government employment exists to deal with the automobile. The same effect followed the appearance of the airplane and the radio (how would access to "channels" be determined, what would stations be permitted to broadcast?). And of course in our own day we have seen the same effect from atomic energy, new drugs, space, and weaponry.

3. Urbanization Increased the Need for Government. City life has its appeals, but also its perils. People cannot live in crowded quarters without police, public health, and other facilities far more complex than those needed in a rural setting. Government has always been an urban phenomenon, and as every nation has urbanized, its reach of government has increased.

4. Unification of the Economy Gave Rise to Additional Problems. Industrialization knits an economy together into a kind of vast, interlocked machinery. An unindustrialized, localized economy is like a pile of sand: If you poke a finger into one side of it, some businesses and individuals will be affected, but those on the other side of the pile will remain undisturbed. The growing scale and specialization of industrial operation turns the sandpile into a rigid structure. You move one side of it, and the entire structure shakes. Problems can no longer be localized. The difficulties of the economy grow in extent: There is a need for a national, not a local, energy program, for national transportation, urban, and educational programs. Government—largely federal government—is the principal means by which such problems have been handled.

5. Economic Malfunction Brought Public Intervention. Seventy-five years ago the prevailing attitude toward the economy was a kind of awed respect. People felt that the economy was best left alone, that it was fruitless as well as ill-advised to try to change its workings. That attitude changed with the Great Depression. In the ensuing collapse the role of government greatly enlarged. The trauma of the Depression and the determination that government had the responsibility to prevent its recurrence were a watershed. Keynes's thinking played a very important part in this transition.

6. A New Philosophy of "Entitlement" Replaced the Older One of "Rugged Individualism." Largely, but not wholly as a consequence of the experience of the Depression, a profound change has been registered in public attitudes toward the appropriate role of government. We no longer live in a society in which old-age retirement, medical expenses, and income during periods of unemployment are felt to be properly the sole responsibility of the individuals concerned. For better or worse, these and similar responsibilities have been gradually assumed by governments in all capitalist nations. Here lie crucial reasons for the swelling volume of state, local, and federal production and purchase.

The Trend in Recent Years

What has happened to the trend toward big government in recent years? In most people's minds, the trend of the past has continued or accelerated. The years since 1950 are popularly regarded as a time when the reach of government has vastly increased.

Has it? In Figure 8(a) we trace the evolution of the public sector over the last 37 years. The first thing that strikes us is the tremendous increase in government purchases. This surely seems evidence of an unprecedented growth of government in modern times. But the upward-sweeping line is not corrected for inflation or real growth. In Figure 8(b) we show the same dollar figures as a percentage of GNP. A completely different picture now emerges. **As a share of the economy, there has been no appreciable growth in government spending for goods and services over the last 37 years.** The shift to "big government" came with the Depression and World War II; since then government has grown along with, but not more quickly than, the economy itself.

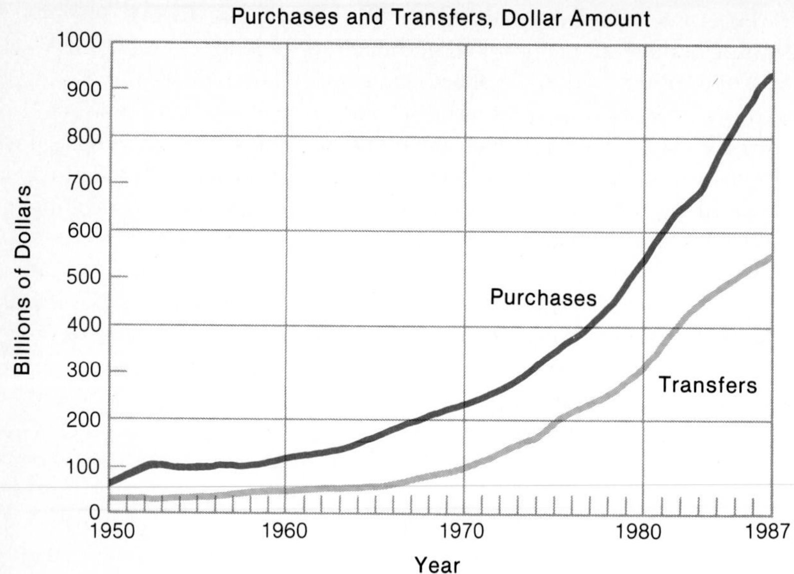

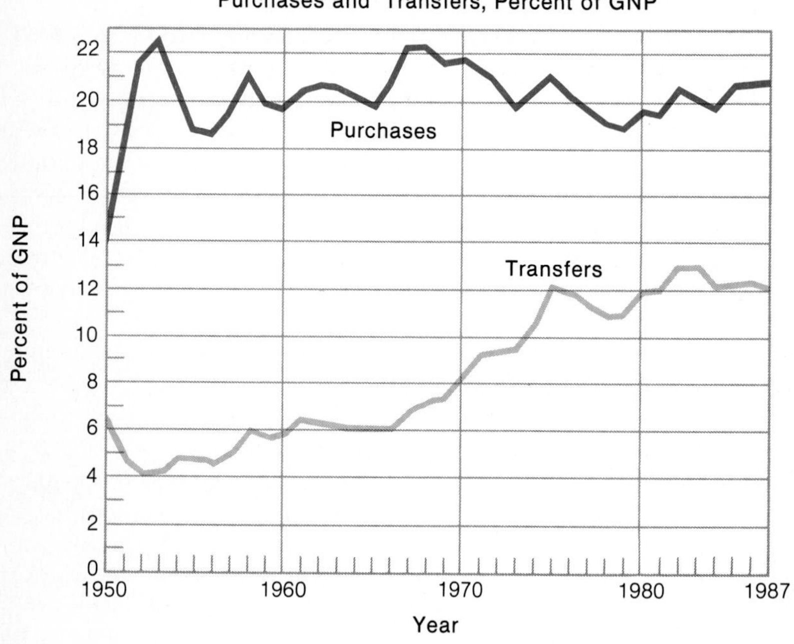

FIGURE 5.8
Government Buying or Spending Since 1950
Government trends are much more stable, as a percentage of GNP, than is apparent in the nominal data.
Source: *Economic Report of the President, 1988.*

The Trend in Transfers

The picture is somewhat different when we look at the growth of government transfers. Here we find a rise not only in the dollar totals but also in the size of transfers compared to GNP. In 1950 transfer payments of all kinds amounted to about 6.3 percent of GNP; in 1986 they had grown to about 12 percent of GNP.

But now we must distinguish between the growth of *programs* and the growth of *expenditures.* The number of welfare programs has not increased, particularly since the Reagan administration's effort to reduce the government's role to one of providing a relatively small "safety net." Expenditures have only grown because the costs of expanding a few large entitlement programs have far outweighed the savings from the abandonment of numerous smaller ones. Primary among these increases in expenditure have been the growth of social security payments, "indexed" to the cost of living, and the very rapid rise in Medicare costs. Together these two transfer programs have increased from $150 billion in 1980 to over $298 billion in 1988. An additional factor has been the mushrooming growth of interest payments on the national debt, up from $52 billion to $148 billion over the same eight years. This is a transfer from taxpayers to bondholders, who, as we have seen, come from the wealthiest stratum of our society.

Growth in Intervention?

Last comes a question that is not so readily answerable by graphs and figures. Has government intervention into the workings of the system followed the rising trend that marked the period from the late nineteenth century to the present?

That is a question we cannot answer because we have recently come through a history-making experiment. A great many regulatory efforts of the past have been undone—for example, the regulation of airline routes and trucking rates and the safety and environmental aspects of enterprise. In the 1980s the United States passed through a period of impatience with government intervention combined with a willingness to let the market mechanism itself serve as the great regulator of the system. It is too early to know how far this movement will go, or how permanent will be the changes it has already brought. This is an issue to which we will return.

LOOKING BACK

KEY CONCEPTS

This chapter has been concerned with the economy in movement—not in quick, month-to-month fluctuations of the kind that will concern us when we study macroeconomics, but in longer-run, year-to-year, or decade-to-decade changes. Here are the most important of them.

Real vs. nominal growth

More inputs and more productive inputs

1 There is a long-term growth pattern to GNP—a pattern that is much more striking in nominal GNP than in real GNP (that is, in figures uncorrected for inflation than in corrected figures), but remarkable even with all adjustments for rising prices. This growth can be attributed mainly to two factors: an increase in the quantity of inputs as our labor force and our stock of wealth have grown, and an increase in the quality and effectiveness of inputs as our productivity has increased. Here is Adam Smith's growth projection in reality.

Rise in incomes but little change in distribution

2 A second main trend is directly connected with the rise in output. It is the rise in dollar incomes for all levels of households—a rise that is, of course, much greater before we adjust for inflation than after. The distribution of income among classes has changed only very slowly, however. Poverty has been gradually eroded, but remains a stubborn problem, recently worsened.

Big-business share of assets has grown, but not its share of individual markets.

3 The share of total assets belonging to the biggest corporations showed a startling increase in the decades of the 1950s and 1960s. However, the increase in the share of sales in different markets going to the biggest firms has shown no significant change. Big firms get bigger by absorbing assets of companies in *different* branches of business, so that their degree of monopoly control within markets shows little change. The main sources of business growth have been technology (recall Chapter 2) and mergers.

A new merger wave in the 1980s may disrupt the corporate scene.

4 Starting in the mid-1980s, an unprecedented merger wave has brought enormous changes to the corporate world. The concentration of overall assets has certainly increased, but it is less certain that market concentrations have also increased. The merger wave has created a considerable threat of financial instability because mergers have often taken place through the issuance of ill-secured new bonds to finance company takeovers.

The reasons for a growing public sector are linked to the attributes of evolving capitalism.

5 The public sector has grown dramatically since the late nineteenth century. Here is a list of the most important causes:

- the growing size of business
- the disruptive effects of technology
- urbanization
- the unification of the economy
- a Keynesian remedy for economic malfunction
- a new philosophy of entitlement

For the last 37 years we have seen stability in the public sector, except for a few big entitlement programs.

6 There has been a striking stability in the trend of the public sector since 1950. The ratio of government spending to GNP has been virtually unchanged, although the dollar amounts are of course much larger. Transfer payments have risen as a fraction of GNP, but this is the result of indexing social security, the growth of Medicare, and higher interest payments on the national debt, not because of a growing number of transfer programs.

Can the trend be reversed?

7 We have recently seen an effort mounted by the Reagan administration to curtail further government growth and to cut back certain government programs. It is still too early to tell whether this effort will succeed, or be reversed under President Bush.

ECONOMIC VOCABULARY

Gross national product 74
Real and nominal GNP 75
Index numbers 77
Productivity 79
Economies of scale 89

QUESTIONS

1. Here are some raw data:

	GNP (Current $Billions)	Price Index (1982 = 100)	Population (Millions)
1970	$ 977	42.0	204
1980	2,633	85.7	227
1985	3,966	280	240
1987	4,486	117.5	—

What is real GNP per capita in 1980 and 1988 in 1982 dollars? In 1988 dollars? *Hint:* You will need a new price index with 1988 = 100.

2. If there were no change whatsoever in technology, do you think that a larger quantity of labor might result in GNP growing faster or slower than the sheer increase of man-hour input? *Hint:* Can people organize their activities better as their numbers change? Does this continue indefinitely?
3. Do you think it might be possible to construct a theory to explain why the pretax, pretransfer shares of income are so fixed? Could there be a kind of pecking order in society? Could different groups establish economic distances that satisfy them? Would they then strive only to retain, not to increase, those differences?
4. Can you imagine an invention that would result in rapid concentration in a very unconcentrated industry—say, the restaurant business? or the laundry business? Can you imagine an invention that could radically deconcentrate an industry? How might a watch-sized CB radio affect the telephone industry? What invention could do the same for Exxon? IBM?

CHAPTER 6

America in the World Economy

A LOOK AHEAD

With a rude shock, Americans have realized that our national economic health depends on events in the wider world. The United States is a trading nation. We have a need for foreign raw materials and a taste for foreign goods. We rely on foreign markets for the products of our agriculture, our aerospace, our capital equipment, and much else. We are affected by drought in the Soviet Union, by war in the Middle East, by depression in Latin America. It used to be said that when America sneezed, Europe caught pneumonia; now it is at least true that when the world economy catches cold, we sneeze.

This chapter is a first look at a problem that will concern us many times as we move through our studies. It focuses our attention on three main problems:

1 What is the position of the United States in the world economy today?
2 What has happened to our traditional competitive advantages?
3 What challenges lie ahead?

THE WORLD ECONOMY

Not many years ago, problems of international economics were largely relegated to the backs of textbooks, including this one, and it was understood that the busy instructor and the overworked student were both to be forgiven for letting them go by. There were two main reasons for this deliberate downplaying of the international side. The first was that America was still generally thought of as a **closed economy,** one that was able to get along quite well without worrying too much about the rest of the world. The second reason was that international economics introduced a new, seemingly unnecessary complication into the economic problem. It necessitated thinking about two kinds of money—ours and theirs.

For better or worse, the closed economy has become wide open. The rest of the world has moved from the backs of textbooks to the front pages of every newspaper. One does not have to be an economist to be aware of the "invasion" of foreign goods into American markets, an invasion that has not been forced on us, but that we have brought about freely by choosing to buy foreign cars, TV sets, shoes, and machine tools. All of us became aware of another aspect of America's international economic problems in August 1982, when Mexico nearly defaulted on its almost $100 billion debt to U.S. and foreign banks. We then realized for the first time the extent of our financial involvement with the rest of the world—we hold over $400 billion of loans, many of them very shaky. And in the years since, the debt problem of the developing countries has deepened and widened, and still seems far from a resolution.

So the era of the "closed" economy—it was never *really* closed—is over. Students and instructors, indeed all American citizens, must learn to think about a world where America's problems are tied into foreign problems, and where even the American dollar has to be understood as just one currency among many. That is what this chapter is about.

A SPECTRUM OF NATIONS

Let us begin by taking a look at the world economy as it might appear to an economist traveling at a planet-encompassing height. The first thing to be noted is that the United States is still the world's wealthiest economy. Our gross national product is about equal, each year, to that of *all* of Western Europe. We produce only a little more per capita than Japan, but more than twice as much overall, since Japan has only half of our population. We are twice as productive, both absolutely and on a per person basis, as our major strategic rival, the Soviet Union. We are 50 times more productive per worker than China, and 10 times more productive overall, since we have only one-fifth of its population. All in all, as Table 1 shows, we still possess the richest and most productive large industrial economy in the world.

TABLE 1
Population, GNP, and GNP Per Capita—Some Recent Figures.

Country	*Population 1987 (Millions)*	*GNP 1984 (Billions of $)*	*GNP per Capita (Actual $)*
Ethiopia	46.7	$ 4.7	$ 111
Bangladesh	107.1	12.6	128
Indonesia	180.3	82	484
Nicaragua	3.3	2.6	788
Mexico	81.8	139.4	1,795
Israel	4.2	21	5,070
USSR	284	1,998	7,035
Italy	57.3	360.7	6,330
Hungary	10.6	77.6	7,277
United Kingdom	56.8	466.4	8,270
Japan	122	1,249	10,237
W. Germany	60.9	674	11,020
Canada	25.8	329.4	13,100
U.S.	243.8	3,640	14,979
Switzerland	6.6	104.5	16,220

Source: *Statistical Abstract of the United States, 1988.*

Other Advanced Nations

Although we are the world's wealthiest nation, we are certainly not the world's only wealthy nation. Japan, for example, has made tremendous strides over the last 40 years. Its best manufacturing industries are second to none in efficiency. Its high rates of household saving and of investment are the envy of the world, and its economic growth rates have for decades averaged over twice our own. If Japan were not a crowded island chain with few natural resources, dependent on the Middle East and Indonesia for energy, on Australia and the Americas for food, and on the United States and Europe to provide markets for its manufacturing production, the Japanese would probably be richer than we are today.

Europe is not short of land or resources, but it has lacked the political and cultural unity that has so favored the development of Japan. Until the twentieth century, Europe was by far the most developed part of the world, dominant in world politics and in world trade. Nationalism, warfare, political upheaval, loss of colonial empires, economic depression, and an inability to integrate narrow national markets into a single economy brought a loss of Europe's competitive edge. But since World War II Europe has been overcoming these obstacles and building a stable, modern, integrated multinational economy. Today Europe is rich, peaceful, and self-sufficient, and looking ahead to full commercial integration in 1992. However, Europe also remains plagued by high unemployment, and worried about whether it can keep up with the Americans and the Japanese.

Among the advanced nations of the world, the Soviet Union is today perhaps the most interesting. Its history in this century up to the 1950s was remarkable—it went from peasant backwardness and war destruction to a capability in sophisticated space technology and impressive programs of social improvement. Then the first signs of a creeping disease became apparent, the disease of advanced bureaucratic arteriosclerosis. First the Russian economy lost momentum, then it stagnated, then it began to run in reverse. But the full story is not yet written. Under the leadership of Mikhail Gorbachev, the Soviet Union has entered the era of *perestroika*—restructuring. President Gorbachev has announced a radical program for dismantling the cumbersome structure of central planning and introducing many of the institutions of a freer—if not quite a free—market. Will these reforms work? Does perestroika mean the nose of the capitalist camel is under the communist tent? These are questions we will look into again in Chapter 38, but we raise them now as part of our first survey of the world economy.

The Third World

Beyond these giants there is the vast diversity of the Third World, where more than 3 billion of the world's people now live. The Third World encompasses every kind of economic experience, as well as every standard of living. Average living standards range from near-starvation (the per capita GNP of Ethiopia is $110 per year) to modest (Brazil, Chile, and Mexico have per capita incomes of $1,500 to $2,000 per year), but these averages are the result of lumping together the incomes of the affluent few and the indigent many. On this basis of averaging rich and poor, a few tiny principalities and sheikhdoms enjoy the highest living standards on the planet—the "average" per capita (not per household) income in the United Arab Emirates was $19,270.

Since 1970, Third World nations have demonstrated their importance in two ways. The first was their ability to extract an enormous flow of wealth from the West when the Organization of Petroleum Exporting Countries (OPEC) boosted oil prices from $2.59 to $11.59 per barrel in 1973 and again from $13.34 to $24.00 in 1979. The resulting transfer of wealth amounted to over $377 billion. It gave a tremendous boost to inflation in the West and produced some economic development in a few countries of the East and South. It also set into motion a spiral of lending, partly to help finance oil imports into countries like Brazil that had few domestic supplies, partly to finance industrialization in oil-exporting countries like Venezuela and Mexico. This lending spree ended in a vast overextension of credit that still hangs over the world. Perhaps most significant of all, OPEC made abundantly clear the vulnerability of all Western economies to any long-lasting interruption of oil supplies. Until the price of oil collapsed in 1986, the political geography of the planet was profoundly changed.

A second impact, less dramatic but no less significant, was the demonstration that the underdeveloped areas could combine low-wage labor with high technology to create export industries capable of challenging the Western economies. New techniques of transportation and communication made it possible to make circuit boards in Hong Kong, TV sets in Taiwan, automobiles in South Korea—achievements utterly impossible only a few years before. These countries soon became principal suppliers for their European and American markets. So far only a few of the underdeveloped countries have achieved this capability, but the more successful among them have become new and, to some, worrisome entrants to the advanced capitalist world.

FITTING INTO THE WORLD ECONOMY

How does the United States fit into this array of national economies? The United States has long been the largest trader in the world. In 1987 we imported $560.1 billion worth of goods, about as much as the entire gross domestic product of Great Britain! (We exported $425.8 billion, more than the whole GNP of Canada.) What's more, the American presence is felt in world trade even where the United States is not a direct party. The American dollar has been the unit of account for world trade since the end of World War II. Today it is estimated that up to a trillion dollars are held by foreigners who use them to finance world trade. Oil moving all over the world is priced in dollars, and the same is true of many other commodities traded on the international markets.

Nonetheless, until recently most Americans were not aware of the role the rest of the world played in their economic lives. That is because our participation in world trade and finance, vast though it was, was still small in comparison with the business we did internally, with ourselves.

Rising U.S. Involvement

But over the past 25 years that has changed. The change seems fairly modest when viewed against *total* GNP. In 1960 exports and imports amounted to only 5 percent of the total value of goods and services produced in the United States. By 1987, exports had risen to 11 percent of GNP and imports to 15 percent.

But look at manufacturing: Today one dollar of every five earned from the sale of U.S. manufactures comes from an export; one dollar of every two spent by Americans on manufactured products is spent on an import. These figures hit home harder when they are made more specific. One out of every three American-made jet planes, about one out of every two oil rigs, and approximately one of every three computers is destined for sales overseas. Taken together, exports are responsible for the jobs of 13 million Americans. At the same time, American consumers have acquired an enormous taste for imported manufactured goods, from automobiles to umbrellas, and American companies have come to rely more and more on raw materials, and intermediate goods such as steel, that are produced abroad. In 1960 foreign cars held only 4 percent of the U.S. market; in 1987 their share was 26 percent. In certain parts of the country, such as California, all the top-selling automobiles are imported. In steel, the share of imports in U.S. production has risen from 4.2 percent to 25 percent since 1960. Similar statistics could be cited for a host of other products—radios, televisions, bicycles and motorcycles, textiles, leather goods, and much more. We get a sense of this by looking at Figure 1.

The Trade Deficit

If our rising involvement in the world economy meant only a greater interweaving of American production and American consumption with world demand and

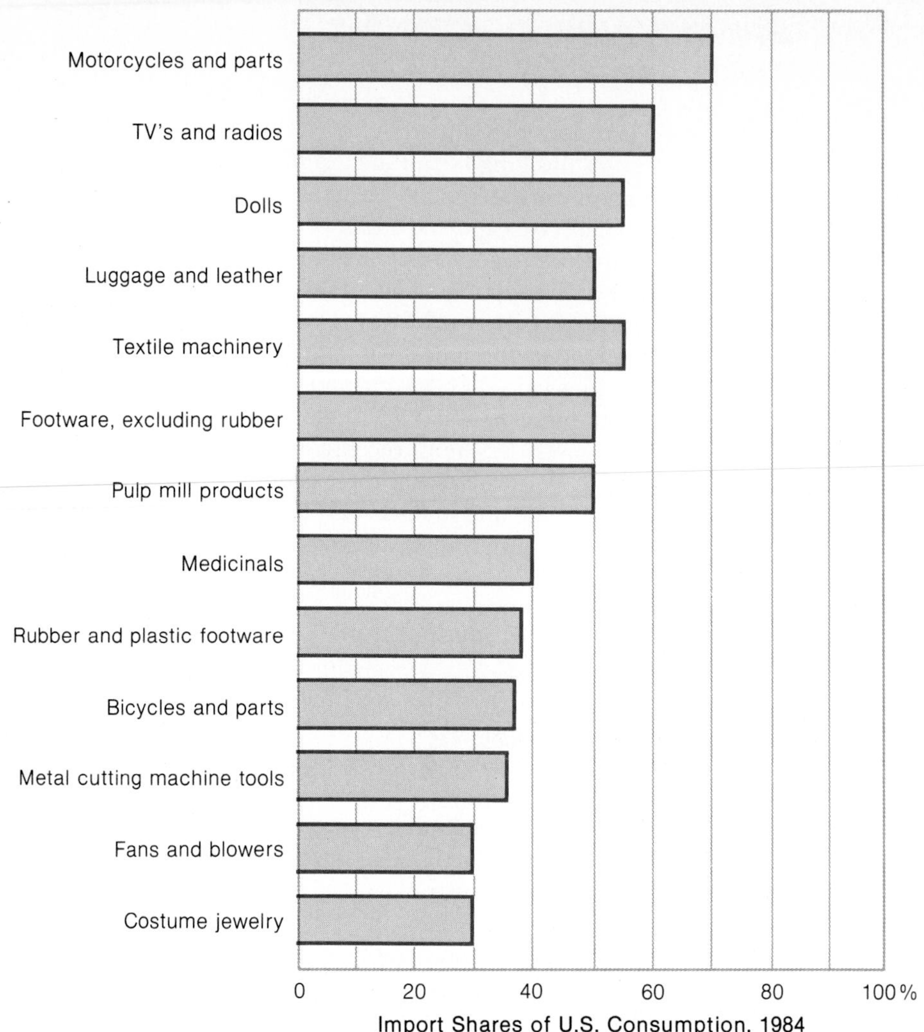

FIGURE 1
Americans Buy Many Foreign-Made Goods, as a recent survey shows.
Source: *Department of Commerce.*

world supply, we might still be able to put the international economy at the back of our textbooks. But something has happened in addition to a globalization of American economic activity. The globalization has taken place unevenly, with our imports rising much more rapidly than our exports.

We can see this in Table 2. Note that up to 1982 our exports were generally larger than our imports, so the *trade balance*—the net difference between what foreigners paid us for American goods and services and what we paid them for their goods and services—showed a sum in America's favor. In 1982, for example, the balance was $19 billion. If we think of the United States economy as a kind of national "firm" trading with (and competing against) other national "firms," that is

TABLE 2
U.S. Exports and Imports
Starting in 1983, there is a striking change in our balance of foreign trade.

	Exports and Imports of Goods and Services		
Period	*Exports*	*Imports*	*Net Exports*
1974	146.2	132.8	13.4
1975	154.9	128.1	26.8
1976	170.9	157.1	13.8
1977	182.7	186.7	−4.0
1978	218.7	219.8	−1.1
1979	281.4	268.1	13.2
1980	338.8	314.8	23.9
1981	369.9	341.9	28.0
1982	348.4	329.4	19.0
1983	336.2	344.4	−8.3
1984	364.3	428.5	−64.2
1985	347.7	441.6	−94.0
1986	377.4	523.2	−145.8
1987	425.8	560.1	−134.3
1988	518.7	611.9	−93.2

Source: *Economic Report of the President.*

the net amount we earned that year. Now look at the years since then. Our purchases have far outrun our sales, so we have run up a very substantial deficit. In effect, we are no longer paying our way.

A Word about Trade Deficits

We now come to one of those complications that we used to skip: A nation is not a firm; and although individual businesses make or lose money in international trade, the nation runs no such profit and loss account. Instead, **a nation earns or loses claims against other countries from its exports and imports.** When we sell American goods abroad, we are paid in dollars by foreigners. Where do they get those dollars? Either from selling goods and services to us, or by borrowing from American lenders, such as investors who will buy their bonds or banks (probably American banks) who will extend them credit in dollars, or by spending any stores of previously earned dollars, called **reserves.**

If we buy more than we sell, we must also find the **foreign exchange**—the needed foreign currencies—to pay for what we have not earned. Where do we get that exchange? Exactly like foreigners, we have no choice but to spend any reserves we have accumulated or to borrow the money from banks who will lend us exchange or from investors who will buy our bonds.

What Table 2 shows is that in six years we have had to pay almost $550 billion more to foreigners than we have earned from them. This means that we have had to borrow that much from foreign banks and other lenders, mainly by selling them United States bonds. Even for a nation as large and wealthy as the United States, a debt of $550 billion to foreigners is beginning to be a serious problem, even though we have large investments abroad. If we go on piling up such debts, at some point our debt will seem so large that foreigners will no longer consider the United States a good risk. They will no longer be willing to buy our bonds or to extend credit for their currencies against IOUs in dollars.

A Trade Crunch

At that point America would have to bring its imports into line with its exports. America would have to "pay its way" because there would be no other source of foreign currencies with which to buy the foreign goods it wanted. We would then experience the same trade crunch that has been felt by countries such as Mexico or Brazil, whose economic plight has made them very poor credit risks.

Because Mexicans or Brazilians cannot borrow foreign currencies, they are forced to limit their imports to the amount that they can sell abroad—minus a very large fraction of those export earnings that must be paid to foreigners as interest on past debts. **The result is a severe fall in the standard of living.** The same result could be felt by this country if, let us say, our foreign debt was $2 trillion, and our ability to get foreign credits vanished. We would then have to bring our imports down to the value of our exports—minus the huge interest payments we would owe on our $2 trillion debt.

It is unlikely that the United States, with its vast strength, will ever experience a trade crunch like that of Mexico or Brazil. But it is not a scenario to be dismissed as "impossible," for that is the direction in which events are moving unless we bring order into our international economic relationships—an order that does not presently prevail.

Behind the Trade Deficit

How did the richest nation in the world become a debtor in the world economy? There is no simple answer, but we should become familiar with two main explanations.

1. The Dollar Was Too High. In the international economy currencies of different countries are constantly being exchanged for one another, and their prices often change dramatically. In the case of the United States, the rate of exchange of the dollar against other main currencies fell in the 1970s, and then moved sharply up after the turn of the decade. In 1980, for example, it cost $2.33 to purchase a British pound. In early 1985 the price of dollars had risen—and the price of pounds had correspondingly fallen—to the point where you could buy a pound for $1.24. Over the same five-year period the **exchange rate** for dollars against two other major European currencies had risen from 4.22 French francs to the dollar to over 10 francs, and from 1.82 German marks to 3.1 marks.

Why was the dollar so high? As with the prices of commodities, we explain movements of currencies in terms of supply and demand. A high price for dollars meant that foreigners were seeking to acquire dollars more than Americans were seeking to acquire other moneys. The main reason foreigners wanted dollars so strongly is that American interest rates became higher, and American inflation rates lower, than the corresponding rates in many European countries. Investors in those countries, or big international companies looking for a place to park their funds, bought dollars in order to purchase U.S. bonds or other investments. As this "portfolio" demand grew, the price of dollars rose.*

What is the effect of a high dollar? We will put ourselves first into the shoes of an American importer, then into those of an American exporter. Suppose we are a department store buyer shopping for sweaters in England. The English manufacturer doesn't quote us a price in dollars; he gives us a price in English pounds—don't forget that he probably sells the greater part of his sweaters to English stores, not American ones. Say that his price is £30. The high dollar becomes a wonderful break for our department store buyer. The higher the dollar goes, the fewer dollars she has to pay to acquire the pounds she needs. In 1980, for example, a £30 sweater would have cost $69.90. By early 1985, the same £30 sweater cost her only $37.20.

So high dollars mean cheap imports. Can you see that for the same reasons high dollars mean expensive exports? A French buyer of computers will be much less eager to pay $1,000 for an American computer when the dollar is high than when it is low, because it will cost him more francs to purchase that thousand dollars.

We have to leave a deeper examination of the exchange rate for Chapter 26. But we have seen one very important reason for the American trade deficit. A high dollar priced us out of a competitive position in exports and lured us into a vast import boom. Most experts believe that the dollar in 1985 was at least 30 percent over its normal relationship to other currencies.

From High Dollars to Low Dollars

Not surprisingly, the dollar began to fall in 1986. In fact, it did not merely fall—it plummeted, at least against the major currencies we use as benchmarks. In two years the price of a German mark rose from 46 cents to 56 cents; of 100 Japanese yen from 59 to 75 cents. As we write these words, the dollar has fallen so far that it is now American goods that are cheap in international trade and foreign goods that are expensive at home.

Then why hasn't the trade balance turned around? Why aren't American exports booming and U.S. imports from abroad shrinking? Part of the answer is that our exports *are* booming, but that our imports are *also* booming, mainly because foreign sellers have trimmed their profit margins to keep their foothold in the American market. Part of the answer is that important potential markets for U.S. goods, especially among the Third World countries, are stagnant because those nations remain trapped in their debt crisis and have no foreign exchange left to buy U.S. goods. Part of the answer may lie in a slow global shift in the location of production, away from former industrial centers to the burgeoning Pacific Rim and other newly industrializing areas.

*Later on we will find that American interest rates have been high because of American monetary and fiscal policy. That is a twist to the story which we must postpone for the moment.

TABLE 3
Manufacturing Productivity
The United States is no longer a world leader in productivity.

	Output per Hour (1983)	*Rate of Growth (%) 1977–1982*
United States	$18.21	0.6%
Germany	20.22	2.1
France	19.80	3.0
Italy	17.72	3.6
Japan	17.61	3.4
Canada	17.03	−0.3
U.K.	11.34	2.7

Source: Lester Thurow, *The Zero Sum Solution* (New York: Simon & Schuster, Inc., 1985), p. 49.

We will have to investigate these matters more carefully later in our book. Here it is enough to note that the falling dollar has not yet been enough to remedy our adverse trade flows, although sooner or later it is very likely to bring things into better balance.

2. PRODUCTIVITY GROWTH WAS TOO LOW. The high dollar is a big factor in the adverse American trade balance, but it is not the only reason for concern about America's position in the world economy. A second type of apprehension stresses real, not monetary, factors.

Behind the Productivity Lag

The data in Table 3 show that U.S. manufacturing productivity had already been bettered by Germany and France in 1983; it has probably further slipped since then. It has also probably been surpassed by a number of smaller European countries such as Sweden, the Netherlands, Switzerland, and Austria. Thus we are no longer the undisputed leader in productivity, at least not in the manufacturing sector. Even more disturbing are the data that show our rate of productivity growth to be slower than of most of our main competitors. We may recall from Chapter 5 how important growth rates are (look back for a moment to the box on page 00). U.S. figures during the five years shown in Table 3 reveal that we have been one of the worst performers in the advanced industrial world.

A country whose productivity is growing more slowly than that of its competitors will slowly find itself priced out of the market, exactly the same as a company whose efficiency is improving less rapidly than that of its competition. Although high exchange rates make our competitive position very difficult in the short run, low productivity growth makes it difficult in the long run.

Too Many Services?

What lies behind this laggard performance? Few important phenomena are less well understood. Some economists believe the reason lies in the failure of the American economy to save and invest as large a fraction of its GNP as its major competitor nations—Japan, for example, invests 28 percent of its GNP, Germany 20 percent—against our 19 percent.

This relatively low investment share in GNP reflects another big change in the U.S. economy—toward a lower share of manufacturing in total employment. We are shifting workers, in effect, from high-productivity-growth manufacturing jobs into lower-productivity-growth service jobs. In Chapter 4 we saw that three out of every four Americans today work in service occupations. These range from highly skilled occupations such as architect and engineer to low-skilled jobs in fast-food operations, but on the average, services produce less GNP per worker per year than either agriculture or manufacturing.

Hence the sheer movement into services pulls down our productivity average. This drift is visible in all advanced countries, but nowhere has it developed to the extent that it has in the United States—in France, Germany and Japan the service sector absorbs only 60 percent of the labor force. Moreover, the distribution of the labor force *within* the service sector is not helpful to the United States. Consider this comparison: For every 10,000 U.S. working people, there are 20 lawyers, 40 accountants, and 70 engineers. In Japan the numbers are 1 lawyer, 3 accountants, and 400 engineers.*

Other Explanations

Another explanation calls attention to our educational system. Much as with our relatively poor showing in capital formation, the United States compares badly with other advanced countries in its formation of human capital. In 19 international tests of educational achievement, Americans never scored at the top, and in 7 tests scored at the bottom.†

And there are still other explanations—adversarial rather than cooperative relations between American management and labor; the absence of a workable consensus on the role of government in the economy; inflexible management styles and failure to take full advantage of the flexible production techniques high technology makes possible; a decline of the old-fashioned work ethic; and more besides.

Moreover, unlike the problem of a high dollar, the productivity problem does not lend itself to a tidy solution. No matter what the root of the problem—capital formation, our occupational mix, our educational system, our labor-management structure—the cure involves our whole society, at every level and in every public and private dimension. **Some form of national policy will be needed to change the underlying configuration of American society in ways that encourage rather than discourage national productivity growth.**

**The New York Times,* December 19, 1982, Sec. 12.

†Barbara Lerner, "American Education: How Are We Doing?" *Public Interest,* Fall 1982, p. 64.

A DEBTOR NATION?

In the summer of 1985 the Commerce Department announced that the United States had become a debtor nation for the first time since 1914. By a debtor nation, we mean that the value of U.S. assets held by foreigners—real plant and equipment, real estate, stocks and bonds, CDs, or just bank balances—exceeded the value of foreign assets of similar kinds held by Americans. Moreover, this net external debt was growing rapidly. By the end of 1985, it had already exceeded $100 billion, making us one of the world's largest net debtors. By the end of 1986, it was $400 billion. At the rate it was growing, our debt would reach $1 trillion by 1990. *The New York Times* called this "the most dramatic transformation in [the United States] financial position since world War I"; it may very well be the most dramatic turnabout in world financial history.*

The basic cause of the startling turnaround lies in our adverse balance of trade. As we know, the only way any nation can import more than it exports is to borrow the foreign exchange needed to pay for its import surplus. Our own borrowing took the form of selling many kinds of United States obligations to foreigners, from Treasury bonds to mutual funds or CDs. All these transactions made foreign currencies available to Americans because foreigners had to sell their own currencies in order to buy U.S. assets. The foreign funds they sold then became available through the banking system to U.S. importers.

Is the net U.S. debt a worrisome thing? There is no simple answer to this question. Insofar as our import surplus stimulates foreign production, our growing debt makes a sizable contribution to world economic growth, from which we

FINDING OUR PLACE

As we move through macro- and microeconomies and into international trade, we will have a chance to consider policies that may help us find a viable place in the world. In this introduction to the problem, let us end as we began, by trying to see the problem as a whole.

An Interdependent World

As we have seen, the importance of the rest of the world for the U.S. economy has risen sharply. Curiously, the importance of the U.S. economy *within* the rest of the world has not. In 1960 it was estimated that the United States accounted for 40 percent of all the production in the world. By 1984 this fraction had fallen to 24 percent. This is even more striking on an industrial basis. In 1960 U.S. steel companies produced 26 percent of the world's steel. In 1985 they produced only 11

benefit as well as others. In addition, the sale of Treasury bonds or bills and other securities to foreigners makes it possible for the United States to incur its own domestic debts, both private and public, without relying exclusively on its own savings. This eases the pressure on interest rates and helps growth at home.

The main danger is that the growth of foreign debt will eventually imperil America's international creditworthiness—its ability to borrow more foreign funds. That depends not so much on the size of our foreign borrowings as on the use to which we put them. In the nineteenth century we borrowed heavily from Europe to build a vast transcontinental railway system. But because foreign savings were put to such productive use, American international credit remained good despite the frequent bankruptcies of the railroads themselves. If our present and future international debt were put to equally productive use, the same optimistic forecast would seem appropriate today. Alas, that does not seem to be the case. Our foreign borrowings have not been earmarked for the creation of productive assets, public or private. Even though our borrowings have helped world economic recovery and have stimulated American growth, there is no reason for foreigners to feel that the value of their American assets is secure because those assets are "real wealth," like railways. The danger is that foreign lenders will appraise the soundness of their investments in the United States by the general condition of the American economy—*including its ability to make its exports pay for its imports.* We will look into these matters again when we study the workings of the Federal Reserve in Chapter 20.

*As we will see when we look into multinational corporations (Chapter 30), the way we measure our international indebtedness is not altogether reliable. But there is no denying the trend.

percent. In 1960 we produced 52 percent of the world's automobiles; 25 years later, only 26 percent.

Up to now we have considered this global shift from America's point of view, where it appears as a formidable problem. But there is also the view of the rest of the world. From this perspective, the relative decline in U.S. importance appears as an opportunity, not a problem. It reflects the success of other nations—some left behind in the nineteenth century, some still in the ninth century—in finding a place in the world economy necessary for their own well-being. American policies in both Europe and the underdeveloped world have tried to stimulate growth. Thus America's relative decline in the world economy represents a political success, even though it presents an economic challenge.

We do not know at all what a truly integrated and well-functioning world economy would look like. Would it be knit together solely by market forces, or would there have to be a political framework of constraint over the whole? Would there be a single world monetary unit, or would each nation, as today, insist on its inviolable right to coin its own money? Would nations continue to define the boundaries of what we call "economies," or would there be such an intermingling of markets that national boundaries would have very little economic significance?

We cannot begin to answer these questions yet. Indeed, we hardly know whether they are the right questions to ask. But they give us some sense of the real significance of the relation between what we call the economy of the United States and the economy of the world.

LOOKING BACK

KEY CONCEPTS

The U.S. is no longer a closed economy.

1 The United States economy is still the richest and most productive economic entity in the world. But it is certainly not a "closed" economy. Both in trade and in finance, it is enmeshed in a world economy.

A spectrum of economies from rich to poor

2 The world economy is made up of a wide range of nations, from the Euro-Japanese group of "Western" economies through the underdeveloped, or Third World, countries where live most of the world's population. The Third World nations have made a significant impact through OPEC and as the location of new high-tech, low-wage industries.

Rising U.S. trade involvement

3 United States involvement in the world economy has been rising steadily in recent years, although, unhappily, imports have expanded much more rapidly than exports. More important is the very high ratio of manufacturing exports and imports: 20 percent of our manufactures are exported; 50 percent of domestic purchases of manufactured goods are imports.

The growing trade deficit

4 The United States has normally exported more goods and services than it has imported. During the last several years, however, it has incurred a very large and growing deficit in its balance of trade.

Deficits require using reserves or borrowing from abroad.

5 A deficit means that a nation has not earned enough from exports to pay for its imports. It must finance the deficit either by using its reserves of foreign exchange or by borrowing from abroad. If deficits become too large, a nation may no longer be able to borrow and will be forced to reduce its exports to the level of its imports—less any payments of interest on its debt abroad.

Our trade deficit began because of the high dollar, which cheapened imports into the United States and made U.S. goods expensive to foreigners.

6 Our trade deficit began because the dollar was too high. When the dollar is high, imports become cheap because we can buy many units of a foreign currency with each dollar; when the dollar falls, it takes more dollars to buy the same amount of foreign currency, and the price of imports goes up. By the same token, a high dollar makes our goods expensive for foreigners, while a lower dollar cheapens our goods in foreign money. The dollar was extremely high in the early 1980s, because of attractive U.S. interest rates.

Imports have remained high, despite the dollar's fall.

7 The cure for an adverse trade balance should be a fall in the exchange rate. But the American dollar dropped precipitously from 1985 to 1987 without remedying our situation. This is probably because of our stubborn propensity to import based on quality differentials and to the failure of world demand to magnify our export boom.

Lagging productivity has weakened the U.S. competitive position. National policy may be needed to correct lagging productivity.

8 A second general explanation for U.S. trade difficulties, especially in manufacturing, is lagging productivity. Numerous reasons have been offered for this lag, among them inadequate capital formation, a shift to low-productivity occupations in the service sector, and a comparatively poor education system. Policy changes affecting our whole society may be needed to bring about a shift in these (or other) causes of our low rate of productivity improvement.

A debtor nation

9 Largely because of our chronic trade deficit, the United States has suddenly become a net debtor to the world. If our trade deficit continues at the present level, we will owe the rest of the world huge amounts within a few years. International debts are not necessarily bad—indeed, they can be very useful when the borrowed money is put to productive use, as in the building of the railways in the nineteenth century. The worry about the present rise of international debt is that it has not been productively used, and that it might end in a panicky flight from the U.S. dollar.

An interdependent world is emerging

10 The United States economy no longer bulks so large in the world economy. This is due to the rise of Europe, Japan, and now some parts of the underdeveloped world to a position of greater well-being. This represents a political gain, even though it poses an economic challenge. What a fully interdependent world would look like we do not know.

ECONOMIC VOCABULARY

Closed economy 102
Reserves 107
Trade deficit 105
Foreign exchange 107
High and low dollar 108
Exchange rate 108

QUESTIONS

1. What do you think are the advantages of an open economy? The disadvantages?
2. Describe what is meant by a trade "deficit." What is a trade "surplus"? If one nation runs a deficit, must another run a surplus?

3. How does the United States manage to buy $130 billion more than it sells? Why cannot a country like Israel run up as large a deficit as the United States?
4. Suppose that it costs 50 francs to produce a bottle of French wine, and that the dollar buys 5 francs. What is the price of wine, ignoring transportation costs, to a New York retailer of wine? Now suppose that the dollar buys 10 francs instead of 5. Do we say that the dollar has gone up or down? Does a higher dollar make French goods cheaper or dearer? Will that increase imports or decrease them? Now put yourself in the shoes of a French importer of American wheat, which sells for $5 a bushel. Again forgetting transportation costs, what will the wheat sell for in Paris if 1 franc buys 20 cents? If 1 franc buys 5 cents? Can you see that a high dollar must mean a low franc? Are high dollars good for American grain exporters? Are high francs? Try to see international transactions as always involving two *differing* points of view.
5. Let us suppose you were convinced that the long-run cause of our trade deficit was a failure to build up our capital. What measures might help remedy this situation? Suppose you thought the trouble lay essentially in our education system. Now what would you recommend to make our performance as good as that of our main competitors?
6. Do you think economic relations tend to unite nations or divide them? Think about the effect on global living standards if there were no trade—and then think about the quarrels and wars that have been fought over economic spoils. Do you think it is possible that economic interrelations serves both to unite and to separate the world?

PART II

SOME BASIC ECONOMICS

CHAPTER 7

Economic Science

A LOOK AHEAD

Now that we have some background in the field, we are ready to take the next step toward becoming economists by learning something of the ways economists think. Here we are dealing with the abstract and analytic aspects of the field that we mentioned in Chapter 1.

Essentially this short chapter tells you that economic theory is about maximizing behavior that takes place against constraints. Acquisitiveness is a good first approximation of the meaning of "maximizing," and "constraints" implies limits, boundaries, or costs.

Economic reasoning consists of puzzling out what happens when rational acquisitors face constraints imposed by nature or society. Keep that in mind and the chapter will unfold step by step.

What is it that we are trying to understand as economists? Certainly it is not the economic attributes of *all* societies. Our first chapters focus on the United States, not merely because we are naturally interested in the economic aspects of our own country, but also because the United States is a kind of society that lends itself to economic analysis. Economic reasoning, we should note at the outset, applies most cogently to market societies, to capitalism.

However, economic reasoning will not try to come to grips with all of society. Our earlier survey paid little attention to vast areas of social life that we call sociological or political, still less to the religious or artistic. Economics mainly is concerned with the facts that bear on only one aspect of our social life: our efforts to produce and to distribute wealth. Boom and bust, inflation and depression, poverty and riches, growth or no growth—all can be described in terms of the production of wealth and its distribution.

MAXIMIZING VS. CONSTRAINTS

Our task, then, is to find some way of explaining production and distribution. Therefore economists observe the *human* universe, much as natural scientists observe the physical universe, in search of data and orderly relationships that may permit them to construct hypotheses.

What do economists see when they scrutinize the world of economic activity? Two attributes of a market society attract their attention:

1. Individuals in such a society display a particular behavior pattern when they participate in economic activities, as consumers or businesspeople. They behave in acquisitive, money-searching, "maximizing" ways.
2. A series of obstacles or constraints stands between the acquisitive drive of marketers and their realization of economic gain. Some are the constraints of nature; some are the obstacles of social institutions.

Thus an extraordinary conclusion begins to dawn. A great deal of the activity of a market society can be explained as the outcome of two interacting forces. One is the force of maximizing behavior—a force we have described in terms of the acquisitive behavior of men and women in a market society. The other is the constraining counterforce of nature or of social institutions—a series of obstacles that holds back or channels or directs the acquisitive drive. This suggests the daring scientific task that economics sets for itself. It is to explain the events of economic reality—even to predict some of the events of future economic reality—by *reasoning based on fundamental hypotheses about maximizing behavior and its constraints.*

HYPOTHESES ABOUT BEHAVIOR

Let us start with the economist's assumption about behavior. We can sum it up in a sentence: People are maximizers.

ACQUISITIVENESS

Remember that we are talking about the kind of behavior that we find in a market society. Perhaps in a different society of the future, another hypothesis about behavior would have to serve as our starting point. People might then be driven by the desire to better the condition of others rather than of themselves.

A story about heaven and hell is to the point. Hell has been described as a place where people sit at tables laden with sumptuous food, unable to eat because they have three-foot-long forks and spoons strapped to their hands. Heaven is described as the very same place. But in heaven, people feed one another.

Maximizing Utilities

What does that hypothesis mean? Essentially, it means that people in market societies seek to gain as much pleasurable wealth from their economic activity as they can. **We call this pleasurable wealth "utility." Thus we hypothesize that men and women are *utility maximizers.***

Note that we define utility as *pleasurable* wealth. Economists do not argue that people try to accumulate the largest amount of wealth possible, regardless of its pleasures. We all know that after a certain point wealth-producing work brings fatigue, or even pain. Therefore we assume that as people work to maximize their wealth, they take into account the pains (or disutilities) of achieving it.

It is impossible to *prove* that people maximize in this fashion. But it seems plausible that most of us do seek wealth either as wage earners or as businesspeople and that we take account of the nuisances and difficulties of achieving it.

Satiable and Insatiable Wants

Economics not only assumes that men and women are maximizers, it also has a hypothesis about why they behave so acquisitively. **The hypothesis is that people's wants are insatiable; that human desires for utility can never be filled.**

Are our wants, in fact, insatiable? Does human nature keep us on a treadmill of striving that can never bring us to a point of contentment? As with maximizing, there is a prima facie plausibility about the assumption. For if we include leisure as well as goods among our aims, more time to enjoy ourselves as well as more income to be enjoyed, it seems true enough that something very much like insatiability afflicts most people. At least this appears true in societies that encourage striving for status and success and that set high value on consumption and recreation.

For example, surveys regularly show that men and women at all economic levels express a desire for more income (usually about 10 percent more than they actually have), and *this drive for more does not seem to diminish as we move up the economic scale.* If it did, we would be hard put to explain why people who are generally in the upper echelons of the distribution of wealth and income work just as hard as, sometimes even harder than, those on the lower rungs of the economic ladder.

There is, however, a very important qualification to the assumption that wants are insatiable for all wealth, including leisure. **The qualification is that economists assume human wants for *particular kinds* of wealth, including leisure, are indeed capable of being satisfied.** This idea of the satiability of *particular* wants will play a key role in our next chapter, when we see how we can derive the concept of demand and demand "curves" from our hypotheses concerning behavior.

Rationality

Equally important is an assumption about the way individuals think and act as they go about striving to fulfill their insatiable wants-in-general or their satiable wants-in-particular. **This assumption is that people are *rational* maximizers.** Economists mean by this that people in a market milieu stop to consider the various courses of action open to them and to calculate in some fashion the means that will best suit their maximizing aims. There may be two different ways of producing a good. As rational actors, people will choose the method that will yield them the good for the smallest effort or cost.

This concept of rational maximizing does not mean that human beings may not wish, on some occasions, to go to more trouble than necessary. After all, people could worship God in very simple buildings or out-of-doors, but they go to extraordinary lengths to erect magnificent churches and decorate them with sculpture and paintings. It is meaningless to apply the word *rational* to pursuits such as these, which may nevertheless have vast importance for society.

But when people are engaged in producing the goods and services of ordinary life, seeking to achieve the largest possible incomes or the most satisfaction-yielding patterns of consumption, the economist assumes that they *will* stop to think about the differing ways of attaining a given end and will then choose the one that is least costly. This is particularly true of businesspeople, whose activities are vital for a capitalist society.

The Economist's View of Humankind

Of course, economists do not believe that men and women, even in business life, are solely rational, acquisitive creatures. They are fully aware that people have many motivations: aesthetic, political, religious. If economists concentrate on the rational and acquisitive elements in people, it is because they believe these to be decisive for most economic behavior; that is, for the explanation of our ordinary productive and distributive activities.

Economic theory is therefore a study of the effects of one aspect of human behavior as it motivates people to undertake their worldly activities. Very often, as economists well know, other aspects will override or blunt the acquisitive, maximizing orientation. To the extent that this is so, economic theory loses its clarity or may even suggest outcomes different from those we find in fact. **But economists think that rational maximizing—the calculated pursuit of pleasurable wealth—is universal and strong enough to serve as a good working hypothesis on which to build their complicated theories.** To put it differently, economists do *not* think that political or religious or other such motives regularly overwhelm maximizing behavior. If that were so, economic theory would be of little avail.

Economists regard maximizing as a potentially useful mode of behavior. Of course they understand that there is a lot more to life than making as much money as possible. But economics allows us to see that maximizing can be a beneficial activity. Business schools exist, in part, to teach people to be better maximizers—that is, more efficient and productive.

HYPOTHESES ABOUT CONSTRAINTS

So far, we have traced the basic assumptions of economic reasoning about behavior. What about constraints? As we have seen, people do not maximize in a vacuum—or, to speak in more economic terms, in a world where all goods are available effortlessly in infinite amounts. Instead, people exert their maximizing efforts in a world where nature, technical limitations, and social institutions oppose those efforts. Goods and services are not free; they must be won by working with the elements of the physical world. Land, resources, and artifacts inherited from past generations are not boundlessly abundant. Laws and social organizations constantly impede our maximizing impulses.

Another way of putting it is that maximizing describes what we *want* to do, while constraints describe what we *cannot* do. Economics thus studies the problems, and sometimes the impossibility, of achieving what we want. That is why economics is often characterized as *maximizing subject to constraints.*

Constraints of Nature

Constraints are obviously very important. But we cannot sum them up as simply as the idea of maximizing.

Let us first think about two constraints on our maximizing desires that are imposed by nature. Later we will study these constraints in greater detail, but this is a good time to become generally familiar with them.

1. Diminishing Returns. Why can't you grow all the world's food in a flowerpot? Because there isn't room, obviously. But the economist sees something of considerable interest in this fact. It is that a *law of diminishing returns* describes what happens to output as you add more and more of one input—let us say seed—to a fixed amount of other inputs—in this case, the flowerpot.

Why is it, after all, that you can't produce ever-larger crops by adding more seed (or more labor or more fertilizer or more of any other single input) to a single field? The answer is that each seed needs to be complemented by a certain amount of soil, labor, and fertilizer; and that adding more and more seed brings you over that point of optimal combination. Thereafter, each additional unit of input yields less and less additional (or *marginal*) output (see Figure 1).

Once it is called to our attention, we find the workings of diminishing returns in many aspects of production. We cannot go on adding workers to a fixed number of machines without experiencing falling marginal (additional) output, once we pass the best mix of labor and machinery. On a larger scale, the Food and Agriculture Organization of the United Nations has noted that in the mid-1930s each additional ton of fertilizer improved output by 15 tons of grain. Forty years later, when annual inputs of fertilizer were far higher than before, each additional ton increased grain yields by only 5.8 tons. Diminishing returns was once more at work.

2. Increasing Cost. The second constraint is less familiar. It has to do with the fact that not all land or labor or resources are alike, so that **as we move from one kind of production to another, we are likely to find it more and more costly to produce each additional unit of the new output.** Costs are measured not in money, but in terms of alternative outputs forgone—what you have to give up in order to get an additional unit of the product whose output you are increasing.

Here a diagram can help us visualize the problem. In Figure 2 we see a community that can produce two kinds of output—milk and grain. If it puts all its labor and all its land into milk production, it can produce an amount of milk that we'll represent by the distance *OA* on the milk axis. If it puts all its land and labor into grain, it will produce *OB* of grain, as represented on that axis.

Now suppose that our community is producing nothing but milk and that it

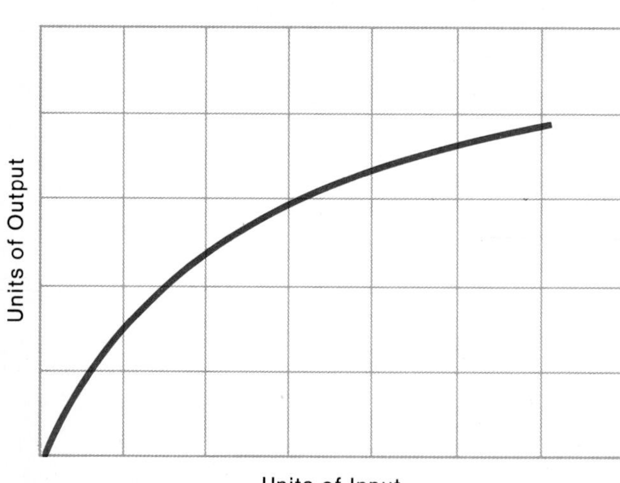

FIGURE 1
Diminishing Returns
A production function shows the relationship between inputs and outputs. When diminishing returns prevail, each additional unit of input yields smaller and smaller additional units of output.

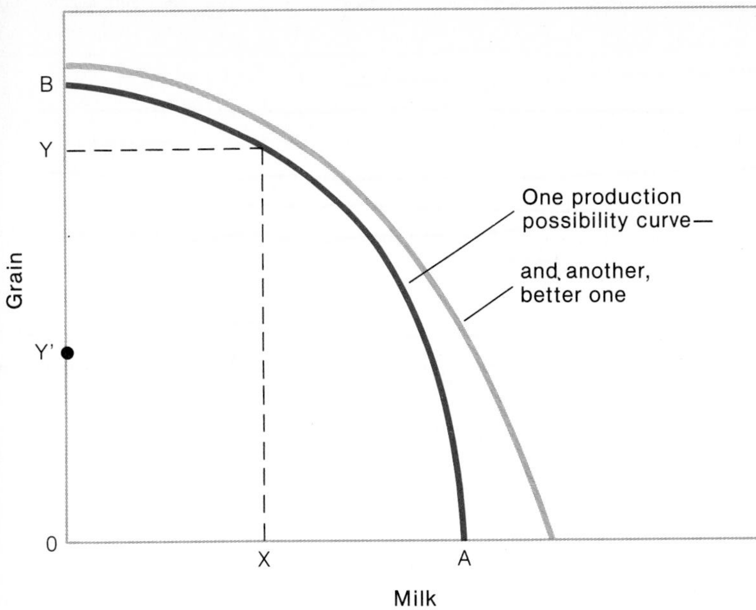

FIGURE 2
Increasing Cost
The curve AB *is called a production possibility curve. It is an imaginary curve here, but it is meant to depict a real-life situation, in which we see how many tons of outputs, like milk or grain, a society could produce by using its resources in various combinations. The dotted line shows how better technology, for instance, could move such a curve out. What would an earthquake do to it? Draw in such a reduced production possibility curve. The curve bows because of the law of increasing cost—that is, because it becomes less and less efficient to move both labor and resources from one use to another. Compare how much grain we get* (OY) *as we cut milk production in half (moving from* OA *to* OX*), with how little we get* (BY) *as we move the remaining half* (OX). *Use a pencil to see if it works the other way around. Start from all grain* (OB) *and zero milk. First chart how much milk you get if you move the economy out of grain (from* OB *to* OY′*). Now eliminate all grain production. How much* additional *milk do you get?*

decides to balance its output. It cuts milk production in half (to *OX*), moving land and labor into grain. We can see that it thereby gains *OY* amount of grain. Now notice what happens if the community moves the remaining half of its land and labor into grain. Output rises only a small amount, *YB*.

Why is the second half of the community investment in land and labor less productive than the first half? Because we have already plowed the best fields and availed ourselves of the most skilled farmers. The last bushels of grain are much harder to win than the first. And of course the same result would take place in reverse if we started from all grain, at *B*, and switched over into milk. **The constraint means that the more of any one product that we want, the more of some other product we have to give up to get it.**

How much of one thing do we have to surrender to get something else? That depends on a host of things—the resources available, the technology we can call on, the energy we can muster. The curve in Figure 2 shows us the grain-milk trade-off in our hypothetical community on some imaginary date, but a new invention, a change in climate, even a new economic system could change the efficiency with which we use our wealth. Thus the curve in Figure 2, which we call a **production possibility curve,** can move—loosening our constraints, as the dotted line shows, or possibly tightening them. We will come back to study this when we take up the subject of economic growth.

Opportunity Cost

Here is a good place to make a very important point about the constraint of cost: **Cost constrains us because it means that we have to give something up to gain wealth.** The cost of the grain in Figure 2 is the milk we had to give up to get it, and the cost of the milk is the grain we had to forgo. That is why economists say "There is no such thing as a free lunch." Even if you did not pay money for it, someone had to produce that lunch, and the actual labor and materials that were used to make it can never be retrieved to make something else.

All costs, to economists, are opportunity costs. They are the utilities we must do without because we have chosen to devote our energies and wealth to creating other utilities. Later on, we will be talking about costs in dollars and cents, which is the way we usually think of cost. But when we say that something costs $10, what we really mean is that it costs us whatever utilities we might have enjoyed if we had spent the $10 on something else.

Have you ever hesitated over whether to buy this *or* that? Then you know what opportunity cost means.

Constraints and Costs

All these properties of nature set the stage for maximizing behavior. People seek wealth through the production and exchange of goods and services, but they do not maximize in a world where goods can be limitlessly and effortlessly obtained. Nature and our given technology offer us their services easily or reluctantly, depending on whether we are trying to maximize output by adding more and more of one kind of input (when we encounter diminishing returns), or whether we are trying to increase the output of one good or service at the expense of others (when the law of increasing cost comes into play).

Needless to say, different societies enjoy different settings in nature—rich or poor soils, cold or warm climates, easily available or scarce mineral deposits. These gifts of nature help establish the limits of productive activity.

Thus constraints will play a basic role in establishing costs or supplies. We return to these considerations in the next chapter, where we encounter a *supply curve*, the counterpart of the demand curve.

Constraints of Society

Perhaps we can already see the makings of a powerful analytic device in the interplay of maximizing drives and constraining influences. Before we move on, however, it is necessary to recognize that nature is not the only constraint on the maximizing force of behavior.

Society's constraints on our behavior are just as effective as nature's. The *law* is a major constraining factor on our acquisitive propensities. *Competition* also limits freedom of action, preventing us from charging as much as we would like for goods or services. The banking system, labor unions, the legal underpinnings of private property, are all *institutions* that operate like the constraints of nature in curbing the unhampered exercise of our maximizing impulse. So is the constraint of our available resources, our *budget.* Like technology, this is partly a constraint imposed by nature, partly one that is the consequence of man.

Not least, constraints affect us by our choice of the *social organization* of our productive efforts, as well as by their technical efficiency. The very same factory may have high or low output depending on whether employees' morale is good or bad.

BASIC HYPOTHESES

Let us briefly review the basic propositions in this first look into economic analysis. They can be summed up very simply.

Because economics generalizes about human behavior and the behavior of nature, it can theorize about, and to some extent predict, the operations of a market society. If we could not begin with the plausible hypothesis that people are rational maximizers and that nature (and social institutions) constrain their behavior in clearly defined ways, we could not hazard the simplest predictive statement about economic society. We could not explain why a store that wants to sell more goods marks its prices down rather than up or why copper costs will probably rise if we try to double copper production in a short period of time.

Economics as a Social Science

Perhaps these simple generalizations about behavior and nature do not seem to be an impressive foundation for a social science. Ask yourself, though, whether we can match these economic generalizations when we think in political or sociological terms. Are there political or social laws of behavior that we can count on with the same degree of certainty we find in laws of economics? Are there constraints of nature, comparable to the laws of production, discoverable in the political and social areas of life? There are not. That is why we are so much less able to predict political or sociological events than to predict economic events.

Although economic prediction has sharp limitations, its underlying structure of behavioral and natural laws gives it unique strength. We must now explore its capabilities. The place to begin must be obvious from our look into economic reality and our first acquaintance with supply and demand. It is the market mechanism.

LOOKING BACK

This chapter covers quite a few technical ideas, such as diminishing returns and increasing costs. Don't try to master them yet. Instead, be sure that you have the following simple conception of economic reasoning firmly in mind.

Economics is about production and distribution. It theorizes from two premises: utility maximizing and constraints.

1 Economic reasoning is mainly about production and distribution of wealth. It constructs hypotheses about this problem from two premises: (a) Men and women are maximizers of utility, and (b) they maximize in the face of well-defined obstacles or constraints.

Maximizing means an insatiable desire for utility in general, not for any one kind of utility.

2 Maximizing behavior means that individuals seek as much pleasurable wealth as possible. This pleasurable wealth is called *utility.* Economists believe that in a market society such as ours there is an insatiable desire for pleasurable wealth in general, although not for each particular kind of pleasurable wealth (after a certain point, more food makes us sick, more leisure is a bore).

Maximizing is guided by rational choice.

3 Economists also assume that individuals pursue their maximizing goals rationally—not in a haphazard, thoughtless way, but by making the best choices they can. Maximizing can therefore be socially useful.

Nature and technology impose two constraints:
- Diminishing returns
- Increasing costs

4 Maximizing behavior has to contend with the obstacles set by nature and by society. Nature and technology together establish two important kinds of constraints:

The law of diminishing returns puts limits on the amount of output we can get from adding any one input—we can't grow all the world's food in a flowerpot.

The law of increasing costs limits our attempts to maximize because not all resources can be applied efficiently to any given purpose: We can't raise dairy cattle in Nevada. We can graph this in a production possibility curve.

Society applies institutional and social constraints.

5 Society imposes other constraints on maximizing—laws, institutional barriers, competition, and the like. Other important limits are imposed by budget considerations and morale.

Costs are missed opportunities.

6 Costs are basically missed opportunities. The term *opportunity cost* makes it clear that costs are not just sums of money, but possibilities for making wealth of various kinds that are forever lost because we have chosen to make wealth of one kind.

Maximizing subject to constraints is the analytic basis for much economics.

7 A powerful social science has emerged from the idea of interplay between maximizing and constraining forces. We shall see a demonstration of its power as we enter into a discussion of supply and demand in the next chapter.

ECONOMIC VOCABULARY

Maximizing 120
Utilities 121
Rationality 122
Constraints 123
Diminishing returns 123
Increasing cost 124
Production possibility curve 125
Opportunity cost 126

QUESTIONS

1. Do you feel like a maximizer? Are you content with your income? If you are not, do you expect that someday you will be satisfied?
2. Do you act rationally when you spend money? Do you consciously try to weigh the various advantages of buying this instead of that, and to spend your money for the item that will give you the greatest pleasure? Consciously or not, do you generally act as a rational maximizer?
3. How valid do you think the laws of economic behavior are? If they are *not* valid, why does economic society function and not collapse? If they *are* valid, why can't economists predict more accurately? (Chapter 9 has more about that!)
4. In what way is competition an institution? Are people naturally competitive? Would there be competition in a society that denied spatial or social mobility to labor, as feudalism did?
5. Can you think of any political activities or limits comparable to economic maximizing or constraints? Are there constraints of national size? Might it be possible to devise an economics of politics? For example, do you think politicians seek to maximize votes?
6. Suppose that you had a very large flowerpot and extraordinary chemicals and seeds. Could you conceivably grow all the world's food in it? Why would you still get diminishing returns?
7. What is the opportunity cost of undertaking a program such as space exploration? Of mounting a vast slum clearance program? Suppose the two cost the same amount of money? Does that mean the opportunity cost is the same?

CHAPTER 8

Supply and Demand

A LOOK AHEAD

In this chapter you come to grips with the most important and powerful tool that economic reasoning gives us. The tool is an understanding of supply and demand and how they drive the market system.

It will help you to keep the following four steps in mind:

1 You will learn exactly what the word *demand* means, and what a "demand curve" represents.

2 You will learn the same thing about supply—what the word means and what a "supply curve" represents.

3 You will put the two together and see how demand and supply give rise to an *equilibrium* price.

4 You will begin to distinguish shifts of supply and demand curves from movements along those curves.

What impresses us first when we study the market as a solution to the economic problem? The striking fact is that the market uses only one means of persuasion to induce people to engage in production or to undertake the tasks of distribution. That means it is neither time-honored tradition nor the edict of any authority.

Prices and Behavior

Thus our first question: How is it that prices take the place of tradition or command, and become the guide to economic behavior?

The key lies in maximization. Through prices, acquisitive individuals learn what course of action will maximize their incomes or minimize their expenditures. This means that in the word *price* we include prices of labor and capital and resources which we call wages, profits, interest, and rent. Of course, within the category of prices we also include those ordinary prices that we pay for the goods and services we consume and the materials we purchase in order to build a home or to operate a store or factory. In each case, the only way that we can tell how to maximize our receipts and minimize our costs is by reading the signals of price that the market gives us.*

Therefore, if we are to understand how the market works as a mechanism—that is, how it acts as a guide to the solution of the economic problem—we must first understand how the market sets prices. For this, two distinct concepts are essential: *demand* and *supply*.

DEMAND

Taste and Income

When you enter the market for goods (almost every time you walk along a shopping street), two factors determine whether you will actually become a buyer and not just a window shopper. The first is your desire for the good. Economists call this "taste." It is your taste that determines whether a good offers you pleasure or utility, and if so, how much. The windows of shops are crammed with things you could afford to buy but which you simply do not wish to own. Perhaps if some of these were cheaper, you might wish to own them; other goods you would not want even if they were free. For such goods, for which your tastes are too weak to motivate you at the price at which they are offered, your demand is zero. The pleasure or utility they afford is not offset, for you, by what they cost. **Thus taste determines your willingness to buy.**

Yet taste is not the only component of demand. Shop windows are also full of

*In the real world reading prices can be very complicated, for it involves not only how much we know about the market, but also how much we *think* we know about it. Here we simplify matters and assume, to begin with, that we all have the knowledge that we need.

goods that you might very much like to own but cannot afford to buy. Thus your "effective demand" for Rolls-Royces is apt to be zero. The demand of the poor for food, shelter, clothing, and other necessities is small, even though their need and desire for such items may be very large. **In other words, demand also hinges on your ability to buy—on your possession of sufficient wealth or income as well as on your own taste.**

Diminishing Marginal Utility

Note that your demand for goods depends on your willingness and ability to buy goods or services *at their going price.* From this it follows that the amounts of goods you demand will change as their prices change, just as it also follows that the amounts you will demand change as your wealth or income changes. There is no difficulty understanding why changing prices should change our ability to buy: Our wealth simply stretches further or less far, our budget is less or more constrained by our income.

But why should our *willingness* to buy be related to price? The answer lies in the nature of utility. People are maximizing creatures, but they do not want ever more of the *same* commodity. On the contrary, as we saw, economists take as a plausible generalization that additional increments of the same good or service, within some stated period of time, will yield smaller and smaller increments of pleasure. **These increments of pleasure are called *marginal utility*, and the general tendency of marginal utility to diminish with rising consumption of any good is called the law of *diminishing marginal utility*.** Remember: Diminishing marginal utility refers strictly to behavior and not to nature. The units of goods we continue to buy are not smaller—it is the pleasure associated with each additional unit that is smaller.

Demand Curves*

In the bar chart on the left of Figure 1, we show the ever-smaller amounts of money we are willing to pay for additional units of some good or service, because each additional unit gives us less utility than its predecessor. In the graph on the right, we have drawn a *demand curve.* You will see that a demand curve generalizes this basic relationship between the quantity of a good we are interested in acquiring and the price we are willing to pay for it.

Figure 1 deserves a careful look. Note that each *additional* unit affords us less utility, so we are not willing to pay as much for the next unit as for the one we just bought. This does not mean that the *total utility* we derive from all 3 or 4 units is less than that we derived from the first. Far from it. It is the *addition* to our utility from the last unit that is much lower than the *addition* from the first or second.

*Anyone unfamiliar with graphs should turn right now to page 167 –168 and learn how to read them and use them. Look as well into the extra word on graphs on page 174–178.

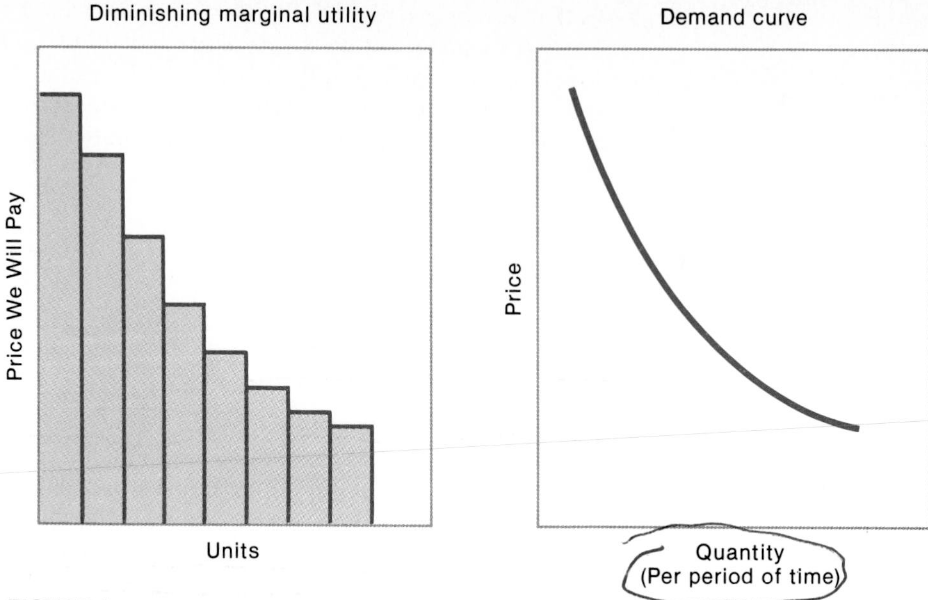

FIGURE 1
Diminishing Marginal Utility and a Demand Curve
Notice, on the left, how the marginal utility of each additional unit of a good diminishes as units are added to a purchase. The curve on the right simply generalizes the fact that each additional unit yields less pleasure than the one before it, and will therefore command a smaller price.

The Puzzle of Bread and Diamonds

The notion of diminishing marginal utility clears up an old puzzle of economic life: Why is it that we are willing to pay so little for bread, which is a necessity for life, and so much for diamonds, which are not? The answer is that we have so much bread that the *marginal* utility of any loaf we are thinking of buying is very little, whereas we have so few diamonds that each carat has a very high marginal utility. If we were locked inside Tiffany's over a long holiday, the prices we would pay for bread and diamonds, after a few days, would be very different from those we would have paid when we entered.

SUPPLY

What about the supply side? Here, too, willingness and ability enter into the seller's actions. As we would expect, they bring about reactions different from those in the case of demand.

At high prices, sellers are more *willing* to supply goods and services because they will take in more money. They will also be more easily *able* to offer more goods because higher prices will enable less efficient suppliers to enter the market, or will cover the higher costs of production that may result from increasing outputs.

Therefore we depict normal supply curves as rising. These rising curves present a contrast to the falling curves of demanders: Sellers respond eagerly to high prices; buyers respond negatively. Figure 2 shows such a typical supply curve. Note that a supply curve, like its demand counterpart, represents a functional relationship: how much we will offer at different prices. Time does not enter into this curve—the curve does not show changes that would require time-consuming activity, such as changing our scale of operation. For this reason it is called a *short-run* supply curve.

Supply and Demand

The idea that buyers welcome low prices and sellers welcome high prices is hardly apt to come as a surprise. What is surprising is that the meanings of the words *supply* and *demand* differ from the ones we ordinarily carry about in our heads. It is very important to understand that when we speak of demand as economists, we do not refer to a single purchase at a given price. **Demand in its proper economic sense refers to a *schedule of quantities* that we are willing and able to buy at different prices at a given time. That relationship is shown by our demand curve.**

The same relationship between price and quantity enters into the word *supply.* When we use the word *supply,* we do not mean the amount a seller puts on the market at a given price. We mean the *differing* amounts offered at *different* prices. Thus our supply curves, like our demand curves, portray the relationship between willingness and ability to enter into transactions at different prices.

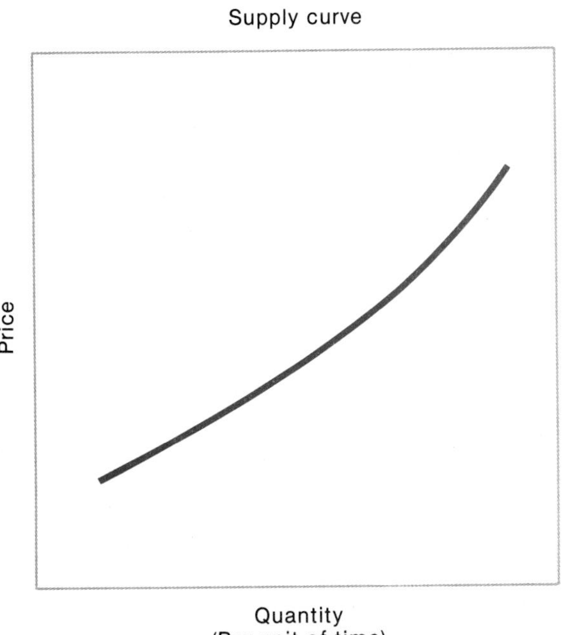

FIGURE 2
The Short-run Supply Curve
A typical supply curve slopes upward because each additional unit tends to be more difficult or expensive to make, at least in the short run.

Balancing Supply and Demand

We are now ready to see how the market mechanism works. Undoubtedly you have already grasped the crucial point on which the mechanism depends. **This is the opposing behavior that a change in prices brings about for buyers and sellers. Rising prices will be matched by an increase in the willingness and ability of sellers to offer goods, but by a decrease in the willingness and ability of buyers to take goods.**

It is through these opposing reactions that the market mechanism works. Let us examine the process in an imaginary market for shoes in a small city. In Table 1 we show the price-quantity relationships of buyers and sellers: how many thousand pairs will be offered for sale or sought for purchase at a range of prices from $50 to $5. We call such an array of price-quantity relationships a *schedule of supply and demand.*

As before, the schedules tell us that buyers and sellers react differently to prices. At high prices, buyers are either unwilling or unable to purchase more than small quantities of shoes, whereas sellers would be only too willing and able to flood the city with them. At very low prices, the quantity of shoes demanded would be very great, but few shoe manufacturers would be willing or able to gratify buyers.

If we now look at *both* schedules at *each* price level, we discover an interesting thing. **There is one price at which the quantity demanded is exactly the same as the quantity supplied.** This price is $25 in our example. At every other price, one quantity—that supplied or demanded—is larger, but at $25 the amounts in both columns are the same: 30,000 pairs of shoes. We call this balancing price the **equilibrium price.** We shall soon see that it is the price that emerges spontaneously in an actual market where supply and demand contend.

EQUILIBRIUM PRICE

How do we know that an equilibrium price will be brought about by the interaction of supply and demand? The process is one of the most important in all of economics, so we should understand it very clearly.

Interplay of Supply and Demand

Suppose in our example above that for some reason or other the shoe retailers put a price tag on their shoes not of $25 but of $45. What would happen? Our schedules show us that at this price shoe manufacturers will be pouring out shoes at a rate of 90,000 pairs a year. But customers would be buying them at the rate of only 5,000 pairs a year. Shortly, the shoe factories would be bulging with unsold merchandise. It is plain what the outcome of this situation must be. In order to unload their stocks, shoe manufacturers will begin to cut their prices. They will do so because this is their rational course—they can make a higher profit, or take a smaller loss, by selling more shoes, even though the price per shoe is lower.

TABLE 1
Demand and Supply Schedules for Shoes
Go down the price schedule and notice that quantities demanded do not equal quantities supplied—until you get to $25. Below $25 they are also unequal. $25 is the equilibrium price.

Price	*Quantity Demanded (thousands)*	*Quantity Supplied (thousands)*
$50	1	125
$45	5	90
$40	10	70
$35	20	50
$30	25	35
$25	30	30
$20	40	20
$15	50	10
$10	75	5
$ 5	100	0

As they reduce the price, their situation will begin to improve. At $40, demand picks up from 5,000 to 10,000, while at the same time the slightly lower price discourages some producers, so that output falls from 90,000 pairs to 70,000. Shoe manufacturers are still turning out more shoes than the market can absorb, but the difference between the quantities supplied and the quantities demanded is smaller than it was before.

Let us suppose that the competitive pressure continues to reduce prices so that shoes sell at $30. Now we have a much more satisfactory state of affairs. Producers will be turning out 35,000 pairs of shoes. Consumers will be buying them at a rate of 25,000 a year. Still there is an imbalance. Some shoes will still be piling up, unsold, at the factory or in stores. Prices will therefore continue to fall, eventually to $25. At this point, the quantity of shoes supplied by the manufacturers—30,000 pairs—is exactly that demanded by customers. There is no longer a surplus of unsold shoes hanging over the market and acting to press prices down.

The Market Clears

Now let us trace the interplay of supply and demand from the other direction. Suppose that prices were originally $5. Our schedules tell us that customers would be standing in line at the shoestores, but producers would be largely shut down, unwilling or unable to make shoes at such a price. Customers, many of whom would gladly pay more than $5, will let it be known that they would welcome a supply of shoes at $10 or even more. They too are trying to maximize—in this case, utilities rather than profits. If enough customers bid $10, a trickle of shoe output begins. Still, the quantity of shoes demanded at $10 far exceeds the available supply. Customers snap up the few pairs around and tell shoe stores they would gladly pay $20 a pair. Prices rise. Now we are getting closer to a balance of quantities offered and bid for. At $20 there will be a demand for 40,000 pairs of shoes, and output will have risen to 20,000 pairs. Still the pressure of unsatisfied demand raises prices further. Finally a price of $25 is tried. Now, once again, the quantities supplied and demanded are exactly in balance. There is no further pressure from unsatisfied customers to force the price up further, because at $25 no customer who can afford the going price will remain unsatisfied. We say that the market "clears."

Characteristics of Equilibrium Prices

Thus the interaction of supply and demand brings about a price at which both suppliers and demanders are willing and able to sell and buy the same quantity of goods. We can visualize the equilibrating process more easily if we now transfer our supply and demand schedules to graph paper. Figure 3 is the representation of the shoe market we have been dealing with.

The graph shows us at a glance the situation we have analyzed in detail. At the price of $25, the quantities demanded and supplied are equal: 30,000 pairs of shoes. The graph also shows more vividly than the schedules why this is an *equilibrium* price.

Suppose that the price were temporarily lifted above $25. If you will draw a horizontal pencil line from any point on the vertical axis above the $25 mark to represent this price, you will find that it intersects the demand curve before it reaches the supply curve. In other words, **the quantity demanded is less than the quantity supplied at any price above the equilibrium price, and the excess of the quantity supplied means that there will be a downward pressure on prices, back toward the equilibrium point.**

The situation is exactly reversed if prices should fall below the equilibrium point. Now the quantity demanded is greater than that supplied, and the pressure of buyers will push the price up to the equilibrium point.

Thus equilibrium prices have two important characteristics:

1. They are the prices that will spontaneously establish themselves through the free play of the forces of supply and demand.

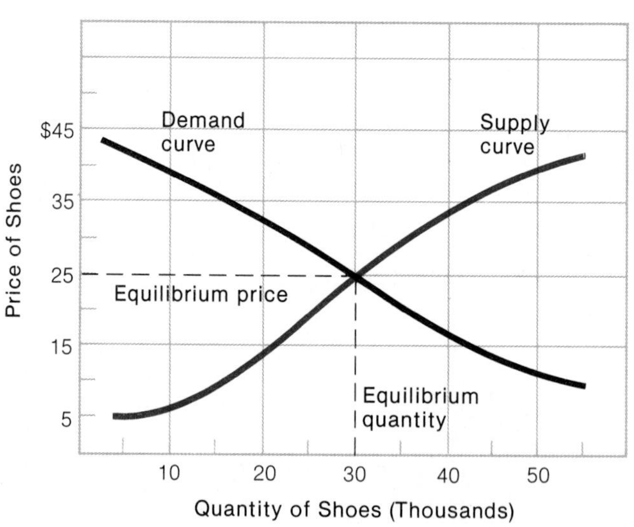

FIGURE 3
Determination of an Equilibrium Price
Demand and supply curves only show what the schedule has already revealed: There is one price at which the two quantities are equal. This is the equilibrium price.

2. Once established, they will persist unless the forces of supply and demand themselves change.

Does "Demand" Equal "Supply"?

There is one last thing to be noted carefully about equilibrium prices. They are the prices that bring about an equality in the *quantities demanded* and the *quantities supplied.* They are not the prices that bring about an equality of "supply and demand."

Probably the most common beginning mistake in economics is to say that supply and demand are equal when prices are in equilibrium. If we remember that both supply and demand mean the *relationships* between quantities and prices, we can see that an equality of supply and demand would mean that the demand schedule and the supply schedule for a commodity were alike, so that the curves would lie one on top of the other. In turn, this would mean that at a price of $50, buyers of shoes would be willing and able to buy the same number of shoes that suppliers would be willing to offer at that price, and the same for buyers at $5. If such were the case, prices would be wholly indeterminate and could race high and low with no tension of opposing interests to bring them to a stable resting place.

Hence we must take care to use the words *supply* and *demand* to refer only to relationships or schedules. When we want to speak of the effect of a particular price on our willingness or ability either to buy or to sell, we use the longer phrase *quantity demanded* or *quantity supplied.*

The Role of Competition

We have seen how stable, lasting prices may emerge spontaneously from the flux of the marketplace, but we have passed over in silence a basic condition for the

SUPPLY AND DEMAND, AGAIN

Here is one of the oldest "puzzles" in economics. Suppose that the price of A.T.&T. stock rises. Because the price rises, the demand for the stock falls. Therefore the price of A.T.&T. must decline. It follows that the price of A.T.&T. should never vary or at least should quickly return to the starting point.

Tell that to your broker. Better, tell it to your instructor and show him—and yourself—with a graph of supply and demand, where the fallacy of this puzzle lies. If you have trouble, think again about the distinction between "demand" and "quantity demanded."

formation of these prices. This is the role played by *competition.*

Competition is often discussed as a somewhat unpleasant feature of economic life. Now, however, we can see that, although competition may well be unpleasant, it is indispensable—if we are to have socially acceptable outcomes for a market process.

Competition is the regulator that "supervises" the orderly working of the market. But economic competition (unlike the competition for prizes outside economic life) is not a single contest. It is a *continuing process.* It monitors a race that no one ever wins, a race where all must go on endlessly trying to stay in front, to avoid the economic penalties of falling behind.

Moreover, unlike the contests of ordinary life, economic competition involves not just a single struggle among rivals, but two struggles. One is between the two sides of the markets; the other is among the marketers on each side. **The competitive marketplace is not only where the clash of interest between buyer and seller is worked out by the opposition of supply and demand, but also where buyers contend against buyers and sellers against sellers.**

SHIFTS IN DEMAND AND SUPPLY

Prices, emerging from the unsupervised competition of buyers and sellers, are now a part of our understanding. These prices, once formed, silently and efficiently perform the necessary social task of allocating goods among buyers and sellers. Yet our analysis is still too static to resemble the actual play of the marketplace, for one of the attributes of an *equilibrium* price, we remember, is its lasting quality, its persistence. Things are different in the real world around us, where prices are often in movement. How can we introduce this element of change into our analysis of microeconomic relations?

The answer is that the word *equilibrium* does not imply changelessness. Equilibrium prices last only as long as the forces that produce them do not change. To put it differently, if we want to explain why any price changes, we must always look for changes in the forces of supply and demand that produced the price in the first place.

What makes supply and demand change? If we recall the definition of those words, we are asking: What might change our willingness or ability to buy or sell something at any given price? Having asked the question, it is not difficult to answer it. If our *incomes* rise or fall, that will clearly alter our *ability* to buy. A change in the *price* of *other* commodities will have a very similar effect: When food goes up, we go to the movies less often. Finally, a change in *tastes* will change our willingness to buy.

On the seller's side, things are a bit more complicated. If we are owners of the factors of production (labor, land, or capital), changes in incomes or tastes will also change our ability and willingness to offer these factors on the market. If we are making decisions for firms, changes in *cost* will be the main determinant.

Shifts in Curves vs. Movements along Curves

Thus changes in tastes or prices or in income or wealth will shift our whole demand schedule. The same changes, plus any change in costs, will shift our whole supply schedule.

Note that this is very different from a change in the quantity we buy or sell when *prices* change. **In the first case, as our willingness and ability to buy or sell is increased or diminished, the whole demand and supply schedule (or curve) shifts bodily. In the second place, when our basic willingness and ability is unchanged, but prices change, our schedule (or curve) is unchanged, but we move back or forth along it.**

Here are the two cases to be studied carefully in Figure 4. Note that when our demand schedule shifts, we buy a *different amount at the same price.* If our willingness and ability to buy are enhanced, we will buy a larger amount; if they are diminished, a smaller amount. Similarly, the quantity a seller will offer will vary as his willingness and ability are altered. Thus demand and supply curves can shift about, rightward and leftward, up and down, as the economic circumstances they represent change. In reality, these schedules are continuously in change, since tastes and incomes and attitudes and technical capabilities (which affect costs and therefore sellers' actions) are also continuously in flux.

Price Changes

How do changes in supply and demand affect prices? We have already seen the underlying process at work for shoes. Changes in supply and demand will alter the *quantities* that will be sought or offered on the market at a given price. An increase in demand, for instance, will raise the quantity sought. Since there are not enough goods offered to match this quantity, prices will be bid up by unsatisfied buyers to a new level. At that level, quantities offered and sought will again balance. Similarly, if supply shifts, there will be too much or too little put on the market in relation to the existing quantity of demand, and competition among sellers will push prices up or down to a new level at which quantities sought and offered again clear.

In Figure 5 we show what happens to the equilibrium price in two cases: first, when demand increases (perhaps owing to a sudden craze for the good in question); and second, when demand decreases (when the craze is over). Quite obviously, a rise in demand, other things being equal, will cause prices to rise; a fall will cause them to fall.

We can depict the same process from the supply side. In Figure 6 we show the impact on price of a sudden rise in supply and the impact of a fall. Again the diagram makes clear what is intuitively obvious: An increased supply (given an unchanging demand) leads to lower prices; a decreased supply to higher prices.

And if supply and demand *both* change? Then the result will be higher or lower prices, depending on the shapes and new positions of the two curves; that is, depending on the relative changes in the willingness and ability of both sides.

Figure 7 shows a few possibilities, where S and D are the original supply and demand curves, and S' and D' the new curves.

Changes in Quantities Demanded or Supplied vs. . . . . .Changes in Demand or Supply

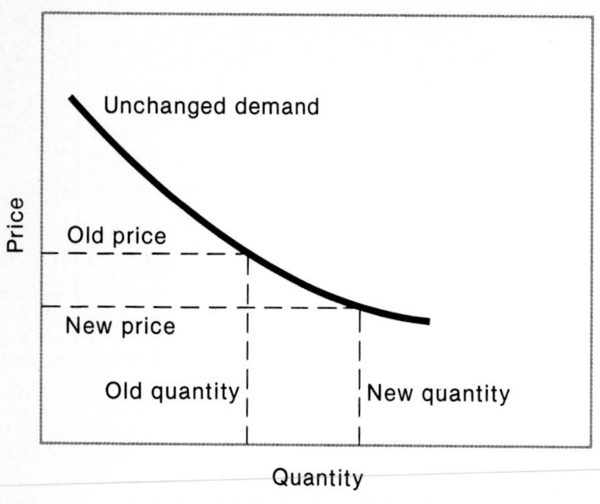

A change in price alone changes the *quantity* we demand.

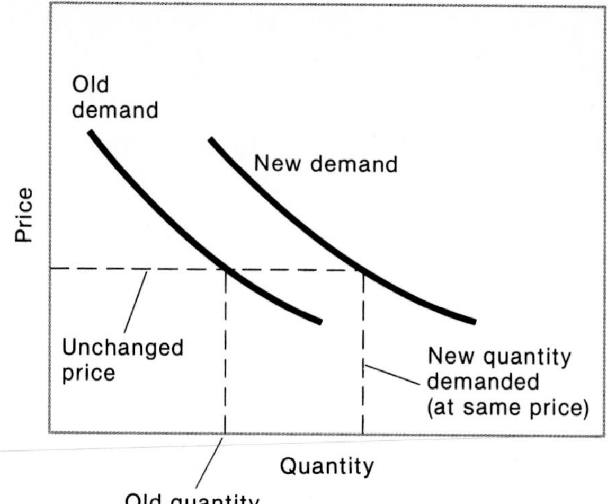

A change in our willingness or ability to buy changes our whole *demand schedule.*

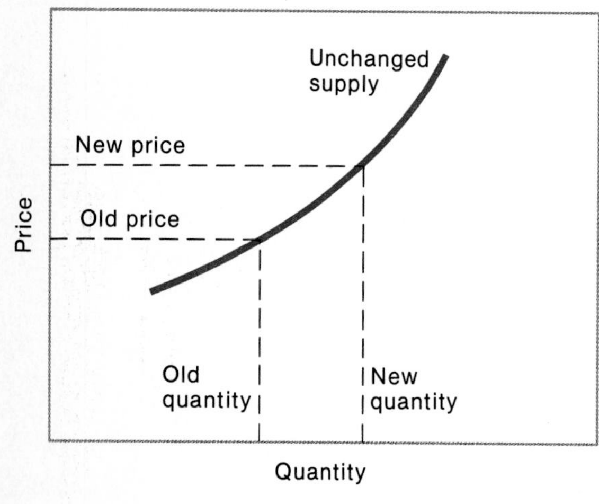

A change in price alone changes the *quantity* we supply.

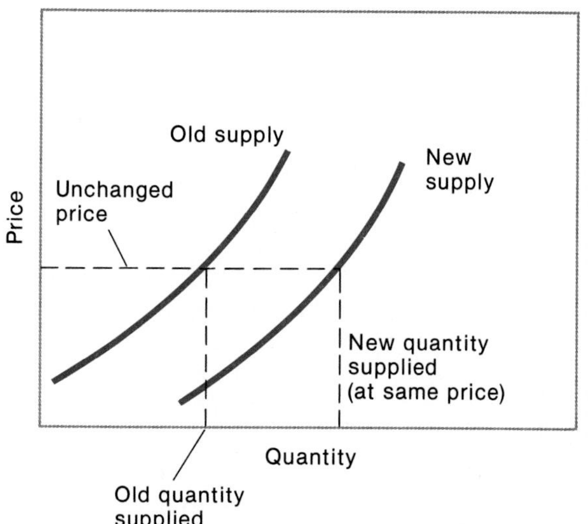

A change in our willingness or ability to sell changes our whole *supply schedule.*

FIGURE 4
Here is where we can see the difference between a change in demand or supply, and a change in the quantity demanded or supplied. This is a graph that should be studied until you fully understand it.

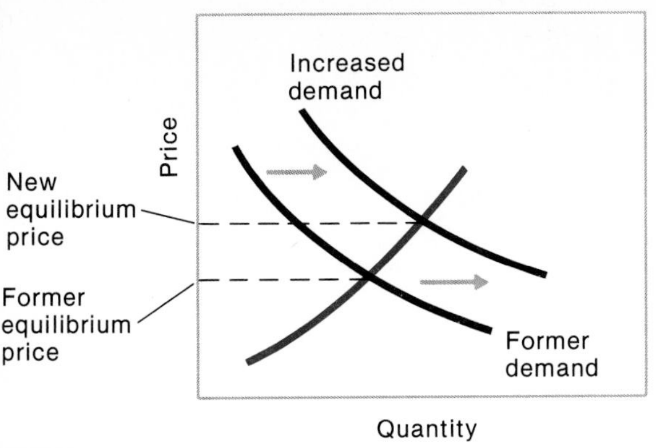

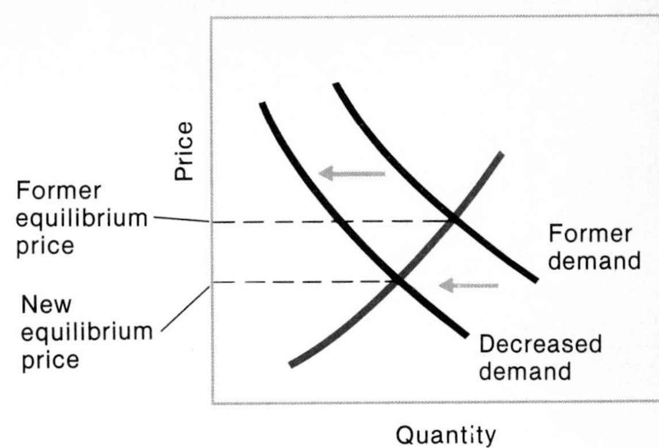

FIGURE 5
Shifts in Demand
An increase or decrease in our demand schedule changes the equilibrium price, raising it in the first case, lowering it in the second.

FIGURE 6
Shifts in Supply
Shifts in supply also change equilibrium prices. Increased supplies lower them; decreased supplies raise them.

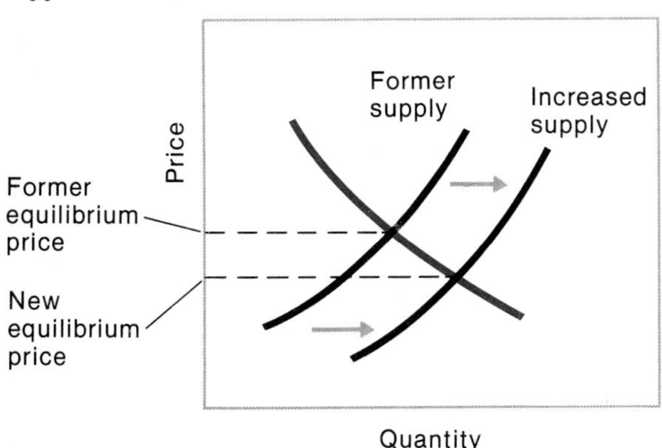

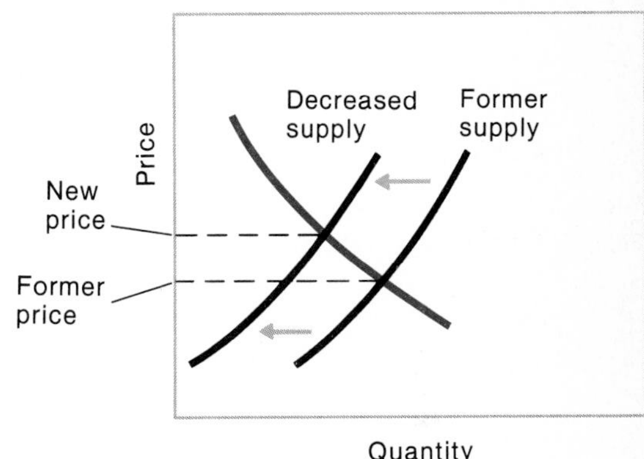

Long and Short Run

There is one point we should add to conclude our discussion of supply and demand. Students often wonder which "really" sets the price—supply or demand. Alfred Marshall, the great turn-of-the-century economist, gave the right answer: *Both do,* just as both blades of scissors do the cutting.

Yet, whereas prices are always determined by the intersection of supply and demand schedules, we can differentiate between the *short run,* when demand tends to be the more dynamic force, and the *long run,* when supply is the more important force. In Figure 8 we see (on the left) short-run fixed supply, as in the instance of

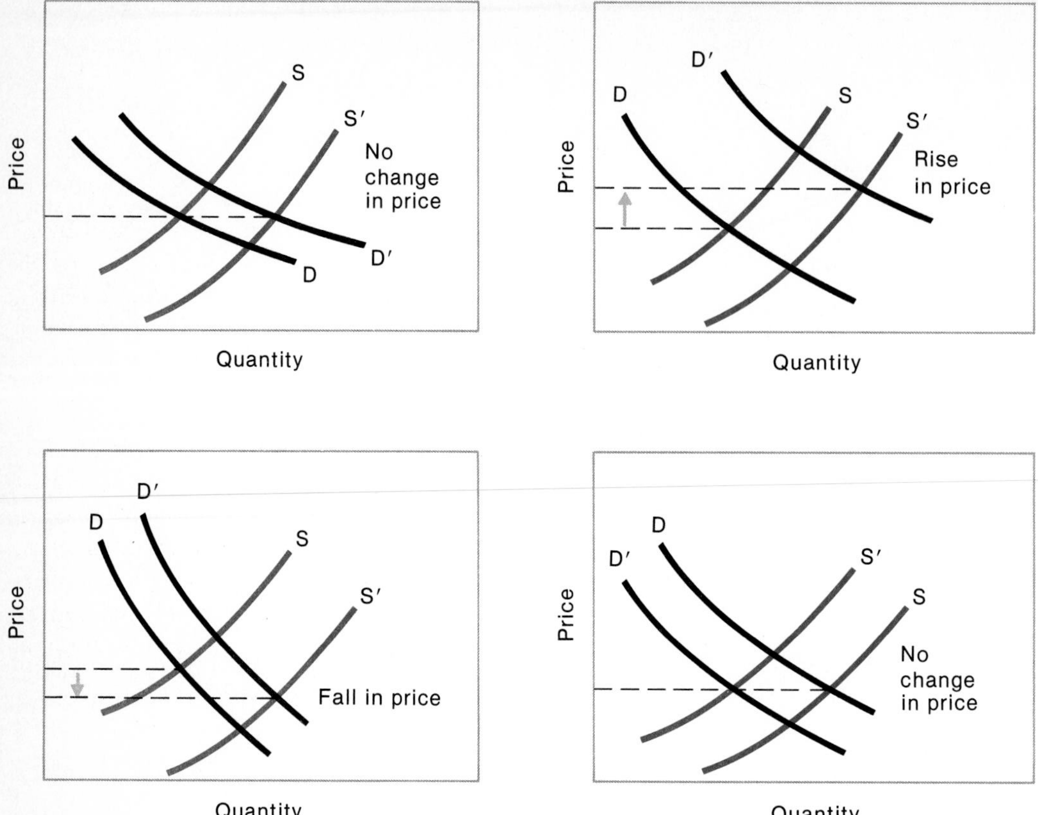

FIGURE 7
Shifts in Both Supply and Demand
When both supply and demand change, prices may rise, fall, or remain unchanged. The outcome is determined by the intersection of both *curves, so that we can never tell what will happen to price if we only know what has happened to one curve, but not to the other. It will help greatly if you try different combinations.*

fishermen bringing a catch to a dock. Since the size of the catch cannot be changed, the supply curve is fixed in place, and the demand curve is the only possible dynamic influence. Broken lines show that changes in demand alone will set the price.

Now let us shift to the long run and draw a supply curve representing the average cost of production of fish (and thus the supply price of fish) in the long run. We make, for the purpose of illustration, a crucial simplifying assumption: that in the long run the unit cost of catching fish does not increase as boats and nets and new fishermen are added to the fleet. Thus the long-run supply curve is horizontal. Fluctuations in demand now have no effect on price, whereas a change in fishing costs that would raise or lower the supply curve would immediately affect the price.

In all cases, do not forget, *both* demand and supply enter into the formation of price. In the short run, as a rule, changes in demand are more likely to

affect changes in prices. In the long run, changes in supply are apt to be the predominant cause of changes in price, as when technology lowers the cost of commercial fishing.

A Last Word on Maximizing

Does the market mechanism bear a relation to the general notion of maximizing? Indeed it does. Buyers and sellers both are *willing* to respond to price signals because they wish to maximize their utilities. But neither can maximize at will. Buyers are *constrained* by their budgets, and sellers are *constrained* by their costs. Thus the *ability* of buyers or sellers to respond to price signals is limited by obstacles of budgets or cost.

In addition, buyers and sellers are both constrained by the operation of the market. A seller might like to sell his goods above the market price, and a buyer might like to buy goods below the market price. But the presence of competitors means that a seller who quotes a price above the market will be unable to find a buyer, and a buyer who makes a bid below the market will be unable to find a seller.

Thus the market mechanism embodies what economists call "maximizing subject to constraints." We will learn more about this in Part Four. Already we can see that the very interaction of the maximizing drives and the constraining

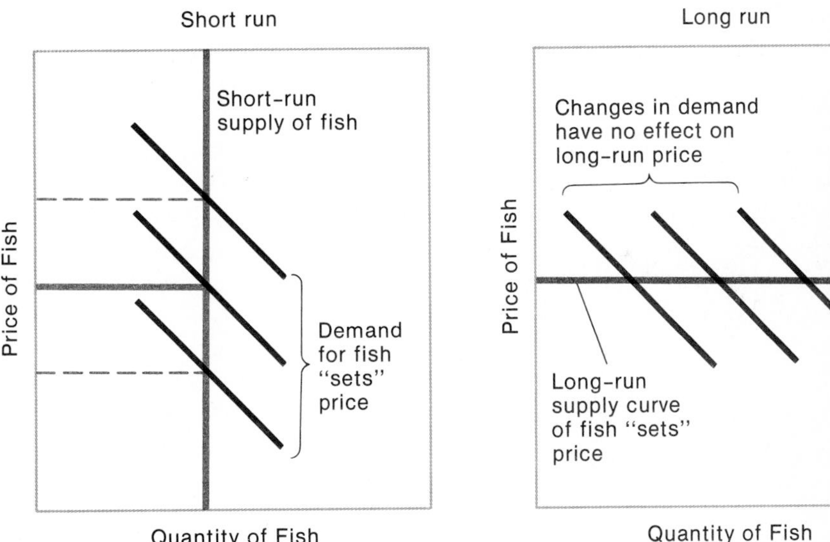

FIGURE 8
Short- and Long-run Supply Curves
Short-run supply is represented by a vertical curve since the same amount is offered no matter what the price. Here, demand "sets" the price, although without the supply curve there would be no price. In the long run, supply is horizontal, and demand has no effect on price. Yet without a demand curve there would be no sales of fish—and therefore no price at all! Both supply and demand are essential for all prices.

obstacles leads the market to establish equilibrium prices. We can also see that if we could know these maximizing forces and constraints beforehand, we would know the supply and demand curves of a market and could actually predict what its equilibrium price would be! In actual fact, our practical knowledge usually falls far short of such omniscience. But often we can use this principle for the next-best purpose, which is to predict the *change* in an existing equilibrium price that will result from particular changes in the forces of supply and demand. We will encounter this mode of analysis in the pages ahead.

LOOKING BACK

KEY CONCEPTS

You can now see that the purpose of this chapter is to show how maximizing subject to constraints works in terms of demand and supply. Here are the main points that you should carry away from what you have read:

Demand is the willingness and ability to buy at a given price.

1 Demand is a central idea of economics. It means the willingness and ability of any person or group of persons to buy a good or service at a particular price. Your demand schedule reflects your desire to maximize your utilities for that good, within the constraint of your budget.

Marginal utility typically falls.

2 Our willingness or ability to buy more of any kind of good reflects the marginal utility that another unit of that good will yield. The marginal utility means the additional utility—the pleasures of the *next* movie, the *next* pair of shoes, the *next* dollar of income—within a given period of time. A basic assumption of economic reasoning is that the marginal utility of any one thing diminishes: The second movie, pair of shoes, or dollar will not give as much pleasure as the first one.

Therefore typical demand curves fall.

3 This gives rise to normal, downward-sloping demand curves, showing that we are only willing to buy more units of the same goods at cheaper prices. These curves represent our schedules in simplified form.

Supply curves typically rise.

4 Supply curves typically rise because suppliers are not able (or willing) to offer more and more goods within a given period of time, except at higher prices.

Supply and demand vs. quantities supplied or demanded

5 Supply and demand refer to the range of goods or services that sellers or buyers will offer at differing prices. At any given price we should refer to the *quantity supplied* or the *quantity demanded.* When we say supply or demand, we mean the whole schedule or the curve that represents that schedule.

The idea of equilibrium where quantities offered are equal to quantities demanded

6 When we compare schedules, or plot two supply and demand curves, we can find out if there is an equilibrium price. This is a price where the quantities offered or supplied are equal to the quantities demanded. Economists are often careless and say that at an

equilibrium price "supply equals demand," but students should watch their language! In an equilibrium price, the *quantities demanded* equal the *quantities supplied,* and the market clears.

How equilibrium prices emerge and persist

7 Equilibrium prices are spontaneously established through the interplay of supply and demand, and they will persist unless the willingness or abilities of buyers and sellers change.

There is a two-sided aspect of competition.

8 There is a double-edged aspect to competition. Competition not only means that buyers oppose sellers, each trying to get the better of the other, but also that buyers have to win out against other buyers and that sellers have to outdo—or do as well as—other sellers.

Changes in supply or demand mean shifts in the entire curves, not movements along them.

9 Changes in price occur when there are shifts in supply and demand—that is, when the quantities that people are willing and able to buy or sell change at a given price. These changes are characterized by shifts in the supply and demand curves rather than by movements along these curves. Thus an increase (decrease) in demand means that we buy more (less) *at the same price.*

The price system

10 Last, bear in mind that you are learning the remarkable way in which an economic mechanism coordinates the very different objectives and activities of buyers and sellers through only one means—the signal of price. Prices inform people how to maximize rationally, given their constraints. The Invisible Hand does the rest!

ECONOMIC VOCABULARY

Demand 132
Taste 132
Effective demand 133
Diminishing marginal utility 133
Supply 134
Schedules 135
Equilibrium prices 136
Demand and supply curves 138
Competition, two aspects 139
Shifts in curves vs. movements along curves 141

QUESTIONS

1. Fill out the schedule below by supplying reasonable numbers to show the quantities demanded and supplied for T-shirts in a small town, at prices ranging from $1 to $10, over a period of, say, one year. (You might assume that there are about 10,000 potential buyers in your market.) Now graph the schedule in the graph space provided. Be sure to indicate the quantities on the horizontal axis.

2. Choose any arbitrary price above the equilibrium. How will maximizing behavior change this higher price back toward equilibrium? Does it require a contest among buyers? Sellers? Both? Either?
3. Now do the same thing with a price below the equilibrium.

SCHEDULE OF SUPPLY AND DEMAND FOR T-SHIRTS, PER YEAR

Price of T-Shirts	*Quantity Demanded*	*Quantity Supplied*
$10		
9		
8		
7		
6		
5		
4		
3		
2		
1		

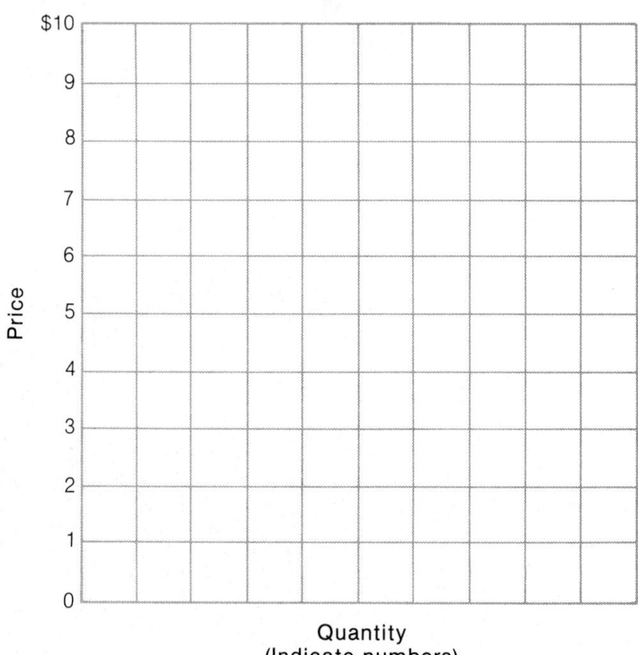

4. Subtract the quantities in your supply schedule from those in your demand schedule. There will be a plus or minus at all prices except one. Why is that? Does that help explain why an equilibrium price clears a market?
5. Whatever quantity is sold must be bought; whatever is bought must be sold. Then how can we say that only one price will clear the market? *Hint:* Look again at your answer to question 2.

6. What changes in your economic condition would increase your demand for clothes? Draw a diagram to illustrate such a change. Show on it whether you would buy more or less clothes at the prices you formerly paid. If you wanted to buy the same quantity as before, would you be willing and able to pay prices different from those you paid earlier?
7. Suppose that you are a seller of costume jewelry. What changes in your economic condition would decrease your supply curve? Suppose that costs dropped. If demand were unchanged, what would happen to the price in a competitive market?
8. Draw a diagram that shows what we mean by an increase in the quantity supplied; another diagram to show what is meant by an increase in supply. Now do the same for a decrease in quantity supplied and in supply. (*Warning:* It is very easy to get these wrong. Check yourself by seeing if the decreased supply curve shows the seller offering less goods at the same prices.) Now do the same exercise for demand.

CHAPTER 9

Why Economists Disagree

A LOOK AHEAD

We have just seen that economics has many science-like aspects. Yet we all know that no two economists ever seem to agree. Why is this the case? This chapter talks about the inherent difficulties of forecasting; about the reasons why predictions concerning human behavior can never have the same degree of accuracy as predictions about natural processes; and about the ways in which our values color our perceptions and lead us to different expectations concerning economic events.

This is certainly not a difficult chapter to read or understand. But it is exceedingly difficult to apply. Indeed, the whole secret of being a good economist lies in the lessons it tries to teach.

Economists are notorious for disagreeing. No two forecasts for the economy are alike. Liberal and conservative economists often seem to be looking at two entirely separate worlds. Different economists will recommend different, and sometimes diametrically opposed, policies as fervidly on one side as on the other. If economics is as analytic a study as we have made it out to be, why don't economists agree more?

Of course there is a quick rejoinder. Doctors disagree. Lawyers disagree. Physicists disagree. Even mathematicians disagree. Evidently there is nothing in the nature of science, or argument, or even abstract logic that forces unanimity of thought on all its practitioners. So an easy response to the question of this chapter is simply that disagreement is a common attritbute of human discourse. If economists didn't disagree, they would be supermen—or fools.

But that is not a wholly satisfactory answer because it does not tell us anything about the *reasons* why economists (or doctors or lawyers or mathematicians) differ. The reasons are interesting because they make us think about the foundations of economics.

ECONOMICS AND FORECASTING

Perhaps the first place where we notice the differences among economic opinions is in the general field of forecasting. We are all familiar with the clash of forecasts put out by the economists of the administration (any administration) and of Congress, or the divergences of views of well-known private economists in bank or industry or foundations.

Why do forecasts vary so frequently and by so much? A good answer is that economists' forecasts differ for exactly the same kinds of reasons as meteorologists'. Meteorologists typically differ as to their predictions, and even the most reliable of them make terrible mistakes. Asking why meteorological forecasting is so often mistaken or at odds with itself deepens our understanding of why economic forecasting is also often wrong. Here are two reasons that apply in both cases: the problem of data and the problem of complexity.

1. The Problem of Data. The meteorologist is often wrong because he or she doesn't have enough data. Moreoever, no meteorologist can ever have enough data. That would require him or her to know everything about the weather at any moment—the temperatures at every point in the country, the direction and intensity of each and every wind current. Thus every meteorologist is forced to make forecasts on the basis of partial information, and that which has been left out may turn out to have been decisive. "Ah! If I'd only know about *that,*" says the weather person when asked why his "sunny day tomorrow" turned out to be a downpour.

The same is true for the economist. No economic forecaster can know the complete state of the economy at any moment. *Indeed, no one knows it.* Of necessity this introduces an element of uncertainty into every forecast. Something is *always* left out. If it is important, the forecast will be wrong.

2. The Problem of Complexity. The second problem is closely allied with the first. Even if the weather person knows each and every fact about today's meteorological conditions, there is no way to combine the data to yield tomorrow's weather with absolute certainty. This is because the "systems" that constitute weather are too complex to be reduced to exact models. For example, atmospheric turbulence cannot be described except in very general terms, whose form is described by the new science of *chaos theory.* Such systems are characterized by the fact that very small errors in data can lead to very large differences in predictions.

The same problem applies to economics. Even if some gigantic computer had stored within it every bit of data concerning individual incomes and tastes, and every last iota of technical information about production techniques, and all the other facts that impinge on economic activity, there would still be no way of putting these billions of items into a precise model of the actual economy. It is not surprising, then, that economists' forecasts differ, because different economists combine—and simplify—the data at hand in different ways.

BEYOND METEOROLOGY

These are obvious reasons why economic forecasting, like weather forecasting, cannot be an exact science. But there are other reasons why economists disagree—reasons that are not to be found in meteorology, or for that matter in any other natural science.

1. Will and Intention. One reason is that the elements of the social world differ from those of the natural world in a very important respect: They possess wills and intentions. When the astronomer predicts the eclipses of the moon, she does not have to worry about how the moon feels about going into eclipse. If she did, astronomy would be a much less reliable science. But wills and intentions are very much part of what economists must constantly worry about. An economist who predicts that prices or GNP will rise has to make assumptions about the behavior of human beings, not of inanimate objects. Because no one can ascertain how the members of a society think or feel at any moment, an economist is forced to assume that human beings will act in the way economic theory assumes to be their normal behavior—as rational, maximizing beings.

But suppose that they do not. Suppose that whims or fads, or patriotic or revolutionary sentiments, sweep the country. Then prices may not behave in textbook fashion because consumers rush for or shun the commodity in question for no "good" reason at all; or GNP may fall because workers go on strike—perhaps "against their best interests." Such kinds of behavior are not an ordinary part of social life—if they were, we would not be able to talk about rational, maximizing behavior as the norm. But as long as individuals have wills and purposes, unexpected behavior will occur. Of course, when it does, forecasts will go wrong.

2. Expectations. But let us suppose that behavior *is* nomal. Can forecasts still go askew?

They can and will if the forecaster does not correctly assess the frame of mind of the economic agents with respect to the future. Forecasting depends critically on *correctly assessing the expectations* of the actors on the marketplace.

This is such an important aspect of economic prediction that we must take a moment to illustrate it. Let us look at the operation of a simple market when the price of a commodity rises (perhaps beause of a rise in the cost of producing it). In Figure 1 we see the result. Price moves from *OA* to *OB;* the quantity bought declines from *OX* to *OY*; and that is that. A new stable equilibrium has been reached.

But now let us introduce the matter of expectations. Suppose that consumers interpret the rise in the price of the commodity as indicating a futher rise to come. They think: "This is only the beginning. Prices will be soon be even higher." **Because of these changed expectations, a rational, maximizing pattern of behavior will lead to a different course of action.** Instead of buying less, consumers will buy more to stock up on the item before its price goes higher. In that case, the same increase in prices will lead to a shift in the demand curve, from *DD to D'D.* The quantity demanded will not fall, but will actually rise, as Figure 2 shows.

Hence a major element in all economic forecasting involves assumptions about the way actors in the market think about the future. Car manufacturers cut prices. Will that lead to a rise in sales? It will, if households expect that prices will rise again in the future, or will at least stay at their new levels. But if buyers read the cut in prices as a forerunner of future cuts, their national maximizing behavior will lead them to hold back and wait for bigger bargains to come. In that case, the price cut will result in a drop in auto sales, not an increase.

One last complication. Expectations not only play a critical role in determining how markets behave, but they are also beyond direct observation. There is no way of knowing what consumers think about the future because expectations are subject

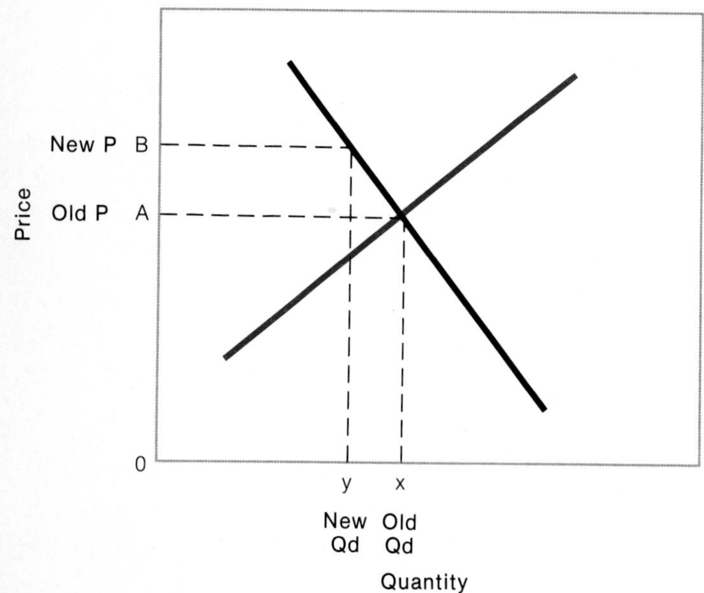

FIGURE 1
A Normal Price Response
A normal response to higher prices is a fall *in the quantity demanded* (Q_d).

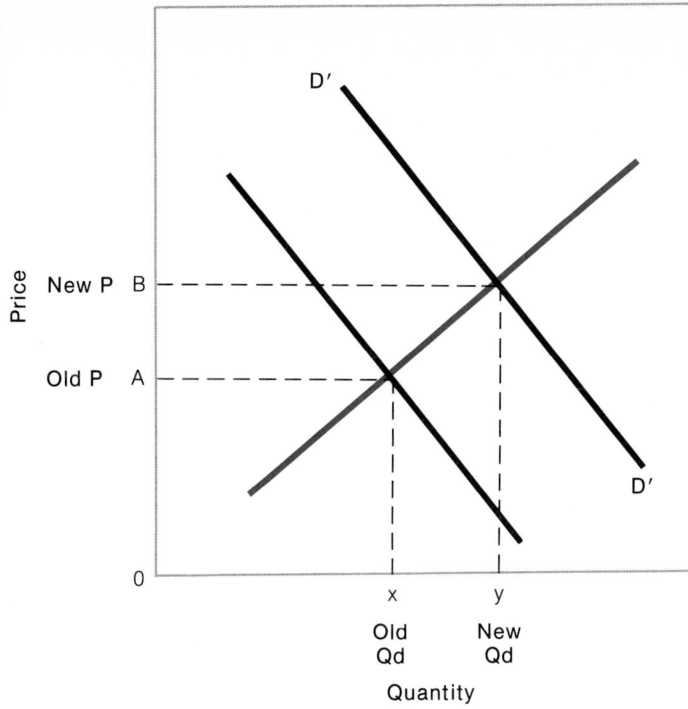

FIGURE 2
How Expectations Change Market Behavior
If expectations move the demand curve out to D′D′, higher prices will result in an increase *in* Q_d.

to lightning changes. One of the biggest difficulties in political polling is that voters change their minds at the last minute—often right in the voting booth. The same problem complicates the "polling" of economic expectations—a complication magnified by the fact that we cast economic votes much more frequently than we do political ones.

3. The Speed of Economic Adjustment. A third problem that plagues economic forecasting involves the speed at which economic changes take place. When scientists predict the outcome of natural processes, they often know very clearly how long it will take for the process under observation to reach its expected conclusion. We know how rapidly the earth spins, the speed at which light travels, and a number of other such constants that involve time. Even then, natural scientists cannot always predict how rapidly changes will occur—the rain predicted for today may arrive tomorrow.

Economists are in a much worse fix because they have no constants that involve time. There are no regularities in economic life by which we can set our clocks. We do not spend our incomes or respond to price changes or even work with clocklike regularity. As a result, economic processes can take place slowly or rapidly. Markets, disturbed by some outside shock like a bad harvest, may restore order in a matter of days or hours, or may fluctuate irregularly for weeks. Workers who have been thrown out of their jobs may rapidly find new work, or may suffer unemployment for long periods of time. Businesspeople may respond to optimistic news quickly or slowly.

The speed at which the economy adjusts to changes—including the very important changes of government policy—profoundly affects forecasting. How many times have we not heard an economist whose predictions have failed to come true say: "Wait!" The difficulty is, of course, that no one can say how long to wait. Yet we can see that the pace of economic adjustment is bound to affect the rightness or wrongness of our economic pronouncements.

FROM PREDICTION TO UNDERSTANDING

It is clear that economic prediction is inherently fraught with problems. No one can foresee with 20-20 vision tomorrow's price of apples or next week's Dow Jones average, or next month's GNP. Indeed, we can see that exact prediction is beyond the capabilities of the science.

Commonsense Prediction

Is all prediction therefore illegitimate for economists? That is certainly not our conclusion. **In a powerful sense, it is impossible not to predict.** When we declare ourselves in favor of, or opposed to, any form of policy—a tax increase or decrease, high tariffs or no tariffs—it is because we are predicting the effect of such a policy on our nation's fortunes. On a smaller scale, when we decide to buy more or less of an item when its price changes, it is because we are predicting that the given change will or will not be followed by further changes in the same direction.

But how can we predict when we have just declared that prediction is beyond the reach of economics? Part of the answer lies in the degree of precision we expect of prediction. Exact prediction is impossible, but not workable predictions on which we can rely with a fair degree of certainty. A good many economic processes display a kind of stability that makes it possible to forecast their course within boundaries that are fairly narrow; others have no such built-in stabilizing properties. No one has yet invented a system for predicting the stock market, which can—and sometimes does—show tremendous jumps or declines. On the other hand, the day-to-day course of GNP cannot fluctuate like the stock market as long as 100 million Americans get up in the morning and go to work (as economist Herbert Stein has put it).

Thus we can make much more reliable forecasts about the course of GNP than about that of the stock market. By the same token, however, our demands for accuracy rise, so that a forecast for GNP a year from now that is 10 percent off is deemed a failure, whereas such a forecast for the stock market would be a triumph.

Prediction vs. Expectations

A second approach to the problem draws a distinction between precise prediction and a general state of reasoned expectations. Even if we cannot predict the movements of the economy with a high degree of accuracy and a strictly fixed time schedule, **we can have informed anticipations of economic developments.** To the degree that we grasp the underlying forces and constraints of economic life, we can understand economic events as parts of a "system." The workings of the economy do not appear as inexplicable events but as happenings that reveal—however deep below the surface—the presence and influence of economic regularities.

Not predictions, but reasoned expectations based on understanding, are therefore the goal of economic science. These reasoned expectations can never attain the precision of an astronomer's calculations, so that two economists telling us what tomorrow's economic weather will be are as likely to disagree as to agree. Indeed, as long as observers differ in their assessments of such noneconomic factors as the nation's frame of mind, or its adaptability to change, or its stability of purpose and intention, they *must* come to different answers about the economic future.

Nevertheless, they will each try to reach reasoned conclusions about the shape of things to come, based on the application of economic laws (such as supply and demand or diminishing return) to the situation as they perceive it. They will talk about the future as emerging from a set of forces and constraints, not as mere chance.

FROM UNDERSTANDING TO ADVOCACY

A great deal of economic preditions is, in fact, economic advocacy. Or to put it the other way around, we often advocate economic policies, such as higher or lower taxes, because we predict that the effect of these changes will be favorable for the system. This introduces the question of values into the question of why economists disagree.

Values

Values are an inextricable part of all social thinking. We are "for" or "against" such things as economic equality among citizens or among nations in much the same way that we are for or against political equality. One can argue endlessly about such matters, but there is no final court of appeal. In the end, values remain—values. They are social arrangements that we prefer, sometimes mildly, sometimes passionately. They are not conclusions that are irrefutably thrust upon us by logic.

Value judgments permeate many of our economic determinations. They deeply affect the manner in which economists perceive the social world, and as a result they also affect the ways in which economists tell us that the economy will behave. Here are a few examples.

Producer vs. Consumer Well-Being

Many economic events affect us in two different ways—for instance, as producers and as consumers. When prices go up, they favor us if we are producers of that commodity, but not if we are consumers of it. When imports are taxed or otherwise restrained, we are grateful if we are workers in an industry whose existence is threatened by foreign competition, but resentful if we want to buy those goods as inexpensively as possible.

Which side of this clash of interests is entitled to preference—workers in American automobile plants or would-be buyers of Nissans and Hondas? As we will see when we look into foreign trade, that is a very hard question to answer. To a large degree it depends on the assumptions we make about how quickly and easily our economy will adjust to imports. If we think the adjustment will be quick and relatively painless, we will favor the consumer side. If not, we are likely to be more sympathetic to the producer side. Since some economists feel one way and some the other, they will disagree as to the policy we ought to follow—and as to the consequences of doing one thing or another.

Concentrated Pains, Diffuse Benefits

Another common case in which economists differ involves situations in which a given policy, or course of economic events, inflicts considerable pain on a few individuals, but benefits the general public. An instance in point might be a reduction in welfare payments that hurts poor families but lightens general taxes, or the lifting of rent controls that penalizes occupants of those apartments but stimulates the construction of new dwellings.

Once again, values come to the forefront. There is no cut-and-dried way of comparing the cost to those individuals who are adversely affected by the events or policies in question with the benefits for those who will gain. As with the opposed interests of producers and consumers, different economists will judge the situation differently, in part depending on their values—their "affinity" for those on each side; in part on their appraisal of how quickly and easily individuals and firms will respond to one set of arrangements or the other. The result is that one economist will be all for reducing welfare payments and easing our tax burdens, while another will be against it; one economist will seek to protect rent control and another will urge getting rid of it.

Values and interests

Of course values enter here, too. There is no purely objective criterion that guides us when we decide whether the pains of unemployment or of relocation are justified by the gains to society. Our value judgments reign in these matters, although they may be buttressed by facts and figures. Yet, as we know from our own experience, there are often facts and figures on the other side too.

In this difficult question we can often rely on one guide. **Our values are frequently, although not always, affected by our interests.** We learn to look with skepticism on the "disinterested" opinion of someone who stands to gain from one side or another of a dispute. The same applies, of course, to economic disputes. It would be a true cynic who declared that our judgments always reflect our selfish interests, but it would be a fool who declared that there was no connection between them. The fact that values normally and naturally incline us to one side or the other of issues adds another degree of clarification to economic disagreements. Does the advocate of a policy stand to gain from its adoption? Do two economists in debate have affiliations with opposing economic groups? To the extent that that is the case, of course they will disagree. The only disreputable aspect of such a disagreement is to conceal one's interest or to pretend that it plays no role in one's judgment.

FROM VALUES TO CONCEPTIONS

Beneath values lies a still more deeply buried substratum on which differences are also based. There are fundamental perceptions about the nature of the economic system itself. We have already seen how differently capitalism looked to Adam Smith and Marx and Keynes. Those deeply divided perceptions continue to the present day, giving rise to many of the differences in economic pronouncements.

What are some of these ground-level disagreements? One of them is of special importance: the inherent stability or instability, self-correcting or self-destroying, property of capitalism.

Is Capitalism Inherently Workable?

Adam Smith certainly believed in the workability of the system. Its success derived, in his view, from the inherent tendency of a market society to grow because of the driving force of its thrust for accumulation, and to adapt to change because of the mobility of its market institutions. Marx believed it was not workable because the very process of expansion, in the absence of any plan, would lead to crises of one sort or another. Keynes thought that capitalism might be workable, provided that government intervened to prevent it from undergoing long-lasting unemployment.

Many economists today strongly believe that Smith was essentially right, and that capitalism will work—if it is left alone. Obviously such economists predict a different outcome for the system than those who believe, along with Keynes, that the economy tends to settle down into a condition of persisting unemployment unless the government steps in to remedy this state of affairs. And neither the Smith-nor the Keynes-oriented economist will expect or predict the same outcome as someone influenced by Marx.

Which view of capitalism is correct? Economists have debated these matters for a long time, and have not come to any agreement. **Moreover, as we see it, one can legitimately perceive the economy from each of these (and perhaps still other) perspectives. There are aspects of the system that are strongly self-stabilizing and corrective, other aspects that are powerfully self-destabilizing and destructive, and still others in which the workability of the system appears to depend on the policies we undertake.**

At any rate, that is the point of view that wil appear in this book, which adheres to no single school of thought. Recognizing the existence—and in our view, the validity—of multiple perspectives sheds still more light on the question of why economists disagree.

A Last Look at Disagreement

So it is clear that economists will continue to disagree. But it should also be clear that what they disagree about is not the nature of economic inquiry itself. Economists of all schools use the same basic tools of inquiry, talk about supply and demand and constraints of various kinds, rely on the idea of "maximizing" as the force that drives the system and of "rationality" as the mind set that guides its actors. **There is, in other words, a language of economics common to all economists—the language we have set out to learn in this introduction to the subject.**

To speak the same language, however, is not to say the same thing. Economists disagree about matters that are fundamentally political or social, matters that are fraught with value suppositions and deeply held views about the economic world that are neither provable nor disprovable. From this point of view, being a good economist requires more than merely speaking the language of economics well. One also has to have a keen sense of what the world is all about. That is a matter no introductory text can teach—nor any advanced one either.

LOOKING BACK

KEY CONCEPTS

Disagreement is commong among scientists.

1 The fact that economics has science-like aspects does not exempt economists from disagreement. Scientists also disagree, as do philosophers and other scholars.

Forecasters often rely on different facts.

2 Economic forecasters often differ for exactly the same reasons as do meteorologists. The data of the economic universe are too numerous to be completely gathered, and too complex to be understandably ordered.

Humans possess wills and intentions and form expectations concerning the future. That also often makes their behavior unpredictable.

3 In addition, economists deal with human beings, whose actions are influenced by wills and intentions and by expectations concerning the future. Expectations can turn our actions around 180 degrees, because our rational maximizing impulse will cause us to hold back when prices fall and to rush in when prices rise—if we expect the fall or rise to worsen. If we expect the price change to be short-lived, our behavior will be just the opposite.

Uneven speeds of adjustment also cloud economic predictions.

4 Further, accurate predictions are made more difficult because there are no constant speeds of behavioral adjustment in economic processes. Markets may move quickly or slowly—making predictions right or wrong, depending on the time frame of the predictor.

Workable predictions are made on the basis of inertia.

5 Nonetheless, we all "predict" economic outcomes, both in our daily lives and as practicing economists. Often we do so on the basis of the natural stability or inertia of social processes. The question then is how accurately we can speak of their future course.

Reasoned explanation is the economists' goal, not exact prediction.

6 Because exact predictions are impossible, the goal of economics might be better described as its ability to form reasoned explanations. These enable us to speak about the future as determined, however inexactly, by the kinds of regularities and processes we have previously looked into.

We often base advocacy on prediction. Values usually enter these decisions, as well as interests.

7 Economic advocacy often involves prediction—we favor certain policies because we expect certain consequences to follow from their adoption. Advocacy also involves value judgments—deep-seated preferences concerning the desirability of various economic (or social) outcomes. Very often these values are revealed in our preferences for one side or another when economic processes benefit some people but not all. In turn, our values are often determined by our interests.

Preconceptions about the workings of capitalism also affect our judgment.

8 As deep as our values are, our basic conceptions about the nature of the economic system itself, in particular about the inherent tendencies of a capitalist system. There is no general agreement among economists as to whether the system has stabilizing, destructive, or correctible aspects. Our own belief is that it contains all three, so that different conceptions are legitimate concerning different aspects of its workings. This, too, introduces a reason for disagreement among economists.

Despite these disagreements, economics provides a language of discourse.

9 Disagreements are therefore built into the nature of economic understanding. Nonetheless, economists have devised a language that enables them to speak in widely shared meanings about the properties of their subject. This language is economics.

ECONOMIC VOCABULARY

Chaos theory 153
Expectations 153
Prediction 156
Values 157

QUESTIONS

1. What is the difference between the "behavior" of an atomic particle and that of a buyer or seller?
2. Describe a scenario in which expectations make prices rise when we would normally expect them to fall. And vice versa.

3. What characteristics would we have to expect of stock traders to give us the grounds for a reliable prediction of stock prices?
4. Can you suggest some general attributes of our economic system that seem to have self-stabilizing tendencies? Self-destabilizing ones? How about sales of commodities like salt for one, and runs on banks for another?
5. Are you aware of your own value-laden preconceptions? For example, do you think that men and women are entitled to equal pay for equal work? That economic inequality is acceptable, but not political inequality?

CHAPTER 10

An Economist's Kit of Tools

A LOOK AHEAD

This is a chapter about concepts and techniques. It isn't about "economics," but about some ideas, simple statistical devices, and other tools with which every economist must be familiar. There is no single, large idea to keep in mind as you go through this chapter. We suspect that for most students it will be very easy; easy or hard, it has to be mastered. Keep a list of the six ideas as they come, and check them off against the review in "Looking Back" after you have finished.

This chapter will give us a series of concepts and techniques that we will use in thinking clearly about economics. Some of them seem very simple but are more subtle than they appear at first. Others look demanding at first, even though they are actually very simple. There are six of these intellectual tools. Try to master them, for we will be using them continuously from now on.

CETERIS PARIBUS

The first concept is the need to eliminate outside influences that might invalidate our efforts to make scientific statements about economic behavior. If we were physicists trying to arrive at the formula for gravitation, for instance, we would have to make allowances for wind or air resistance in calculating the force that gravity really exerts. So in economics we have to eliminate disturbing influences from our observations. We do so by making the assumption that "other things" remain constant while we focus on the particular relationships we're interested in.

This assumption of holding "other things equal" is called by its Latin name, *ceteris paribus.* It is extremely easy to apply in theory and extremely difficult in practice. In our examination of the demand curve in Chapter 8, for example, we assumed that the *income* and *tastes* of the person (or of the collection of persons) were unchanged while we examined the influence of price on the quantities of shoes they were willing and able to buy. The reason is obvious. If we allowed their incomes or tastes to change, both their willingness *and* their ability would also have changed. If prices doubled but a fad for shoes developed, or if prices tripled but income quadrupled, we would not have found that demand decreased as prices rose.

Ceteris paribus is applied every time we speak of supply and demand, and on many other occasions as well. Since we know that in reality prices, tastes, incomes, population size, technology, moods, and many other elements of society are continually changing, we can see why this is a heroic assumption. It is one that is almost impossible to trace in actual life or to correct for fully by special statistical techniques.

Yet we can also see that unless we apply *ceteris paribus,* at least in our minds, we cannot isolate the particular interactions and causal sequences that we want to investigate. The economic world then becomes a vast Chinese puzzle. Every piece interlocks with every other, and no one can tell what the effect of any one thing is on any other. If economics is to be useful, it must be able to tell us something about the effect of changing *only* price or *only* income or *only* taste or any *one* of a number of other things. We can do so solely by assuming that other things are equal and by holding them unchanged in our minds while we perform a particular intellectual experiment.

FUNCTIONAL RELATIONSHIPS

Economics, it is already very clear, is about relationships—relationships of human beings to nature and relationships of individuals to one another. The laws of diminishing marginal utility or diminishing returns or supply and demand are all statements of those relationships, which we can use to explain or predict economic matters.

We call relationships that portray the effect of one thing on another *functional relationships.* Functional relationships may relate the effect of price on the quantities offered or bought, or the effect of successive inputs of the same factor on outputs of a given product, or the effect of population growth on economic growth, or whatever.

STATICS AND DYNAMICS: THE IMPORTANCE OF TIME

Of all the sources of difficulty that creep into economic analysis, none is more vexing than *time.* The reason is that time changes all manner of things and makes it virtually impossible to apply *ceteris paribus.* That is why, for example, we always mean "within a fixed period of time" when we speak of something like diminishing marginal utility. There is no reason for the marginal utility of a meal tomorrow to be less than one today, but good reason to think that this will be true of a second lunch today on top of the first.

So, too, supply and demand curves presumably describe conditions that prevail within a short period of time, ideally at one instant. The longer the time period covered, the less is *ceteris* apt to be *paribus.*

This poses many difficult problems for economic analysis because it means that we must use a "static" (or timeless) set of theoretical ideas to solve "dynamic" (or time-consuming) questions. The method we will use to cope with this problem is called *comparative statics.* We compare an economic situation at one period with an economic situation at a later period, without investigating in much detail the path we travel from the first situation to the second. To inquire into the path requires calculus and advanced economic analysis. We'll leave that for another course.

One important point: Functional relationships are not logical relationships of the kind we find in geometry or arithmetic, such as the square of the hypotenuse of a right triangle being equal to the sum of the squares of the other two sides, or the number 6 being the product of 2 times 3 or 3 times 2. Functional relationships cannot be discovered by deductive reasoning. They are descriptions of real events that we can discover only by empirical investigation. We then search for ways of expressing these relationships in graphs or mathematical terms. In economics, the technique used for discovering these relationships is called *econometrics.*

IDENTITIES

Before going on, we must clarify an important distinction between functional relationships and another kind of relationship called an *identity.* We need this distinction because both relationships use the word *equals,* although the word has different meanings in the two cases.

A few pages ahead we shall meet the expression

$$Q_d = f(P)$$

which we read "Quantity demanded (Q_d) *equals* or *is* a function of price ($=f(P)$)." This refers to the kind of relationship we have been talking about. We shall also find another kind of "equals," typified by the statement $P + S$ or purchases equals sales. $P + S$ is *not* a functional relationship, because purchases do not "depend" on sales. They are *the same thing* as sales, viewed from the vantage point of the buyer instead of the seller. P and S are identities: Q and P are not. The identity sign is $+$.

Identities are true by definition. They cannot be "proved" true or false, because there is nothing to be proved. On the other hand, when we say that the quantity purchased will depend on price, there is a great deal to be proved. Empirical investigation may disclose that the suggested relationship is not true. It may show that a relationship exists but that the nature of the relationship is not always the same. Identities are changeless as well as true. They are logical statements that require no investigations of human action. The signs $+$ and $=$ do not mean the same thing.

Sometimes identities and behavioral equations are written in the same manner with an equal sign ($=$). Technically, identities should be written with an identity sign ($+$). Unfortunately, the sign also reads "equals." Since it is important to know the difference between definitions, which do not need proof, and hypotheses, which *always* need demonstration or proof, we shall carefully differentiate between the equal sign ($=$) and the identity sign ($+$). **Whenever you see an equal sign, you will know that a behavioral relationship is being hypothesized. When you see the identity sign, you will know that a definition is being offered, not a statement about behavior.**

As definitions, identities deserve our attention because they are the way we establish a precise working language. Learning this language, with its special vocabulary, is essential to being able to speak economics accurately.

SCHEDULES

We are already familiar with the next item in our kit of intellectual tools. It is one of the techniques used to establish functional relationships: the technique of drawing up *schedules* or lists of the different values of elements.

We met such schedules in Chapter 8, in our lists of the quantities of shoes supplied or demanded at various prices. **Schedules are thus the empirical or hypothetical data whose functional interconnection we wish to investigate.** As working economists, we would experience many problems in drawing up such schedules in real life. We often use them, however, in economic analysis, as examples of typical economic behavior.

GRAPHS

The depiction of functional relationships through schedules is simple enough, but economists usually prefer to represent these relationships by graphs or equations. This is so because schedules show the relationship only between *specific* quantities and prices or specific data of any kind. **Graphs and equations show *generalized* relationships, relationships that cover all quantities and prices or all values of any two things we are interested in.**

The simplest and most intuitively obvious method of showing a functional relationship in its general form is through a graph. Everyone is familiar with graphs of one kind or another, but not all graphs show functional relationships. A graph of stock prices over time, as in Figure 1, shows us the level of prices in different periods. It does not show a behavioral connection between a date and a price. Such a graph merely describes and summarizes history. No one would maintain that such and such a date *caused* stock market prices to take such and such a level.

On the other hand, a graph that related the price of a stock and the quantities that we are willing and able to buy *at that price, ceteris paribus,* is indeed a graphic depiction of a functional relation. If you look at the hypothetical graph in Figure 2, you will note the dots that show the particular price-quantity relationships. Now we can tell the quantity that would be demanded at any price, simply by going up the price axis, over to the demand curve, and down to the quantity axis. In Figure 2, at a price of $50, the quantity demanded is 5,000 shares per day.*

*Technically, we would need a schedule of survey results showing the quantities demanded for every conceivable price in order to draw a graph. In fact, we obtain results for a variety of prices and assume that the relationship between the unmeasured points is like that of the measured points. The process of sketching in unmeasured points is called *interpolation.*

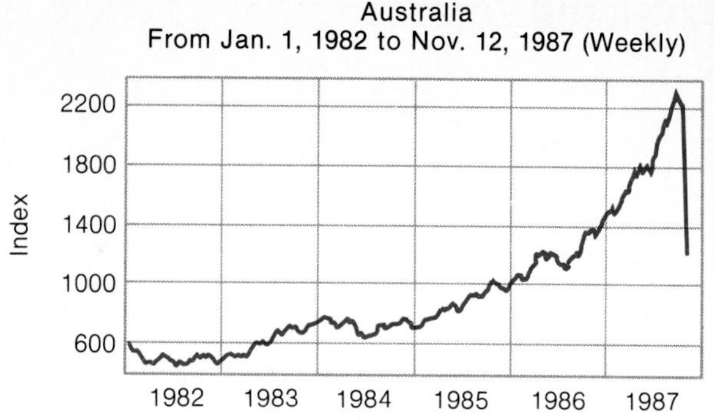

Frankfurt
From Jan. 1, 1982 to Nov. 12, 1987 (Weekly)
Index
700
600
500
400
300
200
1982 1983 1984 1985 1986 1987

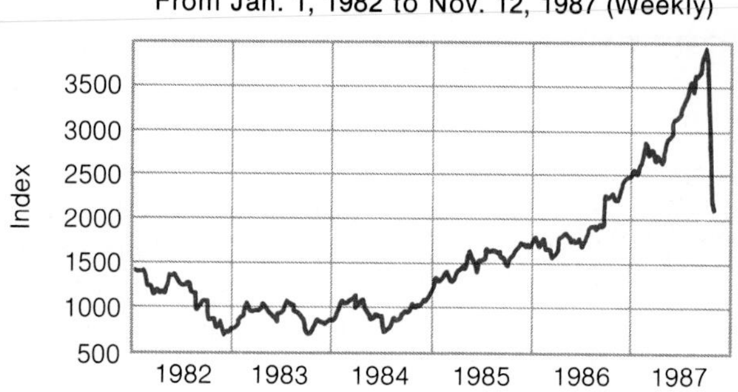

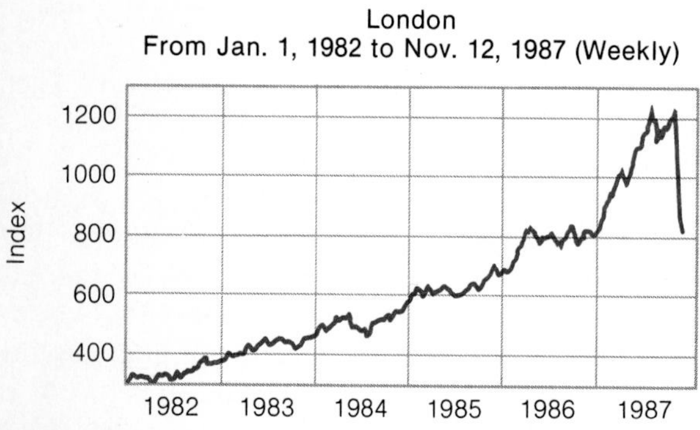

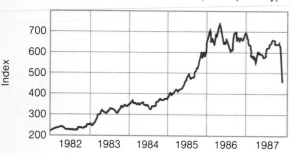

FIGURE 1
Stock Market Prices
Some graphs like these, show how a given variable behaves over time.
Source: *Report of Presidential Task Force on Market Mechanisms.*

UPWARD-SLOPING DEMAND CURVES

Although most demand curves slope downward, in two interesting cases they do not. The first concerns certain *luxury* goods in which the price itself becomes part of the "utility" of the good. The perfume Joy used to be extensively advertised as "the world's most expensive perfume." Do you think its sales would have increased if the price had been lowered and the advertisement changed to read "the world's second-most expensive perfume"?

The other case affects just the opposite kind of good: certain basic staples. Here the classic case is potatoes. In nineteenth-century Ireland potatoes formed the main diet for very poor farmers. As potato prices rose, Irish peasants were forced to cut back on their purchases of other foods to devote more of their incomes to buying this necessity of life. More potatoes were purchased, even though prices were rising, because potatoes were still the cheapest thing to eat.

Such goods have upward-sloping demand curves. The higher the price, the more you (are forced to) buy. Of course, when potatoes reach price levels that compete with, say, wheat, any further price rises will result in a fall in the quantity demanded, since buyers will shift to wheat.

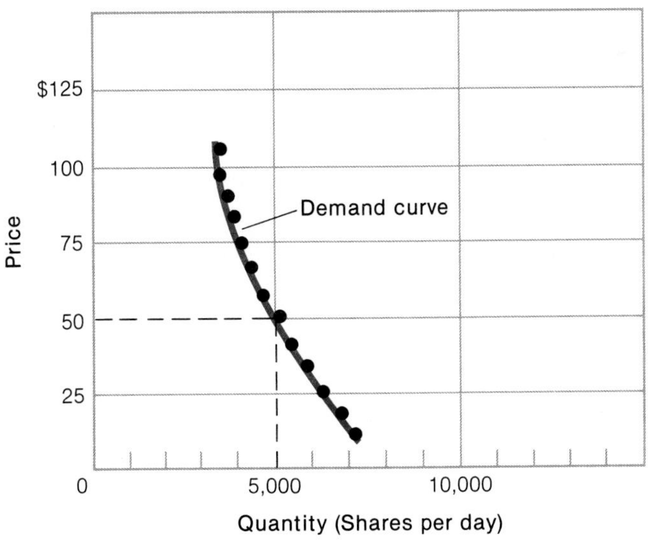

FIGURE 2
Price-Quantity Relationship of a Given Share
Other graphs, like this one, depict relationships. There is more about this in the extra word following this chapter.

EQUATIONS

A third way of representing functional relationships is often used for its simplicity and brevity. **Equations are very convenient means of expressing functional relationships, since they allow us to consider the impact of more than one factor at a time.** A typical equation for demand might look like this:

$$Q_d = f(P)$$

Most of us are familiar with equations but may have forgotten their vocabulary. There are three terms in the equation above: Q_d, f, and P. Each has a name. We are interested in seeing how our quantity demanded (Q_d) is affected by changes in price (P). In other words, our "demand" is dependent on changes in price. Therefore the term Q_d is called the **dependent variable:** "variable" because it changes; "dependent" because it depends on changes in P. As we would imagine, the name for P is the **independent variable.**

Now for the term f. The definition of f is simply **function** or "function of," so that we read $Q_d = f(P)$ as "quantity demanded is a function of price." If we knew that the quantity demanded was a function of both price *and* income (Y), we would write $Q_d = f(P,Y)$. Such equations tell us what independent variables affect what dependent variables, but they do not tell us *how* Q_d changes with changes in P or Y.

The "how" depends on our actual analysis of actual market behavior. Let us take a very simple case for illustrative purposes. Suppose that a survey of consumer purchasing intentions tells us that consumers would take 100 units of a product if its price were zero—that is, if it were given away free—and that they would buy one-half unit less each time the price went up by \$1. The demand equation would then be:

$$Q_d = 100 - .5(P)$$

Thus, if price were \$10, buyers would take $100 - .5 \times 10$, or 95 units.*

We should stop to note one important property of ordinary price-quantity demand or supply functions. It is that they have opposite "signs." A normal demand function is negatively sloped, showing that quantities demanded *fall* as prices rise. A supply function is usually positively sloped, showing that quantities supplied *rise* as prices rise. A survey of producers might tell us that the quantity supplied would go up by 2 units for every \$1 increase in price, or

$$Q_s = 2(P)$$

Note that the sign of the coefficient 2 is positive, whereas the slope of the demand function was negative, −.5.

*Suppose we wanted an equation that would measure the effect on quantity demanded of both price and income (see box page 172). Such an equation might be:

$$Q_d = 100 - .5(P) + .1(Y) \text{ where } Y = \text{income}$$

In this equation the quantity demanded goes *up* by 100 units whenever incomes rise by \$1,000. As before, it goes *down* by ½ unit as prices rise by \$1. If incomes were \$2,000 and P were \$10, the quantity demanded would be $(100 - .5 \times 10 + .1 \times 2{,}000) = 295$ units.

ECONOMIC TECHNIQUES REVIEWED

The basic assumptions that economics makes regarding economic society can be summed up in two sets of general propositions or laws—laws about behavior and laws about production. What we have been learning in this chapter are the *techniques* of economic analysis—the ways in which economics uses its basic premises.

These techniques, as we have seen, revolve around the central idea of functional relationships. Because behavior or production is sufficiently regular, functions enable us to explain or predict economic activity. Their relationships are presented in the form of graphs or equations derived from the underlying schedules of data.

As we have seen, the ability to establish functional relationships depends critically on the *ceteris paribus* assumption. Unless we hold other things equal, either by econometric means or simply in our heads, we cannot isolate the effect of one variable on another.

ECONOMIC FALLACIES

No chapter on the mode of economic thought would be complete without reference to *economic fallacies.* **Actually, there is no special class of fallacies that is called *economic.* The mistakes we find in economic thought are only examples of a larger class of mistaken ways of thinking that we call fallacies.** But they are serious enough to justify a warning in general and some attention to one fallacy in particular.

The general warning can do no more than ask us to be on guard against the sloppy thinking that can make fools of us in any area. It is easy to fall into errors of false syllogisms,* of trying to prove an argument *post hoc, ergo propter hoc* ("after the fact, therefore because of the fact"). An example would be "proving" that government spending must be inflationary by pointing out that the government spent large sums during periods when inflation was present, ignoring other factors that may have been at work.

The gallery of such mistaken conclusions is all too large in all fields. One fallacy that has a special relevance to economics is called the **fallacy of composition.** Suppose we had an island community in which all farmers sold their produce to one another. Suppose further that one farmer was able to get rich by cheating: selling his produce at the same price as everyone else, but putting fewer vegetables into his bushel baskets. It must follow, then, that all farmers could get rich if all cheated.

We can see that there is a fallacy here. Where does it arise? In the first part of our example, when our cheating farmer got rich, we ignored a small side effect of his action. The side effect was that a loss in real income is inflicted on the other members of his community. To ignore that side effect was proper so long as our

*See the questions at the end of this chapter.

EQUILIBRIUM IN EQUATIONS

It is very easy to see the equilibrium point when we have a supply curve and a demand curve that cross. But since equations are only another way of representing the information that curves show, we must be able to demonstrate equilibrium in equations. Here is a simple example:

Suppose the demand function, as before, is:

$$Q_d = 100 - .5(P)$$

and that the supply function is:

$$Q_s = 2(P)$$

The question is, then, what value for P will make Q_d equal to Q_s? The answer follows:

$$\text{If } Q_d = Q_s, \text{ then } 100 - .5(P) = 2(P).$$

Putting all the P's on one side,

$$2(P) + .5(P) = 100, \text{ or } 2.5p = 100. \text{ Solving, } P = 40.$$

Substituting a price of 40 into the demand equation, we get a quantity of 80. In the supply equation we also get 80. Thus 40 must be the equilibrium price.

focus of attention was what happened to the one farmer. But when we broadened our inquiry to the entire community, as we had to in order to examine the effect of widespread or universal cheating, the loss of income should have become a consideration. Everyone loses as much by being shortchanged as he gains by shortchanging. The side effect has become a central effect. What was true for one turns out not to be true for all. Later on, in macroeconomics, we will find a very important example of exactly such a fallacy when we encounter what is called the Paradox of Thrift.

LOOKING BACK

KEY CONCEPTS

This is a chapter about the concepts and techniques of economic analysis, not about the basic assumptions underlying economic theory. We should become familiar with a few of these ideas, or tools.

Ceteris paribus	1 *Ceteris paribus* is the assumption that everything other than the two variables whose relationship is being investigated is kept equal. Without *ceteris paribus* we cannot discern functional relationships.
Functional relationships	2 Functional relationships showing that X depends on Y lie at the very center of economic analysis. They are not logical or deductive relationships but relationships that we discover by *empirical investigation.*
Identities	3 Identities are purely definitional, therefore not subject to proof or to empirical investigation. Such definitions can, however, be very important.
Schedules, graphs, and equations	4 The three techniques used to present functional relationships are: (a) schedules, or lists of data; (b) graphs, or visual representations; and (c) equations.
Independent and dependent variables functions	5 You should know the meaning of three equational terms: the *independent variable,* the causative element that interests us; the *dependent variable,* the element whose behavior is affected by the independent variable; and the *function,* a mathematical statement of the relation between the two. Read the sentence $x = f(y)$ as "x is a function of y." Here, x is the dependent variable; y is the independent variable.
Fallacy of composition	6 Finally, learn to be on guard against economic fallacies, especially against the fallacy of composition.

ECONOMIC VOCABULARY

Ceteris paribus 164
Functional relationships 165
Identities 166
Schedules 167
Independent and dependent variables 170
Functions 170
Fallacy of composition 171

QUESTIONS

1. Suppose you would acquire 52 books a year if books were free, but that your acquisitions would drop by 5 books for every $5 that you had to pay. Can you write a demand function for books?
2. Can you write a hypothetical function that might relate your demand for food and the price of food, assuming *ceteris paribus?*
3. "The quantity of food bought equals the quantity sold." Is this statement a functional relationship? If not, why not? Is it an identity?

4. Here is a schedule of supply and demand:

Price	*Units Supplied*	*Units Demanded*
$1	0	50
2	5	40
3	10	30
4	20	25
5	30	20
6	50	10

Does the schedule show an equilibrium price? Can you draw a graph and approximate the equilibrium price? What is it?

5. How do we read aloud the following? $C = f(Y)$ where C = consumption and Y = income. Which is the independent variable? The dependent?

6. Which of the following statements is a fallacy?

All X is Y
  Z is Y
Therefore Z is X
All X is Y
  Z is X
Therefore Z is Y

Try substituting classes of objects for the *X*s and *Y*, and individual objects for the *Z*s. Example: All planets (*X*s) are heavenly bodies (*Y*). The sun (*Z*) is a heavenly body (*Y*). Therefore the sun (*Z*) is a planet (*X*). Clearly, a false syllogism.

Other fallacies:

If I can move to the head of the line, all individuals can move to the head of the line.

If I can save more by spending less, all individuals should be able to save more by spending less. *Hint:* If all spend less, what will happen to our incomes?

The fact that Lenin called inflation a major weapon that could destroy the bourgeoisie indicates that inflations are part of the communist strategy for the overthrow of capitalism.

AN EXTRA WORD ABOUT

Graphs and Economic Causation

Many students worry a great deal about drawing graphs and worry very little about what graphs show. They are wrong on both counts. The technique of graphing is essentially simple. What graphs show is not.

USES OF GRAPHS

Some graphs show the movement of a variable over time—for example, stock market prices. No one is perplexed by graphs of this kind. But other graphs show relationships. These are the graphs that worry students. Here are some hints to help you to draw these kinds of graphs.

1. Always begin by labeling the axes of a graph. Even the most common supply and demand type of graph should have one label identified as price (or *P*) and another as quantity (or *Q*). No mistake is as frequent as omitting *P*s and *Q*s or whatever identifying symbols are called for on a graph.

2. Each point on a graph represents two variables. Each point shows what value of *X* is related to a given value of *Y*—e.g., what quantity is offered (or bought) at a given price. Therefore every point must always be referred to *both* axes. In Figure 1, for example, point *H* shows 5 units of quantity offered at a price of 6 dollars. 5 units and 6 dollars are called the *coordinates* of point *H.*

3. Curves show how relationships vary. A given dot shows the relation of only one pair of coordinates, such as 5 units and 6 dollars. A curve shows the relationship of many pairs of coordinates for the function we are interested in. The upward curve *FGH* in Figure 1 shows how *P* and *Q* vary for sellers, for instance. Another curve, *ABC,*

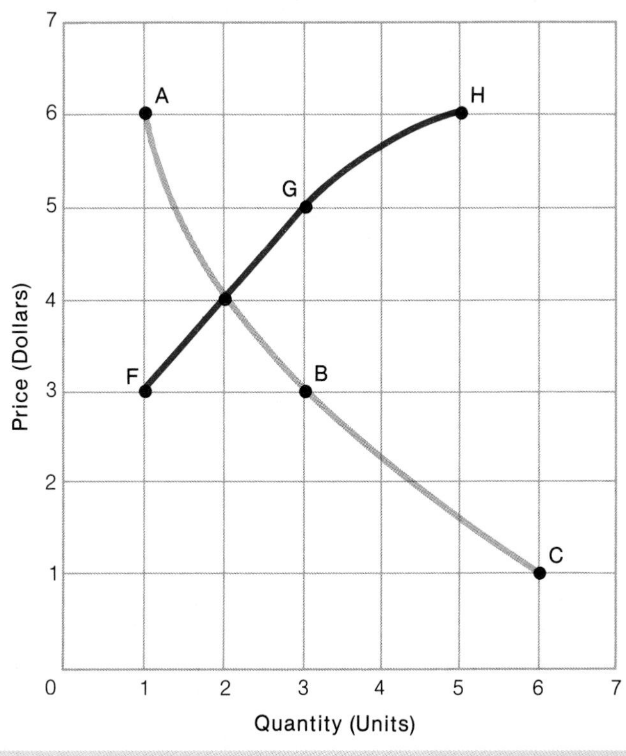

shows a relationship with a downward slope, perhaps for buyers. What are the actual values of *P* and *Q* at points *A, B,* and *C*? What, if any, coordinates are shared by both curves?

4. Graphs should be carefully drawn. Very often a graph represents an important idea visually. It may show that a pair of coordinates lies on *two* curves, as does the equilibrium point in the standard supply-demand graph. Or it may show that one curve touches another at just one point, which also means that the two curves have one pair of coordinates in common. When you draw a curve, you are *describing* a relationship: Be sure you describe it right. Figure 2 gives two freehand examples for you to study.

5. Professor Edwin Dolan writes in *Basic Economics,* "When you come to a chapter in this book that is full of graphs, how should you study it? The first and most important rule is *do not ever memorize graphs."* Professor Dolan is so right! Graphs come last, to capsulize what you know. They never come first, to tell you what you *should* know. Graphs are a pictorial shorthand for ideas, usually ideas about functional relationships (curves) and their interconnections. Learn the economics and the graphs will follow. Learn the graphs—and you will know only geometry.

CORRELATION

That was the easy part of understanding graphs. Now for the hard part. Most students think that graphs "explain" things. They look at a graph of a demand curve and say "The lower price *causes* us to buy more." They look at a graph showing a nice regular pattern between variable *A* and variable *B,* and they assume that this pattern of "correlation" implies an explanation.

Here's an example. On the left side of Figure 3, we have plotted the shoe size and

Note that axes are labeled. This graph shows that there is one point (X), where there is a common pair of coordinates, M and N, for two functions or curves.

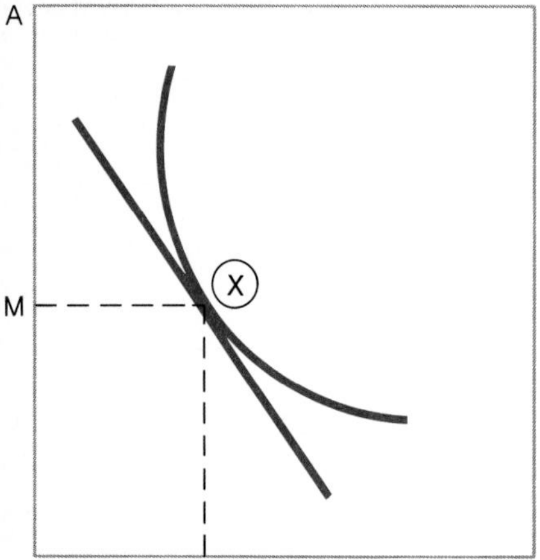

Note axes are not labeled. The graph shows that there is a no point where one pair of coordinates relates to both curves. Is that what you want to show?

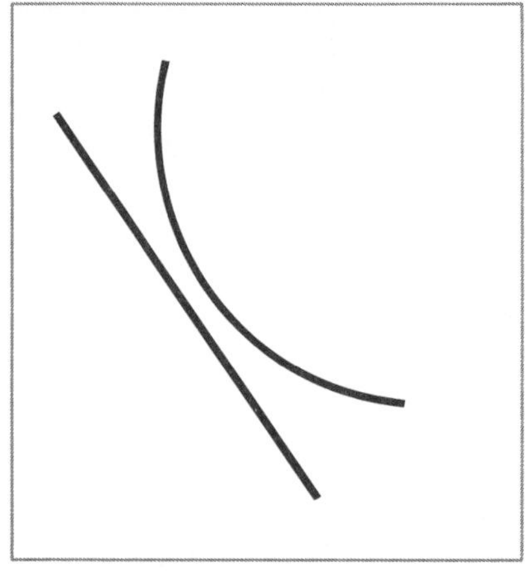

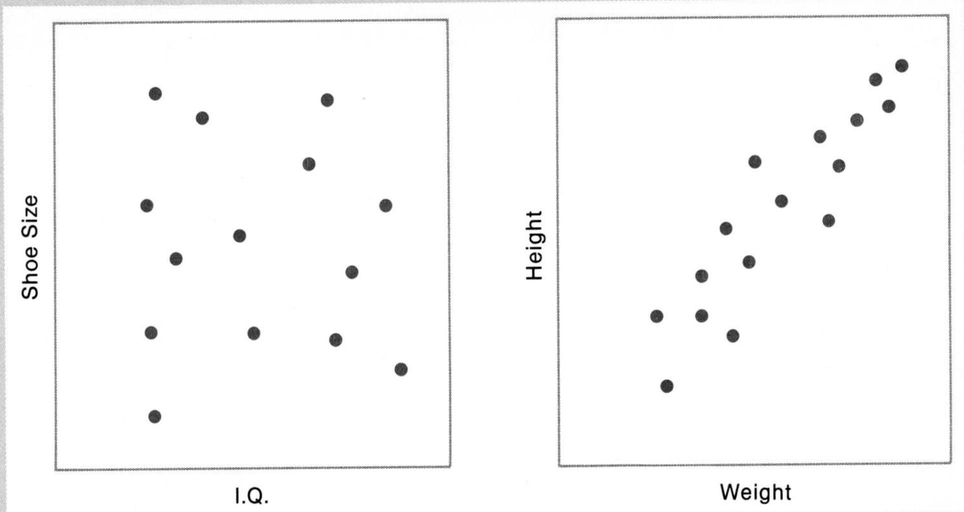

No pattern or correlation exists here. *A clear pattern or correlation is visible.*

the IQs of a group of seniors. No pattern—no "correlation"—is visible.

Hence no one assumes that large shoe sizes cause high IQs. On the right side of Figure 3 we correlate a sample of the heights and the weights of a number of individuals. There is a clearly visible pattern or correlation.

Does this mean that height causes weight to increase? Yes and no. Height is associated with weight, but height *and* weight both depend, in part, on age. Our graph happens to cover a population that includes both infants and adults, and so of course there is a correlation, but it is not purely a causal one. Height is associated with weight partly through the mediating factor of maturity. Lesson: Be very, very careful of jumping to conclusions about causes just from the evidence of associations, or correlations.

Here are a few examples for you to think about.

1. Wrong-way causation. It is a statistical fact that there is a positive correlation between the number of babies born in various cities of northwestern Europe and the number of storks' nests in those cities. Is this evidence that storks really do bring babies? The answer is that we are using a correlation to establish a causal connection the wrong way. The true line of causation lies in the opposite direction. Cities that have more children tend to have more houses, which offer storks more chimneys to build their nests in!

2. Spurious causation. Suppose there was a positive correlation all during the 1970s between the cost of living in Paris and the numbers of Americans visiting there. Does that imply that American visitors were the cause of price increases in that city?

Here at least there is little danger of getting the causal links back to front. Few people would argue that more Americans visited Paris *because* its prices were going up. It would be equally difficult to argue that American tourists were the cause of rising Parisian prices, simply because the total amount of American spending was small in relation to the total amount of expenditure in Paris.

The answer, then, is that the correlation is spurious in terms of causality, although it is real in terms of sheer statistics. The true explanation for the correlation is that the rising numbers of American visitors and the rising costs of living in Paris were both aspects of a worldwide expansion in incomes and prices. Neither was the "cause" of the other. Both were the results of more fundamental, broader-ranging phenomena.

3. The problem of ceteris paribus. Finally, we must consider again the now familiar problem of "other things being equal." Suppose we correlate prices and sales in order to test the hypothesis that lower prices "cause" us to increase the quantities we buy. Now suppose that the correlation turns out to be very poor. Does that disprove the hypothesis? Not necessarily. First we have to find out what happened to income during this period. We also have to find out what, if anything, happened to our tastes. We might also have to consider changes in the prices of other, competitive goods.

As we know, this problem affects all scientific tests, not just those of economics. Scientists cannot test the law of gravitation unless "other things" are equal, such as an absence of air that would cause a feather to fall much more slowly than Galileo predicted. The trouble with the social sciences is that the "other things" are often more difficult to spot—or just to think of—than they are in the laboratory.

WHAT CAN CORRELATION TELL US?

These (and still other) pitfalls make economists extremely cautious about using correlations to "prove" causal hypotheses. *Even the closest correlation may not show in which direction the causal influences are working.*

So, too, the interconnectedness of the economic process often causes many series of data to move together. In inflationary periods, for example, most prices tend to rise, and in depression many indexes tend to fall, without establishing that any of these series was directly responsible for a movement in another particular series.

Finally, economists are constantly on the lookout for factors that have not been held constant during correlation, so that *ceteris paribus* conditions were not in fact maintained.

Is there an answer to such puzzling problems of correlation and causation? There is a partial answer. We cannot claim that a correlation is proof that a causal relationship exists. But every valid hypothesis—economic or other—*must* show a high and "significant" correlation coefficient between "cause" and "effect," provided that we are reasonably certain that our statistical test has rigorously excluded spurious correlations and unsuspected "other things."

This exclusion is often very difficult, sometimes impossible, to achieve with real data. A physicist can hold "other things equal" in his laboratory, but the world will not stand still just so an economist can test his theories. *The net result is that correlations are a more powerful device for disproving hypotheses than for proving them.* All we can say on the positive side is that a causal relationship is likely to exist (or at least has not been shown *not* to exist) when we can demonstrate a strong correlation backed by solid reasoning.

PART III

MACROECONOMICS

CHAPTER 11

GNP—The Nation's Output

A LOOK AHEAD

Here we begin a section of four chapters whose overall purpose is to provide a working knowledge of how the macroeconomy works. We will gain this knowledge in four steps. In Chapter 11 we learn what GNP consists of and how economists describe and define it. In Chapter 12 we move to the question of how GNP is "sustained"—that is, where the purchasing power comes from that enables production to go on year after year. In Chapter 13 we go from sustaining GNP to increasing it, as we look more deeply than before into the sources of economic growth. And finally, in the last chapter we investigate the savings-investment relationship, the critical link in the macroeconomic system of a capitalist economy.

Chapter 11 presents us with two tasks:

1 We learn the vocabulary that economists use in describing GNP components. These definitions should be memorized—you cannot "speak economics" unless you know these words and phrases and their meanings.
2 We look into the question of the degree to which GNP is a reliable indicator of our well-being. This is a more reflective, less exact part of our introduction to GNP, but not a less important one.

What is *macroeconomics?* The word derives from the Greek *macro,* meaning "big," and the implication is therefore that it is concerned with bigger problems than is microeconomics (*micro* = small). Yet microeconomics wrestles with problems that are quite as large as those of macroeconomics. The difference is really not one of scale; it is one of approach, of original angle of incidence. **Macroeconomics begins from a viewpoint that initially draws our attention to aggregate economic phenomena and processes, such as the growth of total output.** Microeconomics begins from a vantage point that first directs our analysis to the workings of the marketplace. Both views are needed to comprehend the economy as a whole, just as it takes two different lenses to make a stereoscopic picture jump into the round. Since we can learn only one view at a time, we now turn to the spectacle of the entire national economy as it unfolds to the macroscopic gaze.

The Macro Perspective

What does the economy look like from the macro perspective? We look down on the economy as from a plane, to see it as a vast landscape stretching from one horizon to the other. We know that this landscape is populated by business firms, households, and government agencies, but from the macro perspective, as from an airplane, it is not these individual features that stand out. Instead, the focus is on a process of central and crucial importance that is more easily perceived from above than from ground level: the activity of production on a national scale; the creation and re-creation of wealth by which the country replenishes, renews, and expands its material life.

OUTPUT

How does this flow of production arise? Later, in microeconomics, we will investigate the motives that lead individual factors of production to offer their services to business firms, and the motives that lead firms to hire factors. A macro perspective studies the market process from a somewhat different standpoint, one that focuses on the stream of output as a whole, rather than tracing it back to its individual springs and rivulets.

It may help us picture the flow as a whole if we imagine that each and every good and service that is produced—each loaf of bread, nut and bolt, doctor's service, car, ship, lathe, or bolt of cloth—can be identified and followed as a radioactive isotope allows us to follow the circulation of certain kinds of cells through the body. Then if we look down on the economic panorama, we can see the continuous combination of land, labor, and capital giving off a continuous flow of "lights" as goods and services emerge in their salable form.

Intermediate Goods

Where do these lights go? Many are soon extinguished. **The goods or services they represent are *intermediate* goods that are incorporated into other products to form more fully finished items of output.** Thus, from our aerial perspective we can follow a product such as cotton from the fields to the spinning mill, where its light is extinguished, for there the cotton disappears into a new product—yarn. In turn, the light of the yarn traces a path as it leaves the spinning mill by way of sale to the textile mill, there to be doused as the yarn disappears into a new good—cloth. Again, cloth leaving the textile mill lights a way to the factory where it will become part of an article of clothing.

A First "Final" Good: Consumption

And what of the clothing? **Here at last we have what the economist calls a *final* good. Why "final"? Because once in the possession of its ultimate owner, the clothing passes out of the active economic flow.** As a good in the hands of a consumer, it is no longer an object in the marketplace. Its light is now extinguished permanently; or if we wish to complete our image, we can imagine it fading gradually as the clothing disappears into the utility of the consumer. In the case of consumer goods like food or of consumer services like recreation, the light goes out faster, for these items are "consumed" as soon as they reach their final destination.* We call the expenditures that are made for private household consumption—not for public consumption, such as education—**personal consumption expenditures.**

We shall have a good deal to learn in later chapters about the macroeconomic behavior of consumers. What we should notice in this first view is the supreme importance of this flow of production into consumers' hands. By this vital process, the population replenishes or increases its energies and ministers to its wants and needs. If the process were halted very long, society would perish. That is why we speak of *consumption* as the ultimate end and aim of all economic activity.

A Second Final Good: Investment

For all the importance of consumption, if we look down on the illuminated flow of output, we see a surprising thing. Whereas the greater portion of the final goods and services of the economy is bought by the human agents of production for their consumption, we also find that a lesser but still considerable flow of final products is not. What happens to it?

If we follow an appropriate good, we may find out. Watch the destination of steel leaving a Gary mill. Some of it, like our cotton cloth, will become incorporated into

*In fact, of course, they are not *really* consumed but remain behind as garbage, junk, wastes, and so on. Economics used to ignore these residuals, but it does so no longer. They are identified as "externalities" and discussed in Chapter 27.

consumer goods, ending up as cans, automobiles, or household articles. But some will not find its way to a consumer at all. Instead, it will end up as part of a machine or an office building or a railroad track.

Now in a way these goods are not "final," for they are used to produce still further goods or services. The machine produces output of some kind; the building produces office space; the rail track produces transportation. Yet there is a difference between such goods, used for production, and consumer goods, like clothing. The difference is that the machine, the office building, and the track are goods that are used by business enterprises as part of their permanent productive equipment. In terms of our image, these goods slowly lose their light-giving powers as their services pass into flows of production, but usually they are replaced with new goods before their light is extinguished.

That is why we call them *capital goods* or *investment goods*, as distinguished from consumer goods. As part of our capital, they will be preserved, maintained, and renewed, perhaps indefinitely. Hence the stock of capital, like consumers, constitutes a final destination for output.

Gross and Net Investment

We call the great stream of output that goes to capital *gross investment.* The very word *gross* suggests that it conceals a finer breakdown; and looking more closely, we can see that the flow of output going to capital does indeed serve two distinct purposes. Part of it is used to replace the capital—machines, buildings, track, or whatever—that has already been used up in the process of production. Just as the human agents of production have to be replenished by a flow of consumption goods, so the material agents of production need to be maintained and renewed if their contribution to output is to remain undiminished. We call the part of gross investment whose purpose is to keep society's stock of capital intact replacement investment, or simply **replacement.**

Sometimes the total flow of output going to capital is not large enough to maintain the existing stock, as for example when we allow inventories (a form of capital) to become depleted, or when we simply fail to replace worn-out equipment or plant. This running down of capital we call **disinvestment,** meaning the very opposite of investment. Instead of maintaining or building up capital, we are (literally) consuming it.

Yet not all gross investment is used for replacement purposes. Some of the flow may *increase* the stock of capital by adding buildings, machines, track, inventory, and so on. **If the total output consigned to capital is sufficiently great not only to make up for wear and tear but also to increase the capital stock, we say there has been new or net investment, or net capital formation.**

A Third Final Good: Government Purchases

While consumption by private households and investment by private firms constitute by far the greater part of the final disposition of goods and services, government also plays a role in the composition of output. Rather, it plays two roles. A small part of final output is *directly produced* by government activity—for example, the electricity produced by the Tennessee Valley Authority and the services produced by firefighters, teachers, and the armed forces. Another part is not directly produced by government but is *bought* by it. Thus the bulk of the equipment used by the armed forces is produced by private contractors. Roads, school buildings, and sewage treatment plants are generally built by private firms, with local, state or federal agencies playing the role of buyer, not producer.

When government itself produces output and sells that output to private individuals or business firms, we treat that product as part of the consumption or investment of the private sector. Thus there is no analytical difference, so far as the GNP accounts are concerned, between TVA power and the electricity supplied by Consolidated Edison to New York.

But when government acts as the final buyer of a product or service, we have another story. There is no private purchaser for the clean water created in a governmental sewage treatment plant, or for the services of firefighters and police. Still less do private firms willingly invest in, say, the antitrust services of the federal Justice Department! In these cases, we say that government is itself the final consumer. **And so we treat government purchases of goods and services as a separate category of final output. Taken in their entirety, public goods and services come to about a quarter of total final production.**

Two Oddities

There are two odd aspects of this government part of final demand. The first is that our system of national accounting does not indicate whether a government purchase is for consumption or investment. Whether government spends its income for such purposes as to provide weather information (it is hard to think of a more fleeting service) or for a vast dam (it is hard to think of a more durable good), it is all one and the same to the statisticians who tot up the national accounts. Both items are lumped under a single category—government purchases—rather than being classified as government investment or government consumption. Later we will see that this has considerable consequences in assessing the national deficit.

The second odd aspect is that a very large flow of government spending does not show up in our final output at all! This is the flow we call **transfer payments,** the most important of which is social security. Why do we not count social security in GNP? *The answer is that transfer payments show up in other categories of final demand.* When a household spends its social security check, that is counted as part of personal consumption expenditures. When a firm, such as a farm, spends a government subsidy (also a transfer payment), that too shows up somewhere in the flow of output, perhaps as the payment for an intermediate good. To count the social security or the subsidy check as a direct part of final output would be to include it twice—once when it was received, and once when it was spent.

Transfer payments are an extremely important form of government policy by which it seeks to redistribute incomes. We will be looking into the use—and abuse—of transfer payments, especially those for welfare purposes, later on. **In the**

meantime, it is important to understand why we do not include welfare, or subsidies, or any other form of transfer as part of our flow of production.

A *Final* Final Good: Net Exports

Finally, let us pay heed to a small flow of production that has previously escaped our notice. This is the net flow of goods and services that leaves the country; that is, the total flow going abroad minus the flow that enters. This international branch of our economy has been playing an increasingly important role in recent years; you already learned something about it in Chapter 6. It will crop up again and again as our analysis unfolds, and then be treated in detail in Part Five. We must give it its proper name, **net exports.** Net exports are a kind of investment (they are goods we produce but do not consume), so we must now rename the great bulk of investment, other than government investment, that remains in this country: We will henceforth call it **gross private domestic investment.***

The Circular Flow

A simple diagram may help us picture the flow of final output we have been discussing. Figure 1 calls our attention to the paramount attributes of the output process:

1. **The flow of output is self-renewing, self-feeding.** This circularity is one of the dominant elements in the macroeconomic processes we will study. Consumption output returns to restore or increase our human capital—our ability to work. Investment output restores or increases our material capital.
2. **Societies must make a choice between consumption and investment.** At any given level of output, consumption and investment uses are rivals for the current output of society. Furthermore, we can see that society can add to its capital only the output that it refrains from consuming. Even if it increases its output, it cannot invest the increase except by not consuming it.
3. **Both consumption and investment flows are split between public and private use.** These are also rival uses for output. A society can devote whatever portion of output it pleases to public consumption or public investment, but only by refraining from using that portion for private consumption or investment.
4. **Output is the nation's budget constraint.** Our output is the total quantity of goods and services available for all public and private uses (unless we want to use up our past wealth). More goods and services may be desired, but if output is not large enough, they cannot be had.

*What about a trade deficit—a *negative* "net export" flow? These are goods that we add to our national consumption, but do not produce. They are a form of *disinvestment!*

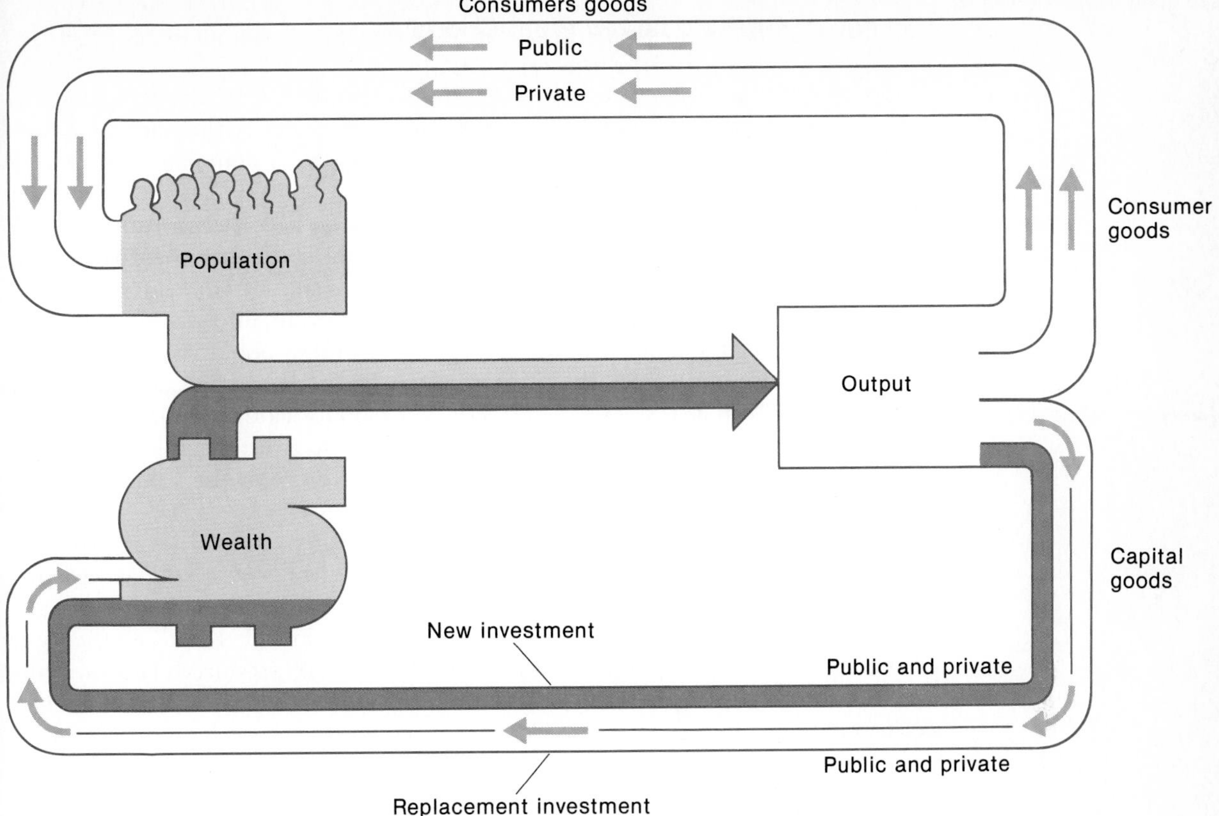

FIGURE 1
The Circular Flow View 1
The first view of the circular flow shows that output divides into two main streams, consumption and investment—consumption replenishing our human capital, investment replenishing our material capital. Note that there are public and private flows in both consumption and investment output.

GROSS NATIONAL PRODUCT

We have had a first view of the overall flow of national output that will play so large a role in our macroeconomic studies. Now we want to look into the flow more closely. Here we can begin by defining gross national product, a term that is already familiar to us from Chapter 5. **We call the dollar value of the total annual output of final goods and services in the nation its gross national product.** The gross national product (or GNP, as it is usually abbreviated) is thus the dollar value of all consumption goods and all investment goods, public and private, produced in a year. We are already familiar with this general meaning; now we must move on to a more precise definition.

Reminder: GNP Measures Final Goods

Remember that we are interested, through the concept of GNP, in measuring the value of the *ultimate* production of the economic system; that is, the total value of all final goods and services enjoyed by its consumers or accumulated as new or replacement capital.

Hence we do not count the intermediate goods we have already noted in our economic panorama. We do not add up the value of the cotton *and* the yarn *and* the cloth *and* the final clothing when we compute the value of GNP. That kind of multiple counting might be very useful if we wanted certain information about our total economic activity, but it would not tell us accurately about the final value of output. When we buy a shirt, the price we pay includes the cost of the cloth to the shirtmaker. In turn, the amount the shirtmaker paid for cloth included the cost of the yarn. In turn again, the seller of yarn included in its price the amount paid for raw cotton. Embodied in the price of the shirt, therefore, is the value of all the intermediate products that went into it.

Thus in figuring the value for GNP, we add only the values of all final goods, both for consumption and for investment purposes. Note as well that GNP includes only a given year's production of goods and services. Therefore sales of used cars and antiques and other used goods are not included, because the value of these goods was picked up in GNP the year they were produced. However, the service provided by the used car or antique dealer *is* included, because that is a new contribution to output. These services are valued at the dealer's income.

Four Streams of Final Output

We now have four streams of final output, each going to a final purchaser of economic output. **Therefore we can speak of gross national product as being the sum of personal consumption expenditure (*C*), gross private domestic investment (*I*), government purchases (*G*), and net exports (*X*), or (to abbreviate a long sentence) we can write that**

$$\text{GNP} \equiv \boldsymbol{C} + \boldsymbol{I} + \boldsymbol{G} + \boldsymbol{X}$$

This is a descriptive identity that should be remembered.

It helps, at this juncture, to look at GNP over the past decades. In Figure 2 we show the long irregular upward flow of GNP from 1929 to 1988, with the four component streams of expenditure visible. Later we will be talking at length about the behavior of each stream, but first we need to be introduced to the overall flow.

GNP AS A MEASURE

GNP is an indispensable concept in dealing with the performance of our economy, but it is well to understand the weaknesses as well as the strengths of this most important single economic indicator.

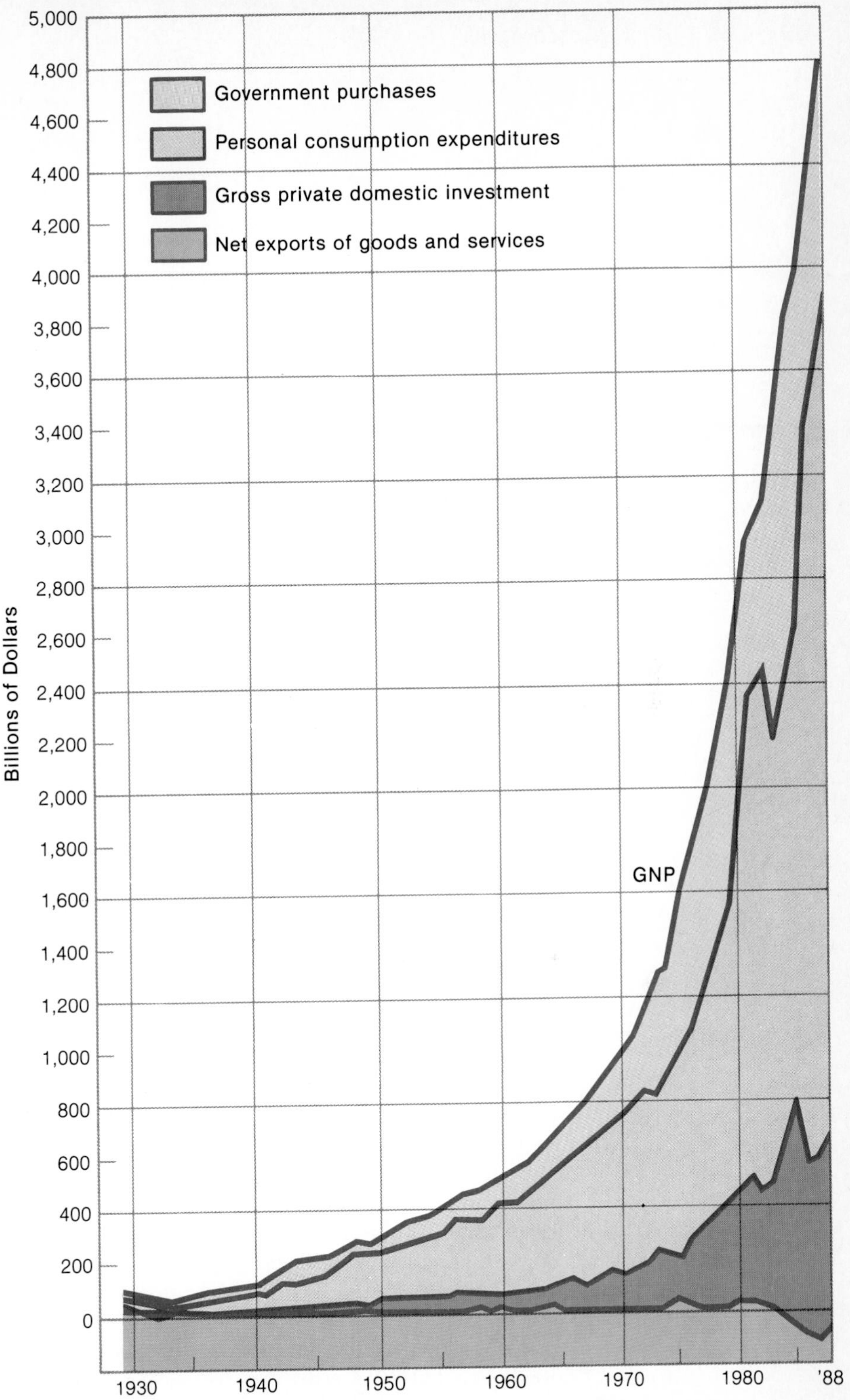

FIGURE 2
GNP and Components, 1929–1988
Here we see the historical record of GNP (a graph we have already met), this time with its component parts added.

PRICE INDEXES

It's worth a moment to review the ideas on pages 188–189.

How do we arrive at a figure for "real" GNP? *The answer is that we "correct" the value of GNP (or any other magnitude measured in dollars) for the price changes that affect the value of our dollars but not the real quantities of goods and services our dollars buy.*

We make this correction by applying a *price index.* Such an index is a series of numbers showing the variation in prices year to year, from a starting or *base year* for which the price level is set at 100. Thus if prices go up 5 percent a year, a price index starting in year 1 will read 105 for year 2, 110.25 + for year 3 (105 × 1.05), 115.8 for year 4, and so on.

In correcting GNP we use a very complex price index called a GNP *price deflator.* This index, constructed by the Department of Commerce, allows for the fact that different parts of GNP, such as consumer goods and investment goods, may change in price at different rates. The present price deflator uses GNP price levels in 1982 as a base. In 1987 the value of the deflator was 117.7, that is, the price index was up 17.7 percent from 1982.

Now let us work out an actual example. *To arrive at a corrected GNP, we divide the current GNP by the deflator for that year, and then multiply by 100.* For example, GNP in current figures was $4,240 billion for 1986; $4,527 billion for 1987;

1. GNP Deals in Dollar Values, Not in Physical Units; We Have To Correct It for Inflation. Trouble arises when we compare the GNP of one year with that of another to determine whether or not the nation is better off. If prices in the second year are higher, GNP will appear higher, even though the actual volume of output is unchanged or even lower!

We could correct for this price change easily if all prices moved in the same direction or proportion. We would then choose any year as a "base year," and we could easily establish an index to show whether GNP in another year was really higher or lower than in the base year, and by how much.

Problems arise, however, when there are changes in relative prices, with some prices rising more rapidly than others. Then the choice of a base year will affect our calculations. There is no correct way of choosing a base year. We just have to be aware that our choice affects our results. In Figure 3 we have used 1982 as our base. **Notice the enormous difference between nominal and real GNP!**

2. Changes in Quality of Output Will Not Show in GNP. The second weakness of GNP also involves its inaccuracy as an indicator of "real" trends over time. The difficulty revolves around changes in the quality of goods and services. In a technologically advancing society, goods are usually improved from one decade to the next or even more rapidly, and new goods are constantly being introduced. In

and $4,861 billion for 1988. The deflators for those years were 114, 118, and 122. Here are the results:

$$1986: \frac{4240}{114} = 37.2 \times 100 = 3720 \text{ billion}$$
$$1987: \frac{4527}{118} = 38.4 \times 100 = 3840 \text{ billion}$$
$$1988: \frac{4861}{122} = 39.8 \times 100 = 3980 \text{ billion}$$

Thus the "real value" of GNP in 1987 was $3,840 billion, *in terms of 1982 prices,* rather than the $4,527 billion of its current value. Two things should be noted in this process of correction. First, the real value of any series will differ, depending on the base year that is chosen. For instance, if we started a series in 1987, the real value of GNP for that year would be $4,527 billion, the same as its money (current) value.

Second, the process of constructing a GNP deflator is enormously difficult. In fact, there is no single accurate way of constructing an index that will reflect all the variations of prices of the goods within GNP. To put it differently, we can construct different kinds of indexes, with different "weights" for different sectors, and these will give us differing results. The point is to be cautious in using corrected figures. Be sure you know what the base year is. And remember that complex indexes, such as the GNP deflator, are only approximations of a change that defies wholly accurate measurement.

an urbanizing, increasingly high-density society, the quality of some goods may fall over time. An airplane trip today, for example, is certainly preferable to one 30 years ago; a subway ride is not. On the other hand, this year's car costs more than last year's car, but it also gets better gas mileage.

How much of the increase in price reflects improvement in quality and how much of the increase is simply an increase in price? It is difficult for anyone to know, but government statisticians try to adjust GNP statistics for just such changes in quality. **Generally speaking, the longer the time period over which comparisons of real GNP are being made, the larger is the quality factor, and therefore the more tentative the results become.**

3. GNP Does Not Reflect the Purpose of Production. A third difficulty with GNP lies in its blindness to the ultimate use of production. If in one year GNP rises by a billion dollars owing to an increase in expenditure on education, and in another year it rises by the same amount because of a rise in cigarette production, the figures in each case show the same amount of growth of GNP. Even output that turns out to be wide of the mark or totally wasteful—such as military weapons that are obsolete from the moment they appear—all are counted as part of GNP.

The problem of environmental deterioration adds another difficulty. Some types of GNP growth directly contribute to pollution—cars and paper or steel

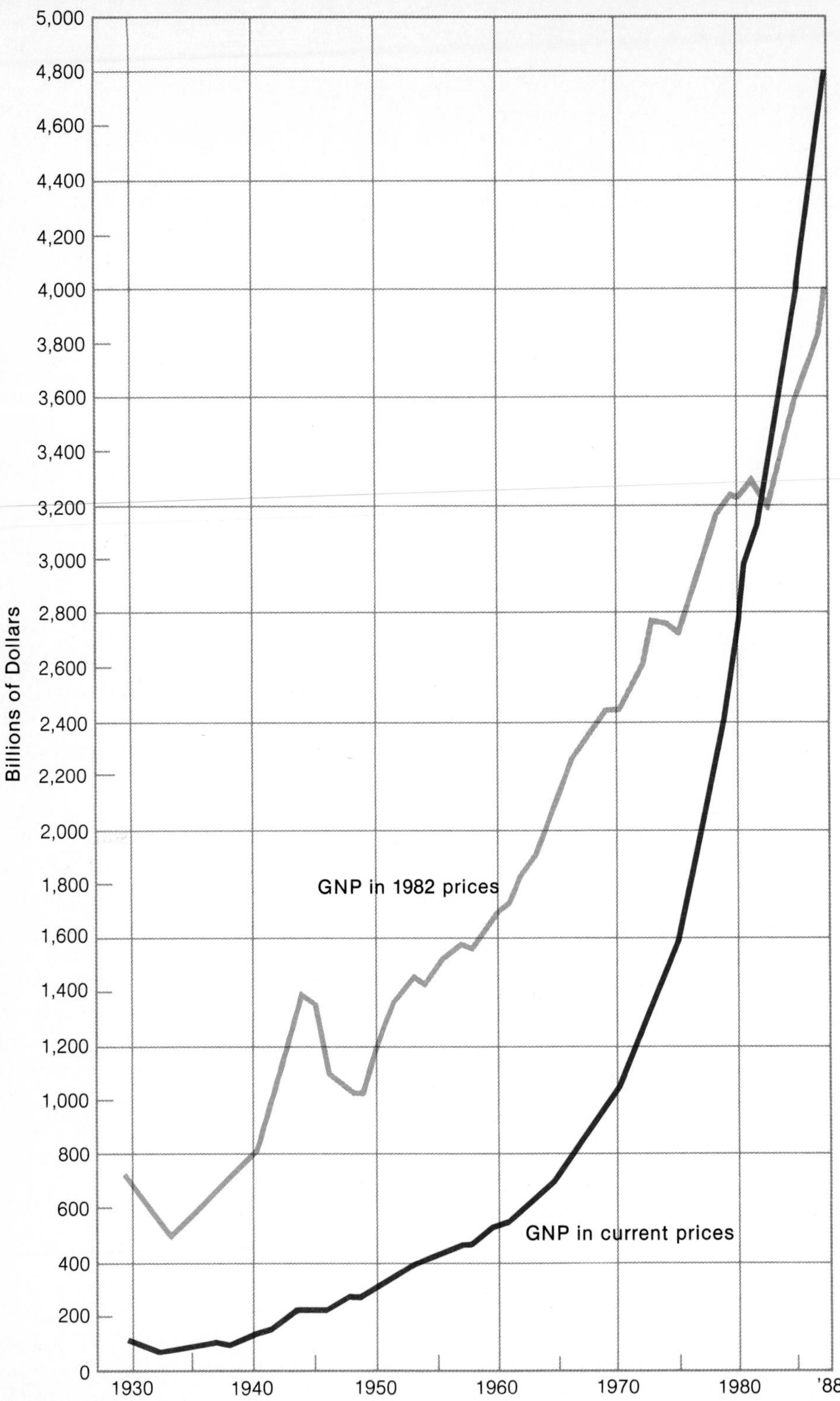

FIGURE 3
GNP in Constant and Current Prices, 1929–1988
We reduce nominal or current GNP—output measured at existing prices—to real GNP by using a price index. Because relative prices change, it matters which year we use as our base. There is no correct year, but our choice affects our comparisons. Here we use 1982 as the base.

production, for example. Other types of GNP growth are necessary to stop pollution—sewage disposal plants or the production of cleaner internal combustion engines. Still other types of GNP have little direct impact on the environment. Most personal services fall into this category.

Our conventional measure of GNP makes no distinction among the uses of outputs. For instance, the cleaning bills we pay to undo damage caused by smoke from the neighborhood factory become part of GNP, although cleaning our clothes does not increase our well-being. It only brings it back to where it was in the first place.

4. GNP Does Not Include Most Goods and Services That Are Not for Sale. Presumably GNP tells us how large our final output is. Yet it does not include one of the most useful kinds of work and chief sources of consumer pleasure—the labor of women in maintaining their households. Curiously, if this labor were paid for—that is, if we engaged cooks and maids and babysitters instead of depending on wives for these services, GNP *would* include their services as final output, since they would be purchased on the market. The labor of wives, being unpaid, is excluded from GNP.*

A related problem is that some parts of GNP are paid for by some members of the population and not by others. Rent, for example, measures the services of landlords for homeowners and is therefore included in GNP. But what of the homeowner who pays no rent? Similarly, what of the family that grows part of its food at home and therefore does not pay for it?

There is no entirely satisfactory solution to such problems. Because no one has devised a way of valuing housewives' services in a manner that appears fair and objective, we just leave the value of these services out of GNP. On the other hand, when it is possible to impute a value to unpaid services, statisticians at the Department of Commerce do so. For instance, they include in GNP an estimate of the value of the rentals of owner-occupied homes and of food grown at home.

5. GNP Does Not Indicate Anything about the Distribution of Goods and Services among the Population. Societies differ widely in how they allocate their production of purchasable goods and services among their populations. A purely egalitarian society might allocate everyone the same quantity of goods and services. Many societies establish minimum consumption standards for individuals and families. Few deliberately decide to let someone starve if they have the economic resources to prevent such a possibility. **Yet to know a nation's GNP, or even to know its average (per capita) GNP, is to know nothing about how broadly or how narrowly this output is shared.** A wealthy country can have many poor families. A poor country can have some very wealthy families.

GNP and Welfare

All these doubts and reservations should instill in us a permanent caution against using GNP as if it were a clear-cut measure of social contentment or happiness.

*An added difficulty here is that we are constantly moving toward purchasing "outside" services in place of home services. Laundries, bakeries, and restaurants all perform work that used to be performed at home. Thus the process of "commoditizing" activity gives an upward trend to GNP statistics that is not fully mirrored in actual output.

Economist Edward Denison once remarked that perhaps nothing affects national economic welfare so much as the weather, which certainly does not get into the GNP accounts! Hence, because the United States may have a GNP per capita that is higher than that of say, Denmark, it does not mean that life is better here. It may be worse. In fact, by the indices of health care or quality of environment, it probably *is* worse.

Yet, for all its shortcomings, GNP is still the simplest way we possess of summarizing the overall level of market activity of the economy. If we want to examine its welfare, we had better turn to specific social indicators of how long we live, how healthy we are, how cheaply we provide good medical care, how varied and abundant our diet is, etc.—none of which we can tell from GNP figures alone. But we are not always interested in welfare, partly because it is too complex to be summed up in a single measure. For better or worse, therefore, GNP has become the yardstick used by most nations in the world. Although other yardsticks are sure to become more important, GNP will be a central term in the economic lexicon for a long time to come.

LOOKING BACK

KEY CONCEPTS

The macro perspective

1 Our introduction to macroeconomics involves a special perspective on the economy, one that emphasizes total output rather than behavior in the marketplace.

Intermediate vs. final goods: consumption and investment

2 Observing the flow of total output, we discover that it can be divided into intermediate goods and final goods. Intermediate goods go *into* final goods. Final goods are those used for consumption or for investment.

Gross investment comprises net investment and replacement.

3 Investment can be further divided into gross and net investment. Gross investment is the sum of output not used for consumption. Part of it is for replacement of worn-out capital goods. The remainder is net investment.

Government purchases have the characteristics of both consumption and investment, but are treated as one category.

4 Government also enters into final output when it produces public goods such as education or when it buys them from private contractors or producers. Although these government purchases may have the characteristics of consumption goods or investment goods, they are conventionally added together as a single category of final output called *government purchases.* Note that these purchases do not include transfer payments, which are picked up as part of consumption or investment or as intermediate flows.

Exports minus imports gives us a last category: net exports.

5 A final category of final demand consists of those goods that we produce at home but ship abroad—our exports—less goods produced abroad and shipped here for final use—imports. These net exports are actually a category of investment, but they are shown as a separate part of final output. Gross investment less net exports is properly called *gross private domestic investment.* The "domestic" calls attention to the fact that exports have been excluded.

Output is a circular flow.

6 The flow of output has four major characteristics: It is circular, replenishing our human or material wealth; it is used for consumption *or* investment (the same item cannot be used for both simultaneously); it has public and private uses, both as consumption and as investment; and it constitutes the budget constraint of the nation.

Gross national product is the value of final output.

7 The annual flow of final output, valued at its market price, is called the *gross national product,* or *GNP.* Note that it includes only final, not intermediate, output.

GNP $\equiv C+I+G+X$

8 The annual output can be described as comprising four distinct flows: (a) a consumption flow, (b) a net export flow, (c) a flow of domestic gross private investment, and (d) a public flow. Together they give us the identity GNP $\equiv C+I+G+X$.

Real GNP is a widely used measure of performance. But GNP does not show quality, usefulness, or nonmarket output, and it ignores income distribution.

9 Gross national product is widely used as a measure of economic performance. However, it suffers a number of deficiencies as such a measure. It has even more difficulties as an indicator of welfare or well-being because:

- Real GNP is not easy to calculate from nominal GNP. And even real GNP (GNP corrected for price changes) does not tell us about the quality, or purpose, or distribution of income. It also ignores nonmarketed output.
- GNP gives a very imperfect indication of the quality of output.
- The size of GNP does not inform us of its purpose or usefulness.
- GNP does not include (or imprecisely includes) any output that is not sold.
- GNP gives us no clue as to the distribution of income.

ECONOMIC VOCABULARY

Macroeconomics 182
Intermediate goods 183
Consumption goods 183
Final goods 183
Personal consumption expenditures 183
Gross and net investment 184
Replacement 184
Disinvestment 184
Capital formation 184
Government purchases 184
Gross private domestic investment 186
Net exports 186
Circular flow 186
GNP formula 188

QUESTIONS

1. Explain how the circularity of the economic process means that the outputs of the system are returned as fresh inputs.

2. What is meant by net investment? How is it different from gross investment? Does the idea of "net consumption" mean anything? (Suppose there is a minimum amount of consumption needed to keep body and soul together?)
3. Why are investment goods considered final goods and not intermediate ones?
4. Do you think that education is a consumption service—or an investment? What about military expenditure? Can you see how one might classify many such expenditures in more than one way?
5. Write the basic formula for GNP.
6. Do you think we should develop measures other than GNP to measure our performance? What sorts of measures?

CHAPTER 12

Buying the National Product

A LOOK AHEAD

So far we have looked into only one side of the national income "accounts ledger," the side concerned with *output*. Now we move to the other side, which is concerned with *income*. We begin our analysis with a central question: How can an economy sustain itself? How can it buy back all its own production?

We will attack the problem by seeing how every item of cost incurred in production becomes someone's income. That is a key part of the answer. Costs are also incomes. But it is not the whole answer: Incomes must thereafter be spent if they are to become demand. And if they are not spent? Then we have trouble such as slowdowns in production or recession.

This chapter is the basis on which rests a great deal of what follows in the study of the macroeconomy. We suggest you read it twice—once quickly to get the point, once very slowly to master each link in the argument.

In the last chapter we talked about gross national product from the supply point of view. That is, we learned to see the great stream of final output as a river that feeds four sectors—a sector of private households that require consumption goods, a sector of firms that need investment goods of various kinds, a sector of government agencies concerned with public goods, and a sector made up of individuals and firms and governments of other countries—the export or foreign sector.

FROM SUPPLY TO DEMAND

Now we must look at that same stream of production from another perspective, that of demand. This brings us to a question whose answer we will soon discover is both simple and surprisingly complex. **The question is where the economy finds the necessary purchasing power to buy the output it has produced.** Specifically, where will households get the money to buy the consumer goods that have been produced? Where will businesses get the funds to buy the investment goods they seek? Where will government find the wherewithal to purchase public goods?*

The question leads us to seek a link between the supply of output and the demand for output. The link is not hard to find. Anyone in business will tell you that the crucial factor in determining the supply of output is the demand for it—that is, the presence of buyers who are willing and able to buy goods or services at prices that sellers are willing to accept.

So demand is necessary to assure supply. But where does demand come from? Here is the surprising twist. **Demand is produced by supply!** Ask any buyers in the marketplace where their incomes come from, and the answer you will get is that their incomes come directly or indirectly from production itself—from the wages or rents or profits or interest that have been received because these buyers have entered the economy on the supply side as factors of production.

Thus output is generated by demand—and demand is generated by output! Our quest for the motive force behind the flow of production therefore leads us to discover a great *circular flow* within the economy.

The Circular Flow

At the top of the circle in Figure 1 we see payments flowing from households to firms or government units (cities, states, federal agencies), thereby creating the demand that brings forth production. At the bottom of the circle we see more payments, this time flowing from firms or governments back to households, as businesses or government agencies hire the services of the various factors in order to carry out production. **Thus we can see that there is a constant regeneration**

*We will not look into the question of where foreigners get the money they need because we are not yet ready to step into the world of international trade and finance. For now, we confine our investigation to an economy that is "closed"—that is, an economy that buys and sells nothing abroad. Later we will make the corrections necessary to bring the foreign sector into the picture.

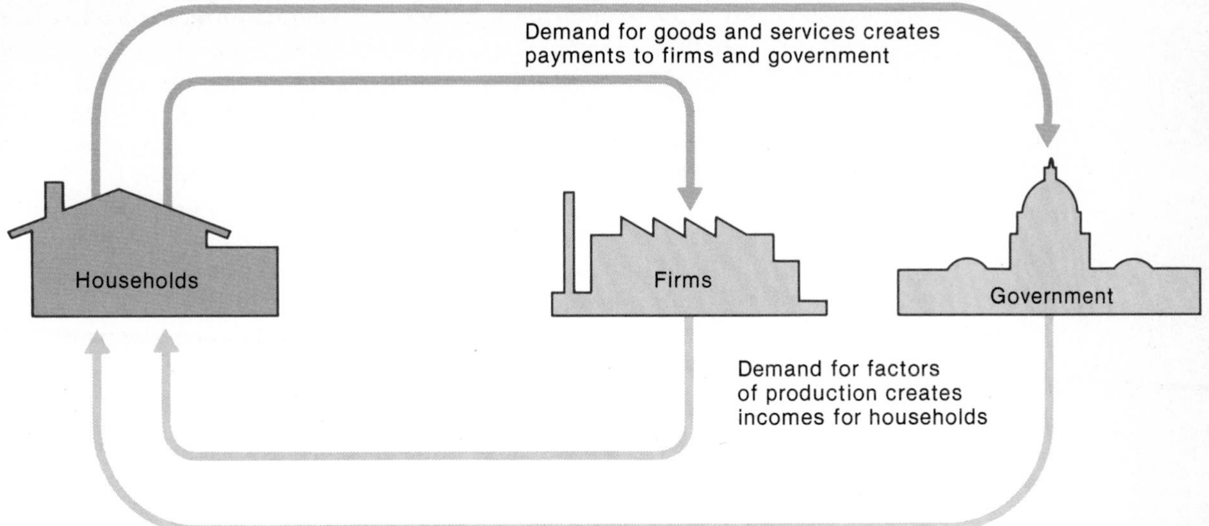

FIGURE 1
The Circular Flow of Supply and Demand
This is the same circular flow concept that we encountered in Figure 1, Chapter 11. Here we use it to emphasize that the demand for output is itself generated by output.

of demand as money is first spent by the public on the output of firms and governments, and then in turn is spent by firms and governments for the services of the public. That is how an economy that has produced a given GNP is able to buy it back.

This is by no means a self-evident matter. Indeed, one of the most common anxieties about the flow of economic activity is that there will not be enough purchasing power to buy everything we have produced—that somehow we may be unable to buy enough to keep up with the output of our factories. So it is important to understand once and for all how an economy can sustain a given level of production through its purchases on the market.

We start with an imaginary economy in full operation. We can, if we wish, imagine ourselves as having collected a year's output, which is now sitting on the economic front doorstep looking for a buyer. What we must now see is whether it will be possible to *sell* this gross national product to the people who have been engaged in producing it. We must ask whether enough income or receipts have been generated in the process of production to buy back all the products themselves.

COSTS AND INCOMES

How does production create income? Business people do not think about "incomes" when they assemble the factors of production to meet the demand for their product. They worry about *cost.* All the money they pay out during the production process is paid under the heading of *cost,* whether it be wage or salary cost, cost of materials, depreciation cost, tax cost, or whatever. Thus the concept of cost offers us a point of entry into the economic chain. **If we can show how all costs become incomes, we will have taken a major step toward understanding whether our gross national product can in fact be sold to those who produced it.**

It may help us if we begin by looking at the kinds of costs incurred by business firms in real life. Since governments also produce goods and services, this hypothetical firm should be taken to represent government agencies as well as business firms. Both incur the same kinds of costs; only the labels differ.

Table 1, a hypothetical expense summary of General Output Company, will serve as an example typical of all business firms, large or small, and all government agencies. (If you examine the year-end statements of any business, you will find that costs all fall into one or more of the cost categories shown.)

Factor Costs

Some of these costs we recognize immediately as payments to factors of production. The item for wages and salaries is obviously a payment to the factor *labor.* The item for interest (perhaps not so obviously) is a payment to the factor *capital;* that is, to those who have lent the company money in order to help it carry on its productive operation. The item for rent is, of course, a payment for the rental of *land* or natural resources from their owners.

Note that we have included profits with rent and interest. In actual accounting practice, profits are not shown as a cost. For our purposes, however, it will be quite legitimate and very helpful to regard profits as a special kind of factor cost going to businesspeople for their risk-taking function. Later we shall go more thoroughly into the matter of profits.

Factor Costs and Value of Output

Two things strike us about these factor costs. *First, it is clear that they represent payments that have been made to secure production.* In more technical language, they are payments for factor inputs that result in commodity outputs. All the useful activity actually carried on within the company or government agency—whether

TABLE 1
General Output Company Cost Summary

Wages, salaries, and employee benefits	$100,000,000
Rental, interest, and profit payments	5,000,000
Materials, supplies, etc.	60,000,000
Taxes other than income	25,000,000
Depreciation	20,000,000
Total	$210,000,000

production or assembly or distribution—all the value it has added to the economy, has been compensated by the payments the company or the agency has made to land, labor, and capital. To be sure, there are other costs, for materials and taxes and depreciation, and we shall soon turn to these. **But the total of factors costs equals the value of the total new output that General Output by itself has given to the economy.**

Factor Costs and National Income

A second striking fact is that **all factor costs are income payments. The wages, salaries, interest, rents, etc., that were costs to the company or agency were income to its recipients. So are any profits, which will accrue as income to the owners of the business.**

From here it is a simple step to add up *all* the factor costs paid out by *all* the companies and government agencies in the economy, in order to measure the total new *value added* by all productive efforts in the year. **This measure is called national income.** As we can see, it is less than gross national product, for it does not include other costs of output—namely, certain taxes and depreciation.

Thus, just as it sounds, national income means the total amount of earnings of the factors of production within the nation. If we think of these factors as constituting the households of the economy, we can see that **factor costs result directly in incomes to the household sector.** If factor costs were the only costs involved in production, the problem of buying back the gross national product would therefore be a very simple one. We should simply be paying out to households, as the cost of production, the very sum needed to buy GNP when we turned around to sell it.

But a glance at the General Output expense summary shows that this is not the case. There are other costs besides factor costs. How shall we deal with them?

Costs of Materials

The next item of the expense summary is puzzling. Called payments for "materials, supplies, etc.," it represents all the money General Output has paid not to its own factors, but to other companies for other products it has needed. We may even recognize these costs as payments for those *intermediate products* that lose their identity in a later stage of production. How do such payments become part of the income available to buy GNP on the marketplace?

Perhaps the answer is already intuitively clear. When General Output sends its checks to, let us say, USX or General Electric or to a local supplier of stationery, each of these recipient firms now uses General Output's payments to pay its own costs. And what are those costs? What must USX or all the other suppliers now do with their checks? The answer is obvious: They must reimburse their own factors and then pay any other costs that remain.

Figure 2 may make the matter clear. It shows us, looking back down the chain of intermediate payments, that what constitutes material costs to one firm are factor and other costs to another. Indeed, as we unravel the chain from company to

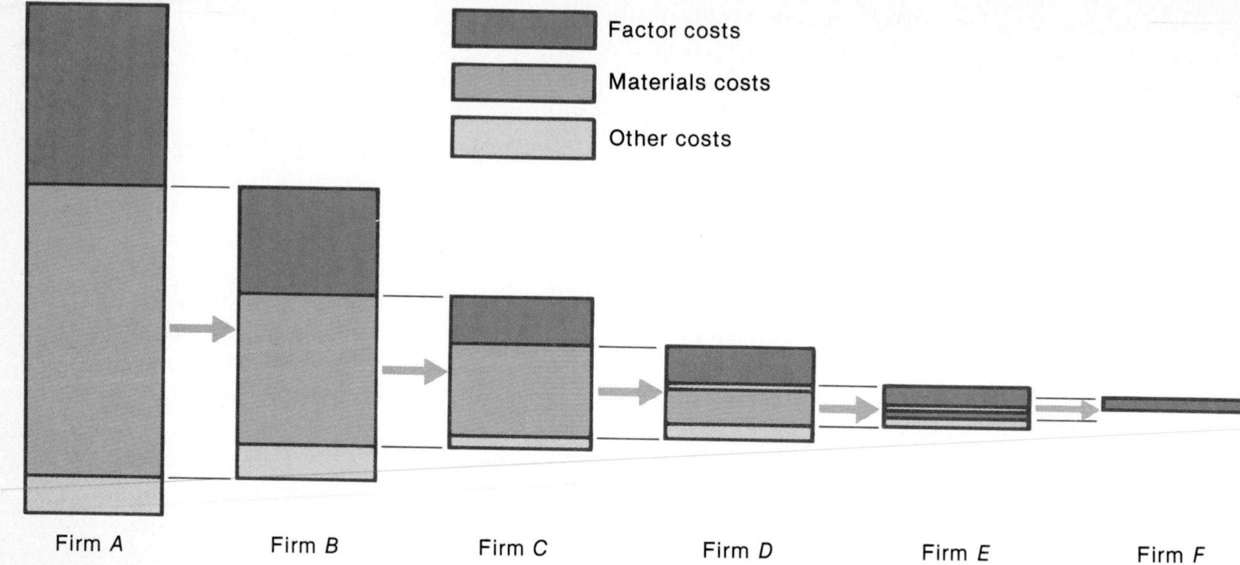

FIGURE 2
How Materials Costs Become Other Costs
The cost of materials to firm A consists of firm B's payments to its factors and other costs, just as firm B's materials cost is made up of firm C's factor and other costs. Eventually all costs of materials reduce to payments for the services of labor, capital and land. After all, what other ultimate costs are there?

company, it is clear that all the contribution to new output must have come from the contribution of factors somewhere down the line. **All the costs of new output—all the value added—must ultimately be resolvable into payments to the owners of land (or natural resources), labor, and capital.**

Another way of picturing the same thing is to imagine that all firms or agencies in the country were bought up by a single gigantic corporation. The various production units of the new supercorporation would then ship components and semifinished items back and forth to one another, but there would not have to be any payment from one division to another. The only payments that would be necessary would be those required to buy the services of factors—that is, various kinds of labor or the use of property or capital—so that at the end of the year, the supercorporation would show on its expense summary only items for wages and salaries, rent, and interest (and, as we shall see, taxes and depreciation), but it would have no item for materials cost.

We have come a bit further toward seeing how our gross national product can be sold. **To the extent that GNP represents new output made during the course of the year, the income to buy back this output has already been handed out as factor costs, either paid at the last stage of production or carried along in the guise of material costs.**

But a glance at the General Output expense summary shows that entrepreneurs incur two kinds of costs that we still have not taken into account: taxes and depreciation. Here are costs employers have incurred that have not been accounted for on the income side. What can we say about them?

Tax Costs

Let us begin by tracing the taxes that General Output pays, just as we have traced its material payments.* In the first instance, its taxes will go to government units—federal, state, and local. But we need not stop there. Just as we saw that General Output's checks to supplier firms paid for the suppliers' factor costs and for still further interfirm transactions, so we can see that its checks to government agencies pay for goods and services that these agencies have produced—goods such as roads, buildings, and defense equipment; services such as teaching, police protection, and the administration of justice. General Output's tax checks are thus used to help pay for factors of production—land, labor, and capital—that are used in the *public sector.*

In many ways, General Output's payments to government units resemble its payments to other firms for raw material. Indeed, if the government *sold* its services to General Output, charging for the use of the roads, police services, and defense protection it affords the company, there would be *no* difference whatsoever. The reason we differentiate between a company's payment to the public sector and its payments for intermediate products is important, however, and worth looking into.

The first reason is clearly that, with few exceptions, the government does *not* sell its output. This is partly because the community has decided that certain things the government produces (education, justice, and most city parks, for instance) should not be for sale, but should be supplied to all citizens without direct charge. In part, it is also because some things the government produces, such as defense or law and order, cannot be equitably charged to individual buyers since it is impossible to say to what degree anyone benefits from—or even uses—these communal facilities. Hence General Output, like every other producer, is billed, justly or otherwise, for a share of the cost of government.

Indirect Taxes

Here is a second reason why we consider that the cost of taxes is a new kind of cost, distinct from factor payments: When business firms have finished paying the factors, they have not yet paid all the sums employers must lay out. Some taxes, in other words, are an addition to the cost of production. These taxes are called *indirect taxes,* and they are levied on the productive enterprise itself and on its actual physical output. Taxes on real estate, for instance, and taxes that are levied on each unit of output (such as excise taxes on cigarettes) and taxes levied on goods sold at retail (sales taxes) are all payments entrepreneurs must make as part of their costs of doing business. *They are an entirely new kind of cost of production, not previously picked up.* As an expense paid out by entrepreneurs, over and above factor costs (or material costs), these tax costs must be part of the total selling price of the goods and services in GNP.

Will there be enough incomes handed out in the process of production to cover

*For simplicity, we also show government agencies as taxpayers. In fact, most government units do *not* pay taxes. Yet there will be hidden tax costs in the prices of many materials they buy. No harm is done by treating government agencies like taxpaying firms in this model.

this additional item of cost? Yes. The indirect tax costs paid out by firms will be received by government agencies who will use these tax receipts to pay income to factors working for the government. Any direct taxes (income taxes) paid by General Output or by its factors will also wind up in the hands of a government. **Thus all tax payments result in the transfer of purchasing power from the private to the public sector, and when spent by the public sector, they will again become demand in the marketplace.**

Direct Taxes

This does not mean that all taxes collected by the government are costs of production. Many taxes will be paid not by the entrepreneurs as an expense of doing business, but by the *factors* themselves. These so-called *direct taxes* (such as personal income taxes) are *not* part of the cost of production. When General Output adds up its total cost of production, it naturally includes the wages and salaries it has paid, but it does not include the taxes its workers or executives have paid out of their incomes. Such direct taxes transfer income from earners to government, but they are not a cost to the company itself.

In the same way, income taxes on the profits of a company do *not* constitute a cost of production. General Output does not pay income taxes as a regular charge on its operations, but waits until a year's production has taken place and then pays income taxes on the profits it makes *after* paying its costs. If it finds that it has lost money over the year, it will not pay any income taxes—although it will have paid other costs, including indirect taxes. **Thus direct taxes, such as income taxes, are not a cost paid out in the course of production that must be recouped, but a payment made by factors (including owners of the business) from the incomes they have earned through the process of production.**

Depreciation

There is still one last item of cost. At the end of the year, when the company is totting up its expenses to see if it has made a profit for the period, its accountants do not stop with factor costs, material costs, and indirect taxes. If they did, the company would soon be in dire straits. In producing its goods, General Output has also used up a certain amount of its assets—its buildings and equipment—and a cost must now be charged for this wear and tear if the company is to be able to preserve the value of its physical plant intact. If it did not make this cost allowance, it would have failed to include all the resources that were used up in the process of production, and it would therefore be overstating its profits.

Yet this cost has something about it clearly different from other costs that General Output has paid. Unlike factor costs or taxes or material costs, depreciation is not paid for by check. When the company's accountants make an allowance for depreciation, all they do is make an entry on the company's book stating that plant and equipment are now worth a certain amount less than at the beginning of the year.

At the same time, however, General Output *includes* the amount of depreciation in the price it intends to charge for its goods. As we have seen, one of the resources used up in production was its own capital equipment, and it is certainly entitled to consider the depreciation as a cost. Yet it has not paid anyone a sum of money equal to this cost! How, then, will there be enough income in the marketplace to buy back its product?

Replacement Expenditure

The answer is that in essence it has paid depreciation charges to itself. Depreciation is thus part of its gross income. Together with after-tax profits, these depreciation charges are called a business's *cash flow.*

A business does not *have* to spend its depreciation accruals, but normally it will, to maintain and replace its capital stock. To be sure, an individual firm may not replace its worn-out capital exactly on schedule. But when we consider the economy as a whole, with its vast assemblage of firms, that problem tends to disappear. Suppose we have 1,000 firms, each with machines worth $1,000 and each depreciating its machines at $100 per year. Provided that all the machines were bought in different years, this means that in any given year about 10 percent of the capital stock will wear out and have to be replaced. It's reasonable to assume that, among them, the 1,000 firms will spend $100,000 per year to replace their old equipment over a ten-year span.*

This enables us to see that insofar as there is a steady stream of replacement expenditures going to firms that make capital goods, there will be payments just large enough to balance the addition to costs due to depreciation. As with all other payments to firms, these replacement expenditures will become incomes to factors, etc., and thus can reappear on the marketplace.

Profits and Demands

One last item remains. During our discussion of the circular flow, we spoke of profits as a special kind of factor cost—a payment to the factor *capital.* Now we can think of profits not merely as a factor cost (although there is always a certain element of risk remuneration in profits), but also as a return to especially efficient or forward-thinking firms who have used the investment process to introduce new products or processes ahead of the run of their industries. We also know that profits accrue to powerful firms that exact a semimonopolistic return from their customers.

What matters in our analysis at this stage is not the precise explanation we give to the origin of profits, but a precise explanation of their role in maintaining a "closed-circuit" economy in which all costs are returned to the marketplace as

*What if the machines *were* all bought in one year or over a small number of years? Then replacement expenditures will *not* be evenly distributed over time, and we may indeed have problems. This takes us into the dynamics of prosperity and recession, to which we will turn in due course. For the purpose of our explanatory model, we will stick with our (not too unrealistic) assumption that machines wear out on a steady schedule and that aggregate replacement expenditures therefore also display a steady, relatively unfluctuating pattern.

demand. A commonly heard diagnosis of economic maladies is that profits are at the root of the trouble, because they cause a withdrawal of spending power or income from the community. If profits are saved or retained within the firm, this can be true. In fact, however, profits are usually distributed in three ways. They may be

1. paid out as income to the household sector in the form of dividends or profit shares, to become part of household spending;
2. directly spent by business firms for new plant and equipment; or
3. taxed by the government and spent in the public sector.

All three methods of offsetting profits appear in Figure 3.

Thus we can see that profits need not constitute a withdrawal from the income stream. Indeed, unless profits are adequate, business will very likely not invest enough to offset the savings of the household sector. They may, in fact, even fail to make normal replacement expenditures.

Thus the existence of profits, far from being deflationary—that is, far from causing a fall in income—is, in fact, essential for the maintenance of a given level of income or for an advance to a higher level. Nonetheless, there is a germ of truth in the contention of those who have maintained that profits can cause an insufficiency of purchasing power. **For unless profits are returned to the flow of purchasing power as dividends that are spent by their recipients, or as new capital expenditures made by business, or as taxes that lead to additional public spending, there will be a gap in the community's demand.** Unspent, hoarded profits are a drag on growth, but invested profits are not.* Thus we can think of profits just as we think of savings—an indispensable source of economic growth or a potential source of economic decline.

The Three Streams of Expenditure

Our analysis is now complete. Item by item, we have traced each category of cost into an income payment, so that we now know there is enough income paid out to buy back our GNP at a price that represents its full cost. Perhaps this was a conclusion we anticipated all along. After all, ours would be an impossibly difficult economy to manage if somewhere along the line purchasing power dropped out of existence, so that we were always faced with a shortage of income to buy back the product we made.

But our analysis has also shown us something more unexpected. We are accustomed to thinking that all the purchasing power in the economy is received and spent through the hands of the people—usually meaning households. Now we can see that this is not true. There is not one, but *three* streams of incomes and costs, all quite distinct from one another (although linked by direct taxes):*

*Here we must distinguish between the individual firm and all firms together. An individual firm that saves its profits will usually put them in a bank and thereby make them available to other firms. But if all firms collectively hold onto their profits, trouble will result.

*For purposes of simplicity, we will again include profits in factor costs.

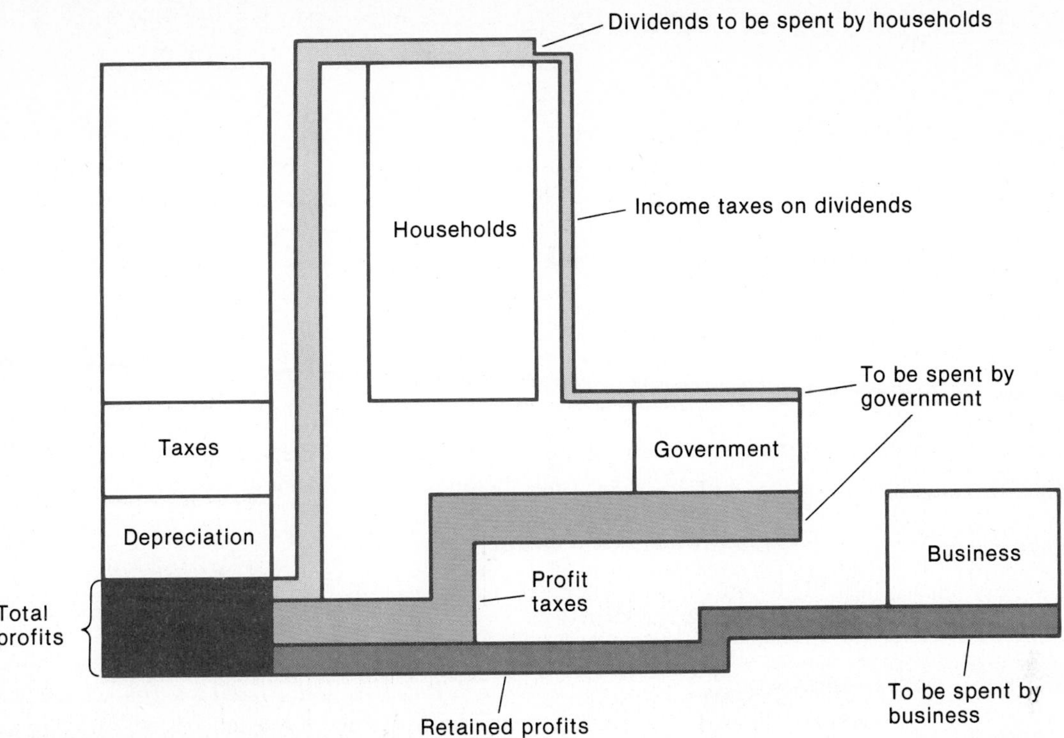

FIGURE 3
Profits in the Circular Flow
There are three ways in which profits can be returned to GNP as expenditure: (1) by being distributed as dividends and spent by households, (2) by being taxed away and spent by government, and (3) by being directly spent by business for new investment.

1. Factor costs → Households → Consumers goods
↘ Direct Taxes ↓
2. Indirect taxes → Government agencies → Government goods
↗ Direct Taxes ↑
3. Depreciation → Business firms → Replacement investment

The one major crossover in the three streams is the direct taxes of households and business firms that go to governments. This flow permits governments to buy more goods and services than they could purchase with indirect taxes alone.

There is a simple way of explaining this seemingly complex triple flow. Each stream indicates the existence of a *final taker* of gross national product: the consumer, government, and business itself. Since output has final claimants other than consumers, we can obviously have a flow of purchasing power that does not enter consumers' or factors' hands.†

†We have not forgotten about the export sector, but we cannot integrate it into the picture until we study international trade.

THE COMPLETED CIRCUIT OF DEMAND

The realization that factor owners do not get paid incomes equal to the total gross value of output brings us back to the central question of this chapter: Can we be certain that we will be able to sell our GNP at its full cost? Has there surely been generated enough purchasing power to buy back our total output?

We have thus far carefully analyzed and answered half the question. **We know that all costs will become incomes to factors or receipts of government agencies or of firms making replacement items.** To sum up again, factor costs become the incomes of workers, managements, owners of natural resources and of capital; and all these incomes together can be thought of as comprising the receipts of the household sector. Tax costs are paid to government agencies and become receipts of the government sector. Depreciation costs are normally accrued within business firms, and these accruals belong to the business sector. Profits go to households, government, and business.

Crucial Role of Expenditures

What we have not yet established, however, is that these sector receipts will become sector expenditures. That is, we have not demonstrated that all households will now *spend* all their incomes on goods and services, or that government units will necessarily *spend* all their tax receipts on public goods and services, or that all firms will assuredly *spend* their depreciation accruals for new replacement equipment.

What happens if some receipts are not spent? The answer is of key importance in understanding the operation of the economy. A failure of the sectors to spend as much money as they have received means that some of the costs that have been laid out will *not* come back to the original entrepreneurs. As a result, they will suffer losses. If, for instance, our gross national product costs $1 trillion to produce but the various sectors spend only $900 billion in all, then some businesses will find themselves unable to sell all their output. Inventories of unsold goods will begin piling up, and businesspeople will soon be worried about overproducing. The natural thing to do when you can't sell all your output is to stop making so much of it, so businesses will begin cutting back on production. As they do so, they will also cut back on the number of people they employ. As a result, business costs will go down; but so will factor incomes, for we have seen that costs and incomes are opposite sides of one coin. As incomes fall, the expenditures of the sectors might very well fall further, bringing about another twist in the spiral of recession.

This is not yet the place to go into the mechanics of such a downward spiral of business. But the point is clear. **A failure of the sectors to bring all their receipts back to the marketplace as demand can initiate profound economic problems. In the contrast between an unshakable equality of costs and incomes on the one hand, and the uncertain connection between incomes and expenditures on the other, we have come to grips with one of the most important problems in macroeconomics.**

From Recession to Inflation

We have raised the problem of recession, of a shortfall in purchasing power and a failure of expenditures to "buy back" all of GNP, because that is a good way to illuminate the circular flow of production. It is a dual flow, as we have seen, of incomes in one direction and expenditures in the other. And when costs and incomes exceed expenditures, the economy can indeed experience the trauma of recession.

What of inflation? It is tempting to find a simple symmetry here, to argue that inflation must stem from an *excess* of expenditures over incomes. We have all heard inflation described as "too much money chasing too few goods." The metaphor, at least, is clear: Such an unbalanced chase must force costs, and so prices, to rise until the cost-value of goods is again equal to the expenditures that are trying to purchase them.

But be wary! We have not yet learned about money, nor about the ways prices are determined. We shall discover in due course that inflation is a complex subject, one that defies easy characterization. But for that we will simply have to wait. We will return to the subject many times.

SOME IMPORTANT DEFINITIONS

We have completed the necessary economic analysis of this chapter, showing how the demand for GNP is generated. But we still need to improve and refine our economic vocabulary. Before we move on, therefore, we must learn some very useful and frequently encountered definitions.

The first of these concerns two ways of looking at GNP. One way is to think of GNP as measuring the value of a year's final output of consumption, investment, government, and net export goods and services. But we also know that the value of this output is a sum of costs: factor costs, indirect tax costs, the costs of depreciation. These costs are identical with the incomes or receipts of sectors. Therefore GNP measures total incomes as well as total costs.

GNP and GNI

To express the equality with the conciseness and clarity of mathematics, we can write two equations. First, GNP as a sum of final outputs:

$$\text{GNP} \equiv C + G + I + X$$

where C, I, G, and X (net exports) are designations of the four categories into which we divide our flow of production.

Next, we write an equation that describes the *same* flow, not as a sum of outputs, but as a sum of costs:

$$\text{GNP} \equiv F + T + D$$

where F, T, and D are familiar to us as factor, indirect tax, and depreciation costs. *But we have also learned that all costs are identical with incomes.* It follows, therefore, that we can speak of the sum of these costs as gross national income, or GNI. Hence the last set of identities:

Gross National Product ≡ Gross National Income or GNP ≡ GNI

or

$$C + G + I + X \equiv F + T + D$$

It is important to remember that these are all accounting identities, true by definition. The National Income and Product Accounts, the official government accounts for the economy, are kept in such a manner as to make them true. As the name implies, these accounts are kept in two sets of books, one on the products produced in the economy and the other on the costs of production, which we know to be identical with the incomes generated in the economy. Since both sets of accounts are measuring the same output, the two totals must be equal.

NNP and National Income

It is now easy to understand the meaning of the two other measures of output. One of these is called **net national product (NNP).** As the name indicates, it is exactly equal to the gross national product minus depreciation. GNP is used much more than NNP because the measures of depreciation are very unreliable. The other measure, **national income,** we have already met. It is *GNP minus both depreciation and indirect taxes.* This makes it equal to the sum of factor costs only. Figure 4 should make this relationship clear. The aim of this last measure is to identify the net income that actually reaches the hands of factors of production. Consequently, the measure is sometimes called the *national income at factor cost.* Its abbreviation is Y.*

The Circular Flow Again

The "self-reproducing" model economy we have now sketched out is obviously still very far from reality. Nevertheless, the particular kind of unreality we have deliberately constructed serves a highly useful purpose. An economy that regularly and dependably buys back everything it produces gives us a kind of benchmark from which to begin our subsequent investigations. We call such an economy, whose internal relationships we have outlined, an economy in **stationary equilibrium,** and we denote the changeless flow of costs into business receipts, and receipts back into costs, a *circular flow.*

We shall return many times to the model of a circular flow economy for insights into a more complex and dynamic system. Hence it is important to summarize two of the salient characteristics of such a system.

*Why not I? Because we keep that letter for "investment."

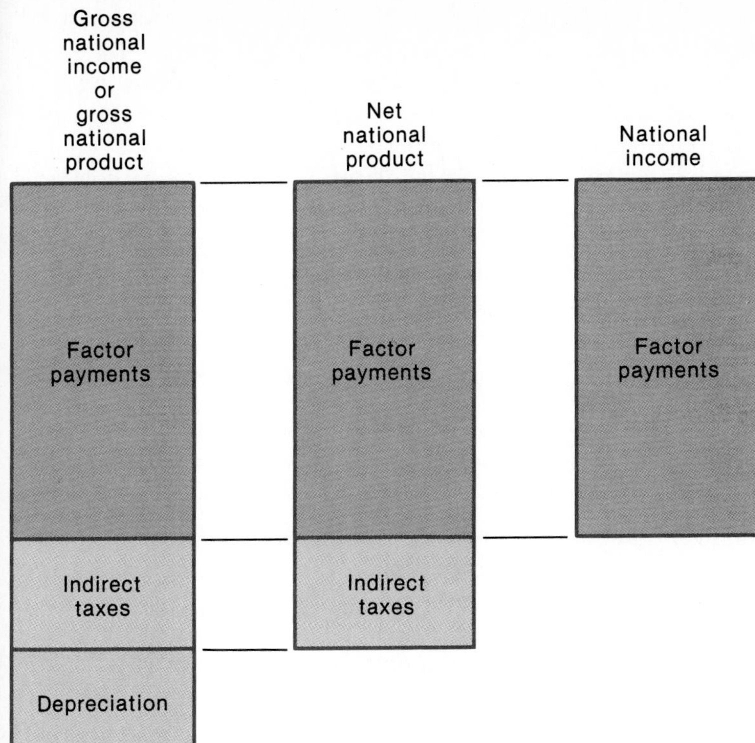

FIGURE 4
GNP, NNP, and NI
GNP, NNP, and NI (or Y) fit into one another like a nest of Chinese boxes. As you can see, the basic unit of measurement of output is national income; net and gross national products are derived by adding specific costs—indirect taxes for NNP and depreciation for GNP.

1. A CIRCULAR FLOW ECONOMY WILL NEVER EXPERIENCE A RECESSION. Year in and year out, its total output will remain unchanged. Indeed, the very concept of a circular flow is useful in showing us that **an economic system can maintain a given level of activity** ***indefinitely,*** so long as all the sectors convert all their receipts into expenditures.

2. A CIRCULAR FLOW ECONOMY WILL NEVER KNOW A BOOM. It will not grow, and its standard of living will remain unchanged. That standard of living may be high or low, for we could have a circular flow economy of poverty or one of abundance. But in either state changelessness will be its essence. Note further that if population rises, per capita income will fall! This follows from the fact that income is unchanged.

The Great Puzzle

What we have demonstrated in this chapter is an exceedingly important idea. There *can* always be enough purchasing power generated by the process of output to buy back that output.

Yet we all know from our most casual acquaintance with economics that in fact there is not always enough purchasing power around, and that on occasion there is too much purchasing power. With too little, we have slumps and recessions; with too much, booms and inflation.

Hence the circular flow sets the stage for the next step in our study of macroeconomics. If there *can be* the right amount of purchasing power generated, why isn't there? Or to put the question more perplexingly: If there *can be* enough purchasing power to buy *any* size output, small or large, what determines how large purchasing power will actually be, and therefore how large output will actually be?

These questions point the way to the next stage of our investigation. We must study the workings of demand much more realistically by removing some of the assumptions that were necessary to create a model of a circular flow system.

LOOKING BACK

KEY CONCEPTS

The demand for GNP is generated in the act of production as firms hire factors.

1 The question to be grasped is how an economy can sustain itself, how it can generate enough demand to buy back its own output. This leads at once to the origin of demand for output, or purchasing power. In turn, we see that purchasing power is generated by the act of production, as firms and government employers hire factors of production. Thus we begin with the concept of a circular flow.

Factor costs are income to the factors of production.

2 When factors are hired, they create costs. It is important to see that all costs are necessarily also incomes. We group all costs—including material costs—into three categories. The first category, factor costs—wages, salaries, interest payments, and the like—are obviously incomes for the factors of production who receive them.

Indirect taxes are costs that become receipts of government agencies. (Note: Income taxes are not costs of production.)

3 In the second category are the costs of indirect taxation. These are not direct income taxes, which are borne by the factors out of their incomes and are not a cost of production. Indirect taxes are simply added onto factor costs as an expense of production. Such indirect taxes become part of the receipts of government agencies.

Depreciation costs accrue to firms. Profits also recirculate.

4 Depreciation costs are the final category of production cost. These costs are received by business firms, which use them to finance replacement investment. Profits also can return to the income stream as dividends or investment spending or via taxation.

Thus all costs are incomes, but all incomes may not become expenditures.

5 Thus there are three separate streams in the economy: (a) factor costs, which go to households, who spend these "costs" (their incomes) for consumption; (b) indirect taxes, which go to government for expenditure on public goods and services; and (c) depreciation costs which accrue to business firms for expenditure as replacement investment. It is important to see that the transition from "cost" to "income" is unbreakable—they are identities. All costs must become someone's income or receipt. This is not so for the transition from cost (or income) to expenditure. Here is a crucial area of potential malfunction.

GNP ≡ GNI

6 We can express GNP in two ways: as a sum of final outputs or as a sum of incomes (receipts). Thus there is an identity between gross national income and gross national product.

A circular flow economy has no growth.

7 The model of a circular flow economy elucidates how such an economy can repurchase its own production. But a circular flow system has no vitality, no growth.

ECONOMIC VOCABULARY

Factor costs 200
National income 201
Direct and indirect taxes 203, 204
Depreciation 204
GNP and GNI 209
Net national product 210
Circular flow 210
Stationary equilibrium 210

QUESTIONS

1. What are factor costs? To what sector do they go? Do all factor costs become personal incomes? Do they become personal expenditures? (Careful about this last: Suppose that a household *saves* part of its income!)
2. What are direct taxes? What is "direct" about them? Why are they distinguished from "indirect" taxes? Why is an indirect tax, such as a sales tax, considered an addition to the value of GNP, whereas an income tax is not? *Think:* Does the value (or cost) of the goods or services you personally create get bigger if you pay a larger income tax? Does the cost get larger if the sales tax is increased?
3. To whom are material costs paid? Why do we not count them as a separate part of GNP?
4. Exactly what is depreciation? Why is it a cost? Who pays it, and how? Who receives it? Is it possible that a firm can pay depreciation to itself? How else would you describe a business that made an allowance at the end of the year for the value of the machinery that had been used up in production?
5. Why is the link between an expenditure and a receipt an identity? Why is the link between a receipt and an expenditure not an identity? Can there be any expenditure without someone receiving it? Can someone receive a payment, but not make an expenditure himself? Be sure you grasp the difference here.

CHAPTER 13

The Growth of Supply

A LOOK AHEAD

We have learned some essential macroeconomic *concepts*, but we have not yet learned much macroeconomic *analysis*. We begin to do so as we move from the idea of a stationary, changeless economy to that of a dynamic, growing one.

In this chapter we take a look at growth. Here we are going to learn more about the two sources of growth that we have already singled out: changes in the quantity and quality of labor and capital inputs. Incidentally, we shall learn how difficult it is to measure those sources precisely, especially with regard to capital.

Our chapter will lead us again to the production possibility curve we first met in Chapter 7. A production possibility curve helps us understand the nature of the limits to, or constraints on, growth in terms of real output. That will pave the way for our next chapter on the dynamics of the growth in income that must accompany growth in output.

In our last chapter we learned how an economy creates the purchasing power needed to buy back its own output. That led to the idea of a stationary equilibrium, in which an economic system produces output and then purchases it year after year, without either increasing or decreasing the volume of its production or the incomes needed to buy that production.

The idea of a circular flow enables us to grasp the connection between costs and incomes, and the link between income and demand. Without a clear idea of how the economy generates demand from supply, and supply from demand, we cannot understand how the macro system works. But of course the picture of a changeless, level flow of economic activity is very far removed from the real world. Here activity normally grows, taking one year with another, as we have already seen. Sometimes it falls, or fails to grow fast enough.

It is these dynamic changes that are the main focus of macroeconomics. In this chapter we return to a historical view of growth, stressing the sources and limits of the *supply of output.* That will ready us for an analysis of the growth of demand in the chapter to follow.

A Quick Review

Macroeconomics is concerned essentially with growth. Chapter 7 opened a discussion of the long upward trend of U.S. output and the reasons for this trend. Recall that our growth trend for nearly 100 years has resulted in an average annual increase in real GNP per capita of about 1.5 percent a year—enough to double per capita income every 47 years.

Now we are going to push forward by learning much more about the underlying trends and causes of growth in the American economy. That will set the stage for the work that still lies ahead, when we will narrow our focus to the present and inquire into the reasons for the problems of our macrosystem—unemployment and inflation, booms and busts.

What determines how fast we have grown in the past and how rapidly we may grow in the future? We already know the basic answer. **Growth comes from increases in the quantity or in the quality of the two major aspects of supply—labor and capital. Of course, it also depends mightily on the resources with which we are endowed and it is influenced by our sheer willingness to work hard. And all of these may be brought into play—or driven out of play—by the state of demand.** Therefore growth is anything but a cut-and-dried subject that can be disposed of by a simple analysis of the inputs of labor and capital. Nevertheless, by looking into these inputs, we will learn a lot.

LABOR

Output depends on work. The first source of growth is therefore the rise in the sheer number of people who work for pay—who *participate* in the national labor force. Figure 1 gives us a picture of the population and the labor force over the past

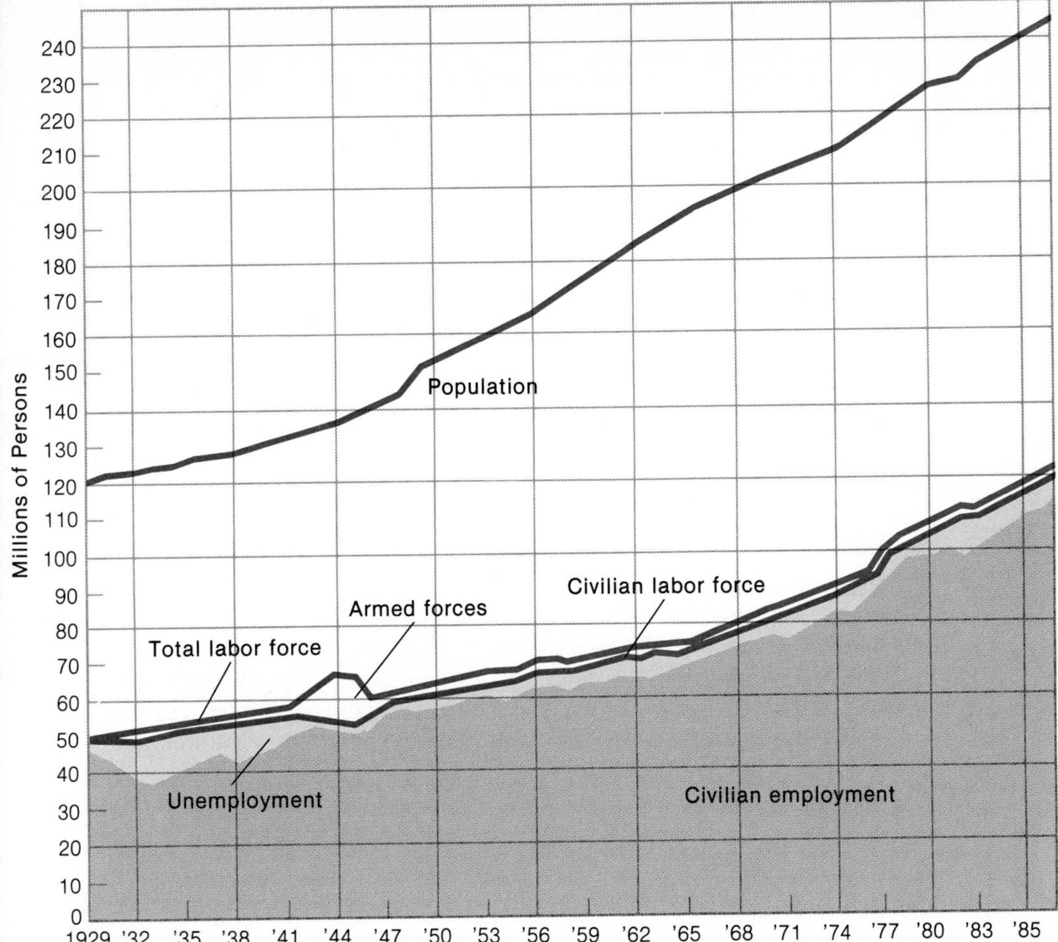

FIGURE 1
United States Labor Force, 1929–1988
Although our eyes cannot easily make it out on the graph, the proportion of the total population seeking work has steadily risen. Today about two-thirds of the working age population is in the labor force—at work or looking for work.

60 years. As we would expect, the size of the labor force has been steadily rising as our population has increased.

But there is more here than quickly meets the eye. One might expect that as our society has grown richer and more affluent, fewer people would seek employment. But that is not the case. If we go back to 1890 or 1900, we find that only 52 out of every 100 persons over age 14 sought paid work. Today about 65 out of every 100 persons of working age seek employment. Looking forward is more uncertain; but if we extend the trend of the past several decades to the year 2000, we can expect perhaps as many as 70 persons out of 100 to be in the labor market by that date.

Participation in the Labor Force

The overall trend toward a larger **participation rate** for the entire population masks two significant changes.

1. Male Participation in the Labor Force Has Fallen. In part, this is because males entering the labor force are older than those who entered in the past. A larger number of young men remain in high school now or go on to college, and the ratio is steadily growing. At the same time, older males show a dramatic withdrawal from the labor force. Almost seven out of ten older males used to work. Now only two or three out of ten work. One reason is the improvement of social security and private pension plans; another, less positive reason is the displacement of older workers in industrial transitions. Will the proportion of older males in the labor force continue to fall? That depends: In recent years cutbacks in social security may be reducing the attractiveness of early retirement to those who can work.

2. There Has Been a Spectacular Rise in Total Female Participation. The mass entrance of women into the labor force accounts for the overall trend toward an increasing search for work. Today 53 percent of all women work outside the home, compared to 34 percent in 1950. Young married women with small children, traditional stay-at-homes, have been the group with the fastest-rising participation rate in recent years. Today even the woman who marries in her early twenties and goes on to raise a family will spend 25 years of her life in paid employment.

Several changing factors in the American scene account for this surge of women into the labor market. Perhaps most important is the desire (and pressure) for the higher living standards and greater income security that two incomes provide—particularly as high-paid manufacturing jobs for men, which were once the ticket to middle-class comfort, become harder to find. Changing family structures—more single-parent households and childless couples—are another reason. The growth of the service sector has also meant more nonmanual relative to manual jobs, and nonmanual jobs are more accessible to women.

These are self-reinforcing factors: The surge of working women has helped to chip away at patterns of educational and employment discrimination, and to foster cultural acceptance of the working woman and the working wife and mother.

Hours of Work

The total supply of labor time depends not only on how many people work but also on how *long* they work—how many hours in a week, how many weeks in a year. Before the rise of factory production, these decisions were governed by the seasons, the crop cycle, and the calendar of religious holidays. Ever since the Industrial Revolution, working men and women have been subject to regulation by a master of their own making: the clock.

Had we asked what determined the length of the working day (or week) in the days of Adam Smith, it would have been relatively simple to answer. Wages were so close to subsistence that someone in the labor force was obliged to work extremely long hours to keep body and soul together. Paid vacations were unknown to the employees of the cotton mills. Unpaid vacations would have been tantamount to starvation.

With the passage of time, the rise of productivity, and the spread of material wealth, working men and women gradually gained higher incomes, and came to realize that a new possibility existed: that of deliberately working less than the physical maximum, using part of their increased productivity to buy leisure for themselves instead of wages.

Thus, beginning in the early nineteenth century, we find that labor organizations (still very small and weak) sought to shorten the workweek. In Chapter 2 we saw that a signal victory was won in England in 1847 with the introduction of the 10-hour day as the legal maximum for women and children. In America, amid the prosperity of the 1920s, the 48-hour week finally became standard; in the 1940s and 1950s, the 40-hour week. Since then, average weekly hours have remained just about constant in the manufacturing sector and in construction. However, average hours in retail trades have declined sharply, from 40 hours in 1950 to just 29 hours in 1987. This reflects another, in some ways less encouraging, trend: the rise of part-time work, (especially for women), which often lacks the stability and benefits that full-time employment provides.

Thus the total supply of labor time has not risen as fast as the labor force because a decline in average hours has offset a rise in participation rates and in population. On balance, the total supply of labor hours has increased, but the supply of labor hours per employee, male and female, has fallen.

From Quantity to Quality

Was the change in the sheer quantity of work hours sufficient to account for the growth of total output? A very simple calculation shows us that it was not. In 1900 our labor force was approximately 30 million men and women who worked approximately 60 hours a week. As a result, they expended 94 billion hours of annual labor. By 1987 the total labor force had grown to almost 120 million. The average workweek was now 35 hours. Total hours of labor input therefore amounted to roughly 210 billion hours of annual labor.*

Total hours of labor input over this 87-year period therefore increased by a little more than twofold. But total economic output over the same period increased by almost tenfold. Clearly the sheer physical increase in the hours of labor was not sufficient to account for more than a small part of our growth trajectory.

Where shall we look for the remaining sources of growth? Our first move will be to examine changes in the quality of our labor hours. The 210 billion hours of labor expended in 1987 were in many cases more skillful, more knowledgeable, more healthy, than the labor hours of 1900. These changes in the quality of our working abilities have come about in two ways.

*This is a very rough calculation, intended for purposes of illustration. Our estimate makes no allowance for strikes, illnesses, or unemployment, although we assume two weeks of vacation in 1987 and none in 1900. This estimate is legitimate enough to make the central point: The *quantity* of labor input cannot possibly account for more than a small portion of our total growth.

1. Growth of Human Capital. By human capital, we mean the skills and knowledge possessed by the labor force. Even though the measurement of human capital is fraught with difficulties, we cannot ignore this vital contributory element in labor productivity. Ferenc Jánossy, a Hungarian economist, has suggested a vivid imaginary experiment to highlight the importance of skills and knowledge.

Suppose, he says, that the populations of two nations of the same size could be swapped overnight. Fifty million Englishmen would awake to find themselves in, say, Nepal, and 50 million Nepalese would find themselves in England. The newly transferred Englishmen would have to contend with all the poverty and difficulties of the Nepalese economy. The newly transferred Nepalese would confront the riches of England. But the Englishmen would bring with them an immense reservoir of literacy, skills, discipline, and training, whereas the Nepalese would bring very low levels of the *kinds* of skills and knowledge needed for an industrial economy. Is there any doubt, asks Jánossy, that production in Nepal, with its new, skilled population, would soon rise dramatically, and that output in England would fall catastrophically?

2. Shifts in the Occupations of the Labor Force. A second source of added productivity results from shifts in employment from low-productivity areas to high-productivity areas. If workers move from occupations in which their productivity is low to other occupations in which output per man-hour is high, the productivity of the economy will rise even if there are no increases in productivity *within* the different sectors.

A glance at Table 1 shows that very profound and pervasive shifts in the location of labor have taken place. What have been the effects of this shift on our long-term ability to produce goods?

The answer is complex. In the early years of the twentieth century, the shift of labor out of agriculture into manufacturing and services probably increased the overall productivity of the economy, since manufacturing was then the most technologically advanced sector. In more recent years, however, we would have to arrive at a different conclusion. Agriculture, although highly productive, is now a very small sector in terms of employment. Moreover, the proportion of the labor force employed in manufacturing is roughly constant, up or down only a few percentage points year to year.

Today growth in employment takes place mainly in the mixture of occupations

TABLE 1
Percent Distribution of All Employed Workers
Notice the long-term shift out of agriculture, through manufacturing and other goods-related occupations, into services.

	1900	*1987*
Agriculture, forests, and fisheries	38.1	2.0
Manufacturing, mining, transportation, construction, utilities	37.7	24.0
Trade, government, finance, professional and personal services	24.2	74.0

Source: Bureau of Labor Statistics, *Employment and Earnings.*

we call the service sector: government; retail and wholesale trade; utilities and transportation; and professions such as the law, accounting, and medicine. The growth of output per capita is less evident in these occupations. Thus the drift of labor into the service sector means that average GNP per worker is growing more slowly today than it would be if labor were moving into manufacturing or agriculture.

Overall Contribution of Labor

Clearly, changes in the *quality* of inputs—in our skills and capacities—far outweigh changes in our quantity of inputs—sheer hours of effort. Knowledge and know-how, energy and initiative, enthusiasm and intelligence, are powerful motors of economic growth. Indeed, economic growth expresses the gradual accumulation of these qualities of humankind much more than it expresses the increase in its sheer volume of exertion.

CAPITAL

What about capital? It must be apparent that without increases in the quantity of capital we could never achieve much growth. The rising labor force would then have to work with the same amount of machines, buildings, transportation equipment and the like, and diminishing returns would soon lower productivity severely. Therefore we have to **widen capital**—to keep the amount of capital at least abreast of increases in the labor force—if we are to have any significant growth.

Actually, a vigorous economy does better than that. It also **deepens capital,** adding to its stock of capital wealth faster than to its labor force, so that each worker has more capital equipment than his or her predecessor, thereby experiencing the same increase in productivity that Adam Smith's workers experienced when new machinery was added to their pin factory.

The Measurement Problem

By how much has our stock of capital grown? Right away we come across a problem that we did not have to face when we considered the labor force. When we seek to measure the effects of changing labor inputs, we can at least count heads, or hours, in comparing past and present. But there is no such convenient unit of measurement when we come to capital. Is a power crane comparable to a shovel? Can we measure the amount of capital used by a bookkeeper today and in 1900 by comparing a computer (or even a calculator) to a pencil?

Such considerations make it plain that we cannot easily distinguish changes in the size of our capital stock from changes in its quality. Occasionally we can directly measure changes in the amount of capital; for instance, we can compare miles of railroad track over time. But even here there are changes in quality embodied in the "same" capital—modern rails are welded, not riveted; roadbeds are different; tracks are electrified. In practice, we estimate the value of our capital stock by adding up the value of new investment, year after year, and subtracting an allowance for the value of capital depreciation. There are many problems in this procedure, but it remains the best we can do.

Total Capital Stock

In 1986, our total national tangible capital amounted to $19.8 trillion, an unimaginably vast sum, almost $200,000 worth of capital for every person in the labor force. This is the value of all the land, structures, and equipment owned by businesses, households, and government—all the resources on or below the ground, all machinery and tools, all the buildings, the inventories, the gold and silver of the nation. It does not include the value of stocks and bonds. Why? Because these are *claims* against our tangible wealth, not wealth in themselves.

This total capital stock is about five or six times as large as the capital stock at the beginning of the century. (Remember: To a large extent we are comparing apples and pears here. The smaller sum was not only less capital of the same kind—fewer miles of railroad track, if you will—but also very different capital: pencils instead of computers.) **One thing is indubitable from this overview: The increase in the quantity and the quality of capital is of critical importance in explaining our national growth. More and better capital are essential elements in increasing productive capacity.**

Investing and Inventing

How do we augment the amount of capital or improve its quality? Actually the two processes generally go hand in hand, for the very act of adding to our capital stock is usually accompanied by improvements. But it is useful to separate the two processes in our minds.

We increase the quantity of capital by withholding resources from consumption—saving them—and by using those resources to build capital goods. This is the process of investment that we studied in the last chapter. A great deal of our macroeconomic studies in the chapters immediately ahead will be about this vital process.

We improve the quality of our capital by a process for which there is no simple name. Let us call it technology. Technology includes inventing and applying new products and processes, and achieving economies of scale—improvements that arise from sheer size.

Sources of Technology

Technology is probably the single most important factor in determining how fast we grow. Yet no one quite understands how technical change comes about. Studies have shown that inventions often follow economic demand—the late-nineteenth-century boom in railroad travel, for example, induced research and development in the expanding industry.* A famous study by Jewkes, Sawers, and Stillerman, *The Sources of Invention,* has revealed that most of the major technological breakthroughs of the mid-twentieth century, from penicillin to the jet engine, were the work of individual inventors and tinkerers and not of organized laboratories.†

How Technology Spreads

Diffusion of new technical knowledge is another matter entirely. The principles of nuclear physics, of aerodynamics, and of digital computing may have been discovered by individuals, but their coming into widespread use reflected a massive commitment of resources. Government has been society's major technological risk-taker, often under the impetus of wartime needs. Sometimes, as in the case of the transistor, invented at the Bell Laboratories, the resources come from a large corporation. More recently, in the expansion of biotechnology and microcomputing, the venture capital market has supplied the resources to support large-scale commercialization of new technologies.

Thus technology has independent sources over which we have little or no control. **But there is no doubt that technical change in our economy can be nurtured by systematic investigation and research and development—R&D in industry, in universities, and under government sponsorship—and by increasing the pace of new investment.** In recent years the share of R&D expenditures has shown a disquieting fall in the United States—a drop of one-fifth, from 3 to 2.5 percent of GNP.

PRODUCTION POSSIBILITY CURVES

We should now have a fairly clear picture of how the growth of output originates. Let us conclude by translating the material we have covered into a production possibility curve—the graphic depiction of potential output that we have already encountered on page 125.

The Production Frontier

Increases in the quantity or quality of labor or capital move our production possibility curve to the right. Do you remember the illustration we used of an economy that produced only milk and grain? In Figure 2 we show how changes in the size of our labor force, in its skills, or in its equipment can alter the production "frontier" for these goods. Panel I shows the results when production of both outputs increases; but II and III make clear that this is not always the case.

*Jacob Schmookler, *Invention and Economic Growth* (Cambridge: Harvard University Press, 1966).

†John Jewkes, David Sawers, Richard Stillerman, *The Sources of Invention* (London: Macmillan, 1960).

Sometimes increases in education, new inventions, or other changes will affect one kind of output and not the other.

Such a two-commodity diagram may seem unreal, but remember that "milk" and "grain" can stand for consumption and investment (or any other choices available to an economy). In fact, with a little imagination we can construct a three-dimensional production possibility *surface* showing the limits imposed by scarcity on a society that divides its output among three uses such as consumption, investment, and government. Such a diagram looks like Figure 3.

Note how the production possibility surface swells out from the origin like a wind-filled sail. Any place on the sail represents some combination of consumption, investment, and government spending that is within the reach of the community. **Any place behind the efficiency frontier represents a failure of the economy to employ all its resources. It is a graphic depiction of unemployment of people or materials.**

Very few economies actually operate on their efficiency frontiers. Most have at least *some* unemployed inputs or are not using their inputs with all possible efficiency. Perhaps only in wartime do we reach the frontiers of our production possibility map, and then only at great sacrifice of other things we value, such as safety and leisure. Nonetheless, we can see that a major job of economic policymakers is to move the economy as close to its frontier as possible under normal conditions, and to move the frontier out as fast as possible. Note, too, that the frontier does not represent a firm, immutable limit to output. It can be changed, not only by the various sources of growth we have looked into, but also by *policies* that increase the quantity or quality of labor or capital.

From Supply to Demand

Everything we have discussed in this chapter relates to the ways in which our total output—our GNP—can grow. Let us emphasize *can.* The production possibility

FIGURE 2
Shifts in the Production Frontier
Changes in the quantity or quality of labor and/or capital make growth possible by pushing out our production frontier. As we can see, they may not affect all kinds of output equally.

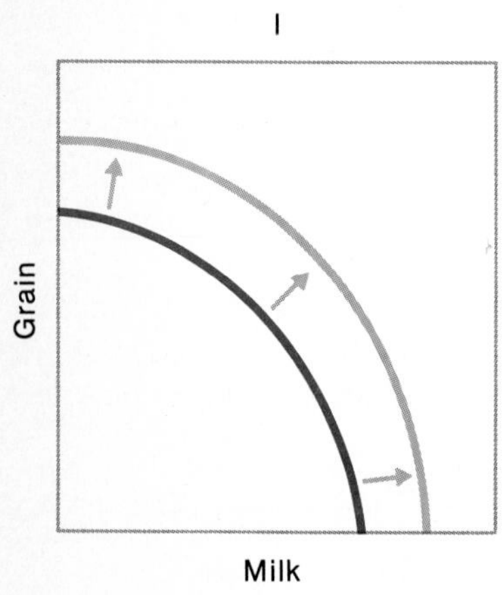

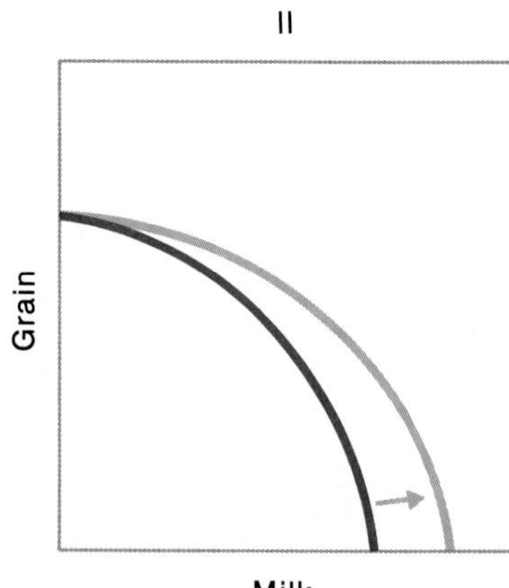

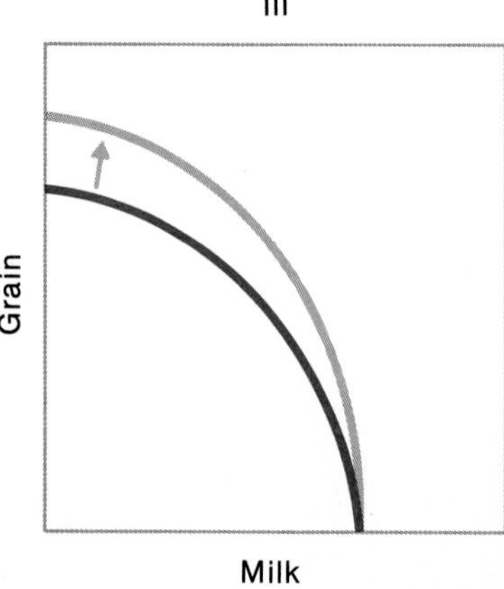

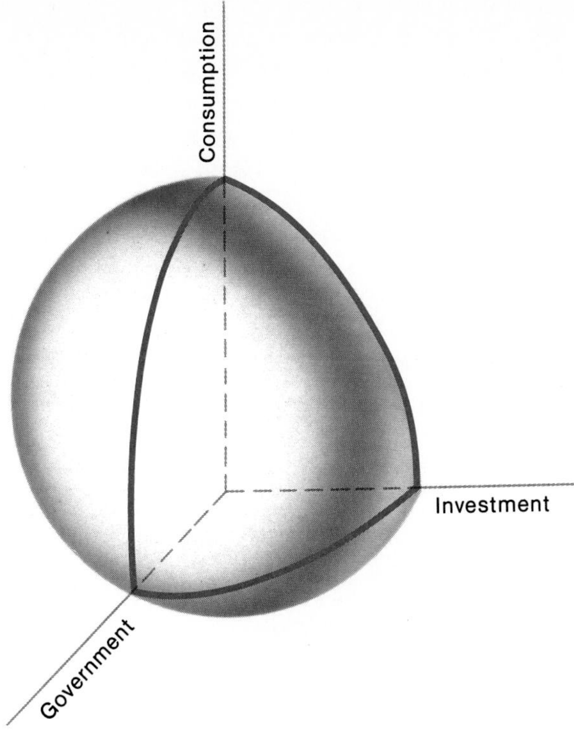

FIGURE 3
A Production Possibility Surface
Actually, there is a frontier for every kind of output, but we have no way of depicting such a fantastic array. Here is a three-dimensional P–P surface that shows the frontier for these crucial outputs: consumption, investment, government.

curve depicts the best we can do, given our labor force and our stock of capital goods. But it does not depict how well we will actually do. That depends on how fully we utilize our productive capacity—how far we drive the economy toward its frontiers.

What determines that? We already know the answer. It is the level of national demand, the volume of aggregate purchasing power, the size of our gross national income. How does income grow to propel the economy to the limits established by its human and material resources? That is the vital question to which we turn next.

LOOKING BACK

KEY CONCEPTS

Growth is the central trend.

1 Growth is the central concern of macroeconomics and it is a central trend of the economy. In this chapter we analyze the growth of supply; in our next, the growth of demand. In Chapter 5 we saw that our real per capita growth has increased at about 1.5 percent a year, plus or minus 10 percent. This doubles real per capita living standards every 47 years.

Increases in labor inputs reflect population

2 Growth comes from increases in the quantity or quality of our main inputs, labor and capital. Increases in the quantity of labor have

growth and changes in participation rates.

resulted from growth in population and a gradual rise in the overall participation rate, especially by women.

Total labor hours have roughly doubled from 1900 to 1980.

3 Weekly work hours have decreased since the turn of the century. Overall, it is likely that total labor hours (labor force times working hours) have slightly more than doubled from 1900 to 1980.

Labor hours today embody more education, but the labor force works in less productive occupations.

4 Changes in the quality of labor are more difficult to measure. They include increases in the amount of education embodied in the labor force and adding to the value of our human capital, and also changes in the kinds of work we do. There has been a long-term shift into service occupations, which have a lower than average rate of productivity and growth.

Total real output is up ten times since 1900. Much of this comes from capital but we cannot measure increases in quantity vs. quality.

5 Total real output between 1900 and today has increased some tenfold. A major portion of this growth must come from capital inputs. However, it is almost impossible to separate changes in the quantity and quality of capital, because capital is always changing.

Investment is the process by which we add to the quantity of capital; technology adds to its quality.

6 Although quantity and quality are almost impossible to separate, we speak of increases in the quantity of capital as arising through investment, and increases in its quality as arising through technology. In fact, an act of saving and investment is the means by which invention or innovation takes place.

R&D is a key activity, recently declining as a percent of GNP.

7 The sources of technology are not clearly understood. Research and development activities are likely a very important source of technological improvement; recently the share of R&D spending has been declining in the United States.

Changes in labor and capital inputs move out the production possibility frontier.

8 Production possibility curves can now be seen as describing provisional constraints on growth. We can move the frontiers out by the changes in labor and capital inputs we have been describing. We must now learn about the impetus that sets growth in motion.

ECONOMIC VOCABULARY

Participation rates 218
Human capital 220
Deepening vs. widening capital 221
R&D 223
Production possibility curves 223
Production frontiers 223

QUESTIONS

1. Set up a production possibilities curve for an economy producing food and steel. Show how some combinations of food and steel cannot be produced, even

though each of the goods lies within the limit of production on its own axis. Explain why the *P-P* curve is bowed. (If you can't, reread page 224.)

2. Think about ways in which education can improve productivity—and ways in which it cannot. Would you think that going or not going to elementary school would have a greater or lesser effect on output per hour than going to college? In what line of work?
3. Try to think of some kinds of capital that have remained essentially unchanged over the last 50 years. How about ordinary tools, such as those that a carpenter uses? Can you picture in your mind's eye the effect of widening this kind of capital to match a growing force of carpenters, as against equipping the force with new kinds of tools such as power saws?
4. Is it possible for an economy that fails to invest to continue to grow? Suppose it works harder? Are there limits to such kinds of growth? Are there limits to the growth that new and better capital will bring?

CHAPTER 14

The Growth of Demand

A LOOK AHEAD

This chapter explains the relationship between the growth of *potential* output and the growth of output that the economy actually enjoys. In the last chapter we learned about the elements that determine how fast we *could* grow—mainly the quantity and quality of labor and capital. We also saw that expenditure was the link in the circular flow that determined how much of our potential output we actually bought.

In this chapter we pursue the matter of expenditure further. Specifically, we gain an understanding of a key process by which saving becomes the necessary condition for investment, or capital formation. The savings-investment relationship is therefore at the heart of this chapter. It is not the whole answer to the growth of demand—that will have to await a study of the monetary system. But the savings-investment link will give us the first deep grasp of how a macroeconomy really "works"—not in a circular flow, but in the dynamic fashion that is its hallmark.

Note: At the end of the chapter, on page 238 there are four questions. Answer them! If you can show, in words or diagrams, that you have mastered these four questions, you are well launched into the study of macroeconomics.

Our model of a circular flow economy which buys back all its output by spending all its receipts begins to explain how our economic system works—and why sometimes it does not work. Yet it leaves us in the dark with respect to the central question of growth, for an economy that merely bought back all its output by spending all its receipts would not grow. It would remain in place, reproducing itself from year to year. If we want to put growth into the picture, we have to add something that has so far been lacking from our exposition.

That missing element is a process central to all capitalist economies—indeed, to all economies whose output tends to expand. It is the process by which some of the factors of production are directed into the making of goods that will enable the economy to break out of its circular flow. As we already know, these output-creating, growth-inducing uses are called *net investment,* or *capital formation,* and the manner in which factors are put to this dynamic use is called the *savings-investment link.* That is the key process we look into in this chapter.

The Meaning of Saving

We begin by making sure that we understand a key word—*saving.* **Saving, for an economist, is not just putting money in the bank. Rather, it is refraining from spending *all or part of income for consumption goods or services.*** It should be very clear then why saving is such a key term. In our discussion of the circular flow it became apparent that expenditure was the critical link in the steady operation of the economy. If saving is not-spending, then it would seem that saving could be the cause of just that kind of downward spiral of which we caught a glimpse in that discussion.

And yet this is clearly not the whole story. The act of investing—of spending money to direct factors into the production of capital goods—requires an act of saving. To say it again, because it is very important, **we must save—that is, not use all our income for consumption—if we are to have the ability to hire factors to build capital goods. A society that did no saving would have no way of breaking out of a stationary circular flow.**

Hence saving is necessary for the process of investment. Now, how can one and the same act be necessary for economic expansion and a threat to an economy's stability?

The Demand Diagram

Let us use a diagram to show how saving can create both a "gap" in demand and an "opening" for investment.

In Figure 1 we trace the flow of expenditure through the economy from left to right. On the left we start with three blocks showing the factor, tax, and depreciation costs that have been incurred by businesses and government agencies as costs of production. Now we are going to follow those costs as they become incomes to different sectors, and thereafter as they are translated into new demand through the act of expenditure.

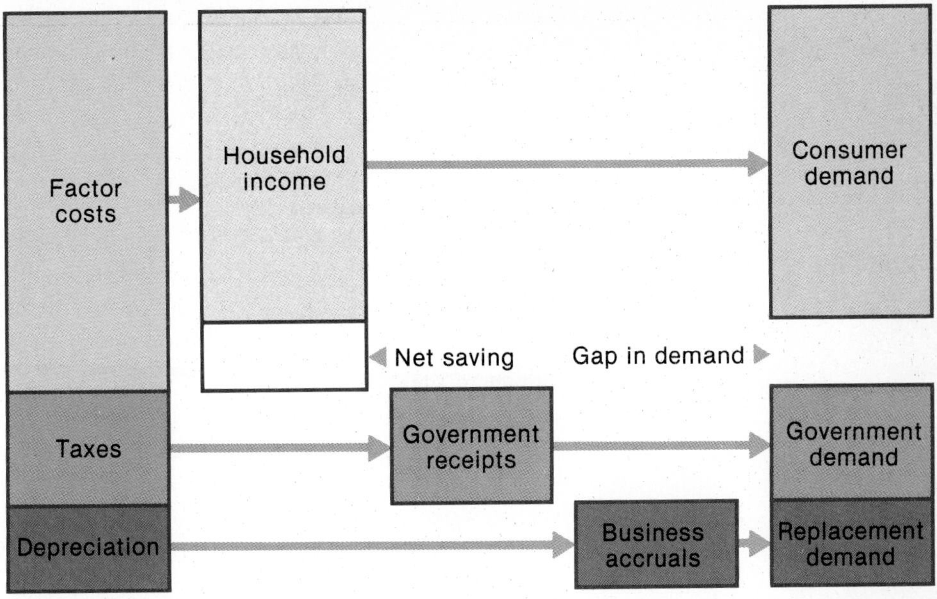

FIGURE 1
The Demand Gap
We have used a circular flow type of diagram to show how a demand gap—and also an opening for investment—can arise. We assume that business and government spend all their receipts. Of course, that assumption may not be true—but it highlights the effects of saving in the household sector, which is the focus of our present investigation.

Look at the blocks for taxes and depreciation first. Here we see that an amount of taxes becomes the exact equivalent amount of government receipts; and thereafter an equal amount of government expenditure. (We could think of this as a sum of indirect taxes that becomes the income of a city government and thereafter is all paid out as salaries to city employees.) Clearly there is no gap in demand here. But neither is there an opening for investment.

The same analysis applies to the bottom block. First we see the cost of depreciation, every penny of which becomes a receipt of the business sector, and all of which is spent as replacement investment. No gap here, and no net investment either.

The Gap

But now look at the top block, representing factor costs. Every penny of those costs becomes factor income, as our diagram shows. This must be the case because all costs, as we know, are incomes. If households now spent all their income, there would be no gap here either, and we would have a stationary, circular flow economy. But our diagram shows that households save a part of their incomes. The result is precisely what we would expect. **There is a gap in demand introduced by the deficiency of consumer spending.** It begins to look as if we are approaching the cause of economic recession and unemployment. Yet whereas we have introduced net saving, we have forgotten about its counterpart, net investment. Cannot the investment activity of a growing economy in some way close the demand gap?

The Dilemma of Saving

This is indeed, as we shall soon see, the way out of the dilemma. But before we trace the way investment compensates for saving, let us draw some important conclusions from the analysis we have made up to this point.

1. Any act of saving, in and by itself, creates a gap in demand, a shortage of spending. Unless this gap is closed, there will be trouble in the economic system, for employers will not be getting back as receipts all the sums they laid out.
2. The presence of a demand gap forces us to make a choice. If we want a dynamic, investing economy, we will have to be prepared to cope with the problems that net saving raises. If we want to avoid these problems, we can close the gap by urging consumers not to save. Then we would have a dependable circular flow, but we would no longer enjoy economic growth.

THE OFFSET TO SAVINGS

How, then, shall we manage to make our way out of the dilemma of saving? The diagram makes clear what must be done. **If a gap in demand is due to the savings of households, then *that gap must be closed by the expanded spending of some other sector.*** There are only two other such sectors: government and business. Thus in some fashion or other, the savings of one sector must be offset by the increased activity of another.

But how is this offset to take place? How are the resources that are relinquished by consumers to be made available to entrepreneurs in the business sector or to government officials? In a market economy there is only one way that resources or factors not being used in one place can be used in another: Someone must be willing and able to hire them.

Whether or not government and business *are* willing to employ the factors that are not needed in the consumer goods sector is a critical matter, soon to command much of our attention. But let us suppose that they are willing. How will they be able to do so? How can they get the necessary funds to expand their activity?

Increasing Expenditure

There are six principal methods of accomplishing this essential increase in expenditure.

1. The business sector can increase its expenditures by *borrowing* the savings of the public through the sale of new corporate bonds.
2. The government sector can increase its expenditures by *borrowing* savings of the other sectors through the sale of new government bonds.
3. Both business and government sectors can increase expenditures by *borrowing* additional funds from commercial banks.*
4. The business sector can increase its expenditures by attracting household savings into partnerships, new stock, or other *ownership* (or *equity*).
5. The government sector can increase its expenditures by *taxing* the other sectors. (We will see later why total spending is likely to increase despite higher taxes.)
6. Both business and government sectors can increase their expenditures by drawing on *accumulated past savings,* such as unexpended profits or tax receipts from previous years.

Claims

The first four of these methods, unlike the last two, operate through the capital markets. They thus give rise to claims, or obligations, that must eventually be honored. And so they reveal from whom funds have been obtained, and on what terms. Bonds, corporate or government, show that savings have been borrowed from individuals, banks, or firms by businesses and governments. Shares of stock (equities) reveal that savings have been obtained on an ownership basis, as do new partnership agreements. Borrowing from banks means the extension of loans, effectively from the depositors of the banking institution. **Claims in the capital market establish the ownership of new capital assets in a growing economy.**

Public and Private Borrowing

The upper diagram in Figure 2 shows what happens when savings are made available to the business sector by direct borrowing from households. Note the claim (or equity) that arises. If the government were doing the borrowing rather than the business sector, the diagram would look like the lower diagram in Figure 2. Notice that the claim is now a government bond.

We have not looked at a diagram showing business or government borrowing its funds from the banking system. (This process will be better understood when we take up the problem of money and banking, in Chapter 19.) The basic concept, however, although more complex, is much the same as above.

Completed Act of Offsetting Savings

We have seen how it is possible to offset "excess" savings in one sector by increasing the funds available to another sector. There remains one last step. That is to *spend*

*Actually they are borrowing from the public through the means of banks. We shall learn about this in Chapter 19.

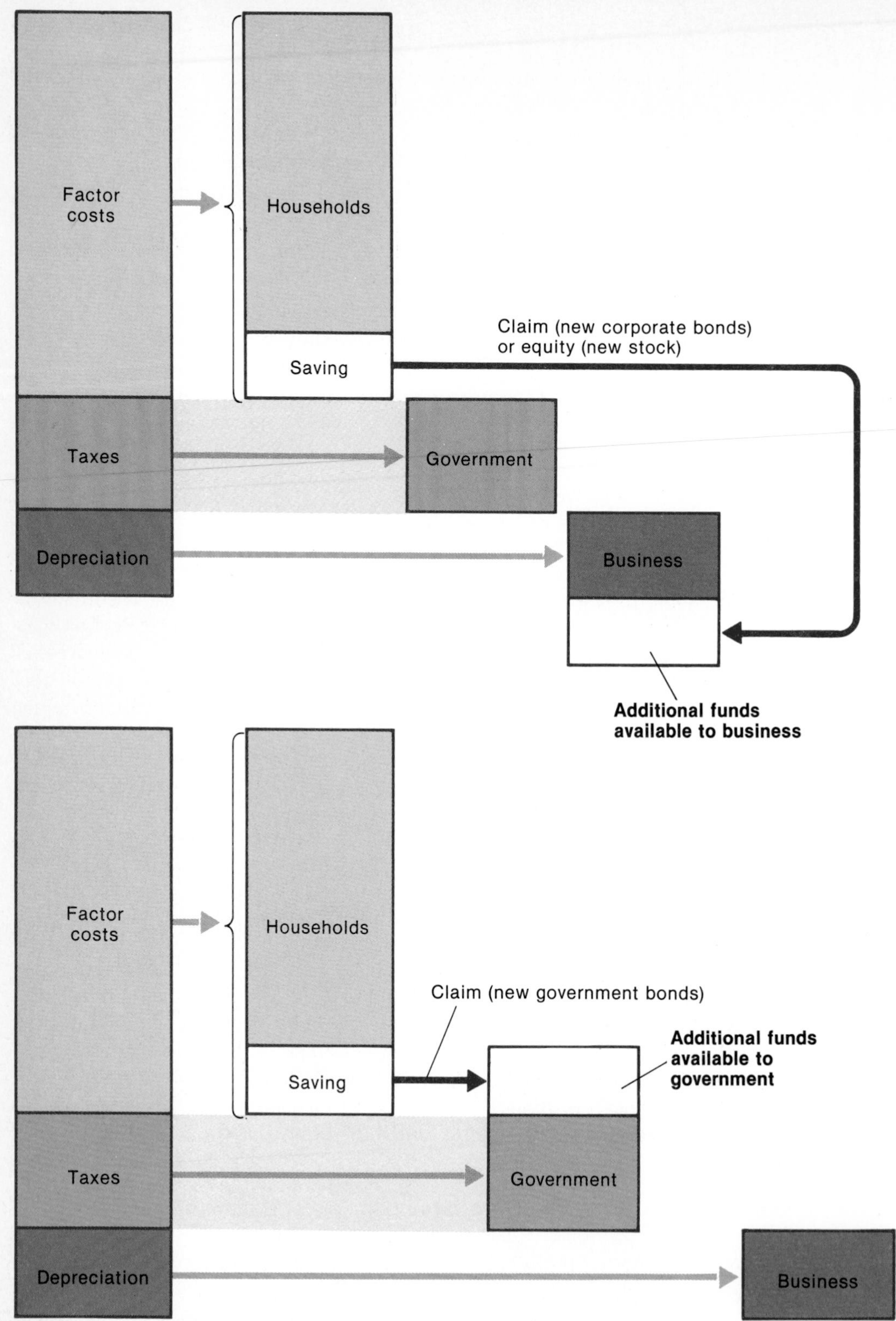

FIGURE 2
Two Ways of Transferring Savings between Sectors
Here we depict the way a demand gap can be closed by transferring the savings of one sector to another that will spend it. Our diagrams show how savings can go to business, in exchange for claims (bonds or stock), or to government, in exchange for government bonds.

those additional funds in the form of additional investment or, in the case of the government, for additional public goods and services. The two completed expenditure circuits appear in Figure 3.

While Figure 3 is drawn so that the new investment demand or new government demand is exactly equal to net saving, **it is important to understand that there is nothing in the economic system guaranteeing that these demands will exactly equal net saving. The desire for new investment or new government goods and services may be either higher or lower than new saving.**

The Savings—Investment Link

An economy which is working normally, in which saving takes place, *must* generate potential demand gaps, and such an economy *must* offset those gaps if it is to function properly. But there is no guarantee that it will do so in practice.

Once this simple but fundamental point is clearly understood, much of the mystery of macroeconomics disappears, for we can then begin to see that an economy in movement, as contrasted with one in a stationary circular flow, is one in which sectors must *cooperate* to maintain the closed circuit of income and output. In a dynamic economy we no longer enjoy the steady translation of incomes into expenditure that, as we have seen, is the key to an uninterrupted flow of output. Rather, we are faced with the presence of net saving and the possibility of a gap in final demand. This savings-investment link is the key to the volume of demand that a market economy will generate. The price of economic growth, in a sense, is the risk of economic decline.

This matter is sufficiently important so that it is worth our while to review it entirely once more. The problem, we recall, was to explain how growth enters the changelessness of a circular flow system. Is it by changes in the quantity and quality of labor and capital that establish the system's production possibility frontier—its potential supply? Or is it through changes in the flows of expenditure of the four great sectors that determine the level of its aggregate demand? The answer is both.

1. ***The stock of our labor and capital resources determine the limits of our growth.*** With all the demand in the world, we cannot grow faster than these real elements allow. But we may not grow as fast as these real factors permit.
2. ***Growth enters the economy when labor and capital are used to produce goods and services that increase our ability to produce.*** Usually these are capital goods. Thus we can think of growth as moving resources and labor from current final consumer goods production into the formation of capital.
3. ***Financial saving is the way in which a market economy carries out these transfers of resources.*** When we save part of our income—for instance, when we put money into a bank—we refrain from using all our potential spending power. The saving that we perform has a counterpart in the labor and capital that we "free up" by not consuming to our full abilities.
4. ***These freed resources are now available for bringing about the changes in supply that will give us more (or better) output.*** Thus savings are the indispensable condition for capital formation and growth. But the act of financial saving creates a problem along with this opportunity. The problem

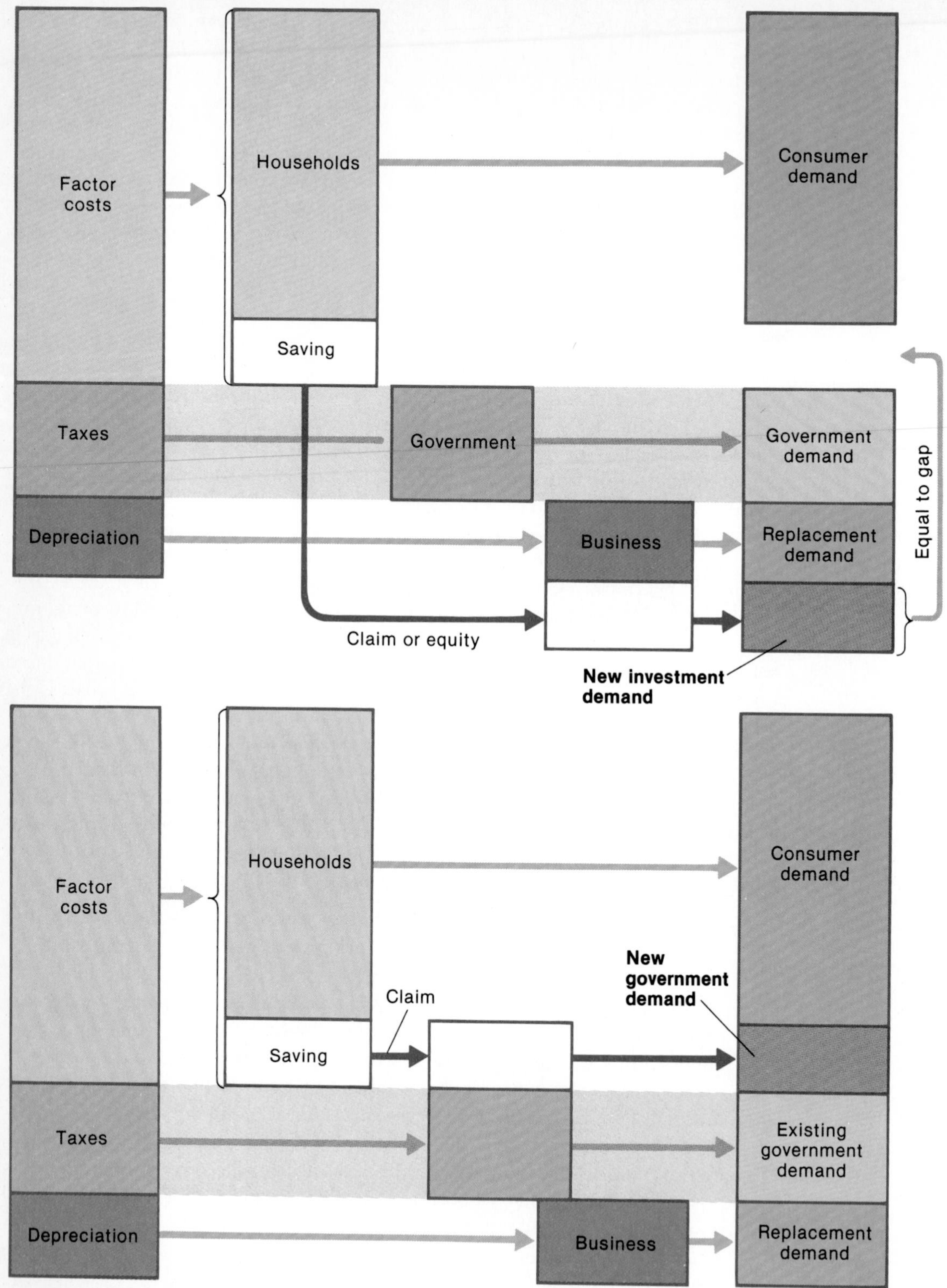

FIGURE 3

Two Ways of Closing the Demand Gap

Here we show how the savings of the household sector, now transferred to business or government, is spent by these latter sectors to offset the gap in demand in consumption. **Note:** *There is no guarantee that the offsets will just balance the savings.*

is the demand gap that must be offset by additional expenditure if GNP is not to decline.

5. ***Even if savings are offset by net investment, there is no guarantee that growth will be adequate.*** The volume of investment spending may fall short of the amount needed wholly to compensate for the diminution of consumer spending. Or the new output may prove unsuited to the market, creating losses for investing firms instead of profits. Or government fiscal or monetary policies may interfere with the growth process.
6. ***Last but not least, there may be more additional business or government spending than the flow of savings can accommodate.*** The pressure of total demand, in that case, may be greater than the value of the existing, or easily available, supply. The result will be inflation as well as growth.

Setting the Agenda

These considerations also establish the agenda for the chapters to come. First, we need to learn more about how savings are generated in the consumer sector and how they are put to use in the business sector. That will occupy us in the chapters immediately ahead. Thereafter we have to look into the public sector—not only because government is itself an absorber of saving, but also because government policies, including unbalanced budgets, are clearly an important part of the total growth problem and process. And that still leaves the question of money. Until we have looked at the operations of the banking system and the relation between the amount of money and the volume of spending, we cannot fully grasp the growth mechanism.

Finally, we must confront a question that will run through all these chapters: *Can we control the growth process?* Can we avoid or mitigate recessions or slow growth? Can we avoid or curb inflationary growth? These are the large questions in macroeconomics, questions to which we will turn in Chapters 23 and 24.

LOOKING BACK

KEY CONCEPTS

The meaning of saving

1 Saving is indispensable for investment. To save means to refrain from using all our income for consumption, thus freeing resources for use as capital wealth.

Saving is necessary for growth, but creates a demand gap.

2 A circular flow economy has no gaps. But if we introduce the act of saving, there will be some purchasing power that is not returned to the economy. Thus the act of saving, which is necessary for growth, creates the necessity to offset the gap it leaves in spending.

Intersectoral transfers of saving against claims

3 Demand gaps can only be offset if another sector increases its spending sufficiently to offset the gap. The second sector can do this by issuing claims or equities—such as bonds or stocks—that attract saving for its use.

Necessity of sectoral cooperation; offsets must balance gaps

4 The essential point is that intersectoral cooperation is necessary in any modern economy that has net saving. Saving creates the conditions for growth—and for decline. There must be offsets to demand gaps if GNP is not to decline. And needless to say, if the offsets are too large, inflation will follow.

Growth requires both adequate supply and adequate demand.

5 Growth is a complicated process that requires changes in the supply of and demand for GNP. Without increases in the quantity or quality of labor and capital inputs, growth is impossible, no matter how large expenditures may be. And without adequate expenditure, growth will not take place, no matter how much labor and capital is available.

Saving releases capital and labor for the purpose of capital formation.

6 Growth takes place because financial saving releases capital and labor from consumption (or other uneconomical) tasks for the purpose of capital formation. Matching the supply of labor and capital with the right amount of demand is the central problem of macroeconomics.

ECONOMIC VOCABULARY

Saving 230
Demand gap 231
Claims 233
Linkage of savings and investment 235
Intersectoral cooperation 235

QUESTIONS

1. Show what we mean by a demand gap in a diagram. (And draw the diagram very, very carefully.)
2. In the same diagram show how this gap can be offset by business investment. Now show how the gap could have been filled by government spending.
3. Why is saving indispensable for investment? Can you think of any way in which a society could gather together the factors of production to undertake investment without performing an act of saving? From this point of view, what does "saving" mean?
4. Can we have an act of saving without an act of investment?

AN EXTRA WORD ABOUT

National Savings

In this chapter, we have discussed the economic meaning of savings as the withholding of resources from current consumption necessary to build for the future. In this extra word, we take a first look at what has happened to savings in the United States in recent years.

National savings are the sum of savings by private individuals and government savings. *Private savings* correspond closely to what we think of as savings in ordinary language: the amounts that individuals set aside from current income, plus whatever businesses set aside out of their current profits.

What does government set aside as savings? The conventional answer is the part of its tax income that is not spent. From this viewpoint, government saving is equal to the government's budget surplus. In recent years government has been continually in deficit rather than surplus, so it follows that the deficit measures negative government saving, or *government dissaving.*

It is important to note, however, that this way of measuring government saving and dissaving is not consistent with the way we measure the same concepts in the private sector. For our measure of government spending *includes current outlays and all expenditures on public investment activities,* whereas private businesses separate their current outlays from investment expenditures. In the private sector, savings are calculated *before* investment expenditures are made, whereas in the public sector we call "savings" what is left *after* investment expenditure has been taken out.

Table 1 shows how we must adjust our conventional accounts to reflect a consistent accounting scheme, on the rough assumption that $100 billion of federal, state, and local government expenditure went for public capital formation in 1988. We see that by the conventional deficit measure, government dissaving (the deficit) came to $93 billion in 1988. But our adjusted measure shows *positive* savings of $7 billion, a figure derived by subtracting all government spending *for purposes other than*

TABLE 1
Saving and Investment in the U.S. Economy, 1988 ($ billions)

	Standard Measure		*Adjusted Measure*	
Consumer saving	+141		+141	
Business saving	+582		+582	
Government saving	−93		+7	
Memo: Spending		−1649		−1549
taxes		+1556		+1556
Total national saving	+641		+741	
Private investment	−765		−765	
Public investment			−100	
Savings shortfall	−135		−135	

Source: Robert Heilbroner and Peter Bernstein, *The Debt and the Deficit,* (New York, Norton, 1989)

investment from all government taxes. This is then accompanied by $100 billion of gross public investment, leaving a total national shortfall of savings of $135 billion, as before.

Table 2 shows the disquieting trends of private saving and "government dissaving" in the United States from 1950 through the first half of 1988. Note that government deficits have doubled as a share of GNP in this decade. Private savings have also taken a sharp decline, from an average of 9.7 percent of GNP to a mere 6.7 percent in the first half of 1988. Thus, total national saving, which was just under 8 percent of GNP in the 1970s, has declined to the 2 to 3 percent range.

Net domestic investment has not, however, fallen nearly so much as national saving. The reason is that *foreign* investment in the United States has risen to over 3 percent of GNP. Thus we are increasingly dependent on foreign capital flows to keep U.S. domestic investment going.

The decline in private savings is not easy to explain. Studies support neither the idea that it is the result of higher rates of consumer indebtedness (the credit card economy of which we hear), nor the suggestion that people are spending against large unrealized capital gains on their stock market investments or their houses. A more serious possibility lies in the effect of high interest rates on pension fund investments, a major component of net savings. Economist Barry Bosworth of the Brookings Institution explains:

> *Contributions to [pension] funds increased sharply in the mid-1970s because the ERISA law required employers to meet minimum funding requirements. Then, in the 1980s much higher market interest rates, used in computing the present value of future liabilities, resulted in many of these plans becoming overfunded, and employer contributions fell off dramatically.*

The fall in personal savings as a share in income remains a troubling problem for

TABLE 2
Net Saving and Investment as a Share of Net National Product, United States, 1951–88:1H percent.

	Percent of Net National Product						
Item	*1951–1960*	*1961–1970*	*1971–1980*	*1981–1985*	*1986*	*1987*	*1988 (prelim)*
Net Saving							
Private saving	8.7	9.4	9.7	8.2	7.4	6.1	6.7
Government saving	−0.7	−1.0	−2.0	−4.6	−5.3	−4.1	−3.6
Total National Investment	8.0	8.4	7.7	3.6	2.1	2.0	3.0
Net foreign investment	0.3	0.7	0.3	−1.3	−3.8	−4.0	−3.3
Net domestic investment	7.7	7.7	7.5	5.0	5.6	5.8	6.1

Source: United States Department of Commerce, *United States National Income and Product Accounts,* Bureau of Economic Analysis.

which no clear solutions have been found. Cutting the budget deficit (for example, by raising taxes) may not succeed in raising total saving, unless offsetting steps (for example, a more expansionary monetary policy) are taken to assure that private incomes, and therefore personal savings, do not fall as public savings are increased. And it makes little sense to try to raise available savings for private purposes by cutting public *capital investment*—it may be that we need the public investments more than we need the private ones. The trick is to raise national income, whence all savings flow. Very likely this will not happen until we have found our way in the international economy; and *that* may have to wait until the world economy itself gets out of the doldrums.

CHAPTER 15

Household Consumption

A LOOK AHEAD

The next three chapters concern the dynamics of the system, approached from the point of view of the major flows that go into GNP. Thus we first study the forces that determine the level of consumption spending; then the forces that act on investment spending; finally those that are paramount in the government sector. These three chapters take us into the heart of macroeconomics by allowing us to understand the manner in which changes in the spending of households, or business firms, or government agencies affect the overall level of GNP.

We begin in Chapter 15 with the household sector.

1 The one essential economic fact in this chapter is the basic passivity of consumption—the fact that consumption has generally followed income and has rarely been an independent economic force of its own.
2 The *propensity to consume* describes how we divide our income between consumption and saving. The *average* propensity to consume describes the division of our *total* income; the *marginal* propensity to consume describes the division of any *changes* in our income.
3 Putting together the propensity to consume and the idea of consumption's passivity we will arrive at a consumption function—a simple mathematical way of depicting how the nation's consumption relates to its income.

With a basic understanding of the crucial role of expenditure and of the complex relationship of saving and investment behind us, we are in a position to look more deeply into the question of the determination of gross national product. For what we have discovered so far is only the *mechanism* by which a market economy can sustain or fail to sustain a given level of output through a circuit of expenditure and receipt. Now we must try to discover the *forces* that dynamize the system, creating or closing gaps between income and outgo. What causes a demand for the goods and services measured in the GNP? Let us begin to answer that question by examining the flow of demand most familiar to us—consumption.

THE HISTORIC PICTURE

Figure 1 shows us the flow of consumption spending since 1929. Certain things stand out.

1. Consumption Spending Is by Far the Largest Category of Spending in GNP. Total consumer expenditures—for **durable** goods such as automobiles or washing machines, for **nondurables** like food or clothing, and for **services** such as recreation or medical care—account for approximately two-thirds of all the final buying in the economy.

2. Consumption Is Not Only the Biggest, but the Most Stable of All the Streams of Expenditure. Consumption is *the* essential economic activity. Even if there is a total breakdown in the social system, households will consume some bare minimum. Further, it is a fact of common experience that even in adverse circumstances, households seek to maintain their accustomed living standards. Thus consumption activities constitute a kind of floor for the level of overall economic activity. **Investment and government spending, as we shall see, are capable of sudden reversals; but the streams of consumer spending tend to display a large measure of stability over time.**

3. In Depression, Inflation, and War, the Share of Consumption in GNP Will Vary. This proportionate fluctuation must reflect changes in the relative importance of investment and government spending. And indeed this is the case. As investment spending declined in the Depression, consumption bulked relatively larger in GNP; as government spending increased during World War II, consumption bulked relatively smaller. **The changing *relative* size of consumption, in other words, reflects broad changes in *other* sectors rather than sharp changes in consuming habits.**

To this broad generalization we must make a partial exception for the behavior of consumption during inflation. As we shall see, consumption can take on a life of its own in periods when consumers buy in advance of their normal needs because they hope to beat expected price rises.

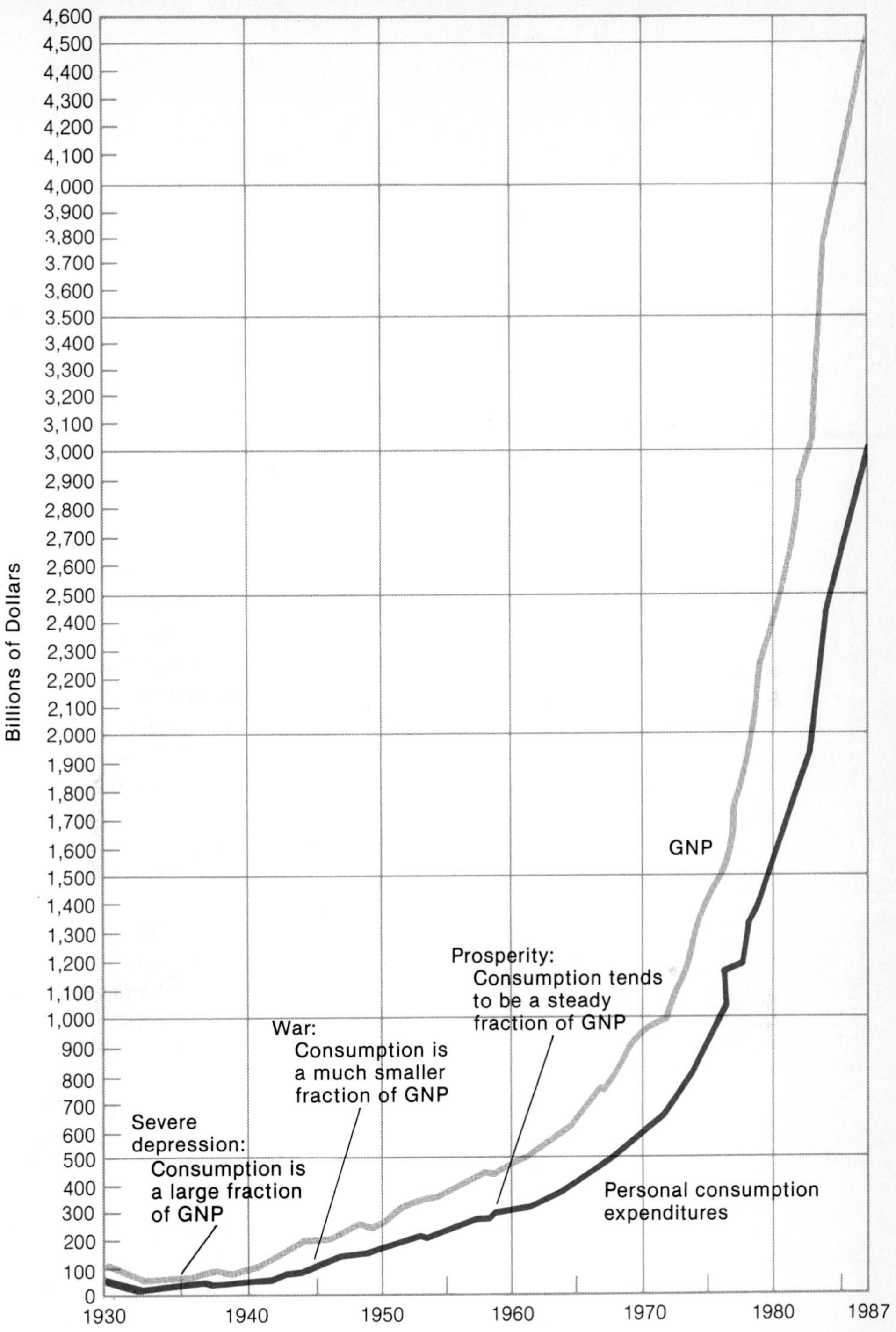

FIGURE 1
The statistics of consumption show that it tends to be a reliably steady share *of GNP. There are two big exceptions to this generalization. Wars roll back consumption to make room for military production, so that consumption falls as a share of GNP. And severe depressions result in a fall in business spending, so that consumption bulks larger as a fraction of GNP.*
Source: *Economic Report of the President, February 1988.*

4. Despite Its Importance, Consumption Alone Will Not "Buy Back" GNP. It is well to recall that consumption, although the largest component of GNP, is still *only* two-thirds of GNP. Government buying and business buying of investment goods are essential if the income-expenditure circuit is to be closed. **During our subsequent analysis it will help to remember that consumption expenditure by itself does not provide the only impetus for demand.**

Consumption, Saving, and Income

This first view of consumption activity sets the stage for our inquiry into the causes of fluctuations in GNP. We already know that the savings-investment relationship lies at the center of this problem and that much saving arises from the household sector. Hence let us see what our knowledge of household consumption can tell us about the supply of saving.

We begin with Figure 2, which shows the relationship of household saving to disposable income—that is, to household sector incomes after the payment of taxes.

We see here two interesting facts. First, in the depths of the Great Depression there were *no* savings in the household sector. In fact, under the duress of unemployment, millions of households were forced to **dissave**—to borrow or to draw on their old savings (hence the negative figure for the sector as a whole). In contrast, we notice the immense savings of the peak war years when incomes were high, consumer goods were rationed, and prices were controlled. Clearly, then, the *amount* of saving is capable of great fluctuation, falling to zero or to negative figures in periods of great economic distress and rising to as much as a quarter of income during the managed economy of wartime.

FIGURE 2
Saving as a Percent of Disposable Income
The ratio of personal savings to disposable income is remarkably steady, war and depression aside. This steadiness will become the basis of an important generalization about the macro behavior of the economy.
Source: *Economic Report of the President.*

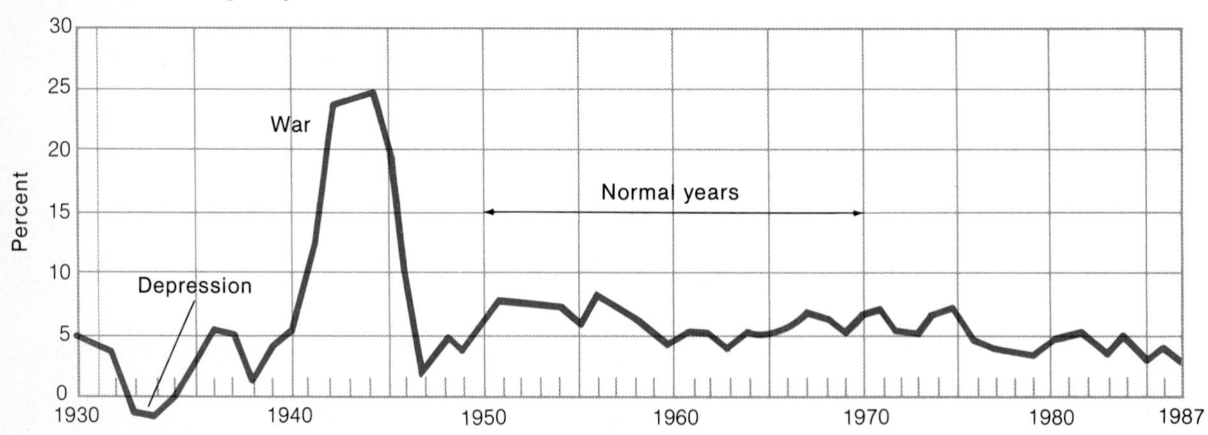

There is another striking fact in this graph, which is that the **savings ratio** shows a considerable stability in normal years. This steadiness is particularly noteworthy in the postwar period. From 1950 to the mid-1980s, consumption has ranged between roughly 92 and 95 percent of disposable personal income—which is, of course, the same as saying that savings have ranged roughly between 8 percent and 5 percent. **If we take the postwar period as a whole, we can see that in an average year we have consumed a little more than 94 cents of each dollar of income and that this ratio has remained fairly constant even though our incomes have increased markedly.**

Long-Run Trends

Looking at the postwar period as a whole, there seems to be a gradual declining trend in the rate of household savings, which were 50 percent higher as a share of income in 1975 than they were 13 years later. Whether this represents a permanent change in behavior patterns, we do not yet know. It worries many economists, who fear that we need to encourage household savings as a source of business investment. Others believe that the problem is better posed the other way around; that higher investment will *create* additional savings by raising our national income. This is an important macroeconomic issue to which we will return.

The long-run trends in the saving ratio interest us for another reason as well. Statistical investigations reveal that rich families tend to save a larger proportion of their incomes than poor ones. Does it not therefore stand to reason that the nation as a whole ought to save a steadily rising fraction of its total income as its wealth increases and as families move from lower to higher income brackets?

Were this so, the economy would face a very serious problem. To sustain higher levels of aggregate income, it would have to match a swelling ratio of savings with an equally fast-growing share of investment. As we shall see in the next chapter, investment is always a source of potential trouble because it is an inherently risky undertaking. If we had to keep on making ever-larger investments compared with GNP to absorb our larger share of savings, we would live in an exceedingly vulnerable economic environment. Yet this is not the case. Our savings ratio, far from rising over time, has displayed a great deal of stability over the last century, and has drifted lower, not higher, in recent years. How do we square this with the fact that our real level of income is much higher than it was, and that almost all families have moved over time from lower to higher income brackets?

Relative Incomes and Saving

The explanation turns on the role of *relative* incomes in determining consumption decisions. That is, individuals set their living standards in relation to the community in which they live—the famous keeping-up-with-the-Joneses syndrome. This habit carries with it an important economic consequence: As income levels rise, so do consumption standards. And so, on average over the whole economy and population, savings rates remain remarkably stable.

For example, a family that earned just the median income in 1989 (about

SAVINGS, INFLATION, AND CREDIT

You will note in Figure 2 a drop in the savings rate starting in 1976 and lasting until 1980 or 1981. This seems to have been a consequence of high inflation rates and easy credit conditions. During the inflation wages did not keep up with prices, mainly because imported goods like oil went up in price much more sharply than domestically produced goods. Moreover, credit was cheap, since inflation meant that borrowings would be repaid in depreciated dollars. So households borrowed heavily. As consumer credit soared, household savings fell.

The "tight money" policy that began in 1979 (coupled with controls put on consumer credit in 1980) broke the back of this borrowing spree. As households found that they were forced to rely more on their incomes, their spending propensities again became more cautious. All in all, the proportion of savings to disposable personal income (income after taxes) rose from 6.8 percent in 1979 to 7.5 percent in 1981. But this effect did not prove durable. By 1985, the personal savings rate had fallen back to 5.1 percent; and by 1987, it had dropped to an all-time low of 3.8 percent.

What caused the drop in personal savings after 1981? One partial explanation lies in the rapid growth of interest due on personal debts, which is a drain on personal savings, and which is up by more than one-half percent of personal disposable income. Another lies in rising net payments to foreigners: also up by about half a percent of income. But perhaps the fundamental reason lies in a growing reliance by consumers on *new debts* with which to finance current consumption. By the end of the 1980s, personal per capita debt levels were at all-time records, with disquieting consequences for the future financial stability of American households.

$30,000) enjoyed a far higher real living standard than a family that earned, say, $3,000 in 1940—despite the fact that in 1940 a $3,000 income put one well *above* the median at that time. But in 1989 our $30,000 family probably saved *less* as a share of income than did our $3,000 family in 1940. Our 1940 family was well-to-do, and saved a share of its income customary for the affluent. But in 1989 our higher living standard made a $30,000 income commonplace; to maintain this standard of living required a higher share of that income. Overall, the requirements of "normal" consumption have seemed to rise about in tandem with income, at least until the emerging credit dependency of recent years.

A similar relative income effect is seen in the savings rates of black families. Since black family incomes are lower than white family incomes, any *given* income has a higher relative position among blacks than it does among whites. Consequently, for any given income level, the average black family saves more than the average white family.

THE CONSUMPTION-INCOME RELATIONSHIP

What we have so far seen are some of the historical and empirical relationships of consumption and personal saving to income. We have taken the trouble to investigate these relationships in some detail since they are among the most important causes of the gaps that have to be closed by investment. But the statistical facts in themselves are only a halfway stage in our macroeconomic investigation. Now we want to go beyond the facts to a generalized understanding of the behavior that gives rise to them. Thus our next task is to extract from the facts certain behavioral *relationships* that are sufficiently regular and dependable for us to build into a new dynamic model of the economy.

If we think back over the data we have examined, one primary conclusion comes to mind. This is the indisputable fact that the *amount* of saving generated by the household sector depends in the first instance upon the income enjoyed by that sector. Despite the long-run stability of the savings ratio, the dollar volume of saving in the economy is susceptible to great variation, from negative amounts in the Great Depression to very large amounts in boom times. Now we must see if we can find a systematic connection between the changing size of income and the changing size of saving.

Propensity to Consume

There is indeed such a relationship. We call it the *consumption function* or, more formally, the *propensity to consume,* a term invented by John Maynard Keynes, the famous English economist, in 1936.* What is this "propensity" to consume? **It means that the relationship between consumption behavior and income is sufficiently dependable so that we can actually *predict* how much consumption (or how much saving) will be associated with a given level of income.**

We base such predictions on a *schedule* that enables us to see the income-consumption relationship over a considerable range of variation. Table 1 is such a schedule.

One could imagine, of course, innumerable different consumption schedules; in

TABLE 1
A Schedule of the Propensity to Consume

A typical propensity to consume schedule shows that savings and consumption both rise as income rises.

Income	*Consumption (Billions of Dollars)*	*Savings*
$100	$80	$20
110	87	23
120	92	28
130	95	35
140	97	43

*See Chapter 3 for more on Keynes.

one society a given income might be accompanied by a much higher propensity to consume (or a lower propensity to save) than in another. But Keynes's basic hypothesis—a hypothesis amply confirmed by research—was that the consumption schedule in all modern industrial societies had a particular basic configuration despite these variations. **The propensity to consume, said Keynes, reflected the fact that, on the average, people tended to increase their consumption as their incomes rose, *but not by as much as their income increased.* In other words, as the incomes of individuals rose, so did both their consumption *and their savings.***

Note that Keynes did not say that the *proportion* of saving necessarily rose. We have seen how involved is the dynamic determination of savings ratios. Keynes merely suggested that in the short run the *amount* of saving would rise as income rose—or to put it conversely again, that families would not use *all* their increases in income for consumption purposes alone. It is well to remember that these conclusions hold in going down the schedule as well as up. **Keynes's basic law implies that when there is a decrease in income, there will be some decrease in the *amount of saving,* or that a family will not absorb a fall in its income entirely by contracting its consumption.**

What does the consumption schedule look like in the United States? We will come to that shortly. First, however, let us fill in our understanding of the terms we will need.

Average Propensity to Consume

The consumption schedule gives us two ways of measuring the fundamental economic relationship of income and saving. One way is simply to take any given level of income and to compute the percentage relation of consumption to that income. This gives us the *average propensity to consume.* In Table 2, using the same hypothetical schedule as before, we make this computation.

The average propensity to consume, in other words, tells us how a society at any given moment divides its total income between consumption and saving. It is thus a kind of measure of long-run savings behavior, for households divide their income between saving and consuming in ratios that reflect established habits and, as we have seen, do not ordinarily change rapidly.

TABLE 2
Calculation of the Average Propensity to Consume
We calculate the average propensity to consume simply by dividing consumption by income.

Income	*Consumption* (*Billions of Dollars*)	*Consumption ÷ Income (Av. Propensity to Consume)*
$100	$80	.80
110	87	.79
120	92	.77
130	95	.73
140	97	.69

Marginal Propensity to Consume

But we can also use our schedule to measure another very important aspect of saving behavior: the way households divide *increases* (or decreases) in income between consumption and saving. This *marginal propensity to consume* is quite different from the average propensity to consume, as the figures in Table 3 (still from our original hypothetical schedule) demonstrate.

Note carefully that the last column in Table 3 is designed to show us something quite different from the last column of the previous table. Take a given income level—say, $130 billion. In Table 2 the average propensity to consume for that income level is .73, meaning that we will actually spend on consumption 73 percent of our income of $130 billion. But the corresponding figure opposite $130 billion in the marginal propensity to consume table (3) is .30. This does *not* mean that out of our $130 billion income we somehow spend only 30 percent, instead of 73 percent, on consumption. It *does* mean that we spend on consumption only 30 percent *of the $10 billion increase* that lifted us from a previous income of $120 billion to the $130 billion level. The rest of that $10 billion increase we saved.

Much of economics, in micro as well as macro analysis, is concerned with studying the effects of *changes* in economic life. It is precisely here that marginal concepts take on their importance. When we speak of the average propensity to consume, we relate all consumption and all income from the bottom up, so to speak, and thus call attention to behavior covering a great variety of situations and conditions. **But when we speak of the marginal propensity to consume, we are focusing only on our behavior toward *changes* in our incomes.** Thus the marginal approach is invaluable, as we will see, in dealing with the effects of short-run fluctuations in GNP.

A Scatter Diagram

The essentially simple idea of a systematic behavioral relationship between income and consumption will play an extremely important part in the model of the economy we shall soon construct. But the relationships we have thus far defined are

TABLE 3
Calculation of the Marginal Propensity to Consume
We calculate the marginal propensity to consume by dividing changes in our consumption by changes in our income.

Income	*Consumption*	*Change in Income*	*Change in Consumption*	*Marginal Propensity to Consume = Change in Consumption ÷ Change in Income*
	(Billions of Dollars)			
$100	$80	—	—	—
110	87	$10	$7	.70
120	92	10	5	.50
130	95	10	3	.30
140	97	10	2	.20

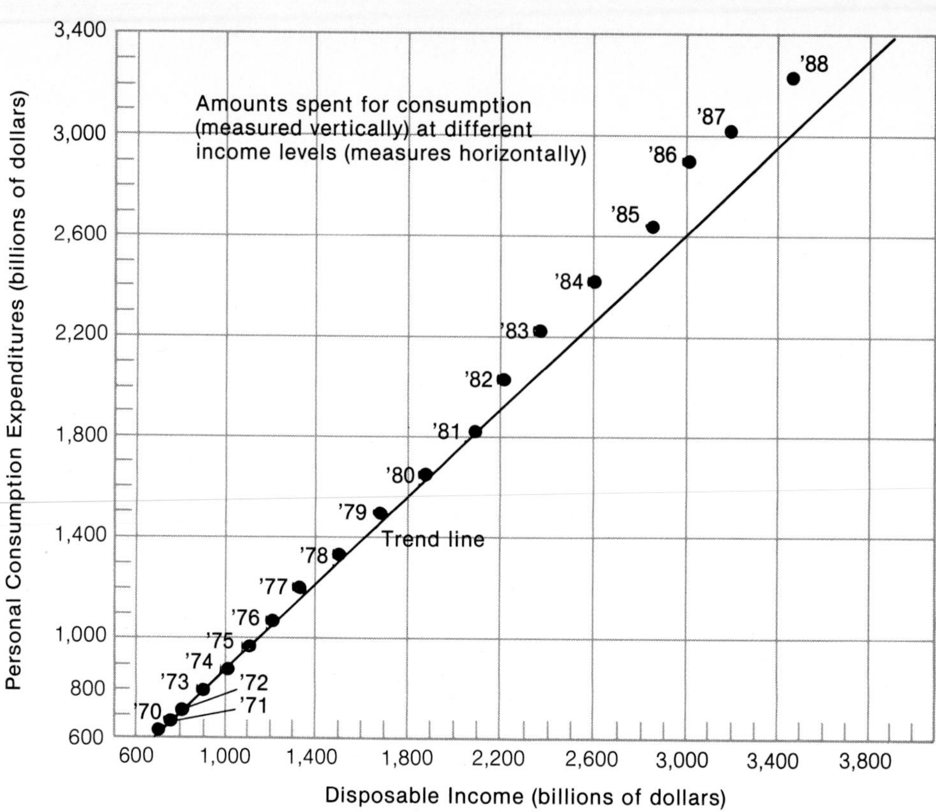

FIGURE 3
U.S. Propensity to Consume, 1970–1988
A scatter diagram shows the functional relationship between two variables—in this case between consumption and income. The trend line is fitted by a statistical technique known as "the least squares method." The trend line shows us the average propensity to consume. We get a very rough (and not very accurate) idea of the marginal propensity to consume by noting the slope of the line between two consecutive years.
Source: *Economic Indicators.*

too vague to be of much use. We want to know if we can extract from the facts of experience not only a general dependence of consumption on income, but a *fairly precise method of determining exactly how much saving will be associated with a given amount of income.*

Here we reach a place where it will help us to use diagrams and simple equations rather than words alone. So let us begin by transferring our conception of a propensity to consume schedule to a new kind of diagram directly showing the interrelation of income and consumption.

The scatter diagram (Figure 3) shows precisely that. Along the vertical axis on the left we have marked off intervals to measure total consumer expenditure in billions of dollars; along the horizontal axis on the bottom we measure disposable personal income (income after direct taxes), also in billions of dollars. The dots tell us, for the years enumerated, how large consumption and income were. For instance, if we take the dot for 1987 and look directly below to the horizontal axis, we can see that disposable personal income for that year was about \$3.2 billion. The same dot measured against the vertical axis tells us that consumption for 1987 was \$3.0 billion. If we now divide the figure for consumption by that for income, we get a value of 93.75 percent for our propensity to consume. If we subtract that from 100, our propensity to save must have been 6.25 percent.*

Returning to the diagram itself, we notice that the black line which fits the trend of the dots does not go evenly from corner to corner. If it did, it would mean that each amount of income was matched by an *equal* amount of consumption—in other words, that there was no saving. Instead, the line leans slightly downward, indicating that as income goes higher, consumption also increases, but not by quite as much.

Does the chart also show us marginal propensity to consume? Not really. As we know, our short-run savings propensities are higher than our long-run propensities. This chart shows our settled position from year to year, after the long-run, upward drift of spending has washed out our marginal (short-run) savings behavior.

Nevertheless, if we look at the movement from one dot to the next, we get some notion of the short-run forces at work. During World War II, as a result of high incomes, price controls, and a shortage of some consumer goods, the average propensity to consume was very low. If our chart went back to those years, the dots would form a bulge below the trend line. After the war the marginal propensity to consume was very high. As a matter of fact, for a few years consumption actually rose faster than income, as people used their wartime savings to buy things that were unavailable during the war. Between 1946 and 1947, for example, disposable income rose by some \$9.8 billion, but personal outlays rose by almost \$18 billion! By 1950, however, the consumption-income relationship was back to virtually the same ratio as during the 1930s.

The Consumption Function in Simple Math

There is another way of reducing to shorthand clarity the propensity to consume. Obviously, what we are looking for is a functional relationship between income (Y) the independent variable, and consumption (C), the dependent variable. In mathematical language we write

$$C = f(Y)$$

and we want to discover what f looks like.

Highly sophisticated and complex formulas have been tried to fit values of C and Y. Their economics and their mathematics are both beyond the scope of this book. But we can at least get a clearer idea of what it means to devise a **consumption function** by trying to make a very simple one ourselves. If we look at statistics, we find that during the Depression years, at very low levels of income, consumption was just as large as income itself. In some years it was actually bigger; as we have seen, there was net dissaving in 1933. From this we can estimate a fixed value that

*It is difficult to read figures accurately from a graph. The actual values are: disposable income, \$3,209 billion; consumption, \$3,012 billion; average propensity to consume, 93.86 percent.

consumption would have *if there were no income at all.* And we might hypothesize that a consumption function for the United States would have a fixed value representing this "bottom," plus some regular fraction designating the fraction of income that would be spent once income rose above zero.

A Generalized Consumption Function

This is a very important hypothesis. **It enables us to describe the consumption function as an amount that represents rock-bottom consumption, to which we add additional consumption spending as income rises. If a is the bottom, and subsequent spending out of additional income is $b(Y)$, where b represents this marginal spending propensity, we can now write the consumption function as a whole as:**

$$C = a + b(Y)$$

Suppose that a is \$50 billion, and we know that our actual spending propensity, b, is about 93 percent. Therefore we can get a *very rough* approximation of consumption by taking \$50 billion and adding to it 93 percent of our disposable income over \$50 billion. In 1987, for example, disposable income was \$3,209 billion. If we add \$50 billion and .93 (3209 − 50), we get \$2938. Actual consumption in 1987 was 2.5 percent more than this.

The process of translating economics into econometrics—that is, of finding ways to represent abstract theoretical relationships in terms of specific empirical relations—is a very difficult one. Hence the formulas that relate C and GNP are much more complex than our simple linear function. Nonetheless, even our simple example gives an idea of what the economist and the econometrician hope to find: a precise way of expressing functional interrelations (like those between consumption and income) so that the relations will be useful in making predictions.

Passivity of Consumption

Throughout this chapter we have talked of the dynamics of consuming and saving. **Now it is important to recall the main conclusion of our analysis, the essential passivity of consumption as an economic process.** Consumption spending, we will recall, is a function of income. This means it is a *dependent* variable in the economic process, a factor that is acted *on,* but that does not itself generate spontaneous action.

To be sure, it is well to qualify this assertion. For one thing, consumption is so large a fraction of total spending that small changes can bring large results. In 1974 and again in 1979 consumers held back on car purchases for fear of gasoline shortages, and the effect on automobile sales had a considerable impact on GNP.

Yet these are exceptions to the rule. During the normal course of things, no matter how intense wants may be, consumers ordinarily lack the cash to translate all their desires into effective demand. Brief swings in consumption—as for automobiles—may give rise to short-run fluctuations in saving. But these swings are short-lived and therefore cannot drive the economy upward or downward for any extended period of time.

Can Consumption Drive the Economy?

This highlights an extremely important point. **Wants and appetites *alone* do not drive the economy upward; if they did, we should experience more demand in depressions, when people are hungry, than in booms, when they are well off.** Hence the futility of those who urge the cure of depressions by suggesting that consumers should buy more! There is nothing consumers would ordinarily rather do than buy more. And let us not forget that they are constantly being cajoled and exhorted to increase their expenditures by the multibillion-dollar pressures exerted by the advertising industry.

The trouble is, however, that consumers cannot steadily buy more unless they have steadily higher incomes. Of course, for short periods they can borrow or sharply reduce their rate of savings or draw on their old savings; but each household's borrowing capacity or accumulated savings are limited, so that once these bursts are over, the steady, habitual ways of saving and spending are apt to reassert themselves.

Thus it is clear that in considering the consumer sector we study a part of the economy that, however ultimately important, is not in itself the source of major changes in activity. Consumption mirrors and, as we shall see, can magnify disturbances elsewhere in the economy; but it does not initiate the greater part of our long-run economic fortunes or misfortunes.

LOOKING BACK

KEY CONCEPTS

Consumption spending is the largest and steadiest flow in GNP. Disposable income is factor earnings after direct taxes.

1 The household sector is the largest of the components of GNP. Household income is called disposable personal income—it is factor earnings minus taxes plus transfers. Household expenditures are called consumption. The main categories of consumption are nondurables, durables, and services. Altogether, consumption spending is the biggest and the steadiest of the GNP flows.

2 Despite its steadiness and size, however, consumption fluctuates and will not buy back GNP.

Long-run savings habits have been very stable at 4–8 percent a year.

3 Savings behavior is very steady over the long run. We tend to save about 4 to 8 percent of our household incomes, except for exceptional periods such as war, depression, or inflation. This long-run stability is probably attributable to the sociological factor known as "keeping up with the Joneses."

The propensity to consume is simply a fraction: C to Y. The hypothesis is that changes in income are always used for both saving and consuming.

4 The relation between saving and income is called the propensity to consume. The words themselves simply mean the ratio into which we divide income between consumption and saving. But the behavior hypothesis of the propensity to consume is that *increases* in income are never entirely spent or entirely saved, but are used for both spending and saving in regular, predictable ways.

Average and marginal propensity to consume

5 The measure of the relation between any given level of income and its associated level of consumption is called the *average* propensity to

consume. The relation between a change in income and the associated change in saving or consumption is called the *marginal* propensity to consume.

C = a + b(Y), where *a* is the "bottom" and *b* is the proportion of *Y* used for consumption.

6 The generally accepted hypothesis about consumption behavior is that there is a "bottom"—a level of consumption that will be maintained (for a while) even if income falls below consumer spending by using up past saving to maintain a minimum standard of living. Additional income over this bottom will be divided in some regular way between consumption and saving. The bottom is designated *a.* The division of income (*Y*) between consumption and saving is designated *b.* Thus we write the consumption function as $C = a + b(Y)$.

Consumption is a dependent variable in the GNP flow.

7 Although changes in consumption can exert considerable effects on GNP because of the size of total consumption, consumption is usually a passive element in the flow. It is *Y* that is the independent variable, not *C.*

ECONOMIC VOCABULARY

Nondurables, services, durables 244, 257
Dissaving 246
Savings ratio 247
Propensity to consume 249
Average propensity to consume 250
Marginal propensity to consume 251
Scatter diagram 251
Consumption function 253
Disposable personal income 257

QUESTIONS

1. Why are some components of consumption more dynamic than others? Why, for instance, does the demand for durables fluctuate more widely than that for services? (Has *durability* something to do with it?)
2. "The reason we have depressions is that consumption isn't big enough to buy the output of our farms and factories." What is wrong about this statement? Is it *all* wrong?
3. Suppose a family has an income of $30,000 and saves $1,500. What is its average propensity to consume? Can you tell from this information what its marginal propensity to consume is?
4. Suppose the same family now increases its income to $32,000 and its saving to $1,750. What is its new propensity to consume? Now can you figure out its marginal propensity to consume?
5. Draw a scatter diagram to show the following:

Family Income	*Savings*
$20,000	$ 0
25,000	250
30,000	750
35,000	1,500
40,000	2,500

From the figures above, calculate the average propensity to consume at each level of income. Can you calculate the marginal propensity to consume for each jump in income?

AN EXTRA WORD ABOUT

The Household Sector

Largest and in many respects most important of all the sectors in the economy is that of the nation's households—that is, its families and single-dwelling individuals (the two categories together are called *consumer units*) considered as receivers of income and transfer payments* or as savers and spenders of money for consumption.

How big is this sector? In 1987 it comprised some 64 million families and some 23 million independent individuals who collectively gathered in $3,780 billion in income and spent $3,209 billion. As Figure 1 shows, the great bulk of receipts was from factor earnings; transfer payments played only a relatively small role. As we can also see, we must subtract personal tax payments from household income (or personal income, as it is officially designated) before we get disposable personal income—income actually available for spending. It is from disposable personal income that the crucial choice is made to spend or save. Notice the presence of savings in the bar on the right. This is the source of a demand gap that other sectors will have to fill.

SUBCOMPONENTS OF CONSUMPTION

Finally we see that consumer spending itself divides into three main streams. The largest of these is for an assortment of expenditures we call consumer services, comprising such things as rent, doctors' or barbers' services, transportation, and other purchases that are not a physical good but work performed by someone or some equipment. Second largest is for **nondurable** goods, such as food and clothing or other items whose economic life is (or is assumed to be) short. Last is a substream

*Remember that the word *transfer* refers to payments made unilaterally—that is, without any service being performed by the recipient. Social security (or any pension) is a transfer payment. So are unemployment insurance and business subsidies and allowances paid to children.

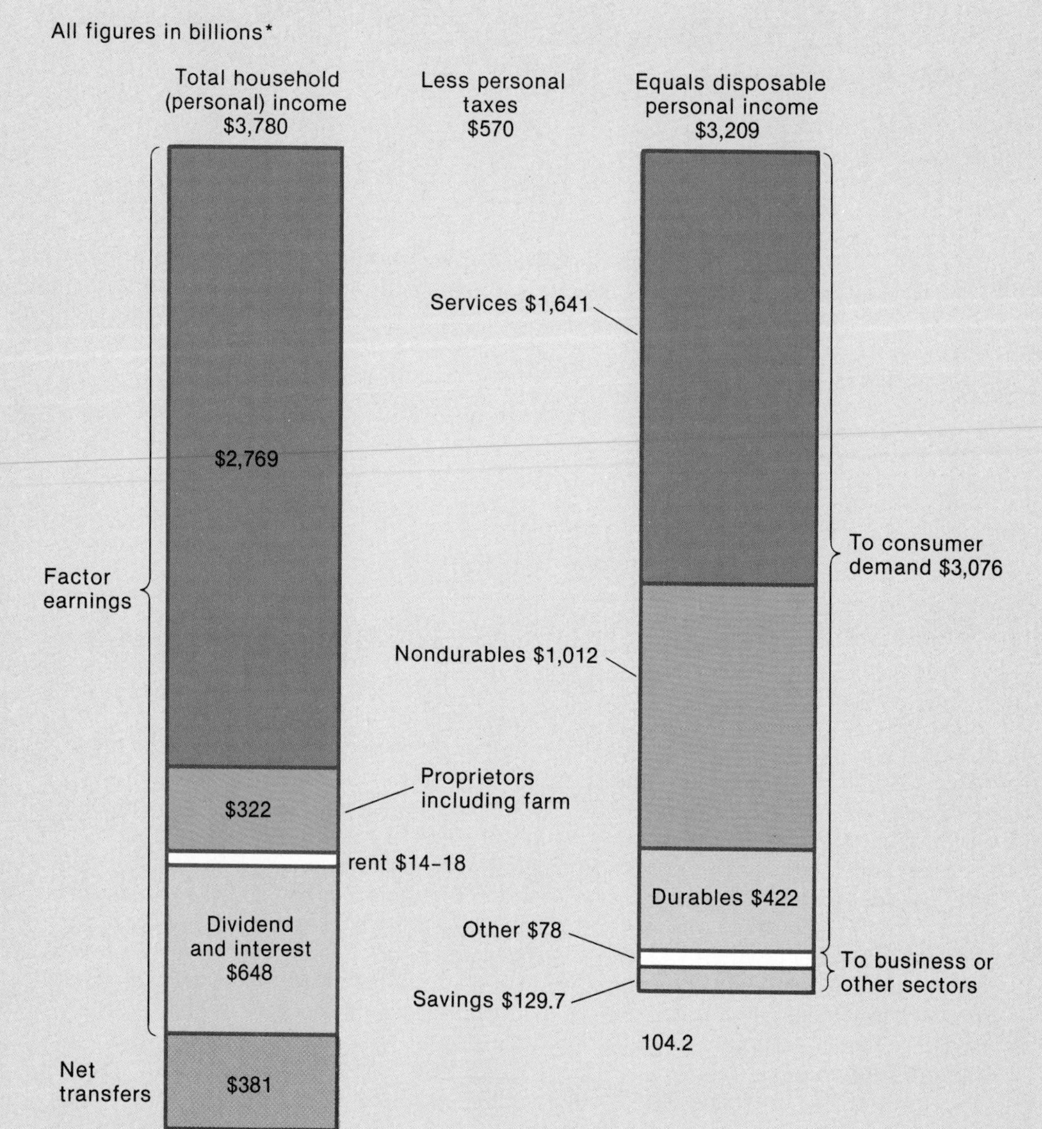

*Totals do not always add, owing to rounding

FIGURE 1
Household Sector, 1987
Notice that the consumption flow chart shows that the sector is a net saver. Here is the source of a demand gap that other sectors must compensate for.
Source: *Economic Indicators.*

of expenditure for consumer **durable** goods, which, as the name suggests, include items such as cars or household appliances whose economic life is considerably greater than that of most nondurables. We can think of these goods as comprising consumers' physical capital.

There are complicated patterns and interrelations among these three major streams of consumer spending. As we would expect, consumer spending for durables is extremely volatile. In bad times, such as 1933, it sank to less than 8 percent of all consumer outlays; in the peak of good times in the early 1970s, it came to nearly double that. Meanwhile, outlays for services have been a steadily swelling area for consumer spending in the postwar economy. As a consequence of the growth of consumer buying of durables and of services, the relative share of the consumer dollar going to soft goods has been slowly declining.

These internal dynamics of the household sector do not affect the basic passive behavior of that sector, but are very important for business planning.

CHAPTER 16

Business Investment

A LOOK AHEAD

Warning! This is also a chapter that ought to be read twice. It contains ideas that are both new and important. What is more, the vocabulary is one that most of us are not used to.

1 The vocabulary: Investment, unlike consumption, is not an activity we are familiar with at first hand; we have to learn to think of it in real terms, not financial ones.
2 There are two new ideas, both much used by economists: (a) The idea of the multiplier. You will want to learn the formula for the multiplier and to understand why it is determined by the marginal propensity to save. (b) The idea of marginal efficiency. Here you need to know about discounting future income—the key to understanding expected profit and the decision-making process behind investment.
3 Most important of all: Investment gives us the first real insight into why the macro system can be unstable. It is not only the key to growth, it is also the key to booms and busts. That's the idea that will unify the pages ahead.

In studying the behavior of the consumption sector, we have begun to understand how the demand for GNP arises. Now we must turn to a second source of demand—investment demand. This requires a shift in our vantage point. As experienced consumers, we know about consumption, but the activity of investing is foreign to most of us. Worse, we are apt to begin by confusing the meaning of investment, as a source of demand for GNP, with "investing" in the sense familiar to most of us when we think about buying stocks or bonds.

Investment: Real and Financial

We should begin, then, by making certain that our vocabulary is correct. **Investing—or investment, as the economist uses the term in describing the demand for GNP—is an activity that uses the resources of the community to maintain or add to its stock of physical capital.** It is the counterpart of the real activity of saving we learned about in Chapter 14.

Investment may or may not coincide with the purchase of a security. When we buy an ordinary stock or bond, we usually buy it from someone who has previously owned it, and therefore our personal act of "investment" becomes, in the economic view of things, merely a *transfer* of claims without any direct bearing on the creation of new wealth. A pays B cash and takes his General Output stock; B takes A's cash and doubtless uses it to buy stock from C; but the transactions between A and B and C in no way alter the actual amount of real capital in the economy. Only when we buy *newly issued* shares or bonds, and then only when their proceeds are directly allocated to new equipment or plant, does our act of personal financial investment result in the addition of wealth to the community. In that case, A buys stock directly (or through an investment banker) from General Output itself, and not from B. A's cash can now be spent by General Output for new capital goods, as presumably it will be.

Thus much of investment, as economists see it, is a little-known form of activity for the majority of us. This is true not only because real investment is not the same as personal financial investment, but also because the real investors of the nation usually act on behalf of an institution other than the familiar one of the household. **The unit of behavior in the world of investment is typically the business firm, just as in the world of consumption it is the household.** Boards of directors, chief executives, and small business proprietors are the persons who decide whether or not to devote business cash to the construction of new facilities or to the addition of inventory; and this decision, as we shall see, is very different in character and motivation from the decisions familiar to us as members of the household sector.

INVESTMENT IN HISTORIC PERSPECTIVE

Let us take a look at the flow of investment not over a single year but over many years, as we did with consumption.

In Figure 1 several things spring to our attention. Clearly, investment demand is not nearly so smooth a flow of spending as consumption. Note that gross investment in the depths of the Depression virtually disappeared—that we almost failed to *maintain,* much less add to, our stock of wealth. (Net investment was, in fact, a negative figure for several years.) Note also that investment was reduced during the war years as private capital formation was deliberately limited through government allocations.

Four important conclusions emerge from this examination of investment spending:

1. **As we have many times stressed, investment is a major vehicle for growth. The upward sweep of investment is a basic explanation of our long-run rising GNP.**
2. **As we have already seen, investment spending contains a component—net additions to inventory—that is capable of drastic, sudden shifts. This accounts for much of the wavelike movement of the total flow of investment expenditure.**
3. **Investment spending as a whole is capable of collapses of a severity and degree that are never to be found in consumption.**
4. **Unlike household spending, investment can fluctuate independently of income. It may rise when GNP is low, perhaps to usher in a boom. It can fall when GNP is high, perhaps to trigger a recession. It is an independent variable in the determination of demand.**

The prime example of such a collapse was, of course, the Great Depression. From 1929 to 1933, while consumption fell by 41 percent, investment fell by *91 percent,* as we can see in Figure 1. At the bottom of the Great Depression in 1933, it was estimated that one-third of total unemployment was directly associated with the shrinkage in the capital goods industry. Conversely, whereas consumption rose by a little more than half from 1933 to 1940, investment in the same period rose by *nine times.*

THE MULTIPLIER

We shall look more closely into the reasons for the sensitivity of investment spending. But first a question must surely have occurred to the reader. For all its susceptibility to change, the investment sector is, after all, a fairly small sector. In 1982 total expenditures for gross private domestic investment came to less than one-seventh of GNP, and the normal year-to-year variation in investment spending in the 1960s and 1970s is only about 1 to 2 percent of GNP. To devote so much time to such small fluctuations seems a disproportionate emphasis. How could so small a tail as investment wag so large a dog as GNP?

Snowball Effect

The answer lies in a relationship of economic activities known as the *multiplier.* **The multiplier describes the fact that additions to spending (or diminutions in**

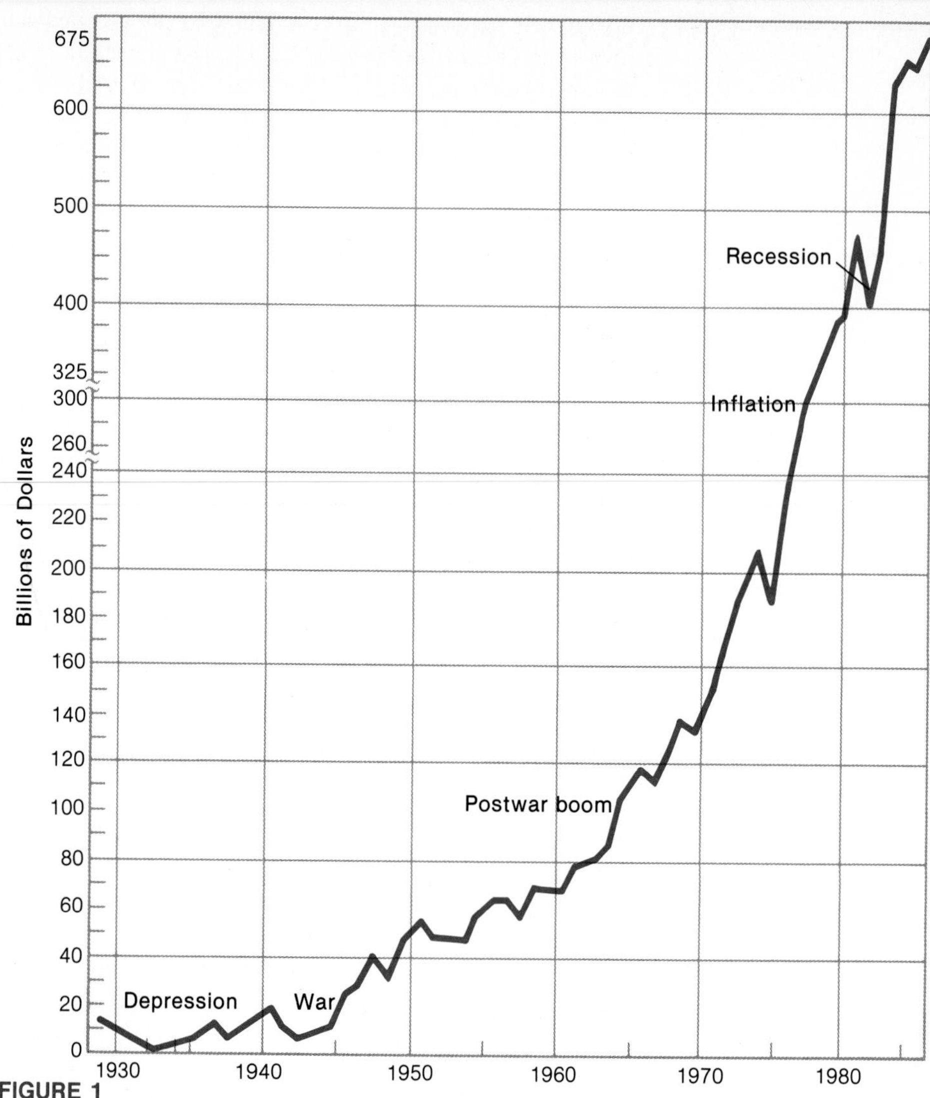

FIGURE 1
Gross Private Domestic Investment 1929–1987
It is evident that investment is a much more volatile item than consumption. Look at the collapse in the Great Depression. The World War II trough was different—investment was pushed aside for war spending. Then came the great postwar boom.
Sources: *Economic Report of the President; Economic Indicators.*

spending) have an impact on income that is greater than the original increase or decrease in spending itself. In other words, even small increments in spending can *multiply* their effects (whence the name).

It is not difficult to understand the general idea of the multiplier. Suppose we have an island community whose economy is in a perfect circular flow, unchanging from year to year. Next, let us introduce the stimulus of a new investment expenditure in the form of a stranger who arrives from another island (with a supply of acceptable money) and proceeds to build a house. This immediately increases the islanders' incomes. In our case, we will assume that the stranger spends $1,000 on wages for construction workers, and we will ignore all other expenditures he may make. (We also make the assumption that these workers were previously unemployed, so that the builder is not merely taking them from some other task.)

Now the construction workers, who have had their incomes increased by $1,000, are very unlikely to sit on this money. As we know from our study of the marginal propensity to consume, they are apt to save some of the increase (and they may have to pay some to the government as income taxes), but the rest they will spend on additional consumption goods. Let us suppose that they save 10 percent and pay taxes of 20 percent on the $1,000 they get. They will then have $700 left to spend for additional consumer goods and services.

But this is not the end of the matter. The sellers of these goods and services will now have received $700 over and above their former incomes, and they too will be certain to spend a considerable amount of their new income. If we assume that their family spending patterns (and their tax brackets) are the same as the construction workers', they will also spend 70 percent of their new incomes, or $490. And now the wheel takes another turn, as still *another* group receives new income and spends a fraction of it.

Continuing Impact of Respending

If the newcomer then departed as mysteriously as he came, we would have to describe the economic impact of his investment as constituting a single "bulge" of income that gradually disappeared. The bulge would consist of the original $1,000, the secondary $700, the tertiary $490, and so on. If everyone continued to spend 70 percent of his new income, after ten rounds all that would remain by way of new spending traceable to the original $1,000 would be about $28. Soon the impact of the new investment on incomes would have virtually disappeared.

But now let us suppose that after our visitor builds his house and leaves, another visitor arrives to build another house. This time, in other words, we assume that the level of investment spending *continues* at the higher level to which it was raised by the first expenditure for a new house. We can see that the second house will set into motion precisely the same repercussive effects as did the first, and that the new series of spendings will be added to the dwindling echoes of the original injection of incomes.

In Figure 2 we can trace this effect. The succession of colored bars at the bottom of the graph stands for the continuing injections of $1,000 as new houses are steadily built. (Note that this means the level of new investment is only being maintained, not that it is rising.) Each of these colored bars now generates a series of secondary, tertiary, etc., bars that represent the respending of income after taxes and savings.

Let us now examine the effects of investment spending in a generalized fashion, without paying attention to specific dollar amounts. In Figure 3 we see the effects of a single *once-and-for-all* investment expenditure (the stranger who came and went)

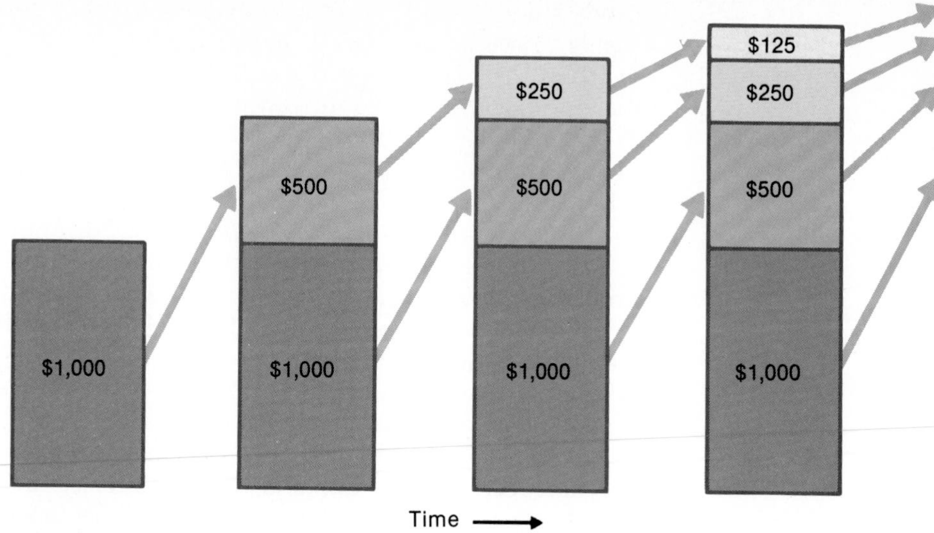

FIGURE 2
The Multiplier
This flow chart shows how respending creates additional income from one period to the next. This addition to income is called the multiplier. The size of the multiplier is the relation between the original new spending ($1,000) and the total new income created ($2,000). In this case, the respending fraction is 50 percent and the multiplier is 2.

FIGURE 3
Once-for-All and Continuing Effects of Investment
A single act of new spending creates a bulge in income that gradually disappears as successive receivers save part of their receipts and therefore do not respend them. A continuing flow of new spending creates a permanent addition to incomes that is larger than the new investment. Here the gradual retirement of new receipts into saving is offset by pumping out fresh additions to income.

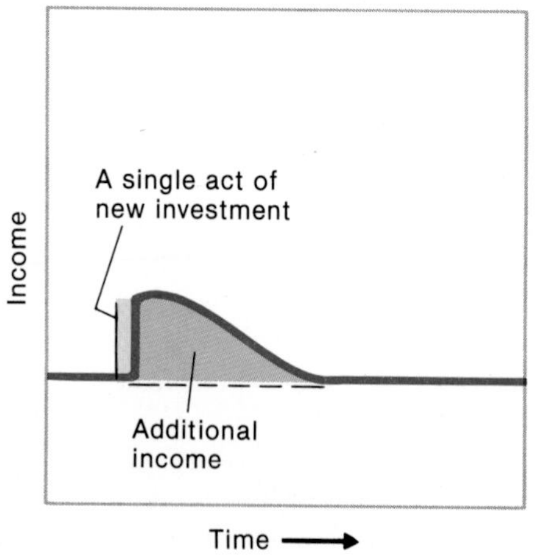

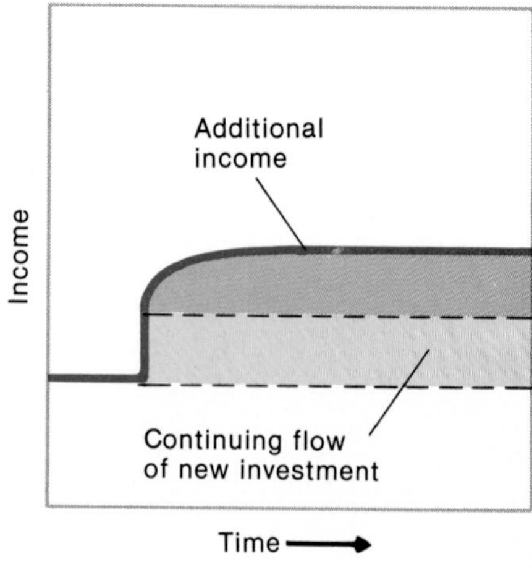

contrasted with the effects of a *continuing* stream of investment.

Our diagrams show two important things:

1. A single burst of investment creates a bulge of incomes larger than the initial expenditure, but a bulge that disappears.
2. A continuing flow of investment creates a new steady level of income, higher than the investment expenditures themselves.

Marginal Propensity to Save

We can understand now that **the multiplier is the numerical relation between the initial new investment and the total increase in income.** If the initial investment is $1,000 and the total addition to income due to the respending of that $1,000 is $3,000, we have a multiplier of 3; if the total addition is $2,000, the multiplier is 2.

What determines how large the multiplier will be? The answer depends entirely on our marginal consumption (or, if you will, our marginal saving) habits—that is, on how much we consume (or save) out of each dollar of additional income that comes to us. Let us follow two cases in Figure 4. In the first, we will assume that each recipient spends only half of any new income that comes to him, saving the rest. In the second case, he spends three-quarters of it and saves one-quarter.

It is very clear that the amount of income that will be passed along from one receiver to the next will be much larger where the marginal propensity to consume is higher. In fact, we can see that the total amount of new incomes (total amount of boxes below) must be mathematically related to the proportion that is spent each time.

What is this relationship? The arithmetic is easier to figure if we use, not the consumption fraction, but the *saving fraction* (the two are, of course, as intimately related as the first slice and the remaining cake). If we use the saving fraction, the sum of new incomes is obtained by taking the reciprocal of the fraction we save. Thus if we save ½ our income, the total amount of new incomes generated by respending will be ½ inverted, or 2 (twice the original increase in income). If we save ¼, it will be the reciprocal of ¼, or 4 times the original change.

Basic Multiplier Formula

We call the fraction of new income that is saved the *marginal propensity to save* (often abbreviated as *mps*). As we have just seen, this fraction is the complement of an already familiar one, the marginal propensity to consume (*mpc*). If our marginal propensity to consume is 80 percent, our marginal propensity to save must be 20 percent; if our mpc is three-quarters, our mps must be one-quarter. *In brief, mps + mpc = 1.*

Understanding the relationship between the marginal propensity to save and the size of the resulting respending fractions allows us to state a very simple (but very important) formula for the multiplier:

change in income = multiplier × change in investment

Case I: Marginal propensity to save, 50 percent. Low multiplier.

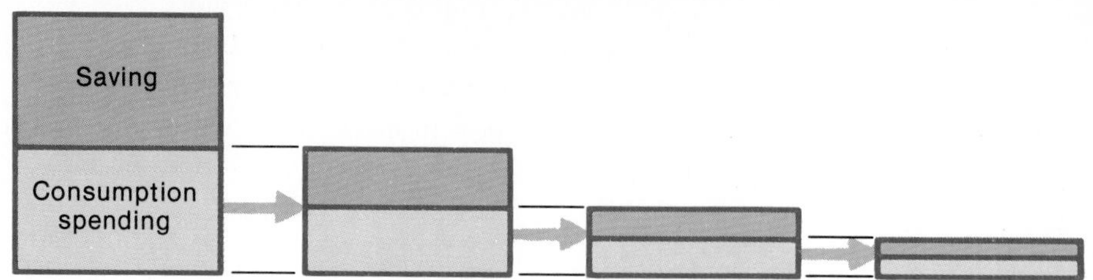

Case II: Marginal propensity to save, 25 percent. High multiplier.

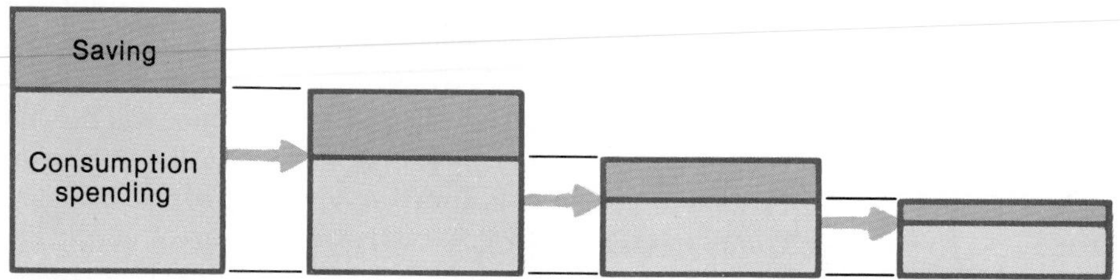

FIGURE 4
Comparison of Two Multipliers
The graph makes visually apparent the obvious fact that the amount we can respend is determined by the amount we save. Therefore the lower our savings ratio, the higher the total of our respending. Or vice versa, high marginal propensities to save result in low multipliers.

Since we have just learned that the multiplier is determined by the reciprocal of the marginal propensity to save, we can write:

$$\textbf{multiplier} = \frac{\mathbf{1}}{\mathbf{mps}}$$

If we now use the symbols we are familiar with, plus a Greek letter **Δ**, delta, that means "change in," we can write the important economic relationship above as follows:

$$\Delta Y = \left(\frac{1}{\text{mps}}\right) \times \Delta I$$

Thus, if our mps is ¼ (meaning, let us not forget, that we save a quarter of increases in income and spend the rest), then an increase in investment of $1 billion will lead to a total increase in incomes of $4 billion:

$$\$4 \text{ billion} = \left(\frac{1}{1/4}\right) \times \$1 \text{ billion}$$

Note that the multiplier is a complex or *double* fraction: it is 1/(¼) and *not* 1/4. If the mps is 1/10, $1 billion gives rise to incomes of $10 billion; if the mps is 50 percent, the billion will multiply to $2 billion. And if mps is 1? This means that the entire increase in income is unspent, that our island construction workers tuck away (or find taxed away) their entire newly earned pay. In that case, the multiplier will be 1 also, and the impact of the new investment on the island economy will be no more than the $1,000 earned by the construction workers in the first place.

LEAKAGES

The importance of the size of the marginal savings ratio in determining the effect additional investment will have on income is thus apparent. Now, however, we must pass from the simple example of our island economy to the more complex patterns of real life. The average propensity to save (the ratio of saving to disposable income) runs around 3 to 4 percent. In recent years, the *marginal* propensity to save (the ratio of additional saving to increases in income) figured over the period of a year has not departed very much from this figure. If this is the case, then, following our analysis, the multiplier would be very high. If mps were even as much as 10 percent of income, a change in investment of $1 billion would bring a $10 billion change in income. If mps were nearer 4 percent—the approximate level of the average propensity to save—a change of $1 billion would bring a swing of over $25 billion. Were this the case, the economy would be subject to the most violent disturbances whenever the level of spending shifted.

Taxes. In fact, however, the impact of the multiplier is greatly reduced because the successive rounds of spending are dampened by factors other than personal saving. One of them we have already introduced into our imaginary island economy. This is the tendency of *taxation* to "mop up" a fraction of income as it passes from hand to hand. This mopping-up effect of taxation is in actuality much larger than that of saving. For every dollar of change in income, federal taxes will take about 20 cents, and state and local taxes another 14 cents.

Business Saving. Another dampener is the tendency of respending to swell *business savings* as well as personal incomes. Of each dollar of new spending, perhaps 10 cents goes into business profits, and this sum is typically saved, at least for a time, rather than immediately respent.

Imports. Still another source of dampening is the tendency of consumers and businesses to increase purchases from abroad as their incomes rise. Historically, increasing imports have diverted 4 to 5 percent of new spending to foreign nations and accordingly reduced the successive impact of each round of expenditure. In recent years this marginal propensity to import has risen sharply, and is now in the 10 to 20 percent range.

The Effect of Leakages. All these withdrawals from the respending cycle are called *leakages,* and the total effect of all leakages together (personal savings, business savings, taxes, and imports) is to reduce the overall impact of the multiplier from an impossibly large figure to a very manageable one. In dealing with the multiplier equation ($\Delta Y = 1/\text{mps} \times \Delta I$), we usually interpret mps to mean the total withdrawal from spending due to all leakages. The combined effect of all leakages brings the actual multiplier in the United States in recent times to a little more than 2 over a period of two years.

To be sure—and this is very important—all these leakages *can* return to the income stream. Household saving can be turned into capital formation; business profits can be invested; tax receipts can be disbursed in government spending programs; and purchases from foreign sellers can be returned as purchases *by* foreigners. What is at stake here is the regularity and reliability with which these circuits will be closed. In the case of ordinary income going to a household, we can count with considerable assurance on a "return expenditure" of consumption. In the case of the other recipients of funds, the assurance is much less; hence we count their receipts as money that has leaked out of the expenditure flow, for the time being.

The Downward Multiplier

The multiplier, with its important magnifying action, rests at the very center of our understanding of economic fluctuations. Not only does it explain how relatively small stimuli can exert considerable upward pushes, but it also makes much clearer than before how the failure to offset a small savings gap can snowball into a serious fall in income and employment.

For just as additional income is respent to create further new income, a loss in income will not stop with the affected households. On the contrary, as families lose income, they will cut down on their spending, although the behavior pattern of the propensity to consume schedule suggests that they will not cut their consumption by as much as their loss in income. Yet each reduction in consumption, large or small, lessens to that extent the income or receipts of some other household or firm.

We have already noted that personal savings alone do not determine the full impact of the multiplier. This is even more fortunate on the way down than on the way up. If the size of the multiplier were solely dependent on the marginal propensity to save, an original fall in spending would result in a catastrophic contraction of consumption through the economy. **But the leakages that cushion the upward pressure of the multiplier also cushion its downward effect.** As spending falls, business savings (profits) fall, tax receipts dwindle, and the flow of imports declines. We shall discuss this cushioning effect when we look into the government sector.

All of these leakages now work in the direction of mitigating the repercussions of the original fall in spending. The fall in business profits means that less will be saved by business and thus less withdrawn from respending; the decline in taxes means that more money will be left to consumers; and the drop in imports similarly releases additional spending power for the domestic market. Thus, just as the various leakages pulled money away from consumption on the way up, on the way down their siphoning effect decreases and in this way purchasing power is restored to consumers' hands. **As a result, in the downward direction as in the upward, the actual impact of the multiplier is about 2, so that a fall in investment of, say, $5 billion will lower GNP by $10 billion.**

Even with a reduced figure, we can now understand how a relatively small change in investment can magnify its impact on GNP. If the typical year-to-year change in investment is around $10 billion to $20 billion, a multiplier of 2 will produce a change in GNP of $20 billion to $40 billion—by no means a negligible figure.

The Multiplier and Inflation

Is the multiplier an inflation-breeding process? It is easy to think so, because the very word *multiplier* suggests inflation.

But that is not the correct way of looking at the question. The multiplier itself only describes the outcome of a basic pattern of economic behavior—the fact that we spend part of any additional income we receive. In itself, respending is not inflationary. But two things could make it so.

1. **If there are no more goods available—if we have reached a ceiling on production—then indeed our efforts to spend more money will only succeed in driving up prices.** Here is really "too much money chasing too few goods." But in that case, the inflation-creating condition is the ceiling on production. The effort to use our income for more enjoyments is still perfectly normal.
2. **If we begin to expect inflation and therefore spend more of our incomes than we ordinarily would, or if we rush to get rid of our income as soon as possible for fear that prices will be higher tomorrow, then indeed our spending pushes us toward inflation.** This kind of panicky spending is a very important perpetuating mechanism for inflation, and we will be considering it more carefully in the chapter devoted to inflation. But even here, it is the *expectations* that are the cause of inflation. The respending itself is a normal part of economic behavior.

THE DEMAND FOR INVESTMENT

Consumption demand, we remember, is essentially directed at the satisfaction of the individual—at providing him with the "utilities" of the goods and services he buys. An increasingly affluent society may not be able to say that consumer expenditure is any longer solely geared to necessity, but at least it obeys the fairly constant promptings of the cultural and social environment, with the result that consumer spending, in the aggregate, fluctuates relatively little, except as income fluctuates.

Profit Expectations

A quite different set of motivations drives the investment impulse. Whether the investment is for replacement of old capital or for the installation of new capital, the ruling consideration is not apt to be the personal use or satisfaction the investment yields to the owners of the firm. **Instead, the touchstone of investment decisions is *expected profit*.**

Note the stress on *expectations*. One firm may be enjoying large profits on its existing plant and equipment at the moment; but if it anticipates no profits from the sales of goods that an *additional* investment would make possible, the firm will make no additions to capital. Another firm may be suffering current losses; but if it anticipates a large profit from the production of a new good, it may launch a considerable capital expenditure. The view is never backward, always forward.

There is a sound reason for this anticipatory quality of investment decisions. Typically, the capital goods bought by investment expenditures are expected to last for years and to pay for themselves only slowly. In addition, they are often highly specialized. If capital expenditures could be recouped in a few weeks or months, or even in a matter of a year or two, or if capital goods were easily transferred from one use to another, they would not be so risky and their dependence on expectations not so great. But it is characteristic of most capital goods that they *are* durable, with life expectancies of ten or more years, and that they tend to be limited in their alternative uses, or to have no alternative uses at all. You cannot spin cloth in a steel mill or make steel in a cotton mill.

The decision to invest is thus always forward-looking. Even when the stimulus to build is felt in the present, the calculations that determine whether or not an investment will be made necessarily concern the flow of income to the firm in the future. These expectations are inherently much more volatile than the current drives and desires that guide the consumer. Expectations, whether based on guesses or forecasts, are capable of sudden and sharp reversals of a sort rare in consumption spending. Thus in its orientation to the future we find a main cause for the volatility of investment expenditures.

The Determinants of Investment

We speak of consumption as a function of income because we know there is a behavior pattern that relates the flow of consumer spending to household incomes. Can we speak of a similar investment function relating capital spending to corporation incomes?

No such simple function exists. This is because the forward-looking nature of investment makes it inherently independent of past influences. Some investment is "induced" by past consumption—inventories, for example, may follow sales—but other investment is "autonomous"—quite independent of consumption. Much investment depends on technology, which is largely unpredictable. And other erratic or unknowable events also bring their effects to bear: the gyrations of the stock market, changes in the inflationary outlook, the ups and downs of foreign relations, and the like.

THE ACCELERATION PRINCIPLE

Nevertheless, investment expenditure is not just a random variable. There are patterns in investment, even though they may be upset by sudden unforeseen shifts in total investment spending.

One such pattern of considerable importance is called the *acceleration principle,* or sometimes just the *accelerator.* The name springs from the fact that investment often depends upon the rate of growth of the economy.

Table 1 is a model that explains this phenomenon. It shows us a firm whose sales rise for six years, then level off, and finally decline. We assume it has no unused equipment and that its equipment wears out every ten years. Also, we will make the assumption that it requires a capital investment of $2 to produce a flow of output of $1.

Now let us see the accelerator at work.

In our first view of the firm, we find it in equilibrium with sales of, let us say, $100 million, capital equipment valued at $200 million, and regular replacement demand of $20 million, or 10 percent of its stock of equipment. Now we assume that its sales rise to $120 million the following year. To produce $120 million of goods, the firm will need (according to our assumptions) $240 million of capital. This is $40 million more than it has, so it must order new equipment. Note that its demand for capital goods now shoots from $20 to $60 million: $20 million for replacement as before, and $40 million for new investment. Thus investment expenditures *triple,* even though sales have risen only 20 percent!

Now assume that in the next year sales rise further, to $130 million. How large will our firm's investment demand be? Its replacement demand will not be larger, since its new capital will not wear out for ten years. And the amount of new capital needed to handle its new sales will be only $20 million, not $40 million as before. Its total investment demand has *fallen* from $60 million to $40.

What is the surprising fact here? It is that *we* can have an actual fall in induced investment, though sales are still rising! In fact, as soon as the *rate of increase* of consumption begins to fall, the *absolute amount* of induced investment declines. Thus a slowdown in the rate of improvement in sales can cause an absolute decline in the orders sent to capital goods makers. This

TABLE 1
A Model of the Accelerator
The accelerator model shows how investment spending can fall even though sales are rising. Compare the total amount of investment in the last column with the change in sales in the second column. In the third year sales are up by $10 million. But investment spending is down by $20 million!

Year	*Sales (Millions)*	*Existing Capital (Millions)*	*Needed Capital (2 × Sales) (Millions)*	*Replacement Investment (Millions)*	*Induced New Investment (2 × Addition to Sales) (Millions)*	*Total Investment*
1	$100	$200	$200	$20	—	$20
2	120	200	240	20	$40	60
3	130	240	260	20	20	40
4	135	260	270	20	10	30
5	138	270	276	20	6	26
6	140	276	280	20	4	24
7	140	280	280	20	—	20
8	130	280	260	—	—	0
9	130	260	260	20	—	20

helps us to explain how weakness can appear in some parts of the economy while prosperity seems still to be reigning in the market at large. It will play a role when we come to explain the phenomenon of the business cycle.

Now look at what happens to our model in the eighth year, when we assume that after several years of increases, to a peak of $140 million, sales slip back to $130 million. Our existing capital ($280 million) will be greater by $20 million than our needed capital. That year the firm will place no new orders for capital goods and may not even make any replacements, because it can produce all it needs with its old machines. Its orders to capital goods makers will fall to zero, even though its level of sales is 30 percent higher than in year 1. The next year, however, if sales remain steady, it will again have to replace one of its old machines. Its replacement demand again jumps to $20 million. No wonder capital goods industries traditionally experience feast or famine years!

There is, in addition, an extremely important point to bear in mind. **The accelerator's upward leverage usually takes effect only when an industry is operating at or near capacity.** When an industry is not near capacity, it is relatively simple for it to satisfy a larger demand for its goods by raising output on its underutilized equipment. Thus, unlike the multiplier, which yields its effects on output only when we have unemployed resources, the accelerator yields its effects mainly when we do *not* have unemployed capital.

Interest Rates and Cost of Investment

There is a second element in the economy that imposes a certain degree of orderliness on investment—the influence of interest rates.

Interest rates affect investment in two ways. The first is to change the costs of investment. If businesses must borrow to make capital expenditures, a higher rate of interest makes it more expensive to undertake an investment. For huge firms that target a return of 15 to 20 percent on investment projects, a change in the interest rate from 10 to 11 percent may be negligible. But for certain kinds of investment—notably utilities and home construction—interest rates constitute an important component of the cost of investment funds. To these firms, the lower the cost of borrowed capital, the more stimulus for investment. The difference in *interest costs* for $1 million borrowed for 20 years at 10 percent instead of 11 percent is $200,000, by no means a negligible sum. Since construction is the largest single component of investment, the interest rate therefore becomes an important influence on the value of total capital formation.

Interest Rates as a Guide to Discounting

The second way interest rates affect investment is as a guide offered to businesses not directly seeking to borrow money for investment, but debating whether to invest the savings (retained earnings) of the firm. This problem of deciding on investments introduces us to an important idea: the discounting of future income.

Suppose that someone gave you an ironclad promise to pay you $100 a year hence. Would you give him $100 *now* to get back the same sum 365 days in the

THE STOCK MARKET AND INVESTMENT

How does the stock market affect business investment? There are three direct effects. One is that the market has traditionally served as a general barometer of the expectations of the business-minded community as a whole. We say "business-minded" rather than "business," because the demand for, and supply of, securities mainly comes from securities dealers, stockbrokers, and the investing public rather than from nonfinancial business enterprises themselves. When the market is buoyant, it has been a signal to business that the "business climate" is favorable, and the effect on what Keynes called the "animal spirits" of executives has been to encourage them to go ahead with expansion plans. When the market is falling, on the other hand, spirits tend to be dampened, and executives may think twice before embarking on an expansion program in the face of general pessimism.

This traditional relationship is, however, greatly lessened by the growing power of government to influence the trend of economic events. Business once looked to the market as the key signal for the future. Today it looks to Washington.

A second direct effect of the stock market on investment has to do with the ease of issuing new securities. One of the ways in which investment is financed is through the issuance of new stocks or bonds whose proceeds will purchase plant and equipment. When the market is rising, it is much easier to float a new issue than when prices are falling. This is particularly true for certain businesses that depend heavily on stock issues for new capital rather than on retained earnings.

Finally, when the market is very low, companies with large retained earnings may be tempted to buy up other companies rather than use their funds for capital expenditure. Financial investment, in other words, may take the place of real investment. This helps successful companies grow, but does not directly provide growth for the economy as a whole.

The Crash of 1987

On October 19, 1987, the Dow Jones stock average dived over 500 points, the largest drop in its history. The crash was echoed more or less around the world, as stocks plummeted in Tokyo, Paris, Hong Kong, and elsewhere. All stock exchanges these days are linked together into one vast market, as price movements in one city rapidly spill over into movements in others.

In the previous great crash in 1929, the greatest immediate damage done by the falling market was inflicted on individual shareowners. Hundreds of thousands of stockholders found themselves bankrupted because they had bought their shares "on margin"—that is, with borrowed money. When the market collapsed, the brokerage houses that had extended these loans dumped their customers' stocks in order to protect themselves as best they could.

In the 1987 crash there was very little "calling" of margin loans. Most customers hung onto their stocks, hoping that eventually the markets would recover from their bottoms, which they did. The great worry on Wall Street and in Washington was what the crash would do to business expectations and to investment spending. People feared that the collapse would start a general bank panic or cause businesspeople to call off investment projects. Fortunately, neither of these worries materialized. The crash came and went, doing relatively little actual damage—but leaving us with a sense of *potential* instability and *potential* damage that will not be quickly forgotten.

---

future? Certainly not, for in parting with the money you are suffering an *opportunity cost,* or a cost that can be measured in terms of the opportunities that your action (to pay \$100 now) has foreclosed for you. Had the going rate of interest been 10 percent, for example, you could have loaned your \$100 at 10 percent and had \$110 at the end of the year. Hence, friendship aside, you are unlikely to lend your money unless you are paid something to compensate you for the opportunities you must give up while you are waiting for your money to return. **Another way of saying exactly the same thing is that we arrive at the *present value* of a specified sum in the future by discounting it by some percentage.** If the discount rate is 10 percent, the present value of \$100 one year in the future is \$100 ÷ 1.10, or approximately \$90.90.

Discounting the Future

This brings us back to the firm that is deciding whether to make an investment. Suppose it could invest \$100,000 in a machine that is expected to earn \$25,000 a year for five years, over and above all expenses, after which it will be worthless. Does this mean that the expected profit on the machine is therefore \$25,000—the \$125,000 of expected earnings less the \$100,000 of original cost? No it does not, for the expected earnings will have to be discounted by some appropriate percentage to find their present value. Thus the first \$25,000 to be earned by the machine must be reduced by some discount rate; and the second \$25,000 must be discounted *twice* (just as \$100 to be repaid in *two* years' time will have to yield the equivalent of *two* years' worth of interest); the third \$25,000, three times, etc.*

Clearly, this process of discounting will cause the present value of the expected future returns of the machine to be less than the sum of the undiscounted returns. If, for example, its returns are discounted at a rate of 10 percent, the firm will find

*The formula for calculating the present value of a flow of future income that does not change from year to year is:

$$\text{present value} = \frac{R}{(1+i)} + \frac{R}{(1+i)_2} + \ldots + \frac{R}{(1+i)_n}$$

where R is the annual flow of income, i is the interest rate, and n is the number of years over which the flow will last.

that the present value of a five-year flow of $25,000 per annum comes not to $125,000, but to only $94,700. This is *less* than the actual expenditure for the machine ($100,000). Hence, at a discount rate of 10 percent, the firm would not undertake the venture.

On the other hand, if it used a discount rate of 5 percent, the present value of the same future flow would be worth (in round numbers) $109,000. In that case, the machine *would* be a worthwhile investment.

Marginal Efficiency of Investment

What rate should our business use to discount future earnings? Here is where the rate of interest enters the picture. Looking out at the economy, the business manager sees that there is a whole spectrum of interest rates, ranging from relatively low rates on bonds (usually government bonds), where the element of risk is very small, to high rates on securities of the same maturity (that is, coming due in the same number of years), where the risk is much greater, such as "low-grade" corporate bonds or mortgages. Along this spectrum of rates, there will be one at which he or she can borrow—high or low, depending on the business's creditworthiness in the eyes of the banking community. By applying that rate, the manager can discover whether the estimated future earning from the venture, properly discounted, is actually profitable or not.

We can see the expected effect of interest rates on investment in Figure 5. Suppose a business has a choice among different investment projects from which it

FIGURE 5
Marginal Efficiency of Capital
A business manager calculates profitability by discounting the expected returns of various ventures. This gives him the marginal efficiency of those ventures. By comparing these marginal efficiencies with the rate of interest for projects of the same degree of risk, he can tell whether the opportunity cost of putting his money into the venture is worthwhile or not.

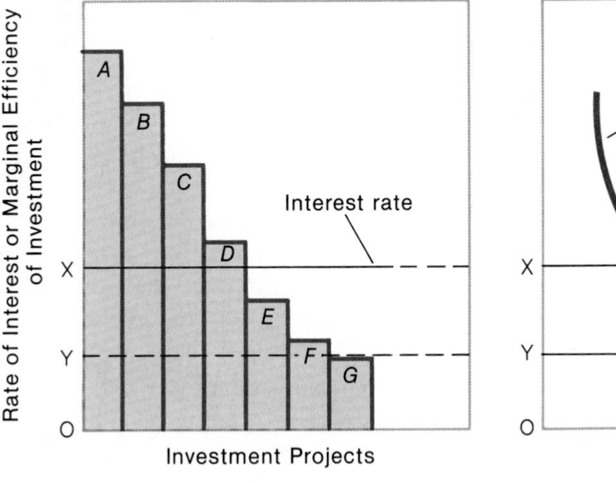

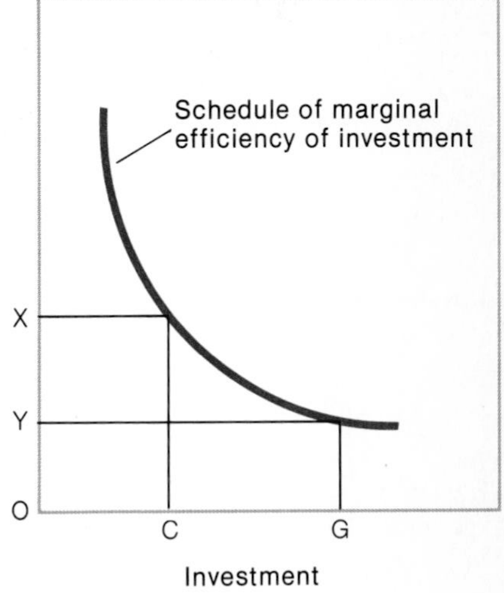

anticipates different returns. The technical name for these discounted returns is the **marginal efficiency of investment.** Suppose those projects are ranked as we have ranked them in Figure 5, starting with the most profitable (A) and proceeding to the least profitable (G). How far down the list should the business manager go? The rate of interest gives the answer. Let us say that the rate (for projects of comparable risk) is shown by *OX*. Then all investment projects whose marginal efficiency is higher than *OX* (investments *A* through *D*) will be profitable, and all those whose marginal efficiency falls below *OX* (*E* through *G*) will be discarded or at least postponed.

Note that if the interest rate falls, more investments will be worthwhile; and that if it rises, fewer will be. As the figure on the right shows in generalized form, a fall in the rate of interest (say from *OX* to *OY*) induces a rise in the quantity of investment (from *OC* to *OG*).

Interest and Investment

Thus, whether we figure interest as a cost or as a guideline against which we measure the expected returns of a capital investment, we reach the important conclusion that low interest rates should encourage investment spending—or in more formal language, that investment should be inversely related to the rate of interest.

To be sure, the fact that a given investment, such as project *B* above, has a marginal efficiency higher than the interest rate is no guarantee that a business actually will undertake it. Other considerations—perhaps political, perhaps psychological—may deter management, despite its encouraging calculations. But assuredly a business will not carry out a project that yields less than the interest rate, because it can make more profit by lending the money, at the same degree of risk, than by investing it.

LOOKING BACK

KEY CONCEPTS

Real vs. financial investment

1 By the term *investment,* economists usually refer to the use of resources to create new capital, not to the use of money to buy assets. Investment is crucial as the key to growth.

Differences of investment and consumption: expectations a key factor

2 Investment is in large degree an independent, not a dependent, variable. It is subject to swings or even collapses of a kind unknown to consumption. Above all, investment is keyed to expectations of future profit, and not to past income.

Investment exerts an upward or downward multiplier, determined

3 Investment exerts a larger effect on GNP than the direct change in investment spending. This is because income created by new investment (or income reduced by a fall in investment) is multiplied. The

by the respending fraction mps = 1 − mpc. Respending in itself is not inflationary.

multiplier depends on the degree to which the original change in investment is respent. This respending fraction is the marginal propensity to consume, or its reciprocal, the marginal propensity to save. Respending is normal, not inflationary. It creates inflation only when there is too little production or when respending becomes panicky.

$$\Delta Y = \frac{1}{mps} \times \Delta I$$

4 The effect of a change of investment on GNP therefore depends on the mpc or the mps. The simplest way to calculate the multiplier is to use the formula Y = 1/mps. Do not forget that mps is itself a fraction: If mps = ¼, then the multiplier is 1 ÷ ¼ = 4.

Leakages:
- savings
- imports
- taxes
- business savings

5 The actual mps is not just determined by our personal savings. Imports, marginal taxes, and business savings also absorb increases in income and therefore lower respending. These are all leakages, which together reduce the actual effect of the multiplier to about 2 over the period of a year.

The acceleration principle links investment to increases in output; investment may fall even though output is still rising.

6 Although investment can be highly unstable, it does have some internal patterns and regularities. One of these is the accelerator or acceleration principle. This is a wavelike pattern that is induced in investment, to the extent that increases in output require ("induce") increases in investment. As output rises, induced investment at first rises faster; then investment may actually fall even though output is still growing.

Interest rates affect investment through cost.

7 Interest rates also influence investment spending. One obvious effect is that interest is a cost of investment.

Future income must be discounted to calculate the marginal efficiency of investment.

8 Interest rates are also a guide to investment profitability. Business managers discount the expected future earnings of investment because future income represents an opportunity cost. Interest rates show the returns available for various kinds of risk. A business compares the discounted earnings of any project—its marginal efficiency—with the interest rate to see if it is worth the opportunity cost.

Low interest rates encourage investment.

9 Whether as a cost or as a guide to marginal efficiencies, interest rates encourage investment when they go down and discourage it when they go up.

ECONOMIC VOCABULARY

Real vs. financial investment 262
Multiplier 263
Marginal propensity to save 267
Multiplier formula 267
Leakages 269
Acceleration principle 272
Discounting 274
Marginal efficiency of investment 277

QUESTIONS

1. If you buy a share of stock on the New York Stock Exchange, does that create an equal amount of investment?
2. Why are inventories subject to such sudden shifts?
3. Why do we face the possibility of a large-scale collapse in investment spending but not in consumption spending?
4. Draw a diagram of boxes showing the multiplier effect of $100 expenditure when the marginal propensity to spend is one-tenth. Draw a second diagram showing the effect when the mps is nine-tenths. The larger the savings ratio, the larger or smaller the multiplier?
5. Calculate the impact on income if investment rises by $10 billion and the multiplier is 2. If it is 3. If it is 1.
6. A simple problem: Income is $500 billion. Inventories decline by $5 billion. The multiplier is 2. What is the new level of income?
7. Suppose you had the following leakages: mps, 10 percent; marginal taxation, 20 percent; marginal propensity to import, 5 percent; marginal addition to business saving, 15 percent. What will be the size of the second round of spending if the first round is $1 billion? What will be the size of the third round? What will be the final total of new spending?
8. Explain the relationship between the marginal propensity to consume and the marginal propensity to save. Why must these two fractions always add up to 1?
9. Complete the following accelerator model, assuming that you need $2 of equipment to produce $1 of output, and that replacement is at 20 percent per year. Check back on page 272 if you need guidance.

Year	*Output*	*Replacement Investment*	*New Equipment Needed*	*Total Investment*
1	100	$40	$ 0	$—
2	120	—	40	—
3	130	—	—	—
4	135	—	—	—

10. If the rate of interest were 10 percent, what would be the present value of $100 due a year hence? Two years hence? Remember: The first year's discounted value has to be discounted a second time.

AN EXTRA WORD ABOUT

The Business Sector

Let us gain a quick acquaintance with the business sector as a whole, much as we did with the household sector.

Figure 1 gives a general impression of the investment sector in a recent year. Note

FIGURE 1
Business Sector, 1987
There is one essential difference between this flow chart and that for consumption. The consumption chart shows net saving—the source of a demand gap. Investment typically shows net spending—an excess of business expenditures over the retained earnings of business.
Sources: *Economic Report of the President; Economic Indicators.*

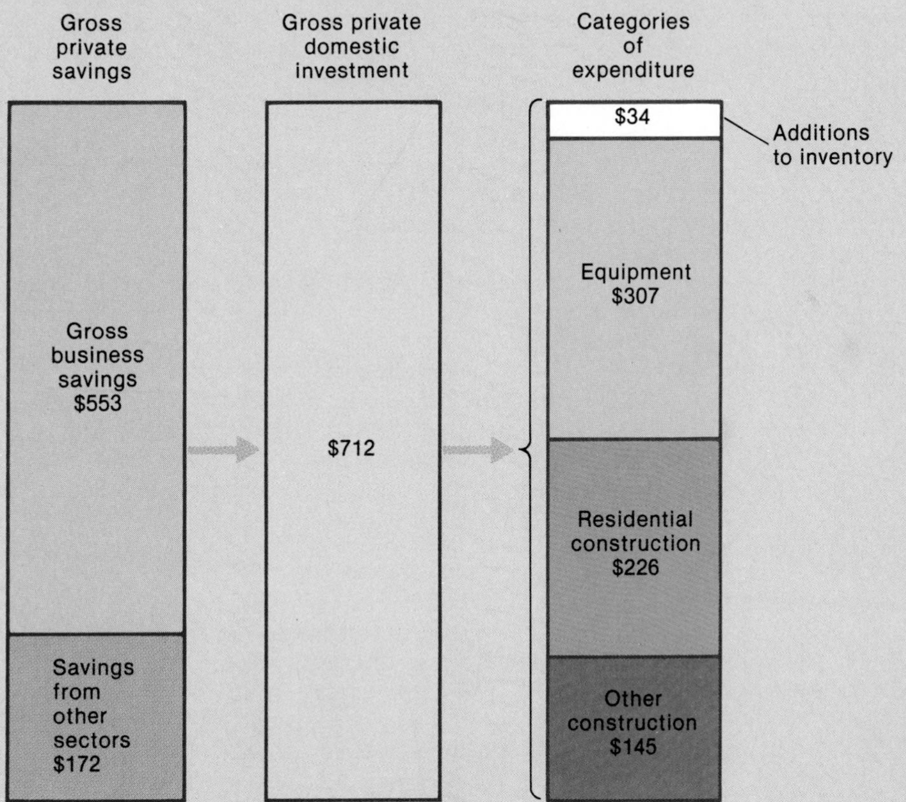

that the main source of gross private domestic investment expenditure is the retained earnings of business; that is, the expenditures come from depreciation accruals or from profits that have been kept in the business. However, as the next bar shows, gross investment *expenditures* are considerably larger than retained earnings. The difference represents funds that business obtains in various ways—mainly by borrowing or issuing new equity.

Our chart enables us to see that most gross investment is financed by business itself from its *internal* sources—retained earnings plus depreciation accruals—and that external sources play only a secondary role. In particular, this is true of new stock issues, which, during most of the 1960s and early 1970s, raised only some 3 to 8 percent of the funds spent by the business sector for new plant and equipment.

CATEGORIES OF INVESTMENT

From the total funds at its disposal, the business sector now renews its worn-out capital and adds new capital. Investment, as we know, is one of the main vehicles for growth. Let us say a word concerning some of the main categories of investment expenditure.

1. Inventories At the top of the expenditure bar in Figure 1 we note an item of $34 billion for additions to inventory. Note that this figure does not represent total inventories, but only *changes* in inventories—upward in this case. If there had been no change in inventory over the year, the item would have been zero even if existing inventories were huge. Why? Because those huge inventories would have been included in the investment expenditure flow of *previous* years when they were built up.

Inventories are often visualized as completed TV sets sitting in some warehouse. While some inventories are completed goods sitting in storage, most are in the form of goods on display in stores, half-finished goods in the process of production, or raw materials to be used in production. When a steel company adds to its stock of iron ore, it is adding to its inventories.

Investments in inventory are particularly significant for one reason. Alone among the investment categories, inventories can be *rapidly* used up as well as increased. A positive figure for one year or even one calendar quarter can quickly turn into a negative figure the next. *This means that expenditures for inventory are usually the most volatile element of any in gross national product.* A glance at Figure 2 shows a particularly dramatic instance of how rapidly inventory spending can change. In the third quarter of 1982, we were reducing inventories at an annual rate of $61 billion a year. Five quarters later, we were building up inventories at a rate of $74 billion, on an annual basis. Thus, within a span of 18 months there was a swing of $135 billion in the rate of spending. Rapid inventory swings, although not quite of this magnitude, are by no means uncommon.

As we shall see more clearly later, this volatility of investment has much significance for business conditions. Note that while inventories are being built up, they serve as an offset to saving—that is, some of the resources released from consumption are used by business firms to build up stocks of inventory capital. But when inventories are being "worked off," we are actually making the demand gap bigger. As we would expect, this can give rise to serious economic troubles.

2. Equipment The next item in the expenditure bar of Figure 1 is more familiar; $307 billion for *equipment.* Here we find expenditures for goods of a varied sort—lathes,

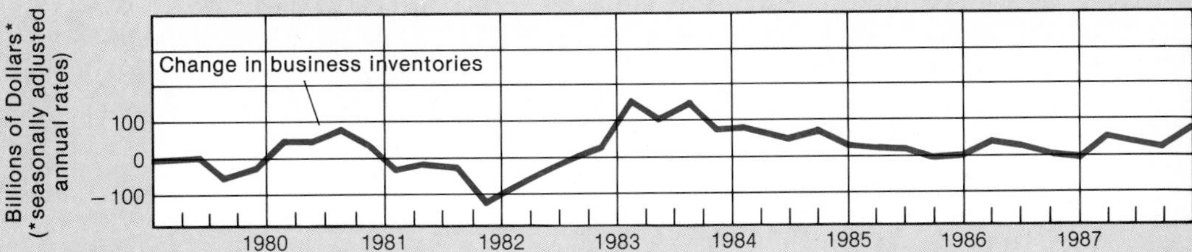

FIGURE 2
Inventory Swings
Inventories are a crucial portion of investment because they can change so rapidly.
Sources: *Economic Indicators; Survey of Current Business.*

trucks, generators, computers, office typewriters.* The total includes both *new equipment* and *replacement equipment.*

New equipment is obviously a very important means of widening and deepening capital—that is, of promoting growth. But let us take a moment to consider *replacement investment.* Exactly what does it mean to "replace" a given item of equipment? Suppose we have a textile loom that cost $100,000 and is now on its last legs. Is the loom replaced by spending another $100,000, regardless of what kind of machine the money will buy? What if loom prices have gone up and $100,000 no longer buys a loom of the same capacity? Or suppose prices have remained steady, but that owing to technological advance, $100,000 now buys a loom with double the old capacity?

Such problems make the definition of "replacement" an accountant's headache and an economist's nightmare. At the moment there isn't even a generally accepted estimate of replacement investment. We need not involve ourselves deeper in the question, but we should note the complexities introduced into a seemingly simple matter once we leave the changeless world of stationary flow and enter the world of invention and innovation.

3. Construction—residential Our next section on the expenditure bar of Figure 1 is *total residential construction,* another big growth item. But why do we include this $226 billion in the investment sector when most of it is represented by new houses that householders buy for their own use?

Part of the answer is that most houses are built by business firms, such as contractors and developers, who put up the houses *before* they are sold. Thus the original expenditures involved in building houses typically come from businesses, not from households. Later, when the householder buys a house, it is an existing asset. His or her expenditure does not pump new incomes into the economy, but only repays the contractor who *did* contribute new incomes.

Actually this is a somewhat arbitrary definition, since business owns *all* output before consumers buy it. However, another reason for considering residential construction as investment is that, unlike most consumer goods, houses are typically maintained as if they were capital goods. Thus their durability also enters into their classification as investment goods.

*But *not* typewriters bought by consumers. Thus the same good can be classified as a consumption item or an investment item, depending on the use to which it is put.

Finally, we class housing as investment because residential purchases behave very much like other items of construction. Therefore it simplifies our understanding of the forces at work in the economy if we classify residential construction as an investment expenditure rather than as a consumer expenditure.

4. Other construction—plant Last on the bar in Figure 1, $145 billion of other construction is largely made up of the "plant" in "plant and equipment"—factories and stores and private office buildings and warehouses. This category does not, however, include public construction such as roads, dams, harbors, or public buildings, all of which are picked up under government purchases.) It is interesting to note that the building of structures, as represented by the total of residential construction plus other private construction, accounts for over half of all investment expenditures. This total would be further swelled if public construction were included. This tells us that swings in construction expenditure can be a major lever for economic change. One reason why high interest rates depress the economy is that the construction business depends heavily on borrowed money.

THE EXPORT SECTOR

The export sector is always added up separately in the calculation of GNP. It is *not* lumped together with investment. Nevertheless, it bears some very important resemblances to investment, so we take a quick look at it here, before we meet it again when we study international competition.

Impact of Foreign Trade We must begin by repeating that our initial overview of the economic system, with its twin streams of consumption and investment, was actually incomplete. It portrayed what we call a "closed" system, an economy with no flows of goods or services from within its borders to other nations or from other nations to itself.

First a word of explanation. Exports are the total value of all goods and services we sold to foreigners. Imports are the total value of all goods and services we bought from foreigners. The difference between the value of the goods we sold abroad and the value of those we bought from abroad is called *net exports,* and it constitutes the net contribution of foreign trade to the demand for GNP.

If we think of it in terms of expenditures, it is not difficult to see what the net contribution is. When exports are sold to foreigners, their expenditures add to American incomes. Imports, on the contrary, are expenditures we make to other countries (and hence that we do not make at home). If we add the foreign expenditures made here and subtract the domestic expenditures made abroad, we will have left a net figure that will show the contribution (if any) by foreigners to GNP. When, as in recent years, we buy more from abroad than we sell in turn, we subtract our negative trade balance from GNP.

The Export multiplier Whether a balance is favorable or unfavorable, we can see that a *change* in that balance, up or down, exerts a multiplier effect, just as does a change in the level of investment. When our export balance increases (remember: *balance* means exports minus imports, not just exports by themselves), the contribution to our incomes from abroad gets respent, exactly as in the parable of the stranger who visits an island and starts the multiplier process going. When our negative balance worsens (not when it "stands still"), we get a downward multiplier, because the new outflow of funds will not go through its normal respending pattern here at home. Thus whenever the foreign trade balance moves, up or down, it exerts a pressure on the level of GNP that is roughly twice as large as the movement itself. That's the export multiplier at work.

CHAPTER 17

Public Spending and Deficits

A LOOK AHEAD

This long and important chapter begins our coverage of the government's role in the economy. Three basic ideas should be kept in mind as you go through the chapter:

1 The nature of the influence public spending exerts on the flow of GNP. Whether one thinks that influence too great or too small, it is vital to know precisely how it works.

2 The meaning of a government "deficit," and the role a deficit plays in the determination of GNP.

3 The confusions that surround the deficit—as a source of growth and as a source of trouble.

We will learn in this chapter that there is no clear and simple rule about deficits. They can be useful—and they can be destructive. The most important task for an economist is to understand that deficits are a tool of fiscal policy, one tool that can be used wisely or unwisely.

THE PUBLIC SECTOR

We became familiar with the general size and shape of the government establishment in Chapters 4 and 5. Now we are going to review and expand that familiarity by taking a careful look at the public sector.

We begin by recalling the general magnitude of government in the economy. In 1929 total government purchases of goods and services were still very small—only half as large as total private investment spending. By 1988, that had changed dramatically; government purchases have long surpassed total private investment. In terms of its contribution to GNP, government is now second only to consumption.

We are, of course, also interested in the composition of public spending, and Table 1 gives us a first look. Note that while the federal government spends more than the state and local governments on transfers, the state and local governments outspend the federal government on purchases.

Measuring the Public Sector

The growth of government activity within the economy has become a matter of political as well as economic importance in recent years. Opinions are sharply polarized by the question of whether or not government is "too big." That is not an issue we will tackle head on—yet. One reason we want to defer it is that people can easily argue at cross purposes if they are not very clear about what they mean when they say that "government" is too big, or possibly not big enough.

One way to gauge the size of government is to measure its total impact on the national economy. We can do this adding its contribution to GNP and its transfer payments, including payments of interest on all government debt. This mixed measure of purchases plus transfers can be thought of as the total contribution of government to the incomes received by its citizens.* In 1987 this contribution was equal to 34.7 percent of GNP.

Table 2 compares this measure of government in several major Western industrial nations. From this comparison, we see that the United States now

TABLE 1
Government Purchases and Transfers, 1987
Note that the states outspend the federal government for purchases, but that the federal government far outspends the states for transfers.

Total Government Expenditures ($ Billions)	*1987*
Purchases	
Federal	373
State and local	531
Transfers	
Federal	414
State and local	118

Sources: *Economic Indicators; Statistical Abstract of the United States.*

*It also includes contributions to incomes of foreign citizens who own U.S. or state bonds or who receive social security payments.

occupies the low position among large capitalist economies. We have a considerably smaller government sector than West Germany or France, where not only are transfers to private citizens larger, but the government also directly owns and operates businesses such as airlines and freight railroads (and in the case of France, a number of other heavy industries). Even Japan's public sector now exceeds ours in relation to total incomes, despite the fact that Japan relies less on government transfers and more on private pensions to support its older citizens than we do.

Effects of the Public Sector

Table 2 also shows us a very important and interesting fact: **There is no relationship between the size of government in a country and the standard of living that country enjoys.** Some countries that we consider to have a very high standard of living have a higher share of government spending, while others that we consider to be very dynamic have a lower share. The size of government does not seem to affect the rate of economic growth.

What effects, then, does government spending have? There are two:

Stabilizing Effects. From an economic standpoint, what distinguishes big-government from small-government countries is not the effects of the size of government per se, but rather the stability or instability the government sector imparts to the stream of total spending. We have already seen that household consumption tends to be a very stable stream of spending, while business investment tends to be much more volatile. Government purchases, in peacetime, tends to be the most stable sector of all. The reason is simple: Government spending is planned by a centralized political process and administered by large bureaucratic agencies that tend to do the same things year after year, unaffected by interest rates or past profits or the state of demand or the climate of expectations.

***Ceteris paribus*, then, we would expect that countries with proportionately larger government sectors would enjoy a higher degree of macro stability than countries with proportionately smaller public sectors. And by and large that is what we seem to find.**

TABLE 2
A Comparison of Government Size and Per Capita Incomes
Table 2 shows two things: (1) The U.S. ratio of total government spending to GNP is somewhat lower than in most other major capitalist economies; and (2) there is no relation between the share of government and the level of per capita GNP.

Country	*Total Government Spending (% of GNP, 1987)*	*Per Capita Income (US $, 1986)*
United States	34.7	$16,494
Japan	34.8	11,803
West Germany	48.6	12,179
France	51.5	11,445
United Kingdom	47.2	10,915
Canada	46.8	15,223

Source: *OECD Historical Statistics.*

Countercyclical Effects. A second key fact about government spending is that its variations tend to run counter to the movements of spending in the private economy. That is because many government programs are entitlements, whose outlays are related to need. Thus when GNP declines and the unemployment rate rises, unemployment compensation rises automatically, along with outlays for food stamps, aid to dependent children, and other relief programs. In 1982, for example, when unemployment neared 11 percent, total federal outlays were $25 billion higher than they would have been if unemployment had been only 5 percent. That $25 billion helped offset the drop in private spending caused by the recession.

We call this tendency for government spending to rise or fall countercyclically an *automatic stabilizer*. An even more powerful automatic stabilizer is the tax system. The mechanism is very obvious. Because income tax rates are higher on big incomes than on small ones, the national tax bite rises faster than national income. When income falls, it works the other way around; the tax flow decreases faster than income does.

Note that government of any size can have automatic stabilization built into the way it functions; however, the larger the size of government, the smaller the proportionate change in all government spending has to be in order to achieve a given stabilizing effect.

THE DEFICIT

Now we turn to the great issue of the budget deficit, central to the macroeconomic role of the public sector in the twentieth century. Under what conditions will deficit spending help the performance of the economy? When will it hurt? How long can large-scale deficit spending be sustained? What will happen if it continues for too long?

Let us begin by understanding what the budget deficit is. **The federal budget deficit is defined as the difference between all federal spending and all federal tax revenues.** For the purposes of calculating the deficit and its economic effects, we disregard the distinctions between government purchases, transfers, grants, and interest and their differing effects on GNP, and count them all together as spending. Likewise, we aggregate all tax revenues, whether general-purpose (like the income tax) or special-purpose (like the payroll tax that finances social security outlays). We pay no heed to whether government spends money for warfare or welfare, for consumption purposes or to build capital. We are concerned only with the difference between these two gross concepts—total outlays and total receipts.*

*This method of calculating the budget deficit, which lumps together regular-budget items, such as normal tax revenues and expenditures, and "off-budget items," such as Social Security Trust Fund income and outlays, is called the national income and products account method. We mention this because sometimes the deficit is calculated without either social security income (payroll taxes) or expenditures. The difference in dollars is already considerable, but projections indicate that there will be a very large *surplus* in the social security account by the mid to late 1990s. In that case, it would make a big difference which method of calculation we used. Most economists, including ourselves, favor the national income and product accounts method because it includes all the inflows and outflows that affect GNP.

The Deficit and the Debt

The government raises the cash to bridge the difference between outlays and receipts by selling bonds to the public, which increases the outstanding stock of the federal debt. The debt is therefore the sum of all outstanding past borrowings. Table 3 shows us the trend in both debt and deficit from 1960 to the present—and into the near future.

Is the deficit a danger? Is the debt too large? These are obviously questions for which we are eager to have the answers. But we cannot rush into the questions unprepared. For the moment, then, let us rein our impatience until we have mastered the mechanics of deficit spending.

The Mechanics of the Deficit

Deficits are caused in the first place because the government needs revenues, over and above taxes, to finance its expenditures. But deficits do not arise only because governments need more revenues than taxes provide. **Deficits also serve the purpose of stimulating the economy. A government can choose to incur a deficit as part of its fiscal policy, deliberately setting expenditures above taxes, or arranging matters so that expenditures will automatically rise and taxes automatically fall under certain economic conditions, such as a recession. As such, deficits are a key tool of fiscal policy.***

TABLE 3
The Deficit and the Debt ($ Billions)
The table shows the rise in both debt and deficit over the last quarter century. The estimate for 1994 comes from the Congressional Budget Office and is based on a "current services" concept. The table shows the gross federal debt, which includes that part of the debt held by federal agencies such as the Social Security Trust Fund. In 1987 the debt held by the public was about $1,897 billion.

Year	*Deficit*	*Gross Federal Debt*	*Debt Held by Public*
1960	.3	$ 291	$ 225
1970	-2.8	383	263
1975	-53.2	544	397
1980	-73.8	914	596
1981	-78.9	1,004	678
1982	-127.9	1,147	895
1983	-207.8	1,382	1,044
1984	-185.3	1,577	1,256
1985	-222.2	1,841	1,515
1988	-121	2,581	2,031
1994	-121		2,806

*What is *fiscal* policy? As the word suggests, it is any policy affecting the overall level of operation of the economy that involves the government's *fisc,* or treasury. All spending or taxing measures are "fiscal" tools of the government. The other great branch of government economic influence is monetary policy. This tool uses government's powers of money creation.

The basic idea behind the stimulative function of the deficit is simple enough. We have seen that economic recessions have their roots in a failure of the business sector to offset the savings of the economy through sufficient investment. If savings or leakages are larger than intended investment, there will be a gap in the circuit of incomes and expenditures. That gap can cumulate downward, at first by the effect of the multiplier, and thereafter, even more seriously, by further decreases in investment brought about by falling sales and gloomy expectations.

But if a falling GNP is caused by an inadequacy of expenditure, corresponding to a surplus of saving in one sector, our analysis suggests an answer. Could not the public sector serve as a supplementary avenue for the transfer of savings into expenditure?

Filling in the Demand Gap

As Figure 1 shows, a demand gap can indeed be closed by transferring savings to the public sector and spending them. The diagram shows savings in the household sector partly offset by business investment and partly by government *deficit spending.* It makes clear that at least so far as the "mechanics" of the economic flow are concerned, the public sector can serve to offset savings or other leakages as well as the private sector.

How is the transfer accomplished? It is accomplished much as business does it, by offering bonds that individuals or institutions may buy with their savings. (Unlike business, government cannot offer stock because it is not run as a profit-making enterprise). Thereafter, the proceeds of the bonds are deposited into the government's checking accounts, where they enable the government to pay its bills by writing checks against those accounts.

UNDERSTANDING DEFICITS

Thus the sheer mechanics of government deficit spending are almost exactly like that of business investment spending. This parallel now enables us to go a little deeper into the pros and cons of deficit spending. Let us begin to inquire into the safety or dangers of a government deficit by asking whether business can also afford to incur deficits.

Deficits vs. Losses

There is one kind of deficit that a private business *cannot* afford: a deficit that comes from spending more money on current production than it will realize from sales. This kind of deficit is called a *business loss;* and if losses are severe enough, a business firm will be forced to discontinue its operations.

But there is another kind of deficit, although it is not called by that name,

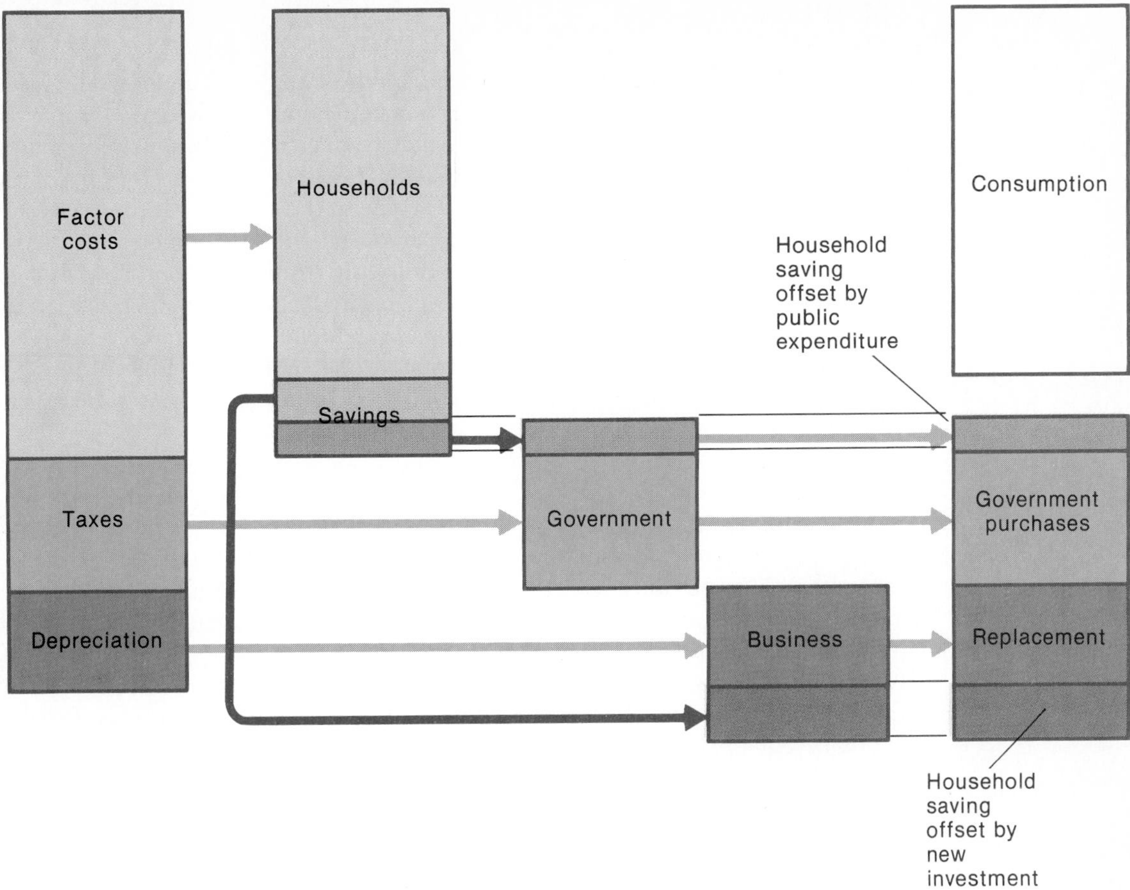

FIGURE 1
Public Expenditure and the Demand Gap
The economics of filling a demand gap by government spending are exactly like those of investment spending. The politics are not.

in the operations of a private firm. This is an excess of expenditures over receipts brought about by spending money on *capital assets*. When the American Telephone and Telegraph Company or the Exxon Corporation uses its own savings or those of the public to build a new plant and new equipment, it does not show a loss on its annual statement to stockholders, even though its total expenditures on current costs and on capital may have been greater than sales. Instead, expenditures are divided into two kinds, one relating current costs to current income, and the other relegating expenditures on capital goods to an entirely separate capital account. Instead of calling the excess of expenditures a deficit, they call it investment.*

*Investment does not *require* a deficit, since it can be financed out of current profits. But many expanding companies do spend more money on current and capital account than they take in through sales, and thereby incur a deficit for at least a part of their investment.

Debts and Assets

Can AT&T or Exxon afford to run deficits of the latter kind indefinitely? The surprising answer is yes! To be sure, after a stated number of years, AT&T's or Exxon's bonds will come due and must be paid back. Perhaps the companies can do that out of their accumulated earnings. Usually, however, when a bond becomes due, a corporation issues *new* bonds equal in value to the old ones. It then sells the new bonds and uses the money it raises to pay off its old bondholders.

Many big corporations do, in fact, continuously "refund" their bond issues, paying off old bonds with new ones, and never paying back their indebtedness as a whole. AT&T, for instance, increased its total indebtedness over tenfold between 1929 and 1985. Exxon ran up its debt from $170.1 million in 1929 to over $5 billion in 1985. And the credit rating of both companies today is as good as, or better than, it was in 1929.

Government Assets

Can government, like business, borrow indefinitely? The question is important enough to warrant a careful answer. Let us begin by comparing government borrowing and business borrowing.

One difference that springs quickly to mind is that businesses borrow in order to acquire productive assets. That is, matching the new claims on the business sector is additional real wealth that will provide for larger output. From this additional wealth, business will also receive the income to pay interest on its debt or dividends on its stock. But what of the government? Where are its productive assets?

We have already noted that the government budget includes dams, roads, housing projects, and many other items that might be classified as assets. During the 1960s federal expenditures for such civil construction projects alone averaged about $5 billion a year. Thus the total addition to the public debt during the 1960s (it rose from roughly $240 billion in 1960 to $279 billion in 1969) could be construed merely as the financial counterpart of the creation of public assets.

Between 1970 and 1987, when debt held by the public rose from $285 billion to $1.9 trillion, assets also kept pace. Total assets owned by government rose from $537 billion in the earlier year to over $2 trillion in 1985. Of these $2 trillion in assets, slightly more than half were tangible wealth of various kinds, such as public buildings, structures, equipment, and land. The remainder were financial assets—mortgages, loans due the government, gold, and cash in the government's own checking accounts.

Why do we not treat the government's debt the way we do a corporation's, weighing assets against liabilities? The reason is simply that the United States national income accounts lump together all public expenditures, without regard to purpose. In some European countries public capital expenditures are sharply differentiated from public current expenditures. If we had such a system, the government deficit on capital account could then be viewed as **the public equivalent of a business deficit on capital account.** As government spends money on capital assets like dams or roads or schools, the nation's productivity rises. During the mid-1980s, when record deficits were being chalked up, the actual addition to nonmilitary public capital—not only roads and dams, but research and development and federal contributions to education as well—were in many years as large as, or larger than, the recorded deficit!* As a result of this government-financed rise in national productivity, tax revenues also rise, just like the sales of a company that has invested shrewdly.

Such a view of government spending, which stresses its potential usefulness—or wastefulness—in terms of the effects on tax revenues would greatly improve the level of discussion concerning government's finance.

Government's Power of Taxation

There is an additional, much more powerful argument that applies to federal deficits. It is that national governments, unlike the biggest corporations—and unlike states or municipalities—have the ability to "capture" the spending power of their citizens through taxation.

Thus even if government does not use its expenditures to increase the productive assets of a nation—even if it squanders the money—the expenditures themselves remain within its reach in a manner not enjoyed by a spending entity that does not have the power of national taxation. **Whatever goes into the income stream is always available to government as a source of revenue, whereas whatever goes into the income stream from a corporation's expenditures is not available to it in the same way.** In normal circumstances the federal government will recover about one-half to two-thirds of its expenditures in this way through normal taxes.†

This reasoning helps us understand why federal finance is different from state and local government finance. An expenditure made by New York City or New York State is apt to be respent in many other areas of the country. Thus taxable incomes in New York will not, in all probability, rise to match local spending. As a result, state and local governments must look on their finances much as an individual business does. The power of full fiscal recapture belongs solely to the federal government.

Internal and External Debts

This difference between the limited powers of recoupment of a single firm and the relatively limitless powers of recoupment of a national government lies at the heart of the basic difference between business and government deficit spending. It helps us understand why the government has a capacity for financial operation that is inherently of a far higher order of magnitude than that of business. We can sum up this fundamental difference in the contrast between the ***externality of business debts*** **and the** ***internality of national government debts.***

*For a searching exploration of the deficit, see Robert Eisner, *How Real Is the Federal Deficit?* (New York: The Free Press), 1986.

†We can make a rough estimate of the multiplier effect of additional public expenditure as 2 and of the share of an additional dollar of GNP going to federal taxes as about ⅓ (see page 228). Thus $1 of public spending will create $2 of GNP, of which 67 cents will go back to the federal government.

What do we mean by the externality of business debts? Simply that business firms owe their debts to someone distinct from themselves—someone over whom they have no control—whether bondholders or the bank from which they borrowed. To service or to pay back its debts, business must transfer funds from its own possessions into the possession of outsiders. If this transfer cannot be made, if a business does not have the funds to pay its bondholders or its banks, it will go bankrupt.

The government is in a very different position. Its bondholders, banks, and other people or institutions to whom it owes its debts belong to the same community as that whence it extracts its receipts.* In other words, the government does not have to transfer its funds to an outside group to pay its bonds. It transfers them instead from some members of the national community over which it has legal powers (taxpayers) to other members of the *same* community (bondholders).

The contrast is much the same as that between a family that owes a debt to another family, and a family in which the husband has borrowed money from his wife; or again, between a firm that owes money to another, and a firm in which one branch has borrowed money from another. **Internal debts do not drain the resources of one community into another, but merely redistribute the claims among members of the same community.**

To help bring home the point, imagine that you and your roommate exchange $1,000 IOUs. Each of you now has a $1,000 asset (an IOU from the other person) *and* each of you also has a $1,000 liability (the IOU each owes the other). The total debt of the room is now $2,000. But is your room richer or poorer, or is any individual in the room richer or poorer? The answer is obviously no. No one is better or worse off than before. And what happens if you now each pay off your IOUs? Once again, no one is richer or poorer than before. The same thing is true at the national level. The national debt makes us neither richer nor poorer, since we (as taxpayers) owe it to ourselves (as bondholders).

The Inflation Factor

Last but by no means least, there is a tendency to view the deficit and the debt unrealistically by failing to apply an inflation correction to their size. Do you remember the tremendous difference in the growth of GNP before and after the figures were scaled down from nominal to real magnitudes? (See pages 000–000.) The same is true of the debt and deficit. Inflation has steadily multiplied the number of dollars of both figures, but their real growth is much less. In Table 4 we show the debt held by the public before and after correcting for inflation.

The Growth Factor

Thus inflation seriously distorts the real size of the debt. But even inflation-proof figures do not reflect another necessary correction—the fact that our real GNP

*Except for foreigners, who owned about 14 percent of the national debt in 1988.

TABLE 4
Nominal and Real Debt
The nominal debt increased by more than ninefold from 1960 to 1987. The real debt, measured in 1982 dollars, rose by less than twofold.

	Nominal Debt (Billions of Current Dollars)	*Real Debt (Billions of 1982 Dollars)*
1960	225	728
1970	263	626
1980	596	695
1982	895	895
1984	1,266	1,166
1986	1,746	1,530
1987	1,897	1,614

Source: *Report of the President*

rises, along with our real debt, so that debt as a proportion of GNP grows even more slowly than debt corrected for inflation alone.

We can best see the effects of this second correction by looking at Table 5. Here we see figures for both the national debt and annual deficits, as a percentage of GNP.

These figures may come as a surprise. They show that the national debt, as a percentage of GNP, is hardly above the level of the 1960s. This is because we greatly enlarged our debt in the 1940s to finance World War II, and our growth in real GNP by 1960 had not yet reduced the debt to the proportion to which it would fall by early 1980s.

Nevertheless, in recent years our deficits have been very large, and our ratio of debt to GNP has again risen. In 1960 we actually ran a small surplus. In the early 1970s, our deficits averaged about 1 percent of GNP. But starting in 1982, deficits began to soar, until by 1984 and 1985, they had risen to around 5 percent of GNP. From 1985 to 1988, the deficit stabilized and even declined in relation to GNP, but it remains very large by recent historical standards.

Is that increase alarming? Has deficit spending now become a source of danger for our economy? We are back to the questions that impelled us into a study of

TABLE 5
Deficits, Debts, and GNP
Relating debts and deficits to GNP is the best way of judging their real magnitude, for this corrects for both inflation and real growth.

	Deficits as % of GNP	*National Debt Held by the Public as % of GNP*
1965	0.2	38.9
1970	.3	28.8
1975	3.5	26.8
1980	2.8	26.8
1985	5.4	38.3
1988 (est.)	2.5	41.8

Source: Congressional Budget Office.

federal finance some pages back, but now we are in a position to consider the problem much more knowledgeably.

DEFICITS AND GROWTH

The overall answer is probably already clear to you. **Deficits can indeed be too big—and they can also be too small. There is no absolute magnitude that separates a useful deficit from a useless or even dangerous one.**

Two overall considerations have to be borne in mind before we can judge the positive or negative effects of any deficit, large or small:

1. The Impact of the Deficit Will Depend on the Kinds of Government Goods and Services for Which It Is Used. A deficit that is mainly incurred to create public assets—or public growth-producing services such as education—will clearly have a different significance from one that is incurred to produce war material that will never (we hope) be used, or one that is the result only of transfer payments that help to sustain demand, but do not increase productivity.

The trouble is that government spending is normally a mixture of growth-producing and non-growth-producing expenditures, so it is difficult or impossible to attribute the deficit just to one set of programs. Because we do not have a national capital budget, we can only bear in mind that some portion of public spending is indeed the equivalent of capital investment. When we argue about the ways of using the public sector, we should not overlook its contribution to economic growth.

2. The Impact of the Deficit Will Also Depend on the Level of Aggregate Demand. When the sum of all private spending—households, businesses, and foreign demand—is not enough to bring the economy to a high level of employment, deficit spending can use the public sector to increase demand. As we have now seen, the mechanism of public spending is exactly the same as that of private investment. Each helps to offset a demand gap with additional expenditure. The only difference, from this point of view, is that private investment spending increases our stock of capital wealth, whereas public spending may or may not do this, depending on the purposes for which it is used.

But will not public expenditure be inflationary if it is added to private expenditure? Indeed it may be, if we are at the borderline where added spending affects prices as strongly as (or more strongly than) it affects employment and output. **But in that case, the same inflationary effects would also follow from more private spending!** There is no inflationary difference between an additional dollar spent by the Treasury or by General Motors. The only difference lies in the effects of each expenditure on our productivity. By and large, public spending probably adds less to productivity, dollar for dollar, than private investment spending. But this is not necessarily so. General Motors' investment will not exert a strong effect on growth unless there are good roads on which to run its cars. Public expenditure for basic research will boost growth in the long run more than private expenditure for luxury hotels.

PUBLIC CAPITAL AND PRIVATE PROFITS

We have all heard about the need to rebuild America's **infrastructure:** the roads, bridges, airports, railways, and water and sewer works that it is the function of government to provide. The interstate highway system alone requires some 2,000 miles of reconstruction *every year.* It is estimated that one of every five bridges in the United States needs to be rebuilt. And the problems of inadequate water treatment return to haunt us every summer in polluted beaches and rivers. Estimates of the cost of meeting these needs run as high as $400 billion through the end of the present century alone.

But what difference does this make for the economy? A recent study by the Federal Reserve Bank of Chicago offers some interesting answers.

The Federal Reserve study points out that there has been a drastic decline in the public components of capital formation over the past 35 years. This is shown in Figure 2, which presents estimates of the public and private capital stocks, per worker. Since 1971 the amount of public capital per worker has actually fallen, from $15,576 to $14,226 in 1984. Public net investment was as high as 2.3

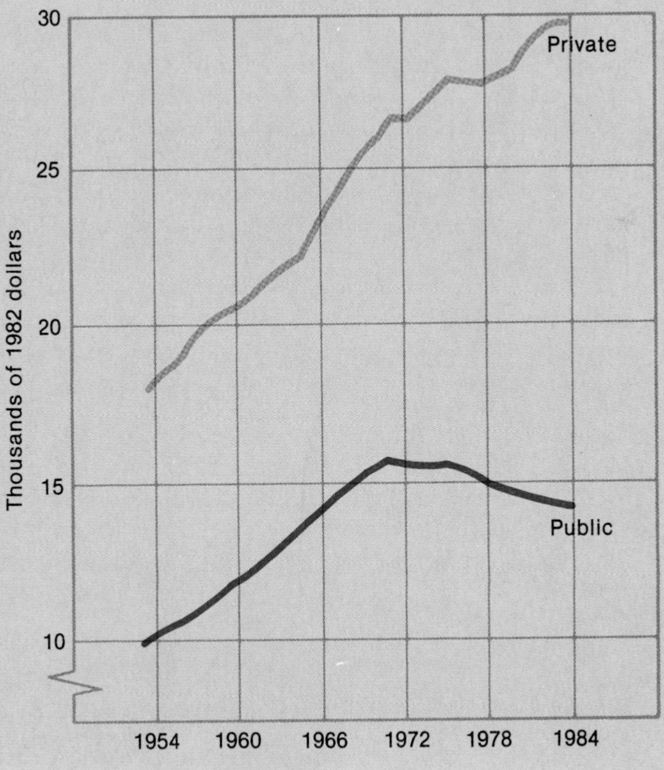

FIGURE 2
Capital Stock per Worker

percent of GNP in 1965–1969, but by 1980–1984 it had fallen to a mere 0.4 percent.

The study argues that the decline in public capital formation has paralleled a decline in the rate of profit on private investment. The reason is that as the public sector retreated from its responsibilities, private investors found that *their costs* were higher for transportation, water, and so on. Thus a deficiency of *public* investment hurts the *private* sector!

The Chicago Federal Reserve study concludes that the rates of return are now higher on public than on private investment. And if public capital formation were to return to its 1953–1969 average of 2.1 percent of GNP, private profitability would rise by over 2 percentage points. The total national capital stock would be higher, and the economy would be more productive.

Source: David Alan Aschauer, "Is the Public Capital Stock Too Low?," *Chicago Fed Letter,* October 1987.

DEFICIT DANGERS

Up till now we have mainly stressed the constructive aspects of deficit spending and sought to take away some of the fears that get in the way of an intelligent discussion of fiscal policy. Yet the last impression that we wish to leave with a reader is that deficits are always useful or that there is nothing to worry about when expenditures exceed revenues. We have made the point that under the right conditions, deficits are useful or even necessary for economic growth. Now let us make the complementary point—under different conditions, deficits are useless and even detrimental for growth.

We have already made clear what those conditions are. **If we are at or near full employment of labor and full utilization of resources, additional government spending will add to demand—but cannot add to supply.** Additional spending will therefore push the economy out of equilibrium. Three possibilities may follow.

1. Crowding Out. The first possibility is *crowding out.* This means that the effect of excess total demand is felt primarily through an intense competition for capital in the financial markets. Business will be seeking funds to invest, and the government will be seeking funds to cover the gap between intake and outgo. As the total demand for funds rises, interest rates may also rise,* and consequently

*Here is an interesting complication introduced by the emerging global economy. Economists used to fear that crowding out would produce a sharp rise in interest rates because the pool of national savings was relatively fixed. But it has become increasingly evident that there is an international pool of savings that seeks investments such as United States' (or German or Japanese) private and public bonds. Therefore the U.S. Treasury has a vastly larger number of potential buyers than American citizens alone. As a result, the crowding-out effect has been much less severe than once seemed likely, although we pay the price of increasing our foreign indebtedness (see below).

private business will curtail its investment plans (remember our analysis of the marginal efficiency of investment?).

Public needs will "crowd out" private ones, and business growth will suffer. This might be accepted if we were all of one mind that public needs were more important than private ones, as is usually the case during wars. But in peacetime there is no such agreement. Crowding out is then regarded with unease as enforcing a priority for public spending that may not be in accord with our public sentiments.

2. INFLATION. The fear of crowding out has been much talked about by economists contemplating the huge budget deficits expected for the rest of the century. But notice that the fear rests on the assumption that competition for funds occurs exclusively in the capital markets, and does not spill over into the markets for real goods, precipitating a general rise in prices. Suppose that instead of merely competing for funds in the capital markets, governments, business, and households actually go out and collectively spend more dollars than the maximum value of output the economy can produce. Then we have a simple case of too many dollars chasing too few goods: Prices will rise.

Here an unpleasant reality must be faced. We have seen that the carrying capacity of the United States for its national debt is limited only by the taxing power of the government on national income. But now we must also recognize another possibility: *Inflation can be used as a substitute for taxation in "servicing" the national debt.*

If inflation increases, tax revenues will rise, and the government will have more dollars in revenue with which to pay the interest on its debts. At the same time, the bonds that make up the debt will have lost real purchasing power over goods and services. Thus the debt will have *depreciated* by the amount of the inflation. This is another way in which governments can ensure that they always have the wherewithal to repay their debts. This mechanism is known to economists as the **inflation tax.**

Needless to say, this is a very unjust and potentially dangerous method of financing a debt. Nevertheless, as long as inflation persists, it is a means of financing that has been used by all governments to some extent, including our own.

3. FOREIGN INDEBTEDNESS. A third possibility is to borrow the needed extra savings from foreigners. This was the course adopted by the United States in the 1980s. High interest rates made it very attractive for foreigners to seek dollar-denominated assets like Treasury bonds. Foreigners bought $267 billion of U.S. debt (public *and* private) in 1987, 56 percent of that year's government deficit and 14 percent of the national debt.

Running up a foreign debt is a time-honored way to have your cake and eat it too—to spend in excess of production while avoiding inflation or crowding out. But can it last? That depends on how productive the investments being made with the money prove to be. In the 1870s the United States opened the West with borrowed money—U.S. railroad bonds, sold in the markets of London and Paris. This was perhaps the most lucrative investment—in terms of physical if not financial rewards—any nation has ever made. But in the 1970s many Latin American countries tried to do the same thing and fell flat on their faces when the markets for their oil and copper and other commodities collapsed in the recession of 1979–1982. Were the dollars borrowed by the American government in the

1980s put to productive use in building infrastructure that would increase American productivity? We know they were not.

4. THE EXTERNALITY RISK. This brings us back to the problem of the internality and externality of debt that we discussed on page 000. We can see that externality becomes a major problem if we do not use our foreign borrowing productively, because we will not then generate the additional income needed to pay the interest we owe to foreigners. And as we know, we cannot tax foreigners to service the debt they own, the way we can tax our own citizens.

An even greater burden would fall on us should we begin to issue debts denominated in foreign currencies—say, Treasury bonds payable in Swiss francs. Then we would truly begin to get into a position of owing obligations over whose ultimate value we had no control. This is the road down which Argentina, Mexico, Brazil, and Poland traveled in recent years when they issued bonds payable, not in their currencies, but in dollars. When the dollar became very expensive, they found they could no longer afford to buy the dollars they needed to repay the interest they owed. Defaults, or hairbreadth escapes from defaults, followed, with painful results for the borrowers, who were then unable to obtain any further credit abroad. The United States is still very far from such a grim end, but the recourse to foreign borrowing should make us aware that the risk exists.

A LEGISLATED BALANCED BUDGET?

Because of these arguments there exists a considerable body of public opinion firmly opposed to federal budget deficits under any conditions. This opinion has been mobilized behind a suggested amendment to the Constitution requiring Congress to enact a balanced budget except during emergencies such as war or a severe recession.

Would a balanced budget amendment be useful? It must be apparent from our discussion that we do not think so. Nor does the great majority of the economics profession, which has registered its opposition to such a proposed amendment in a message conveyed to President Reagan from the American Economic Association. To enact such an amendment, most economists fear (and we with them), would place a straitjacket on our ability to use the federal sector effectively, not only as a means of creating and financing national capital projects, such as roads or buildings that normally require financing through borrowing, but also in mounting programs to sustain purchasing power when recessions shrink private activity.

The Gramm-Rudman Approach

Despairing of finding a consensus to reduce expenditures, and faced with President Reagan's adamant opposition to any tax increase, Congress passed the Gramm-Rudman Balanced Budget Act in 1985. Under this act, budgets must be progressively reduced each year by scheduled percentages until a balanced budget is attained in 1993. If the President and Congress do not agree on the spending cuts or tax increases needed to achieve the mandated reductions, the cuts are to be imposed by law "across the board," with certain limited exceptions. In actual practice, it has had little effect. But its very existence raises the question: Should Congress try to specify a rigid track toward a balanced budget?

The Deficit Outlook

Economic prognostication is a treacherous business. Nevertheless, we here venture a few observations on the future of the deficit as we see it.

1. The Base Case. According to the Congressional Budget Office (CBO), the overall deficit is expected to decline both absolutely from $148 billion to $121

PERSONAL DEBTS AND PUBLIC DEBTS

In view of the fact that our national debt today figures out to over $8,000 for every man, woman, and child, it is not surprising that we frequently hear appeals to "common sense," telling us how much better we would be without this debt and how our grandchildren will groan under its weight.

Is this true? We have already discussed the fact that internal debts are different from external debts, but let us press the point home from a different vantage point. Suppose we decided that we would pay off the debt. This would mean that our government bonds would be redeemed for cash. To get the cash, we would have to tax ourselves (unless we wanted to roll the printing presses), so that what we would really be doing would be transferring money from taxpayers to bondholders.

Would that be a net gain for the nation? Consider the typical holder of a government bond—a family, a bank, or a corporation. It now holds the world's safest and most readily sold paper asset from which a regular income is obtained. After our debt is redeemed, our families, banks, and corporations will have two choices: (1) They can hold cash and get *no* income, or (2) they can invest in other securities that are slightly *less* safe. Are these investors better off? As for our grandchildren, it is true that if we pay off the debt they will not have to carry its weight. But to offset that, neither will they be carried by the comfortable government bonds they would otherwise have inherited. They will also be relieved from paying taxes to meet the interest on the debt. Alas, they will be relieved as well of the pleasure of depositing the Treasury checks for interest payments that used to arrive twice a year.

billion between 1989 and 1994, and in relation to GNP from 2.7 to 1.7 percent. Underlying this projection are two sharply divergent trends: a rising *"on-budget" deficit,* from $199 billion to $234 billion, and an even more rapidly rising *"off-budget" surplus* in the Social Security trust funds, from $39 billion to $121 billion. This projection rests on two critical assumptions: that the economy will grow on a steady path, and that there will be no major changes in spending or tax policy.

2. THE CRUCIAL ROLE OF BOOM OR RECESSION. Changes in economic conditions can vitally affect the above forecast. If real economic growth is higher than assumed by 1 percentage point per year for six years, the 1994 deficit would be $138 billion smaller! Interest rates matter too: An increase of just 1 point each year above the forecast can raise the deficit by $27 billion in 1994. If there is an unpredicted recession, the budget results could be a disaster: deficits above $300 billion.

3. POLICY CHANGES. The CBO baseline deficit assumes no change in tax laws and an eventual leveling off of federal expenditure growth in real terms. We think both assumptions are implausible. Federal spending has historically grown at just about the same real rate as the economy itself—around 3 percent per year—and we expect that it will continue to do so. Why? Because there are needs that cannot be ignored: for health care, environmental protection, housing, education, and infrastructure. We expect that Congress and the administration will have to address those needs in the years ahead. At the same time, we expect that taxes will be raised, in part to reduce the deficit and in part to fund new programs. In deficit terms, however, the result could be a wash: Higher taxes would nearly offset new spending initiatives, leaving the CBO baseline estimates close to target.

Table 6 presents the CBO's budget outlook as of August 1988.

The Public Sector as a Balancing Force

Is it imperative to balance the budget at all costs? If there is any single lesson we should like to drive home, it is that the government sector must be considered in conjunction with the private sectors before any intelligent judgment can be passed on its size, or on whether it should show a surplus, be in balance, or run a deficit.

There may be sound arguments to diminish the size of government spending or to increase it—arguments based on national security considerations, or on feelings about the proper role of the government with regard to poverty, or on convictions respecting the influence that government exerts on the private sector. These arguments may incline their holders to advocacy of a large, moderate, or small government presence.

But in our view, the decision to run a government sector deficit or not hinges entirely on the fact that it is the only part of the economy that is directly under our control. To repeat what we have said before, we cannot (and do not want to) command the households of the nation to save or spend, nor can we force businesses to invest or not. We can tempt both private sectors with tax and other incentives, but in the end a free enterprise system will do as it wishes. That

TABLE 6
Baseline Deficit Projections and Targets (by Fiscal Year)

	Actual	*Estimate*	*Projections*					
	1987	*1988*	*1989*	*1990*	*1991*	*1992*	*1993*	*1994*
			In Billions of Dollars					
Baseline projections								
On-budget deficit	170	194	199	199	206	212	220	234
Off-budget surplus*	20	39	52	63	74	86	99	113
Total deficit	150	155	148	136	131	126	121	121
Deficit targets	†	144	136	100	64	28	0	†
			As a Percentage of GNP					
Baseline projections								
On-budget deficit	3.8	4.1	3.9	3.7	3.6	3.4	3.3	3.3
Off-budget surplus*	0.4	0.8	1.0	1.2	1.3	1.4	1.5	1.6
Total deficit	3.4	3.2	2.9	2.5	2.3	2.0	1.8	1.7
Deficit targets	†	3.0	2.7	1.8	1.1	0.5	0	†

*Social security (Old-Age and Survivors Insurance and Disability Insurance Trust Funds).
†The Balanced Budget and Emergency Deficit Control Reaffirmation Act of 1987 established targets for 1988 through 1993.
Source: Congressional Budget Office.

leaves only the public sector to serve as a balancing mechanism. We do not preach that the mechanism be used in a particular way. But we must teach what it means when that mechanism is used to create a surplus or a deficit.

LOOKING BACK

KEY CONCEPTS

Understanding the makeup of the public sector

1 The public sector can usefully be thought of in two ways. One of them is as a flow of expenditures that contributes to GNP. In this view, state and local governments are more important than the federal government. The other is as the source of transfer payments plus purchases. Here the federal government plays a crucial role. Neither as a provider of GNP nor of incomes is the U.S. public sector large compared with other capitalist nations.

Not size but stability is important.

2 There is no clear relationship between the size of the public sector and the size of GNP per capita. What counts is the stability or instability the public sector imparts to the economy as a whole.

Automatic stabilizers lend stability to the overall economy.

3 Stability is enhanced by the tendency of government to serve as an automatic stabilizer. This results from the tendency of taxes to rise or fall faster than GNP because individuals move into higher or lower brackets. This slows down booms and cushions recessions. The "countercyclical" flows of certain transfers such as unemployment benefits and farm subsidies have the same effect.

Debt and deficit

4 Deficits refer to excesses of government expenditures over tax revenues. The amount of the deficit must be borrowed, and the sum of borrowings constitutes the national (or state or local) debt.

Public spending can be used to fill demand gaps.

5 The mechanics of the public sector show that government spending can be used to offset a demand gap exactly as the business sector can. The difference is that the public sector can be deliberately used to manage the economy in a way that the private sector cannot.

Corporation deficits are safe if they create earning assets. Government deficits can also create assets.

6 Are public deficits safe? A comparison with private corporations is useful. Corporations run two kinds of excesses of expenditures over receipts. One of these is a loss. No corporation can withstand prolonged losses. The other is capital investment. This is a form of "deficit spending" that can be maintained indefinitely if the assets built by the corporation are profitable. A government does not keep its books in the same way. But it too has assets—dams, roads, schools—that also create revenues for it by increasing GNP.

Real vs. nominal debts and deficits

7 Debts and deficits must be corrected for inflation and real growth. In real terms, the national debt is much reduced in size, but deficits have shown a real increase.

The difference internality makes

8 The government has one power that corporations do not. It can recapture its own expenditures through taxation. As long as its debts are internally held—held by U.S. citizens—it can always tax the revenues needed to pay interest or repay bonds. That is a power possessed only by the federal government, not by states or localities or businesses.

Deficits can be useful or dangerous.

9 Deficits can be useful in generating demand. They can be dangerous in generating excess demand—more demand than can be satisfied by the supply capabilities of the economy at going prices.

Three dangers: crowding out (high interest); inflation and the inflation tax; and the need for foreign borrowing

10 Three possibilities then impend. One is crowding out, which forces up interest rates as the public sector competes for funds with the private sector. The second possibility is inflation, as public and private demands force up prices. The rise of prices serves as an inflation tax, to help service the debt. The third is the need to borrow from foreign borrowers. This can be useful—but it also makes debt an external and not an internal burden.

A balanced budget amendment has been suggested to avoid these risks and the Gramm-Rudman Act seeks to enforce balanced accounts within five years. Most economists oppose such straitjacket measures.

11 Because of these dangers, there exists considerable public sentiment for a balanced budget amendment to the Constitution or for legislation to enforce budgetary balance within a stated time period. Most economists, including ourselves, oppose such measures. We need the ability to run deficits *when they are useful,* which a balanced budget amendment would very probably deprive us of. The public sector, with all its problems, remains a powerful means for influencing our economy, a means that we would not wish to see disappear.

ECONOMIC VOCABULARY

Automatic stabilizers 290
Deficits and debts 291
Internal and external debts 295
Crowding out 300
Inflation tax 301

QUESTIONS

1. What is the "size" of government? Can you distinguish the economic effects of government purchases from transfers? Are the effects of regulation counted in the GNP?
2. We have seen that the "size" and the "growth" of government are not related to the size or the growth of GNP. Do you feel that the size of government affects economic well-being in other ways? Are these effects desirable, undesirable, or neutral? Explain your reasoning.
3. Show in a diagram how increased government spending can offset a demand gap. Can you show how decreased taxation can do the same?
4. Show how the automatic stabilizers might work if we have a rise in unemployment of 1 million and a corresponding fall of production of 3 percent. Assume that (a) at the outset expenditures and taxes are both $600 billion; (b) every unemployed worker receives $5,000 in (tax-free) unemployment compensation; (c) every point drop in production reduces taxes by 1.5 percent; and (d) the multiplier is 2.
5. If the government is going to go into debt, does it matter whether it spends money for roads or relief? Weapons or education? Distinguish short-run income effects from long-term wealth-generating effects.
6. If the government invests in an aircraft carrier that is deemed necessary to the national defense, is that different from a company investing in a new headquarters deemed necessary for efficient operations? How are the two actions treated in their respective governmental and corporate accounts?
7. Suppose that you were a member of the Council of Economic Advisors and that the president wanted the opinion of the Council on the effect of a deficit totaling 5 percent of GNP. What facts would you take into consideration before recommending whether such a deficit would be growth-producing or not?
8. How would you answer someone who claimed that deficits were always bad because: (a) "The government, just like a household, can't live beyond its means." (b) "You can't spend what you don't have." (c) "Debts are the royal road to bankruptcy."

AN EXTRA WORD ABOUT

Controlling the Domestic Deficit

As these words are being written, the deficit in the federal government budget is approximately $150 billion and the nation is in a mood to get rid of it.

CAPITAL BUDGETS AS A CHOICE

Two big issues are at stake here. The first is whether we really want to get rid of the deficit at all! Here the question concerns how we define the deficit itself. We would strongly urge against cutting federal expenditures for capital-building purposes—federal office buildings, roads, research, aid to education, and the like. In our opinion, and in that of many economists, such growth-promoting expenditures ought to be segregated in a *capital budget,* not mixed in an overall budget with ordinary operating expenditures. If we had such a capital budget we would then only have to balance the normal operating budget, except in times of severe recession, when we might wish to run a deficit for stimulatory purposes.

BALANCING THE OPERATING BUDGET

If we had a capital budget, the problem of balancing the remaining (operating) budget would be much simpler than balancing a budget that included both operating and capital expenditures.* Easier or not, the problem of deciding which expenditures to trim or which taxes to raise remains the same. Here are our thoughts on the matter.

Could we just get rid of the military? The American people would not stand for that. Then could we deeply cut entitlement programs, such as social security and Medicare? No one would stand for that. Then suppose we reduced all the other costs of government—congressional and diplomatic expenses, the array of Washington agencies, Amtrak, space exploration, and the rest. To balance the budget at the expense of these items would virtually wipe them out altogether. There would be nothing left.

Then how about a mixture of all three? It is just the failure to produce such a mixture that has put us where we are—unable to agree on acceptable cuts, and bowing our heads to the Gramm-Rudman ax.

THE TAX SIDE

Then how can we reduce a deficit if it is too large? It seems to us that the best way out of this dilemma is to raise taxes substantially. This would not only reduce the deficit, but would also lower interest rates because government's need to borrow would be cut. Lower interest rates, in turn, would spur investment and diminish the cost of interest on the debt. Not least, increased government revenues would make it

*Items on a capital budget would be depreciated year by year, just as they are on a corporate capital budget. These annual depreciation charges would be included in the normal operating budget.

possible to preserve a level of public expenditure that seems to us necessary to improve the quality of both public and private life.

But what taxes? There is the rub. To raise the needed revenues from income taxes might well be the fairest way, especially now that income tax reform has given us a simpler, less loophole-ridden, and still reasonably progressive income tax system. But higher income tax rates seem to be the least attractive option for many politicians. An effort to raise a large sum by a much higher payroll tax would also encounter stiff opposition, since such taxes are dedicated (for political reasons) to the social security funds, and since they fall far more heavily on the low-paid worker than on the more highly paid one.

Some economists have advocated adopting a European-style *value-added tax*—a sales tax paid by businesses on the value they add to the commodities they handle. Value-added taxes are passed along from business to business and are finally paid by the consumer. But VATs have serious drawbacks. Among them: (1) They are about as regressive as the payroll tax; (2) they impart a inflationary shock to prices when they are introduced; and (3) they compete for the same tax base that many states and localities now rely on.

A WAY OUT?

So raising taxes is easier said than done. Nevertheless, if we are to bring the budget into manageable shape, we believe it is the best way out of our present fix. Therefore we favor tax increases large enough to change the present budgetary picture in a dramatic way, but not so large as to pose impossible political or dangerous economic strains.

How large should such tax increases be? The size of the tax hike cannot be specified precisely because it will vary with the state of the economy. If we are experiencing a severe recession when these words are read, we would not favor any tax increase at all. The full deficit would then be needed to sustain our level of employment and expenditure. If we should be enjoying a strong boom, we would favor a tax rise that might even produce a surplus in the operating budget, for the advantages of reducing government borrowing would become greater the stronger the investment spending of the private sector. In such a strong economy, however, revenues would be higher, and the deficit smaller, to begin with.

THE CRITERION OF FAIRNESS

Where would the additional tax revenues come from? Political expediency suggests a multiple-source approach, combining higher oil and gasoline taxes, heavier "sin" taxes on cigarettes and alcohol, and a higher upper-bracket rate for the income tax. We believe that a better policy is to adjust income tax rates to get an additional 1 percent of GNP in revenue. This would require raising each marginal rate by about 3 percentage points, leaving a top rate still below 35 percent. Such a tax rise should be accompanied by a sharp reduction in interest rates, so as to assure that it does not slow the pace of growth in the economy overall. We strongly believe that such a tax increase will be perceived as fair and necessary. That is one of the advantages of writing a textbook! It gives us a soapbox from which to talk.*

*We get back on the soapbox in the extra word on "Fair Taxation," in Chapter 31.

CHAPTER 18

Aggregate Demand and Supply

A LOOK AHEAD

We have gradually assembled the parts of the puzzle. It remains only to piece them together to get a picture of how GNP is determined. That is what we do in this chapter.

1 We will show how the three sectors we have studied—consumption, investment, and government spending—together make up *aggregate demand,* a sum total of spending in the economy.
2 We will show how aggregate demand interacts with *capacity,* or the potential to produce, to determine an *equilibrium* level of real GNP.
3 We will show how a true supply curve for GNP can be introduced, so that with supply and demand together we can jointly determine the equilibrium level of real GNP and the rate of inflation.

We are near the destination toward which we have been traveling for several chapters. We are now almost in a position to understand how to determine the actual level of GNP that confronts us in daily life—"the state of the economy" that affects our employment, our incomes, our sense of security, our economic well-being and satisfaction or dissatisfaction. By the end of this chapter we will have arrived at this destination, and will even have taken a step beyond it, to examine how real GNP is determined in relation to prices.

THE UTILIZATION OF POTENTIAL

In Chapter 13 we examined the sources of growth in the capacity to produce, including the contributions of labor and capital and of improvements in technology. These gave us the abstraction of the production possibility frontier, which indicates the upper limit (at any given time) of our ability to generate GNP. Of course the production possibility frontier is always shifting outward as time goes on. But what determines whether, at any given moment, one is on the production possibility curve or within it? Put another way, what determines whether one is using, or not using, the capacity or potential to produce that actually exists? That is the first subject of the analysis in this chapter.

The Identity of Costs and Incomes

By restricting our focus to the *use of potential output,* we simplify our problem dramatically. What we must analyze is the relationship between *spending,* or aggregate demand for goods and services, on the one hand, and *incomes* on the other.

We know from Chapter 12 that incomes are identically equal to the *costs* of production. And we also know that costs of production are identically equal to the *value* of production: $F+T+D = GNP$. **Every dollar going into production must become the income of some individual or institution.** The value of GNP produced must therefore be identical with the value of GNP earned!

We can show this identity in Figure 1, which makes clear that the resulting relationship is a 45 degree line. Study this figure and make sure you understand why an identity between costs and incomes *must* be such a line. Do you see that each dollar by which we increase output must add a dollar to income?

So every dollar spent will be dollar earned. But how much spending will there be? That is the great unanswered question.

Aggregate Demand

We discover the answer in two steps. First, in Figure 2, we construct a schedule of *desired* spending by adding together the components that make up GNP: consumption, investment, and government. Note that of the three components of spending

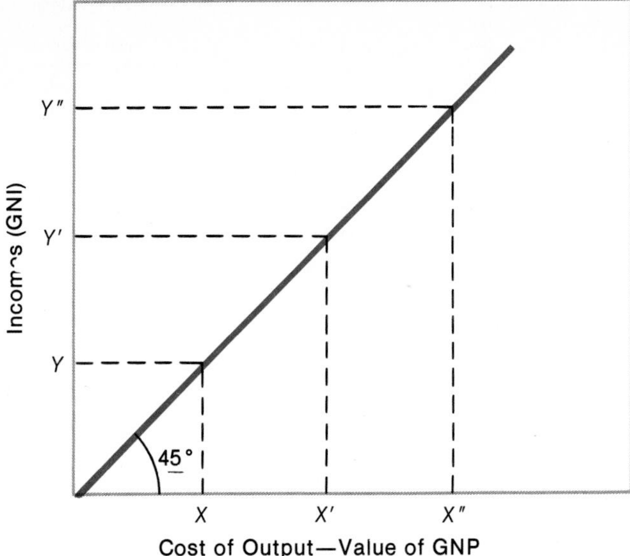

FIGURE 1
Identity of Incomes and Costs
Here we illustrate the identity between output (C + I + G + X) and income (F + T + D). Every unit of output generates incomes that exactly match its costs. This identity gives rise to a 45-degree line, which lies equidistant between the two axes at all points.

only consumer spending rises sharply when output rises. This is enough to give the *aggregate demand function* in panel IV its characteristic upward slope.

It now remains to relate this aggregate demand function to the actual value of output. This is done in Figure 3. **The point of intersection of the aggregate demand function with the 45 degree line gives us an equilibrium value of gross national product. It shows us how much of our capacity we will use at any given time. At levels of GNP below the equilibrium value, aggregate spending is higher than the value of actual output and GNP will tend to rise. At levels of GNP above the equilibrium value, output is higher than desired spending, there is a demand gap, and GNP will tend to fall. Only at the equilibrium value do spending and the value of output just match.**

Note that our equilibrium does not necessarily occur at the point where all of potential capacity is used. It may well occur far short of that point, leaving factories idle and workers unemployed. If so, the only remedy is to shift the aggregate demand curve upward until the intersection (and equilibrium) occurs at capacity or full employment. How is this to be done? By changing any of the components of aggregate demand—by altering spending for consumption, for investment, or by government. Here is the basic mechanism of **demand management policy.**

ANOTHER VIEW OF EQUILIBRIUM

Saving and Investment

Equilibrium is a complicated subject, so let us fix the matter in our minds by going over the problem once more from a different point of view. Suppose that by means of a questionnaire we are going to predict the level of GNP for an island

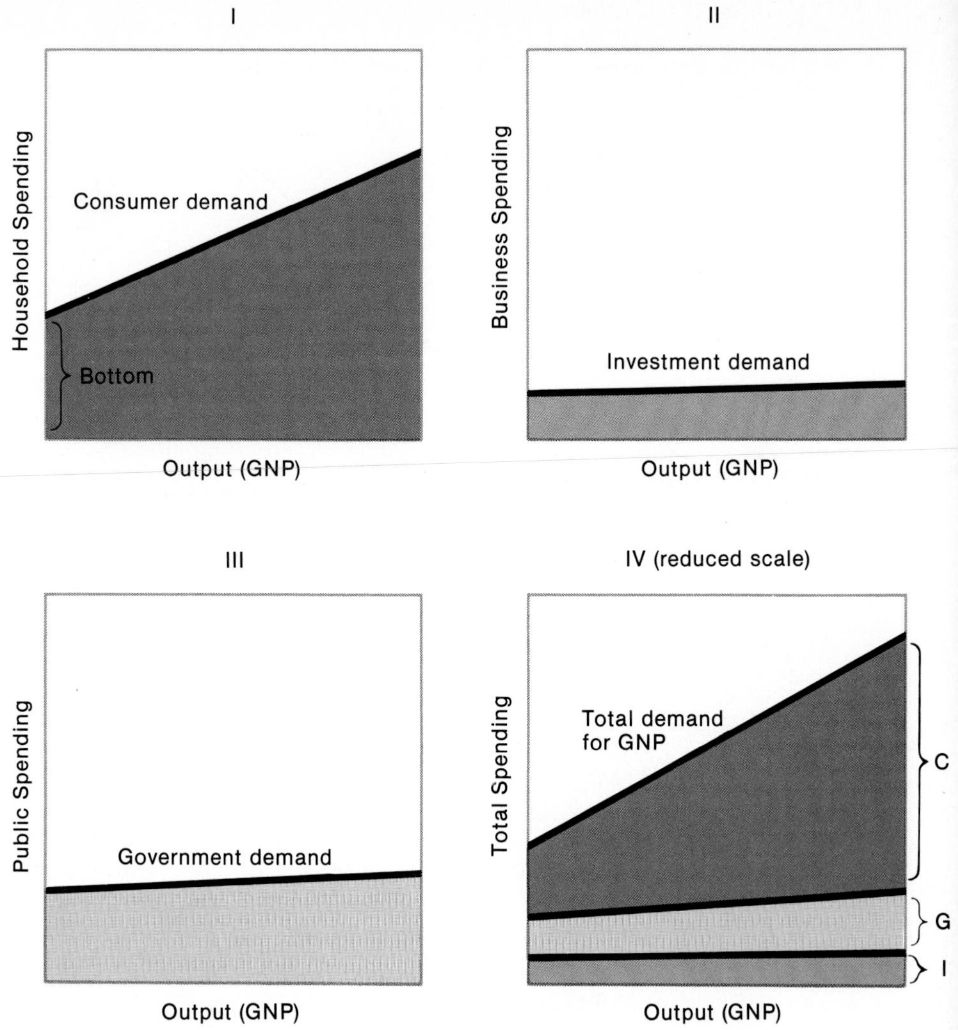

FIGURE 2
The Aggregate Demand Function
These panels show the amounts of spending that will take place in each sector (and then the three combined) as the degree of ultilization increases. Spending rises in the household sector because of the propensity to consume. The accelerator and various governmental "propensities" give a slight positive slope to spending in those sectors as well, but they are not strictly necessary to our analysis.

community. To simplify our task, we will ignore government and exports so that we can concentrate solely on consumption, saving, and investment.

We begin by interrogating the island's business community about their intentions for next year's investment. We know, of course, that some investment will be induced and that therefore investment will partly be a result of the island's level of income; but again for simplification, we assume that businesses have laid their plans for next year. They tell us they intend to spend $30 million for new housing, plant, equipment, and other capital goods.

TABLE 1
The interplay of saving and investment reveals the equilibrium output just as schedules of supply and demand show an equilibrium price.

Income	*Consumption* (in Millions)	*Saving*	*Investment*
$100	$75	$25	$30
110	80	30	30
120	85	35	30

Next our team of pollsters approaches a carefully selected sample of the island's householders and asks them what their consumption and savings plans are for the coming year. Here the answer will be a bit disconcerting. Reflecting on their past experience, our householders will reply: "We can't say for sure. We'd *like* to spend such-and-such an amount and save the rest, but really it depends on what our incomes will be." Our poll, in other words, will have to make inquiries about different possibilities that reflect the island's propensity to consume."

Now we tabulate our results and find that we have the schedule shown in Table 1.

Interplay of Saving and Investment

If we look at the last two columns of Table 1, those for saving and investment, we can see a powerful cross play that will characterize our model economy at different levels of income, for the forces of investment and saving will not be in balance at all levels. At some levels, the propensity to save will outrun the act of purposeful investment; at others, the motivation to save will be less than the investment expenditure made by business firms. In fact, our island model shows that at only one level of income—$110 million—will the saving and investment schedules coincide.

What does it mean when intended savings are greater than the flow of intended

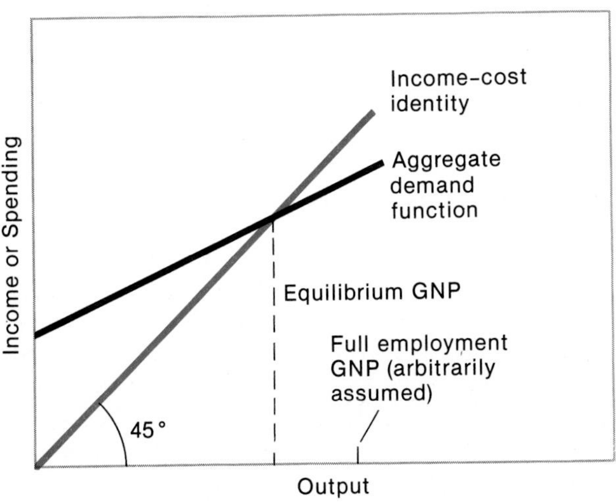

FIGURE 3
Determination of GNP
Here the 45-degree line shows the amount of income associated with different amounts of output. They are identical. The aggregate demand function shows the amount of spending at different levels of output. Where spending equals income we have an equilibrium level of GNP. Note that this is not *necessarily the level corresponding to full employment.*

investment? It means that people are *trying* to save out of their given incomes a larger amount than business is willing to invest. Now if we think back to the exposition of the economy in a circular flow, it will be clear what the result must be. The economy cannot maintain a closed circuit of income and expenditure if savings are larger than investment. This will simply give rise to a demand gap, the repercussions of which we have already explored.

But a similar lack of equilibrium results if intended savings are less than intended investment expenditure (or if investment spending is greater than the propensity to save). Now business will be pumping out more than enough to offset the savings gap. The additional expenditures, over and above those that compensate for saving, will flow into the economy to create new incomes—and out of those new incomes, new savings.

Income and output will be stable, in other words, only when the flow of intended investment just compensates for the flow of intended saving. Investment and saving thus conduct a tug of war around this pivot point, driving the economy upward when intended investment exceeds the flow of intended saving; downward when it fails to offset saving. In Figure 4 we show this cross current in schematic form. Note that as incomes fall very low, householders will *dissave.*

Injections vs. Leakages

We can easily make our graph more realistic by adding taxes *(T)* and imports *(M)* to savings, and exports *(X)* and government spending to investment. The vertical axis in Figure 5 now shows all *leakages and injections.*

We recall that leakages are any acts, such as savings, increased taxes, profits, or imports, that reduce spending. Similarly, injections are any acts, such as investment or higher government spending or rising exports or even a spontaneous jump in consumption, that lead to higher spending. And just to introduce another feature of the real world, we will tilt the injection line upward, on the assumption that induced investment will be an important constituent of total investment. The leakages curve will not be exactly the same shape as the savings curve, but it will

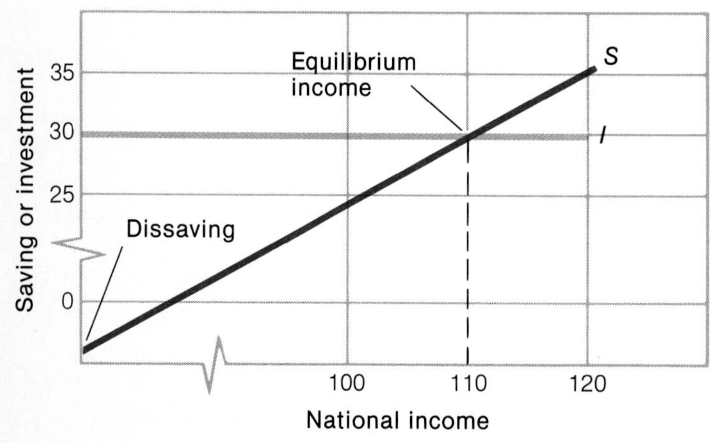

FIGURE 4
Saving and Investment
Here we simply put into graphic form the schedules of saving and investment (or leakages and injection). The equilibrium point is easy to see.

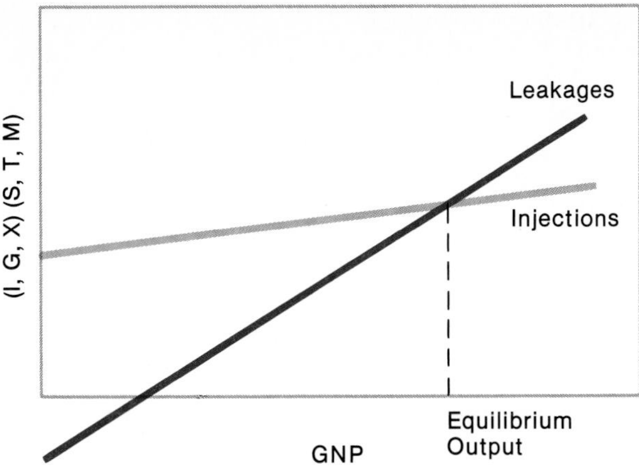

FIGURE 5
Leakages and Injections

reflect the general tendency of savings and imports and taxes to rise with income.

The careful reader may have noted that we speak of *intended* savings and *intended* investment as the critical forces in establishing equilibrium. This is because there is a formal balance—an identity—between *all* saving and investment (or all leakages and all injections) at every moment in the economy. In the same way, purchases in any market must exactly equal sales at each and every moment, but that does not mean the market is in equilibrium at all times.

Economists distinguish between the formal identity between total saving and investment (or between all leakages and all injections) and the active difference between *intended* savings and investment (or *intended* saving, *intended* imports, *intended* business saving, etc., and *intended* additional expenditures of all kinds).

What matters in the determination of GNP is the *actions* people are taking—actions that lead them to try to save or to invest or that make them struggle to get rid of unintended inventories or to build up desired inventories. These are the kinds of activities that will be moving the economy up and down in the never-ending "quest" for its equilibrium point. **The fact that at each moment past savings and investment are identical from the viewpoint of the economy's balance sheet is important only insofar as we are economic accountants. As analysts of the course of future GNP, we concentrate on the inequality of future, intended actions.**

The Paradox of Thrift

The fact that income must always move toward the level where the flows of intended saving and investment are equal leads to one of the most startling—and important—paradoxes of economics. **This is the so-called paradox of thrift, a paradox that tells us that the attempt to increase intended saving may, under certain circumstances, lead to a fall in actual saving.**

The paradox is not difficult for us to understand at this stage. An attempt to save, when it is not matched by an equal willingness to invest or to increase government expenditure, will cause a gap in demand. This means that business will not be getting back enough money to cover costs. Production will be curtailed or costs will be slashed, with the result that incomes will fall. As incomes fall, savings will also fall, because the ability to save will be reduced. Thus, by a chain of activities working their influence on income and output, the effort to *increase* savings may end in an actual *reduction* of savings.

This frustration of individual desires is perhaps the most striking instance of a common situation in economic life: the incompatibility between some kinds of individual behavior and some collective results. An individual farmer, for instance, may produce a larger crop in order to enjoy a bigger income; but if all farmers produce bigger crops, farm prices are apt to fall so heavily that farmers end up with less income. So, too, a single family may wish to save a very large fraction of its income for reasons of financial prudence; but if all families seek to save a great deal of their incomes, the result—unless investment also rises—will be a fall in expenditure and a common failure to realize savings objectives. The paradox of thrift, in other words, teaches us that the freedom of behavior available to a few individuals cannot always be generalized to all individuals.*

THE MULTIPLIER

There remains only one part of the jigsaw puzzle to put into place. This is the integration of the *multiplier* into our analysis of the determination of GNP.

We remember that the essential point about the multiplier was that changes in investment, government spending, or exports resulted in larger changes in GNP because the additions to income were respent, creating still more new incomes. Further, we remember that the size of the multiplier effect depended on the marginal propensity to consume, the marginal propensity to tax, and the marginal propensity to buy imports as GNP rises. Now we have to show how this basic analytic concept enters into the determination of equilibrium GNP.

Let us begin with the diagram that shows injections and leakages, and let us now draw a new line showing an increase in injections (Figure 6). Notice that the increase in GNP is larger than the increase in injections. *This is the multiplier itself in graphic form.*

Slope of the Leakage Curve

Both diagrams also show that the relation between the original increase in injections and the resulting increase in GNP depends on the *slope* of the leakage line. Figure 7 shows us two different injections—GNP relationships that arise from differing slopes.

*The paradox of thrift is actually only a subtle instance of a type of faulty reasoning we discussed earlier called the *fallacy of composition.* The fallacy consists of assuming that what is true of the individual case must also be true of all cases combined. The flaw in reasoning lies in our tendency to overlook "side effects" of individual actions (such as the decrease in spending associated with an individual's attempt to save more, or the increase in supply when a farmer markets his larger crop), which may be negligible in isolation, but which are very important in the aggregate.

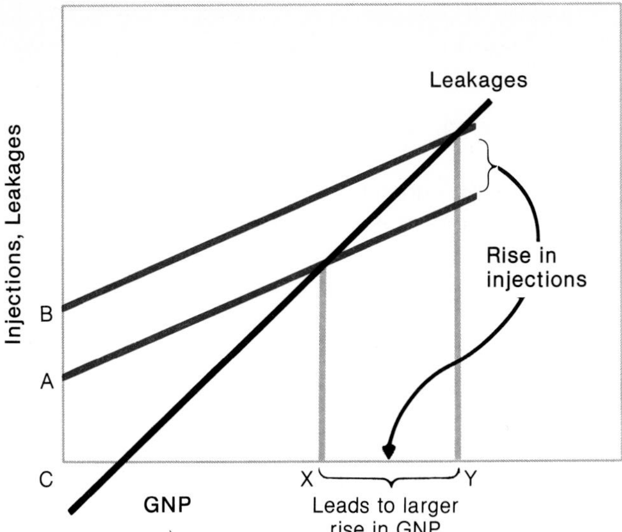

FIGURE 6
Multiplier in Graphic Form
An increase of injections of AB leads to a larger increase in GNP, XY. This is a graphic presentation of the multiplier. It is important to understand why AB creates XY. The reason is that the leakage curve slopes. And why does it slope? Because its slope represents the marginal propensity to save. And that is the cause of the multiplier.

Notice how the *same* increase in spending (from *OA* to *OB* on the injections axis) leads to a much smaller increase in panel I GNP (from *OX* to *OY*), where the leakage slope is high, than in panel II (from *OX′* to *OY′*), where the slope is more gradual.

Why is the increase greater when the slope is more gradual? The answer should be obvious. The slope represents the marginal propensity to save, to tax, to import—in short, all the marginal propensities that give rise to leakages. If these propensities are high—if there are high leakages—then the slope of the leakage

FIGURE 7
Two Multipliers
Here is another chance to relate the graphics of the multiplier to the underlying behavior that causes the multiplier. The two differently sloped leakage curves generate different multipliers. This is because their different slopes picture different patterns of spending and saving.

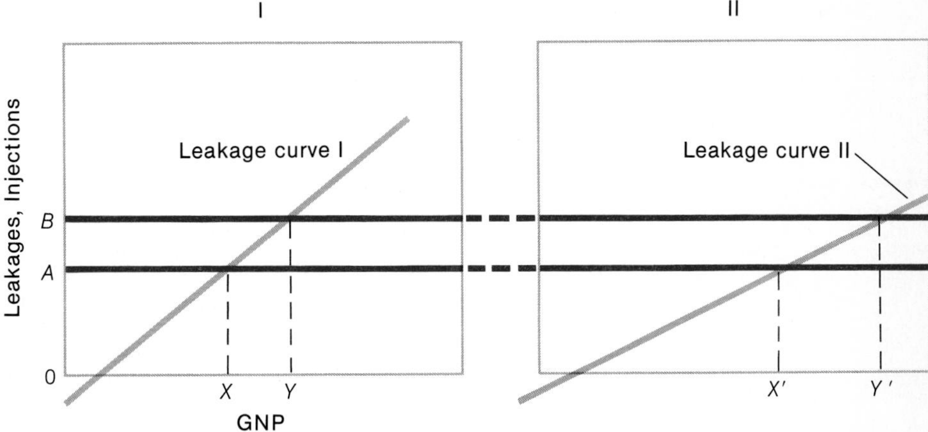

curve will be high. If it is low, the leakage curve will be flat, and the increase of GNP will be greater for any given amount of stimulus to spending.

A Last Look at Equilibrium

Thus we finally understand how GNP reaches an equilibrium position after a change in demand. It is worth repeating, however, that the word *equilibrium* does not imply a static, motionless state. Nor does it mean a desired state. We use equilibrium only to illustrate that *given* certain behavior patterns, there will be a determinate point to which their interaction will push the level of income; and *as long as the underlying patterns of injections and leakages remain unchanged, the forces they exert will keep income at this level.*

In fact, of course, the flows of spending and saving are continually changing so that the equilibrium level of the economy is constantly shifting, like a ping-pong ball suspended in a rising jet of water. Equilibrium can thus be regarded as a target toward which the economy is constantly propelled by the push-pull between leakages and injections. The target may be attained but momentarily before the economy is again impelled to seek a new point of rest. What our diagrams and the underlying analysis explain for us, then, is not a single determinate point at which our economy will in fact settle down, but the *direction* it will go in quest of a resting place as the dynamic forces of the system exert their pressures.

Aggregate Supply and Price

Our presentation of the determination of equilibrium GNP up to now has been carefully and deliberately circumscribed. We have asked only how the level of GNP is determined, in the short run, for an economy with a given, fixed potential to produce. We have not at all investigated how the *price level* of that GNP is set. To do so, we need to move beyond the simplified 45 degree line analysis and introduce proper curves for the "supply" and "demand" for aggregate GNP.

Here is a demonstration of the manner in which the "price" of GNP—that is, the average price level of total output—interacts with the quantities of output that are produced.*

To understand this analysis, it is helpful to visualize the economy itself divided between two broad classes of economic actors: those who supply goods and services and those who demand them. Let us imagine that both groups wake up one morning and go to market knowing only what yesterday's output levels and prices were. They do not know what today's outputs and price levels will be, though they may have an idea in their heads about how they will react to various prices they may see. The question we ask is: How will they behave when they get to market, and what will the equilibrium value and prices of output be? As we can see, if this situation is the image of a market, magnified to encompass the entire economy.

*We are grateful to Professor James Devine of Loyola Marymount College for persuading us that a simplified version of the aggregate supply/aggregate demand framework familiar to advanced students can be made accessible in our text, and for permission to incorporate his ideas into this work.

The Demand for GNP

Figure 8 shows the demand and supply curves of the two classes of actors—demanders and suppliers. The demand curve *DD* shows the reactions of demanders to the prices they may find. For example, if prices seem unusually low, buyers will seek to stock up on goods, and the quantity of real GNP demanded will be higher. Conversely, if prices seem unusually high, the quantity of GNP demanded will be reduced. This gives the demand curve for GNP its downward slope in relation to price. (Meanwhile, in the background, the aggregate demand function we have already studied tells us where the *position* of the *DD* curve will be: A higher aggregate demand curve in Figure 3 will correspond to an upward, or rightward, shift of the *DD* curve to *D′D′* in Figure 8.)

The Supply of GNP

For suppliers, the relationships between price and output supplied are reversed. If the price level seems high, suppliers will be happy to work overtime or to reach into inventory to supply a high level of current output. If prices seem low, supplies will be withdrawn and commodities will become scarce. Thus the supply curve for output has its characteristic upward slope.

FIGURE 8
Supply and Demand for GNP
The aggregate supply and aggregate demand curves jointly tell us what the equilibrium rate of output and the equilibrium price level will be. Note the shape of the SS *curve.*

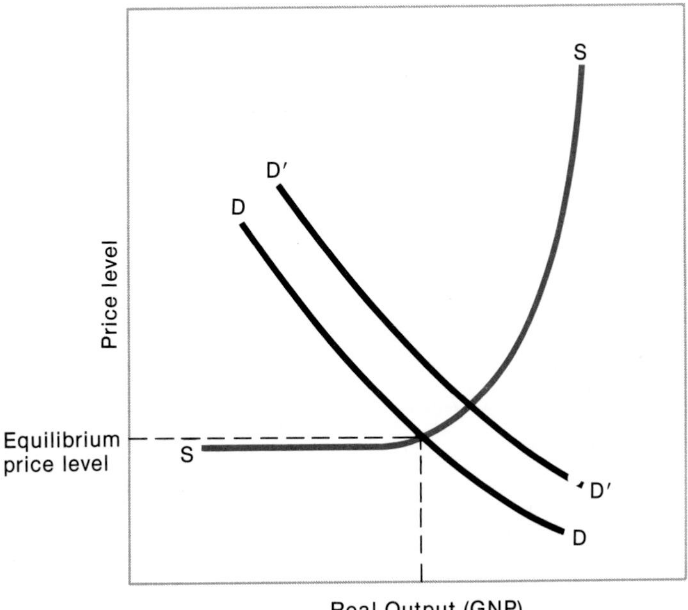

Note, too, that suppliers are limited by physical conditions. To the left of Figure 8, where levels of output are low, there is little change in price as we increase output. This is because unemployed factors can be put to use as demand for output grows, and suppliers are kept from pushing up prices by intense competition. But as we approach full employment, it becomes more difficult to mobilize factors and the supply price of real GNP begins to rise. Finally, as we scrape the limits of capacity, supply curves become nearly vertical, and increases in the demand for GNP bring virtually no more output, only higher prices. We are at the production possibility frontier—a situation not unlike that faced by an economy at war.

Expected Prices and Supply

We have examined the shape of the *SS* curve. What determines its position? The answer is: *expected prices* or inflation. Suppliers of goods and services come to market with an idea of the rate of inflation that will prevail over the market day. And they will set their "offer" prices at rates that compensate them for the expected rise in the general level of prices. *If the expected rate of inflation rises, the whole* SS *curve shifts vertically upward.* You can see that this must have the effect of reducing real GNP, unless the *DD* curve shifts up as well, reflecting a corresponding increase in money incomes and the desire to spend. Figure 9 shows such offsetting shifts in *SS* and *DD*.

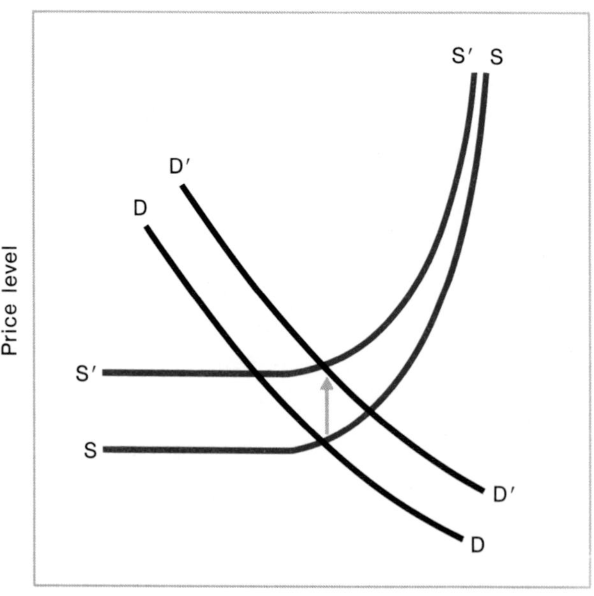

FIGURE 9
Shifts of *SS* and *DD*
An upward shift of aggregate supply, caused by a price shock, will be inflationary if it is not accommodated by a corresponding outward shift in aggregate demand. What will happen if the demand curve does not shift? Can you see how that will result in the condition known as "stagflation"—inflation with recession?

Dynamics of Supply and Demand

We can also analyze the movements of *SS* and *DD* separately.

Look first at the aggregate demand curve, *DD*. Suppose that changes because a sudden increase or decrease in investment brings increases or decreases in spending. We can see that the effects of these shifts in demand will have relatively little impact on the price level of GNP as long as the *DD* curve intersects with the "flat" portion of the *SS* curve, but that changes in demand are likely to bring marked changes in price when *DD* intersects with the rising portion of the *SS* curve. We will be looking into this output-price relationship in our inflation chapters ahead.

But the *SS* curve also shows something else. The flat portion can be thought of as representing average costs of production in rather slack times. The diagram shows that any forces that raise the "flat" part of the curve will raise the supply price of GNP even if there is a high level of unemployment. This is a graphic depiction of the kind of inflation we associate with upward wage "drift," or with external cost shocks such as the famous OPEC oil boosts of the 1970s.

We can also see that the SS *curve can move rightward, giving us more output at the same price level, to the extent that we enjoy rising productivity.* Here is the growth associated with an expansion of the production possibility frontier. Thus we see how the basic outline of the aggregate supply/aggregate demand framework can serve to bridge our transition from the formal model of macroeconomic relationships into the real world of output and prices to be tackled in Chapter 23.

LOOKING BACK

KEY CONCEPTS

Actual output depends on the degree of utilization of human and other resources.

1 The potential output of the economy is determined by its production possibilities. But the amount actually produced depends on how close we can get to the production possibility frontier. This depends on the degree to which we utilize our human and other resources.

Aggregate demand relates spending and output.

2 The degree of utilization depends on the demand for GNP. The demand for GNP is determined by the amounts the sectors will want to buy at different levels of utilization.

The identity of cost and income means that the supply curve will be a 45 degree line.

3 We use the identity between costs and incomes to show that at all levels of utilization output will generate incomes equal to its cost. The relation of identity between cost and income means that the supply curve of GNP will be a 45 degree line. Whatever the level of output, the supply of income (or spending power) will be identical with the cost of producing that output.

Equilibrium GNP is most easily shown as the

4 Equilibrium GNP is determined by the position of the aggregate demand function. It is easily depicted in terms of the interaction of the

level of output where $S = I$, or leakages equal injections.	savings and investment, or leakage and injection, schedules. At equilibrium, saving must equal investment, and leakages must equal injections.
Investment or injection determine the level of income, via the multiplier. Attempts to increase S without increasing income will fail.	**5** In the interplay between S and I (or leakages and injections), it is investment (or injections) that play the critical role in establishing the equilibrium level of output. Saving or leakages are dependent, passive variables in the process. Changes in intended investment will lead, via the multiplier, to changes in income that permit the economy to save the amount that matches intended investment. Attempts to save more, without boosting income first, are doomed to failure—the paradox of thrift.
Equilibrium GNP may not be full-utilization GNP.	**6** An equilibrium GNP may not be a socially satisfactory GNP. The economy may be at rest although it is well behind its production frontiers.
Aggregate supply and demand jointly determine prices and GNP.	**7** We can construct a framework that models both the demand and supply sides of the determination of GNP. This framework helps us see the relationship between an aggregate demand curve, an aggregate supply curve, and both the level of GNP and the rate of inflation.

ECONOMIC VOCABULARY

Utilization 312
Aggregate demand function 313
Demand management policy 313
Injections vs. leakages 316
Intended and unintended S and I 317
Paradox of thrift 317
Expected rate of inflation 322

QUESTIONS

1. Suppose an economy turns out to have the following consumption and saving schedule (in billions). Fill in the missing numbers.

Income	*Saving*	*Consumption*
$400	$50	$350
450	—	395
—	60	440
550	70	—
600	85	—

Now suppose that firms intend to invest $60 billion. What will be the level of income? If investment rises to $85 billion, what will be the new level of income? What will be the multiplier?

2. Diagram the model above assuming that $I = 60$, then that $I = 85$.
3. Show in the diagram that the multiplier is determined by the slope of the leakage curve. What does this slope represent?
4. Copy Figure 3 showing the curves that establish where equilibrium GNP will be. Now draw a new, higher demand curve, and drop a perpendicular line to the horizontal axis to show where the new equilibrium GNP will be. Measure the distance showing the rise in the demand for GNP and the distance showing the change in equilibrium GNP. Can you see that GNP will increase by more than the rise in demand? And that this is simply another way of showing the multiplier? And that, as in Figure 7, the multiplier will depend on the slope of the leakage curve, here depicted as its twin, the marginal propensity to spend?
5. Here is a question to be thought about very carefully. Why does GNP have to increase if we are to maintain a given level of employment? Would this be true if the size of the labor force were constant and if people did not expect to improve their levels of consumption? How does growing productivity figure into the picture? If the population grows at 1 percent a year, if people strive for an increase in real living standards of 2 percent a year, and if productivity grows by 2 percent, by how much will *real* aggregate demand have to grow?

CHAPTER 19

Money and Banking

A LOOK AHEAD

This next section of four chapters is focused on the subject of money. We will tackle it in stages. First, in Chapter 19, we learn the ABCs of money—what it is, and what we call the "money supply." Next, in Chapter 20, we learn how the Federal Reserve, together with the banking system, regulates the supply of money. In Chapter 21 we study money in action—the impact of changes in the money supply on the level of the macrosystem. And finally we turn to the Great Debate about money—how important is it in moving the economy?

In this chapter we begin by studying two things:

1 What is money, and how is it created by the banking system?

2 How do banks work?

This is another chapter to read twice. The basic ideas are not hard to get, but it takes some time until the practice of banking becomes clear. The questions at the back will help.

We have almost completed our analysis of the major elements of macroeconomics, and soon we can bring our analysis to bear on some major problems of the economy. But first there is a matter we must integrate into our discussion. This is the role that money plays in fixing or changing the level of GNP, along with the other forces that we have come to know.

Actually, we have been talking about money throughout our exposition. After all, one cannot discuss expenditure without assuming the existence of money. But now we must look behind this unexamined assumption and find out exactly what we mean when we speak of money. This will entail two tasks. In this chapter we investigate the question of what money *is*—for money is surely one of the most perplexing inventions of human society. In our next chapter, once we have come to understand what currency and gold and bank deposits are and how they come into being, we will look into the effect money has on our economic operations.

THE DEFINITION OF MONEY

Let us begin by asking "What is money?" Coin and currency are certainly money. But are checks money? Are the deposits from which we draw checks money? Are savings accounts? Government bonds?

The answer is somewhat arbitrary. Basically, money is anything with which we can make purchases. But there exists a spectrum of financial instruments that serve this purpose—a continuum that varies in liquidity or the ease with which it can be used for purchasing. By law, coin and currency are money because they are defined by law as "legal tender": A seller *must* accept them as payment. Checks do not have to be accepted (we have all seen signs in restaurants saying "WE DO NOT ACCEPT CHECKS"), although in fact checks are overwhelmingly the most prevalent means of payment.

Thus a variety of things can be counted as money. By far the most important general definition is the sum of all cash in the hands of the public (including traveler's checks) and checkable deposits. This amount is called M1 by the Federal Reserve, which also keeps track of M2 (M1 plus dollar balances abroad, money market funds, and savings accounts), and M3 (M2 plus large savings deposits and some other special types of accounts), up to L, M3 plus all other liquid assets. The difference is very large—in 1987, for instance, M1 was $753; M2 was $2,894; M3 was $3,661; and L was $4,330 billion.

Which is the correct figure? That depends on many things. For our purposes, which are to learn about our monetary system, we will settle for M1, meaning cash in the hands of the public plus checking accounts. This is the figure that most people are primarily concerned about.

Currency

In 1987, for example, M1 was $753 billion, of which $200 billion was currency held by the public and $292 billion was the total of ordinary checking accounts, or **demand deposits,** to give them their technical name.

CREDIT CARDS

Money serves as a mechanism for storing potential purchasing power and for actually purchasing goods and services. Since cash and personal checks are the principal means for making these purchases, money has come to be defined as cash outside banks plus checking accounts. But what about credit cards? Shouldn't they be considered money?

Credit cards clearly can be used to make purchases, so they appear on the surface to have a vital attribute of money. But a moment's reflection shows that in fact they *substitute* for the cash or checks in which payment is finally made. The moment you pay your credit card bill, or the moment the credit card company pays the local merchant, the credit card is replaced by standard money. Thus credit cards play the role of money only to the extent that credit bills are unpaid!

In this role credit cards are not unique. Any unpaid bill or charge account is like money, in that you are able to purchase goods and services in exchange for your personal IOU. In a sense, each person is able to "print" money to the extent that he can persuade people to accept his IOUs. For most of us, that extent is very limited.

From an economist's point of view, the value of all outstanding trade credit (unpaid bills, unpaid charge accounts, or credit cards) *should* be considered money, but it is not included in the official statistics for two reasons. First, it is difficult or impossible to figure how much trade credit is outstanding at any moment. Second, fluctuations in trade credit do not have a big impact on the economy. Ordinarily, the value of trade credit does not vary much, and therefore trade credit does not give rise to substantial changes in the effective money supply.

Of the two main kinds of money, currency is the most familiar to us. Yet there is a considerable mystery even about currency. Who determines how much currency there is? How is the supply of bills or coins regulated?

We often assume that the supply of currency is set by the government that issues it. Yet when we think about it, we realize that the government does not just hand out money, and certainly not coins or bills. When the government pays people, it is nearly always by check.

Then who does fix the amount of currency in circulation? You can answer the question by asking how you yourself determine how much currency you will carry. If you think about it, the answer is that you cash a check when you need more currency than you have, and you put the currency back into your checking account when you have more than you need.

What you do, everyone does. **The amount of cash that the public holds at any**

time is no more and no less than the amount it *wants* to hold. When it needs more—at Christmas, for instance—the public draws currency by cashing checks on its own checking accounts; and when Christmas is past, shopkeepers (who have received the public's currency) return it to their checking accounts.

Thus the amount of currency we have bears an obvious, important relation to the size of our bank accounts, for we can't write checks for cash if our accounts will not cover them. Does this mean, then, that the banks have as much currency in their vaults as the total of our checking accounts? No, it does not. But to understand why not, let us follow the course of some currency that we deposit in our banks for credit to our accounts.

Demand Deposits

When you put money into a checking account, you have the right and the ability to take your money back out—all of it—at any time; hence the term *demand deposit.* Yet the bank does not hold that money for you as a pile of specially earmarked bills or as a bundle of checks made out to you from some payer. The bank takes notice of your deposit simply by crediting your account, a computer entry recording your present balance. After the amount of the currency or check has been credited to you, the currency is put away with the bank's general store of vault cash and the checks are sent to the banks from which they came, where they will be charged against the accounts of the people who wrote them.

There is probably no misconception in economics harder to dispel than the idea that banks are warehouses stuffed with money. In point of fact, you might search as hard as you pleased in your bank, but you would find no money that was yours other than a computer entry in your name. This seems like a very unreal form of money. And yet, the fact that you can present a check at the teller's window and convert your computer entry into cash proves that your account must nonetheless be real.

But suppose that you and all the other depositors tried to convert your accounts into cash on the same day. You would then find something shocking. There would not be nearly enough cash in the bank's till to cover the total withdrawals. In 1987, for instance, total demand deposits in the United States amounted to about $292 billion. But the total amount of coin and currency held by the banks was only $26 billion!

At first blush, this seems like a highly dangerous state of affairs. But second thoughts are more reassuring. After all, most of us put money into a bank because we do *not* need it immediately, or because making payments in cash is a nuisance compared with making them by check. Yet there is always the chance—more than that, the certainty—that some depositors *will* want their money in currency. How much currency do the banks need then? What is a proper reserve for them to hold?

Federal Reserve System

For many years the banks themselves decided what reserve ratio constituted a safe proportion of currency to hold against their demand deposits. Today, however, most large banks are members of the Federal Reserve, a central banking system established in 1913 to strengthen the banking activities of the nation. Under the Federal Reserve System, the nation is divided into 12 districts, each with a **Federal Reserve Bank** owned (but not really controlled) by the member banks of its district. In turn, the 12 Reserve Banks are themselves coordinated by a seven-member Federal Reserve Board in Washington. Since the president, with the advice and consent of the Senate, appoints members of the board for 14-year terms, they constitute a body that has been purposely established as a formally autonomous monetary authority.*

One of the functions of the Federal Reserve Board is to establish reserve ratios for different categories of banks, within limits set by Congress. Historically these reserve ratios ranged between 13 and 26 percent of demand deposits for city banks, with a somewhat smaller reserve ratio for country banks. Today reserve ratios are determined by size of bank and by kind of deposit, and they vary between 18 percent for the largest banks and 7 percent for the smallest. The Federal Reserve Board also sets reserve requirements for time deposits (the technical term for those savings deposits that, like certificates of deposit, have a specific expiration date and cannot be withdrawn on demand). These range from 1 to 6 percent, depending on the ease of withdrawal.

The Banks' Bank

Yet here is something odd! We noticed that in 1987 the total amount of deposits was $292 billion and that banks' holdings of coin and currency were only $26 billion. This is much less than the 16 percent average reserve against deposits established by the Federal Reserve Board. How can this be?

The answer is that cash is not the only reserve a bank holds against deposits. Claims on other banks are also held as its reserve.

What are these claims? Suppose, in your account in bank A, you deposit a check from someone who has an account in bank B. Bank A credits your account and then presents the check to bank B for payment. Bank A does not expect to be paid coin and currency, however. Instead bank A and bank B settle their transaction at still *another* bank where both bank A and bank B have their own accounts. These accounts are with the 12 Federal Reserve Banks of the country, where all banks who are members of the Federal Reserve System (and this accounts for banks holding most of the deposits in our banking system) *must* open accounts. Thus at the Federal Reserve Bank, bank A's account will be credited and bank B's account will be debited, in this way moving reserves from one bank to the other.†

The Federal Reserve Banks serve their member banks in exactly the same way as the member banks serve the public. Member banks automatically deposit in their Federal Reserve accounts all checks they get from other banks. As a result, banks are constantly clearing their checks with one another through the Federal Reserve System, because their depositors are constantly writing checks on their own

*The independence of the Federal Reserve is a perennially controversial issue. See the extra word at the end of Chapter 20.

†When money is put into a bank account, the account is credited; when money is taken out, the account is debited.

banks payable to someone who banks elsewhere. **Meanwhile, the balance that each bank maintains at the Federal Reserve—that is, the claim it has on other banks—counts, as much as any currency, as part of its reserve against deposits.**

In 1987, therefore, when demand deposits were $292 billion and cash in the banks only $26 billion, we would expect the member banks to have had heavy accounts with the Federal Reserve banks. And so they did—$23 billion in all. Thus total reserves of the banks were $49 billion ($26 billion in cash plus $23 billion in Federal Reserve accounts), enough to satisfy the legal requirements.

Fractional Reserves

Thus we see that our banks operate on what is called a *fractional reserve system.* That is, a certain specified fraction of all demand deposits must be kept on hand at all times in cash or at the Federal Reserve. The size of the minimum fraction is determined by the Federal Reserve, for reasons of control that we shall shortly learn. It is *not* determined, as we might be tempted to think, to provide a safe backing for our bank deposits. For under *any* fractional system, if *all* depositors decided to draw out their accounts in currency and coin from all banks at the same time, the banks would be unable to meet the demand for cash and would have to close. We call this a "run" on the banking system. Needless to say, runs can be terrifying and destructive economic phenomena.*

Why, then, do we court the risk of runs, however small this risk may be? What is the benefit of a fractional banking system? To answer that, let us look at our bank again.

Loans and Investments

Suppose its customers have given our bank $1 million in deposits and that the Federal Reserve Board requirements are 20 percent, a simpler figure to work with than the actual one. Then we know that our bank must at all times keep $200,000 either in currency in its own till or in its demand deposit at the Federal Reserve Bank.

But having taken care of that requirement, what does the bank do with the remaining deposits? If it simply lets them sit, either as vault cash or as a deposit at the Federal Reserve, our bank will be very "liquid," but it will have no way of making an income. Unless it charges a very high fee for its checking services, it will have to go out of business.

And yet there is an obvious way for the bank to make an income while performing a valuable service. **The bank can use all the cash and check claims it does not need for its reserve to make *loans* to businesses or families or to make financial *investments* in corporate or government bonds. It will thereby not only earn an income, but will also assist the process of business investment**

*A "run" on the banking system is no longer much of a threat as in the past because the Federal Reserve could supply its members with vast amounts of cash. We shall learn how later in this chapter.

and government borrowing. Thus the mechanics of the banking system lead us back to the concerns at the very center of our previous analysis.

INSIDE THE BANKING SYSTEM

Fractional reserves allow banks to lend, or to invest in securities, part of the funds that have been deposited with them. But that is not the only usefulness of the fractional reserve system. It works as well to help enlarge or diminish the supply of investible or loanable funds, as the occasion demands. Let us follow the workings of this process. To make the mechanics of banking clear, we are going to look at the actual books of the bank—in simplified form, of course—so we can see how the process of lending and investing appears to the banker.

Assets and Liabilities

We begin by introducing two basic elements of business accounting: *assets* and *liabilities.* Every student at some time or another has seen the balance sheet of a firm, and many have wondered how total assets always equal total liabilities. The reason is very simple. Assets are all the things or claims a business owns. Liabilities are claims against those assets—some of them the claims of creditors, some the claims of owners (called the *net worth* of the business). Since assets show everything that a business owns, and since liabilities show how claims against these self-same things are divided between creditors and owners, it is obvious that the two sides of the balance sheet must always come to exactly the same total. **The total of assets and the total of liabilities are an identity.**

T Accounts

Businesses show their financial condition on a *balance sheet* on which all items on the left side represent assets and all those on the right side represent liabilities. By using a simple two-column balance sheet called a T account (because it looks like a T), we can follow very clearly what happens to our bank as we deposit money in it or as it makes loans or investments (see Table 1).

TABLE 1
Original Bank
T accounts always balance because liabilities show claims on assets.

Assets	*Liabilities*
$1,000,000 (cash and checks)	$1,000,000 (money owed to depositors)
Total $1,000,000	**Total $1,000,000**

We start off with the example we have just used, in which we open a brand new bank with $1 million in cash and checks on other banks. Accordingly, our first entry in the T account shows the two sides of this transaction. Notice that our bank has gained an asset of $1 million, the cash and checks it now owns, and that it has simultaneously gained $1 million in liabilities, the deposits it *owes* to its depositors (who can withdraw their money).

As we know, however, our bank will not keep all its newly gained cash and checks in the till. It may hang on to some of the cash, but it will send all the checks it has received, plus any currency that it feels it does not need, to the Federal Reserve for deposit in its account there. Table 2 shows the resulting T account.

Excess Reserves

Now recall from our previous discussion that our bank does not want to remain in this very liquid, but very unprofitable, position. **According to the law, it must retain only a certain percentage of its deposits in cash or at the Federal Reserve—20 percent in our hypothetical example. All the rest it is free to lend or invest.** As things now stand, however, it has $1 million in reserves—$800,000 more than it needs. Hence let us suppose that it decides to put these *excess reserves* to work by lending that amount to a sound business risk. (Note that banks do not themselves lend the excess reserves. These reserves, cash and deposits at the Fed, remain right where they are. Their function is to tell the banks how much they may loan or invest.)

Making a Loan

Assume now that the Smith Corporation, a well-known firm, comes in for a loan of $800,000. Our bank is happy to lend it that amount. **But making a loan does not mean that the bank now pays the company in cash out of its vaults. Rather, *it makes a loan by opening a new checking account for the firm* and by crediting that account with $800,000.** (Or if, as is likely, the Smith firm already has an account with the bank, it will simply credit the proceeds of the loan to that account.)

Now our T account shows some interesting changes (see Table 3).

There are several things to note about this transaction. First, our bank's reserves

TABLE 2
Original Bank
This is how the T account looks after checks have been cleared through the Federal Reserve. If you examine some bank balance sheets, you will see these items listed as "Cash and due from banks." This means cash in the bank's own vaults plus their bank's balance at the Federal Reserve.

Assets		*Liabilities*	
Vault cash	$100,000	Deposits	$1,000,000
Deposit at Fed	900,000		
Total	**$1,000,000**	**Total**	**$1,000,000**

(its cash and deposit at the Fed) have not yet changed. The $1 million in reserves are still there.

Second, notice that the Smith Corporation loan counts as a new asset for the bank because the bank now has a legal claim against the company for that amount. (The interest on the loan is not shown in the balance sheet; but when it is paid, it will show up as an addition to the bank's cash.)

Third, deposits have increased by $800,000. Note, however, that this $800,000 was not paid to the Smith firm out of anyone else's account in the bank. It is a new checking account, one that did not exist before. As a result, the supply of money is also up! More about this shortly.

The Loan Is Spent

Was it safe to open this new account for the company? Well, we might see whether our reserves are now sufficient to cover the Smith Corporation's account as well as the original deposit accounts. A glance reveals that all is well. We still have $1 million in reserves against $1.8 million in deposits. Our reserve ratio is much higher than the 20 percent required by law.

It is so much higher, in fact, that we might be tempted to make another loan to the next customer who requests one, and in that way further increase our earning capacity. But an experienced banker shakes his head. "The Smith Corporation did not take out a loan and agree to pay interest on it just for the pleasure of letting that money sit with you," he explains. "Very shortly, the company will be writing checks on its balance to pay for goods or services; and when it does, you will need every penny of the reserve you now have."

That, indeed, is the case. Within a few days we find that our bank's account at the Federal Reserve Bank has been charged with a check for $800,000 written by the Smith Corporation in favor of the Jones Corporation, which carries its account at another bank. Now we find that our T account has changed dramatically. Look at Table 4.

Let us see exactly what has happened. First, the Smith Corporation's check has been charged against our account at the Fed and has reduced it from $900,000 to $100,000. Together with the $100,000 cash in our vault, this gives us $200,000 in reserves.

Second, the Smith Corporation's deposit is entirely gone, although its loan agreement remains with us as an asset.

TABLE 3
Original Bank
The bank has used its excess reserves to make a loan. The loan itself is a signed IOU which is a new asset for the bank. The corresponding liability is the new deposit opened in the name of the borrower.

		Liabilities	
Cash and at Fed	$1,000,000	Original deposits	$1,000,000
Loan (Smith Corp.)	800,000	New deposit (Smith Corp.)	800,000
Total	**$1,800,000**	**Total**	**$1,800,000**

TABLE 4
Original Bank
The borrower uses the loan, and its deposits fall to zero. But the assets (and deposit liabilities) of another bank have risen.

Assets		*Liabilities*	
Cash and at Fed	$ 200,000	Original deposits	$1,000,000
Loan (Smith Corp.)	800,000	Smith Corp. deposits	0
Total	**$1,000,000**	**Total**	**$1,000,000**

Second Bank

Assets		*Liabilities*	
Cash and at Fed	$800,000	Deposit (Jones Corp.)	$800,000
Total	**$800,000**	**Total**	**$800,000**

Now if we refigure our reserves, we find that they are just right. We are required to have $200,000 in vault cash or in our Federal Reserve account against our $1 million in deposits. That is exactly the amount we have left. Our bank is now fully "loaned up."

Continuing Effects

But the banking *system* is not yet fully loaned up. So far, we have traced what happened only to our bank when the Smith Corporation spent the money in its deposit account. Now we must trace the effect of this action on the deposits and reserves of other banks.

We begin with the bank in which the Jones Corporation deposits the check it has just received from the Smith Corporation. Another look at Table 4 will show you that the Jones Corporation's bank now finds itself in exactly the same position as our bank was when we opened it with $1 million in new deposits, except that the

TABLE 5
Second Bank
(after the Brown Company spends the proceeds of its loan)
Here is a repetition of the same process, as the second bank uses its lending capacity to finance the Brown Company.

Assets		*Liabilities*	
Cash and at Fed	$160,000	Deposits (Jones Corp.)	$800,000
Loan (to Brown Co.)	640,000	Deposits (Brown Co.)	0
Total	**$800,000**	**Total**	**$800,000**

Third Bank
(after Black Co. gets the check of Brown Co.)

Assets		*Liabilities*	
Cash and at Fed	$640,000	Deposit (Black Co.)	$640,000
Total	**$640,000**	**Total**	**$640,000**

addition to this second-generation bank is smaller than the addition to the first-generation bank.

As we can see, our second-generation bank has gained $800,000 in cash and in deposits. Since it needs only 20 percent of this for required reserves, it finds itself with $640,000 excess reserves, which it is now free to use to make loans as investments. Suppose that it extends a loan to the Brown Company and that the Brown Company shortly thereafter spends the proceeds of that loan at the Black Company, which banks at yet a third bank. The two T accounts in Table 5 show how the total deposits will now be affected.

As Figure 1 makes clear, the process will not stop here but can continue from one bank to the next as long as any lending power remains. Notice, however, that this lending power gets smaller and smaller and will eventually approach zero.

EXPANSION OF THE MONEY SUPPLY

If we now look at the bottom of Figure 1, we will see something very important. **Every time any bank in this chain of transactions has opened an account for a new borrower, *the supply of money has increased.*** Remember that the supply of money is the sum of currency outside the banking system (i.e., in our own pockets), plus the total of demand deposits. As our chain of banks kept opening new accounts, it was simultaneously expanding the total check-writing capacity of the economy. Thus money has materialized, seemingly out of thin air.

Now how can this be? If we tell any banker in the chain that he has "created" money, he will protest vehemently. The loans he made, he will insist, were backed at the time he made them by excess reserves as large as the loan itself. Just as we had $800,000 in excess reserves when we made our initial loan to the Smith Corporation, so every subsequent loan was always backed 100 percent by unused reserves when it was made.

Our bankers are perfectly correct when they tell us that they never, never lend a penny more than they have. Money is not created in the lending process because a banker lends money he or she doesn't have. **Money is created because you and I generally pay each other by checks that give us claims against each other's bank.** If we constantly cashed the checks we exchanged, no new money would be created. But we do not. We deposit each other's checks in our own bank accounts; and in doing so, we give our banks more reserves than they need against the deposits we have just made. These new excess reserves make it possible for our banks to lend or invest, and thereby to open still more deposit accounts, which in turn lead to new reserves.

The Expansive Power of Money

This all sounds a little frightening. Does it mean that the money supply can go on expanding indefinitely from a single new deposit? Wouldn't that be extremely inflationary?

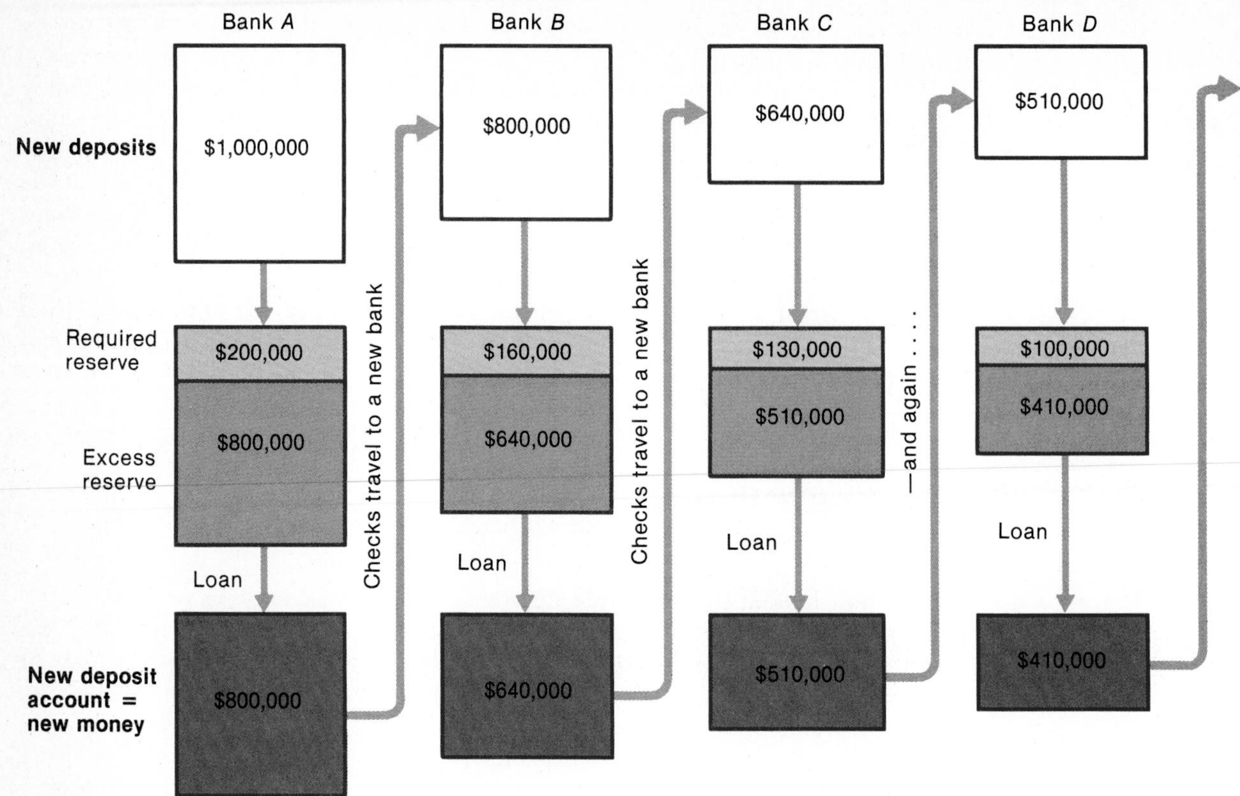

FIGURE 1
Expansion of the Money Supply
As the relending process continues, successive banks add to their deposits, and the money supply increases. Note the resemblance to the multiplier process.

In our next chapter we will tackle the relation between the money supply and the level of prices directly. But we ought to say a preliminary word here. **Clearly bank reserves have an inflationary potential in a fractional reserve system, simply by virtue of the fact that they are capable of creating a multiple of themselves. That is why economists pay careful attention to the volume of reserves when they are considering the extent of the inflationary dangers facing an economy.**

But the fact that bank reserves *can* become the basis for inflation is not at all the same as saying that inflation is directly caused by bank reserves. It merely tells us that the existence of a flexible money supply poses a problem for monetary management—the theme of Chapter 21.

But monetary management quite aside, we must also understand that there are powerful forces preventing the creation of a single new deposit from expanding indefinitely throughout the system. Here are five very important counterforces that must be borne in mind.

MONEY AND DEBT

All this gives us a fresh insight into the question of what money is. We said before that it is whatever we use to make payments. But what do we use? The answer is a surprising one. We use *debts*—specifically, the debts of commercial banks. Deposits are, after all, nothing but the liabilities that banks owe their customers. Furthermore, we can see that one purpose of the banking system is to buy debts from other units in the economy, such as businesses or governments, in exchange for its own debts (which are money). For when a bank opens an account for a business to which it has granted a loan or when it buys a government bond, what else is it doing but accepting a debt that is *not* usable as money in exchange for its deposit liabilities that *are* usable as money. And why is it that banks create money when they make loans, but you or I do not when we lend money? Because we all accept bank liabilities (deposits) as money, but we do not accept personal or business IOUs to make payments with.

Limits on Expansion

1. Not Every Loan Generates an Increase in Bank Deposits. If our bank had opened a loan account for the Smith Corporation at the same time that another firm had paid off a similar loan, there would have been no original expansion in bank deposits. In that case, the addition of $800,000 to the Smith account would have been exactly balanced by a decline of $800,000 in someone else's account. Even if that decline had taken place in a different bank, it would still mean that the nation's total of bank deposits would not have risen, and therefore no new money would have been credited. **Thus only net additions to loans have an expansionary effect.** We will shortly see how such net additions arise in the first place.

2. There Is a Limit to the Rise in Money Supply from a Single Increase in Deposits. As Figure 1 shows, in the chain of deposit expansion each successive bank has a smaller increase in deposits, because each bank has to keep some of its newly gained cash or checks as reserve. Hence the amount of *excess* reserves, against which loans can be made, steadily falls.

Further, we can see that the amount of the total monetary expansion from an original net increase in deposits is governed by the size of the fraction that has to be kept aside each time as reserve. **In fact, we can see that, just as with the multiplier, the cumulative effect of an increase in deposits will be determined by the reciprocal of the reserve fraction.** If each bank must keep one-fifth of its increased deposits as reserves, then the cumulative effect of an original increase in deposits, when it has expanded through the system, is five times the original increase. If reserves are one-fourth, the expansion is limited to four times the original increase, and so on.*

3. The Monetary Expansion Process Can Work in Reverse. Suppose the banking system as a whole suffers a net loss of deposits. Instead of putting $1 million into a bank, the public takes it out in cash. The bank will now have too few reserves, and it will have to cut down its loans or sell its investments to gain the reserves it needs. In turn, as borrowers pay off their loans, or as bond buyers pay for their securities, cash will drain from other banks that will now find *their* reserves too small in relation to their deposits. In turn, they will have to sell more investments or curtail still other loans, and this again will squeeze still other banks and reduce their reserves, with the same consequences.

Thus, just as an original expansion in deposits can lead to a multiple expansion, so an original contraction in deposits can lead to a multiple contraction. The size of this contraction is also limited by the reciprocal of the reserve fraction. If banks have to hold a 25 percent reserve, then an original fall of $100,000 in deposits will lead to a total fall of $400,000, assuming that the system was fully loaned up to begin with. If they had to hold a 20 percent reserve, a fall of $100,000 could pyramid to $500,000.

4. The Expansion Process May Not Be Fully Carried Through. We have assumed that each bank in the chain always lends out an amount equal to its excess reserve, but this may not be the case. The third or fifth bank along the way may have trouble finding a creditworthy customer and may decide—for the moment, anyway—to sit on its excess reserves. Or borrowers along the chain may take out cash from some of their new deposits and thereby reduce the banks' reserves and their lending powers. Thus the potential expansion may be only partially realized.

5. The Expansion Process Takes Time. Like the multiplier process, the expansion of the money supply encounters many "frictions" in real life. Banks do not instantly expand loans when their reserves rise; bank customers do not instantly spend the proceeds of bank loans. The time lags in banking are too variable to enable us to make an estimate of how long it takes for an initial increase in new deposits to work its way through the system, but the time period is surely a matter of months for two or three rounds.

Why Banks Must Work Together

There is an interesting problem concealed behind this crisscrossing of deposits that leads to a slowly rising level of the money supply. Suppose that an imaginary island economy was served by a single bank (and let us forget about all complications of international trade, etc.), and this bank, which worked on a 20 percent reserve

*If M is the money supply, D is net new deposits, and r is the reserve ratio, then $\Delta M = 1/r \times \Delta D$. Notice that this formula is exactly the same as that for the multiplier.

ratio, was suddenly presented with an extra $1 million worth of reserves—let us say newly mined pure gold. Our bank could, of course, increase its loans to customers. By how much? By *$5 million!*

In other words, our island bank, all by itself, could use an increase in its reserves to create a much larger increase in the money supply. It is not difficult to understand why. Any borrower of the new $5 million, no matter where he spent his money on the island, would only be giving his checks to someone who also banked at the single, solitary bank. The whole $5 million, in other words, would stay *within* the bank as its deposits, although the identity of those depositors would, of course, shift. Indeed, there is no reason why such a bank should limit its expansion of the money supply to $5 million. Such a bank could create as much money as it wanted through new loans, counting each corresponding deposit as a reserve—though to do so would quickly produce, as we will see, a runaway price inflation.

The imaginary bank makes it plain why ordinary commercial banks *cannot* expand deposits beyond their excess reserves. Unlike the monopoly bank, they must expect to *lose* their deposits to other banks when their borrowers write checks on their new accounts. As a result, they will also lose their reserves, and this can lead to trouble.

Overlending

This situation is important enough to warrant taking a moment to examine. Suppose that in our previous example we had decided to lend the Smith Corporation not $800,000 but $900,000, and suppose as before that the Smith Corporation used the proceeds of that loan to pay the Jones Corporation. Now look at the condition of our bank after the Smith payment has cleared (Table 6).

Our reserves will now have dropped to 10 percent! Indeed, if we had loaned the company $1 million, we would be in danger of insolvency.

Banks are, in fact, very careful not to overlend. If they find that they have inadvertently exceeded their legal reserve requirements, they quickly take remedial action. One way a bank may repair the situation is by borrowing reserves for a short period (paying interest on them, of course) from another bank that may have a temporary surplus at the Fed; this is called borrowing *federal funds.* Or a bank may quickly sell some of its government bonds and add the proceeds to its reserve account at the Fed. Or again, it may add to its reserves the proceeds of any loans that have come due and deliberately fail to replace these expired loans with new loans. Finally, a bank may borrow reserves directly from its Federal Reserve Bank

TABLE 6
Original Bank
A bank that lends an amount larger than its excess reserve will be in trouble. Its reserves will fall below the level required by law.

Assets		*Liabilities*	
Cash and at Fed	$ 100,000	Original deposits	$1,000,000
Loan (Smith Corp.)	900,000	Smith Corp. deposit	0
Total	**$1,000,000**	**Total**	**$1,000,000**

and pay interest for the loan. We shall shortly look into this method when we talk about the role of the Federal Reserve in regulating the quantity of money.

The main point is clear. A bank is safe in lending only an amount that it can afford to lose to another bank. But of course one bank's loss is another's gain. That is why, by the exchange of checks, the banking system can accomplish the same result as the island monopoly bank, whereas no individual bank can hope to do so.

Investments and Reserve

If a bank uses its excess reserves to buy securities, does that lead to the same multiplication effect as a bank loan?

It can. When a bank buys government securities, it usually does so from a securities dealer, a professional trader in bonds.* Its check (for $800,000 in our example) drawn on its account at the Federal Reserve will be made out to a dealer, who will deposit it in his or her bank. As a result, the dealer's bank suddenly finds itself with an $800,000 new deposit. It must keep 20 percent of this as required reserve, but the remainder is excess reserve against which it can make loans or investments as it wishes.

Is there a new deposit, corresponding to that of the borrower? There is: the new deposit of the securities dealer. Note that in the dealer's case, as in that of the borrower, the new deposit on the books of the bank has not been put there by the transfer of money from some other commercial bank. The $800,000 deposit has come into being through the deposit of a check of the Federal Reserve Bank, which is not a commercial bank. Thus it represents a new addition to the deposits of the private banking system.

Let us see this in the T accounts. Table 7 shows what our first bank's T account looks like after it has bought its $800,000 in bonds (paying for them with its Federal Reserve checking account).

As we can see, there are no excess reserves here. But look at the bank in which the seller of the government bond has deposited the check he has just received from our bank (Table 8). Here there are excess reserves of $640,000 ($800,000 less 20 percent reserve set-aside) with which additional investments can be made. It is possible for such new deposits, albeit diminishing each time, to remain in the

TABLE 7
Original Bank
Excess reserves can be used to buy bonds as well as to finance loans.

Assets		*Liabilities*	
Cash and at Fed	$ 200,000	Deposits	$1,000,000
Government bonds	800,000		
Total	**$1,000,000**	**Total**	**$1,000,000**

*The dealer may be only a middleman who will in turn buy from, or sell to, corporations or individuals. This doesn't change our analysis, however.

TABLE 8
Second Bank
When the seller of the bond deposits his check, the same money-expanding process will be set into motion.

Assets		*Liabilities*	
Cash	$800,000	New deposit of bond seller	$800,000
Total	**$800,000**	**Total**	**$800,000**

financial circuit for some time, moving from bank to bank as an active business is done in buying government bonds.

Yields

Meanwhile, however, the very activity in bidding for government bonds is likely to raise their price and thereby lower their rate of interest.

This is a situation you will probably be faced with in your personal life, so you should understand it. A bond has a *fixed* rate of return and a stated face value. If it is a 9 percent, $1,000 bond, this means it will pay $90 interest yearly. If the bond now sells on the market for $1,200, the $90 yearly interest will be less than a 9 percent return ($90 is only 7.5 percent of $1,200). If the price should fall to $900, the $90 return will be more than 9 percent ($90 is 10 percent of $900). **Thus the *yield* of a bond varies inversely—in the other direction—with its market price.**

When the price of government bonds changes, all bond prices tend to change in the same direction. This is because all bonds are competing for investors' funds. If the yield on "governments" falls, investors will switch from governments to other, higher-yielding bonds. But as they bid for these other bonds, the prices of these bonds will rise—and their yields will fall, too!

In this way, a change in yields spreads from one group of bonds to another. A lower rate of interest or a lower yield on government securities is quickly reflected in lower rates or yields for other kinds of bonds. In turn, a lower rate of interest on bonds makes loans to business look more attractive. Thus, sooner or later, excess reserves are apt to be channeled to new loans as well as new investments. Thereafter, the deposit-building process follows its familiar course.

LOOKING BACK

KEY CONCEPTS

The supply of money is usually defined as cash in the public's hands plus demand deposits.

1 The supply of money is generally defined as the cash in the possession of the public (not the cash in bank vaults) plus checking deposits, technically known as demand deposits. The total is called M1. Other measures of money include savings accounts and other liquid assets.

Banks must keep stated fractions of reserves against their deposits: These reserves are cash or accounts at a Federal Reserve Bank. Banks can lend or invest sums equal to excess reserves.

2 Banks are required by the Federal Reserve Act to maintain stated proportions of actual cash (in their own vaults) or claims on other banks as reserves against their deposits. These reserves are largely maintained as accounts with one of the 12 Federal Reserve banks of the country. This is called the fractional reserve system. It permits banks to make loans or investments equal in amount to their excess reserves.

Banks make loans by opening deposits for the borrower. These deposits, when spent, become new deposits for other banks, enabling them in turn to expand their loans or investment.

3 When a bank makes a loan against its excess reserve, it opens a deposit in the name of the borrower. That deposit is normally used for business purposes, and thereby becomes a new deposit in some other bank. In turn, that bank must keep a legal reserve to cover part of its new deposit, but is free to lend or invest an amount equal to its excess reserve.

The process of successive relending expands the money supply. The banking system can increase M, although no bank by itself could long do so.

4 The successive spending of loans creates additional deposits through the system, acting like a multiplier. These new deposits are additions to the money supply. No single bank on its own would dare to expand the total of deposits, but working together as a system, the member banks can increase this supply to the extent that fractional reserve requirements permit.

The expansion process has limits, set by the reserve fraction. It applies only to net loans, and it may work in reverse.

5 The money expansion has several limits: Only net loans create new money, not loans that are offset by repayments; expansion is controlled by the reserve fraction, just like the multiplier process; monetary expansion can work in reverse if repayments exceed new loans; the expansion process may not be carried all the way through; and the process takes time.

Using excess reserves to buy bonds also increases the money supply.

6 A bank that uses its excess reserve to buy bonds also creates new deposits when the seller of the bond deposits a check. This too can expand the money supply.

As bond prices change, bond yields also change. The higher the price, the lower the yield.

7 As bonds are bought and sold, their price changes. Because bonds have fixed interest obligations, a higher or lower price for a bond changes its yield. As bond prices rise, yields fall, and vice versa.

ECONOMIC VOCABULARY

Money supply 328
Demand deposits 330
Federal Reserve System 330
Fractional reserves 332
Assets and liabilities 333
T accounts 333
Excess reserves 334
Overlending 341
Yields 343

QUESTIONS

1. Why do we not count cash in the tills of commercial banks in the money supply? When you deposit currency in a commercial bank, what happens to it? Can you ask for your particular bills again? If you demanded to see "your" account, what would it be?
2. What determines how much vault cash a bank must hold against its deposits? Would you expect this proportion to change in some seasons, such as Christmas? Do you think it would be the same in worried times as in placid times? In new countries as in old ones?
3. What are excess reserves? Suppose a bank has $500,000 in deposits and a reserve ratio of 30 percent is imposed by law. What is its required reserve? Suppose it happens to hold $200,000 in vault cash or at its account at the Fed. What, if any, is its excess reserve?
4. If the bank above wanted to make loans or investments, how much would it be entitled to lend or invest? Suppose its deposits increased by another $50,000. Could it lend or invest this entire amount? Any of it? How much?
5. If a bank lends money, it opens an account in the name of the borrower. Now suppose the borrower draws down his new account. What happens to the reserves of the lending bank? Show this in a T account.
6. Suppose the borrower sends his check for $1,000 to someone who banks at another bank. Describe what happens to the deposits of the second bank. If the reserve ratio is 20 percent, how much new lending or investing can it do?
7. If the reserve ratio is 20 percent and the original addition to reserves is $1,000, what will be the total potential amount of new money that can be created by the banking system? If the ratio is 25 percent?
8. Suppose you own a $1,000, 10 percent bond from the U.S. government that you bought for $1,000. Now suppose that the rate of interest for comparable securities rises from 10 to 20 percent. Would you be able to sell your bond for $1,000? Suppose the rate of interest sank to 5 percent. Would you be able to get more than $1,000 for your bond? Think about this question very carefully. We will take it up again in detail in Chapter 21.

CHAPTER 20

The Federal Reserve

A LOOK AHEAD

In the last chapter we learned what money was and how the money supply could be increased. But we have not yet investigated the methods by which the national government exercises control over the money supply: We shall do this here.

1 First we look into the workings of the Federal Reserve System, particularly with respect to the three ways in which it can loosen or tighten the monetary strings. This brings us to the question of how the Fed is involved in the international exchange market.
2 Second, we look into gold and paper money. Where do those famous "printing presses" get into the money question?
3 Third, we look again at the involvement of the United States in the world economy and ask to what extent we can still speak of "our own" money supply.

We have now seen how a banking system can create money through the creation of excess reserves. But the key to the process is the creation of the *original* excess reserves, for without them the cumulative process will not be set in motion. We remember, for example, that a loan will not result in an increase in the money supply if it is offset by a decline in lending somewhere else in the banking system; neither will the purchase of a bond by one commercial bank if it is only buying a security sold by another. **To get a net addition to loans or investments, a banking system—assuming that it is fully loaned up—needs an increase in its reserves.** Where do these extra reserves come from? That is the question we must turn to next.

ROLE OF THE FEDERAL RESERVE

In our example we have already met one source of changes in reserves. When the public needs less currency and deposits its extra holdings in the banks, reserves rise, as we have seen. When the public wants more currency, it depletes the banks' holdings and thereby lowers their reserves. In the latter case, the banks may find that they have insufficient reserves behind their deposits. To get more currency or claims on other banks, they will have to sell securities or reduce their loans. This might put a very severe crimp in the economy. Hence, to allow bank reserves to be regulated by the public's fluctuating demand for cash would be an impossible way to run our monetary system.

But we remember that bank reserves are not mainly currency; in fact, currency is a relatively minor item. Most reserves are the accounts that member banks hold at the Federal Reserve. If these accounts could somehow be increased or decreased, we could regulate the amount of reserves—and thus the permissible total of deposits—without regard to the public's changing need for cash.

This is precisely what the Federal Reserve System is designed to do. Essentially, the system is set up to regulate the supply of money by raising or lowering the reserves of its member banks. When these reserves are raised, member banks find themselves with excess reserves and are thus in a position to make loans and investments by which the supply of money will increase further. Conversely, when the Federal Reserve lowers the reserves of its member banks, they will no longer be able to make loans and investments, or they may even have to reduce loans or get rid of investments, thereby extinguishing deposit accounts and contracting the supply of money.

Monetary Control Mechanisms

How does the Federal Reserve operate? There are three ways.

1. Changing Reserve Requirements. It was the Federal Reserve itself, we will remember, that originally determined how much in reserves its member banks should hold against their deposits. By changing that reserve requirement for a given level of deposits, it can give its member banks excess reserves or create a shortage of reserves.

This has two effects. First, *it immediately changes the lending or investing capacity of all banks.* In our imaginary bank we have assumed that reserves were set at 20 percent of deposits. Suppose now that the Federal Reserve determined to lower reserve requirements to 15 percent. It would thereby automatically create extra lending or investing power for our *existing* reserves. Our bank with $1 million in deposits and $200,000 in reserves could now lend or invest an additional $50,000 without any new funds coming in from depositors. On the other hand, if requirements were raised to, say, 30 percent, we would find that our original $200,000 reserve was $100,000 short of requirements, and we would have to curtail lending or investing until we were again in line with requirements.

Second, *the new reserve requirements raise or lower the reserve multiplier*—expanding or contracting the limits of the flexible money system. Because these new reserve requirements affect *all* banks, changing reserve ratios is a very effective way of freeing or contracting bank credit on a large scale. But it is an instrument that sweeps across the entire banking system in an undiscriminating fashion. It is therefore used only rarely, when the Federal Reserve Board feels that the supply of money is seriously short or dangerously excessive and needs remedy on a countrywide basis.

2. CHANGING DISCOUNT RATES. The second means of control uses interest rates as the money-controlling device. Recall that member banks short on reserves have a special privilege, if they wish to exercise it. *They can borrow reserve balances from the Federal Reserve Bank itself and add them to their regular reserve account at the bank.*

The Federal Reserve Bank, of course, charges interest for lending reserves, and this interest is called the discount rate. By raising or lowering this rate, the Federal Reserve can make it attractive or unattractive for member banks to borrow to augment reserves. In contrast with changing the reserve ratio itself, changing the discount rate is a mild device that allows each bank to decide for itself whether it wishes to increase its reserves.

Although changes in the discount rate can be used as a major means of controlling the money supply, and are in some countries, they are not used for this purpose in the United States. The Federal Reserve Board does not allow banks to borrow whatever they would like at the current discount rate. The discount "window" is a place where a bank can borrow small amounts of money to cover a small deficiency in its reserves, but it is not a place where banks can borrow major amounts of money except in an emergency. **As a result, the discount rate serves more as a signal of what the Federal Reserve would like to see happen than as an active force in determining the total borrowings of banks.**

3. OPEN MARKET OPERATIONS. Most frequently used is a third technique called open market operations. This technique permits the Federal Reserve Banks to change the supply of reserves by buying or selling U.S. government bonds on the open market.

How does this work? Suppose the Federal Reserve authorities wish to increase

HOW THE FEDERAL RESERVE BOARD CAN CREATE MONEY

HOW THE FEDERAL RESERVE BOARD CAN CREATE MONEY

Start

The Federal Reserve Board's open market committee instructs Alan R. Holmes of the Federal Reserve Bank of New York to purchase Government securities.

Mr. Holmes writes a check to buy $100 million in Treasury Bills from Salomon Brothers.

Salomon Brothers has $100 million more cash, but correspondingly less in Treasury Bills.

Salomon Brothers deposits $100 million in Citibank.

Citibank puts $15 million back in Fed as "Reserve Requirement" and loans $85 million to United States Steel.

USX has $85 million more cash, but a debt to Citibank.

U.S. Steel deposits $85 million in the Pittsburgh National Bank.

Pittsburgh National puts $13 million in its reserve account at the Fed and uses remaining $72 million to buy notes of the City of Boston.

Boston has $72 million more cash, but a debt to Pittsburgh National.

Finish

The process continues until, with a 15 percent "Reserve Requirement," The New York Fed's original check for $100 million adds more than $600 million to the total of bank deposits in the nation.

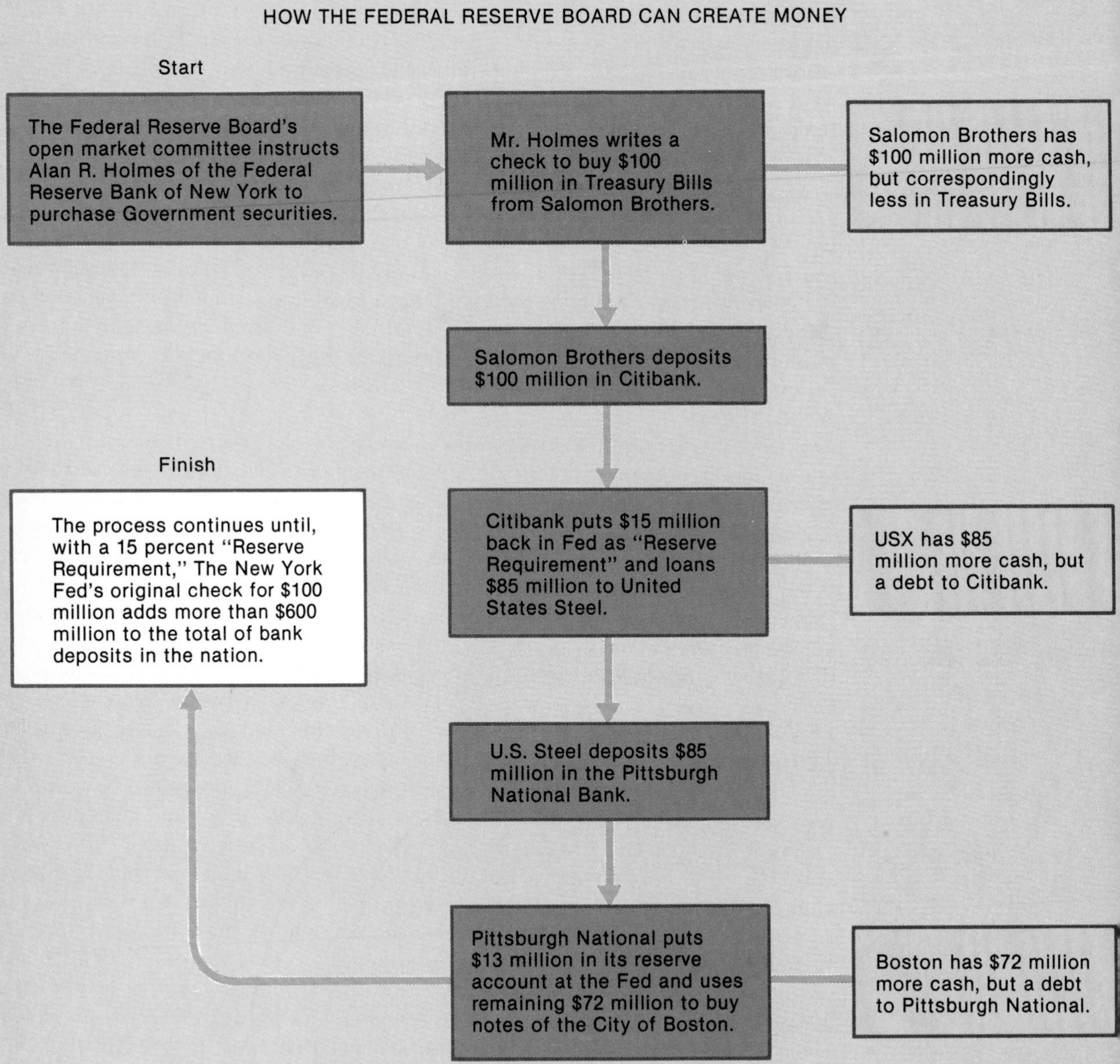

the reserves of member banks. They will begin to buy government securities from dealers in the bond market, and they will pay these dealers with Federal Reserve checks.

Notice something about these checks: *They are not drawn on any commercial bank!* They are drawn on the Federal Reserve Bank itself. The security dealer who sells the bond will deposit the Federal Reserve's check, as if it were any other check, in his own commercial bank; and his bank will send the Federal Reserve's check through for credit to its own account, as if it were any other check. *As a result, the dealer's bank will have gained reserves, although no other commercial bank has lost reserves.* On balance, then, the system has more lending and investing capacity than it had before. In fact, it now has *excess* reserves and these, as we have seen, will spread out through the system. **Thus by buying bonds the Federal Reserve has, in fact, deposited money in the accounts of its members, thereby giving them the extra reserves that it set out to create (see box page 350).**

Conversely, if the authorities decide that member banks' reserves are too large, they will sell securities. Now the process works in reverse. Security dealers or other buyers of bonds will send their own checks on their own regular commercial banks to the Federal Reserve in payment for these bonds. This time the Fed will take the checks of its member banks and charge their accounts, thereby reducing their reserves. **Since these checks will not find their way to another commercial bank, the system as a whole will have suffered a diminution of its reserves.** By selling securities, in other words, the Federal Reserve authorities lower the Federal Reserve accounts of member banks, thereby diminishing their reserves.

Isn't this, you might ask, really the same thing as raising or lowering the reserve ratio? If the Fed is really just putting money into member bank accounts when it buys bonds and taking money out when it sells them, why does it bother to go through the open market? Why not just tell the member banks that their reserve requirements are larger or smaller?

Analytically, you are entirely right. But there are cogent reasons for working through the bond market. The open market technique allows banks to *compete* for their share of the excess reserves that are being made available or taken away. Banks that are good at attracting depositors will thereby get extra benefit from an increase in the money supply. Thus, rather than assigning excess reserves by executive fiat, the Fed uses the open market as an allocation device.

A FLEXIBLE MONEY SUPPLY

There are many important questions to be examined with regard to the problem of controlling the money supply. We shall look at them in some detail in our next chapter. But at this point, where we are still learning about how the Fed works, we must examine a question we have heretofore passed over in silence. We have taken for granted that we need a larger supply of money in order to expand output. But why should we? Why could we not grow just as well if the supply of money were fixed?

Theoretically we could. If we cut prices as we increased output, a given amount of money (or a given amount of expenditure) could cover an indefinitely large real output. Furthermore, as prices fell, workers would be content not to ask for higher wages (or would even accept lower wages), since in real terms they would be just as well or better off.

It is not difficult to spot the flaw in this argument. In the real world, prices of many goods cannot be cut easily. If the price of steel rose and fell as quickly and easily as prices on the stock exchange or if wages went down without a murmur of resistance or if rents and other contractual items could be quickly adjusted, then prices would be flexible and we would not require any enlargement of the money supply to cover a growing real output.

In fact, as we know, prices are extremely "sticky" in the downward direction. Union leaders do not look with approval on wage cuts, even when living costs fall. Contractual prices cannot be quickly adjusted. Many big firms administer their prices and carefully avoid price competition: Note, for example, that the price of many customer items is printed on the package months before the item will be sold.

An Economic Straitjacket

Thus we can see that a fixed, unchanging, supply of money would put the economy in a straitjacket. As output tended to increase, businesses would need more money to finance production, and consumers would need more money to make their larger expenditures. If businesses could get more money from the banks, all would be well. But suppose they could not. Then the only way they could get a larger supply of cash would be to persuade someone to lend the money, and persuasion would be in the form of a higher rate of interest. But this rising interest rate would discourage other businesses from going ahead with their plans. Hence the would-be boom would be stopped dead in its tracks.

A flexible money supply avoids this economic suffocation. The fact that banks can create money (provided they have excess reserves) enables them to take care of businesses that wish to make additional expenditures. The expenditures themselves put additional money into the hands of consumers. And the spending of consumers in turn sends the enlarged volume of purchasing power back to business firms to complete the great flow of expenditure and receipt.

THE FEDERAL RESERVE AND FOREIGN EXCHANGE

There is one further function of the Federal Reserve that we must understand. It concerns the role of the Federal Reserve in the foreign exchange market.

Perhaps you recall from our early discussion of America in the world economy (Chapter 6) that exporting and importing required the participation of banks as well as producers or merchants or transportation companies. If an American automobile importer wants to bring Hondas into this country, someone has to find the yen with which to pay the Japanese exporter, and if a Japanese importer wants to bring American wheat into Japan, someone has to find the dollars to pay the American grain merchant. Banks provide the needed foreign exchange in both cases. But where do banks acquire their supplies of other countries' currencies?

In part the answer is that banks participate in foreign trade to help both importers and exporters, and thereby acquire claims on foreign currencies. But the answer also involves the Federal Reserve—or more correctly, all central banks. **Central banks are agencies of their governments in the international currency markets.** When the Federal Reserve buys yen or francs, it pays out dollars and builds up deposits of foreign money. When it sells foreign exchange, it exchanges these foreign reserves for dollars. Central banks are therefore potential sources and absorbers of foreign exchange for their own banks.

For example, if the Chase Manhattan Bank finds it has deposits of 10 million more yen in its Tokyo branch than it can use there, it can exchange those extra yen (at the going exchange rate) for a credit in dollars to its dollar account at the Federal Reserve. The Federal Reserve then holds the yen as part of its Japanese reserve account. In the same way, a Japanese bank with more dollars in its New York branch than it knows what to do with can do the same thing with its central bank, the Bank of Japan. The Bank of Japan will transfer the unwanted dollars to its own dollar reserve account, giving the Japanese bank a credit in yen.

What the Federal Reserve Can—and Cannot—Do

As a result, the Federal Reserve, like all central banks, becomes a repository for **international reserves**—the supplies of foreign exchange that establish the international creditworthiness of a nation. As a central bank, it therefore plays a very important role in the market in which the exchange rate for dollars is established. By selling its reserves of marks or yen, it tends to lower the price of the currencies it sells and to *raise* the price of the dollar. And by selling dollars, it tends to *lower* their price and to raise the exchange rate for foreign currencies.

How does the Fed sell dollars? Exactly the same way it "sells dollars" when it buys bonds on the open market. The Federal Reserve simply buys yens or francs or marks, instead of bonds, paying for them with checks written on itself—just as it does at home.

Limits on the Fed

Can the Federal Reserve thereby establish any price it wants for the dollar? It would be very nice for the United States if it could, because then the Fed could serve as a powerful means of boosting exports or discouraging imports just by buying or selling foreign exchange.

As you might imagine, however, things are not that simple. To begin with, the Federal Reserve is not the only central bank in the world, and unless it acts in concert with other central banks, such as the Bank of England and the German and

French and Japanese central banks, its own purchases or sales may be swamped by the contrary actions of others. In addition, all the central banks in the world do not by any means control the worldwide market for foreign exchange. A glance at the box on page 350 shows the magnitude of the flows concerned. Central banks are only a small group of players, who by no means dominate the market for international finance.

Finally, there are problems that affect the Fed because of the very large amount of America's foreign debt and its still uncertain position in the world economy. For example, seeing the Federal Reserve embark on an operation of dumping dollars—buying other currencies right and left by writing checks on itself—private investors, domestic and foreign, might become nervous about the dollar's value. To some extent, they would worry about the direct effects of the Federal Reserve's actions—but *mostly they would worry about each other.* If the dollar is going to fall, who wants to be the last person holding dollars? With such a psychology, even a small commitment to exchange rate intervention could, at any moment, turn into a stampede. In that case, the dollar might fall by much more than desired or planned.

What would happen if the dollar did fall precipitously? As foreign depositors removed their dollars *en masse,* many United States banks might find themselves in a precarious position, exactly as they would if many domestic depositors closed their accounts. However, in the international case, the withdrawn dollars might not be redeposited in another American bank, but might instead end up in a foreign country. The Federal Reserve could therefore be forced to lend reserves to member banks—possibly in massive amounts—to prevent a domestic credit crunch.

No doubt we could weather such a crisis. But in a year or so we would confront a different problem. United States exports, suddenly more competitive, would rise; and United States imports, suddenly more expensive, would fall. Thus the trade deficit would shrink—and that would be a good thing. But if domestic markets were tight, the rising prices of imports might well lead to rising prices of domestically produced goods, and thereafter to rising wages as workers tried to offset the fall in their standard of living. Inflation could return via rising costs and expenditures.

The Internationalization of Finance

Scenarios such as these make it clear that the power of the Federal Reserve, vast though it is, is limited. Together with its sister institutions in other countries, the Federal Reserve is a major force in international finance. But its power of action is constrained by the immensely greater forces of the international financial network of exchange. At best, the Federal Reserve can mobilize a few billions of foreign exchange to put on the market. But the average value of a day's trading in foreign currencies around the world is estimated to come to $180 billion! Thus the impact of the Federal Reserve is primarily psychological, not economic.

Indeed, the power of the Federal Reserve is limited not only in the international financial markets, but at home as well. To a very large extent, there is now only one international financial market in the world, established by the collective and uncoordinated operations of the world's financial institutions—including its central banks, its commercial banks, and its markets in stocks, bonds, and other securities.

International Banking

This internationalization of finance is the consequence of many developments. One of them is the greatly expanded activities of multinational corporations, which maintain very large bank balances in many nations, switching them around to earn the highest possible rate of return on their funds. This creates a constant flow of "hot money" across national frontiers, as money rushes in to take advantage of an interest rate edge or an expected rise in the exchange rate, and then rushes out if the interest edge becomes negative or the currency threatens to devalue.

Equally significant is the rise of international banking. In 1965 the 20 biggest U.S. banks had a total of only 211 branches around the world. By 1972 the number of branches had grown to 627, and today the number is well over 1,000. This same multiplication of banking facilities has taken place in other major nations: In New York City alone there are branches of at least 100 foreign banks listed in the telephone directory.

These banks create an international money mechanism that also ties together capitalist economies. Using electronic techniques, banks lend money literally around the world for a few hours at a stretch, so that deposits that are not "working" in Citibank after banking hours can be loaned overnight to a bank in Hong Kong or New York, where they will serve as deposit reserves until Hong Kong shuts down and New York opens up, and the deposits are "returned."

The international integration of money markets means that other asset markets, such as for stocks and bonds, are now closely tied together as well. Suppose, for example, that interest rates in the United States rise. Normally, this will prompt U.S. investors to sell stocks, and stock prices will fall. But with internationalization the effects may be different. If the rise in U.S. interest rates leads to an expectation that the value of the U.S. dollar will rise, all U.S. assets may be more attractive to foreigners than they were before. A flow of foreign capital to U.S. asset markets can begin, offsetting the expected domestic effects.

More dangerously, shocks to a market can now be transmitted around the world in minutes or hours. The stock crash of October 19, 1987, the largest one-day drop in prices in history, began in New York. But within hours it had spread around the world, so that prices fell by nearly equivalent amounts in every foreign stock market from Rotterdam to Singapore.

PAPER MONEY AND GOLD

Finally, let us clear up one last mystery of the monetary system—the mystery of where currency (coin and bills) actually comes from and where it goes. If we examine most of our paper currency, we will find that it has "Federal Reserve

Note'' on it: That is, it is paper money issued by the Federal Reserve System. We understand, by now, how the public gets these notes: It simply draws them from its checking accounts. When it does so, the commercial banks, finding their supplies of vault cash low, ask their Federal Reserve district banks to ship them as much new cash as they need.

And what does the Federal Reserve Bank do? It takes packets of bills ($1 and $5 and $10) out of its vaults, where these stacks of printed paper have *no monetary significance at all,* charges the requisite amount against its member banks' balances, and ships the cash out by armored truck. So long as these new stacks of bills remain in the member banks' possession, they are still not money! But soon they will pass out to the public, where they will be money. Do not forget, of course, that as a result the public will have that much *less* money left in its checking accounts.

Could this currency-issuing process go on forever? Could the Federal Reserve print as much money as it wanted to? Suppose the authorities at the Federal Reserve decided to order a trillion dollars' worth of bills from the Treasury mints. What would happen when those bills arrived at the Federal Reserve banks? The answer is that they would simply gather dust in their vaults. There would be no way for the Federal Reserve to "issue" its money unless the public wanted cash. And the amount of cash the public could want is always limited by the amount of money in its checking accounts.

Thus the specter of "rolling the printing presses" has to be looked at skeptically. In pre-Hitler Germany, where most individuals were paid by cash, not by check, it was easier to get the actual bills into circulation than it would be in a highly developed check money system such as ours. The roads to inflation are many, but the actual printing of money is not likely to be one of them.*

The Gold Cover

Are there no limitations on this note-issuing or reserve-creating process? Until 1967 there *were* limitations imposed by Congress, requiring the Federal Reserve to hold gold certificates equal in value to at least 25 percent of all outstanding notes. (Gold certificates were a special kind of paper money issued by the U.S. Treasury and backed 100 percent by gold bullion in Fort Knox). Prior to 1964 there was a further requirement that the amount of gold certificates also be sufficient to give a 25 percent backing as well to the total amount of member bank deposits held by the Fed. Thus the legal obligation not to go beyond this 25 percent gold cover provided a strict ceiling on the amount of member bank reserves the Federal Reserve System could create or on the amount of notes it could ship at the request of its member banks.

All this presented no problem in, say, 1940, when the total of member bank

*We have all seen pictures of German workers in the 1920s being paid their wages in wheelbarrow loads of marks. The question is this: Why didn't the German authorities simply print paper money with bigger denominations, so that someone who was paid a billion marks a week could get ten 100 million mark notes, not ten thousand 1 million mark notes? The answer is that it takes time to go through the bureaucratic process of ordering a new print run of higher-denomination notes. Imagine a young economist at the finance ministry suggesting to his chief that they ought to stock up on billion-mark notes to be put into circulation six months hence. His superior would certainly be horrified. "You can't do that," he would protest. "Why, an order for billion mark notes would be—inflationary!"

reserves plus Federal Reserve notes came to only $20 billion, against which we held gold certificates worth almost $22 billion. Trouble began to develop, however, in the 1960s when a soaring GNP was accompanied by a steadily rising volume of both member bank reserves and Federal Reserve notes. By 1964, for example, member bank reserves had grown to $22 billion, and outstanding Reserve notes to nearly $35 billion. At the same time, our gold stock had declined to just over $15 billion. With $57 billion in liabilities ($22 billion in member bank reserves plus $35 billion in notes) and only $15 billion in gold certificates, the 25 percent cover requirement was clearly imperiled.

Congress thereupon removed the cover requirement from member bank reserves, leaving all our gold certificates available as backing for our Federal Reserve notes. But even that did not solve the problem. Currency in circulation continued to rise with a record GNP until it exceeded $40 billion in 1967. Our gold stock meanwhile continued to decline to $12 billion in that year and threatened to fall further. The handwriting on the wall indicated that the 25 percent cover could not long be maintained.

There were basically two ways out. One would have been to change the gold cover requirements from 25 percent to, say, 10 percent. That would have made our gold stock more than adequate to back our paper money (and our member bank deposits, too). The second way was much simpler: *eliminate the gold cover entirely.* With very little fuss, this is what Congress did in 1967.

Gold and Money

Does the presence or absence of a gold cover make any difference? From the economist's point of view, it does not. Gold is a metal with a long and rich history of

GOLDFINGER AT WORK

Some years ago a patriotic women's organization, alarmed lest the Communists had tunneled under the Atlantic, forced an inspection of the gold stock buried at Fort Knox. It proved to be all there. An interesting question arises as to the repercussions had they found the great vault to be bare. Perhaps we might have followed the famous anthropological example of the island of Yap in the South Seas, where heavy stone cartwheels are the symbol of wealth for the leading families. One such family was particularly remarkable insofar as its cartwheel lay at the bottom of a lagoon, where it had fallen from a canoe. Although it was absolutely irretrievable and even invisible, the family's wealth was considered unimpaired, since everyone knew the stone was there. If the Kentucky depository had been empty, a patriotic declaration by the ladies that the gold really was in Fort Knox might have saved the day for the United States.

hypnotic influence, so there is undeniably a psychological usefulness in having gold behind a currency. But unless that currency is 100 percent convertible into gold, *any* money demands an act of faith on the part of its users. If that faith is destroyed, the money becomes valueless; so long as it is unquestioned, the money *is* "as good as gold."

Thus the presence or absence of a gold backing for currency is purely a psychological problem so far as the value of a domestic currency is concerned. But the point is worth pursuing a little further. Suppose our currency *were* 100 percent convertible into gold—suppose, in fact, that we used only gold coins as currency. Would that improve the operation of our economy?

A moment's reflection should reveal that it would not. We would still have to cope with a very difficult problem that our bank deposit money handles rather easily. This is the problem of how we could increase the supply of money or diminish it as the needs of the economy changed. With gold coins as money, either we would have a frozen stock of money (with consequences we shall trace in the next chapter), or our supply of money would be at the mercy of our luck in goldmining or the currents of international trade that funneled gold into our hands or took it away. And incidentally, a gold currency does not preclude inflation, as many countries have discovered when the vagaries of international trade or a fortuitous discovery of gold mines increased their holdings of gold faster than their actual output.

Money and Belief

How, then, do we explain the worldwide fascination with gold? The economist can offer no rational explanation for this phenomenon. There is nothing in gold itself that possesses more value than silver, uranium, land, or labor. Indeed, judged strictly as a source of usable values, gold is rather low on the spectrum of human requirements. **The sole reason why people want gold—rich people and poor people, sophisticated people and ignorant ones—is that gold has been for centuries a metal capable of catching and holding our fancy, and in troubled times it is natural enough that we turn to this enduring symbol of wealth as the best bet for preserving our purchasing power in the future.**

Will gold in fact remain valuable forever? And if so, how valuable? There is absolutely no way to answer such a question. As we cautioned at the outset, money is a highly sophisticated and curious invention. At one time or another nearly everything imaginable has served as the magic symbol of money: whales' teeth, shells, feathers, bark, furs, blankets, butter, tobacco, leather, copper, silver, gold, and (in the most advanced nations) pieces of paper with pictures on them, or simply numbers on a computer printout. In fact, anything is usable as money provided there is a natural or enforceable scarcity of it, so that people can usually come into its possession only through carefully designated ways. Behind all the symbols, however, rests the central requirement of faith: **Money serves its indispensable purposes as long as we believe in it. It ceases to function the moment we do not. Money has well been called "the promises men live by."**

LOOKING BACK

KEY CONCEPTS

The Federal Reserve is the source of most of the net increases (or decreases) in deposits.

1 The volume of demand deposits can increase only if there is an increase in deposits that is not matched by a decrease elsewhere. This net increase in deposits and reserves mainly comes from the Federal Reserve system. In the same way, the money supply will contract only if a fall in deposits at one bank is not balanced by a rise elsewhere. Again, the Federal Reserve is the source of such net decreases.

The Fed's three methods of changing the money supply:
1. Raising or lowering reserve requirements is a powerful but undiscriminating weapon.

2 The Fed has three methods by which it can change the net total of deposits. The first is by changing the reserve requirement. This directly freezes or frees a portion of the reserves of each bank and also changes the deposit multiplier. It is a potent means of bringing about large changes in money supply, but it exerts its effect across the board in an undiscriminating fashion.

2. Changing discount rates signals a policy of tighter or easier money.

3 The Federal Reserve can also change discount rates—the rate at which member banks can borrow. This action not only directly encourages or discourages member-bank borrowing, but is widely regarded as a signal to the financial world that the Fed is eager to make money tight or easier.

3. Open market operations are an important week-to-week means of control. When the Fed buys government bonds it creates net deposits; selling bonds reduces total deposits.

4 Most important in week-to-week activities are open market operations. These operations are the buying and selling of government bonds conducted by the New York Federal Reserve Bank in the bond market. When the Fed buys bonds, it pays for them by its own check. This check, when deposited in a bank, creates a new deposit that is not gained from another bank. It is a net increase in money supply. Selling a bond withdraws deposits in the same way. Open market operations enable banks to compete for their share of the new deposits that will be created.

A flexible money system is necessary for an economy with sticky prices.

5 A flexible monetary system is necessary because prices are sticky. This is the consequence of long-term contracts, wage agreements, and similar institutional rigidities that make it impossible for prices to fall so that a fixed money supply could finance a growing volume of real output.

The Federal Reserve acquires foreign exchange; its power of intervention is, however, limited.

6 The Federal Reserve, like all central banks, buys and sells foreign exchange. All national banks can "unload" unwanted exchange on their central bank, where they become part of the central bank reserves of foreign exchange. Thus the Fed can affect the exchange value of dollars by buying or selling its reserves. It cannot greatly lower the price of dollars, however, without the danger of an international flight from American banks.

The internationalization of money

7 This limited power of the Fed is one aspect of the degree to which an internationalized money supply has constrained the power of all banks. National money supplies are now international—especially around the fringes.

Paper money has no gold backing. It only passes into use when the public converts its demand deposits into cash.

8 Printed money is not actually money until it passes into the hands of the public. The amount depends on the demand for cash and the size of checking accounts. There is no longer a gold cover behind printed money.

Gold is valuable because of its long symbolic importance.

9 Gold has long held a special place in the human imagination, and this accounts for its value. There is no way of knowing whether gold will continue to hold that special place.

ECONOMIC VOCABULARY

Changing reserve requirements 348
Discount rates 349
Open market operations 349
International reserves 353
Gold cover 356

QUESTIONS

1. Suppose that a bank has $1 million in deposits, $150,000 in reserves, and is fully loaned up. Now suppose the Federal Reserve System lowers reserve requirements from 15 to 10 percent. What happens to the lending capacity of the bank? What happens to the deposit multiplier?
2. The Federal Reserve banks buy $100 million in U.S. Treasury notes on the open market. How do they pay for these notes? What happens to the checks? Do they affect the reserves of member banks? Will buying bonds increase or decrease the money supply?
3. Now explain what happens when the Fed sells Treasury notes. Who buys them? How do they pay for them? Where do the checks go? How does payment affect the accounts of member banks at their Federal Reserve bank?
4. Suppose you had $1,000 in the bank. Would you be more willing to invest it if you could earn 5 percent or 8 percent? What factors could make you change your mind about investing all or any part at, say, 8 percent? Could you imagine conditions that would make you unwilling to invest even at 10 percent? Other conditions that would lead you to invest your whole cash balance at, say, 3 percent?
5. Suppose the going rate of interest is 7 percent and the monetary authorities want to curb expenditures and act to reduce the quantity of money. What will the effect be in terms of the public's access to cash? What will the public do if it feels short of cash? Will it buy or sell securities? What would this do to their

price? What would thereupon happen to the rate of interest? To investment expenditures?

6. Suppose the monetary authorities want to encourage economic expansion. What are the general measures it will take? What problems might arise because of the international character of money?
7. Why do you think gold was a monetary standard for so long?

A (CONTENTIOUS) EXTRA WORD ABOUT

Independence of the Federal Reserve

The Federal Reserve Board is a regulatory agency established on the quasi-judicial principles of the Progressive era. It is run by seven governors, each appointed to a 14-year term and protected from removal except for wrongdoing. Thus, although fiscal policy is located in the executive and legislative branches of the government, effective power over monetary policy is vested in an independent board.

The initial justifications for this arrangement were a deep distrust by Congress of the presidency. The Progressive era was a time when Congress delegated numerous functions to agencies that would not be under the control of the executive branch, hoping thereby to remove major areas of policy from the realms of politics and of patronage. More recently, it has been said that the continuing independence of the Federal Reserve is necessary for technical reasons, to preserve the necessary freedom to make rapid changes of policy in today's volatile financial climate.

Are these reasons still valid? Some economists think so; others, including ourselves, think not. The arguments about insulation from the political process depend, at bottom, on one's view of democracy, where values rather than science reign supreme. Our political view is that the monetary authorities should be accountable to the president, the Congress, and ultimately to the voters. There is a curious inconsistency, moreover, in the insulation of monetary policies, while fiscal policies must be made through the executive/legislative process. This inconsistency means that the two policies are often made in accordance with divergent *principles*—a dangerous and self-defeating practice.

It is true that day-to-day changes in monetary policy—the business of open market operations—cannot be undertaken by Congress. But there is no reason why such actions cannot be vested wholly in the executive branch, as decisions to intervene in the foreign exchange markets actually are. In most of the world's governments (prominently Japan and France), central banking is subordinate to treasury or finance ministries, and this does not pose any technical problems.

As is true of most institutional debates, dramatic change is unlikely, but there is some hope for a more democratic direction in our monetary management. Congress now expects to be briefed every six months on the Federal Reserve's monetary objectives and forecasts for the growth of GNP and of inflation. Bills have also been introduced into Congress to integrate the Federal Reserve with the executive branch more fully by making the term of the Fed chairman run concurrently with that of the president. In this way, each new president could be assured of a Federal Reserve chairman who would be prepared to work with the administration's economic policies rather than possibly at cross purposes.

CHAPTER 21

Money and the Macro System

A LOOK AHEAD

In our last chapters we learned what money was and how the money supply could be increased. Now we turn to the much more complicated question of how money affects the macro system. Here we encounter two distinct and opposing views. The first is probably the most famous theory in economics—the quantity theory of money, which holds that the key relationship is between *money* and *prices.* The opposing view, associated with John Maynard Keynes, holds that the key relationships are between *money* and *interest rates* and between *interest rates* and *demand.*

In this chapter we will:

1 Learn the old-fashioned quantity theory of money.
2 Find out what was missing from that theory.
3 Learn the alternative Keynesian theory.

We will take up some newer approaches to money, especially the "monetarist" view, in the next chapter.

THE QUANTITY THEORY OF MONEY

One relation between money and economic activity must have occurred to you by now. It is that the quantity of money must have something to do with *prices.* Does it not stand to reason that if we increase the supply of money, prices will go up, and that if we decrease the amount of money, prices will fall?

Quantity Equation

Something very much like this belief lies behind one of the most famous equations (really identities) in economics. The equation looks like this:

$$MV \equiv PT$$

where

M = *quantity of money* (currency outside banks plus demand deposits);

V = *velocity of circulation,* or the number of times per period or per year that an average dollar changes hands;

P = *the general level of prices,* or a price index;

T = *the number of transactions made in the economy* in a year, or a measure of physical output.

If we think about this equation, its meaning is not hard to grasp. What the quantity equation says is that the amount of *expenditure* (*M* times *V*, or the quantity of money times the frequency of its use) equals the amount of *receipts* (*P* times *T*, or the price of an average sale times the number of sales). Naturally, this is an identity. In fact, it is our old familiar circular flow. What all factors of production receive *(PT)* must equal what all factors of production spend *(MV)*.

Just as our GNP identities are true at every moment, so is the quantity theory of money true at every instant. The two merely look at the circular flow from different vantage points. And just as our GNP identities yielded useful economic insights when we began to inquire into the functional relationships within those identities, so the quantity theory can shed light on economic activity if we can find functional relationships concealed within its self-evident "truth."

Assumptions of the Quantity Theory

To move from identities to functional relationships, we need to make assumptions that lend themselves to investigation and evidence. In the case of the GNP = $C + G + I + X$ identity, for instance, we made a critical assumption about the propensity to consume that led to the multiplier and to predictive statements about the influence of injections on GNP. In the case of $MV = PT$, we need another assumption. What will it be?

The crucial assumptions made by the economists who first formulated the quantity theory were two: (1) The velocity of money—the number of times an average dollar was used per year—*was constant;* and (2) transactions (sales) *were always at a full employment level.* If these assumptions were true, it followed that the price level was a simple function of the supply of money:

$$P = \frac{V}{T} \cdot M$$
$$P = kM$$

where k was a constant defined by V/T.

If the money supply went up, prices went up; if the quantity of money went down, prices went down. Since the government controlled the money supply, it could easily regulate the price level.

Testing the Quantity Theory

Is this relation true? Can we directly manipulate the price level by changing the size of our stock of money?

The original inventors of the quantity equation, over half a century ago, thought this was indeed the case. And of course it *would* be the case if everything else in the equation held steady while we moved the quantity of money up or down. In other words, if the **velocity of circulation,** V, and the number of transactions, T, were fixed, changes in M would have to operate directly on P.

Can we test the validity of this assumption? There is an easy way to do so. Figure 1 gives us a first clue as to what is wrong with a purely mechanical interpretation of the quantity theory. In it we show how many times an average dollar was used to help pay for each year's output.* We derive this number by dividing the total expenditure for each year's output (which is, of course, the familiar figure for GNP) by the actual supply of money—currency plus checking accounts—for each year. As the chart shows, the velocity of circulation of money fell by 50 percent between 1929 and 1946, only to rise above the 1929 level over the postwar years.

We shall return later to inquire why people spend money less or more quickly, but it is clear that they do, and this has two important implications for our study of money. First, it gives a very cogent reason why we cannot apply the quantity theory in a mechanical way, asserting that an increase in the supply of money will *always* raise prices. For if people choose to spend the increased quantity of money more slowly, prices may not change at all. If they spend the same quantity of money more rapidly, prices can rise without any change in M.

Second, and more clearly than we have seen, the variability of V reveals that money itself can be a destabilizing force—destabilizing because it enables us to do two things that would be impossible in a pure barter economy. We can:

1. Delay between receiving and expending our rewards for economic effort.

*Note that final output is not quite the same as T, which embraces *all* transactions, including those for intermediate goods. But if we define T so that it includes only *transactions that enter into final output, PT* becomes a measure of gross national product. In the same way, we can count only those expenditures that enter into GNP when we calculate MV. It does no violence to the idea of the quantity theory to apply it only to final output, and it makes statistical computation far simpler.

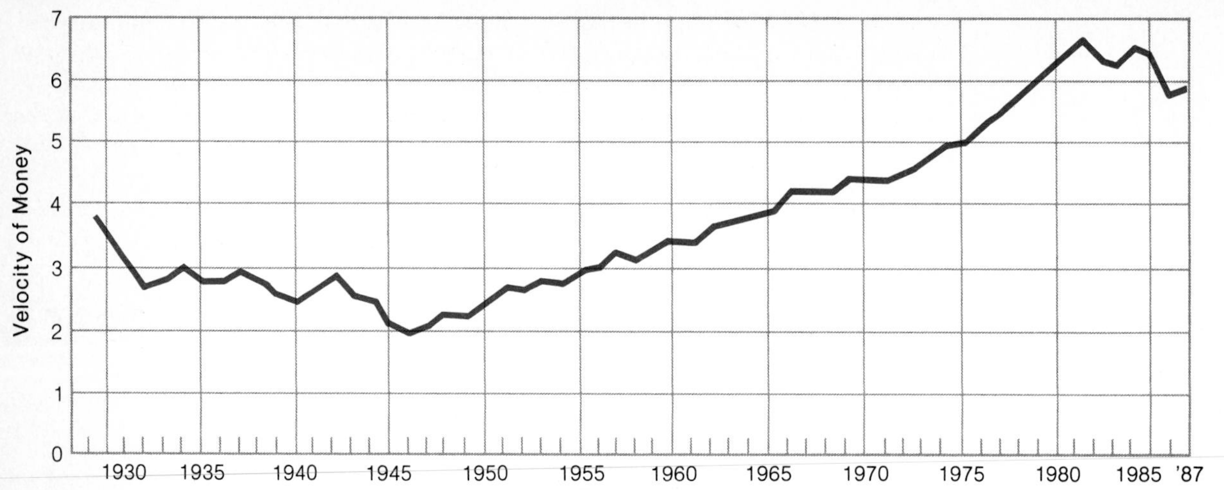

FIGURE 1
Velocity of Money
Velocity is an important source of change. The more quickly we spend money, the more dollars we spend chasing after goods.
Sources: *Statistical Abstracts of the United States.*

2. Spend more or less than our receipts by drawing on, or adding to, our cash balances.

Classical economists used to speak of money as a "veil," implying that it did not itself play an active role in influencing the behavior of the economic players. But we can see that the ability of those players to vary the rate of their expenditure—to hang onto their money longer or to get rid of it more rapidly than usual—makes money much more than a veil. Money (or rather people's wish to hold or to spend money) becomes an independent source of change in a complex economic society. **To put it differently, the use of money introduces an independent element of uncertainty into the circular flow.***

Changes in *T*

Now we must turn to the last and perhaps most important reason why we cannot relate the supply of money to the price level in a mechanical fashion. This reason lies in the role played by *T;* that is, by the volume of output.

Just as the early quantity theorists thought of *V* as essentially unvarying, so they thought of *T* as a relatively fixed term in the quantity equation. In the minds of nearly all economic theorists before the Depression, output was always assumed to be as large as the available resources and the willingness of the factors of production would permit. While everyone was aware that there might be minor variations from this state of full output, virtually no one thought they would be of sufficient

*As the standard economic definition of money puts it, money is both a means of exchange and a store of value. It is the latter characteristic that makes money a potentially disturbing influence.

importance to matter. **Hence the quantity theory implicitly assumed full employment or full output as the normal condition of the economy.** With such an assumption, it was easy to picture *T* as an unimportant term in the equation and to focus the full effect of changes in money on *P*.

The trauma of the Great Depression effectively removed the comfortable assumption that the economy naturally tended to full employment and output. At the bottom of the Depression, real output had fallen by 30 percent. Whatever else the Depression taught us, it made it unmistakably clear that changes in the volume of output (and employment) were of crucial importance in the overall economic picture, and that the economy does *not* naturally gravitate to full employment levels.

Output and Prices

It is clear, then, that the old-fashioned quantity theorists were mistaken. (For an explanation of *why* they erred, see the box on this page).

What should we put in the place of the original $MV = PT$ theory? That is a very important question, but we shall postpone it for a moment. For there are still things to be learned about how money works, and we cannot tackle monetary theory until we have learned them.

The first thing to understand is how our modern emphasis on the variability of

WHY THE OLD QUANTITY THEORISTS ERRED

Modern economists can easily show that the velocity of money is not constant and that the volume of transactions (GNP) is not always at full employment. But it should not be thought that the originators of the quantity theory were stupid or too lazy to look up the basic data. Most of the numbers on which economists now rely were simply not in existence then. The national income, for example, was not calculated until the early 1930s, and the GNP was not "invented" until the early 1940s. You cannot calculate the velocity of money unless you know the national income or the gross national product.

Neither did the original quantity theorists have accurate measures of unemployment or capacity utilization. They used the only method available to them: direct observation of the world, a method that is notoriously inaccurate when one's view is much smaller than "the world." The idea of mass involuntary unemployment required the idea of an equilibrium output that would be less than a full employment output, an idea completely foreign to pre-Keynesian thought.

T—that is, of output and employment—fits into the overall question of money and prices. The answer is very simple, but very important. **We have come to see that the effect of more money on prices cannot be determined unless we also take into account the effect of spending on the volume of transactions or output.**

It is not difficult to grasp the point. Let us picture an increase in spending, perhaps initiated by a business launching a new investment program or the government a new public works project. These new expenditures will be received by many other entrepreneurs as the multiplier mechanism spreads the new spending through the economy. But now we come to the key question: What will entrepreneurs do as their receipts increase?

It is at this point that the question of output enters. For if factories or stores are operating *at less than full capacity,* and if there is an *employable supply of labor available,* the result of their new receipts is almost certain to be an increase in output. That is, employers will take advantage of the rise in demand to produce and sell more goods and services. They may also try to raise prices and increase their profits further. But *if their industries are reasonably competitive, it is doubtful that prices can be raised very much.* Other firms with idle plants will simply undercut them and take their business away. An example is provided by the period 1934 through 1940, when output increased by 50 percent while prices rose by less than 5 percent. The reason, of course, lay in the great amount of unemployed resources, making it easy to expand output without increasing prices.

Full Employment vs. Underemployment

This is a very important finding for macroeconomics, for it helps us see that policies that make sense in one economic situation make no sense in another. This is particularly true with policies that promote spending of any kind—public spending or private spending, spending out of earned income or deficit spending. If an economy is suffering from large numbers of unemployed workers and from large amounts of underutilized capacity, it *must* spend more if it is to move back to its production frontiers. As we learned in Chapter 12, expenditure is the necessary precondition for output. Unless we spend more, we are doomed to remain permanently underemployed.

But spending more will not bring us more output if we are at, or close to, the production frontier. Then more spending—for consumption or investment, for private use or public use—can only send prices higher, with little or no effect on the volume of output.

Until recently, this distinction between the beneficial effects of expenditure when unemployment was high and the bad effects of expenditure when unemployment was low was a central premise of modern macroeconomics. Today the distinction is not as sharp as it was once, for we seem to have moved into a condition in which spending sends prices up even though we are certainly not in a state of full employment or utilization. This is a problem that greatly complicates the management of the nation's money supply. We will look into it more fully in Chapter 23.

THE KEYNESIAN THEORY

The quantity theory of money reigned supreme until the 1930s, when it first became apparent that the assumption of full employment was not a satisfactory basis for a theory of the price level. John Maynard Keynes set about to construct an alternative view of the role of money that could fit into an economic system in which unemployment and underemployment might be the normal or equilibrium conditions.

Keynes's solution was published as his *General Theory of Employment Interest and Money* in 1936. The title gives away the heart of his argument. Keynes simply threw away the quantity theory, and with it the notion that the principal effects of a change in money are on *prices.* Not so, said Keynes: **Changes in the money supply affect not prices, but the rate of interest.** Changes in the rate of interest, in turn, affect the demand for investment spending—as we saw in our chapter on the investment sector—and hence the *level of aggregate demand.* Any effects on prices depend on the level of employment and unemployment, as we have just noted.

The Demand for Money

The bold innovation of Keynes's theory was the idea that there was a demand schedule for money—that actors did not merely accept the volume of money supplied by the authorities, but actively sought to acquire more money, or to get rid of money they did not want or need. Once the idea was entertained that individuals could have changing needs for money, it was a short step to the idea that individuals would pay a price to satisfy their needs. The price was the rate of interest.

But what sorts of needs and wants could give rise to a demand curve for money? Keynes distinguished two separate kinds of demands: transactions and financial.

1. Transactions Demand. The first and most evident reason for individuals to want more or less money, said Keynes, was that they required different amounts to finance their regular purchases and sales. When business was brisk and consumption demand ran high, individuals would ordinarily require larger deposits in their bank accounts. As a result, they would be willing to turn other kinds of assets, such as stocks or bonds, into money by selling them. In doing so, they would have to give up the income that those other investments offered. Cash is very useful for meeting payrolls or for paying other bills, but cash on hand (or in a bank) will not pay you the return you can get from bonds or many other forms of wealth.

2. Financial Demand. A second, quite different, motive for holding money, said Keynes, arose from financial rather than transactional considerations. Keynes saw that the demand schedule for cash for financial purposes related the quantity of cash wanted to the opportunity cost of acquiring that amount of cash. The cost was the income that had to be sacrificed by giving up earning typs of assets for ready

INTEREST RATES AND BOND PRICES

Most bonds are a promise to pay a certain stated amount of interest and to repay the principal at some fixed date. To simplify things, forget the repayment for a moment and focus on the interest. Suppose that you paid $1,000 for a perpetual bond that had a "coupon"—an interest return—of $100 per year with no date of repayment. And suppose that you wanted to sell that bond. What would it be worth?

The answer depends wholly on the current market rate of interest for bonds of equal risk. Suppose this rate of interest were 10 percent. Your bond would then still be worth $1,000, because the coupon would yield the buyer of the bond 10 percent on his money. But suppose interest rates had risen to 20 percent. You would now find that your bond was worth only $500. A buyer can go into the market and purchase other bonds that wil give him a 20 percent yield on his money. Therefore he will pay you only $500 for your bond, because your $100 coupon is 20 percent of $500. If you want to sell your bond, that is the price you will have to accept.

On the other hand, if interest rates have fallen to 5 percent, you can get $2,000 for your bond, for you can show the buyer that your $100 coupon will give him the going market return of 5 percent at a price of $2,000. (If you were to buy a *new* $1,000 bond at the going 5 percent interest rates, it would carry a coupon of only $50.)

These calculations also show that it can be very profitable at times to hold money. When interest rates are rising, bond prices are falling. Therefore the longer you wait before you buy, the bigger your chances for a capital gain if interest rates turn around and go the other way. This means that we tend to get "liquid" whenever we think that interest rates are below normal levels and bonds are too high; and that we tend to get out of money and into bonds whenever we think that interest rates are above normal levels, and therefore bonds are cheap. The trick, of course, is being right about the course of interest rates before everyone else.

cash.* It followed that the higher the rate of interest—that is, the larger the income available from bonds—the greater the cost of holding cash. As interest rates rose, therefore, Keynes reasoned that individuals or firms would seek to minimize their cash holdings. We have seen dramatic confirmation of this relationship in the years of sky-high interest rates in the early 1980s, when companies and

*In Keynes's day, commercial banks did not pay interest on checking accounts. Today a checking account may earn interest, but it is usually much less than the interest available from bonds or other nonliquid assets.

households put every available cent into money market funds and interest-bearing CDs (certificates of deposit) rather than allowing funds to sit idle in checking accounts.

All these financial considerations lead individuals or firms to seek to hold more cash when interest rates are low than when they are high, and more when business is brisk than when it is slack. In all cases, however, the common consideration is how **liquid** or **illiquid** the economic actor wants to be—that is, how he wishes to divide his assets between cash or bonds and other kinds of holdings.

The Supply and Demand for Money

From these motives, we can construct a demand schedule for money. Like other normal demand curves, the demand for money is a downward-sloping curve: In general, the lower the rate of interest, the greater the demand for money. And what is the supply curve of money? It is very simple: It consists of the actual quantities of money made available at any moment by the monetary authorities. It will be drawn, therefore, as a vertical line, like the supply curve for milk on page 125.

If we now put together the supply and demand curves for money, we have a result that looks like Figure 2. Our diagram shows that at interest rate *OA*, there will be *OX* amount of money demanded for transactions purposes and *OY* amount for various liquidity purposes. The total demand for money will be *OM* (= *OX* + *OY*), which is just equal to the total supply at interest rate *OA*.

Changing the Supply of Money

Let us suppose the monetary authorities reduce the supply of money. We show this in Figure 3. Now we have a curious situation. The supply of money has declined from *OM* to *OM′*. But notice that the demand curve for money shows that firms and

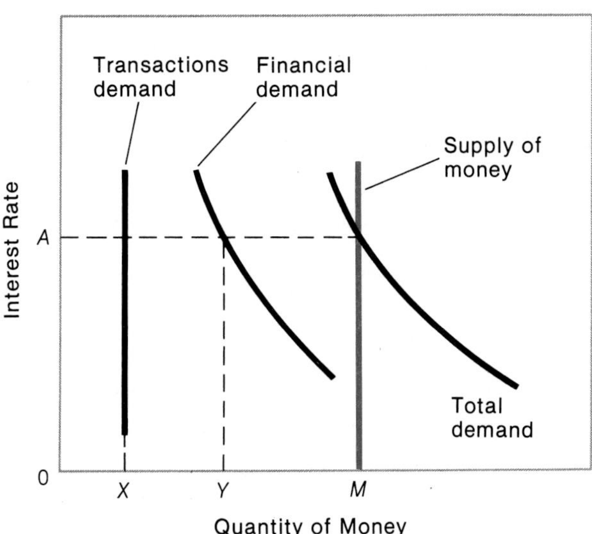

FIGURE 2
Transactions and Financial Demands for Money
The demand for money has a negative slope, whether we want money to spend or to hold as a liquid investment. The lower interest rates fall, the more money we will seek. The supply of money, as we can see, is a fixed quantity in the short run.

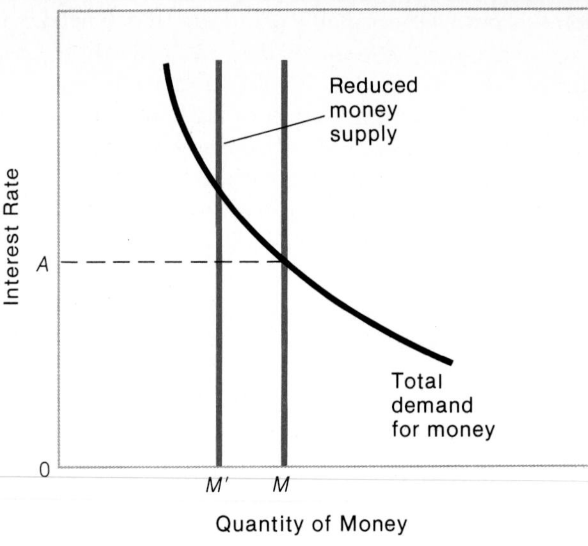

FIGURE 3
Reducing the Supply of Money
The Fed reduces the money supply from OM to OM′. OA is no longer a price for money that will clear the market. Now see Figure 4.

individuals want to hold *OM* at the given rate of interest *OA*. *Yet they cannot hold amount OM, because the monetary authorities have cut the supply to OM′*. What will happen?

The answer is very neat. As bank reserves fall, banks will tighten money—raise lending rates and screen loan applications more carefully. Individuals and firms will be competing for a reduced supply of loans and will bid more for them. At the same time, individuals and firms will feel the pinch of reduced supplies of cash and will try to get more money to fulfill their liquidity desires. The easiest way to get more money is to sell securities, to get out of bonds and into cash. **Note, however, that selling securities does not create a single additional dollar of money. It**

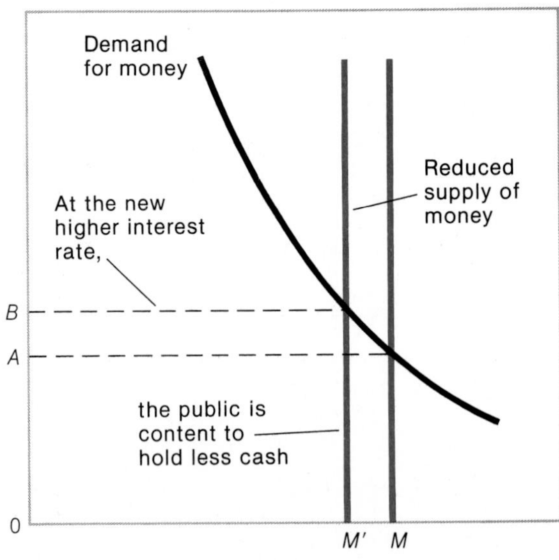

FIGURE 4
Determination of New Equilibrium
When the quantity of money shrinks, the public will try to acquire money by selling bonds. As they do so, bond yields rise. As yields rise, the demand for money falls. The market now finds a new clearing price (OB) for its smaller quantity of OM′.

simply transfers money from one holder to another. But it does change the rate of interest. As bonds are sold, their price falls; and as the price of bonds falls, the interest yield on bonds rises (see p. 370).

Our next diagram (Figure 4) shows what happens. Because interest rates have risen, the public is content to hold a smaller quantity of money. Hence a new interest rate, *OB,* will emerge, at which the public is *willing* to hold the money that there *is to hold.* The attempt to become more liquid ceases, and a new equilibrium interest rate prevails.

Suppose the authorities had increased the supply of money. In that case, individuals and firms would be holding more money than they wanted at the going rate of interest. They would try to get out of money into bonds, sending bond prices up and yields down. Simultaneously, banks would find themselves with extra reserves and would compete for loans, also driving interest rates down. As interest rates fell, firms and individuals would be content to hold more money until a new equilibrium was again established. Figure 5 shows the process at work.

Determination of Interest Rates

This gives us the final link in our argument. We have seen that interest rates determine whether we wish to hold larger or smaller balances. But what determines the interest rate itself?

The Federal Reserve can, of course, raise or lower the discount rate, and big banks from time to time can announce a new *prime rate*—the rate at which they will lend to their best customers. But neither the Fed nor the biggest bank could make a rate stick if there were no bidders for money at that level, or conversely, if everyone converged on the bank for a loan. Although rates are announced by the monetary authorities or by big banks, they must match the forces of the marketplace if they are to hold steady. And we can now see that the forces of the marketplace are

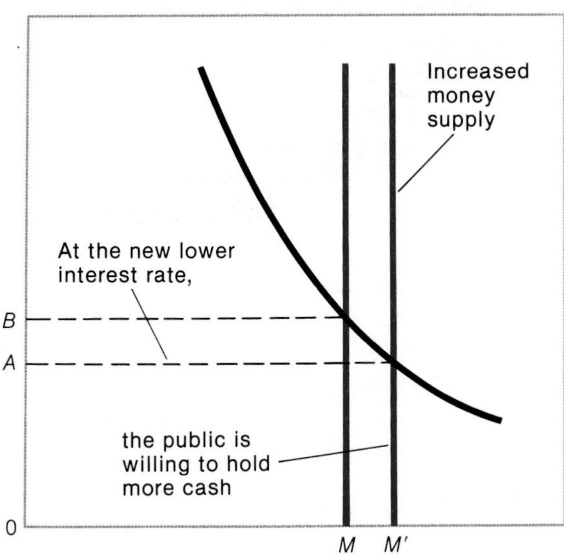

FIGURE 5
Increasing the Supply of Money
Here is the opposite story. The Fed increases M to OM′. Individuals do not want more money at the old price (OB). They use the new supply of money to but bonds. Bond prices rise, yields fall. At a lower interest rate (OA) the public will be willing to hold OM′.

summed up in the interplay of supply and demand we have been discussing.

Our demand for money is made up of our transactions demand curve and our financial demand curve. The supply of money is mainly controlled by the monetary authorities. The price of money—interest—is therefore determined by the demand for, and supply of, money, exactly as the price of any commodity is determined by demand and supply.

Money and Its Effects: A Review

What our analysis enables us to see is that once the interest rate is determined, it will affect the use to which we put a given supply of money. Now we begin to understand the full answer to the question of how changes in the supply of money affect GNP. Let us review the argument, and supply the last link.

1. Suppose the monetary authorities want to increase the supply of money. They will lower reserve ratios or (more likely these days) buy government bonds on the open market.
2. Banks will find that they have larger reserves. They will compete with one another and lower lending rates.
3. Some of the money will come to rest in rising financial balances as interest rates fall, and will have no further financial or real effects. But this typically will not be a large part of the total increase in the supply of money.
4. Here is the last link: Lower lending rates will cause investors to reevaluate the investment projects they have before them. (Recall the schedule of the marginal efficiency of investment we learned about in Chapter 16.) They will discover newly profitable projects, will place new orders with companies that supply equipment and materials, and will take on new workers. The total level of demand will rise, and with it the transactions demand for money.
5. A new equilibrium will be reached at which the total demand for money will just come to equal the supply.

KEYNES VS. THE QUANTITY THEORY

Finally, back to the quantity theory. What is the essential difference between the old *MV-PT* view of the relation between money and prices and the Keynesian view?

There are two ways of describing the difference. The first is that Keynes recognized *two kinds* of needs for money—one for carrying on business, the other for being more or less liquid so that wealth was protected. The older economists made no such distinction; all money was considered as a transaction requirement by them, and the level of transactions, as we have noted, was always considered to be one corresponding to full employment. *Thus there was no demand curve for money.* Individuals or firms simply used all the money available to carry on their affairs. They did not consider whether or not they wanted to economize on money because the interest rate was high, and consequently, the cost of being "in" money also high. So one way of describing Keynes's contribution is that he introduced a financial calculation into the money equation—making it more complicated, but much more realistic.

The other way of describing the difference between Keynes and the Classical economists is that Keynes's demand for money hinges on *expectations.* It is future interest rates, more than present interest rates, that establish liquidity preferences. If we expect rates to go higher, we will want to be more liquid than we are today. If we expect them to fall, we will want to be less liquid. Thus expectations—our imperfectly formed, uncertain, almost surely incorrect views about the future—become a central force in the economic mechanism. This explanation of the working of the world is correspondingly less tidy, but also correspondingly closer to the way things really happen.

LOOKING BACK

KEY CONCEPTS

Originally the quantity theory was formulated as $MV \equiv PT$, where P and T were taken as fixed. We know that they are not.

1 The quantity theory, in its original formulation, directly related increases in M, the stock of money, to increases in P, the price level. The formula for the theory was $MV \equiv PT$, where V, velocity, and T, transactions (output) were assumed to be unchanging.

2 Empirical evidence, not available at the time of the original formulation, has made it clear that V and T are both variables, not constants. This is particularly the case with T, which can no longer always be assumed to tend to full utilization levels.

More spending should not send up prices when unemployment is high.

3 As a general rule, increases in spending will generate additional output, with or without price increases, as long as there is large unused capacity in the labor and capital markets. But additional spending, private or public, will generate only price rises and no more output as we reach full employment.

Bond prices rise and fall to make their yields equal to the going interest rate.

4 Bonds are promises to pay fixed amounts at stated periods until the bond matures. Basically, the price at which you can sell a bond on the market depends on the going rate of interest. If your bond will pay $10 per year, and the going rate of interest is 5 percent, the value of the bond—regardless of what you paid for it—will be the price that gives its buyer a 5 percent return. That will be $200, because the $10 interest payment is a 5 percent return on $200. If the market rate of interest rises, say to 10 percent, the value of the bond on the market will fall to whatever price again makes $10 a year equal to the interest rate. At 10 percent, this new price will be $100. Thus as interest rates rise, bond prices fall, and vice versa.

The rate of interest is set by S and D for money.

5 By changing the stock of money, the authorities create more or less money than the public wants to hold at existing interest rates. The public will buy bonds to get out of money or sell them to get into cash.

Buying and selling will not change the amount of money, but it will change bond yields. Thus interest rates are determined by the supply of and demand for money.

Transactions and financial demands for money
The importance of expectations

6 Keynes's contributions were two: First, he differentiated the financial uses of money from their transactional uses. This was a considerable advance from older views, which made no such differentiation. Second, he introduced the notion of expectations, with all its uncertainties, into the very heart of macroeconomics. Looking forward is the most difficult of all economic tasks, but it is the one on which the trend of things depends.

ECONOMIC VOCABULARY

Quantity equation 364
Quantity theory 364
Velocity of circulation 365
Transactions demand 369
Financial demand for money 369
Bond prices 370
Liquidity 371

QUESTIONS

1. Why is the quantity equation a truism? Why is the interpretation of the quantity equation that M affects P not a truism?
2. If employment is full, what will be the effects of an increase in private investment on prices and output, supposing that everything else stays the same?
3. Suppose you had $1,000 in the bank. Would you be more willing to invest it if you could earn 5 percent or 8 percent? What factors could make you change your mind about investing all or any part at, say, 8 percent? Could you imagine conditions that would make you unwilling to invest even at 10 percent? Other conditions that would lead you to invest your whole cash balance at, say, 3 percent?
4. Suppose that the going rate of interest is 7 percent and that the monetary authorities want to curb expenditures and act to reduce the quantity of money. What will the effect be in terms of the public's access to cash? What will the public do if it feels short of cash? Will it buy or sell securities? What would this do to their price? What would thereupon happen to the rate of interest? To investment expenditures?
5. You hold a bond that pays $80 a year, for which you paid $1,000. What is its percentage return or "yield"? If the market rate of interest is 8 percent, at what price could you sell the bond to someone else? Suppose the market rate rose to

15 percent. Will people still give you $1,000 for your bond? What would they give you—what price would make its $80 coupon worth 15 percent? Suppose the market rate fell to 7 percent? How much will the bond then bring on the market?

6. Suppose that the monetary authorities want to encourage economic expansion. What are the general measures they will take? What problems might changing liquidity preference interpose?
7. Do you unconsciously keep a "liquidity balance" among your assets? Suppose your cash balance rose. Would you be tempted to spend more?
8. Show in a diagram how a decrease in the supply of money will be reflected in lower transactions balances and in lower financial balances. What is the mechanism that changes these balances?
9. Do you understand (a) how the rate of interest is determined; (b) how it affects willingness to hold cash? Is this in any way different from the mechanism by which the price of shoes is determined or the way in which the price of shoes affects our willingness to buy them?

CHAPTER 22

The Debate about Monetary Policy

A LOOK AHEAD

In our last chapter we looked into the difference between the old quantity theory and Keynes's views as to the role of money in determining output, employment, and the price level. In this chapter we explore the modern debate on this issue, perhaps the most important policy question in macroeconomics today.

1 First we take a look at monetarism, the view of monetary policy largely inspired by Professor Milton Friedman. This is a powerful attempt to resurrect the quantity theory on the basis of a new explanation of economic behavior called *rational expectations.*
2 Second, we explore the objections to the monetarist thesis.
3 Finally, we try to discover what the fuss is ultimately about: Can we control the direction of economic affairs?

Where do we stand today with respect to the theory of money? We know that the old mechanical quantity theory is inadequate because it assumes that V is a constant, which is not the case, and because it assumes that T—output—is also fixed. Do we have something to put in its place?

There is probably no area of macroeconomics where there is less consensus. Some economists firmly believe that money is the key variable in the determination of prices (and hence of the dollar value of GNP); others believe that it is only one of many variables, and not necessarily the most important. We cannot resolve that often technical debate here. But we would like to present the arguments on both sides of the case, as we see them.

MONETARISM

In the 1960s and 1970s much controversy was generated by an approach to monetary management called *monetarism,* originally advanced by Nobel Laureate Milton Friedman. Monetarism, at its base, is part of a larger view of the self-correcting, self-propelling nature of our economic system that has long characterized one major strand of economic thinking. But monetarism has three specific, and highly interesting, propositions about monetary management that we should study now.

1. Monetarists Claim That Changes in the Supply of Money Affect Spending Directly, Not through Indirect Effects on the Rate of Interest and the Demand for Investment. Monetarists claim that an increase in the lending capabilities of banks—for that is what an increase in the supply of money comes down to—must result in an increase in bank loans. As these loans are spent, MV will rise, even though there has been no previous drop in interest rates.

The original monetarist formulation did not explain why there would be a *demand* for additional loans without a fall in interest. It simply asserted that a larger supply of money would give rise to more spending: "Money matters" became a kind of monetarist slogan. In the 1970s a new theory of "rational expectations" put a causal foundation under the slogan. We shall shortly see what it is.

2. Monetarists Hold That Monetary Policy Exerts No Lasting Effect on Output. Behind this claim is a belief, much like that of the Classical economists, that money is only a "veil" thrown over the real forces in the economy. These real forces are expressed in what Friedman has called the economy's **natural rate of unemployment.** This is the rate that reflects the willingness of individuals to work, given the prevailing real wage. An injection of money, by raising money wages, may tempt people to seek work in the belief that real wages have also risen. But they will soon discover their error and withdraw from the labor market, since they will find that money prices and wages have risen equally, leaving the real wage unaffected.

Thus the economy will gravitate toward a rate of growth that reflects people's natural desire to work (at a given wage). Changes in the money supply may cause short-lived flurries, but cannot change this real growth-setting pacemaker. Booms and busts will therefore be transient—more often than not the result of futile interventions into the economy. In the long run the economy will express the energy and drive of its working force and its managerial talent, and these guiding forces will not be substantially or permanently affected by changes in the supply of money.

3. The Lasting Effect of Monetary Policy Is on the Price Level. Although monetarism has scant belief in the power of the monetary authorities to change the pace of the economy, it has a profound belief in the importance of money management in determining the nominal prices at which output will be sold. Here the reasoning is very much like that of the old quantity theory. A belief in a natural rate of unemployment is much like a belief in an unvarying level of T in the $MV = PT$ formulation. Increases in spending *(MV)* will therefore drive up prices, but not production. It follows that if the government spends more money by borrowing, it may succeed in capturing a larger share of the total flow of spending, but only at the expense of private spending.

As a consequence, monetarists see no merit in Federal Reserve policies that aim to reduce interest rates or stimulate demand. Any efforts in this direction, they argue, will only create more money than needed at the existing level of prices. No effort to bring unemployment below the level to which it naturally gravitates can have any lasting effect, except to flood the economy with money—and to raise prices.

Monetarist Policy

This seems like a prescription for inaction. But that is not quite the monetarist proposal. Rather, Friedman advocates that **the supply of money should be expanded by an unvarying percentage that corresponds with the growth of the real productive capacity of the economy.** That way, he asserts, the supply of money will accommodate the need for growing payrolls and inventories and loans, but with no risk of inflation.

Moreover, the very steadiness of monetary growth will serve to keep the economy on the track. If we find ourselves headed into a recession, let us say because of a downturn of confidence and investment, the steady increase in the money supply will add to banks' reserves, encouraging them to lower interest rates, expand their loans, and thereby move us out of recession. On the other hand, if we experience a surge of inflation, the same steady and unchanging rate of growth of bank lending capability will act as an automatic curb, holding down the banks' ability to finance the inflation-swollen demands of their customers, thereby mitigating the inflationary pressure.

Rational Expectations

One of the questions monetarism originally left unanswered was how an increase in the money supply became an increase in incomes and spending. To put it concretely, if the Federal Reserve decided to buy bonds, why should this result in individuals spending more? For if individuals did not spend more, monetarism would be without the crucial link between an increase in *M* and an increase in *P*.

Keynes, of course, did supply such a link. As we have seen, he believed that an increase in *M* would lead to a fall in the rate of interest, and that this in turn would stimulate investment spending. But in Keynes's answer to the question, money is no longer "neutral"—merely a veil. A change in the supply of money is not like an incoming tide that lifts all boats; it is like the opening of a sluiceway, forcing some boats along and leaving others alone.

The missing link in monetarism was provided in the 1970s by a group of economists who argued that individuals continually form "rational expectations" about the future and guide their behavior accordingly. The theory of rational expectations does not mean *correct* expectations. Rather, it means that people are always thinking about the future and that they apply their best available economic knowledge to predict how things will go. This process would lead individuals to foresee the likely consequences of government policies in a way that is correct *on average,* although not in every instance.

Essentially the theory lays the basis for a belief that government policy cannot affect the economy because people anticipate its effects and thereby annul them. Suppose, for instance, that people read about efforts of the Federal Reserve to increase the money supply in order to stimulate demand. Will not a rational shopkeeper immediately put up his prices, anticipating the new purchasing power? In that case, the effects of the new money creation will be only inflation, with no increase in production or employment.

Many economists, including ourselves, take a skeptical view of the theory of rational expectations, which rests on far-reaching claims as to the knowledge individuals possess and on the competitive nature of markets. It seems very clear, for instance, that the market for stenographers or steelworkers does not react with the quick omniscience of the market for stocks or bonds. Unquestionably, however, rational expectations has been useful in reminding economists that they are not the only predictors in a market system. The theory may overstate the case seriously when it goes on to claim that because everyone is in the forecasting business to some degree, government can never change the way individuals perceive the economy—and therefore the way they act.

ANTIMONETARISM

Can the propositions of monetarism be proved? Here is where the economics profession is still deeply divided. Let us consider the rejoinders antimonetarists offer to the three points we have enumerated above.

1. Do Changes in the Money Supply Directly Affect Expenditure? Antimonetarists believe they do not. They do not believe the Federal Reserve "controls" the money supply the way the monetarists claim it does. The monetarists assert that when the Federal Reserve increases *M, P* goes up. This means that the direction of causality runs from *MV* to *PT*, thus $MV \rightarrow PT$. But that is not the way the world works, say the antimonetarists. In real life the causal influence runs the other way, $MV \rightarrow PT$

How could this be? The answer, according to the antimonetarists, is that the monetarists fail to understand the overriding aim of the Federal Reserve (or any central bank). That purpose, they say, is not to control inflation or interest rates, or to stimulate or hold back the economy. It is to be sure that the banks have enough reserves to be able to cover their deposits as required by law.

The critics charge that monetarists speak as if the monetary authorities first decided how large the lending capacity of the banking system should be, after which the banks went around looking for customers. But the realities are quite the other way around. Half of all new business loans are made to big corporations under credit lines the companies have negotiated with their bankers, legally entitling them to borrow agreed-upon amounts. As one officer of the New York Federal Reserve has put it, "In the real world, banks extend credit . . . and look for reserves later. In one way or another, the Federal Reserve will accomodate them."

2. Antimonetarists Doubt That the Economy Tends to Full Employment or Even to a Steady "Natural" Rate of Unemployment. Far from regarding the business cycle as transient and unimportant, antimonetarists think of fluctuations in the rate of growth as an intrinsic part of the capitalist mechanism. Many of these cycles, they willingly admit, are short and limited in scope, but others are deep and protracted. In 1973, for example, the United States experienced a depression that lasted six long years. In 1893 a depression brought an unemployment rate of 14 percent that lasted for four years. And of course in 1930 the economy went into a veritable tailspin in which GNP dropped by 30 percentage points and unemployment almost touched 25 percent. That depression was still with us, although in milder form, in 1940.

Were these depressions only transient phenomena, or the product of ill-advised monetary policy? Four years, six years, or ten years is too long to be called transient, say the critics of monetarism. Moreover, the earlier depressions, at least, cannot be blamed on the actions of the Federal Reserve, because there *was* no Federal Reserve in 1873 or 1893.

In 1932 the Federal Reserve did indeed pursue a wrong policy of keeping money tight (it was afraid that the gold flowing into the United States would create an inflation!). But later, when it came to its senses and turned its policy around, it could not raise prices and turn the exonomy around. "You can't push with a string" is the way antimonetarist economists describe the failure of the Federal Reserve to get banks to offer loans, or businesses to seek them, in the climate of terrible pessimism to which the Depression gave rise.

Thus to antimonetarists the record of the past is ample disproof of the proposition that money matters to te exclusion of everything else: The Federal Reserve cannot be blamed for starting depressions that occurred before it existed, and it cannot be credited with curing a depression that proved indifferent to its expansionary monetary policy.

3. Antimonetarists Argue That the Price Level Can Be Influenced by Many Nonmonetary Factors. Antimonetarists hold that prices are above all determined by *costs*. Thus any number of influences can affect the price level: a shock to the price of oil, an inertial spiral of wages and prices, a massive Soviet wheat purchase, the disappearance of anchovies off the coast of Peru (once an essential component of animal feedstocks), or a change in the value of the dollar on foreigh exchange markets. Perhaps a too-easy monetary policy will have inflationare effects.* But antimonetarists argue that to assign to every change in price level a monetary cause stretches the concept of causality—and the responsibility of the central bank to maintain a stable price level—past a resonable limit. Hence antimonetarists argue (as we will in Chapter 23), for a wide range of alternative anti-inflation policies.

For a Discretionary Money Policy

Antimonetarists therefore reject the goal of a stable increase in the money supply. It would perhaps be nice to live in a world that was free of supply shocks, wage explosions, commodity cycles, and technological revolutions—a world in which a steady increase in money might assompany a steady increase in output. However, we do not live in such a world, antimonetarists say, and so it is pointless, and perhaps counterproductive, to conduct policy as though we did.

Antimonetarists point to two situations in particular in which the rule of a steady growth in the money supply leads to an undesirable result. The first is a change in the demand for money. Suppose, for example, that as a result of a drop in the inflation rate, the public decides it would like to hold more cash and demand deposits (M) in relation to the given volume of transactions (T). What happens? Under a monetarist growth rule, no accommodation would be made. But if Vdoes not rise, P or Tmust fall. **Antimonetarists argue that shifting demands for money balances can cause wholly unnecessary fluctuations in output under a money growth rule.**

Second, suppose the economy is hit with an external shock, such as the OPEC oil price increases of the 1970s, which suddenly raises the value of P relative to M and V. Under a monetarist rule, again, there can be no accommodation,. and so T—output—must fall. Antimonetarists argue that this is unnecessary: **M should be increased in such a situation so as to stabilize output at the new level of prices.**

FROM ECONOMICS TO POLITICS?

Is it possible to say which side is right in this dispute? It must be evident that our own judgments incline us to the antimonetarist position. But we would be the first

*Recently, there has been growing skepticism even about this point. During 1985–1987 the money supply grew very repidly, and monetarists warned that the inflation rate would turn up as a consequence. Instead, the inflation rate fell! There were, of course, many reasons why inflation did not worsen—cheaper imports, falling oil prices, easier wage bargains. But don't forget—monetarism has claimed that *only* an increase in money would give rise to inflation, and also that an increase in money would *always* give rise to inflation. The increase took place, but not the expected result; or at least it was delayed until mid-1989 when rising inflation began to emerge once again as a serious problem.

to stress the importance of the contribution the monetarists have made in insisting that money matters. Money does indeed matter. Our position is that money does not always matter in precisely the way the monetarists believe; and that not *only* money matters.

Beyond that is a more serious issue. Monetarist policies seem to us to be most effective in ordinary times, when the actions of the Fed can indeed urge on a mildly lagging system or curb a slightly overheated one. **In our view, however, monetary policies act least well when we most need effective measures, namely in deep depressions and dangerous inflations. In depressions, easy money may not create the desire to spend and invest; and in bad inflations, tight money operates unevenly and in a very costly manner.**

That last matter seems crucial. A tight money policy, applied in the United States from 1979 to 1982 and in England for an even longer period, did indeed succeed in its main objective, which was to bring down the rate of inflation. Inflation rates fell because tight money policy slowed down borrowing, greatly intensified competitive pressures, forced unions to accept lower wage raises, and businesses to accept lower profits.

Costs vs. Benefits

Is that not a very convincing proof that monetary policies work, even if some parts of the system escape the noose? The problem is that it is very hard to compare costs and benefits. For while inflation rates were cut in half, unemployment rates were almost doubled. Bankruptcies soared to levels that had not been experienced since the Great Depression. Indeed, the high cost of money, combined with other problems of the system, brought about the most serious depression since the 1930s. Was monetary policy a success, then, or a failure?

The trouble is that the answer will not be gained by a simple calculus of dollars and cents. Inflation and unemployment involve considerations of equity as well as performance—that is, considerations of what we consider to be fair and just as well as what we deem to be economically effective. The balance between good and bad policies is determined more often than not by considerations of political and moral preference rather than by economic judgments alone.

The Core of the Issue

Is monetarism simply a technical disagreement over the working of the monetary system? That is certainly part of the issue, but not the crux of it. At the core of monetarism is a profound belief in the natural tendency of a capitalist economy to grow in an orderly manner *if it is not interfered with by government.* At the core of the antimonetarist stance is an equally profound conviction that a capitalist economy, left to its own devices, will encounter serious difficulties that require government intervention to cure. That fundamental disagreement—a disagreement that harks back to the views of Adam Smith and of Marx or Keynes—is at the crux of the controversy.

What can we say about this philosophical disagreement? Perhaps we can venture two conclusions that award something to both sides and yet present the issue as we see it.

1. Unquestionably We Are Going to Pursue Interventionist Economic Policies Both in the Short and the Long Run. The interventionists argue that we no longer have the social or political option of not intervening. In the great depressions of the past, the public accepted a passive government response because it believed that government had no capacity (as well as no right) to deal with economic misfortunes. That point of view is now dead, the interventionists insist. When growth stalls or inflation speeds up, the public now demands that government "do something." To be told that doing nothing is the best response to economic trouble is an answer that the American electorate will not accept. Just as the Reagan administration was forced to ease its policies in response to the deep recession of 1981–1982, so might the Bush administration find itself forced into activism in a crisis of either inflation or recession. Government intervention is demanded, the interventionists say, and the arguments of those who advocate strict noninterventionism are simply irrelevant.

This argument seems correct. The noninterventionist position is a *long-run* point of view. It requires a degree of patience that we do not think modern democracies will (or should) display. There is no doubt in our minds that some form of active policy will be followed whatever the ideology of the president.

2. Our Policy Determinations Will Be Seriously Hampered by the Kinds of Problems Raised by the Noninterventionists. Thus we are going to try to improve our short-run economic performance. But how well will we succeed in doing so? The objections raised by the noninterventionists suggest that efforts to accelerate or decelerate, redirect or guide, the economy will be much more difficult than we once believed. It was not so very long ago that economists spoke of "fine tuning" the economy as if it were a vast stereo set that could be regulated with precision by turning the knobs labeled "fiscal policy" and "monetary policy." We now know that this cannot be done. Some knobs are stuck; others turn without much affecting the quantity or quality of sound; still others seem to set up feedback that distorts the results we seek.

But this is not to say that we cannot regulate the economy at all. Our own belief is that we can intervene to our collective benefit, provided that we have realistic expectations of what it lies within our power to do. Modern industrial economics are very complex systems, and we should not expect that we can fiddle with them like radios. But some success is better than none—and some success seems possible.

LOOKING BACK

KEY CONCEPTS

Monetarism has three tenets:

1 An important perspective in the controversy over the relation between money and output (and prices) is known as monetarism.

Changes in *M* directly affect spending.

2 Monetarism has three basic tenets. The first is that changes in the supply of money do not affect the economy via their effect on interest

rates and investment. Rather, changes in the money supply—in the banks' ability to make loans—result directly in changes in expenditure.

There is a natural rate of unemployment that controls the rate of growth.

3 The second tenet concerns the effect of *M* (or *MV*) on output. One of the basic beliefs in monetarism is that the economy naturally gravitates to a rate of growth that reflects the natural rate of unemployment—the willingness of individuals to work, given the prevailing wage. Changes in expenditure *(MV)* may result in bursts of activity, but will not budge that fundamental controlling force. Hence attempts to accelerate growth through increasing the supply of money or government spending will only "crowd out" private activity. The system will return to its natural path. So, too, booms and busts will be transient—indeed, they are more often caused than cured by government intervention.

Changes in *M* affect *P*.

4 Where money matters most is in its effect on the price level. An increase in *M* leads to an increase in *MV;* but because the level of output is "fixed" by the natural rate of unemployment, its effects will be felt in changes in *P*. It is these changes that are the only source of rising or falling prices.

Monetarist policy calls for a steady increase in *M*.

5 The monetary policy urged by Friedman and other monetarists is a steady increase in *M*, geared to the economy's natural rate of productivity growth. This rate would not vary. If circumstances tended to push the economy ahead faster than the fixed rate of growth of *M*, the steady rate would hold it back. If the economy lagged for any reason, the steady increase in *M* would stimulate it to grow up to its natural rate.

Rational expectations link *M* and *MV*.

6 Rational expectations round out monetarism by providing a causal link between *M* and *MV*. Rational expectations theory asserts that all individuals are guided by commonsense predictions about the future. When they read that the authorities are increasing *M*, they expect *P* to rise. Therefore they spend their incomes more quickly to "beat" the coming price rise. As intuitive monetarists, they make monetarist theory come true.

Antimonetarists contend that $MV \leftarrow PT$.

7 The antimonetarists contest all these tenets. First, they deny that the Fed controls the money supply as the monetarists state. Rather, they suggest that the demand for money (for transactions needs) forces the Fed to change the money base. The linkage runs $MV \leftarrow PT$, not $MV \rightarrow PT$.

They deny a natural rate of unemployment or the uselessness of intervention, and assert that costs, not *M*, determine *P*.

8 They doubt that there is a natural rate of unemployment or that depressions are caused by government intervention. They point to very deep depressions that occurred before there was a Federal Reserve, and to the inability of the Federal Reserve to raise prices during the Depression of the 1930s. And they argue that cost, not the quantity of money, is the fundamental element in establishing the price level. The bases for inflation, they state, are such changes as supply shocks and changes in wages.

A discretionary monetary policy

9 Therefore antimonetarists favor a discretionary monetary policy that will try to fit the supply of money to changing needs.

Interventionism vs. noninterventionism

10 Beneath the dispute over monetarism lies a deeper disagreement over the possibilities for intervention in the economy. Essentially monetarism is based on a belief that the economy manifests behavior that cannot easily be turned around by government policy, at least in a free market system. Interventionists argue that policy can indeed make a difference—although often it falls short of the policymaker's hopes, for the very reasons suggested by the noninterventionists.

ECONOMIC VOCABULARY

Monetarism 380
Natural rate of unemployment 380
Rational expectations 381

QUESTIONS

1. Why would a monetarist object to Keynes's view that increases in M affect the economy via the interest rate? *Hint:* Think of the natural rate of unemployment. Doesn't this require that money be "neutral"?
2. Do you think there is a "natural rate" of unemployment? If an unemployed engineer refuses even to inquire about a "Help Wanted" sign in a supermarket, does this show that he prefers not to work at the prevailing wage? How could you test the idea that there was, or was not, a "natural rate" of unemployment? (For one answer, see the section on involuntary unemployment in Chapter 35.)
3. What is "tight" about a tight money policy? How does it bring down inflation? Can you describe how such a policy works in terms of the $MV = PT$ formulation?
4. What would be an antimonetarist policy to lower inflation? Would direct price controls be such a policy? What might a monetarist assert about the efficacy of such controls?
5. If wages rise, will that necessarily push up prices? Does the answer depend on productivity? Suppose that wages rise faster than productivity. Then must they push up costs? What would a monetarist argue about the effect of rising costs on P? Might he assert that the good which now cost more would simply "crowd out" other goods because PT was fixed? Fixed by what?

CHAPTER 23

Inflation

A LOOK AHEAD

In this last section of our macro studies, we take up the challenges that macroeconomists face. They are two: the stubborn problem of inflation—at times an immediate danger and at others a long-term chronic tendency; and, in Chapter 24, the challenge of growth itself, the fundamental necessity and uncertainty of the macro process.

In this chapter we take up inflation in a long-term historical perspective. This leads us to ask the question that underlies the whole chapter: Why has capitalism, in the late twentieth century, shown an inflationary tendency that it never manifested before?

At the same time we examine a number of more technical issues:

1. We learn about the famous Phillips curve, a way of relating the level of unemployment and the rate of inflation.
2. We stop to think about the actual costs and risks of inflation—whom it threatens and why people fear it.
3. We look into the possibility that the inflationary wave has spent its force and that we may possibly be moving into a more stable price environment.

And in the extra word at the conclusion of the chapter we examine ways and means of bringing inflation under control, if the tendency becomes once again acute.

INFLATION IN RETROSPECT

Let us begin our investigation into inflation by setting it in historical perspective. Inflation is both a very old problem and a very new one. If we look back in history, we discover many inflationary periods. Diocletian tried in vain to curb a Roman inflation in the fourth century A.D. Between 1150 and 1325, the cost of living in medieval Europe rose fourfold. Between 1520 and 1650, prices doubled and quadrupled, largely as a result of gold pouring into Europe from the mines of the New World. After the Civil War, the American South experienced a ferocious inflation. And during World War I, prices in the United States rose 100 percent.

Now we focus on the American experience up to 1960, shown in Figure 1. Two things should be noted about this chart. First, **major wars are regularly accompanied by inflation.** The reasons are obvious enough: War greatly increases the volume of public expenditure, but governments do not often curb private spending by an equal amount through taxation. Invariably, wars are financed largely by borrowing, so the total amount of spending, public and private, rises rapidly. Meanwhile, the total amount of goods available to households is cut back to make room for war production. The result fits the classic description of inflation: too much money chasing too few goods. Only in two instances, World War II and the Korean War, has this pattern been largely avoided, by a combination of price

FIGURE 1
Inflation in Perspective
Looking back in history, we can see inflation is a chronic consequence of war. But in the past it was always short-lived.
Source: *Historical Statistics of the United States.*

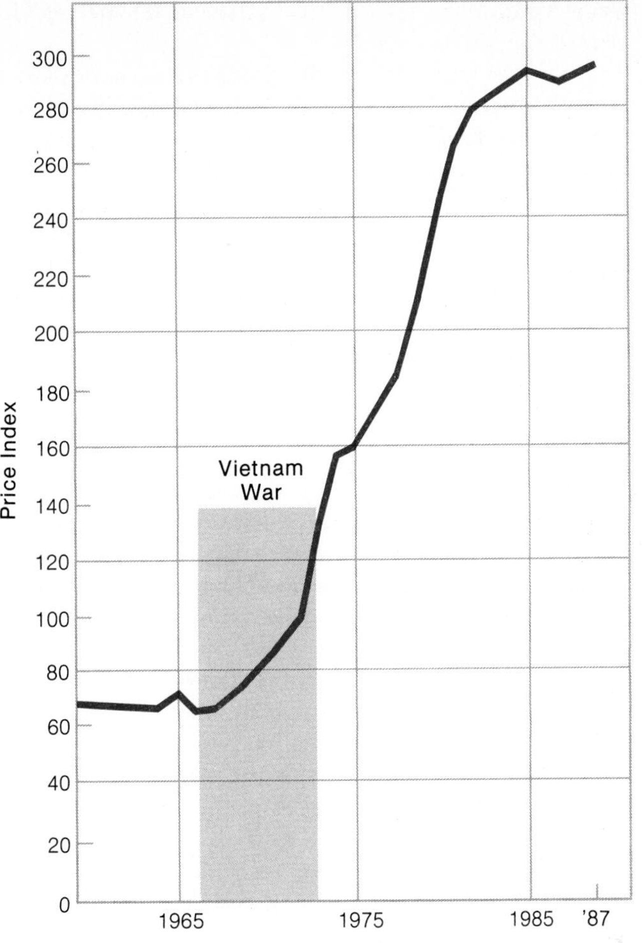

FIGURE 2
Producers' Prices Since 1960
With the Vietnam War, the pattern changed. Inflation became chronic and persistent until broken by the deep recession of 1981–1982. Is it now rising again?
Sources: *Historical Statistics of the United States; Economic Report of the President, 1986.*

controls and rationing that effectively forced households to save their sharply rising incomes rather than spend them.

Second, **U.S. inflations have always been relatively short-lived in the past.** Notice that prices fell during the long period 1866 to 1900, and again from 1925 to 1933. The 100-year trend, although generally tilted upward, is marked with long valleys as well as sharp peaks.

Postwar Inflationary Experience

Figure 2 shows the record of U.S. price changes since 1960. Once again, we notice that the outbreak of a war—the Vietnam War in 1965—brought price rises. But in a vital way, contemporary experience differs from that of the past. Peaks of wartime inflation were not followed by long, gradual declines. Instead, inflation continued after the war wound down and seemed to become a chronic element in our system. It took two severe recessions, in 1974–1975 and 1979–1982, with unemployment rising to double digits, before inflation fell back to levels considered customary before the Vietnam War.

A second novel aspect of recent inflation has been the appearance of rising unemployment side by side with rising inflation. The firmly held belief that inflation could not appear in the face of considerable unemployment was shown to be untrue. In the 1960–1965 period, for instance, unemployment was running at the average rate of 5.5 percent—a rather high rate, historically speaking, so that it came as no surprise to find inflation at the very mild rate of under 2 percent. But by the early 1980s, when unemployment approached 10 percent, the rate of inflation, instead of declining, had grown to 9 percent. This combination of stagnation in employment and a rising price level became known as **stagflation,** the malady of the modern world.

The Phillips Curve

A good way to approach the problem of modern stagflation is through the Phillips curve, a relation between wages and prices first explored by A. W. Phillips, a New Zealand engineer at the London School of Economics, in 1958. Phillips noted that there seemed to be a clear-cut relationship between the level of employment and the rate of change in wages: As employment grew "tighter," wages tended to rise more rapidly. This was soon broadened into a relationship between *prices* (since wages are always an important component of prices) and the level of *unemployment.* As the Phillips curve was first envisaged, there was an unmistakeable "trade-off" between inflation (the change in the price level) and the level of unemployment. We can see this in Figure 3. The lower the level of unemployment, the higher the rate of inflation.*

The trouble began as we entered the 1970s, when it became apparent that the relation between unemployment and inflation was not as stable as we had thought. In Figure 4 we see the relationship plotted through 1988. There is no longer any predictable association. Look particularly at the unemployment range from about 4.5 to 8.5 percent. Annual inflation rates since 1970 have varied from barely more than 3 percent to over 10 percent!

More disconcerting yet, the combination of unemployment and inflation appeared unstable over time. Figure 5 shows the pattern that appears if we connect the inflation-unemployment pairs from year to year. The pattern "explodes" outward, displaying a more and more unsatisfactory state of the economy, and then "implodes."

EXPLAINING INFLATION

Can we explain this modern inflationary propensity? A warning is in order. There is no general consensus among economists as to the causes or even the mechanisms of inflation comparable to the consensus that exists about many other kinds of

*The idea of the Phillips curve is also behind the upward-sloping supply-price of output shown in chapter 18, Figure 8.

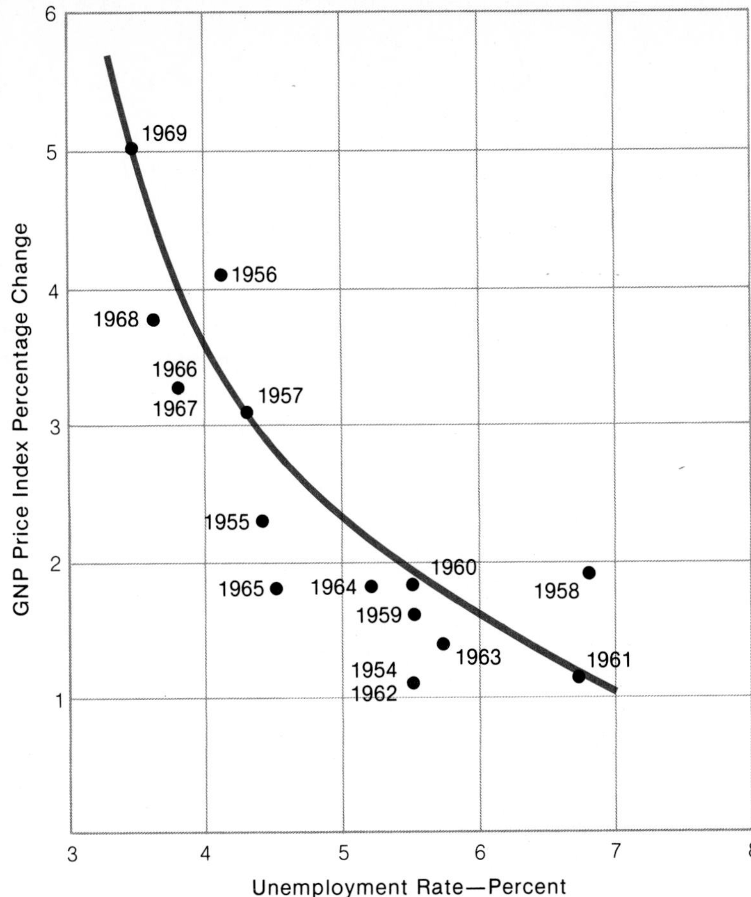

FIGURE 3
Unemployment-Inflation Relation 1954–1969
Until 1969, the Phillips curve looked very clear.
Source: *Historical Statistics of the United States.*

problems. What follows, therefore, we loudly and clearly state, is *our* diagnosis of the nature of the inflationary phenomenon. It is to be thought about, and perhaps argued with. We hope that it will shed light; we cannot promise total illumination.

Basic Market Instability

Our argument begins with a simple but essential fact: It is that market systems are easily disturbed. Wars, changes in political regimes, resource changes, new technologies, shifts in demand—all disturb the equilibrium of the market system as stones cast ripples in a pond.

These unsettling events have caused different kinds of disturbances at different periods in capitalism's political and economic development. For economists, the most important of these disturbances has been the tendency of the market system to develop instabilities in production and prices and employment. We have already encountered these instabilities in the form of business cycles and tendencies to recession. Now we meet them in the form of the inflationary propensities of recent years.

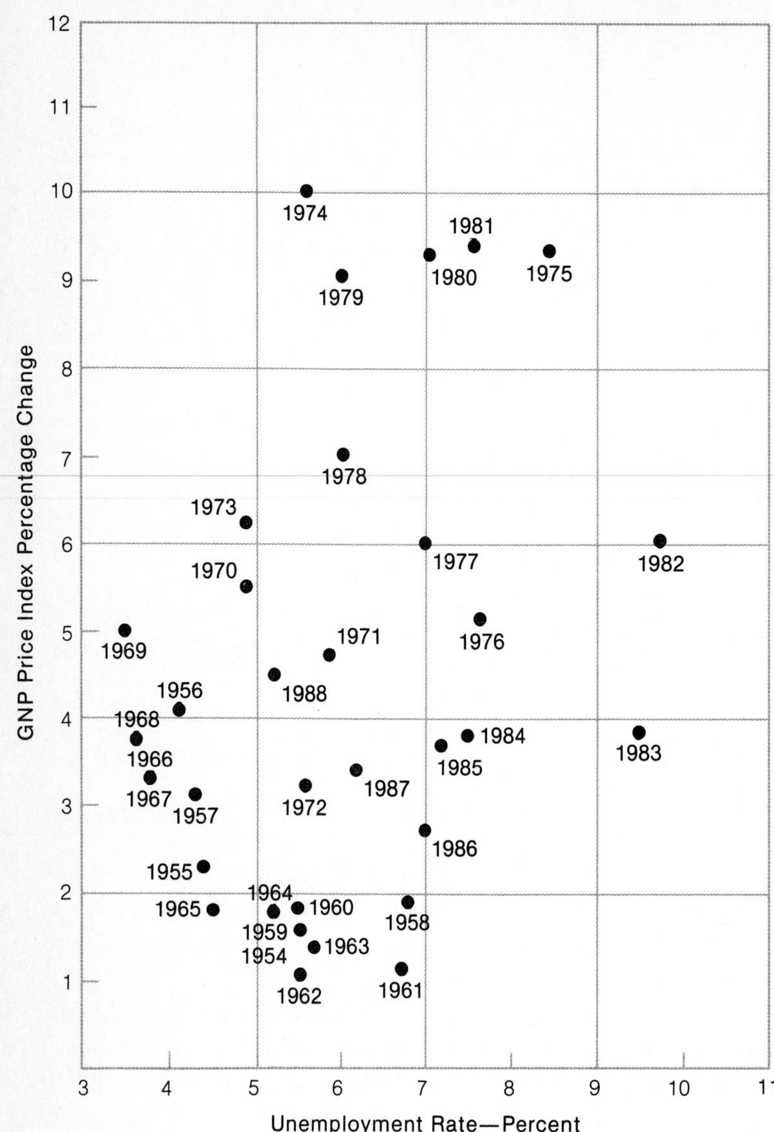

FIGURE 4
Unemployment-Inflation Relation Reexamined
Recent experience makes it clear that there is no reliable unemployment-inflation relation within the "normal" range of unemployment.
Sources: *Historical Statistics of the United States; Economic Report of the President, 1986.*

It may not seem important to begin from a stress on this deep-seated vulnerability characteristic of capitalist systems. But once we place the fact stage center, a striking question immediately faces us: How does it happen that nowadays the vulnerability so often results in inflation, and not depression or some other malfunction? For when we think of it, it was not inflation but other kinds of dysfunctions that troubled capitalism in previous periods—think of the collapse of the 1930s.

From this perspective, inflation appears as the way in which the capitalist system responds to shocks and disruptions in the institutional setting of the late twentieth century. Take, for example, the impetus given to inflation by the oil price rises of 1973 or 1979. Suppose an exactly comparable shock had been administered a century earlier, say by the Pennsylvania coal companies banding together as a coal cartel and suddenly announcing a fourfold increase in coal prices. Would such a coal cartel have produced inflation? The question is ludicrous. It would have brought on a massive depression. Coal mines would have closed, steel mills shut down, car loadings fallen. That imaginary but unchallengeable scenario then puts the right question: **What happened between 1873 and 1973 so that the same shock—an abrupt rise in energy prices—would have produced depression in one era and did produce inflation in another?**

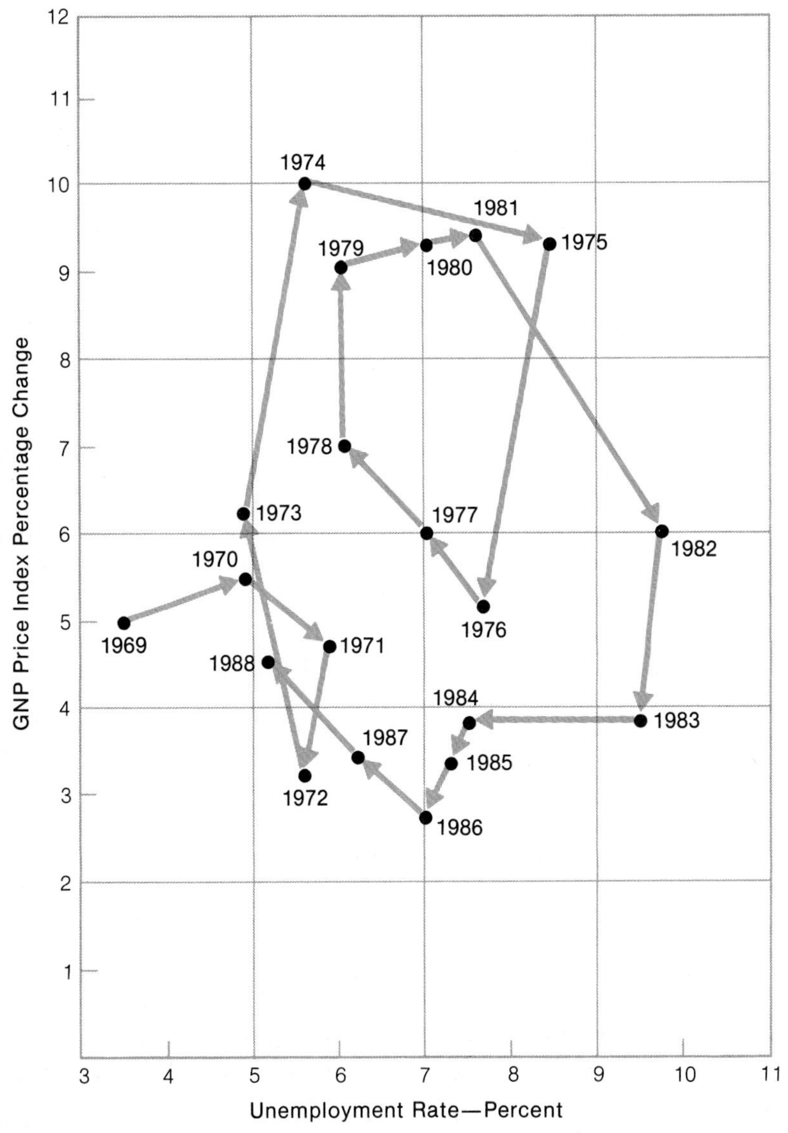

FIGURE 5
The "Exploding" Unemployment-Inflation Relation
As we can see, the unemployment-inflation combination seemed to worsen until 1983. Then it "imploded" in 1988.
Sources: *Historical Statistics of the United States; Economic Report of the President, 1986.*

Public Barriers against Depression

We know the answer. Far-reaching changes have taken place within the social structure of accumulation all over the world. Of these, by far the most visible and important has been the emergence of large and powerful public sectors. In 1890 government expenditures were less than 7 percent of GNP in the United States, the same in Germany, and less than 5 percent in Great Britain. In 1983 the ratio had risen to 38.1 percent in the United States, 48.6 percent in West Germany, and 47.2 percent in Britain.* In Sweden it was an astonishing 62.2 percent.†

Whatever else their significance, these public expenditures provide a floor for economic activity that did not exist before. In itself that is enough to shift a depression-prone world toward an inflation-prone one.

The floors of public expenditure do not prevent the arrival of all recessions, as we know from recent experience. The difference is that a market system with a core of public spending does not easily move from recession into ever-deeper depression. The downward tendency of production and employment is limited by the support of government spending such as social security and unemployment insurance. **Cumulative, bottomless depressions are changed into limited, although persisting, stagnations.**

Increased Private Power

A second aspect of the sea change that has come over capitalism in the last century is the rise in private power. We see it in the vast organizations—the icebergs—that dominate the waters of business and labor.

The emergence of massive institutions of private power makes an important contribution to our inflationary propensity. A striking difference between today and yesterday is that in the past, inflationary peaks were regularly followed by long deflationary periods. Prices trended irregularly *downward* over most of the last half of the nineteenth century. Why? One reason is that the economy was much more heavily agricultural in those days, and farm prices have always been more volatile, particularly downward, than the prices of manufactured goods. Hence an industrial economy, just by virtue of being dominated by manufactures, is much less likely to have price declines than a farming economy.

The second reason is that the character of the manufacturing sector has also changed. In the early decades of the twentieth century, it was not unusual for big companies to announce across-the-board wage cuts when times were bad. In addition, prices declined as a result of technological advances and as a consequence of the price wars that continually broke out among industrial competitors.

That is all part of a chapter of economic history largely ended. Agriculture is now only a small part of GNP. True, technology continues to lower costs, sometimes dramatically—look what has happened to the price of computers during the last decade!—but these lower industrial costs have been offset by the "ratchet tendency" shown by wages and prices since World War II. **A ratchet**

***OECD Historical Statistics*, 1985. Table 6.5.

†1982 data for Sweden.

IS THERE A NATURAL RATE OF UNEMPLOYMENT?

The collapse after 1969 of the short-run Phillips curve led many economists to the view that the "true" Phillips curve was not a curve, but a vertical line. Such a line implies that there exists in the economy a single unemployment rate, dubbed the **natural rate of unemployment,** that is the one consistent with a stable, unchanging rate of inflation. (See Figure 6.)

The natural-rate hypothesis has radical implications for economic policy, undermining the prescriptions of Keynesian economics. For example, if government policy attempted to reduce unemployment below the natural rate, the consequence would be not merely higher inflation, as the stable, upward-sloping Phillips curve had seemed to show. Rather there would be *accelerating inflation.* If government persisted in this policy, *hyperinflation* and economic collapse would result.

The existence of a natural rate of unemployment has come to be widely accepted among American economists, though it has had much less influence elsewhere in the world and virtually none on policymakers. It accords particularly well with the theory of *rational expectations*—that is, people will correctly *anticipate* government policy through their reading of current news, thus beating the government to the punch, as it were (see Chapter 22). If economic actors do indeed operate on rational expectations, then it is likely that the economy does have a natural rate of unemployment.

But in recent years the hypothesis has come under increasing criticism. Two reasons account for the newly critical views. First, empirical estimates of the "natural" rate have shown it to be unstable: It appears to rise in recessions and decline in booms. This means that there is no simple, reliable way to predict just

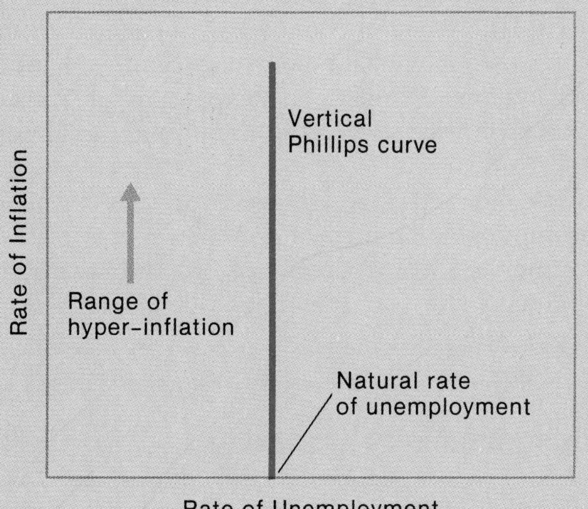

FIGURE 6

when a declining unemployment rate will lead to accelerating inflation—something that one would hope the natural rate would explain.

Second, there is increasing skepticism about the applicability of the rational expectations model to the real economy. In a labor market where contracts prevail, rather than untrammeled perfect competition, and where reliable information about the economy is very costly and difficult for ordinary people to obtain, the rational expectations theory is not a reliable guide and a natural rate of unemployment may well not exist after all.

tendency means that prices and wages go up, but rarely or never come down—always excepting technological revolutions or market debacles. In normal times and normal business, we see the ratchet at work. Concentrated business and union power, coupled with a general abhorrence for the tactics of cutthroat competition, mean that nominal wages and prices generally move in one direction only—up. These tendencies also add to our inflationary drift.

Demand-Pull and Cost-Push

These changes help us understand why we live in a world that, in distinction to that of our fathers, has become inflation-prone. We "catch" inflation the way capitalism of the late nineteenth and early twentieth centuries caught deflation.

But inflation susceptibility is one thing, its actual advent is another. Just like the depressions of bygone eras, our inflationary experience had its origin in specific events that started the process off. Inflation probably received its initial impetus from the boost to spending that resulted from the Vietnam War. A powerful stimulus to inflation in *other* countries then resulted from the manner in which the United States used its global power to force other nations to accept our dollars in lieu of gold, building up inflationary expansions of credit abroad that eventually fed back on our own price levels. And then came the famous oil shocks of 1973 and 1979.

Directly or indirectly, the average American consumer spends 10 cents out of every consumption dollar on energy. When energy prices doubled, this increase, all by itself, generated a 10 percent rise in the cost of living. In contrast to the inflation-inducing effects of spending, called *demand-pull,* these boosts to inflation are called *cost-push.*

Transmitting Inflation by Indexing

We have already reflected on the difference between the inflation-creating effects of the 1973 oil shock and the depression-creating effects that would have accompanied an imaginary "coal shock" in 1873. Now we must pay heed to a very important institution that made the higher prices of the oil shock so contagious. This is the presence of indexing arrangements in social security and many wage contracts. Higher prices no longer serve as a deterrent to buying, as they would have in 1873. **Under indexing, the additional income needed to cover the higher-cost items is automatically provided by COLAs (cost-of-living adjustments) or by social security and other indexed payments.**

When prices rise suddenly, as a consequence of oil shock or wage shock or any other cost increase, the economy momentarily shudders as sales lag and employment declines. But then the higher oil or wage or other costs show up in a higher cost-of-living index number, and as the index rises, so do the checks that go to social security recipients and the wage adjustments paid out on indexed contracts. This serves the excellent purpose of short-circuiting recession. But it also greases the skids for further inflation.

Expectations

With this inflation-transmitting change in institutions comes an even more dangerous inflation-transmitting change in the way people think. In the old days the prevailing point of view about economic life was summed up in the adage, "What goes up must come down," so that booms and price rises typically (although not always) generated a salutary degree of caution. Today attitudes have changed. When we learn that a commodity is going up, our first reaction is that it will probably continue to go up, maybe faster, so we had better get in there while the getting is good. **Thus the very expectation of higher prices becomes an inflation-sustaining mechanism, much the way bad times were stretched out during the Depression because businesses *expected* them to go on and on.** Expectations are self-fulfilling.

In the inflationary process, the widespread and unchallenged belief that "Next year's prices will be 10 percent higher" leads to the very kind of buy now, pay later behavior that guarantees that next year's prices will be 10 percent higher.

An Inflation-Prone Economy

All this allows us to see that many of the conventional explanations of inflation play some role in sustaining the chronic malfunction of our economy. Government is indeed responsible for inflation, insofar as it has introduced floors under the economy, indexed important payments, and bolstered security to the point where our expectations and attitudes are much more aggressive than formerly. The massing of union and business power also contributes to inflation through the ratcheting of wages and prices. And most of the other villains can be seen at work in the background or the foreground.

The difference in our perceptions is that these various explanations can now be seen as taking their various places within an overall coherent framework of understanding. Inflation—our kind of chronic inflation accompanied by a sagging undertow of recession—comes about because capitalism exerts its nervous, thrusting, expansive energy in a changed social environment. Capitalism is now government-supported capitalism, power-bloc capitalism, a capitalism of high public expectations. This is its mid-twentieth century social framework, the milieu within which growth takes place.

THE DANGERS OF INFLATION

Why is inflation widely regarded as such a threat? As we shall shortly see, it cannot be for the reason that inflation makes us poorer—even though we may *feel* poorer. Indeed, one of the perplexing things about inflation is that it is not an economic process that brings a clearly identifiable loss to the nation's wealth.

Recession vs. Inflation

This fact is important enough to warrant very careful attention. In recessionary times incomes fall; unemployed individuals especially suffer real losses in purchasing power. Moreover, there is no gain to set against the loss. The purchasing power given up by an unemployed person does not appear in someone else's pocket. Not so during inflation. Here the decline in the buying power of one unlucky person is *always* offset by a rise in the buying power of another. *This is because a rise in prices always creates a rise in someone's income.* Perhaps the gainer is a strategically placed group of workers enjoying higher wages. Perhaps it is a group of businesspeople for whom higher prices mean higher profits. Perhaps it is a cartel of domestic enterprises and foreign governments that collectively monopolize the supply of a strategic commodity. Whoever may gain, higher prices for one person always mean a higher income for another.

Thus inflation is a zero-sum game—a game of redistribution in which you win what I lose, or vice versa. Recessions, on the other hand, are not zero sum, but negative sum: Losses incurred by some individuals will not be transferred to others as income.

Winners and Losers

In analyzing the economic costs of inflation, therefore, we always have to look for winners and losers. And here we encounter the first of many puzzles in this area. It is very hard to identify economic winners and losers from inflation in any systematic way. From 1970 to 1984, our real GNP grew by $553 billion in 1982 dollars during a period of substantial, though highly variable, inflation. Someone had to be receiving that larger real income, and the inflation—we suspect—had a lot to do with just precisely who. So who was it? The very rich? The oil companies? Municipal workers? The elderly? The answer is: All of us. While there is some evidence that upper-income groups have done particularly well in the years since 1981, there is no evidence at all linking this not-very-dramatic shift of income shares to inflation—nor, for that matter, to disinflation.

THE REAL COSTS OF INFLATION

The difficulty of isolating inflation's winners and losers forces us to ask whether there are economic costs of inflation to the system *in general,* costs that are shared in common by all who experience inflation, even though the measurable effects on any one household's or company's real income may be small. Economists have sought to define a number of such systemic economic costs.

Information Costs

One real cost stems from the fact that inflation tends to upset the normal relationships among prices. Real estate typically soars; commodities often go through the roof (and then sometimes through the floor); speculative fevers are endemic. The sober consequence is that rational forward planning becomes more difficult. Economists speak of this as *raising the cost of information* about prices. The practical effect is that businesses are less able to count on established price relationships in projecting costs and incomes. It becomes increasingly necessary to allow for inflationary distortions. All this raises the degree of business uncertainty and depresses business confidence. As a consequence, investment and productivity are both likely to decline.

This is assuredly a real cost of inflation, but it is a cost that is very difficult to measure because we can never know what investment or productivity growth would have been if business confidence had been greater.

Misallocation and Disincentive Effects

A second real cost concerns the effect of inflation in bringing about *uneconomic behavior.* Firms and households both typically become hoarders—rationally trying to build up stores of supplies before prices go higher. It is never possible to build up enough supplies to ride out the inflation for good, and the effort to protect oneself against the immediate future simply sends out wrong signals to the economy and ties up purchasing power in unused materials.

More serious than the effects on inventories are the consequences of inflation on work. If inflation begins to show serious cumulative tendencies, workers may find that they can do better for themselves wheeling and dealing than working at steady jobs, and businesses may decide they can make more by putting out money in short-term loans at very high rates of interest than in carrying on their normal affairs. During the terrible German inflation of the 1920s, many workers left the factories to roam the countryside, seeking to exchange their work for food rather

MORE ON WINNERS AND LOSERS

It is always surprising to discover that inflation's winners and losers are much harder to find than we imagine. Here are a few additional facts:

Pensioners: The conventional wisdom has always held that pensioners on fixed incomes would suffer most in inflation. No doubt that is true. But today pensioners largely have indexed incomes. Between 1972 and 1988, the average social security recipient found his or her real income improved, not worsened.

Stockholders: We were once brought up to believe that stocks were a "hedge" against inflation because the value of company assets would rise as prices rose. In fact, between 1970 and 1982, prices doubled, but stocks remained unchanged. The real purchasing power of portfolios was halved during that period! Not until 1982 did the market finally begin to make up for lost time. Then came boom—followed by bust. Would an investor who held onto a portfolio of "average" shares through thick and thin have come out all right by the end of 1987? Looking all the way back to 1970, yes. The cost of living would have climbed by 293 percent; his portfolio by 352 percent. If we look

than for nearly worthless currency. Such misallocations and disincentives can have uncountably high costs: They can bring an economy to ruin.

Cumulative Tendencies

There is one further aspect of inflation that figures large in everyone's assessment of its consequences. This is the fear that inflation may run away.

There is a reason behind this fear. Inflation has a built-in tendency to worsen because it is a process in which individuals try to get ahead of inflation—and in so doing, worsen it. Union leaders, for example, will normally try to win a pay increase for their constituencies higher than the going rate of inflation. Suppose the going rate is 5 percent. Union leaders may try to win a real increase of 3 percent, which means that they will bargain for 8 percent—5 percent to stay even with inflation, 3 percent to get ahead of it. But if all union leaders do this, the inflation rate is very likely to rise from 5 to 7 or 8 percent. The next year, union leaders will have to ask for 10 or 11 percent to stay even and get their 3 percent real raise.

There is no question that one of the most disturbing aspects of inflation has been its tendency to accelerate. As we have seen, a pattern of irregularly accelerating inflation can be discovered in most parts of the world. In the ten leading industrial nations the price level rose by about 2.5 percent a year during the 1950s; by not quite 3.5 percent a year in the 1960s; by over 9 percent in the 1970s. We can see back only to 1982, when the stock market finally broke out of its 1970s doldrums, our investor would have fared still better: cost of living up only 25 percent, stock holdings up 217 percent. Thus the stock market now seems to do dramatically better in noninflationary times.

Workers: Have working families suffered from inflation? Many workers were badly hurt during the inflationary years, as the steel and auto industries declined, as imports came flooding in, and as food and energy prices soared. But steel, auto, and foreign trade problems cannot be blamed squarely on inflation; and the rise in food and oil prices came about largely because of foreign economic developments.

All of Us: Then why do we all feel hurt by inflation? One reason is that we are aware of prices rising all through the year as we go shopping. We are unaware—except perhaps once a year—that our incomes are also rising! When we get a pay raise, we feel we have earned it—*forgetting that part of the raise is simply a cost-of-living allowance given to us to keep up with inflation.* As our total raise is nibbled away at by constantly rising prices, we feel cheated. No one keeps books to show us that at the end of the year we are still ahead in real terms. By that time we feel battered and bruised. We complain that inflation robs us. We have forgotten about that *inflated* pay raise.

this irregularly upward-tending pattern in Figure 6. (The sharp spike in 1974 is the result of the OPEC price boost. If you cover the spike with your finger, you can see the upward trend more clearly, together with the general subsidence after 1981.)

The Political Cost of Inflation

We cannot call the endemic cumulative tendency of inflation a "cost." It is better understood as a *threat:* a threat that the economic process of inflation will exact its last and most terrible true cost—political chaos.* For most Europeans, for whom the political experience of the twentieth century is living history, the evil of inflation is axiomatic: Inflation destroys constitutional regimes. It does so, as Keynes wrote in 1919, by a process of pernicious and arbitrary redistribution, by turning the ordinary business of economic life into a lottery that deprives the individual of control over his economic fate, and hence undermines faith in the justice of the system.

*We put a very important point into a footnote. True runaway inflations—called *hyperinflations*—are very rare. They are almost always the consequence of previous military or social collapse, such as the demoralization of the German economy following World War I or of the American South after the Civil War. They remain, quite properly, vivid examples of inflation's ravages, but they should be seen for what they are—political breakdowns with hideous economic consequences. Note that the very severe inflations we have seen in Latin America—up to 1,000 percent a year—are *not* runaways. People learn to live with them, although their costs are huge. True hyper-inflations cannot be lived with.

Keynes's argument likened the effects of inflation to those of a political revolution. In *The Economic Consequences of the Peace*—a polemic against the Versailles Treaty that ended World War I on harsh terms for Germany—Keynes wrote:

> *The sight of this arbitrary rearrangement of riches strikes not only at the security, but at the confidence in the equity of the existing distribution of wealth. Those to whom the system brings windfalls, beyond their deserts and even beyond their expectations or desires, become "profiteers," who are the object of the hatred of the bourgeoisie, whom the inflationism has impoverished, not less than of the proletariat. As the inflation proceeds . . . all permanent relations between debtors and creditors, which form the ultimate foundation of capitalism, become so utterly disordered as to be almost meaningless, and the process of wealth-getting degenerates into a gamble and a lottery.*

Then comes the famous passage:

> *Lenin was certainly right. There is no subtler, no surer means of overturning the existing basis of society than to debauch the currency. The process engages all the hidden forces of economic law on the side of destruction, and does it in a manner which not one man in a million is able to diagnose.*

FIGURE 7
Global Patterns of Inflation 1966–1987
All around the world inflation is diminishing, mainly owing to tight money and economic slowdown.
Source: *The Economic Report of the President, 1988.*

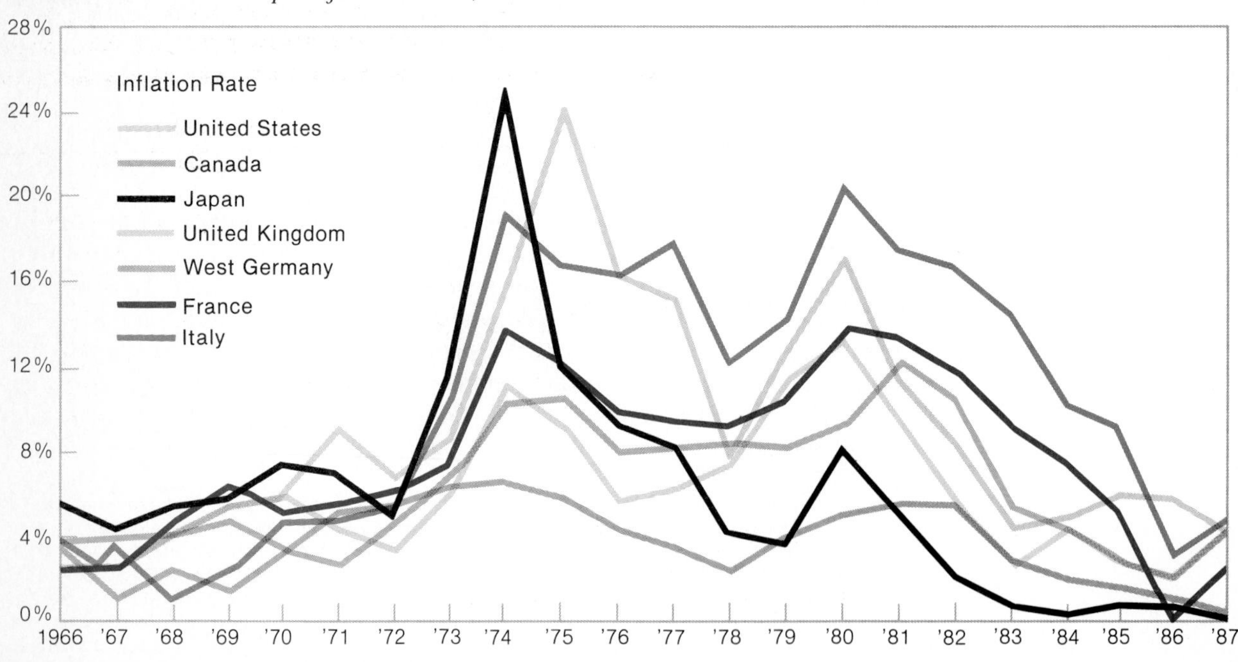

CONTROLLING INFLATION

Can we put an end to the threats and costs of the inflationary process? The question is certainly not an easy one, for we *have* got rid of a great deal of our inflation—but perhaps not of our inflationary tendency. Let us look into the matter carefully.

Disinflation

From 1980 through 1985, the United States economy, and to a lesser extent the economies of Europe, underwent a very deep and rapid process of disinflation—a slowing down of the inflationary process. In March 1980 inflation in the United States was running at a 14 to 15 percent rate. By the end of 1985, the index of producers' prices had ceased to rise, and the consumer price index was increasing at a rate of under 4 percent. This was a massive decline in the inflation rate, all the more dramatic because it was unexpected.

What accounted for this remarkable turnabout? Economist Allen Sinai has identified five main reasons. First, there were *the back-to-back recessions of 1980 and 1981–1982*—recessions brought about by tight money. These created heavy unemployment and large underutilization, and greatly weakened the self-reinforcing tendencies of the wage-price spiral. Second, there was a *change in the oil situation.* Oil prices began to fall in 1983 and collapsed in late 1985, giving us a downward oil shock in place of an upward one. Third, the long, hard recessionary period *changed the pattern of wage negotiations.* Many unions agreed to "givebacks." In important industries union agreements broke old forms in a search for wage scales that would improve U.S. foreign competitive abilities. Not least, the very fact of declining inflation allowed union leaders to lower their bargaining demands because they did not have to anticipate as much inflation as before. Fourth, the *deregulation of a number of strategic industries,* such as transportation, increased competition and lowered the costs of doing business. And finally, *the flood of imports* served as a powerful force for disinflation by bringing in cheaper foreign goods.*

Will Inflation Reappear?

As we write these pages, that long process of "wringing" inflation out of the economy has come to a halt. By the beginning of 1987, prices were beginning to show signs of "firming up." The price of oil stopped falling. An incipient export boom, which gathered momentum, provided an expansive push to the economy. Most important of all, the rate of unemployment showed a steady decline. All these tendencies, welcome in themselves, sparked fears that inflation could not be far around the corner—not the roaring inflation of the late 1970s and early 1980s, but an inflation rate pushing 6 or 7 percent, just high enough to be worrisome.

*Allen Sinai, "The Soaring Dollar Did It," *Challenge,* September–October 1985.

A Permanent Inflationary Propensity?

Will inflation now gather force once again? Does the economy face the prospect of having to choose between prolonged recessions and disquieting inflations? That is perhaps the single most important—and the single most uncertain—question economists face at the end of the 1980s.

It is a question to which we will not know the answer for some time. Our own prognosis lies somewhere between the two extremes. We do not think we will soon go through another recessionary episode like that of the early 1980s. *This is because we think it very unlikely that inflation will quickly become so threatening as to warrant a repetition of the tight money policies that brought on those recessions. At the same time, in the absence of a tight money restraint, we would expect the inflationary propensity of modern capitalism to reassert itself.* As we see it, we are doomed to live with inflation *worries* and some actual worsening of inflation, but not yet with a repeat of the inflationary disaster of ten years ago.

LOOKING BACK

KEY CONCEPTS

Inflations, in our view, stem from instability that is blocked in a downward direction but not in an upward one. Indexing transmits inflationary expectations through the economy. The system is inflation prone.

1 Inflation, in our belief, stems from the instability of capitalist economic systems. That this instability no longer creates cumulative depressions is due to the intervention of the government sector. Increased institutional rigidity also limits downward price adjustments. In this new situation shocks to the economy create only mild recessions; and upward tendencies in costs, transmitted by indexing, result in inflationary expectations. The new social structure of accumulation makes the system inflation-prone, much as the old social structure, without a large public sector, was depression-prone.

Stagflation is a new economic phenomenon.

2 Unlike inflations in the past, contemporary inflation has persisted beyond the end of war and despite the presence of unemployment. Hence it is called stagflation—stagnation combined with inflation.

Inflation and unemployment are no longer clear trade-offs.

3 Stagflation is reflected in the "exploding" Phillips curve. It used to be thought that inflation and unemployment were trade-offs—that an increase in unemployment was accompanied by a decrease in inflation rates. During the 1970s, that relation largely disappeared.

Inflation is a zero-sum game. Actual income distribution has not changed much as a result of inflation.

4 Inflation is a redistributive process, a zero-sum game. Actually, it has not significantly redistributed money incomes among the main classes of income receivers.

Inflation imposes both costs and fears.

5 Inflation poses real but not easily measurable economic costs to the system. One of these is the loss of reliable guides to price relationships. This adds risk to business investment. A second real cost is the tendency to hoard, and at worst, to speculate or scrounge instead of working.

The most serious inflationary problem is its built-in cumulative tendency.

6 Inflation has an endemic cumulative tendency. An important source of this is the effort of union leaders to win wage increases greater than existing inflation. When generalized throughout the system, this simply pushes up prices. Western experience since World War II shows a marked cumulative pattern, but it has not ended in a runaway hyperinflation. Nor does this seem likely to happen. The runaway tendency raises a real fear, but is not itself a true cost of inflation.

Political disillusion is the ultimate cost of inflation.

7 The most damaging of all the costs of inflation is political: It is the loss of political faith in a system that has replaced the norms of economic conduct with mere chance.

Disinflation from 1982 to 1987 has been followed by some signs of reinflation.

8 We experienced a sharp disinflation from 1982 until 1987, largely because of tight money policies that deliberately created unemployment and slow growth. Today we have resumed economic growth and unemployment has declined. The first signs of a renewed tendency to inflation may be at hand. This tendency may continue, but we do not foresee a dramatic burst of inflation or another severe disinflation.

ECONOMIC VOCABULARY

Stagflation 392
Phillips curve 392
Demand-pull 398
Cost-push 398
Indexing 398
Zero-sum game 400
Information costs 401
Disinflation 405

QUESTIONS

1. Is war spending *inherently* inflationary? Would this be true if it were fully financed by taxes?
2. What is the difference between inflation, stagnation, and stagflation?
3. How does the Phillips curve "work"—in theory? How would you explain its curious tendency to show such a clear-cut relationship for the 1960s and such a confusing one for the 1970s?
4. Capitalism in the 1880s was certainly not plagued by constant inflationary tendencies. Yet that seems to be the case in the 1980s. How do you explain the difference?
5. Do you think the day will come when you will buy a 4 percent U.S. bond, payable in 20 years, and be perfectly content that you will not be a loser because of inflation? What sorts of changes in institutions do you think might be needed to instill that frame of mind?

6. How does indexing transmit inflation? Spell out carefully the difference in the scenario of a "coalpec" in the 1870s and an OPEC in the 1970s.
7. What is meant by a zero-sum game? Is chess such a game? The stock market? Is being successful in economic life such a game? Why is inflation considered to be zero sum and recession to be negative sum?

AN EXTRA WORD ABOUT

Restraining Inflation

Can we restrain inflation? Of course we can. The question is: Can we restrain it without plunging the economy into a recession? We think we can do that too. Here are five broad policy proposals that suggest the kinds of steps we could take.

1. DEINDEXING

Indexing has been spreading through the economy for over a decade now, and in each instance a case can be made for it. Workers who sign three-year contracts argue that it is only fair that they be protected against unforeseeable price increases during the life of their contract. Social security recipients argue that old people living on retirement incomes ought not to be penalized because of inflation. Middle and upper classes who benefit from the indexation of income taxes believe they should not be hit with higher tax rates due to "bracket creep"—higher money (not real) incomes that raise them into stiffer tax brackets.

All these arguments have merit, but they ignore one big problem. It is that indexing, which is supposed to protect us against inflation, in fact tends to increase the likelihood of inflation. Do you recall how the OPEC oil shock of 1973 gave us an inflationary impetus, whereas our imaginary "coal shock" of 1873 did not? That is an instance of the way that indexing greases the inflationary skids—*by matching increased costs with increased incomes.*

For these reasons, *a systematic deindexing of many parts of the economic system*—wage contracts, the income taxes, and federal entitlement and retirement programs—*could contribute to the reestablishment of a more price-stable system.* Need we add that this is a suggestion that would be difficult to put into practice? Everyone is for deindexing those parts of the economy that do not affect him or her, but not so quick to accept it for those that concern his or her income. A young wage earner wouldn't object too strenuously to deindexing social security, but would fight like a steer against taking out the COLA (cost-of-living adjustment) clause in his own wage contract. His elderly relatives would likely feel just the other way. The lesson, of course, is that the economic aspects of inflation control are a lot easier to design than their political aspects.

2. INCOMES POLICY

Another way of improving the inflation picture is to institute a voluntary *incomes policy*—an agreement freely entered into by unions and corporations to limit wages or dividend payments in accord with some standard such as a productivity index. Then, if national productivity showed an increase of, say, 3 percent, wages or dividend payments would rise by no more than that amount. In addition, corporations would have to agree not to raise prices unless they could demonstrate that costs had increased for reasons beyond their control. If everyone would agree to such a guideline, the inflation-producing momentum would immediately drop *and no one would be any worse off.* Such a collective decision would halt the escalator, but would not change our respective positions on it.

The idea of such a voluntary incomes policy is very attractive, but the difficulty is how to make the policy stick. For if everyone does not cooperate, the scheme will not work. Just as it helps everyone see the game on the football field if all remain seated (and just as no one sees better if everyone stands), so an incomes policy will only work if everyone "sits," that is, abides by the productivity standard. But again, just as at a football game where the few who stand *will* see better (thereby tempting others to rise), anyone who disregards the voluntary limitations on income will gain, so that soon everyone will be leaving his or her seat.

3. TIP PLANS

Because of this weakness in voluntary schemes, a number of clever plans have been suggested that would retain the voluntary element of a freely accepted incomes policy, but would add inducements and incentives that would increase the likelihood of its effectiveness. Among these are *tax incentive plans (TIPs)* that would levy tax penalties against companies that gave wage settlements in excess of guideline rates. **TIPs have generated considerable interest, but like all incomes policy ideas, they encounter formidable obstacles. They would put the government at the collective bargaining table in a way that would seem, to workers, to favor the employer. And they would require the establishment of a monitoring bureaucracy that would surely seem, to employers, to be an unwarranted intrusion of the tax system into business decisions.** For these and other reasons, TIPs have not yet caught on.

4. PROFIT SHARING

A related idea, which has been advanced in various forms by Professor Martin Weitzman at MIT* and by Professor Daniel J. B. Mitchell of UCLA, would urge corporations to change the way in which they pay wages to synchronize rises in workers' incomes with rises in productivity. To do this would entail scrapping the system of fixed hourly wages in favor of a system of *wages plus profit sharing* or *revenue sharing,* in which workers would be paid a fixed proportion of what the company earns.

In good years earnings would automatically rise, and in bad years they would fall.

**The Share Economy* (Cambridge: Harvard University Press, 1984).

Weitzman argues that such a system would help bring price stability with full employment because it would make variations in earnings, not variations in employment, the balance wheel that would bring supply and demand for labor into equilibrium.

Like TIP schemes, profit-sharing plans seem worth exploring—they are one of the ways that Japan manages to combine low inflation and high employment rates. In the United States, profit-sharing plans have not, as a rule, been greeted with much enthusiasm by labor or management. That may now change. Still, it seems unlikely that so large a change in labor-management relations will rapidly become generalized across the business world.

5. MANDATORY CONTROLS

What about controls, such as legal ceilings on prices and wages? These are drastic measures, although they have a long history in the United States. In the present century they have been imposed four times: in World War I, World War II, the Korean War, and during the period August 1971 through January 1973.

Do controls work? They do—for a time. They were certainly applied successfully during World War II and the Korean War, and helped bring inflation down quite sharply while they were in effect in 1971 to 1973, despite a lack of wartime spirit or enforcement resources.

Controls do not work well over extended periods, however. We are not prepared to place wage and price authority in the hands of government on a permanent basis, with all the bureaucratization and loss of efficiency such a step would entail. Especially during peacetime, controls—when kept in place too long—foster evasion: Black markets, shortweighting, quality deterioration, product differentiation to get around legal categories, and still other control-evading strategems become more prevalent as time goes on.

On the other hand, controls have one major benefit. They halt the inflationary spiral more effectively than any other measure. The halt may be only temporary, but it does provide a breathing space in which more durable anti-inflation reform can be put into effect, such as deindexing or changes in wage-setting institutions. If inflation returns, therefore, and if other measures fail to contain it, we may yet again turn to this last remedy.

BACK TO POLITICS

Can policies such as these control our inflationary propensity? Perhaps. Each of the suggested measures makes economic sense. The question is whether any of them make political sense. For there is no magic *economic* cure for inflation. The objective in all anti-inflationary policies is to find measures that will change people's attitudes and actions. This is difficult because all effective anti-inflation measures require individuals to accept some kind of restraint over their *own* incomes, not just over others' incomes. It is easy to agree that wages should be restrained—if you are not a worker yourself.

Successful anti-inflation policy therefore requires the ability to convince individuals to put the general interest ahead of their own in the short run, as the only way to advance their own interest in the long run. To win such forward-looking agreement is the very essence of effective economic policy in a democracy. Economists can suggest ways and means toward such an agreement, but that is child's play compared with the business of winning the active trust of the community itself.

CHAPTER 24

Prospects for Long-Term Growth

A LOOK AHEAD

Perhaps we remember the great problem with which our study of macroeconomics began. It was the problem of growth—how it originates, how it is sustained, how it can be influenced by government. It is not surprising that this is the problem to which we return at the end of our macroeconomic study, for growth remains the central problem for all capitalist economies.

In this "challenge" chapter we first look at two growth problems that we have heretofore ignored. One of these is the tendency of a market system to develop business cycles—cyclical fluctuations—as it follows its growth path. The other is the possibility that capitalist economies may develop tendencies toward stagnation—not cycles, but long-lasting decelerations in rate of growth. That will prepare the way for a consideration of our long-term growth prospects.

Let us begin by taking a moment to reexamine the patterns of our national economic growth as shown in the first three figures of Chapter 5. These long-run charts impress us with their sense of an uninterrupted momentum, save only for the severe dips associated with great depressions or the superbooms that accompany wars.

But if we look at these charts under a magnifying glass, so to speak, we find that the smooth-seeming historic trend is in fact marked by many sharp rises and falls. Take the years 1895 to 1905. As Table 1 below reveals, these years were anything but the steady climb they appear to be in the charts.

Or let us examine a more recent period, not year by year, but in groups of years. As we can see in Figure 1, the rate of growth has varied greatly over the last 60 years. At times, such as the severe recessions of 1974–1975 and 1981–1987, the economy has even shown negative rates of growth. These episodes may appear only as small dips in the graph of our long-term advance, but they have meant suffering and deprivation for millions of people who were robbed of work or income as a consequence.

BUSINESS CYCLES

This sequence of ups and downs, periods of growth followed by doldrums, introduces us to the question of business cycles. For if we inspect the profile of the long ascent carefully, we can see that its entire length is marked with irregular tremors or peaks and valleys. Indeed, the more closely we examine year-to-year figures, the more of these tremors and deviations we discover, until the problem becomes one of selection: Which vibrations shall we consider significant, and which shall we discard as uninteresting?

The problem of sorting out the important fluctuations in output (or in statistics of prices or employment) is a difficult one. Economists have actually detected dozens of cycles of different lengths and amplitudes. Cycles vary from the very short rhythms of expansion and contraction that can be found, for example, in patterns of inventory accumulation and decumulation, to large background pulsations of 17 or 18 years in the housing industry. In addition, there may be swings of 40 to 50 years in the path of capitalist development as a whole, called *Kondratief cycles* after their Russian discoverer.

TABLE 1
U.S. Rates of Growth 1895–1905

1895–1896	−2.5%	1900–1901	+11.5%
1896–1897	+9.4	1901–1902	+ 1.0
1897–1898	+2.3	1902–1903	+ 4.9
1898–1899	+9.1	1903–1904	− 1.2
1899–1900	+2.7	1904–1905	+ 7.4

Source: *Long-Term Economic Growth* (U.S. Dept. of Commerce, 1966), p. 107.

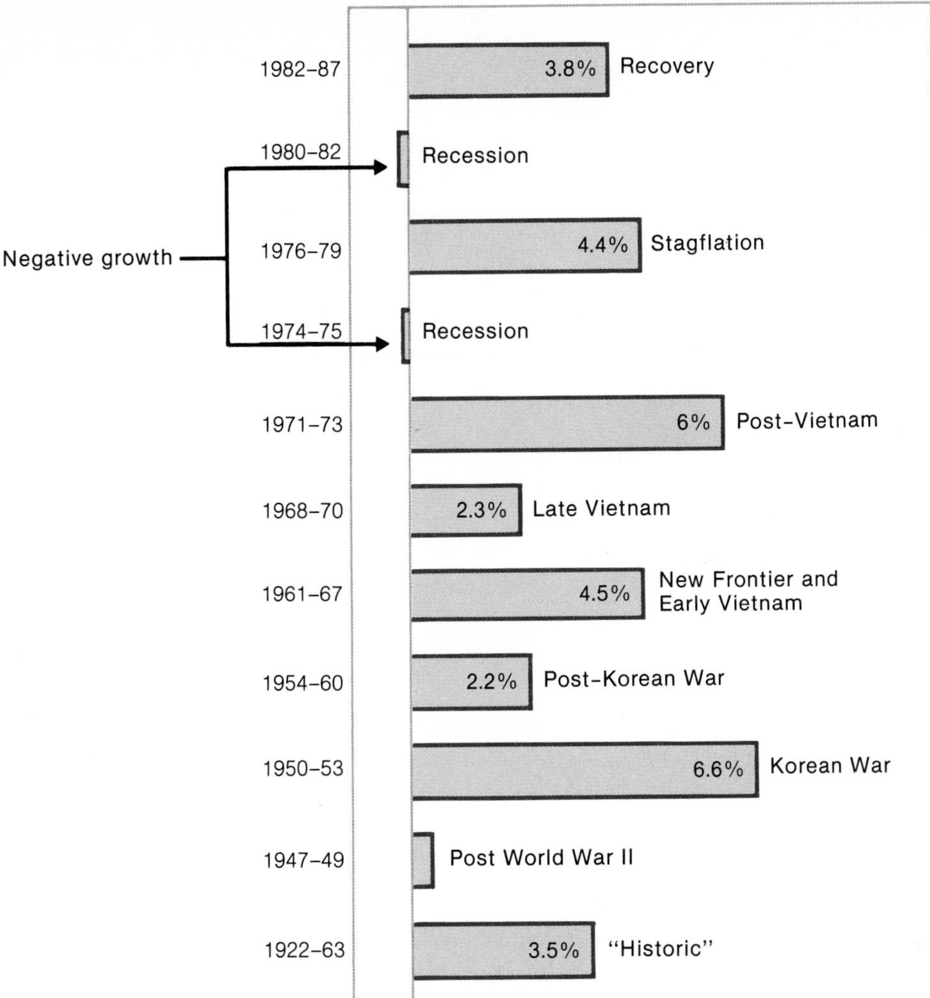

FIGURE 1
Short-Term Variations in the Rate of Growth
Except in periods of real recession, such as 1974–75 or the 1980s, the economy always shows growth. But the rate of growth varies considerably, as we can see.

Generally, however, when we speak of the business cycle, we refer to a wavelike movement that normally lasts (in peacetime years) from 2.5 to 5 years, averaging 46 months. We have had 25 such peacetime cycles between 1854 and 1987.* This major oscillation of the American economy stands forth very clearly in Figure 2, for the chartist has eliminated the underlying tilt of growth so that the profile of economic performance looks like a cross section at sea level rather than a cut through a long incline.

*Victor Zarnowitz, "Recent Work on Business Cycles," *Journal of Economic Literature*, June 1985, Table 1.

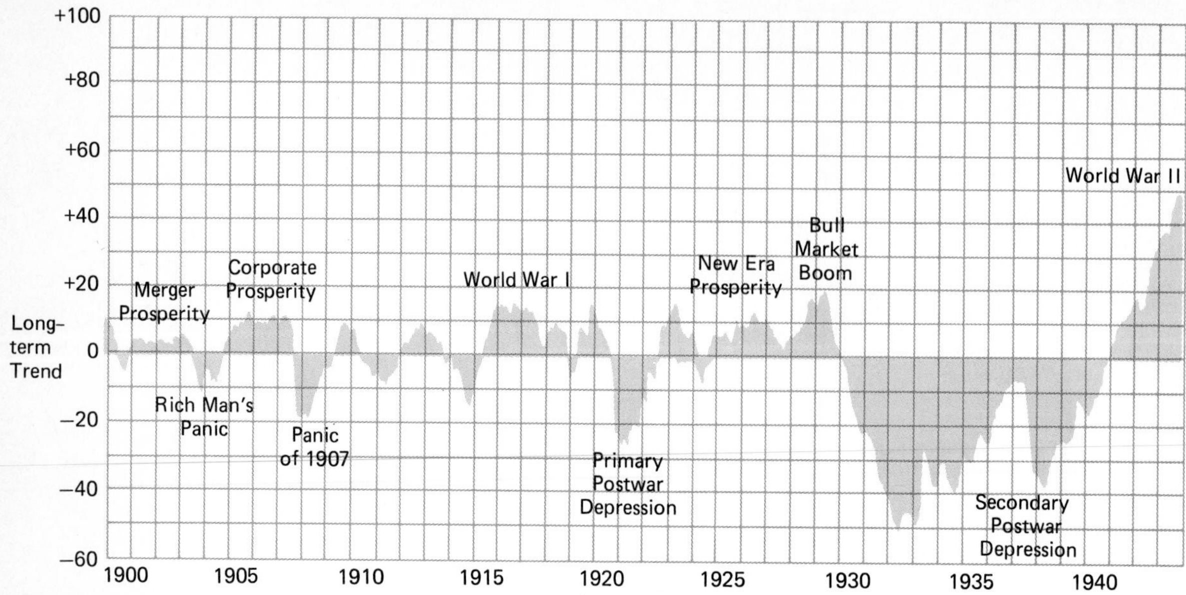

Courtesy AmeriTrust Corporation, Cleveland, Ohio

FIGURE 2
The Business Cycle
This chart, prepared by the AmeriTrust Corporation, vividly shows our swings. Note that the swings lie around a base line called "long-term trend." That is actually an upward-tilting line reflecting our long-term growth rate of 1.5 percent per capita.

Stylized Cycles

In a general way, we are all familiar with the meaning of business cycles, for the alternation of "boom and bust" or prosperity and recession is part of everyday speech. It will help us to study cycles, however, if we learn to speak of them with a standard terminology—**peak, contraction, trough, recovery (or expansion).** We can do this by taking the cycles from actual history, superimposing them, and drawing the general profile of the stylized cycle that emerges. It looks like Figure 3. This model of a typical cycle enables us to speak of the length of a business cycle as the period from one peak to the next or from trough to trough. If we fail to measure from *similar* points on two or more cycles, we can easily get a distorted picture of short-term growth—for instance, one that begins at the upper turning point of one cycle and measures to the trough of the next. Much of the political charges and countercharges about growth rates will be clarified if we examine the starting and terminating dates used by each side.

Causes of Cycles

What lies behind this more or less regular alternation of good and bad times?

Many theories, none of them entirely satisfactory, have been advanced to explain the business cycle. A common business explanation is that waves of optimism in the

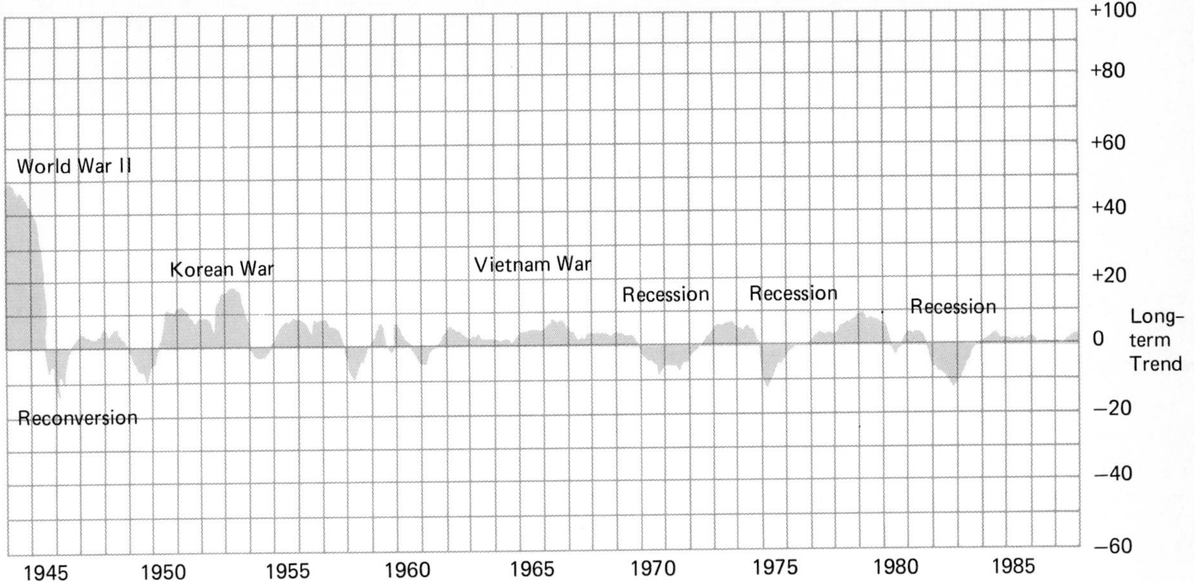

world of affairs alternate with waves of pessimism—a statement that is true enough, but that describes the sequence of events rather than their cause. Hence economists have tried to find the underlying cyclical mechanism in firmer stuff than an alternation of moods. One famous late-nineteenth-century economist, W. S. Jevons, explained business cycles as the consequence of sunspots—perhaps not as occult a theory as it might seem, since Jevons hypothesized that the sunspots caused weather cycles that caused crop cycles that caused business cycles! The trouble was that subsequent investigation showed that the periodicity of sunspots was sufficiently different from that of rainfall cycles to make the connection impossible.

Other economists have turned to causes closer to home: to variations in the rate of gold mining (with its effects on the money supply), to fluctuations in the rate of invention, to the regular recurrence of war, and to yet other factors. There is no doubt that many of these events can induce a business expansion or contraction. The persistent problem, however, is that not one of the so-called underlying causes itself displays an inherent cyclicality—much less one with a periodicity of 2.5 to 5 years.

The Multiplier-Accelerator Cycle

Then how do we explain cycles? **Economists no longer seek a single explanation of the phenomenon in an exogenous (external) cyclical force. Rather, they tend to see cycles as our own eye first saw them on the growth curve—as variations in the rate of growth induced by the dynamics of growth itself.**

We can gain considerable insight into this uneven pace of growth if we combine our knowledge of the multiplier and the accelerator—the latter, we recall, showing us the investment induced by the growth of output.

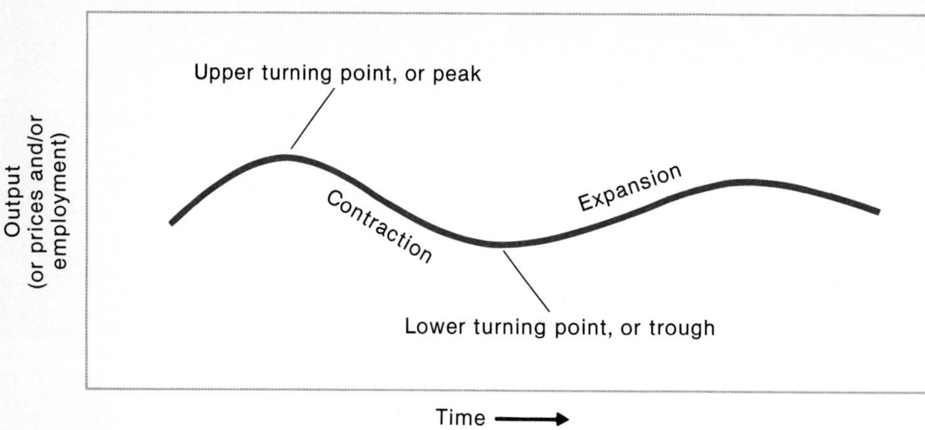

FIGURE 3
The Stylized Cycle
An idealized cycle serves to give us standard nomenclature, so that we can compare two or more cycles.

Boom and Bust. Let us assume that some stimulus such as an important industry-building invention has begun to increase investment expenditures. We can easily see how such an initial impetus can generate a cumulative and self-feeding boom. As the multiplier and accelerator interact, the first burst of investment stimulates additional consumption, the additional consumption induces more investment, and this in turn reinvigorates consumption. Meanwhile, this process of mutual stimulation serves to lift business expectations and to encourage still further expansionary spending. Inventories are built up in anticipation of larger sales. Prices firm up, and the stock market rises. Optimism reigns. A boom is on.

What happens to end such a boom? There are many possible reasons why it may peter out or come to an abrupt halt. It may simply be that the new industry gets built and thereafter an important stimulus to investment is lacking. Or even before it is completed, wages and prices may begin to rise as full employment is neared, and the climate of expectations may become wary. ("What goes up must come down," is an old adage in business too.) Meanwhile, perhaps tight money chokes off spending plans or makes new projects appear unprofitable.

Or investment may begin to decline because consumption, although still rising, is no longer rising at the earlier *rate* (the acceleration principle in action). We have already noticed that the action of the accelerator, all by itself, could give rise to wavelike movements in total expenditure (see page 273). The accelerator, of course, never works all by itself, but exerts its upward and downward pressures within the flux of economic forces and in this way can give rise to an underlying cyclical impetus.

Contraction and Recovery. It is impossible to know in advance what particular cause will retard spending—a credit shortage, a very tight labor market, a saturation of demand for a key industry's products (such as automobiles). But it is all too easy to see how a hesitation in spending can turn into a general contraction.

Perhaps warned by a falling stock market, perhaps by a slowdown in sales or an end to rising profits, business begins to cut back. Whatever the initial motivation, what follows thereafter is much like the preceding expansion, only in reverse.

The multiplier mechanism now breeds smaller rather than larger incomes. Downward revisions of expectations reduce rather than enhance the attractiveness of investment projects. As consumption decreases, unemployment begins to rise. Inventories are worked off. Bankruptcies become more common. We experience all the economic and social problems of a recession.

But just as there is a natural ceiling to a boom, so there is a more or less natural floor to recessions. The fall in inventories, for example, will eventually come to an end, for even in the severest recessions merchants and manufacturers must have *some* goods on their shelves and so must eventually begin stocking up. The decline in expenditures will lead to easy money, and the slack in output will tend to a lower level of costs; both factors will encourage new investment projects. Meanwhile, the countercyclical effects of government fiscal policy will slowly make their effects known. Sooner or later, in other words, expenditures will cease falling and the economy will bottom out.

Government-Caused Cycles

We have spoken about business cycles as if they were initially triggered by a spontaneous rise in investment or by a natural cessation of investment. But our acquaintance with the relative sizes of the components of GNP should make us wary of placing the blame for recessions solely on industry. More and more, as government has become a major source of spending, cycles have resulted from variations in the rate of government spending, not business spending. Cycles these days, more often than not, are made in Washington.

Take the six recessions (periods of decline in real GNP lasting at least six months) since World War II. Every one of them can be traced to changes in government budget policies. The first four recessions—in 1949, 1954, 1957–1958, and 1960–1961—resulted from changes in the military budget. In each case, the federal government curtailed its rate of military expenditure without taking compensatory action by increasing expenditure elsewhere or by cutting taxes. The result in each instance was a slackening in the rate of growth.

The 1969–1970, 1974–1975 and the 1980–1982 recessions are even more interesting. They represent cases in which the federal government deliberately created a recession through fiscal and monetary policies aimed at slowing down the economy. The purpose, as we know, was to dampen inflation. The result was to reverse the trend of growth. Thus it is no longer possible, as it once was, to discuss business cycles as if they were purely the outcome of the market process.

There is no doubt that the market mechanism has produced cycles in the past, and would continue to produce them if the government were miraculously removed from the economy. But given the size of the public sector these days, we often need to look first to changes in government spending as the initiating source of a cycle.

FROM CYCLES TO STAGNATION

Cycles, as we have described them, resemble the oscillations of a pendulum—years of boom alternating with years of bust. But the pendulum does not suggest another aspect of the challenge of growth. This is the possibility that our growth trend fails to give us a large enough GNP over the long pull. Economists call this deeper problem *stagnation.* Stagnation does not mean that the economy stands still; rather, it refers to a chronic tendency to underachieve—to grow too slowly to reach reasonably high levels of employment and robust prosperity.

Loss of Potential Output

Do we face a condition of stagnation in the United States today? The evidence is not clear. Figure 4 shows us one possible measure of stagnation—the amount by which our potential output ran behind our actual output. We derive **potential growth** by

FIGURE 4
Potential and Actual GNP
The graph shows the difference between what we could have produced at "full" employment and what we did produce.
Source: *Congressional Budget Office*

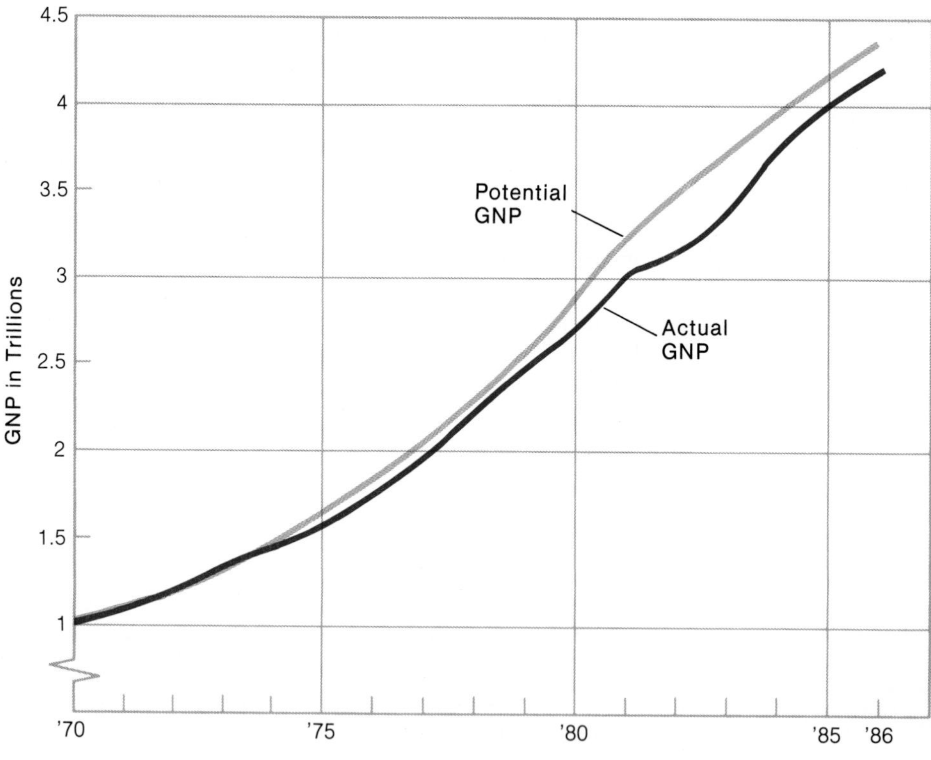

multiplying the rising labor force (adjusted for normal unemployment) by an index of its growing productivity. As the figure shows, this potential output far outpaced actual output during the recession year of 1974 and then narrowed during the recovery that followed.

But the stunning loss came during the two recessions that followed. Here actual GNP fell far below the level of potential GNP. The gap over the years 1980–1986 can be estimated at almost $400 billion—some $6,400 per family. Only at the end of 1988, when unemployment fell nearly to 5 percent, did the economy approach its potential output.

The Trend in Unemployment

Next, let us look at the data for unemployment. Table 2 gives the record of recent years, as well as some benchmark years for further comparison.

The terrible percentages of the Great Depression years speak for themselves. At the very depth of the Depression, a quarter of the work force was jobless at a time when unemployment insurance and welfare were largely nonexistent. Note, too, that massive unemployment persisted until 1940. Only the advent of World War II finally brought unemployment below 1929 levels.

The record of the 1960s and 1970s is mixed. During the early 1960s, unemployment was at a level considered to be uncomfortably high—roughly between 5 and 6 percent of the labor force. This percentage dropped in the second half of the decade, partly as a consequence of higher spending on armaments.

TABLE 2
Unemployment in the United States
Unemployment reached its worst level in 1933. But it was still severe up to World War II. The record throughout the 1970s was poor, and in the 1980s, terrible.

Year	*Unemployed (Thousands)*	*Percent of Civilian Labor Force*
1929	1,550	3.2
1933	12,830	24.9
1940	8,120	14.6
1944	670	1.2
1960–65 av.	4,100	5.5
1965–70 av.	3,117	3.9
1970	4,993	5.9
1980	7,637	7.1
1981	8,273	7.6
1982	10,678	9.7
1983	10,717	9.6
1984	8,539	7.5
1985	8,312	7.2
1986	8,237	7.0
1987	7,425	6.2
1988	6,720	5.4

Source: *Economic Report of the President.*

TABLE 3
Total Number of Weeks of Unemployment
A measure of unemployment that multiplies the number of those without work times the length of time they have been jobless presents a much graver picture of the impact of unemployment in the 1980s.

Period	*Unemployment Rate*	*Number Unemployed (Thousands)*	*Average Duration (Weeks)*	*Total Weeks of Unemployment (Millions)*
1979	5.8%	6,137	10.8	66.3
1980	7.1	7,637	11.9	90.9
1981	7.6	8,273	13.7	113.3
		. . .		
1982	9.7	10,678	15.6	166.6
1983	9.6	10,717	20.0	214.3
1984	7.5	8,539	18.2	155.4
1985	7.2	8,312	15.6	129.7
1986	7.0	8,237	15.0	123.5
1987	6.2	7,425	14.5	107.6
1988	5.4	6,701	13.5	90.5

Sources: *Economic Report of the President; Employment and Earnings.*

It is the record of the 1970s and 1980s that is disturbing. First we watched the unemployment rate rise from 5 percent in 1970 to almost 8 percent in 1980—an increase of 60 percent. Then, as the recessions began to take their toll, we saw unemployment rates reach the alarming figure of 10 percent for several months in 1982–1983. Finally, we witnessed a decline in unemployment as the recovery of 1983 began to gather momentum, but the rate of joblessness did not fall below 6 percent until 1988.

A level of unemployment that would have been considered unacceptable a decade or so earlier had become the best the economy could do despite four years of vigorous growth.

Even these figures may understate the severity of the problem. Paul Manchester, staff economist for the Joint Economic Committee of Congress, has proposed as a truer measure of labor market distress the number of the unemployed multiplied by the average length of unemployment. This yields a figure of the *total number of weeks of unemployment.* As Table 3 shows, that number increased alarmingly as the semi-depression was prolonged through 1982.

PROSPECTS FOR THE FUTURE

How well will the American economy fare over the next decade? As we write, the shape of things to come is uncertain. Perhaps that is always the case, but the uncertainties loom larger today, or perhaps we are more conscious of them. Here are the main issues on which the trajectory of growth will hinge, as we see it.

1. Locating the United States in the World Economy

Perhaps no single problem so clouds the future as the manner in which the American economy will dovetail into the world economy. We have all become painfully conscious of the "openness" of our economy to the forces of international competition during the decade of the 1980s, but it is not yet clear what will be the pattern of world trade and production in the 1990s and beyond. What products will the United States export; and what products will it import? That was a question to which it used to be simple to give an answer: We would export our agricultural surpluses and our mass-production commodities, and import raw materials and whatever goods in which other nations enjoyed a particular advantage—French wines and German binoculars as examples.

That international division of labor, on which all industrial nations relied to chart their general headings, has been knocked into a cocked hat by advances in technology and in organizational forms. We can no longer count on selling our food output to Europe (or even to much of Asia); we now drink our own wines; we buy our binoculars from Taiwan; and mass-produced commodities are being made in low-wage countries. Such developments make it exceedingly difficult to foresee what America's place will be in the world economy of the 1990s, and until that location becomes clearer, we simply do not know whether we will enjoy a decade of vigorous growth or one of relative stagnation.

2. Technological Stimulus

All economists agree that the motor of capitalist growth is capital accumulation, to use Adam Smith's term for the saving and investing process by which the system works. But what determines the volume of accumulation? What makes capitalists eager to risk vast sums in one period, and unwilling to do so in another? **One explanation lays the basic cause for vitality and stagnation at the doorstep of technology. Economists such as Joseph Schumpeter (1883–1950) attribute the momentum of long booms to technological breakthroughs that create entire new horizons for profitable expansion.** The era of railroad construction in the mid-nineteenth century was one such achievement that literally required the building up of an entirely new underpinning for the economies of the West. Railroads were thus, in Schumpeter's view, the basic cause of the buoyancy of the 1850–1870 period, and the saturation of the railroad network was the fundamental cause for the absence of momentum that lengthened the downturns of 1873 and 1893 into full-scale depressions.

That same argument provides a cogent explanation for the upswing that followed in the early twentieth century. Its technological stimulus came from two sources: the introduction of electricity into the home, with the consequent building of huge utility systems; and the perfection of the gasoline-driven internal combustion engine that gave us the automobile, perhaps the most capital-generating invention in history. And as before, the "completion" of the first huge wave of utility and automotive investment helps account for the stagnant tendencies that dragged out the Depression of the 1930s.

So technology—or rather, the absence of a strong enough technological stimulus—helps explain why growth lags from time to time. It is at least plausible that the recurrent periods of history when booms were short and slumps dragged on—the troughs of the Kondratief "long waves" we mentioned earlier—can be attributed to the absence of an adequate technological stimulus.

Technological Prospects. Is it possible to hazard a guess as to technological prospects today? In one sense, that question is answered more easily today than it could have been historically. By general assent, the achievements and promise of modern science are dazzling. The taming of the nuclear force, the adventure into space, the beginning of genetic engineering, and the ubiquitous computer have begun an era of scientific and technical advance that bids fair to change life as deeply and widely as did the first Industrial Revolution. *Ceteris paribus,* that should supply the preconditions for a long investment boom.

But *ceteris* are not quite *paribus* with respect to the impact of modern technology. Also by common consent, the new technology brings unprecedented threats. It is hugely destructive (nuclear explosives), risky (genetic engineering), of dubious profitability (space), and possibly disruptive—the arrival of the automated office and the robotized assembly line, for example, may swell the ranks of the unemployed with displaced white-collar as well as blue-collar workers.*

So the verdict on the *economic* impact of the new technology must remain guarded. That we will witness remarkable scientific progress seems beyond question. That this process will be translated into strong economic growth of output and employment is less certain. It is very likely that the new technology will require brand-new safeguards and safety nets. Perhaps the conclusion to which we are led is that the new technology may provide the basis for a long boom—*if we succeed in controlling it.* More on this later.

3. Wages and Profits

A third area in which to look for clues about our long-term prospects directs our attention to an aspect of the economic process we have not considered since we looked into Adam Smith's and Karl Marx's theories in Chapter 3. This is the crucial relation between wages and profits. If wages are too high, Smith pointed out, profits will be squeezed and accumulation will be choked off. If wages are too low, Marx stressed, the system will suffer from the consequences of **underconsumption** because workers will not be able to match the supply of output with enough demand.

Thus, like a number of other economic variables such as the flow of savings and the supply of money, wages can interfere with economic growth by being too high—or too low! It is probable, for example, that the Great Depression was brought on, in part, because wages lagged behind productivity during the 1920s;

*See the Extra Word section following this chapter.

and it is equally likely that the end of the post-World War II boom was hastened by the pressure of wage costs against business.†

Business profitability, then, clearly depends to a considerable degree on the *wage bargain.* How is this crucial bargain determined? In the past, the level of wages has been largely left to the play of market forces, the supply of and demand for labor. Yet as both Smith and Marx made clear, the wage bargain was never left to these forces operating in an economic vacuum. On the contrary, we saw in Smith's theory that population pressure played a critical background role in preventing wages from encroaching too deeply on profits, and in Marx's theory we found a similar disciplining force in the continuous displacement of labor by laborsaving machinery.

Negotiating the Wage Bargain. And in the modern world? Population growth no longer plays a significant role in setting wage levels, at least in the advanced industrial nations. The displacement of labor by machinery still exerts its pressure on wages, but this pressure is greatly tempered by the existence of unemployment insurance and welfare benefits that act as wage-supporting, not wage-depressing, forces. Nonetheless the level of wages is not left to the free play of supply and demand, like the price of wheat. In every capitalist nation the critical variable of wage levels is arrived at by a process of *negotiation,* quite a different matter from pure competition.

In many capitalist nations the wage negotiation has become a main item on the national agenda. In Japan, for instance, in an annual meeting, labor leaders, employers' representatives, and government officials work out the wage bargain for the coming year. In Sweden, a national labor union and a unified employers' federation do the same thing, but without direct government intervention. In West Germany, cost-of-living increases are outlawed and the main labor unions and big businesses conduct their negotiations under the watchful eye of the government. In the United States, the process of negotiation is much less unified or supervised, but even here both labor's and capital's objectives are considerably influenced by public policy.

All these differing institutional forms of arriving at the wage bargain ultimately have the same objective—to find a middle course between a level of wages so low as to create an undertow of inadequate demand, and a level so high as to choke off investment. What institutional arrangement will best attain this goal? The question leads us to the next element in the prospects for growth.

4. The Social Structure of Accumulation

That last element in our macroeconomic prospects brings us to what labor economist David Gordon has called *the social structure of accumulation.* By this term Gordon means, first, the manner in which employers deploy and supervise their work forces—a relationship that is an immediate determinant of the productivity

†These wage costs include the transfer payments that constitute a considerable portion of total workers' remuneration—not only fringe benefits, but also the unemployment compensation, health payments, and retirement benefits payable to labor. So-called *social wages* are 5 to 15 percent higher than direct wages, and in a number of European countries are a considerable burden on business.

and profitability of labor. But Gordon extends the concept outward from the factory floor to include the relationship of business to government, equally important in establishing the milieu in which profits are made; and from the government into the general relationship between business and the public; and then into the world economy itself.

All these levels and layers of institutions, Gordon suggests, shape the capital-accumulating process, opening up profitable horizons for business or closing them down. Furthermore, Gordon puts forward the idea that a social structure of accumulation that works very successfully in one period may be unsuccessful in another. Like a river that becomes silted up, a given combination of labor, government, public, and world relationships will eventually lose its capacity to serve as a conduit for the accumulation process. When that happens, accumulation slows, and we enter a period of malfunction during which business and government leaders seek new ways of making the system work.

The Coming of the Mixed Economy

We have already noted two periods in history when the social structure of accumulation played a decisive role in establishing the general tenor of economic growth. The first of these was the period preceding the Great Depression. The immediate cause of that depression was a stock market crash that triggered a wave of bankruptcies and a general collapse of confidence. This was worsened by a Federal Reserve policy that tightened credit, rather than loosening it, and by a general belief that the remedy for a slump was "budget balancing."

Underneath these immediate causes, however, were deeper weaknesses—a lagging wage and farm sector (which gives support to an underconsumptionist view) and the cresting of the great automotive boom. But the inability of the economy to regain its former momentum was testimony to a still deeper problem: **This was the vulnerability of an economic system that had embarked on a long accumulation boom of private growth,** *without laying in any support system in the event that growth failed.*

In the nineteenth century America was still a small-town, small-business, heavily rural economy where economic setback was self-limited by virtue of the high degree of independence of so many of its citizens. By the end of the great upswing that ended in 1929, small-business America had become big-business America, small-town America was dwarfed by big-city America, and farming America was decisively displaced by factory and office America.

When the Great Crash came, therefore, it toppled a vast interlocked structure of business and finance in a social setting that was no longer even modestly self-sufficient. With no underpinning for the banks, no dependable stream of expenditures for business, no floors under household income, the economy simply went into free fall.

From the wreckage business and government leaders gradually assembled a structure of institutions that significantly altered the way in which capitalism worked. **Beginning with the New Deal and ending with its endorsement in the mid-1950s by Republican President Dwight D. Eisenhower, a new form of**

capitalism came into being, distinguished from its previous form by the much larger role played by government as a provider of demand. This is a development we are familiar with. But now we can see the evolution of the "mixed economy" and the "welfare state" as a process of transformation whose purpose was to create a milieu in which the accumulation drive would once again take place.

The Long Boom

Did the new social structure of accumulation create a setting in which investment would again flourish? There can be no doubt that it did. The period of economic growth from 1950 to 1973—the year in which the OPEC oil shock dealt the first destabilizing blow to the long boom—was the most buoyant, least interrupted, and most widely shared period of economic expansion capitalism had ever known. Throughout the world, capitalist nations were consciously aware that they had left behind a long history of financial insecurity and meager comforts for the majority of their populations and entered upon an era in which something like a modest affluence was attained by perhaps three-fifths of their citizens. A degree of well-being and social assurance unimaginable in the 1920s (not to mention the nineteenth century) became generalized throughout the West. During the 1950–1973 boom, modern capitalism virtually eliminated dire poverty and provided a previously unknown level of material comfort to its older people, its middle-class citizens, and most important of all, its working classes.

The rise in the general standard of well-being was both the cause and the effect of the rising social wage we previously discussed. The increase in real output made possible higher real wages and a larger volume of welfare transfers, and these in turn helped to sustain the buying power that supported the boom.

The End of the Boom

What happened then? The question brings us back to the macroeconomic issues and challenges of our text. As often before, the new social structure began to produce unforeseen and negative consequences. It changed the momentum of growth into an inflationary spiral. In ways that we do not fully understand, the new milieu seems to have sapped the sources of productivity all over the Western world, not just in the United States. The new social structure brought government more deeply than ever before into the direction of economic affairs, but it did not match the increased involvement of government with a clear agreement as to how public power should be used. It promoted an internationalization of economic life, but no intergovernmental means capable of dealing with the problems. It brought unprecedented advances in government and private scientific exploration, but no clear idea of how to control its own laboratory products.

When we look into the prospects for the future, the organization of our social structure of accumulation seems to take center stage. The way in which we will encourage, winnow, and monitor our technological thrust, the manner in which the all-important wage bargain will be worked out, the success we will have in coping with inflation, productivity, and our national and the international deficits—all these seem finally to hinge not so much on this or that specific policy as on the overall framework within which policies will be made.

What will that framework look like? Will it be characterized by an increasing reliance on the extraordinary mechanism of the self-adjusting market, or on the development of new instruments of control over the market? Will it be distinguished from the present social structure by the emergence of vast international business enterprises that provide the global regulation we require, or will new international government agencies be set into place to stabilize trade and currency flows? Will government play a larger or a smaller role in determining the level of investment, the supply of money, and the degree of protection given to threatened industries?

We cannot answer these questions, although our general predilections and expectations have been spelled out more than once in this text and will be made explicit again at the very end of the book. But it is useful to end our overview of the prospects ahead by returning to the central issue of the political framework within which economic life unfolds. Macroeconomics thereby takes on its proper importance—not just as a "subject" to be dutifully learned, but as an effort to understand how our society copes with the problem of pushing its way through history, like a great ship opening a channel in ice-filled seas.

LOOKING BACK

KEY CONCEPTS

The business cycle exhibits the fluctuating rhythm of economic growth.

1 Growth is not an even process, but is marked by fluctuations that we designate as a business cycle. There are many kinds of cycles, of varying periodicities (durations). We speak of their phases as four: upper turning point or peak, contraction, lower turning point or trough, and expansion.

The 2.5- to 5-year cycle is analyzed in terms of a multiplier-accelerator interaction, often triggered by government.

2 No entirely satisfactory explanation has been found for the 2.5- to 5-year periodicity of the principal business cycle. Economists analyze the alternation of boom and bust mainly in terms of the interaction of the multiplier and accelerator. The cause of the cyclical pattern lies as much in government actions as in the spontaneous behavior of the business economy.

Potential growth focuses on the output that full employment would yield.

3 The attention of economists today is focused less on cycles than on the difference between potential and actual growth. Potential growth is the trend of output that would result from the continuous full employment of the labor force. Actual growth is the value of GNP in fact produced. In recent years there has been a serious growth gap.

Stagnation, or inadequate growth, may be a problem of our time.

4 There is some evidence, not yet clear, that our economy has been displaying signs of stagnation, or growth too slow to reach healthy levels of output.

Four preconditions for sustained growth

5 The future remains unpredictable. But we can identify four important preconditions for sustained and vigorous growth: (a) locating the United States in the world economy, (b) technological stimulus, (c) a wage bargain that avoids underconsumption or profit squeeze, and (d) a favorable social structure of accumulation.

ECONOMIC VOCABULARY

Business cycles 414
Peak, contraction, trough, recovery 416
Multiplier-accelerator 417
Potential growth 420
Stagnation 420
Underconsumption 424
Social structure of accumulation 425

QUESTIONS

1. Explain how the interaction of the multiplier and the accelerator can give rise to cycles. Why does not such a multiplier-accelerator interaction shed light on the question of periodicity? Suppose that capital goods tended to wear out in about three years. Would this give rise to a cycle if their replacement were bunched in time?
2. What facts would you have to know to calculate potential growth? In addition to the size of the labor force, would you need information on productivity? How would you calculate this?
3. How would you design a research program to decide whether capitalism is essentially a stagnation-prone system marked by bursts of prosperity, or a prosperity-prone system marked by interruptions of depression? Can you think of some ways of deciding which of the two tendencies is more "fundamental"? (Remember this is a question about which economists sharply disagree. All the more reason to think hard about it.)
4. Can you write a scenario in which the technical breakthroughs of our day create an industrial boom comparable to that produced by the railroads or autos? What sorts of economic effects would the new breakthroughs have to exert? Why do some inventions, like helicopters, have virtually no impact on economic growth, while others, like the airplane, have a great effect?
5. Consider the problem of "underconsumption." Do you think it likely that there would be high investment if workers were paid starvation wages? Would there be high investment if workers were paid astronomical wages? What do you think the *optimal* wages would be, from the viewpoint of encouraging investment? Would you have to know something about wages as a component of total spending and wages as a component of costs?

AN EXTRA WORD ABOUT

Technology and Unemployment

Unemployment caused by the introduction of machines is a problem that vexes and worries us, partly because it is real, partly because we do not understand it very well. Technology can be a source of job creation, especially when it brings whole new industries into being. But machines can also displace people from established jobs—and may not create new industries to absorb them.

Looking back over the history of the United States, it seems that machines have steadily pushed people out of the agricultural sector, through the factory, and into the office. Fifty years ago it took almost 40 percent of the work force to feed us; today it takes only 3 percent. The proportion of the labor force that works in manufacturing has been falling very slowly over the last 50 years. It is service employment that has burgeoned, employing 74 percent of our labor force today, compared with 25 percent in 1900.

ROBOTIZATION AND OFFICE AUTOMATION

One of the more disquieting technological trends of the last few years has been the development of "robotization," the fancy term for machines that display humanlike capacities for "recognizing" objects, handling and orienting their tools in complex ways, and obeying long and often complex series of built-in commands. As is often the case with new levels of technology, ominous projections have accompanied the appearance of the new robots: In March 1982 *Business Week* took seriously one estimate that the computer revolution would, over 30 years, do away with more than 80 percent of all manufacturing jobs.

Office automation can have the same effect on white-collar workers as robots have on blue-collar workers. In the automated office there will be much less need for people. Machines will do much of the typing, filing, accounting, and other paper-shuffling jobs that occupy so many of us now.

Robotization and office automation bring into play a new level of technological sophistication, but the economic problem they raise is not new. Technology affects production in two ways. It may introduce a new *product,* in which case its effect on employment is to increase the number of jobs in the new areas it opens, and to decrease employment in other fields from which purchasing power is withdrawn. Alternatively, technology may affect the *process* by which goods or services are brought into being. In such cases, the technology will not be introduced unless it cheapens the cost of making the item. If—as in the case of robotization—the new machines perform tasks formerly undertaken by men and women, the technology is called laborsaving. If it undertakes more effectively tasks formerly performed by other kinds of machinery or equipment, we call it capital-saving.

Does laborsaving technology reduce employment? Initially the effect is precisely the same as when new techniques create a brand-new good or a new way of making an old good. The new "robotized" product will be cheaper, because it would not otherwise pay to use the new technology. Because it is cheaper, more of it will be demanded; and if demand is price-elastic, this will tend to reemploy some of the labor that has been pushed aside by machinery. **But as before, the additional demand that is directed to the cheaper product must be taken from some other good or service. The effect of labor-saving technology, in the first instance then, is to rearrange consumer spending—not to increase or decrease it.** Its effect on employment will depend on such matters as the wage levels in the newly robotized process compared with those in the product from which demand has been withdrawn.

THE ROLE OF INVESTMENT

That is not the end of the matter, however. The crucial effect of technology on employment comes through its impact on investment spending. When technology creates a new product that displaces an older one, the new product will require investment in factories for its production. This will be employment-generating because more labor is needed to build a new factory (or a whole new industry) from scratch than was required merely to maintain the older factory or industry whose knell has been sounded. The same is true with a process-cheapening technology, like robotization or word processing. If the new robot-produced items are much cheaper than the old ones, investment may boom in the robotized industry. This may well create more employment than the unemployment created in the industries whose products have been crowded out by the new competition.

Can we then predict what will happen if robotization arrives on a major scale? We cannot, unless we can foretell whether the new technologies will bring into being new kinds of products, or much cheaper products that will give rise to large investment expenditure. It is entirely possible that robots will create new "needs" or new possibilities for expenditure that will easily provide a high level of employment.

And if not? Several alternatives are open. One is to use incentives of various sorts to expand private demand. This is a remedy we have often discussed. Its availability depends first and foremost on our ability to control the inflation that a program of stimulation might cause. A second, quite different tack, has been suggested by Nobelist Wassily Leontief. He suggests that we may adapt to a high level of technological unemployment by reducing the workday or the workweek. This has been a historic mode of adjustment that for some reason has become "stuck" in modern times. Last, we can launch a program of public employment designed to offer work to those who cannot find it in the private sector. The critical factor, once again, would be our ability to control the inflationary tendency the program would be likely to create.

In the long run, robotization and office automation are the very ingredients that lead to higher levels of productivity and higher standards of living. They are no different in terms of their impact than the railroad or electricity. Railroads could deliver the same freight with many fewer workers than were needed in the age of horses and carts. Electricity let us do things that could not previously be done. In both the past and the present, if each of us can produce more because we are working with better machinery, then each of us can achieve a higher material level of consumption. That is, in fact, the only way we can enjoy a higher standard of living. There is no other way.

The difficulty, now as before, is to balance the gains over the long run with the costs in the short run. How to move from an existing structure of social and material life into a new one, with a minimum of wrenching dislocation and a maximum of lasting benefits, is a problem capitalism has never handled very well. Neither has any other social system. Even before the life-rearranging powers of technology, our capacity for reasonable and orderly social adaptation was terribly lacking.

PART IV

THE REST OF THE WORLD

CHAPTER 25

The Gains and Strains of Trade

A LOOK AHEAD

In these last chapters we look again at America in the world economy: first, in terms of our economic relationships; at the end, in a broader, historic perspective.

Chapter 25 takes another look at the economics of international exchange. This will introduce us to one of the most useful ideas in all of economics—that exchange can yield gains in productivity. In order to understand this, we will have to master the principle of comparative advantage—the way in which trade can benefit two nations (or regions or individuals), even though one of the two is more productive than the other in everything it does! The answer to this seeming paradox, we shall see, lies in the efficiency of specializing productive effort. After we have learned about the gains from trade, we review the pros and cons of free trade.

By now we are certainly aware of the importance of the world economy for American economic prospects. Nevertheless, we have not yet analyzed the central problem of international economic relations. That central problem is the gains from trade—and the strains of trade. Until we have understood these crucial issues, we cannot grasp the underlying issue of international economics: the bias of nationalism.

The Bias of Nationalism

The bias of nationalism is the curious fact that relationships and propositions that are perfectly self-evident in the context of "ordinary" economics suddenly appear suspect, not to say downright wrong, in the context of international economics.

Suppose that the governor of an eastern state—let us say New Jersey—wanted to raise the incomes of his constituents and decided that the best way to do so was to encourage some new industry to move there. Suppose furthermore that his son was very fond of grapefruit and suggested to him one morning that grapefruit would be an excellent addition to New Jersey's products. The governor might object that grapefruit needed a milder climate than New Jersey had to offer. "That's no problem," his son might answer. "We could protect our grapefruit by growing them in hothouses. That way, in addition to the income from the crop, we would benefit the state from the incomes earned by the glaziers and electricians who would be needed."

The governor might murmur something about hothouse grapefruit costing more than ordinary grapefruit, so that New Jersey could not sell its crop on the competitive market. "Nonsense," his son would reply. "We can subsidize the grapefruit growers out of the proceeds of a general sales tax. Or we could pass a law requiring restaurants in this state to serve state grapefruit only. Or you could bar out-of-state grapefruit from New Jersey entirely."

"Now, my boy," the governor would return, "in the first place, that's unconstitutional. Second, even if it weren't, we would be making people in this state give up part of their incomes through the sales tax to benefit farmers, and that would never be politically acceptable. And third, the whole scheme is so inefficient it's just downright ridiculous."

But if we now shift our attention to a similar scene played between the prime minister of the small nation Nova Jersia and his son, we find some interesting differences. Like his counterpart in New Jersey, the son of the prime minister recommends the growing of hothouse grapefruit in Nova Jersia's chilly climate. Admittedly, that would make the crop considerably dearer than that for sale on the international markets. "But that's all right," he tells his father. "We can put a tariff on foreign grapefruit, so none of the cheap fruit from abroad will undersell ours."

"My boy," says the prime minister after carefully considering the matter, "I think you are right. It is true that grapefruit in Nova Jersia will be more expensive as a result of the tariff, but there is no doubt that a tariff looks like a tax on them and not on us, and therefore no one will object to it. It is also true that our hothouse grapefruit may not taste as good as theirs, but we will have the immense satisfaction of eating our *own* grapefruit, which will make it taste better. Finally, there may be a few economists who will tell us that this is not the most efficient use of our resources, but I can tell them that the money we pay for hothouse grapefruit—even if it is a little more than it would be otherwise—stays in our own pockets and doesn't go to enrich foreigners. In addition to which, I would point out in my television appearances that the reason foreign grapefruit are so cheap is that foreign labor is so badly paid. We certainly don't want to drag down the price of our labor by making it compete with the cheap labor of other nations. All in all, hothouse grapefruit seems to me an eminently sensible proposal, and one that is certain to be politically popular."

Source of the Difficulty

Is it a sensible proposal? Of course not, although it will take some careful thinking to expose all its fallacies. Will it be politically popular? It may very well be, for economic policies that would be laughed out of court at home get a serious hearing when they crop up in the international arena. Here are some of the things that many of us tend to believe.

Trade between two nations usually harms one side or the other.

Rich countries can't compete with poor countries.

There is always the danger that a country may sell but refuse to buy.

Are these fears true? One way of testing their validity is to see how they ring in our ears when we rid them of our unconscious national bias by recasting them as propositions in ordinary economics.

Is it true that trade between businesses or persons usually harms one side or the other?

Is it true that rich companies can't compete with poor ones?

Is it true that one company might only sell but never buy—not even materials or the services of factors of production?

What is the source of this curious prejudice against international trade? It is not, as we might think, an excess of patriotism that leads us to recommend courses of action that will help our own country, regardless of the effect on others. For, curiously, the policies of the economic superpatriot, if put into practice, would demonstrably injure the economic interests of his own land. The trouble, then, springs from a root deeper than mere national interest. It lies in the peculiarly deceptive problems posed by international trade. What is deceptive about them, however, is not that they involve principles that apply only to relations between nations. All the economic arguments that elucidate international trade apply equally well to domestic trade. The deception arises, rather, for two other reasons.

1. **International trade requires an understanding of how two countries, each dealing in its own currency, manage to buy and sell from each other in a world where there is no such thing as international money.**
2. **International trade requires a very thorough understanding of the advantages of, and arguments for, trade itself.**

Gains from Trade

In a general way, of course, we are all aware of the importance of trade. *It is trade that makes possible the division and specialization of labor on which our productivity is so*

TABLE 1
Unspecialized Production: Case 1
Wooltown and Cottontown each put half their populations to work at wool and cotton, with these results.

Production	*Wooltown*	*Cottontown*
Wool (lbs)	5,000	2,000
Cotton (lbs)	10,000	20,000

largely based. **If we could not exchange the products of our specialized labor, each of us would have to be wholly self-supporting, and our standard of living would thereupon fall to that of subsistence farmers. Thus trade (international or domestic) is actually a means of *increasing productivity,* quite as much as investment or technological progress.**

The importance of trade in making possible specialization is so great that we should take a moment to make it crystal clear. Let us consider two towns. Each produces two goods: wool and cotton; but Wooltown has good grazing lands and poor growing lands, while Cottontown's grazing is poor, but growing is good. Suppose, moreover, that the two towns had equal populations and that each town employed half its people in cotton and half in wool. The results might look like Table 1.

As we can see, the same number of grazers in Wooltown turn out two and one-half times as much wool as they do in Cottontown, whereas the same number of cotton farmers in Cottontown produce double the amount of cotton that they do in Wooltown. One does not have to be an economist to see that both towns are losing by this arrangement. If Cottontown would shift its woolworkers into cotton, and Wooltown would shift its cotton farmers into wool, the output of the two towns would look like Table 2 (assuming constant returns to scale).

Now, if we compare total production of the two towns (see Table 3), we can see the gains from specialization.

In other words, specialization followed by trade makes it possible for both towns to have more of both commodities than they had before. No matter how the gains from trade are distributed—and this will depend on many factors, such as the relative elasticities of demand for the two products—both towns can gain, even if one gains more than the other.

Unequal Advantages

If all the world were divided into nations, like Wooltown and Cottontown, each producing for trade only a single item in which it has a clear advantage over all others, international trade would be a simple matter to understand. It would still present problems of international payment, and it might still inspire its prime ministers of Nova Jersia to forgo the gains from trade for political reasons that we will examine at the end of this chapter. But the essential rationale of trade would be simple to understand.

TABLE 2
Specialized Production
They move all their labor force to the more productive task, with these results.

Output	*Wooltown*	*Cottontown*
Wool	10,000	0
Cotton	0	40,000

TABLE 3
The Gain From Specialization
Comparing the output of the two towns together, before and after, shows the gains from specialization.

Output	*Mixed*	*Specialized*	*Gain from Specialization*
Wool	7,000	10,000	3,000
Cotton	30,000	40,000	10,000

It is unfortunate for the economics student as well as for the world that this is not the way international resources are distributed. Instead of giving each nation at least one commodity in which it has a clear advantage, many nations do not have such an advantage in a single product. How can trade possibly take place under such inauspicious circumstances?

To unravel the mystery, let us turn again to Cottontown and Wooltown, but this time call them Supraville and Infraville, to designate an important change in their respective abilities. Although both towns still enjoy equal populations, which are again divided equally between cotton and wool production, in this example Supraville is a more efficient producer than Infraville in *both* cotton and wool, as Table 4 shows.

Is it possible for trade to benefit these two towns when one of them is so manifestly superior to the other in every product? That seems out of the question. But let us nonetheless test the case by supposing that each town began to specialize.

Trade-off Relationships

But how to decide which trade each town should follow? A look at Figure 1 may give us a clue. Production possibility diagrams are familiar to us. Here we put them to use to let us see the results of trade.

What do the diagrams show? First, they establish maximums that each town could produce if it devoted all its efforts to one product. Since we have assumed that the labor force is divided, this means that each town could double the amount of cotton or wool it enjoys when it divides its workers 50-50. Next, a line between these points shows the production frontier that both towns face.* We see that Supraville is located at point *A,* where it has 5,000 pounds of wool and 20,000 pounds of cotton, and that Infraville is at *B,* where it has 3,000 pounds of wool and 10,000 pounds of cotton.

But the diagrams (and the figures in the preceding table, on which they are based) also show us something else. It is that each town has a different "trade-off" relationship between its two branches of production. When either town specializes in one branch, it must, of course, give up the output of the other. **But each town**

*Why are these lines drawn straight and not bowed, as in Chapter 7? As we know, the bowing reflects the law of increasing cost, which makes the gains from a shift in resource allocation less and less favorable as we move from one extreme of allocation to another. Here we ignore this complication for simplicity of exposition. We have also ignored the problem of variable returns when we assumed that each town could double its output of cotton or wool by doubling its labor force.

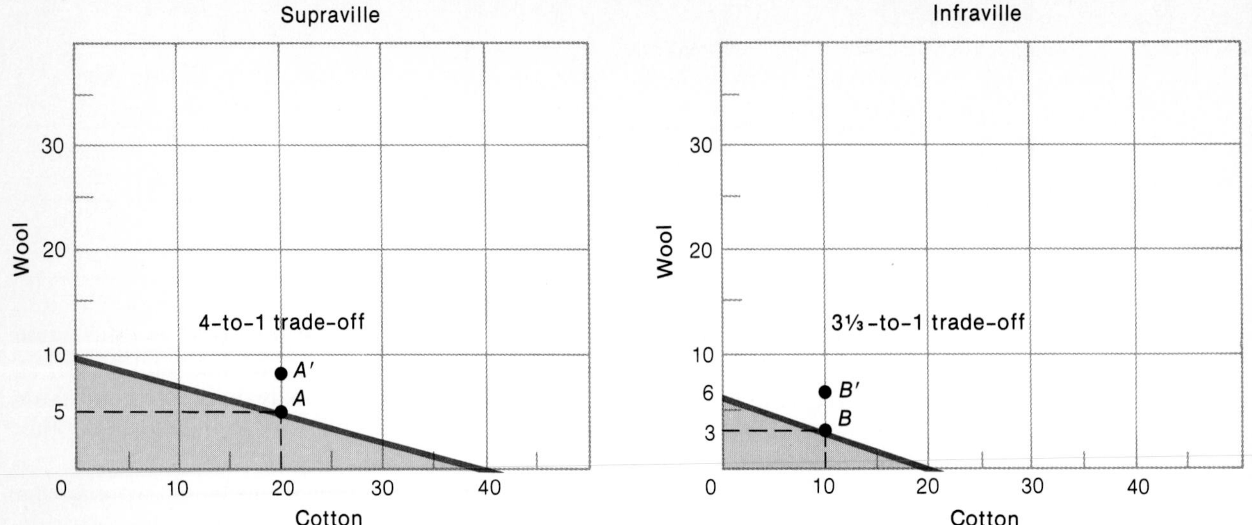

FIGURE 1
Production Possibilities in Two Towns Before Trade
Production possibility curves are graphic depictions of tradeoffs or (same thing) of opportunity costs. Supraville enjoys a wool cotton income at point A, Infraville at point B. Note that points A′ and B′ are out of reach for the two towns.

swaps one kind of output for the other in different proportions, as the differing slopes of the two $p - p$ curves show. Supraville, for example, can make only an extra pound of wool by giving up 4 pounds of cotton. That is, it gets its maximum potential output of 10,000 pounds of wool by surrendering 40,000 pounds of cotton. Infraville can reach its production maximum of 6,000 pounds of wool at a loss of 20,000 pounds of cotton. Thus, rather than having to give up 4 pounds of cotton to get one of wool, it gives up only 3.3 pounds. Therefore, in terms of opportunity cost—how much cotton has to be given up to get a pound of wool—wool actually costs less in Infraville than in Supraville!

Not so the other way round, of course. As we would expect, cotton costs Supraville less in terms of wool than it costs Infraville. In Supraville we get 40,000 pounds of cotton by relinquishing only 10,000 pounds of wool—a loss of a quarter of a pound of wool for a pound of cotton. In Infraville we can get the maximum output of 20,000 pounds of cotton only by a surrender of 6,000 pounds of wool—a loss of approximately ⅓ pound of wool rather than ¼ pound of wool for each unit of cotton.*

Comparative Advantage

Perhaps the light is beginning to dawn. Despite the fact that Supraville is more productive than Infraville in terms of output per man in both cotton and wool, it is *relatively* more productive in cotton than in wool. And despite the fact that

*It takes long practice to master the arithmetic of gains from trade. It is important, first, to get the idea; the calculations can be mastered later.

TABLE 4
Unspecialized Production: Case II
In this case, one country is better than the other not just in one activity, but in both.

	Supraville	*Infraville*
Wool output	5,000	3,000
Cotton production	20,000	10,000

Infraville is absolutely less productive than Supraville, man for man, in both cotton and wool, it is *relatively* more productive in wool. To repeat, it requires a bigger sacrifice of wool to get another pound of cotton in Infraville than in Supraville.

We call this kind of relative superiority *comparative advantage.* It is a concept that is often difficult to grasp at first, but that is central to the reason for trade itself. When we speak of *comparative* advantage, we mean, as in the case of Supraville, that among *various* advantages of one producer or locale over another, there is one that is better than any other. *Comparatively* speaking, this is where its optimal returns lie. But just because it must abandon some lesser opportunity, its trading partner can now advantageously devote itself in the direction where *it* has a comparative advantage.

This is a relationship of logic, not economics. Take the example of the banker who is also the best carpenter in town. Will it pay him to build his own house? Clearly it will not, for he will make more money by devoting all his hours to banking, even though he then has to employ and pay for a carpenter less skillful than himself. True, he could save that expense by building his own house. But he would then have to give up the much more lucrative hours he could be spending at the bank!

Now let us return to the matter of trade. We have seen that wool is *relatively* cheaper in Infraville, where each additional pound costs only 3.3 pounds of cotton, rather than 4 pounds, as in Supraville; and that cotton is *relatively* cheaper in Supraville, where an additional pound costs but ¼ pound of wool, instead of ⅓ pound across the way in Infraville. Now let us suppose that each side begins to specialize in the trade in which it has the comparative advantage. Suppose that Supraville took half its labor force now in wool and put it into cotton. Its output would change as in Table 5.

Supraville has lost 2,500 pounds of wool but gained 10,000 pounds of cotton. Now let us see if it can trade its cotton for Infraville's wool. In Infraville, where productivity is so much less, the entire labor force has shifted to wool output, where its greatly inferior productivity can be put to best use. Hence its production pattern now looks like Table 6.

Infraville finds itself lacking 10,000 pounds of cotton, but it has 3,000 *additional* pounds of wool. Clearly, it can acquire the 10,000 pounds of cotton it needs from Supraville by giving Supraville *more* than the 2,500 pounds of wool it seeks. As a result, both Infraville and Supraville will have the same cotton consumption as

TABLE 5
Supraville uses specialization to boost cotton production at the expense of wool.

	Before the Shift	*After the Shift*
Wool production	5,000	2,500
Cotton production	20,000	30,000

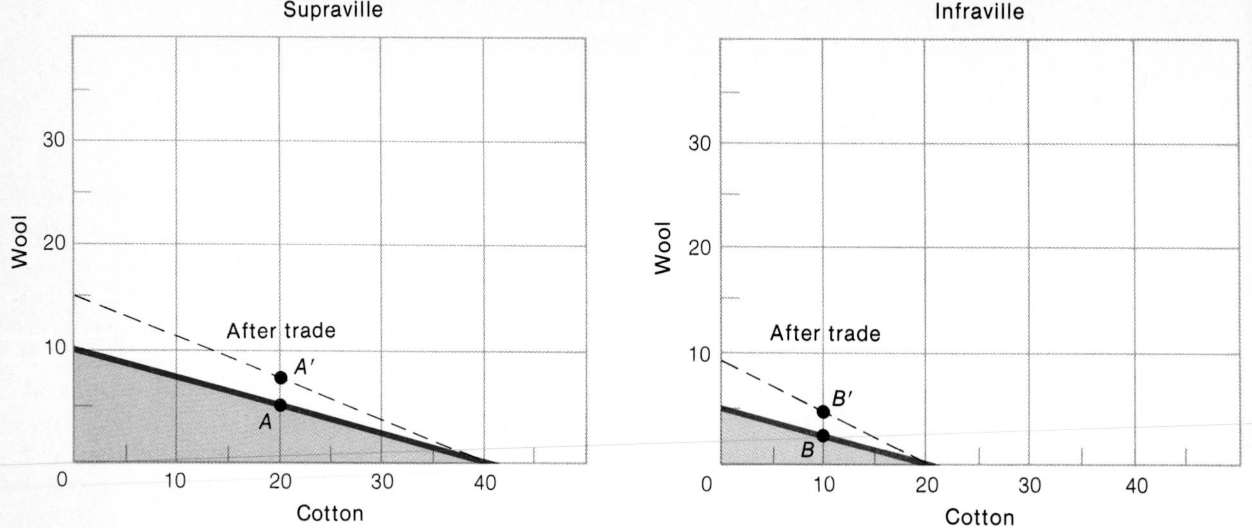

FIGURE 2
Production Possibilities in Two Towns After Trade
Specialization has made more wool available. This is like moving the PP curve outward along the wool axis. Points A′ and B′, formerly out of reach, are now accessible to the two towns. (For clarity's sake, the graph shows a gain much larger than the 500 pounds described in the text.)

before, but there will be a surplus of 500 pounds of wool to be shared between them. As Figure 2 shows, both towns will have gained by the exchange, for both will have moved beyond their former production frontiers (from *A* to *A′* and from *B* to *B′*).

This last point is the crucial one. The nature of production possibility curves is such that any point lying outside the production frontier is simply unattainable by that society. In Figure 2, points *A′* and *B′* lie beyond the pretrade *PP* curves of the two towns, but trade has made it possible for both communities to enjoy what was formerly impossible.

Opportunity Cost

Comparative advantage gives us an important insight into all exchange relationships, for it reveals again a fundamental economic truth we have mentioned more than once before. It is that *cost, in economics, means*

TABLE 6
Specialization is concentrated in wool in Infraville's case.

	Before the Shift	*After the Shift*
Wool	3,000	6,000
Cotton	10,000	—

opportunities that must be foregone. The real cost of wool in Supraville is the cotton that cannot be grown because workers are engaged in wool production, just as the real cost of cotton is the wool that must be gone without. In fact, we can see that the basic reason for comparative advantage lies in the fact that opportunity costs vary, so that it "pays" (it costs less) for different parties to engage in different activities.

If opportunity costs for two producers are the same, then it follows that there cannot be any comparative advantage for either; and if there is no comparative advantage, there is nothing to be gained by specializing or trading. Suppose Supraville has a two-to-one edge over Infraville in *both* cotton and wool. Then, if either town specializes, neither will gain. Supraville may still gain 10,000 pounds of cotton for 2,500 pounds of wool, as before, but Infraville will gain only 2,500 pounds of wool (not 3,000) from its shift away from cotton. Thus the key to trade lies in the existence of *different* opportunity costs.

Are opportunity costs usually different from country to country or from region to region? For most commodities they are. As we move from one part of the world to another—sometimes even short distances—climate, resources, skills, transportation costs, capital scarcity, and abundance all change; and as they change, so do opportunity costs. There is every possibility for rich countries to trade with poor ones precisely because their opportunity costs are certain to differ.

Exchange Ratios

But we have not yet fully understood one last important aspect of trade—the *prices* at which goods will exchange. Suppose that Supraville and Infraville do specialize, each in the product in which it enjoys a comparative advantage. Does that mean they can swap their goods at any price?

A quick series of calculations reveals otherwise. We remember that Supraville needed at least 2,500 pounds of wool for which it was going to offer some of its extra production of cotton in exchange. But how much? What price should it offer for its needed wool, in terms of cotton?

Suppose it offered 7,500 pounds of cotton. Would Infraville sell the wool? No, it would not. At home it can grow its own 7,500 pounds of cotton at a "cost" of only 2,273 pounds of wool, for we recall that Infraville traded off 1 pound of wool for 3.3 pounds of cotton (7,500 ÷ 3.3 = 2,273).

Suppose, then, that Infraville counteroffered to sell Supraville 2,500 pounds of wool for a price of 12,000 pounds of cotton. Would Supraville accept? Of course not. This would mean the equivalent of 4.8 pounds of cotton for a pound of wool. Supraville can do better than that by growing its own wool at its own trade-off ratio of only 4 pounds to 1.

We begin to see, in other words, that the price of wool must lie between the trade-off ratios of Infraville and Supraville. Infraville wants to import cotton. If it did not trade with Supraville, it could grow its own cotton at the cost of one pound of wool for every 3.3 pounds of cotton. Hence, for trade to be advantageous, Infraville seeks to get *more* cotton than that, per pound of wool.

Supraville is in the opposite situation. It seeks to export cotton and to import wool. It could make its own wool at the sacrifice of 4 pounds of cotton per pound of wool. Thus it seeks to gain wool for a *lower* price than that, in terms of cotton. Clearly, any ratio between 3.3 and 4 pounds of cotton per pound of wool will profit both sides.

The Role of Prices

Let us put this into ordinary price terms. Suppose that cotton sells for 30 cents per pound. Then wool would have to sell between 99 cents and $1.20 (30 cents × 3.3 and × 4) to make trade worthwhile.* Let us say that supply and demand established a price of $1.10 for wool. Supraville can then sell its 10,000 pounds of extra cotton production at 30 cents, which will net it $3,000. How much wool can it buy for this sum? At the going price of $1.10 per pound, 2,727 pounds. Therefore Supraville will end up with the same amount of cotton (20,000 pounds) as it had before specialization and trade, and with 227 *more* pounds of wool than before (2,500 pounds produced at home plus 2,727 pounds imported from Infraville—a total of 5,227 pounds). It has gained by trade an amount equal to the price of this extra wool, or $249.70.

How has Infraville fared? It has 3,273 pounds of wool left after exporting 2,727 pounds to Supraville from its production of 6,000 pounds, and it also has 10,000 pounds of cotton imported from Supraville in exchange for its wool exports. Thus it, too, has a gain from trade—the 273 pounds of wool (worth $300.30) over the amount of 3,000 pounds that it would have produced without specialization and trade. In brief, *both* sides have profited from the exchange. To be sure, gains need not be distributed so evenly between the trading partners. If the price of wool had been $1, trade still would have been worthwhile, but Supraville would have gained almost all of it. Had the price of wool been $1.19, both sides again would have come out ahead, but now Infraville would have been the larger beneficiary by far. The actual price at which wool would sell would be determined by the supply and demand schedules for it in both communities.

THE CASE FOR FREE TRADE

Would the prime minister of Nova Jersia be convinced by these arguments? Would his son? They might be weakened in their support for hothouse grapefruit, but some arguments would still linger in their minds. Let us consider them.

1. "Our Workers Cannot Compete with Low-Wage Workers Overseas." This is an argument one hears not only in Nova Jersia, but in every nation in the world, save only those with the very lowest wage rates. Swedish workers complain about "cheap" American labor; American workers complain about sweatshop labor in Hong Kong. And indeed it is true that American labor is

*Obviously, these prices are used for illustrative purposes only. And once again, let us reassure you: These calculations are easy to follow, but not easy to do by yourself. Familiarity will come only with practice.

paid less than Swedish and that Hong Kong labor is paid a great deal less than American. Does that not mean that American labor will be seriously injured if we import goods made under "sweatshop" conditions, or that Swedish labor is right in complaining that its standard of living is undermined by importing goods from "exploited" American workers?

Like the answers to so many questions in economics, this one is not a simple yes or no. The American textile worker who loses his job because of low-priced textile imports *is* hurt; and so is the Swedish worker in an electronics company who loses his job because of American competition. We will come back to their legitimate grievances later. But we must note that both workers would also be injured if they lost their jobs as a result of domestic competition. Why do we feel so threatened when the competition comes from abroad?

Because, the answer goes, foreign competition isn't based on American efficiency. It is based on exploited labor. Hence it pulls down the standards of American labor to its own low level.

There is an easy reply to this argument. The reason Hong Kong textile labor is paid so much less than American textile labor is that *average* productivity in Hong Kong is so much lower than *average* productivity in America. **To put it differently, the reason that American wages are high is that we use our workers in industries where their productivity is very high. If Hong Kong, with its very low productivity, can undersell us in textiles, then this is a clear signal that we must move our factors of production out of textiles into other areas where their contribution will be greater; for example, in the production of aircraft.** It is no coincidence that aircraft—one of the highest-wage industries in America—is one of our leading exports, or indeed that more than 75 percent of our manufactured exports are produced by industries paying hourly wage rates above the national average for all manufacturing industries. In fact, all nations tend to export the goods that are produced at the highest, not lowest, local wages! Why? Because those industries employ their labor most effectively.

But suppose Hong Kong accumulated large amounts of capital and became a center for the manufacture of heavy equipment, so that it sold *both* garments and electrical generators more cheaply than we sold them. We are back to Supraville and Infraville. There would still be a *comparative* advantage in one or more of these products in which we would be wise to specialize, afterward trading with Hong Kong for our supplies of the other good.*

Many readers may say, "That is exactly the situation that faces us today! Are you telling us there is no problem in facing low-wage competition from Asia?" No, we are not saying that. But the problem involves helping displaced workers and businesses find alternative employments. The idea of comparative advantage tells us only that there is *some form* of employment in which our *comparative* productivity will be greater than that of Hong Kong, simply because our resources and opportunity costs are different. Perhaps it lies in developing new technologies. But just suppose that there were no such opportunities. Could Hong Kong then wipe out all American industry? Doubtful. What would they get paid with? How would

*Newspapers in Southeast Asia carry editorials seeking protection from American imports because, they say, we do not use labor in our production, and it is unfair to ask their citizens to compete with our machines that do not have to be paid wages.

we earn Hong Kong dollars to buy their goods unless we sold goods to the East for American dollars?

2. "Tariffs Are Painless Taxes Because They Are Borne by Foreigners." This is a convincing-sounding argument advanced by the prime minister of Nova Jersia (and by some other prime ministers in their time). But is it true? Let us take the case of hothouse grapefruit, which can be produced in Nova Jersia only at a cost of 50 cents each, whereas foreign grapefruit (no doubt produced by sweated labor) can be unloaded at its ports at 25 cents. To prevent his home industry from being destroyed, the prime minister imposes a tariff of 25 cents on foreign grapefruit—which, he tells the newspapers, will be entirely paid by foreigners.

This is not, however, the way his political opponent (who has had a course in economics) sees it. "Without the tariff," she tells her constituency, "you could buy grapefruit for 25 cents. Now you have to pay 50 cents for it. Who is paying the extra 25 cents—the foreign grower or you? Even if not a single grapefruit entered the country, you would still be paying 25 cents more than you have to. **In fact, you are being asked to subsidize an inefficient domestic industry.** Not only that, but the tariff wall means they won't ever become efficient because there is no pressure of competition on them."

Whether or not our economic candidate will win the electoral battle, she surely has the better of the argument. Or does she? For the prime minister, stung by these unkind remarks, replies:

3. "But at Least the Tariff Keeps Spending Power at Home. Our Own Grapefruit Growers, Not Foreigners, Have Our Money." There are

HIGH WAGES?

How do you tell whether a country is a high-wage country or a low-wage country? If German workers are paid 8 marks per hour, are their wages high or low compared to ours? Clearly, you cannot tell without knowing the exchange rate. If 8 marks can be traded for $1, then German workers are paid the equivalent of $1 per hour. We can then compare the German rates relative to the American. If the average American wage is $4 per hour, we would conclude that German wages are low. If, however, 1 mark can be traded for $1, then German workers earn the equivalent of $8 per hour. In this case, German workers are highly paid *relative* to American workers.

We cannot really tell whether a country is high-wage or low-wage until we understand exchange rates and what determines them.

two answers to this argument. First, the purchasing power acquired by foreigners can be used to buy goods from efficient Nova Jersia producers and will thus return to Nova Jersia's economy. Second, if productive resources are used in inefficient, low-productivity industries, then the resources available for use in efficient, high-productivity industries are less than they otherwise would be, and the total output
of the country falls. To keep out foreign grapefruit is to lower the country's real standard of living. The people of Nova Jersia waste time and resources doing something they do not do very well.

4. "BUT TARIFFS ARE NECESSARY TO KEEP THE WORK FORCE OF NOVA JERSIA EMPLOYED." This is the time to remember our investigation of macroeconomic policies. As we learned in macroeconomics, the governments of Nova Jersia and every other country can use fiscal and monetary policies to keep their resources fully employed. If grapefruit workers become unemployed, governments can expand aggregate demand and generate domestic job opportunities in other areas.

THE CASE FOR TARIFFS

Are *all* arguments against tariffs? No. But it is essential to recognize that these arguments take full cognizance of the inescapable costs of restricting trade. They do not contest the validity of the theory of free trade, but the difficulties of its application. Let us familiarize ourselves with them.

Mobility

The first difficulty concerns the problem of mobility. When Hong Kong textiles press hard against the garment worker in New York, higher wages in the high-tech plants in California are scant comfort. The garment worker has a lifetime of skills and a home in New York, and she does not want to move to another state, where she would be a stranger, and to a new trade, in which she would be only an unskilled beginner. She certainly does not want to move to Hong Kong! Hence the impact of foreign trade often brings serious dislocations that result in persistent local unemployment, rather than in a flow of resources from a relatively disadvantaged to a relatively advantaged industry.

Transition Costs

Second, even if free trade increases the incomes and real living standards of each country participating in trade, **this does not mean that it increases the income and real living standards of each individual in each country.** The laid-off Michigan auto worker may find himself with a substantial reduction in income for the rest of his life. He is being economically rational when he resists "cheap" foreign imports and attempts to get his congressman to impose tariffs or quotas.

There is, it should be noted, an answer to this argument—an answer, at any rate, that applies to industrial nations. Since the gains from trade are generally spread across the nation, the real transition costs of moving from one industry, skill, or region to another should also be generally spread across the nation. This means that government (the taxpayers), rather than the worker or business, should bear the costs of relocation and retraining. In this way we spread the costs in such a manner that a few need not suffer disproportionately to win the benefits of international trade that are shared by many.

We should also be aware of the possibility that transition costs may actually exceed the short-term benefits to be derived from international trade. Transition costs thus place a new element in the system, since the standard analysis of competitive systems—national or international—ignores them. A country may be wise to limit its international trade if it calculates that the cost of reallocating its own factors is greater than the gains to be had in higher real income. Remember, however, that transition costs tend to be short-lived and that the gains from trade tend to last. Thus it is easy to exaggerate the costs of transition and to balk at making changes that would ultimately improve conditions.

Full Employment

Third, the argument for free trade rests on the very important assumption that there will be substantially full employment.

In the mid-nineteenth century when the free trade argument was first fully formulated, the idea of an underemployment equilibrium would have been considered absurd. In an economy of large enterprises and "sticky" wages and prices, we know that unemployment is a real and continuous object of concern for national policy.

Thus it makes little sense to advocate policies to expand production via trade unless we are certain that the level of aggregate demand will be large enough to absorb that production. **Full employment policy therefore becomes an indispensable arm of a free trade policy.** Trade gives us the potential for maximizing production, but there is no point in laying the groundwork for the highest possible output unless fiscal and monetary policy are also geared to bringing about a level of aggregate demand large enough to support that output.

National Self-Sufficiency

Fourth, there is the argument of nationalism pure and simple. This argument does not impute spurious economic gains to tariffs. Rather, it says that free trade undoubtedly encourages production, but it does so at a certain cost. This is the cost of the vulnerability that comes from extensive and extreme specialization. This vulnerability is all very well within a nation where we assume that law and order will prevail, but it cannot be so easily justified among nations where the realistic assumption is just the other way. Tariffs, in other words, are defensible because they enable nations to attain a certain *self-sufficiency*—admittedly at some economic cost. Project Independence, the United States effort to gain self-sufficiency in energy, was exactly such an undertaking.

In a world always threatened by war, self-sufficiency has a value that may properly override considerations of ideal economic efficiency. The problem is to hold the arguments for national defense down to proper proportions. When tariffs are periodically adjusted in international conferences, an astonishing variety of industries (in all countries) find it possible to claim protection from foreign competition in the name of national "indispensability."

Infant Industries

Equally interesting is the nationalist argument for tariffs advanced by so-called infant industries, particularly in developing nations. These newly formed or prospective enterprises claim that they cannot possibly compete with the giants in developed countries while they are small; but that if they are protected by a tariff, they will in time become large and efficient enough no longer to need a tariff. In addition, they claim, they will provide a more diversified spectrum of employments for their own people, as well as aiding in the national transition toward a more modern economy.

The argument is a valid one if it is applied to industries that have a fair chance of achieving a comparative advantage once grown up (otherwise one will be supporting them in infancy, maturity, and senility). Certainly it is an argument that was propounded by the youthful industries of the United States in the early nineteenth century and was sufficiently persuasive to bring them a moderate degree of protection (although it is inconclusive as to how much their growth was ultimately dependent on tariff help). And it is being listened to today by some underdeveloped nations who feel that their only chance of escaping from poverty is to develop a nucleus of industrial employment at almost any cost in the short run.

Producer vs. Consumer Welfare

The policy of free trade versus the policy of protectionism ultimately resolves into a choice between the well-being of two groups. **Free trade favors the welfare of consumers. Protectionism favors the welfare of producers.**

To be sure, consumers are producers and producers are consumers, so that in a frictionless, perfect world there would be little to choose between the two. But in a world where frictions are an important part of economic life, it matters very greatly whether we favor policies that benefit almost everyone to some degree, or policies that help or hurt a few people to a considerable degree. That is, in fact, the trade-off when we weigh the gains from trade that accrue as lower prices for textiles or shoes or cars against the impact of protectionism on the jobs of textile workers or shoemakers or auto workers.

In a way, the difficult choice that we face reminds us of the cost of inflation, felt by all, versus the cost of unemployment, borne by a few. The difference is that the political voice aroused by inflation drowns out the voice aroused by unemployment, whereas the injuries of those affected by foreign competition tend to override the murmur of consumers who would benefit from lower prices.

PROTECTIONISM

It is clear that when we add up the costs of a free trade policy, pursued in a world that is *not* prepared to undertake a full employment policy because of inflation fears, that is *not* much concerned about the costs of unemployment, and that *is* deeply interested in securing its national self-sufficiency, the classical arguments in favor of free trade lose a good deal of their force. The limitation of trade through tariffs or quotas or any other form of protectionism may indeed cut down the level of production, but that loss seems much less serious in the circumstances of modern industrial competition.

Is protectionism therefore justifiable as a policy? The question is an academic one, for in fact protection is to some degree the policy in all nations. The United States, for example, limits by agreement the number of cars the Japanese ship to us; has enacted a "trigger" pricing mechanism that automatically puts on a tariff when steel imports exceed a certain level; allows industries to appeal if they can establish "unfair" competition (usually export subsidies from foreign governments); and has other protective institutions. Indeed, protection in the 1980s grew more rapidly in the United States than in any other industrial nation, so that the proportion of imports restricted by one device or another rose from 9 to 15 percent, according to the World Bank.

The Special Case of the Underdeveloped World

One immediate need is to find a way of improving economic relations between the advanced, industrialized world and the backward underdeveloped regions. Free trade has long been preached as a doctrine that would shed its benefits on all alike. In fact, however, it has not worked that way so far as the underdeveloped nations have been concerned. Many of these nations have been until fairly recently colonial possessions of the developed countries. As such, their economic structures were originally shaped to serve as useful adjuncts to the economy of their "home" countries. The result, a typical attribute of underdeveloped economies, was an extreme tilting toward monoculture—one crop such as bananas or coffee, or one product such as tin or copper—and the systematic discouragement of industrial sectors that might have offered competition with their colonial masters.

This has placed the underdeveloped world in a difficult economic situation for which free trade has given no remedy. As sellers of raw commodities, they face a highly inelastic demand for their goods. Like the American farmer, when they produce a bumper crop, prices tend to fall precipitously and demand does not rise

TRANSPORTATION COSTS

If every industry must have a comparative advantage in one country or another, how can there be steel industries (or any other) in more than one country? The answer, quite aside from considerations of nationalism, lies in *transportation costs,* which compensate for lower production costs in many products and thereby allow a relatively inefficient industry to supply a home market.

Transportation costs also explain why some industries, such as brick-making, are spread out in many localities, whereas others, such as diamond cutting, are concentrated in one place. If diamonds were very bulky or bricks very light, the first industry would become more dispersed, and the second less so.

proportionately. At the same time, the prices of the industrial materials they buy in exchange tend to be firm or to rise over the years.

Terms of Trade. Thus the terms of trade—the actual *quid pro quo* of goods received against goods offered—have tended to move against the poorer nations, who have given more and more coffee for the same amount of machinery. In some years, when commodity prices have taken a particularly bad tumble, the poor nations have actually lost more in purchasing power than the total amount of all foreign aid they received. In effect, they subsidized the advanced nations! As an example, it has been estimated that falling prices cost the African nations more, in the first two decades after World War II, than all foreign funds given, loaned, or invested there.

It is possible—we do not yet know—that the internationalization of finance and production may create more new industrialized countries (called NICs), such as Hong Kong, Korea, Singapore, and Taiwan, the four great success stories of development in the 1980s. Already the value of U.S. trans-Pacific trade exceeds that of the trans-Atlantic: The United States economy today faces to the West, not to the East. It is imaginable that the center of industrial life will move away from its historic European-American center into an Asian or Latin American base.

At best, however, that is a distant prospect. Today the underdeveloped world is burdened with debts, and struggling to meet—much less raise—the needs of its vast populations. With 70 percent of the world's peoples, the poorest regions of the world still mount only 10 percent of its total output. In this situation of vastly unequal power, an insistence on free trade is more likely to reproduce the existing tension-ridden relationships of inequality than to lead to a more equitable and mutually rewarding division of the world's production and distribution.

As a consequence, most of the underdeveloped countries have sought to arrange commodity agreements—the international counterparts of the arrangements that support agricultural (and sometimes mining) prices and that regularize marketing in the developed, capitalist world. The developed world has not, however, been quick to respond to the plight of the poorer world. Here lies a source of serious economic and political friction in the present and for the future.

LOOKING BACK

KEY CONCEPTS

Bias of nationalism

1 The bias of nationalism is deep and pervasive. It leads us to assume that gains from trade, which we take for granted within a country, do not apply between countries.

Gains from trade stem from the specialization of labor.

2 The gains from trade essentially stem from the improvement in productivity that results from specialization or a better division of labor. Trade is an indirect means of enhancing productivity.

Principle of comparative advantage gives gains to trading partners even when one is more productive in all activities.

3 The principle of comparative advantage shows that trade is profitable even when one trading partner is more productive in all lines of endeavor than another. This is because it is possible for the superior partner to increase production in the activity that is comparatively best for itself, thus more than making up any loss from shifting resources out of the activity that is comparatively less advantageous.

Specialization allows countries to go beyond their former *PP* curves.

4 By specializing production, the two trading partners gain a combined output that is larger than they could get by producing without specialization and trade. This is true as long as opportunity costs are not the same in both countries, which is almost always the case. Then specialization allows both countries to go beyond their former *PP* curves.

Prices, or exchange ratios, must lie within the ratios of trade-off.

5 Exchange ratios, or prices, must lie within the trade-off ratios of actual output. Otherwise the comparative advantages of the two nations would be lost.

The case for free trade is a case for maximizing productivity and consumer well-being.

6 The case for free trade stresses the gains for the entire society that come from maximizing production. By allowing "cheap" imports to come in without tariffs, we force labor to move away from low-productivity to high-productivity industry, and we benefit consumers.

Free trade also imposes costs.

7 The case for free trade hinges on a willingness to pursue full employment and to compensate the damages of competition. This seems unlikely to be realized.

Protectionism, in some degree, appears in all industrial nations exposed to modern intensified international competition.

8 Some degree of protectionism appears inescapable in a world of greatly intensified international production and competition. All industrial nations practice some degree of protectionism policy. The goal is to steer between the division of labor and the disruptions of unmanageable competition.

Free trade does not shed its benefits equitably when the structure of trade is distorted, as is the case with the underdeveloped world.

9 The arguments for free trade do not take into account the historical circumstances under which the underdeveloped nations' economies were formed. These tend to be monocultures of agriculture or mining, selling products that are highly price inelastic. Most of these nations seek commodity agreements that are the international counterpart of U.S. (or European) farm subsidies or marketing arrangements.

ECONOMIC VOCABULARY

Trade-off relationships 439
Comparative advantage 440
Opportunity cost 442
Mobility 447
Transition costs 447
Self-sufficiency 448
Infant industries 449
Producer vs. consumer welfare 449
Protectionism 450
Terms of trade 451

QUESTIONS

1. What do we mean when we say that trade is "indirect production"?
2. Suppose that two towns, Coaltown and Irontown, have equal populations but differing resources. If Coaltown applies its whole population to coal production, it will produce 10,000 tons of coal; if it applies them to iron production, it will produce 5,000 tons of iron. If Irontown concentrates on iron, it will turn out 18,000 tons of iron; if it shifts to coal, it will produce 12,000 tons of coal. Is trade possible between these towns?
3. In which product does Coaltown have a comparative advantage? How many tons of iron does a ton of coal cost her? How many does it cost Irontown? What is the cost of iron in Coaltown and Irontown? Draw a production possibility diagram for each town. Show where the frontier lies before and after trade.
4. If iron sells for $10 a ton, what must be the price range of coal? Show that trade cannot be profitable if coal sells on either side of this range. What is the opportunity cost of coal to Irontown? Of iron to Irontown?
5. Is it possible that American watchmakers face unfair competition from Swiss watchmakers because wages are lower in Switzerland? If American watch workers are rendered unemployed by the low-paid Swiss, what might be done to help them—impose a tariff?
6. Is it possible that mass-produced, low-cost American watches are a source of unfair competition for Switzerland? If Swiss watchmakers are unemployed as a result, what could be done to help them—impose a tariff? Is it possible that a mutually profitable trade in watches might take place between the two countries? What kinds of watches would each probably produce?

7. Are the duties on French wines borne by foreigners or by domestic consumers? Both? What, if any, is the rationale for these duties? How would you go about estimating the transition costs if we were to abolish the tariff on all wines and spirits? Who would be affected? What alternative employment would you suggest for the displaced labor? The displaced land?
8. Let us suppose that the Japanese perfect a new model of car that will do a hundred miles on the gallon. The car threatens to wipe out General Motors and to deprive 500,000 auto workers of their jobs. What measures, if any, would you advocate with respect to importing the new vehicle? Suppose the Japanese agreed to buy GM's main plants and produce it here. Would you object to that?

CHAPTER 26

Buying and Selling Abroad

A LOOK AHEAD

Our focus shifts from problems at home to problems in the international arena. This chapter:

1. Clarifies what we mean when we say that the dollar is falling or rising.
2. Teaches us the basic elements of international exchange.
3. Introduces us to the problems of fixed and flexible exchange rates.

We have already come to grips with some of the problems of international trade and finance. We have not yet, however, systematically investigated the mechanisms by which foreign trade is carried out in a world of many currencies. That is what we will do in this chapter.

The Foreign Value of the Dollar

When the dollar rises or falls in the international money markets, it does not mean that a dollar will buy more or less American goods. That is a very important point to bear in mind. **When we speak of the dollar in foreign trade, it means only one thing: A dollar will buy more or less foreign money**—German marks, French or Swiss francs, Swedish krona, or whatever. As a result, it becomes cheaper or dearer for us to buy foreign goods and services.

The Rate of Exchange

Let us review what we mean by this. Suppose you enjoy French wine. French wine is sold by its producers for francs, the currency in which French producers pay their bills and want their receipts. Let us suppose they price their wine at 20 francs the bottle.

How much would 20 franc wine cost in America? The answer depends on the rate at which we can exchange dollars for francs—that is, it depends on the price of francs. We discover this price by going to banks, who are the main dealers in foreign currencies of all kinds, and inquiring what the dollar-franc *exchange rate* is. Let us say we are told it is 5 francs to the dollar. To buy a bottle of French wine, then (ignoring transportation, insurance, and other costs), will cost us \$4.00 (20 francs ÷ 5 = \$4.00).

Now suppose that the dollar rises. This means that the dollar becomes dearer on the market for foreign money. It follows, of course, that francs will become cheaper in terms of dollars. Instead of getting 5 francs for a dollar, we now get 10. Meanwhile, the price of wine hasn't changed—it still costs 20 francs. But it now costs us \$2, not \$4, to purchase 20 francs. **A rising dollar therefore lowers the price of foreign goods in terms of American money.**

Conversely, a falling exchange rate would raise it. Imagine we were contemplating a trip to Germany. We inquire into the prices of German hotels, German meals, and the like, and we are told that we can do it comfortably for (let us say) 100 marks per day. "How much is that in American money?" we ask. The answer depends, of course, on the exchange rate. Suppose the rate is 3 marks to the dollar. Then 100 marks would be the equivalent of \$33 a day. But if the dollar happened to be falling, we could be in for an unpleasant surprise. Perhaps by the time we were ready to leave, it would have fallen to 2 marks to the dollar. It still costs 100 marks a day to travel in Germany, but it now costs \$50 to buy 100 marks, not \$33.

We must remember, however, that international economics must always be viewed from both sides of the ocean. When the dollar rises, foreign goods or services become less expensive for us. But for a German, just the opposite is true. A

German tourist coming to America might be told that he should allow $50 a day for expenses. "How much will that cost me in marks?" he asks his bank. The answer, again, hangs on the exchange rate. If it costs only 2 marks to buy a dollar, it will obviously be cheaper for the German tourist than if it costs 3 marks. Notice that this is exactly the opposite of the American tourist's position.

THE MARKET FOR DOLLARS

International economics asserted its importance in the early 1980s, when the dollar was very high. We know now that this means that the price of dollars, on the market for foreign currencies, must have been rising. Why did the dollar rise? As with all price changes, our first task is to look at the supply and demand situation. And that requires us to investigate the nature of the market for dollars and other currencies.

Here we can best begin by mentally grouping all the kinds of dealings in which dollars and other currencies change hands into two basic markets. **One is the market for currencies to carry on current transactions. The other is the market for currencies to carry on capital transactions.** You will have no trouble following the story if you bear these two markets in mind.

Current Transactions

The first market in which currencies are bought and sold is that in which the current transactions between firms, individuals, or governments are carried out. Here *the demand for dollars* comes from such groups as foreigners who want to import U.S. goods and services, and who must acquire dollars to purchase them; foreign tourists who need dollars to travel in the United States; foreign governments who must buy dollars to maintain embassies or consulates in America; and firms abroad (American or foreign) that want to send dividends or profits to the United States in dollars. All these kinds of transactions require that holders of marks or francs or yen offer their currencies on the foreign exchange market in order to buy U.S. dollars.

And, of course, there are similar groups of Americans who *supply dollars* to the foreign exchange market for exactly the opposite reasons. Here we find American importers who want to bring in Japanese cameras and must offer dollars in order to acquire the yen to make their purchases; American or foreign firms that are sending dividends or profits earned in the United States to a foreign branch or headquarters; Americans or foreign residents who sell dollars in order to buy lire or drachmas or kronor to send money to friends or relatives abroad; and the American government, which uses dollars to buy foreign currencies to pay diplomatic living expenses or to make military expenditures abroad.

Taken all together, these supplies and demands for dollars establish what we call our balance on current account. As Figure 1 shows, this balance took a tremendous fall after 1982.

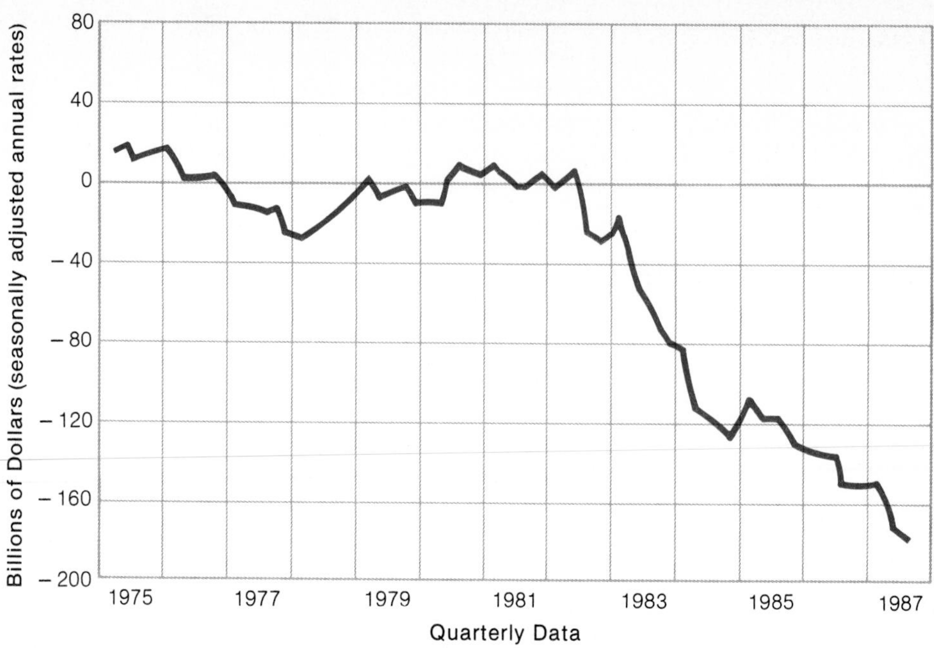

FIGURE 1
Balance on Current Account, 1987
The balance on current account sums up all the supplies and demands for dollars needed for trade, travel, remittances of profits, government expenses, and the like. Until recent years, the market for current account almost always showed a favorable balance. This is no longer the case.
Source: *Department of Commerce.*

Behind the Trade Deficit

What happened to turn the balance from black to red? The answer, as we know from Chapter 6, involves two quite separate reasons. The first is that the dollar rose very sharply on the international money markets, beginning in the early 1980s. We will look very shortly into the causes for this rise, but for the moment we can simply take the rise itself as an important element behind our falling balance of trade.

We have just seen what happens to trade when a currency rises: The high-currency country finds it cheap to buy abroad and low-currency countries find it expensive to buy in the high-currency nation. This is exactly what happened to the United States. Between 1979 and 1985, the French franc fell from 4 francs to a dollar to 10; the German mark from 1.8 to a dollar to 3.3; the British pound from \$2.08 to \$1.09. Tourists went on specially arranged charter flights to London to pick up tweeds and woollens at half their normal prices. Our imports began to rise sharply—from a level of over \$300 billion in the early 1980s to a level of nearly \$450 billion in 1985. (The exact figures are in Table 2 in Chapter 6). Imports also rose because our domestic recovery provided U.S. citizens with more dollar incomes, a considerable portion of which they devoted to buying foreign goods—the propensity to import at work.

THE MARKET FOR CAPITAL

If we think about it, we have now deepened the mystery. Americans were eagerly buying foreign currencies (and selling dollars to get them) to finance the great import boom. Foreigners were unwilling or unable to buy American exports because they were so expensive. One would think that the large supply of dollars offered by Americans and the small demand for dollars stemming from foreigners would lead the dollar to *fall* in price, not rise.

And that is, in fact, exactly what *would* have happened if the only source of supply and demand in the exchange market were the needs of traders of commodities, tourists, and the like. But there is another source of supply and demand that arises to fulfill a set of needs different from those of current transactions. This is the supply and demand for dollars that arises for *capital purposes*—building or buying plants and equipment in another country, or buying stocks and bonds denominated in another country's currency.

The first of these capital flows is called **direct investment.** It arises from the efforts of American firms (mainly multinationals) to expand their ownership of plants and equipment abroad, and from the corresponding efforts of foreign companies to do the same thing here.

The second part of the capital market is made up of American or foreign individuals or firms who want to add to their overseas **portfolio investments** of stocks and bonds. Here we have Americans who buy stock in a Swedish firm or who buy German government bonds, and foreign investors who buy General Motors stock or U.S. Treasury bonds.

The Capital Inflow

If the dollar in the early 1980s was high despite the excess of imports over exports, the net demand for dollars on capital account must have been larger than the net supply of dollars on current account. Why should that demand have been so large? The answer lies in the relatively high rate of real return offered by United States financial assets—such as Treasury bonds—compared with their equivalents abroad.

In 1985 American nominal interest rates, although well beneath their 1980 peaks, were still very high by historical standards: One could buy 10-year Treasury bonds that paid 10 percent interest (in 1960 they paid only 4 percent!). From this yield, an investor would mentally subtract the inflation rate in 1985 of roughly 3.5 percent. The result was a real return of over 6 percent—perhaps half again as much as that obtainable in comparable bonds abroad. As a consequence, foreign capital poured into the United States in such vast quantities that the dollar—despite the worsening trade balance—rose by 47 percent from 1980 to 1985.*

This inflow of dollars could not go on indefinitely. At some point investors would

*The inflow of foreign funds helped finance our domestic budgetary deficit by buying 13 percent of Treasury bonds issued that year. We have seen that this helped us to finance the deficit without the "crowding out" that had been anticipated and feared. It also saddled us with a substantial external debt for the first time in a century.

hesitate before putting their funds in a nation whose ability to earn foreign exchange was in question. And even before that point, the damage caused by the high rates to our trade balance was a powerful incentive for the United States government to act. Act it did, in September 1985, by convening the major economic powers in a five-nation conference. There it was announced that measures would be taken by *all* the central banks to bring the dollar into a more sustainable relation to other currencies. This meant that the Federal Reserve would add to its reserves of foreign currencies and that other central banks would sell dollars to reduce their reserves.

From 1985 through 1987, the dollar's value declined sharply in relation to the yen, the deutschemark, and the other major currencies, until by early 1987 it was only a little above its value in 1980. And, within a year, U.S. exports began to recover. In 1987 and 1988 the real volume of U.S. exports rose over 15 percent, and some of our exporting industries moved close to their full capacity to produce.

Did the dollar's decline solve the U.S. trade problem? Sadly, it did not. For during the period of the high dollar, U.S. consumers had developed an insatiable appetite for imported manufactured goods. And so imports continued to rise as the dollar fell, even though they were becoming increasingly expensive. As we go to press, the pressure on the dollar continues, and we expect that this pressure will not let up until a full adjustment has occurred.

Finding a Balancing Rate

What does this imply for American policy with respect to the exchange rate? The main objective of that policy is not difficult to explain. Essentially the United States—like all other nations—must try to find a rate of exchange that will balance out the supplies and demands for its currency. The aim of our foreign economic policy can therefore be very simply stated. It is to establish a price for American dollars that will result in an "equilibrium" between America's needs for foreign currencies and foreigners' needs for our own.

Consider what happens if a country does not have such an equilibrium relationship. If the rate is too high, there will be a stimulus for the country to buy imports and a deterrent for its exports. The result will be unemployment in its export industries and, as a consequence of the multiplier, unemployment elsewhere. That was the American problem in the early 1980s, when our overvalued dollar was a major cause of a loss of 1.6 million jobs in exporting industries.

But an undervalued exchange rate also brings problems. Now there is an incentive for foreigners to buy the cheap exports or assets of country A. Foreign money will flow into A's banks, raising the money supply. (Foreign deposits increase *M* because the new deposits do not come from another domestic bank.) As the money supply increases, inflationary pressures also increase. The country will suffer from rising prices.

Thus we can present the problem of exchange rates that are too high or too low in this fashion:

Undervalued (too low) exchange rates lead to inflation.
Overvalued (too high) exchange rates lead to unemployment.

WHAT CAN BE DONE?

What can we do to bring about a better balance between the supply of and the demand for dollars? What can any nation that finds itself in a balance of payments squeeze do to right the balance?

Flexible Rates

Here we must first ask whether a nation in balance of payments difficulties need do anything. For let us not forget that a powerful force exists to right the imbalance by itself. This is the force of the marketplace—the pressure of buying and selling that arises spontaneously from the advantages and disadvantages open to traders on the international marketplace.

Imagine for a moment that we did not have a massive inflow of capital on portfolio account. In that case, as we have already noted, the excess of American demands for foreign currency (to finance imports) over the foreign demand for American dollars (to finance imports into *their* countries) would result in a fall in the price of dollars, exactly as if the dollar were a commodity such as shoes, for which the supply were greater than the demand. As the dollar fell, American goods would become cheaper for foreign buyers; conversely, foreign goods would become dearer. In this way, a system of "flexible" (changeable) exchange rates automatically tends to establish a balance in the supplies of and demands for currencies.

Speculative Flows

As we have seen, the difficulty arises from flows of portfolio capital that enter and leave countries for reasons quite unconnected with the prices of imports or exports. The treasurer of a multinational corporation is not interested in the foreign trade balance of a nation, but in the expected future price of its currency. If he thinks its price will appreciate (go up), it will be to his advantage to buy that nation's currency and wait for gain. If he expects it to fall, he will draw his funds out before the decline in exchange rates costs him money.

Two bad effects follow from this state of affairs. First, the flows of speculative capital prevent currencies from responding to market pressures and reaching prices that will "clear" the market. Second, the key importance of expectations makes capital flows highly unstable, and capable of reversing themselves overnight. Under conditions of a panicky flight, a currency can descend in a matter of weeks or days from "too high" to "too low." This is as disruptive for international trade as it would be if the value of domestic currency were arbitrarily changed from one city to the next, so that we never knew what the purchasing power of New York dollars was going to be in Chicago.

Exchange Controls

Is there not some way of preventing these speculative capital movements? One way that has been used many times is to institute an elaborate system of *exchange controls.* Under such a system, anyone who seeks to buy foreign currency must specify the reason for doing so. An importer of machinery is likely to get all the foreign exchange he or she wants, but an importer of luxury cars or a would-be tourist is not. Similarly, a foreign corporation seeking dollars to build or buy a plant abroad will have no trouble with the authorities, whereas a corporation seeking only to park excess funds may not get permission to do so.

Most economists regard exchange controls as a poor way to prevent speculative disruptions. By their nature, controls are cumbersome, bureaucratic, and arbitrary. They require decisions as to what kinds of imports are useful and what kinds are not—decisions in which private opinion takes priority over market preferences. They must differentiate between liquid capital that will be used in the receiving country for the financing of new investment and liquid balances that are here only for speculative purposes. These are difficult, perhaps impossible, decisions to make rationally. Thus exchange controls are always regarded as a last resort, never a first one. We mention them because many nations, hard pressed to achieve a healthy balance of payments, have been forced to institute such controls.

Fixed Exchange Rates

How else can we achieve the equilibrium rate of exchange we seek? Many economists have begun to ask whether there should not be a return to a different system of international currency exchange—*fixed,* rates rather than the flexible rates we now have.

We had such a system of fixed rates for many years after World War II under the Bretton Woods Agreement, signed in 1945 among the major powers. Under this agreement, all major countries announced the value of their currencies with respect to gold (or to other key currencies, such as the dollar.) The dollar, for example, was officially valued at one thirty-fifth of an ounce of gold, or $35 per ounce. These announced rates thereupon regulated the price at which all countries bought or sold foreign exchange. Under special circumstances a nation in international economic difficulties could alter its fixed rate with the permission of the International Monetary Fund (a branch of the United Nations established by the Bretton Woods Agreement to serve as a kind of world central banker), but this was the exception, not the rule.

The Trouble with Fixed Rates

Why did fixed rates not last? The reason must be apparent. Although flows of speculative capital were much less unsettling under the fixed rates system, because they did not affect exchange rates, **there was no automatic self-corrective market mechanism to help keep the balance of payments in equilibrium.**

In those days, the United States was still a major world exporter and ran a large surplus on its current account. As a result, the dollar should have risen, helping to bring the export surplus to an end. But since the dollar was fixed and could not rise, other countries were forced to devalue—lower their exchange rates—to achieve a viable balance with the United States. These devaluations were unsettling and demoralizing. Thus the system of fixed exchange rates became unpopular precisely because it was fixed and inflexible. Economists welcomed the eventual end of the fixed exchange system because very few of them foresaw the destabilizing effects that would follow from a system of flexible rates.

International Currency Reform

Is there some manner of having the best of both worlds—a system that permits market pressures to keep exchange rates in some sort of balance, while preventing disruptive capital flows? In the air today are many plans to attempt to do just that. Most of them envisage a new form of international agreement under which exchange rates will be fixed *within a reasonably wide band,* allowing them to respond to normal market pressures, but preventing the wild swings that have proved so destructive.

These plans are not easy to devise, for a new fixed-flexible system must allow the limits of the band to change if a nation's international situation changes—for example, if its productivity lags behind or races ahead of that of its competitors. With all its difficulties, however, some such general reform seems likely to come onto the agenda in the coming years. It is not only our own serious position of disequilibrium that must be put to rights, but the general economic stability of the world economy.

LOOKING BACK

KEY CONCEPTS

A rising or falling dollar means that dollars buy more or less foreign currency, not more or less U.S. goods.

1 A rising or falling dollar has a different meaning in international trade than in a domestic economy. Domestically, a rising or falling dollar means that prices have changed, so that a dollar can buy more or less goods. In international exchange, it means only that a dollar can buy more foreign currencies. From the international point of view, when the dollar rises, the exchange value of the currency it is traded against must fall.

Two markets for foreign exchange: current and capital

2 There are two separate markets for dollars (or any other currency). One is made up of the supplies and demands for current transactions—mainly imports and exports—and the other comprises supplies and demands for dollars (or other currencies) wanted for capital purposes, whether direct or portfolio investment.

The adverse balance on current account arises mainly from high exchange rates.

3 The U.S. trade deficit reflects an excess of supply over demand in the current market. This is the result of our import surplus. In turn, the import surplus can be traced to the effects of the high dollar and to the loss of international competitiveness.

The demand for portfolio investment has dominated the market, as foreign funds have sought high U.S. real interest rates.

4 The demand for dollars for capital purposes has been sufficiently large as to overbalance the trade deficit. This demand for foreign capital does not so much reflect an influx of direct investment as portfolio investment, taking advantage of very high U.S. real rates of interest.

Dangers of an exchange rate that is too low—or too high. The ideal rate balances total supplies and demands.

5 We can generalize the international exchange rate problem in this way: A rate that is too high (like the U.S. rate in the mid-1980s) brings an excess of imports and unemployment. A rate that is too low brings an excess of exports and an impetus toward inflation. The ideal of foreign economic policy is therefore to find a price for one's currency that equilibrates the demand for it for all purposes with its supply for all purposes.

Flexible rates balance current accounts but allow speculative inflows to interfere with equilibrium.

6 Under a flexible exchange rate system such as we now have, the excess of demand over supply (or vice versa) tends to bring about an equilibrium exchange rate in the balance on current account. But flexible rates are the source of much trouble from speculative capital flows. There is a strong temptation to control speculative flows with exchange controls—a bureaucratic and inefficient measure of last resort.

Fixed exchange rates avoid speculative problems but bring problems of their own.

7 Fixed exchange rates establish durable exchange rates that greatly reduce the damage from speculative inflows. These fixed rates are changeable downward (devaluation) or upward (revaluation) only through international agreement. Devaluations have also been disruptive of foreign trade.

International currency reform will probably try to gain the advantages of both systems.

8 Many economists today hope for a new currency system that will keep rates flexible within bounds but prevent wide swings as a consequence of capital movements.

ECONOMIC VOCABULARY

Current and capital account 457
Direct investment 459
Portfolio investment 459
Exchange controls 461
Flexible and fixed exchange rates 461–62

QUESTIONS

1. If the rate of exchange falls, does this make traveling abroad cheaper or more expensive? Does it make American exports more or less attractive to a foreign buyer? U.S. Treasury bonds more or less attractive to a German investor?
2. Explain why a fall in the exchange rate of the dollar against francs must be exactly the same as a rise in the exchange rate of francs against dollars.
3. If you were the treasurer of an international corporation, would you seek to find the place of highest return for your liquid capital? Why would the inflation rate enter into your calculations? Would you be concerned about the possible wider repercussions of your business decision? Do you think you could be—and still be an effective treasurer?

CHAPTER 27

Where Are We Headed?

A LOOK AHEAD

At the end of our book, we step back for a long historic overview.

1 This leads us first to consider the astonishing turnaround in expectations over the last 50 years. Half a century ago, capitalism was widely considered to be a dying economic system, socialism a rising one. Neither expectation has been fulfilled.

2 The reason for this turnabout lies partly in the issues we have covered in this book; namely, the evolution of macro and micro policies within capitalism to ward off or contain its most self-destructive features. To an equal or even greater degree it lies in unforeseen difficulties within socialist economic planning.

3 The Soviet Union and China are today embarked on programs of deep restructuring that will bring back many elements of capitalism, especially the widespread use of a free market.

4 What does this mean for the prospects for capitalism? We hazard a risky look toward the future.

In this last chapter we come back to the theme of the first—the trajectory of economic history. This time, however, we face toward the future rather than the past, to ask not where capitalism came from, but where it is going.

This is a question conventional economics does not generally address, and for good reason; the question goes far beyond the competence of economists as such. In the end, it will likely be considerations of political wisdom, of social morale, and of institutional adaptability that will determine the future of the United States, Japan, and the European nations that make up most of the capitalist world. The same is true for the future of the Soviet Union, China, and the East European countries that make up the socialisms of the world. And it is true once again for the Third World: the Brazils and Mexicos and Indias and Egypts that are struggling to find their place in the economic sun, some as capitalist economies, some as socialist ones, and some—we instance Iran—as neither.

All the knowledge of the historian, the political scientist, and the philosopher will not allow us to foretell this immense story in detail. Nevertheless, economics may teach us a few lessons that bear on—even if they do not allow us to predict—the shape of things to come.

A LOOK BACK OVER RECENT HISTORY

Yesterday's Outlook . . .

Let us start by reviewing an extraordinary turnabout in the way we perceive economic history itself. Here we must look back to the late 1930s—a mere blink of the eye as historic chronologies usually unfold. The direction of world economic change seemed very clear in those days: World capitalism appeared to be on the way out; world socialism on the way in. Without a single exception, the Western capitalist nations had gone through, or were still embroiled in, the most devastating economic depression in history. Ahead lay a world war whose outcome, most observers quite correctly foresaw, would be the destruction of capitalist colonial empires abroad and the emplacement of "socialistic" welfare schemes at home. Who could entertain optimistic expectations for capitalism in the face of such events and prospects?

Meanwhile, the fortunes of socialism were rising as dramatically as those of capitalism seemed to be fading. The Russian Revolution had seized the imagination of much of the world. In the old colonial regions, socialist parties and leaders were already preparing to reorganize the lands of Asia and Africa under the banner of national planning, whose galvanizing force had been made evident by the Soviet example. The coming war seemed to the Third World a great turning point, signaling the end of the old order and the beginning of the new. With such expectations, who would not have painted the socialist future in bright colors?

. . . And Today's

Need we say that things have not turned out that way? Capitalism is very much alive today, though not, as we know, in perfect health. More striking, socialism is in the midst of a transformation that is deliberately introducing into its midst many aspects of the capitalist system.

Perhaps most surprising of all, the Koreas and Mexicos and Third World countries generally have not left the fold of the capitalist system but have become even more enmeshed in it. Some of that entanglement is the result of their financial indebtedness to their former political and military opponents and masters. But perhaps more significant, the entanglement also proceeds from the emergence of new centers of industrial production in many countries that were certainly not capitalist 50 years ago—Hong Kong, Singapore, Taiwan, South Korea—and the strong signs of further capitalist development elsewhere—Brazil, Mexico, India. In the face of these events, who would today declare that capitalism is dying or that socialism is the wave of the future?

Why History Changed Course

Can we explain this astonishing change of historic course? Two generalizations will help us think about what has happened.

1. Capitalism Has Changed. Capitalism is very much a vital economic force today, but it is not the same capitalism as that to which the gloomy predictions of the past applied. The nature of the change has been spelled out in the pages of this book and does not need to be reviewed here. At its core is the introduction into every advanced capitalist nation of measures to cushion the social (and political) effect of economic malfunction. We can summarize the change by saying that macroeconomic policies to improve and maintain economic growth, however imperfect, have effectively prevented the disaster of another Great Depression.

As every reader of this book must know, that certainly does not mean that capitalism is free of serious problems. Nonetheless, it helps explain the profound change that marks off capitalism's present self-assessment from that of the not-so-distant past. **The outlook for the future, at least in the major capitalist nations, no longer appears to be a choice between capitalism and socialism.** Rather, it concerns the *kind* of capitalism most likely to work well. The debates we have followed in our text—debates over Keynesian policies, welfare, government deficits, protectionism, industrial regulation—are taking place within a general consensus about the viability of capitalism very different from that of 50 years ago.

2. Socialism Has Revealed Unexpected Economic Difficulties. By and large, the early enthusiasts for socialism laid their bets on two aspects of a planned economic system. One was its capacity to move a backward, moribund economy off dead center. The other was its potential to eliminate the inefficiencies and wastefulness of capitalism. One of those bets paid off, at least in part. The other did not.

The bet that paid off was the ability of central planning to bring backward nations into the modern world. This was most dramatically evidenced in the Soviet Union (into whose history we shall shortly look) and in China. No one can compare the old Tsarist empire or the hopelessly inefficient Chinese landlord system with the societies created by the Soviets and the Chinese communists and not recognize that an unprecedented transformation has taken place, however horrendous the cost.

Getting a society off dead center is one thing; keeping it going is another. Here is the bet that socialism lost. **Without exception, the impressive socialist "take-offs" were followed by increasingly disappointing, and finally disastrous, economic performance.** Moreover, the reason for the failure was the same in every case—the vitality of the early stage of mobilization was followed by the inertia, then by the downright disorganization, of bureaucratization. The unexpected lesson of socialism was that planning was an easy word to spell, but a hard one to spell out. Planning was intended to be the remedy for the ills of capitalism; it became a remedy in many cases worse than the disease.

THE RUSSIAN EXPERIENCE

Let the reader be warned that this is not a final balance sheet on the outlook for either capitalism or socialism. Before we attempt that, we need to look a little more closely into the actual problems the two systems have confronted. From our preceding chapters we know something of the difficulties that capitalism has faced and the remedies it has devised and is still devising. But we have not yet had the chance to look at socialism, either as a historical success or as a failure. Hence let us follow its story in a thumbnail review of the single most important socialist state, the Soviet Union.

1. Planning under Lenin

Many of the problems of early Soviet history sprang from a total unawareness on the part of the original revolutionaries of the staggering difficulties of *actually running* an economy. In a famous passage in *State and Revolution,* Lenin wrote that the task of planning a socialist system would be mere child's play—no more than the "extraordinarily simple operations of watching, recording, and issuing receipts, within the reach of anybody who can read and who knows the first four rules of arithmetic."

Things quickly turned out to be considerably more difficult than that. As a result of disdain for "bourgeois" precepts about efficiency and because of the abolition of normal market relationships, industrial output declined precipitiously. By 1920 it had fallen to *14 percent* of prewar levels. As manufactured goods became scarce, peasants became unwilling to part with their output for worthless money. The result was a wild inflation followed by degeneration into an economy of semibarter. For a while, toward the end of 1920, the socialist system was at the brink of complete collapse.

To forestall the impending disaster, Lenin instituted a New Economic Policy, the so-called NEP. This was, in effect, a partial reconstitution of capitalism. Retail trade was reopened to private ownership and small-scale private businesses were allowed to resume their undertakings. Most important, farm output was no longer requisitioned by the state for distribution to urban workers, but was sold at regular market prices. Only the "commanding heights" of large-scale industry and finance remained in government hands.

SOCIALISM AND COMMUNISM

What is the difference between *socialism* and *communism?* In the West, *socialism* implies an adherence to democratic political mechanisms, whereas *communism* does not. But within the socialist bloc there is another interesting difference of definition. Socialism there represents a stage of development in which it is still necessary to use "bourgeois" incentives in order to make the economy function; that is, people must be paid in proportion to the "value" of their work. Under communism, a new form of human society will presumably have been achieved in which these selfish incentives will no longer be needed. Then will come the time when society will be able to put into effect Karl Marx's famous description of communism: "From each according to his ability; to each according to his need." In a true communist economy—the final terminus of economic evolution envisioned by Marx—the necessary but humdrum tasks of production and distribution will be done through the voluntary cooperation of all citizens, and society will turn its serious attention to matters of cultural and humanistic importance.

NEP recussitated the economy, but ushered in a period of intense debate. The debate was not over the basic aim of the Soviet government—that was still to replace private ownership in both industry and agriculture by state ownership and direction. The critical question was how fast to proceed. A slow pace of socialization meant that the institutions and psychology of private property and private enterprise would become more and more deeply embedded; a fast pace threatened to bring another spell of peasant resistance that might again throw the economy into turmoil. The question over which the debate raged was therefore the degree to which the peasant had to be "appeased" while the nation was inching toward socialism.

The argument was never truly resolved. In 1927 Stalin moved into command and cut the Gordian knot by forcibly collectivizing most peasant holdings—at gunpoint.

Forced collectivization solved in one swoop the question of how to get food from the country to the city, but it did so at frightful cost. Many peasants slaughtered their own livestock rather than have it commandeered by the government; others practiced sabotage to lower their crop yields. The Communist authorities reacted with brutal force. An estimated 5 million "kulaks" (rich peasants) were executed or put into labor camps, while in the cities an equally merciless discipline was used to secure industrial output. Workers were summarily ordered to the tasks required by the authorities; the right to strike was abolished; trade unions were reduced to impotence. Not surprisingly, living conditions fell to very low levels.

Nevertheless, in a very important sense, Stalinist policies "worked." Under Stalin's iron hand the Russian economy was transformed into a kind of war machine directed against the economic enemy of backwardness, as rail lines, electric power networks, steel complexes, and other essential elements of a modern economy were forcibly brought into being. Later this same war machine was used to sustain the Russian forces that finally turned the tide against Hitler's invading army.

A different way of putting it is that Stalinist planning was essentially directed at achieving "extensive" growth—growth through the addition of more manpower-hours of labor and capital inputs. Lacking was any interest in "intensive" growth—growth that emerged from higher productivity per worker, usually the consequence of new machinery or technological advance. Seweryn Bialer, a renowned expert on Russia, notes that 90 percent of the economic growth of the United States in the twentieth century was achieved through intensive growth, only 10 percent through extensive growth. In the Soviet Union, it was the other way around.*

3. The Postwar Period

Stalinism "worked" again in the years following World War II, when the ravaged Russian economy was rebuilt in a storm of energy resembling that of the early 1930s. Now, however, the problems of socialism began to change. For once the essential work of rebuilding had been accomplished, the main task of planning changed from construction to coordination. The challenge facing the planners was no longer to bring into being the basic framework of a modern industrial state but to make such a framework function effectively.

That proved to be much more difficult than the earlier effort. Under Stalin's successors, especially in the late years of Leonid Brezhnev, the system began to show alarming signs of failure. According to U.S. government estimates, real Soviet gross national product grew at an average annual rate of about 6.5 percent between 1965 and 1980, but from 1980 to 1985 it grew only by only 1.8 percent per year. In a few parts of the economy, where no expense was spared and where the bureaucracy was subordinated to the highly demanding requirement of special "consumers," the system had its triumphs—the Soviets launched the first space shot, built impressive military planes and tanks, and created whole new cities in strategic regions. But in other areas, where the special interests were not in a position to dominate the bureaucracy, very different results followed.

Bialer gives a few examples:

1. The Soviet Union produces twice as much steel as the United States, but there is a chronic shortage of steel. Why? Because Russia wastes steel in both capital and consumer goods, using much more than is employed in comparable items in the West.
2. The U.S.S.R. is the largest shoe producer in the world, but perhaps the worst—an average shoe may fall apart in a few weeks. Consequently, huge inventories of unwanted shoes rot in Soviet warehouses.

*Seweryn Bialer, "Gorbachev's Program of Change: Sources, Significance, Prospects," in Seweryn Bialer and Michael Mandelbaum, *Gorbachev's Russia and American Foreign Policy* (Westview Press, 1988), p 235.

3. Soviet educational facilities graduate three times as many engineers as American universities, but few of them qualify for U.S. jobs (if they emigrate here) because their training is so narrow.
4. The U.S.S.R. is the world's largest lumber producer, but it utilized only 30 percent of its timber by weight. In Canada, Sweden, and the United States, the utilization rate is 95 percent.*

These examples bear most sharply on the quality of consumer goods, and on the quality of consumer life. Civilian housing is so scarce that married couples often wait years for their own apartment. The level of civilian medical care has declined so sharply that life expectancy has actually declined in recent years. In 1985 only 23 percent of urban and only 7 percent of rural families had a telephone.

SOVIET PLANNING . . . AND PERESTROIKA

Why has Russian planning been an increasingly evident failure? Let us answer the question by learning how planning actually works—or at least how it worked until the present era of perestroika (restructuring), to which we will shortly turn.

The "Old" Soviet Planning System

Until recently, Soviet planning was carried out in successive stages. It began at the center, where the Gosplan, the official state planning agency, laid out the basic guidelines for a five-year effort. This five-year plan dictated such crucial matters as the rates at which consumption and investment would grow, the foreign trade balance with the Soviet Union's satellite states, and the priorities for basic research.

The five-year plan was then broken down into one-year plans. These one-year plans, specifying the output of major sectors of industry, were transmitted to various government ministries concerned with, for example, steel production, rail transportation, and lumbering. In turn, the ministries referred the one-year plans further down the line to the heads of large industrial plants, to experts and advisers, and so forth. Thus the overall design was unraveled into its constituent parts, until finally the threads were traced back as far as possible along the productive process—right to the officials in charge of factory operations.

Thus the factory manager of, say, a coking operation would be given a set of instructions to make his operations dovetail with those of the industries to which his output would flow and from which his inputs would arrive. The manager would then confer with his staff of production engineers and plant supervisors and would transmit up the line his requirements for meeting his "targets"—perhaps an authorization to hire more workers, or to order additional machines. In this way, "demand" requirements flowed down the chain of command and constraints of "supply" flowed back up, all coming together in a giant production blueprint (actually a vast series of computer printouts) in the Gosplan offices.

*Bialer, "Gorbachev's Program of Change," p. 242.

Success Indicators

As we can imagine, the coordination and integration of these plans was a fantastically complicated task. Even with the most sophisticated planning techniques, the process was slow, cumbersome, and mistake-prone. To get around the constant shortages that cropped up (bringing things to a grinding halt), factory managers were given strong financial incentives to *surpass* their planned output.

But this only introduced yet another problem. For the "success indicators" by which plan achievements were measured invariably produced their own bottlenecks and distortions. If the target for a textile mill were specified in yards of cloth, there was obviously a strong temptation to weave the cloth as loosely as possible to maximize the yardage from a given input of thread. If the success indicator was a measure of weight, the temptation was to skimp on quality or design. A cartoon in the satiric magazine *Krokodil* showed a nail factory proudly displaying its "record output"—one gigantic nail suspended by an immense gantry crane. The economic system was, in fact, soon heavily dependent on so-called *tolkatchi*—wheelers and dealers who arranged for shipments to be rerouted, shortages filled, and excess inventories disposed of—all behind the authorities' backs (but sometimes with their tacit permission).

Perestroika

It was to remove these suffocating inefficiencies that Mikhail Gorbachev began to speak of perestroika—the fundamental restructuring of the economic system—in 1985.

What is perestroika? We do not yet know because it still exists more in intention than in fact. Not until 1991 will we have the first five-year plan under the new arrangements about which Gorbachev has written and spoken. So we must content ourselves with a few central aims of the new system, some of which will surely be achieved in full, more of which will be achieved in part, and some of which will perhaps not be achieved at all.

1. There will still be five-year plans, but they will more closely resemble the general objectives of many European economies; specifying targets for GNP, for regional development, for levels and kinds of taxation, social policy, and the like. **With respect to the greater part of consumer output, virtually all planning will go.** Academician Nikolai Shmelev, an architect of perestroika, states that within a few years 70 percent of Soviet output will be subject to market disciplines and free prices. Old-style planning will remain only in strategic areas such as military production and perhaps for such important outputs as steel.
2. The Gosplan will continue, but the ministries of production that oversaw the production of nuts and bolts, shoes and sealing wax, will largely disappear or will play greatly reduced roles. **Production will be increasingly entrusted to the decisions of plant managers whose "success indicators" will be the profitability of their operations.**
3. So that they can earn profits, plant managers will be permitted to make their

own arrangements for delivery and for shipment. That is, instead of having inputs delivered to them as part of a plan, they will *buy* their inputs from whomever they please; and instead of shipping their outputs according to plan, they will have to *sell* their outputs as best they can. **This means that the economy will begin to be linked up by a market system instead of by a blueprint.**

4. **Managers will also be free to hire and to fire workers.** This will introduce the previously unknown element of labor discipline into the system. Today absenteeism is rife because workers know that they cannot be dismissed from their jobs for minor infringements.
5. **Many kinds of small businesses will be encouraged**—restaurants, small retail stores and wholesale establishments, automobile repair shops, and the like. More important, agricultural output will be increasingly (although not totally) provided by household plots or cooperatives (not collectives) selling their output on the market.

Can Perestroika Succeed?

Will perestroika attain its bold ends? The answer probably depends more on political than strictly economic factors. Perestroika will cost people jobs—not least the bureaucrats in the various production ministries whose work will be abolished and who will have to relocate themselves in the new economic structure. It will bring anxiety, perhaps some hardship, to workers who will not be able to count on assured employment. It will introduce the sweet taste of success for those who open profitable stores—and the sour taste of failure for those whose enterprises do not make the grade. It will require new attitudes that may bring down the charge of being "antisocialist" on the heads of those who hold them.

All this means that perestroika cannot possibly be an overnight success. The improvement in efficiency and consumer well-being is likely to come slowly; the pains of transition are likely to come more quickly. Seweryn Bialer reports that a major victory for perestroika would mean that 10 to 15 years from now the Soviet Union would cease *falling behind* the West!*

The new spirit of *glasnost* (openness) that is the political counterpart of restructuring means that those whose incomes or livelihoods or values are hurt will voice their protests freely and even vehemently.

So it would be foolhardy to assume that the economic (or the political) course of Russian socialism will abruptly change. But it would be even more foolish not to recognize perestroika as an epoch-making attempt to create a new and more efficient socialist economy, along with a new and more democratic socialist polity. It may be a decade before we will be able to evaluate the successes and failures of this historic experiment.

* Bialer, "Gorbachev's Program of Change," p. 272.

A MATTER OF NUMBERS

One gets a glimpse into the problems of perestroika in unexpected ways. A high-ranking Soviet economist called on one of the authors of this book, as we were writing this section, to talk about problems and prospects for "deplanning" the Soviet system. He was full of enthusiasm. "Do you realize," he asked, "that in three years we hope to reduce the number of planned prices from over *two million* to less than one thousand!"

The author was considerably impressed. But then he began to think. The two million prices included the price tag for each and every size of nail and screw, each and every cut of shirt and blouse, every item on the menus of the state's restaurants. This did indeed require a staggering number of price decisions, but the decisions did not profoundly affect the allocation of Soviet resources. The same could not be said about the "less than one thousand" prices that would remain under control, for they would doubtless include steel, coal, basic chemicals, and the like. Thus a number that signifies a free economy to someone who has lived in a controlled system still sounds like a planner's nightmare to someone accustomed to a market society.

MEANWHILE, IN CHINA

The Soviet Union is not the only socialist economy in which we find a turn toward the market. Equally stunning was the Chinese turnabout. Although far less industrialized than the Soviet Union, China has also suffered from bureaucratic sclerosis. Hence as early as 1956 Mao Zedong decided that China had to undertake a reform to decentralize the management of its economy.

The initial changes were not promising. Decision-making power shifted back and forth between Beijing and the provinces, bringing a cycle that the Chinese themselves described as "Relax control and get chaos; recentralize and get inertia." As with Gorbachev's perestroika, ending the impasse required the adoption of a bold new plan, proposed in 1979. Its nickname was DPRR, for "Delegate Power and Relinquish Revenues."

As its name suggests, DPRR aimed to release the Chinese economy from the paralytic effects of centralized planning. Hence it included a number of startling innovations to counterbalance the inertia of planned activity. The collective farm system was abandoned in favor of household production from land *rented* by peasant families! Small-scale private enterprise and cooperative undertakings were encouraged, and 80 million off-the-farm jobs were created in the agricultural sector. Local authorities were given autonomy over the expenditures of their share of tax revenues. And perhaps most significant, China opened its doors to foreign enterprise, taking the risk of becoming infected with the capitalist virus in exchange for the transfusion of Western technology. As with the Soviet system, key parts of the economy remained under state control, but here, too, an effort was made to encourage innovative and profit-seeking management.

Was DPRR a success? As a matter of economics, it is too soon to say. China did enjoy one of the highest growth rates in the world in the early 1980s. But economic liberalization sparked strong demands for political freedom, and this the regime was not prepared to grant. The brutal massacre of pro-democracy protesters in Tiananmen square in June of 1989 discredited China's government in the world community, and may have slowed or even stopped, for a time, progress toward a workable economic system.

Market Socialisms

Other departures from central planning can be found in the socialist world. In Yugoslavia much of the economy is today run in a "capitalistic," profit-seeking manner. At the same time, an effort has been made to bring socialist democracy "inside" these capitalist-like firms by establishing workers' councils that determine, together with the manager, how profits will be used, how wage scales will be set, and—at least in theory—whether the manager himself will be kept on! In Hungary more than 10,000 new small private enterprises were formed in 1980 with the approval of the authorities. During the next few years the entire growth of Hungarian national product came from these firms, not from the 1,000 large-scale state and cooperative enterprises. In Czechoslovakia, Bulgaria, and Poland similar kinds of experiments are under way, their successes or failures still to be determined.

What is important is that "market socialisms" of one kind or another have become the norm for socialist economies, taking the place of the centralized structures that were the norm only a decade ago. Market socialisms have not yet worked as their designers hoped. A sluggish core of central planning remains. Yet the political authorities are loathe to surrender central planning, lest the market mechanism become what many fear it will be—the nose of the capitalist camel under the socialist tent.

Thus, in all these new socialist systems we find a tension between the *economic* arguments of efficiency and the *political* arguments of social planning. In our view, this tension will not be easily resolved. The socialist governments will not permit a transition to a fully capitalist system. But neither do they want a return to the failed model of a centrally planned system. As a result, we are likely to see mixed socialist systems—generally free, capitalist-like consumer good sectors, with some kind of continuing government supervision of output and management in the central core of industrial production. Agreements will no doubt be concluded with foreign capitalist firms that will introduce new technologies and perhaps add the stimulus of competition, but it is doubtful that socialist economies will open themselves to world trade on a purely market basis. The rhetoric of socialism will surely persist—along with the siren songs of capitalism's life style. As far ahead as we can see—just to the horizon of the new edition we hope to produce three or four years hence—we picture socialism as a society with these conflicting tendencies.

PROSPECTS FOR CAPITALISM

The drift of planning toward markets in socialist countries raises a question of fundamental importance. Why plan at all? Why not let the market take over the task of coordination that has proved to be such a formidable hurdle for socialism, for is not the market itself a "planning" mechanism?

The question brings us back to the trajectory of history. If, as is surely the case today, the momentum of socialism is dampened, can we anticipate that the market system now has a clear field? Will capitalism continue, at least in the advanced Western societies, indefinitely?

Capitalism's Problems

That is the question with which the worldly philosophers wrestled, and as we recall from Chapter 3, they came to different conclusions. We cannot provide a resolution of their differences, and it is not within our abilities to answer the question itself more convincingly than they. Yet our economic studies, and now our brief survey of the problems of socialism, allow us to suggest a way of thinking about this all-important, but extraordinarily difficult, problem.

Let us begin by asking if there is one central difficulty that threatens capitalism in the same manner that the bureaucratic disease threatens socialism. The answer must surely spring to our minds from the topics we have covered in this book. As we would expect, it is the opposite of the problem of centralized planning: Planning's nemesis is its inability to break away from a plan. Capitalism's nemesis is its inability to formulate one. By "plan" we do not mean a blueprint for the entire economy. We mean the formulation of social objectives other than those that arise from the workings of the marketplace itself.

It is certainly easy to remind ourselves of the manner in which this difficulty appears. Perhaps the most egregious example is the tendency of market systems to tolerate poverty because they do not generate nonmarket mechanisms of distribution adequate to the needs of the poor. Another problem is the failure of capitalisms to pay sufficient attention to the quality of life, turning a blind eye to the deficiencies and excesses (urban blight side by side with conspicuous consumption) that emerge in a society following the guidance of the market. Yet a third are the malfunctions generated by the workings of capitalism itself—its succession of booms and busts, its persisting inability to provide employment for all who seek it, its tendency to generate huge enterprises that defy the very power of the nation-state itself.

The Rise of Capitalist Planning

These difficulties are as deeply rooted in the workings of the market system of capitalism as the difficulties of socialism are rooted in the workings of its system of central allocation. Moreover, just as the problems of socialism could be ignored during its early stages, when the full force of the planning operation was working its mobilizing miracles, so the drawbacks of the market mechanism could be ignored in the early phases of capitalism, while the system was availing itself of the tremendous capacity of the market to match output to market demand.

But as a market society becomes more advanced, its requirements change, just as do those of a socialist society. These latter, as we have seen, desperately need the flexibility and adaptability that central planning cannot give. And capitalisms begin to need the presence of public guidance that the market cannot provide. **The result is that just as we see socialisms turning toward the market, we have seen capitalisms turn toward the state.**

Central planning, to repeat, is not the answer. The planning mechanisms of capitalism comprise the whole range of measures by which it intervenes in, seeks to change the course of, and tries to overcome the problems that arise from the unhindered market. Planning in capitalism therefore embraces its taxes, its fiscal policy and monetary policies, its programs of public investment, its measures of income support and redistribution, its regulation of big business—in short, the gamut of public activities whose various forms and modes of application we have followed in the pages past. Now, however, we no longer view these policies piecemeal, but see them as a response of the system to its problems, similar, in mirror fashion, to the quite opposite response of socialism to its chief functional difficulty.

Politics vs. Economics

Will these measures guarantee the longevity of capitalism? That question can no more be answered with assurance than the same questions directed at socialism. We know from past experience that the malfunctions of capitalism can be very grave. We believe these malfunctions can be made socially tolerable, even if not removed. But here, too, we have no alternative but to await the verdict of history.

One last word must be said with respect to this verdict. We spoke in the opening paragraphs of this chapter about capitalisms and socialisms, not capitalism and socialism. It is wise to return to this careful phrasing as we reach the end of our book. It is likely that there will be successful capitalisms and unsuccessful ones, just as it is probable that some socialisms will flourish and some will not. "In the end," to repeat the words of our opening page, "it will likely be considerations of political wisdom, of social morale, and of institutional adaptability that will determine the futures of the . . . nations that make up most of the capitalist world. The same is true for the . . . countries that make up the socialist world."

Common Problems

That final emphasis brings us to one last generalization about the future. It is that we have spoken of the great differences between the two great world systems, but have ignored their equally great common concerns. Three in particular deserve our attention.

1. Control Over Technology. All modern societies tend to find that their technological capabilities are constantly increasing, while the social, political, and moral institutions by which those capabilities are controlled cannot

match the challenges with which they are faced. Television, for example, is an immense force for cultural homogenization; medical technology changes the composition of society by altering its age groups and life expectancy; rapid transportation vastly increases mobility and social horizons; and the obliterative power of nuclear arms casts a pervasive anxiety over all of life. All these technologically rooted developments fundamentally alter the conditions and problems of life, but we do not know what social, political, and moral responses are appropriate to them. As a result, all modern societies—socialist and capitalist—experience the feeling of being at the mercy of a technological and scientific impetus that shapes the lives of their citizens in ways that cannot be accurately foreseen nor adequately controlled.

2. The Problem Of Democracy. The second problem derives from the first. Because advanced societies are characterized by high levels of technology, they are necessarily marked by a high degree of organization. The technology of our era depends on the cooperation of vast masses of people, some at the levels of production, some at the levels of administration. The common undergirding of all advanced industrial societies lies not alone in their gigantic instrumentalities of production, but also in their equally essential and vast instrumentalities of administration, whether these be called corporations, production ministries, or government agencies.

The problem, then, is how the citizen is to find a place for his or her individuality in the midst of so much organization; how he or she is to express his or her voice in the direction of affairs, when so much bureaucratic management is inescapable; how he or she is to participate in a world whose technological structure calls for ever more order and coordination. This is a matter which, like the sweeping imperative of technology, affects both capitalism and socialism. In both kinds of societies, individuals feel overwhelmed by the impersonality of the work process, impotent before the power of huge enterprises—above all, the state itself—and frustrated at an inability to participate in decisions that seem more and more beyond any possibility of personal influence.

No doubt much can be done to increase the feeling of individual participation in the making of the future, especially in those nations that still deny elementary political freedoms. But there remains a recalcitrant problem of how the quest for increased individual decision-making and participation can be reconciled with the organizational demands imposed by the technology on which all advanced societies depend. This is a problem that is likely to trouble societies—capitalist or socialist—as long as technology itself rests on integrated processes of production and requires centralized organs of administration and control.

3. The Problem Of The Environment. All industrial nations may be facing an era in which economic growth begins to absorb resources at rates faster than we are able to provide them with new technologies; **and all industrialized societies—indeed, the whole world—may soon enter a time in which environmental limitations come into conflict with expectations of growth.**

In this period industrial socialist and capitalist nations again seem likely to share common problems—not only in overcoming environmental limits to growth, but also in achieving social harmony under conditions of increasing resource diversion

A PERSONAL VIEW ABOUT PLANNING

For reasons that are strewn throughout these pages, we expect that the long-term trend in most capitalist nations will be toward some kind of "planning." There are many such kinds, and that which works in one capitalist nation, such as Japan, may be totally inapplicable to another, like Italy or Canada or ourselves. Each nation must find its own way of devising macro and micro policies.

Thus we do not predict any particular direction of kind of planning for the United States. What we do expect is that the problems and market forces and technological capabilities of our age will blur the present distinction between "public" and "private" spheres, moving us, together with other capitalisms, in a direction that will have more business-government integration, more labor-management coordination, perhaps more national insulation against international competition.

This is a view which is deplored by the Left and denounced by the Right. Beyond that, both declare that planning does not work. They are certainly correct that planning does not work very well. What clearer evidence could there be for that than the universal presence of a crisis in all capitalist nations, despite the drift into planning of various kinds? But this objection misses a key consideration. It is that no manner of guiding society, from the most centralized to the most laissez-faire, can be expected to produce a smoothly working system in the face of today's social, political, and technological forces. The very elements that underlie our contemporary troubles—the tensions that divide the rich and poor nations, the impact of technologies of awesome power, the narrowing of ecological tolerances, the disappearance of the public fatalism of the past—must trouble any kind of economic system and any kind of government. It is not capitalism alone that is in crisis, but all modern industrial society. **A realistic attitude toward planning is not that it should work well, but that it should work *well enough*.** That seems a goal within reach.

toward public rather than private goods. Here, too, similar social and political problems may override differences in economic institutions and ideologies.

Envoi

In a larger sense, then, we go beyond economics to the common human adventure in which economic systems are only alternate routes conducting humanity toward a common destination. Perhaps it is well that we end our survey of economics with the recognition that the long history of the market system does not project us onto a final stage in social history. Rather, we arrive at a state in which some kinds of problems—the pitifully simple problems of producing and distributing goods—find resolution, only to reveal vastly larger problems springing from the very technology and organization that supplied the earlier answers.

LOOKING BACK

The end of a long book is a time for celebration, not homework. This is a chapter to think about, not to "learn." It does not lend itself to neat summaries and vocabulary items. We hope, rather, that it will bring the study of economics to a conclusion on a high note rather than a low one, and that it will leave you with the feeling that a subject of immense interest and importance awaits further exploration—by you.

Glossary

Accelerator effect The effect—sometimes stimulating, sometimes depressing—exerted on investment by changes in consumption expenditure. Also *acceleration principle.*

Antitrust legislation Legislation designed to minimize or prevent monopolistic behavior or monopolistic market structures.

Appreciation of exchange A rise in the ability of one nation's currency to buy the currency of another nation.

Average productivity The contribution to output of the average unit of any input. This is obtained by dividing total output by the number of units of the input. It is not the same as the contribution of the last, or marginal unit.

Average propensity to consume The relation between consumption and income, C/Y. It differs from the marginal propensity $\Delta C/\Delta Y$ because the latter is concerned only with spending out of marginal incomes.

Average propensity to save The relation between saving and income S/Y. It differs from the marginal propensity $\Delta S/\Delta Y$ because the latter is concerned only with saving out of marginal income.

Automatic stabilizers Institutional provisions that result in automatic stimulation of the economy in recession times and dampening of it in boom times. The counter-cyclical flows of unemployment insurance or farm subsidies, and the effect on consumption of the graduated income tax are key elements in these stabilizers.

Backward-bending supply curve A supply curve of labor services that displays a preference for fewer hours of labor (more leisure) when the price of labor rises above a certain level.

Balance of payments A set of accounts that records transactions between two countries. (See *Balance on capital* and *Current accounts.*)

Balance on capital account The net sum of demands and supplies for foreign exchange for all items on capital account, mainly direct and portfolio investment.

Balance on current account The net sum of demands for and supplies of foreign exchange for all items on current account, mainly merchandise exports and imports and similar transactions.

Bonds Obligations issued by private or public institutions with fixed dates of repayment and stated interest rates or coupons. (See *Yields.*)

Budget The amount of spending power possessed by an economic actor.

Business cycles The more or less regular recurrence of recession and prosperity.

Capital Wealth in an abstract form produced by capitalism. Also often used to refer to a financial sum of wealth.

Capital goods Final output used for production, not consumption. (See *Investment.*)

Capitalism An economic system oriented toward the accumulation of capital (or generalized, abstract wealth), coordinated by a market system in which land, labor, and capital have become "factors of production."

Capital/output ratio Relationship between the values of the capital stock and the flow of output of a firm, industry, or nation. Marginal capital/output ratios relate increases in output to increases in the capital stock.

Ceteris paribus Latin phrase meaning "other things being equal." The phrase refers to the need to allow for variations in the conditions that affect an experiment or an observation. For example, *ceteris paribus* requires us to make allowance for changes in income or taste when we are seeking to establish the relation of quantity demanded and price.

Circular flow The continuous circuit of spending, from households to firms and from firms back to households.

Claims Legal rights on income or wealth.

Clearing markets A market condition in which quantities demanded just balance quantities supplied.

Comparative advantage The relative edge enjoyed by one nation (or region or economic actor) in producing one commodity compared to another. A country can have a comparative advantage in producing a commodity even if its absolute productivity in that commodity is less than that of its trading partner.

Competition The vying of buyers and sellers in a marketplace. Competition has two aspects: (1) the contest of buyers against sellers, (2) the mutual rivalry of sellers against sellers and buyers against buyers.

Concentration The degree of market control enjoyed by the largest firms in an industry. Concentration ratios often measure the percentage of industry sales enjoyed by the largest four or eight firms.

Constraints Barriers or boundaries to desired behavior.

Consumption Use of output for purposes of private enjoyment.

Cost Cost in everyday speech refers to the expenses incurred in production. In economics it refers to missed opportunities—opportunities foregone because resources are committed to a given use. This is called opportunity cost. (See also *Sunk cost.*)

Cost push An explanation of inflation that stresses increases in factor prices such as higher real wages, or the increase in cost of resources or other inputs. (See *Demand pull.*)

Credit crunch A severe restriction of bank credit, forcing the drastic curtailment of bank lending to businesses or consumers.

Crowding out Rising interest rates resulting from government borrowing on the credit market.

Deepening capital Increasing the value of capital per worker.

Deficit spending Spending financed not by current tax receipts, but by borrowing or by drawing on past reserves.

Demand Willingness and ability to buy. Demand is a schedule that relates the quantities demanded with differing prices. (See also *Quantity demanded.*)

Demand gap The shortfall in demand that arises when the spending of the combined sectors is not enough to maintain a given level of GNP, or a necessary rate of growth of GNP.

Demand pull An explanation of inflation that stresses the effect of spending on the price level. Demand pull is usually focused on the effects of government or business spending. (See *Cost push.*)

Dependent variables Quantities whose value is determined by the value of another "independent" variable, contained in the equation.

Depreciation The decline in the value of capital goods over time. The term is also used to designate funds set aside to replace the worn-out capital.

Depreciation of exchange A fall in the ability of one nation's currency to buy the currency of a foreign nation.

Devaluation A policy deliberately intended to cheapen the exchange value of a currency in order to encourage exports. (Technically, devaluation means cheapening a currency in terms of gold.)

Direct investment Investment in plant and equipment, as contrasted with financial investment.

Direct taxes Taxes levied by local, state, or federal governments on incomes.

Discounting Application of an interest rate to calculate the present value of a sum of money expected to be received or held in the future. At a rate of discount of 10 percent, $100 due a year hence is worth $90 today.

Discount rate The term applied to the interest rate charged by the Federal Reserve banks or loans made to their member banks.

Diseconomies of scale Increases in unit cost resulting from inefficiencies of technology or organization at rising levels (scales) of output.

Disinvestment A failure to create investment equal to the wear and tear on existing capital. Disinvestment means a diminution of capital wealth.

Disposable personal income Factor earnings plus transfers less direct taxes. Disposable personal income therefore defines aggregate household spending power.

Dissaving Expenditure that exceeds income. Dissaving requires that a dissaver use past savings, or borrowing, to finance the additional expenditure.

Distribution The process of allocating output or income among the population. Also used to refer to the results of this process, for example when we say that "income distribution is very unequal."

Efficiency Relation of output to input.

Endogenous Influences internal to a system. The rise in income that results from the multiplier effect is endogenous to the determination of GNP.

Entry The ability to move into a market or line of production.

Equations Mathematical statements usually involving dependent and independent variables in a functional relationship.

Equilibrium A self-correcting and self-perpetuating level of prices or economic activity. Equilibrium prices equate quantities demanded and supplied, and thereby "clear" markets. Equilibrium flows of output, such as GNP, balance opposing tendencies of savings and investment to create a self-perpetuating flow.

Equimarginal rule The general guide to optimization through equalizing the marginal returns of all factors.

Equity Ownership, usually stock ownership.

Eurodollars Supplies of dollars held by foreign or American banks outside the U.S.

Ex ante The view looking forward. Ex ante refers to economic activity that has not yet taken place. Ex ante quantities or values may therefore differ from ex post figures, after the event.

Excess reserves Bank reserves (cash or deposits at the Federal Reserve) over the required amount.

Exchange rate The price of foreign currencies in terms of one's own currency.

Exogenous Influences originating outside the system. An exogenous influence on GNP would be a change in the weather, or a war.

Ex post The view looking backward. Ex post refers to economic activity that has already happened. (See *Ex ante.*)

External debts Debts owed by members of one community, usually a nation, to another community or nation. (See *Internal debts.*)

Externalities Effects (good or bad) imposed by the act of production, or consumption, for which no price is charged. A typical bad or negative externality is the pollution imposed on the public by smoke from a factory.

Factor market The market in which the services of labor, land, or capital are sold. Factor markets regulate wages, rents, and interest rates.

Factor of production The name given to the main kinds of inputs, land, labor, and capital, in a market society.

Federal Reserve banks One of the 12 federally created central banks. Commercial banks may become members of the Federal Reserve System, but are not themselves Federal Reserve banks.

Federal Reserve system The formal institution of central banking in the United States, structured around 12 Reserve banks and governed by a Board of Governors.

Final goods Goods that have reached the end of the production process. Typically these are of four kinds: consumption goods, investment or capital goods, government or public goods, and exports.

Fiscal policy Government efforts to control the level of employment or prices by spending and taxing, rather than by monetary policy.

Fixed exchange rates Exchange relationships between currencies fixed by government agreement and maintained by the action of central banks.

Foreign exchange Supplies of foreign currencies held by the banks or government of any nation.

Fractional reserves The legal permission to hold reserves equal to less than 100 percent of bank deposits. Fractional reserves multiply the effect of new deposits on the money supply.

Full employment budgets Calculation of the impact on GNP of government receipts and expenditure flows assuming that receipts and expenditures are at the levels corresponding to full employment.

Functional relationships Relationships in which the value of one variable is determined by another.

GNP (gross national product) The dollar value of the final output of the economy for a fixed period, usually a year. GNP is the sum of consumption, gross domestic investment, government purchases, and net exports.

Graphs Visual representations of functional relationships or of the movements of variables through time.

Gross investment The use of resources to create capital, whether as an addition to existing wealth or as a replacement for worn-out capital.

Gross national income The sum of factor incomes, tax receipts, and depreciation accruals. GNI is always identical with GNP.

Growth Increase in output. (See *Nominal growth* and *Real growth.*)

Human capital The money value of skills or education.

Identities Mathematical statements of definition.

Imperialism Domination by a highly developed, powerful nation. Specifically used to describe the penetration of capitalist nations into the underdeveloped world.

Incidence of taxation The pattern of impact of taxation. The incidence of taxation attempts to discover where the burden of a tax ultimately falls.

Incomes policy Anti-inflation measures that depend on voluntary acceptance of income limitations, such as moderated wage demands.

Increasing cost The tendency of cost per unit to rise as the volume of output exceeds the point of greatest efficiency. (See *Law of increasing cost.*)

Increasing returns The initial tendency of output to rise faster than input, as one factor is added to fixed amounts of other factors.

Independent variables Quantities whose value is determined independently—that is, outside the equation.

Indexing Adjustment of nominal payments in accordance with a price index.

Indirect taxes Taxes levied by local, state, or federal government on the value of output. Cigarette or gas taxes are instances of indirect taxes.

Industrial policy The use of government policies to encourage (or discourage) industries, especially in international trade.

Infant industries Newly founded industries, especially in developing nations, that require tariff protection in order to achieve competitive scale.

Inflation A process in which prices in nearly all markets display a chronic upward tendency.

Inflation tax The effect of inflation in lessening the cost of a national debt.

Injections Any expenditures that raise the flow of income. The main injections are net investment, deficit spending, an excess of exports over imports, or a consumer spending wave, financed by drawing on past saving or on credit.

Interest The price of the factor capital.

Intermediate goods Goods or services that enter into final goods. For example, wheat is an intermediate good entering into bread.

Internal debts Debts owed by members of a community, usually a nation, to one another.

Intersectoral offsets Spending by one sector, usually business or government, used to offset the insufficient spending of another sector.

Inventories Goods on raw materials that have been produced but not yet sold to final purchasers. All increases in inventories are counted in the national accounts as net investment.

Investment The act of building capital. (See *Real vs. financial investment.*)

Invisible hand A famous phrase used by Adam Smith to indicate that individuals who followed their private self-interest would in fact fulfill a larger purpose, as if "led by an Invisible Hand."

Kondratieff cycle A cyclical pattern of roughly 25 buoyant and 25 stagnant years that may describe capitalist history. Its mechanism and even its existence are uncertain.

Law of increasing cost Eventual tendency of costs of a given output to rise as additional inputs of all factors (not just one) are used to produce it.

Leakages Channels through which additional income is diverted from respending by households. The four main leakages are private saving, business profits, taxes, and imports.

Liquidity Condition of having immediately spendable resources, such as cash or very easily salable securities, such as very short-term government notes.

Liquidity preference The differing proportions of one's wealth that one seeks to hold in liquid form at differing interest rates. High interest rates impose high opportunity costs on holding cash. Therefore, usually we prefer to be less liquid when we can use our cash to earn high interest. Conversely, we seek more liquidity when the opportunity cost is low. Risk also plays an important part in determining our willingness to be liquid or illiquid.

M1 (See *Money supply.*)

Macroeconomics That portion of economics concerned with large-scale movements of the economy, such as growth or decline, inflation or deflation.

Marginal Additional, incremental (plus or minus).

Marginal efficiency of investment The value of the expected returns of new investment discounted to the present.

Marginal propensity to consume The relation between additional income and additional spending: $\Delta C/\Delta Y$. (See *Average propensity to consume.*)

Marginal propensity to save The relation between additional income and additional saving: $\Delta S/\Delta Y$. (See *Average propensity to save.*)

Market socialism Socialist economies that continue to use markets as allocation mechanisms or as incentive systems, in addition to central planning of major elements such as investment.

Market system The structure of exchange relations of buying and selling that sustains the economic process of capitalism.

Maximizing The driving force of economic activity described as the pursuit of the largest possible amount of pleasurable wealth.

Mercantilism The prevailing mode of economic organization in the period between late feudalism and early capitalism, characterized by a highly regulated domestic economy and an effort to achieve a surplus of exports over imports.

Microeconomics That portion of economics concerned with the activity of individuals and firms, mainly with regard to the allocation of resources.

Mixed economies Economies that combine attributes of capitalism, such as private property and market mechanisms, with elements of socialism, in particular welfare structures and some degree of government control over economic activity.

Mobility The capacity to change economic location or function.

Monetarism The body of theory that stresses the importance of the quantity of money in determining the rate of inflation and the level of activity.

Money stock (See *Money supply.*)

Money supply There are many ways of calculating the money supply. Perhaps the most common is cash held by the public, plus demand deposits at commercial banks. This is designated M1. Various other definitions (M1, M2, M3) expand the basic definition by adding other liquid assets.

Multinational corporations Corporations that derive a substantial proportion of their income or sales from overseas production, as contrasted with exports.

Multiplier-accelerator The joint interaction of the multiplier effect, which creates additional income from an injection, and the accelerator effect, which creates additional investment from a rise in consumption.

Multiplier effect The tendency of injections to create increases in income larger than the original injections. The multiplier effect results from the marginal propensity to consume.

National income The total amount of factor incomes earned over a period of time. National income does not include transfer payments.

Nationalization Purchase or seizure by the government of a privately owned firm.

Net investment The use of resources to create additional capital goods.

Net national product Gross national product minus depreciation. Net national product is also national income (factor earnings) plus the value of indirect taxes.

Nominal growth Increase in output measured in current dollars, without allowance for changes in the purchasing power of dollars. If we compare the GNPs of two years, without deflating the dollar amounts, we are comparing nominal growth.

Nominal values The values or prices of objects in current terms with no adjustment for changes in the value of the monetary unit.

Open-market operations The buying or selling of government bonds by the Federal Reserve, as a means of expanding or contracting the reserves of commercial banks.

Opportunity cost The wealth or enjoyments that cannot be obtained because resources or inputs are already committed to a given purpose. All economic activities entail opportunity cost. Every act of consumption or production rules out the possibility of some alternative action.

Optimization The search for the most efficient allocation of wealth or resources.

Overhead cost Costs associated with administration or sales, rather than with direct factory-floor production.

Participation rate The proportion of the population of working age that is actively seeking work.

Per capita GNP Gross national product divided by the population.

Perestroika The restructuring of the Soviet economy by enlarging the sphere of private decision making.

Phillips curve The presumed statistical correlation between unemployment and inflation first pointed out by A. W. Phillips.

Physiocracy A school of economic thought developed by Francois Quesnay (1694–1774) that stressed the productive power of the land.

Portfolio investment Financial investment, as opposed to real investment in plant and equipment.

Price index A statistical measure of price levels in which one year is chosen as a base, and the other years expressed as a percentage of that base.

Production The use of labor and resources to create wealth.

Production possibility curve A graphic depiction of the total outputs available to a society. Production possibility curves are usually bowed outward because of the law of increasing cost.

Production possibility frontier The outer limit of production possibilities as we move resources from one use to another. (See *Production possibility curve.*)

Productivity A measure of output per unit of input over a given period of time, such as yearly or hourly output per worker or per machine.

Progressive incidence A pattern of taxation that imposes proportionally heavier burdens on high income groups than on low income groups.

Propensity to consume The relation between consumption and income: C/Y. (See also *Marginal propensity to consume.*)

Propensity to save The relation between saving and income: S/Y. (See also *Marginal propensity to consume.*)

Proportional incidence A pattern of taxation that imposes equal percentage burdens on all income levels.

Psychic income The value of nonmonetary income in terms of utilities.

Public goods Outputs provided by the public sector and not allocated by the price mechanism.

Purchasing power The ability to buy.

Quantity demanded The amount of a commodity or service that we are willing and able to buy at a given price. (See also *Demand.*)

Quantity equation $MV = PT$. (See *Quantity theory.*)

Quantity supplied The amount of a commodity or service that we are willing and able to supply at a given price. (See also *Supply.*)

Quantity theory The theory that relates the level of prices solely to the quantity of money.

R&D Research and development. Research can be basic—inquiry that has no immediate commercial or economic orientation, or applied—inquiry directed at shaping knowledge for a given purpose. Development refers to commercial readying of goods or processes.

Rational expectations The tendency of markets to foresee and anticipate actions intended to alter market outcomes.

Rationality The assumption that people can intelligently adapt their actions (means) to their purposes (ends).

Rationing The distribution of resources according to some allocation mechanism. The mechanism may be the price system, or it may be a nonmarket system, such as coupons.

Real growth Increases in output corrected for changes in the purchasing power of the currency.

Real vs. financial investment Real investment is the act of devoting resources to capital formation. Financial investment denotes the purchase of equities, claims, or other instruments that channel personal savings into banks or businesses.

Regressive incidence A pattern of taxation that imposes proportionally larger burdens on low income groups than on high ones.

Replacement investment Investment that is designed to renew worn-out capital. Replacement investment plus net investment equals gross investment.

Reserve requirement The proportion of deposits that must be kept in vault cash or at a Federal Reserve bank. Reserve requirements are set by the Board of Governors of the Federal Reserve System.

Reserves Deposits that may not be loaned or invested. Reserves must be held in cash or at a Federal Reserve bank.

Saving The act of not using income for consumption. Saving is a financial act when we put money in a bank, but its real meaning is to relinquish a claim on resources.

Scatter diagram Graphic representation of two variables showing their associated pairs.

Schedule A list of different values of a variable, such as quantities or prices.

Sector A division of the economy with common characteristics. Usually we speak of the public and the private sector; of the consumption, investment, and government sectors; or of the agricultural, industrial, and service sectors.

Shortage The failure of a market to clear when the price is below equilibrium levels and there are unsatisfied buyers at the going price.

Stagflation An economic condition of simultaneous inflation and stagnation—that is, rising prices and inadequate growth.

Sticky prices The tendency of many prices to remain unchanged despite changes in demand and supply. This may be the consequence of contracts (a wage or rent contract) or of institutional inertia.

Stocks Legal instruments of ownership in corporations.

Substitution The capacity of one commodity to provide the utilities of another. Increases in the price of a commodity result in increases in the demand for its substitutes.

Supply Willingness and ability to sell. Supply is a schedule that relates the quantities offered with differing prices. (See also *Quantity supplied.*)

Supply-side economics Policies seeking to use taxes or deregulation to impart a strong momentum to the economy.

Surplus The failure of a market to clear when the price is above equilibrium levels and there are unsatisfied sellers at the going price.

Terms of trade A comparison of the quantities of goods that are required to gain a given amount of goods in return. For example, the Brazilian terms of trade could measure the number of sacks of coffee needed to "buy" a computer.

Tight money A condition, associated with restrictive monetary policy, that makes it difficult for borrowers to obtain bank loans.

Tradeoff An exchange relationship denoting how much of A is needed to obtain a unit of B.

Transactions demand The amount of cash we need to carry on normal economic transactions. At higher levels of economic activity there is normally a higher demand for transactions balances, for such purposes as meeting payrolls or financing ordinary expenditures.

Transfers Any payment from one person or institution to another made for purposes other than to remunerate work. Social security is a transfer payment; so is the payment of an allowance to a minor, or a charity payment.

Unemployment Inability to find acceptable work at the going wage level.

Utility Pleasure or well-being.

Variable proportions See (*Law of variable proportions.*)

Velocity of circulation The number of times a unit of currency is used during a period of time, usually a year. The velocity of circulation is calculated by dividing output (GNP) by the money supply.

Wealth Production that yields utilities.

Widening capital Matching additional workers with amounts of capital equal to those used by previously employed workers.

Yields The income paid by a bond compared with its market value. A bond issued at a price of $1,000 with a "coupon" of $100 (interest payable annually) will have a yield of 20 percent if the bond can be bought on the market at $500. It will have a 10 percent yield if its price is the original issue price. Its yield will fall to 5 percent if the market price of the bond rises to $2,000.

Zero-sum game A contest in which every gain is matched by an exactly equivalent loss.

Index